Jacob Encountering Rachel

The image on the cover and above is of an 1836 painting in oil on canvas by the Bohemian artist Joseph von Fuehrich (1800–1876). Fuehrich was a member of the Nazarenes, a group of nineteenth-century Romantic painters who were dedicated to reviving honest expressions of spirituality in religious art. The image depicted here shows Jacob and Rachel at the well among her father's herds. The image illustrates the first encounter of Jacob and Rachel as described in Genesis 29:9–11. Image provided by Erich Lessing/Art Resource, NY.

Acknowledgments

Thank you to the following individuals who reviewed this work in progress:

Dr. Bernhard A. Asen
Saint Louis University
Saint Louis, Missouri

Dr. Harry P. Nasuti
Fordham University
Bronx, New York

Dr. Chris Franke
College of Saint Catherine
Saint Paul, Minnesota

Dr. Dan Scholz
Cardinal Stritch University
Milwaukee, Wisconsin

Dr. Claire Mathews McGinnis
Loyola College
Baltimore, Maryland

Dr. Kenneth G. Stenstrup
Saint Mary's University
Winona, Minnesota

Dr. Pauline A. Viviano
Loyola University
Chicago, Illinois

*Special thanks to Jerry Windley-Daoust for his work
in the initial development of this text.*

Encountering Ancient Voices

A Guide to Reading the Old Testament

Corrine L. Carvalho
The University of Saint Thomas,
Saint Paul, Minnesota

Saint Mary's Press®

The publishing team included Leslie M. Ortiz, general editor; John B. McHugh, director of college publishing; Erich Lessing/Art Resource, NY, cover and half-title page image; Zev Radovan/www.BibleLandPictures.com, interior images; prepress and manufacturing coordinated by the prepublication and production services departments of Saint Mary's Press.

Printed in the United States of America

Printing: 9 8 7 6 5 4 3 2 1

Year: 2014 13 12 11 10 09 08 07 06

ISBN-13: 978-0-88489-911-2
ISBN-10: 0-88489-911-X

Library of Congress Cataloging-in-Publication Data
Carvalho, Corrine L.
    Encountering ancient voices : a guide to reading the Old Testament / Corrine L. Carvalho.
        p. cm.
Includes bibliographical references and index.
ISBN-13: 978-0-88489-911-2 (pbk.)
ISBN-10: 0-88489-911-X (pbk.)
    1. Bible. O.T.—Textbooks. 2. Bible. O.T.—Criticism, interpretation, etc. I. Title.
BS1194.C38 2006
221.6'1—dc22

                                                                2006025472

CONTENTS

Introduction for the Instructor

Why Another Old Testament Textbook?

You may be asking yourself the same question I've been asking: do we really need another textbook for the Old Testament? And yet, every year when I wander through the book display at the annual meeting of the Society of Biblical Literature, I find that many of the current textbooks have a similar format. They tend to be "passive" in nature, providing students with information that they are meant to read and recall. Many focus on the historical background of the text, while others simply retell the biblical texts, adding in social and cultural information. Some focus on literary issues and others on theological matters.

The best textbooks out there are too difficult for my students, who are undergraduate students taking the course as part of their general requirements. The texts presume too much background and give too much detail. Rather than encouraging students to read the Bible on their own, the texts discourage students, who conclude that there is no way they'll ever know enough to understand the Bible on their own.

One of my primary goals as a teacher is to empower students to read the Bible. I hope that after they leave my class, they will not be afraid to open the Bible and read it on their own. I tell them that eventually many of them will be parents and that it's very likely that someone eventually will ask them to lead a catechism class. I want them to feel confident about reading the text on their own and seeking reliable resources of information when necessary. It's a simple goal, really, one less concerned with comprehensive coverage and more focused on reading strategies.

Therefore, in order to achieve my goal, I designed the textbook using five strategies:

> I wrote the book in such a way that the focus of the class will center on the text. I tried to avoid retelling the stories, as much as possible, in order to encourage students to read the Bible.

> I used active learning techniques wherever possible. This has been difficult, since most active learning occurs when the teacher gets out of the way of student learning. Here I have done that by providing questions that, when applied on a regular basis, help the student develop good reading skills. In addition, each chapter:

>> **Includes materials that help students to learn** about the social and cultural contexts out of which these texts were produced.

>> **Provides a legitimate variety of interpretations** of the text, in order to encourage students to cultivate some ownership of their own interpretations.

>> **Actively acknowledges contemporary approaches** to reading and interpretation. While classical methods, such as source criticism, are taught, the book also recognizes the post-modern context of our current students. It tries to respect where they are, because I have found that students are intensely interested in theological questions when teachers can connect those questions to the students' world.

Except for the first chapter, which deals with broader background issues, each chapter begins with introductory material. This material usually provides an overview of the book or genre in question and provides historical and cultural information that will aid the students' reading.

This introductory section is followed by guided close readings of key biblical texts. I would not expect these texts to be the only ones that a student would read in class, nor would I expect a teacher to assign all of the texts. However, the supplied texts provide representative examples of how to read material in that book or genre. These close readings have the following format:

> Each reading starts with **a brief introduction** to the passage that often poses a question or issue for students to think about.

- Then, a section called **"In Case You Were Wondering"** highlights unfamiliar words or customs.

- Next, students **read the biblical passage**.

- After the biblical passage, questions follow in a section titled **"Looking Closely at the Text"** that will help students focus on the important details of the text.

- Finally, there is a **discussion of the text,** either highlighting the issues students were to consider or suggesting ways they could address the questions posed.

At the end of each chapter I provide a summary of the material covered in the chapter, so as to pull together information and major themes. In addition, there are study questions at the end of the chapter and a brief bibliography ("For Further Reading") for those times when students need more information. I have tried to pick material that is accessible to them, rather than providing cutting-edge scholarship.

Each chapter also includes a number of sidebars. These recognize the fact that instructors of introductory courses often have quite diverse backgrounds themselves. Some of us are biblical scholars, while others are systematic theologians, people with a religious studies background, ethicists, and so on. The sidebars allow different instructors to focus on different aspects of the text.

Every chapter has the following two sidebars:

- **"Focus on Method,"** which introduces a different method of biblical interpretation to the students. Instructors can pick and choose which methods to introduce. If you don't like the order provided (I've tried to link them to texts where they work best), you can easily skip around, using them as self-contained units.

- **"The Bible in the Christian Tradition,"** which focuses on some prominent interpretive traditions within Christianity. These are tied to the content of the chapter and demonstrate how particular traditions of interpretation have developed. I hope that those instructors who are more versed in the Christian tradition will use these sidebars as a jumping-off place for larger hermeneutical discussions.

In addition to these two standard sidebars, others will appear that focus on the ancient near-eastern background of the biblical material. For those instructors who want to provide a fuller treatment of a topic, such as the Gilgamesh epic, these sidebars can be used as a starting point. Other sidebars might address Jewish interpretation of texts, historical background in more detail, or the ways contemporary reading communities approach texts.

The order of the chapters reflects the way that I teach the course. I have experimented with different structures over the years, and each one has its advantages and challenges. I struggle with the best place to introduce poetry, where to put the wisdom material, and how to teach the creation narratives. Recognizing that we all use different structures, I have tried to write some of these units in a way that would make them self-standing. Instructors can feel comfortable moving the units around to fit their own course. You will occasionally see comments in the body of the textbook indicating material that can be more easily moved.

At the end of the textbook you will also find a glossary of key terms and an appendix with maps.

I have kept the writing style of the textbook informal. I hope that this narrative voice can serve as a model for students. Seeing the writer of the textbook struggling with some of the same interpretive issues that they do may help empower students to accept that struggle. It also allows me to be honest about my own presuppositions, a strategy that cuts against those of so many other textbooks where the narrator is the expert and the interpretation is "objective."

I know that this is not a textbook that will suit every instructor; no textbook can do that. But I hope that if you, like me, teach our curious undergraduate students, few of whom will ever go on to do graduate work in theology, Scripture, or religion, you will find this book a useful tool to get your students to read the Bible.

1 CRACKING OPEN A DUSTY OLD BOOK

So they read from the book, from the law of God, with interpretation.
They gave the sense, so that the people understood the reading.
(Neh 8:8)

CHAPTER OVERVIEW

This chapter will introduce you to some basic concepts concerning the Old Testament that you should know before beginning to read the texts. You will find that this chapter contains a lot of information, some of which you may need to return to throughout the course. The following questions will be addressed.

▶ Why study the Old Testament?

▶ What is the Old Testament?

▶ Where was ancient Israel located, and who were its neighbors?

▶ What is the general outline of Israelite history?

▶ How did we get a Bible in the first place?

▶ Are there proper ways to interpret the Bible?

These introductory matters will explain the approach to the Bible that this book will adopt.

Different Names for the Old Testament

This textbook is written from a Christian perspective, so I am using the name for this collection that most Christians use: the Old Testament. This is not, however, the only name for this collection. Modern Jews often call this material either the Tanakh (for the three divisions of their Bible) or simply the *Hebrew Bible* (since their entire Bible is written in Hebrew). Some Christians prefer to use the term *Hebrew Bible* since it is more descriptive and does not imply that this collection is "old," "outdated," or in need of something "new" or "better." Catholics and Orthodox Christians have trouble with the term *Hebrew Bible,* since their Old Testament canon includes books not originally written in Hebrew. Scholars have tried to find other terms that could be acceptable to all religious groups, such as *First Testament* or *Jewish Scriptures.* However, these terms have not yet become widely accepted. Since this textbook looks at the Old Testament within the context of Christian theology, I will continue to use "Old Testament."

WHY STUDY THE OLD TESTAMENT?

That's a question many people ask. The Bible is so familiar within contemporary American culture that we often forget that it is actually a collection of ancient writings. Would you expect to be able to pick up a collection of ancient Egyptian literature and understand it right away? And yet, this is often what people today expect to be able to do with the Bible. Because they have this expectation, they often misinterpret the material that they find there. Therefore, it is important to study the Bible, first and foremost, so that we might understand it.

But why do people want to read the Bible in the first place? People have many reasons for reading the Old Testament or Hebrew Bible. Some want to understand more about the Bible and the stories they may have heard in church or synagogue. Some Christians want to know what Bible Jesus read so they can understand better the images he used. People interested in contemporary culture recognize that the Bible has been very influential in American society, so they want to be familiar with its contents. Still others read the Bible because they are taking a course on it. There are obviously many other reasons for reading the text than those I have listed here.

One problem with many Christians' experience of the Bible is that it is based solely on what they hear in church. If their church uses a lectionary (a preselected set of biblical readings for daily or weekly church services), then these readings will only give a partial exposure to the Old Testament. The lectionary for Roman Catholics contains less than one third of the Old Testament. For example, the lectionary readings concerning Abraham depict God's covenant with Abraham, as well as his near-sacrifice of his son, Isaac. This selection presents a very positive view of Abraham as a model of faith. However, when the whole cycle of stories about Abraham is considered, the picture of Abraham is noticeably different.

Why Read This Textbook?

If you've ever tried to read the Bible on your own, you might know what a difficult task this can be. As a starting point, take a moment to look at one sample text.

Open Your Bible

Read Genesis 6:1–4. Take about three minutes to list what you would need to know to better understand these verses.

The aim of this textbook is not to replace your own reading of the Bible. Requiring you to read a textbook without reading the Bible would be a little like requiring you to read a book about Shakespeare's *Romeo and Juliet* without requiring you to read the play. The goal of this book is to *help* you to read the Old Testament and to give you the kind of information you need to understand many parts of the Bible. No book can answer every question you may have about the Old Testament, but it can give you important background information on the life and culture of the community that produced it. It can also give you ways to think about some of the bigger religious issues that the texts raise.

Let's return to our first example. When I teach this passage, I find that students often have some of the following questions:

> ❯ Who were the "sons of God," and what were they doing wandering around the earth?

> ❯ Who were the "Nephilim," and what does it mean to call them "heroes"?

> ❯ Why does the Bible have a story about heavenly beings having intercourse with human women? Isn't this a pagan idea?

It may be helpful to know that many people who lived in and around ancient Israel believed that, when God first created the world, there was not an impassable separation between heaven and earth. Heavenly beings could walk the earth and even have children with humans. One way that the ancient texts depicted this was to talk about an age of "giants" or, in Hebrew, "Nephilim." Some scholars conjecture that these stories arose to explain large dinosaur bones that people had discovered but couldn't explain.

This helps us today to understand why Genesis 6:1–4 would have made sense to the ancient Israelites. If a person believed that there was a "primordial time" when heaven and earth were not separated, then this story is not surprising. But it does not answer all of the questions one might have about the text. For instance, it does not tell us why God would have let this interaction happen, or where these "sons of God" came from.

Even if we could reconstruct all of what the original audience would have thought about these verses, we still have not even begun to think about the biggest question of all: why should we read or care about this story today? I have to admit, when it comes to Genesis 6:1–4, the immediate "pay-off" may be remote. But I do find that considering that the Israelites may have been trying to understand the presence of dinosaur bones within a divinely created world helps me to appreciate Genesis's view of God's role in creation.

Ultimately, this textbook is meant to help you think about this "bigger" picture, by pointing out where and how the Bible expresses its main themes. At first glance Genesis 6:1–4 seems to have little to do with creation, one of the major themes of Genesis, but it is, in fact, part of an Israelite creation account.

What Is the Old Testament?

What is the Old Testament? The simplest answer is that it is a collection of sacred literature produced by the ancient Israelites. This definition of the Old Testament ("a collection of sacred literature produced by the ancient Israelites") suggests that a study of the Bible has six components:

▸ **Collection.** If this is a collection, then each component must be read as a distinct piece of literature. We should explore the various kinds of literature in the Old Testament and think about how this affects our reading of it. Do we read poetry, for instance, differently from history?

▸ **Sacred.** This means we must think about how the text was produced, how it was handed down, and how it is understood by churches and synagogues today.

▸ **Literature.** What were the literary forms back then? How is reading a piece of poetry, for instance, different from reading a set of laws?

Navigating the Bible

People have struggled throughout the ages to find a standard way to make easy reference to parts of the Bible. Since Bibles have always come in different sizes and shapes, you can't refer to a page number, like you might in a modern novel. At first, when only the most learned people actually read the Bible, people simply quoted the verse, assuming that the audience knew where a particular verse was located. Eventually, however, the biblical books were divided into chapters, and then into smaller units within the chapters, called verses. The addition of chapter and verse numbers did not happen until hundreds of years after the books were written. Chapter and verse numbers, then, are not part of the original text, but they are an aid to help people more easily find things in the Bible.

Since then it has become a tradition to refer to a particular passage from the Bible "by chapter and verse," meaning by referring to the exact chapter and verse number where a quote is located. There are a few variations on this tradition to be aware of. Don't try to memorize them now, but refer back to this section if you are ever confused:

- **Genesis 4: If the name of the biblical book is followed by a number, this means you should read all of chapter 4 in the book of Genesis**

- **Genesis 4—5: If there is more than one number, but no colons, then read all of chapters 4 and 5 in the book of Genesis.**

- **When I say, "Read Genesis 6:1–4," this means you should start reading the book of Genesis at chapter 6, verse 1, and read until the end of chapter 6, verse 4.**

- **Genesis 4:5–6:7: When there are 2 colons, this means you should start reading Genesis at chapter 4, verse 5, and continue until you have read chapter 6, verse 7.**

- **Genesis 4:5–6, 9–10: One colon and a comma signify that you should read chapter 4, verses 5 and 6, then skip to verses 9 and 10.**

- **Genesis 4:5–6; 7:8–9: Semicolons separate different references. This means that you should read chapter 4, verses 5 to 6, and then skip to chapter 7, verses 8 to 9.**

Last, just to make things a little more confusing for you, Europeans do not use colons in references to the Bible. Instead, wherever Americans have a colon, they have a period.

There are standard abbreviations used for most biblical books that can be found in the front of most Bibles. The abbreviations are used whenever *both* chapter and verse numbers are cited (unless the citation begins a sentence). There is no period after the abbreviated name of the biblical book.

See if you can answer the following questions by looking up the references given.

1. Many people know about the talking serpent in the Garden of Eden, but what is the only other talking animal in the Bible (Num 22.28–30)?

2. Who sees "the writing on the wall" (Dan 5:1–9)?

3. How many people did Elisha feed with only a few loaves of bread and some corn (2 Kgs 4:42–44)?

4. How did David's son, Absalom, die (2 Sam 18:9–17)?

5. Who won the first beauty contest in the Bible (Esth 2)?

6. What do the following verses all have in common: Psalm 2:4; 37:13; 59:9?

7. What can bird droppings cause and a fish's gall cure (Tob 2:10; 6:9)?

8. What barley farmer allowed a woman named Ruth to work in his field (Ruth 1:22—2:3)?

	American Style	European Style
Read Genesis chapter 4, verses 1 to 4.	Genesis 4:1–4	Genesis 4.1–4
Read Genesis chapter 4, verses 1 to 2 and verses 5 to 6.	Genesis 4:1–2, 5–6	Genesis 4.1–2, 5–6

> ▶ **Produced.** How and why were the literary pieces written? Why can it be so difficult to identify the authors of texts?

> ▶ **Ancient.** The historical and cultural contexts provide important background information that helps us to appreciate the Bible. We will learn to ask what historical events may have influenced the way a text expresses an idea. Similarly, we may find biblical characters acting in ways that seem strange to us today. At that point, we need to ask what customs they had in their society that we do not have today.

> ▶ **Israelites.** Who were the Israelites? Where did they live? Who were their allies? Who were their enemies?

I am going to start with this last question: who were the ancient Israelites? Then I will move on to the question of how different religious groups arrived at different collections of texts.

WHERE WAS ANCIENT ISRAEL LOCATED?

Ancient Israel was located in the same general vicinity as modern Israel: on the western edge of the continent of Asia, bordering the Mediterranean Sea. Today we refer to that part of the world as the "Middle East," but historians of the ancient world call it the "Near East." The reasons for the shift from "near" to "middle" are too complex to address here. You can simply remember that the "Middle East" is the same thing as the "Near East."

THE LAND

Ancient civilizations were utterly dependent on agriculture. Cities could only thrive near fields which were large and fertile enough to feed the city dwellers who did not work the land. Ancient agriculture was dependent on fresh water sources, provided either through rain or irrigation from prominent rivers. In the ancient Near East, there was an area of land along the rivers that formed a kind of arch, where enough food could be produced to support city life. This area is called the Fertile Crescent. It extends from the Persian Gulf, along the twin rivers of Mesopotamia (the Tigris and the Euphrates), down along the Mediterranean coast, and over to the Nile valley in North Africa. Trade, technology, and intellectual ideas linked these civilizations.

ISRAEL'S NEIGHBORS IN THE FERTILE CRESCENT

The two most prosperous regions within this area were the Nile River Valley, and Mesopotamia. Israel's fate was often determined by the politics of the three super powers that lived in these areas: Egypt, Assyria, and Babylon.

EGYPT

Egypt arose on the continent of Africa along the Nile, the land we often associate with the great pyramids. It had a very stable economy, counting as it could on the annual flooding of the Nile to provide fresh, rich soil. The deserts that surrounded Egypt provided natural protection from most foreign invaders. By the time Israel arrived on the scene, the pyramids were more than 1500 years old.

ASSYRIA AND BABYLONIA

Mesopotamia is the area in the Middle East around and between two great rivers, the Tigris and the Euphrates. Irrigation projects allowed for rich agricultural production in an otherwise dry land. Many different civilizations arose along the Tigris and Euphrates rivers. The two most important civilizations for biblical history are those of the Assyrians and the Babylonians. These nations were interested in expanding their control beyond Mesopotamia to the whole Fertile Crescent.

ISRAEL'S NEIGHBORS IN THE LEVANT

Israel was located in an area referred to as the Levant, that is, the inhabitable land along the coast of the Mediterranean Sea. All of the countries in the Levant were dependent on annual rainstorms that came in from the Mediterranean. The amount of rainfall, however, was not the same every year. In some years there would be plenty of water to grow fine grapes and good barley. In other years there would be severe drought, and the whole area would suffer. Israel's neighbors in the Levant included the following:

AMMON, MOAB, AND EDOM

Ammon, Moab, and Edom were across the Jordan River. The land in these countries was drier than in Israel, and, therefore, they sustained fewer cities. However, the Israelites viewed these people as related to them.

PHOENICIA

Phoenicia lay to the north of Israel. Of the countries of the Levant, Phoenicia had the best harbors to develop significant trade along the Mediterranean. Therefore, of all the countries in the Levant, Phoenicia was economically the strongest; Israel was relatively insignificant compared to Phoenicia. Biblical texts usually refer to Phoenicia by its two major cities: Tyre and Sidon.

PHILISTIA

Philistia was located southwest of Israel along the coast. The Philistines were not originally from the Levant but had come from islands in the Mediterranean Sea. Their culture differed from the culture of other countries in the Levant. The Philistines proved to be a powerful threat to the existence of Israel, especially during the early monarchy.

BEYOND THE FERTILE CRESCENT

References to places outside the Fertile Crescent are rare in the Old Testament. Some of these areas, such as parts of Persia, Africa, and southern Europe, appear during certain periods of Israelite history, but they were not permanent influences on Israel throughout the Old Testament period.

PERSIA

The Persians lived in modern-day Iran, east of the Fertile Crescent. They conquered the Babylonians and supported the Israelites' return to the Promised Land. Old Testament texts convey Israelite gratitude for this support.

AFRICA

The ancient Israelites had some interaction with Africans outside of Egypt. Primarily, these would be the people of modern-day Ethiopia and Sudan. Throughout the early part of Israel's monarchy, these peoples controlled the throne of Egypt, and Israelite soldiers were hired by the Egyptians in their fights to win back the Nile valley.

SOUTHERN EUROPE

The most prominent civilizations in Europe with which Israel interacted were first Greece and then Rome. Greek thought influenced the ideas of some Old Testament books, such as the Wisdom of Solomon. However, Israel's primary interactions with Greece and Rome occurred after most of the Old

Testament books had been written, so there are few references to Greece and Rome in the Old Testament.

ISRAEL AND ITS SHIFTING BORDERS

Within Israel, the most fertile area and, therefore, the largest cities were in the plain between the coastal land and the hills that rose along the Jordan River. Jerusalem was the most important Israelite city, from the period of the monarchy on. Creating a map of ancient Israel, however, is quite difficult. Israel's borders changed throughout its history, depending on the strength of a given king or the power of other forces pressing upon Israel. Within Israel, tribal boundaries also had a degree of fluidity. Some, like Ephraim, were rather stable. Others migrated and even disappeared. For instance, the tribe of Dan first settled near the sea, but then it migrated to the northern-most area of the nation. Simeon appears to have been absorbed into the tribe of Judah. The primary reason for this fluctuation was the fact that Israel was at the mercy of greater national powers throughout its history.

In summary, because Israel was dependent on rainfall, the nation was not as prosperous or powerful as other nations in the Fertile Crescent. Greater powers often determined Israel's history. Along with conflict came trade, and with trade came a shared culture, shared ideas. This broad intellectual culture of the Fertile Crescent encompasses the whole Old Testament.

THE HISTORY OF THE BIBLE

WHEN WAS THE OLD TESTAMENT WRITTEN?

If we define "nation" as an independent, self-ruling government, then Israel was a nation from approximately 1020 BCE to 587 BCE.

Before 1020, there was a group that the Egyptians identified as "Israel," but they were not yet organized under a central government. In 587, the Babylonians destroyed the central government. After 538, Israel again appeared as a country, but, except for a brief period, other larger nations, such as Persia, Greece, and Rome, ruled Israel. The period from 1020–587 BCE is the period called the monarchy, because the central ruling agent was a king. If you remember no other dates related to the Bible, remember these, because they form the central time frame from which all biblical material proceeded. Let me explain.

Counting Backward

What year is it? The number you just thought of is a number counted forward from the date of the birth of Jesus. We call the calendar that we use the Gregorian calendar, because it was finalized by Pope Gregory XIII in 1582. In this Christian-based calendar, dates after the birth of Jesus are referred to as AD, which is an abbreviation for the Latin phrase *anno domini*, meaning "in the year of the Lord." Moreover, if we want to be picky, the AD should be placed before the year number. Let me give an example: John F. Kennedy became president in AD 1960, that is, in the year of the Lord, 1960 years (after Jesus' birth). According to the Gregorian calendar, years before the birth of Jesus are counted backwards, and are designated by the abbreviation BC, meaning "before Christ."

Modern biblical scholars use different abbreviations for these eras, however. Not all biblical scholars are Christian. This is especially true for the study of the Old Testament, since this is the sacred collection for Jews as well as Christians. Biblical scholars use a more neutral designation for years. The term "Common Era" or "CE" has come to replace the more confessional "AD," while BCE ("Before the Common Era") replaces BC ("Before Christ"). As an introduction to the academic study of the Bible, this textbook uses these more standard abbreviations.

The events in the Old Testament occurred before the birth of Jesus. For instance, Alexander the Great, a Greek general, defeated the Persians 333 years before the birth of Jesus, so this date is referred to as 333 BCE. The city of Jerusalem was conquered by the Babylonians 587 years before the birth of Christ, that is, in 587 BCE. So in BCE, or backwards time, 587 comes *before* 333. Most of the dates in this book will be in "backwards time," that is, they will be "BCE," so try not to get confused.

First, Israelite histories are all told with the reality of the nation as a starting point. There never would have been a history of Israel unless there was a nation of Israel. Once that nation became established, the people began to reflect on what events in the past had been particularly important for their emergence.

Second, the nation was ultimately destroyed by the Babylonians. The Israelites were forced to live in exile, and, even after they returned to the land, their political independence remained a thing of the past. The Israelites rethought their history and preserved their literature in light of these events. Some texts show the marks of people struggling with the question of why such disaster befell them. Other literature appears to be the result of an attempt to preserve and revitalize old traditions. Still other literature looks for the hope of some future glory, either in this world or the next.

Biblical texts presume that the reader knows the history of Israel. Prophets will refer obliquely to past events, knowing that their audience understands the allusion. If I said to you today, "Go, look at Pearl Harbor. Did its floating army save it?," it would be much the same as Jeremiah telling the people of Judah to look at Shiloh if they want to know what the fate of

Jerusalem will be (Jer 7:12). Modern readers have to work to catch up with the ancient audience.

Each piece of literature that is preserved in the Old Testament has its own literary history. Some pieces were written during the monarchy. Some were written during the Exile, some during the Persian period, and so on. Some contain accounts preserved in an oral tradition that stretches back before there was a monarchy. Most biblical texts, however, were rewritten and edited all through Israel's history.

Let me give an example from the book of Genesis. There were probably many oral traditions about the founders of the tribes that were eventually written down. Perhaps they were retold at sacred festivals throughout the land. The basic outline of Genesis probably attained a written shape during the united monarchy. However, this written account was reworked, first after the split of the two kingdoms, again when the northern kingdom fell, and yet again during the exile. It was not until the Persian period that the book reached a form similar to what is preserved in the Bible. This reflects common practice at this time. In the ancient Near East, people who wrote books expected that future scribes would rework the material to keep it alive and make sure it continued to address the needs and concerns of the people. We see this in Mesopotamia, just as we see it in the Bible.

How Did We Get a Bible?

Have you ever wandered through the Bible section at a bookstore? If you have, you may have noticed how many different Bibles there are. Some of the differences in these Bibles are purely cosmetic; a Bible bound with a fancy leather cover might not differ at all from a cheaper paperback version. What sometimes distinguishes these Bibles isn't the words of the Bible itself, but the notes that are provided by scholars to help people understand the texts that they are reading. (Always remember that the footnotes in a Bible are not part of the Bible itself; they are aids for the readers.)

Sometimes, however, the differences between Bibles on the bookstore shelf really do affect what is inside. If you look carefully, you will see, for instance, that some Bibles are called "Catholic Bibles," and some are identified as "Protestant"; Some say they contain the "Apocrypha," and others are referred to as "Jewish" Bibles. These differences don't come from modern needs but from ancient traditions about what texts constitute a Bible.

As we said earlier, the Bible is a collection of ancient texts (which today we call "books") that were considered to have some kind of religious

Scrolls and Books

Did you know that books were not "invented" until after Jesus was born? Instead, in ancient Israel, people wrote on "scrolls," which were long sheets of parchment (a form of paper made from reeds) or prepared leather. Scrolls were divided into columns, similar to pages, and wound around two sticks at either end. As a person read, he or she would unwind only one "page" or column at a time. After reading this column, she or he would roll to the next one.

If the scroll became too long, the parchment would tear easily, so scrolls were kept to a manageable length (usually less than thirty-five feet). This meant a book like Genesis would fit on one scroll. Exodus would be on another scroll, and so on. Sometimes really long books, such as Samuel, would have to take up two scrolls.

There was a traditional place to divide the material, and so now we have 1 Samuel and 2 Samuel, even though they really form one book. Other books were so short that they were combined with other books to form one scroll. For instance, there were twelve short prophetic books that made up the one scroll of the Minor Prophets.

When we talk about the "order" of biblical books (for example, Genesis "comes before" Exodus), this really only applies after books were invented and all of these texts were printed together. As long as there were scrolls, their order was a bit more fluid. Once books were created, however, the order of biblical books, and therefore the canon, became more fixed.

The Isaiah Scroll, dated to approximately 100 BCE, is the longest and oldest of the Dead Sea Scrolls found in the caves of Qumran in the 1940s. Scrolls containing almost every book of the Old Testament were found in Qumran.

authority by the ancient communities who collected them. The term *canon*, which originally meant "rule," is sometimes used to refer to these texts. Thus canon is a term used to connote that these particular texts have religious authority.

The books were first used individually at temple and synagogue services for prayer and to teach people about God. The process of canonization entailed gathering groups of these sacred texts together under various categories. A book such as Proverbs, for instance, would have been used for quite a while before it became part of a canon collected at a later date.

The process of collecting these different books started about 2400 years ago, when the ancient Israelites first started referring to certain books as "the torah." This word, which often is translated "law," really means something more like "teaching." The torah for Jews is the collection that Christians call the Pentateuch, and it includes all the laws that have formed the basis for Judaism. The torah forms the core of every Bible everywhere. Its formation was supplemented over the next 600 years by other groups of books that were later viewed as sacred. The Old Testament's formation occurred in at least three distinct stages: the Pentateuch or *torah* came together around 400 BCE; the Prophets, which included some historical books, around 200 BCE; and the Writings, which contain many different kinds of books, including the Psalms, perhaps as late as 100 CE.

These stages reflect the traditions of Jews living in and around what is today the modern country of Israel. However, there were large Jewish populations living in Egypt, Babylon, Greece, and Rome, from perhaps as early as 700 BCE. Over time, these communities could not read or understand Hebrew. The Jews living in Alexandria, Egypt, for instance, only knew Greek. They began translating the Bible into their own language, just as we do today. They arranged this collection differently, dividing the books into four categories: the Pentateuch, History, Wisdom, and Prophecy. They also continued to add books to the collection of their Bible, which the Jewish communities in Judea did not include.

Christianity took hold among Greek-speaking communities, so the Bible that Christians used from the beginning was the longer collection of these Greek-speaking Jews. Their collection was called the Septuagint, to which Christians eventually added the books of the New Testament. This Bible was the basis for Jerome's official translation of the Bible into Latin, called the Vulgate. Meanwhile, Jews had adopted the smaller Israelite collection called the Hebrew Bible Thus, the Christian Old Testament and the Jewish Bible ended up being not exactly the same.

Much later, in the late Middle Ages, there was a movement among some Christians to officially reform the Old Testament so that it matched the Bible being used by the Jews living then. Martin Luther, who is the founder of the Protestant Reformation, was one of these Christians. One of his "reforms" was to exclude the extra books in the Christian Old Testament from the canon. He called the extra books, which are in the Septuagint but not in the Hebrew Bible, the Apocrypha, and he maintained that they had religious value, but not religious authority. Protestant churches, even those not founded by Luther, follow him on this idea.

The result of this abbreviated history is what we have today:

▸ A Jewish Bible contains only the Old Testament, which Jews call the Tanakh or Hebrew Bible, arranged in three sections (Torah or Law, Nevi'im or Prophets, and Ketuvim or Writings).

▸ The Protestant Bible has the Old and New Testaments and sometimes a section called the Apocrypha. The Old Testament has four sections (Law, History, Wisdom, and Prophecy) but only contains the books in the Hebrew Bible.

> ❯ Catholic and eastern Orthodox Bibles have Old and New Testaments but never a section called the Apocrypha. The Old Testament has four sections (Law, History, Wisdom, and Prophecy), containing all of the books of the Septuagint.

This process demonstrates an important principle. How did churches know what books to put in the Bible? It wasn't because there was some committee in charge, which drew up lists and rules. It wasn't because there were some people who "picked" only books with which they agreed or that had the same ideas and themes. These collections grew up among people who read them in the synagogue and the church. They were the books people turned to again and again, because they could hear God's word in them. Early Christian writers, such as Augustine, also tell us that these were the books read by Christian churches "everywhere," that is, not just in Rome or in some powerful place, but also in little towns in North Africa, small communities in modern-day Turkey, and churches in France and Spain.

Didn't God Write the Bible?

Sometimes people will claim that to be a "Christian" means that you must believe that everything the Bible says is true. It is an attractive position, isn't it? Either the Bible is true, or it's not! And we know what "truth" is: it means that the text tells us *exactly what happened.* How much simpler could it be? Many Christian churches, however, including the Catholic Church, would say there are many problems with this view, beginning with how we define the notion of "truth."

Let me give you an obvious example. In Psalm 23, we read: "The Lord is my shepherd. I shall not want. He makes me lie down in green pastures." Well, that can't be literally true. First, God is not a physical shepherd; that statement is a metaphor (God is *like* a shepherd). And, I don't know about you, but I've never been made to "lie down in green pastures," although I do believe God leads and protects me. This is a silly example, because this is obviously a poem, full of metaphors and images, meant to be read poetically. The "truth" of Psalm 23 is not in its literal meaning, but in the truth of those metaphors. Therefore, the Catholic Church's first objection to a literalist interpretation is that it does not recognize all the different kinds of texts the Bible may contain.

One of the arguments that divide Christian denominations is the way that they answer the question, who wrote the Bible? While most Christians would

Focus on METHOD

Texts, Versions, and Translations

There is no single ancient copy of the Bible. In fact, until the last century, the oldest copy of the complete Hebrew Bible that we had dated from the fifteenth century. Archaeological discoveries of the past century, such as the Dead Sea Scrolls, have provided us with much earlier witnesses to the biblical texts, but these witnesses show that there was rarely a single version of a text in circulation.

Think about it. There were no printing presses in the ancient world. Texts were produced by hand. The scribes who copied the texts were also those who interpreted the text. They had the freedom to adapt the text if they felt it would make more sense to their audience, or if they had variant traditions among which they had to decide. Scribes were not human copy machines.

One of the first things that biblical scholars do when they confront a biblical text is to consider the different ancient witnesses to that text. This is called textual criticism. It used to be that text critics sought the "original form" of the text, but text critics today are more interested in uncovering the various witnesses to a pericope (or section of the text). Sometimes they will conclude that one version is "older" than another, but this does not necessarily mean that the older version is more authoritative.

You will not be doing text criticism, since most of you probably do not know Hebrew, Greek, Aramaic, Syriac, Latin, and so on. However, you can take into account various English translations of the Bible. The translation of the Bible into contemporary languages became common with the Protestant Reformation. Luther had the Bible translated into German; Catholics translated the Bible into English, producing the Douay-Rheims version in 1609. Today's translations, such as the New Revised Standard Version (NRSV), New English Bible (NEB), and the New American Bible (NAB), take into account the many manuscript discoveries of the past century. Translations in this textbook are taken from the NRSV.

Students who do not know Hebrew can compare various English translations. By taking note when the translations are widely different, students can recognize places where the Hebrew text is unclear. Some English versions will provide footnotes that tell the reader when the Hebrew is uncertain or when the Septuagint has a different reading, and so on.

say that texts in the Bible were written by both a human and a divine author, the model for how this interaction played out can differ significantly. Some Christians hold to a model of divine dictation: God told the human author what to write. Others think of God's role more as an object for reflection than as an active agent in writing. Each religious tradition deserves careful study to understand how its view of human-divine authorship, or inspiration, fits in with its views on creation, natural reason, and so on. Obviously, there is neither time nor space to do that here. What I can provide, however, is the model that informs my reading as a Catholic biblical scholar. In many ways, it will be compatible with many Protestant and Jewish understandings of inspiration.

The question of how to read the Bible stems in part from the question of the authorship of the Bible. When we use the word *author* today, we usually mean the person who actually took up pen and paper (or computer and printer) and physically, purposefully, wrote the words we read. If we restrict the word *author* in this way, then God did not write the Bible, because God did not physically come to earth and write. But Jews and Christians would say that God is an "author" of the Bible. How can this be?

The Christian discussion of biblical authorship started early in church history when people wrote in Latin. The Latin word for *author* can mean the actual physical writer, but it can also mean something like "the authorizing agent"; in fact, it is at the root of the word *authority*. In this broader sense, the author is the person who guarantees the "authenticity" of the material.

The Bible, then, has levels of authorship: the physical, human author and the divine author who authorizes the material. Most churches throughout the world believe that the Bible is the product of the interaction of divine and human authors. *Inspiration* is a term used to express the fact that the writing of biblical texts entailed an interaction of divine and human author. In summary, the canon (the fixed list of sacred scripture) is the list of those texts which were divinely inspired (had a human and divine author).

So why do churches disagree so much about the Bible? For instance, why do some Christian denominations insist that the Bible's account of creation contradicts views of evolution, while other churches find the accounts compatible? The discord happens because churches disagree on how human and divine authors interact. More to the point, they do not all agree that human authors act as independent, autonomous writers in the process of producing texts.

Let me give you a specific example. The Catholic Church believes that the human authors of the biblical texts act as any human author would in producing the texts. The theological reasons for this teaching are complex but profound. To oversimplify, Catholics believe that God, who has created the world, can use that creation as a vehicle for divine revelation. Put simply, Catholics define "revelation" as God's self-disclosure to humanity. Scripture is one primary way we come to know about God; that is, it is a primary source of revelation. People also come to know something about God by observing God's created world. Humans are part of that creation and, therefore, can reveal something about God through their own nature. Human authors who have written the biblical texts do so as products of God's creation. As such, God does not have to somehow "fix up" or obliterate human nature, which was created by God, in order for scripture to contain revelation.

Some people say that the Bible is inerrant, that is, "free from error". Fundamentalist Christians would say that everything in the Bible is inerrant; so if the Bible says that the world was created in seven days, they would interpret that to mean that it was created in seven calendar days. Catholic teaching is purposefully worded differently. Catholic teaching states that the Bible is inerrant in matters of "salvation." This means that, when the Bible communicates things that people need to know to live a life that leads to salvation, they can count on the fact that the Bible contains no error. For example, Catholics would contend that salvation does not depend on how long it took the world to be created, but that it does depend on knowing that God is the sole creator, that the process of creation has a purpose and design, and that what God created is good.

Let me summarize using the terms you have learned here: the word *Revelation* describes God's act of imparting true knowledge about the divine nature. One way we know God's revelation is through texts written by humans who have been divinely inspired so that what they say really can lead us to salvation. The divinely inspired texts form the canon. Christians call this canon the Bible or Scriptures.

The Bible in the CHRISTIAN TRADITION

Biblical Authority

Perhaps one of the biggest things that divide Christian denominations is their view of the Bible. For example, evangelical Christians have a very precise definition of biblical inerrancy, while Roman Catholics view inerrancy as applicable only to those matters that affect faith and salvation. Moreover, although Protestant churches do have a tradition of interpreting the Scriptures, this tradition does not have the same authority as it does within Roman Catholicism or Orthodox Christianity.

Often people misunderstand the role of Tradition within the Roman Catholic Church. For Catholics, Tradition and Scripture go hand in hand, as two witnesses to the same God and the same revelation. Both are authoritative. Scripture is maintained as an independent witness to God's revelation, apart from Tradition.

The Catholic Church provides guidance in understanding the theological meaning of the sacred Scriptures. This guidance comes through the Church's passing on of its Tradition—its doctrines, teachings, and worship. The Church's magisterium, comprised of the world's bishops together with the pope, has the task of "giving an authentic interpretation of the Word of God, whether in its written form or in the form of Tradition" (CCC, 85). This is to ensure that the faith handed down by the Apostles since the time of Jesus is preserved, passed on, and understood from age to age. But the magisterium has provided a definitive interpretation of very few Old Testament texts. Since the 1940s the magisterium has affirmed and promoted the use of modern methods of biblical scholarship as an aid in interpreting the Scriptures.

What does that mean for Catholics when they read Scripture? It means that they use all of the same tools to understand the Bible as do many other Protestants, Jews, and secular biblical scholars.

How Should We Interpret Scripture?

If human authors acted as human authors when creating the text, then we must use every means available to us to understand that text within its historical-cultural context. There are many things that complicate our ability to understand these texts. Remember our example from Genesis 6:1–4, with which we started this chapter? Modern readers have to learn many things in order to make sense of that story. But even when we think we know what is going on in a story, we may be missing things that would have been obvious to the first readers of the text.

The fact is that some of the Bible can be quite puzzling to modern ears. We may not understand the circumstances in which the texts were written or the meaning originally intended by the authors. Some of the material may seem contradictory. The actions of biblical characters may appear immoral if we do not learn about their laws. We may not recognize a metaphor if we don't understand biblical literature. These are just some of the potential problems.

These texts were written long ago, in a culture quite unlike ours and in a foreign language. To understand the text, we must "translate" it, not just the words but also the images and ideas. In a literal sense, the Bible *has* been translated from the Hebrew and Greek into a number of English versions. But we are speaking here of a different kind of translation—translation aimed at discovering the original intent of an author in writing a given scriptural text.

Scripture scholars do much of that "translation" for us—not just the obvious kind, from the ancient Hebrew and Greek to modern languages, but the more challenging kind that deals with what the authors really meant. Scholars delve into the history, archaeology, literary forms, and culture surrounding the development of the texts to help us understand their intended meanings. Of course, even the best Scripture scholars disagree on certain findings and theories, and many questions are still open to debate (such as when a given scriptural text was written or who wrote it). However, by and large, biblical scholarship has shed great light on a modern understanding of the Bible.

Modern Methods of Biblical Interpretation

Scripture scholars ask a variety of questions about the biblical text in order to understand it better. We call these kinds of questions "methods" of biblical interpretation. The information sought by each method is distinct, and scholars learn to match the method to the kind of information that they want to investigate. Here are a few examples:

▶ Source criticism looks for evidence that an author has used written sources to compose his or her work.

▶ Form criticism originally investigated vestiges of oral traditions in the text.

▶ Redaction criticism focuses on the way the author has put earlier material together.

▶ Literary criticism highlights the artistry of the written text.

▶ Contextual criticism recognizes the importance of the reader's cultural context in interpretations of the Bible.

We will examine methods more closely as we proceed through the biblical text.

How Is the Textbook Arranged?

This book is designed to help you read the Bible. One way it helps is by supplying the historical and literary context of the material in the Old Testament. Another way is to provide examples of ways to read the Old Testament carefully.

Each chapter of this book corresponds to a section of the Bible, sometimes to a single book, sometimes to texts that have a common purpose. Each chapter begins by giving you some general information that will help your own reading of that material. Sometimes that information will be historical information, sometimes a general overview of a book, but often it will be "cultural" information. In other words, I will explain why people in the Bible act like they do, how they lived their lives, and what they expected from a good story, poem, or history.

After this general information, I will take some sample texts and provide close readings, which apply the general information to specific material. These close readings have the following format:

▶ Each reading starts with a **brief introduction** to the passage that often poses a question or issue for you to think about.

▶ Then a section called **"In Case You Were Wondering"** highlights words or customs that may be unfamiliar to you.

> ❯ Next, you **read the biblical passage**.

> ❯ Questions then follow in a section titled **"Looking Closely at the Text"** that will help you focus on important details of the text.

> ❯ Finally, there is a **discussion of the text,** either highlighting the issues you were to consider or suggesting ways you could address the questions posed.

The Old Testament is so long that one textbook obviously cannot cover all the material, but I hope to provide you with a model you can use to try out your own skills at reading other parts of the Bible. Among the sample passages are some of the texts of the Bible that have had the most influence on many readers.

Sometimes there are ancillary topics that can be of interest to students but that are not strictly necessary for understanding the text. These issues are addressed in sidebars. Each chapter also includes a focus on a particular method of biblical interpretation. By studying these along the way, you will develop many reading skills. Last, some students want to better understand how different traditions and theological ideas have developed within Christianity. Each chapter will have a section devoted to a different theological issue or interpretive tradition.

This textbook is designed to help you "study" the Bible. It is an introduction to the academic study of the Bible; it assumes that most students are not majoring in religion or theology. The text does not presume that all its readers are Christian, but it helps explain what Christians believe about the Bible. Your study of the Bible should help you understand how the Bible is read and used in various communities, including the academic community.

FOR REVIEW

1. Why is it important to know the names and locations of the major countries in the Fertile Crescent?

2. What is the Levant?

3. Why is it difficult to create a map of ancient Israel?

4. What affected the location of ancient cities?

5. What is the central time frame of Israel's history, and why?

6. Why is the exile important for the way the Israelites told their history?

7. Why did Israelite scribes rewrite and rework earlier material?

8. What are differences between Jewish, Catholic, and Protestant Old Testaments? Why are the versions different?

9. What do Catholics mean by "inerrant"? How does it differ from a Fundamentalist Christian definition?

FOR FURTHER READING

In this section I will list a few resources that are geared to nonscholars. You can use these resources to learn more about a given topic or as the start to a research project.

Because this is an introductory chapter, I first want to list a few general resources that you can use for a variety of topics. In subsequent chapters, I will list resources for that particular topic.

GENERAL RESOURCES

There are a number of one-volume commentaries on the Bible. A commentary will follow the biblical text verse by verse, providing information on the text. One that I have had my students use is *The Collegeville Bible Commentary,* edited by Diane Bergant (Collegeville, MN: Liturgical Press, 1992). However, your instructor may have other suggestions.

There are also some very good Bible dictionaries available. One of the best is *The Anchor Bible Dictionary,* edited by David Noel Freedman (New York: Doubleday, 1992). It lists entries alphabetically.

You may also want to know more about different methods of biblical interpretation; you'll see that there is a section on this in each of the following chapters. There are all kinds of guides to biblical interpretation. Fortress Press has a series of small books, each one dedicated to a different method of interpretation; the series is titled "Guides to Biblical Scholarship." Two volumes that address contemporary developments of these methods are John Barton's *Reading the Old Testament* (rev. ed.; Louisville, KY: Westminster John Knox, 1996) and Steven L. McKenzie and Stephen R. Haynes's *To Each Its Own Meaning: An Introduction to Biblical Criticisms and Their Application* (rev. ed.; Louisville, KY: Westminster John Knox, 1999).

RESOURCES FOR CHAPTER 1

There are several excellent histories of ancient Israel. Two of the newest are *The Oxford History of the Biblical World,* edited by Michael D. Coogan (New York/Oxford: Oxford University Press, 1998) and *Ancient Israel: From Abraham to the Roman Destruction of the Temple,* edited by Hershel Shanks (rev. ed.; Upper Saddle River, NJ: Prentice Hall; Washington, DC: Biblical Archaeology Society, 1999). If you want to know more about the nations surrounding Israel, you may want to look at *Civilizations of the Ancient Near East,* edited by Jack M. Sasson (New York: Scribner's, 1995; reprinted by Peabody, MA: Hendrickson, 2000).

There are also many books that address issues of biblical theology. Each one will reflect the denominational context of their author. I have presented the Catholic view of inspiration as outlined in the document written by the Pontifical Biblical Commission, entitled "Interpretation of the Bible in the Church." You can find this online, but there is an edition by Joseph Fitzmyer that provides a commentary on this complex work (The Biblical Commission's Document *"The Interpretation of the Bible in the Church": Text and Commentary* [Subsidia Biblica 18; Rome: Pontifical Biblical Institute, 1995)]. There have also been a number of studies on the formation of the canon. You might want to look at *The Canon Debate,* edited by Lee M. McDonald and James A. Sanders (Peabody, MA: Hendrickson, 2002).

2 THE PATRIARCHS AND MATRIARCHS

Your wife Sarah shall bear you a son, and you shall name him Isaac.
I will establish my covenant with him as an everlasting covenant
for his offspring after him.
(Gen 17:19)

CHAPTER OVERVIEW

The following chapters will have two major parts. First, they will present background material to help you read the Bible. Second, they will guide you through close readings of some important texts.

In this chapter we will look at the stories of the patriarchs and matriarchs. To help us understand these stories, the first part of the chapter will provide the following:

▶ An overview of the book of Genesis, including a definition of patriarchs and matriarchs

▶ An examination of the history behind the text, the historical evidence for the patriarchs and matriarchs, and the history of the text's production

▶ A discussion of the social and political relationships of the time as seen through the lens of marriage

The second part of the chapter will examine key texts about Abraham, Isaac, and Jacob, including the covenants God makes with them and their families.

Genesis at a Glance

The Bible begins with the book of Genesis. *Genesis* is an ancient Greek word for the origin or birth of something; not surprisingly, Genesis is all about beginnings: the origin of the world, the human race, national groups, and the people of Israel. The book of Genesis can be divided up into three sections.

> Genesis 1—11 contains Creation accounts, stories of how God created the world, and how humanity was divided into national groups. This section is also called the Primeval History.

> Genesis 12—36 plus chapter 38 tells the story of the founding fathers and mothers of the nation of Israel. It also explains how other nations around Israel came to be.

> Genesis 37, 39—50 focuses on the story of Joseph, one of the founders of Israel who was sold into slavery but, through God's help, saved his people from starvation.

Each of these sections has its own literary style.

There are a couple of reasons why I do not start with the creation stories. First, although Genesis 1—11 sets the world stage on which the history of Israel plays out, it presumes that the reader already understands the history and culture of ancient Israel. Even medieval theologians did not recommend starting one's study of the Bible there. Second, I have found that my students are better able to understand Israelite history and society by starting at Genesis 12. The background knowledge that Genesis 12 presents helps them understand the subsequent biblical texts. Third, I have found that fewer people have strong opinions about the Abraham material than they do about the creation accounts. Their objectivity allows them to be more open to considering various ways to think about the text. Fourth, the creation material, being the result of speculative thought, is more like the wisdom material than the narratives of the patriarchs. Therefore, this textbook will discuss the creation narratives in the context of the wisdom material.

Your instructor, however, may want to start with the creation material, and that is fine. This textbook is adaptable to a variety of uses. So if you're asked to read material from the chapter dealing with the wisdom material, don't panic that you won't understand it. Those sections were written to stand on their own.

These three parts have been woven together to form the first book of the Bible, Genesis, which tells the history of the world from creation, through the period of the patriarchs and matriarchs. The book closes with the ancestors of the nation residing not in the land God promises to Abraham but in Egypt.

Who Are the Patriarchs and Matriarchs?

The patriarchs and matriarchs are the founding fathers and mothers of the tribes of Israel. Although some people tend to think of the twelve tribes of Israel as counties or states, a tribe is actually a kinship group or large family. It consists of all the people who can trace their family tree back to some common ancestor. In the case of the Bible, each of the tribes is named for one of these ancestors. The portrayals of the ancestors embody the author's understanding of that group's character.

According to Genesis, all of the patriarchs were related. Abraham was the first patriarch, and he married Sarah. Their first son, Isaac, married Rebekah. Their second son, Jacob, had several wives, who gave birth to twelve sons and at least one daughter. Jacob's name is eventually changed to Israel, and so he is the patriarch of the nation of Israel. One of his sons, Joseph, has two more sons, and together these various offspring of Jacob became the founding fathers of the twelve tribes of Israel. They were called by their god to possess a particular land, sometimes referred to as the Promised Land. This land is also known as Canaan, since the Canaanites controlled the area before the nation of Israel arose. The geographical name for the area is the Levant, a term that I will use in this textbook

---

A Family Tree

```
              by Hagar----   ----Abraham----------by Sarah
         Ishmael                           Isaac-----------by Rebekah
                                              Esau
              by Leah (& Zilpah)----  ----------Jacob-----------------by Rachel (& Bilhah)
         Reuben, Simeon, Levi, Judah, Issachar,          Dan, Naphtali, Benjamin
            Zebulun, Gad, Asher, Dinah                   Joseph (Manasseh, Ephraim)
```

The Story behind the Story

When Did the Patriarchs and Matriarchs Live?

It is not clear when the patriarchs and matriarchs lived. These are accounts of people who built no buildings and owned no land, except for one burial plot. There is no way to find evidence of any individual figure in the text.

Many scholars agree that the final author has set the stories sometime around 2100–1700 BCE. Archaeologically this is known as the Middle Bronze Period. Archives from the Fertile Crescent shed some light onto the general features of the world that the author imagines. During this period there was a general movement of peoples across the Fertile Crescent, especially among peoples living in Mesopotamia and the Levant. Abraham and Sarah's travels would not have been unusual at this time.

The Life of Tribal Nomads

Societies in the Fertile Crescent consisted of both nomads and city dwellers. Nomads in the time of Abraham and Jacob followed their flocks and herds to various grazing spots, traveling as whole families accompanied by servants. While some nomads who lived in very dry deserts wandered continually, most nomads stayed close to the cities that depended on their flocks for meat and dairy products. These people are called semi-nomads. Some of the journeys of the patriarchs and matriarchs reflect this semi-nomadic lifestyle.

It is natural that nomadic groups defined who they were, not by where they lived, since this changed, but by family descent. Since group identity came from extended family relationships, family ties were often reinforced through marriage. Although people could marry outside of their own tribe, marriage within the tribe was preferred.

Tribal Religion

The religious life of the ancient Israelites, especially before the monarchy, was quite different than it is for modern Christians or Jews. The Israelites themselves portray the religious life of the patriarchs and matriarchs as something "old" and different from the religion of the period of the monarchy.

Who Do They Say That I Am?

The Book of Genesis uses a variety of names to refer to God. Some of these names go back to very ancient practices; a few can be found in pre-Israelite texts from the area. The two most common names are *Elohim* and *Yahweh*. The word *Elohim* is simply the word "god," although the Israelites used it like a name. When you see "God" in your Bible, you know that the Hebrew word is *Elohim*.

The second name, *Yahweh*, is used for God's proper name. Many Jews have a tradition that the divine name should not be pronounced. Instead, whenever the divine name occurs in a text, Jews will substitute the Hebrew word for "lord." Many Bibles respect this tradition, using the term "LORD" (with small capital letters) whenever the Hebrew text has *Yahweh*.

There is a third tradition when referring to God in this time period: "the God of Abraham, Isaac and Jacob." Here the word for "God" is not *Elohim*, but the shorter form *El*. This was a way to designate the family god. This family god protected the group, and, in return, they owed this god their sole allegiance.

At the time referred to in these texts, the Israelites did not think that Yahweh was the only god. They still believed that gods of other nations and families existed. They did believe, however, that they should worship Yahweh alone.

ANGELS AND GOD

One of the distinct elements in these narratives of Israel's early history is the appearance of what today we might call angels. Early Israelite texts do not clearly distinguish between the appearance of God and the appearance of an angel. Were angels understood as heavenly creatures who served God? Were they minor deities? Were they manifestations of the one God on earth? The texts in Genesis are not clear on this point. Later Israelite texts will have a more developed understanding of angels.

SACRIFICE, ALTARS, AND STONES

Most religious activity in the time of the patriarchs and matriarchs took place within the family. Families and clans would gather at places sacred to their group. Sometimes an ancestor had set up a special stone to mark the place, as Jacob does in Genesis 35:9–15. At other places an ancestor had used earth and stone to build an altar at a sacred place. These altars were not like those in a modern church. An altar was a place for offerings, especially those offerings which were burnt as a symbol of their ascent to God in heaven. Incense was burnt on small incense altars, but the large altars of earth and stone were for animal sacrifices. Some of these altars became sites for later temples. In addition, nomads would carry portable shrines with them. These shrines included "household gods," symbols of the god(s) that the family worshipped.

WHEN WERE THESE STORIES WRITTEN DOWN?

No one has ever assumed that the stories of the patriarchs were written down soon after their lifetime. Throughout much of history Christian and Jewish scholars assumed that Moses had written the whole Pentateuch. This would mean that the stories of the patriarchs and matriarchs would have been written

Pictured are the pillars of stone at the Canaanite "High Place" in Gezer, a city located close to the road from Egypt to Mesopotamia. Gezer was conquered by Joshua in the twelfth century BCE (Josh 16:10).

Shown here is a bronze figurine of Baal, perhaps the most notable of the Canaanite gods and goddesses. The name means "lord."

down at least 450 years after the events they described. As early as the Middle Ages, however, the assumption of Mosaic authorship began to be questioned, primarily because of the many anachronisms found there.

Today biblical scholars recognize that the production of a complex work such as the Pentateuch required a settled population able to support the work of ancient authors called *scribes*. This means that the accounts contained in the book of Genesis could not have been written down until the period of the monarchy at the earliest.

ORAL STORIES, WRITTEN NARRATIVES

This does not mean that whoever wrote Genesis just made it all up. Nomadic people and settled societies for whom formal education is sparse, even today, maintain oral histories of their families. The book of Genesis contains written versions of oral traditions from different groups and families. These oral traditions were gathered together to form larger cycles of material.

Canaanite Religion

Religion is always influenced by culture. The images that people use to describe God, the way that people worship and pray, the music and art that they produce to honor God reflect their cultural context. This was as true for the ancient Israelites as it is today.

The religion of the Canaanites had a significant impact on the religious language of Israel. Sometimes Israelites borrowed the music or images of the Canaanites and adapted them to address Yahweh. Other times they refuted the Canaanites' religious language. Biblical scholars have found that understanding Canaanite religion helps us understand the Bible.

Most of our knowledge of Canaanite religion (more properly called West Semitic religion, since it encompasses many groups in that area) comes from the ancient city of Ugarit. Ugarit was located in modern-day Lebanon and was destroyed around 1200 BCE. When the site was discovered in 1928, archaeologists found many texts, including myths.

The Ugaritic gods resembled a royal family and its court. There were parents and children, rulers and servants, reflecting both social and celestial hierarchies. The gods explicitly mentioned in the Bible include the following:

- **El was the head god who ruled and judged. He sat on a throne and presided over a divine council.**

- **Asherah was El's consort. She fed the wild animals of the steppe.**

- **Ashtart was a young goddess who may have been El's daughter. She is associated with fertility. (There was also a similarly named male god, but most references to Ashtart in the Bible are to this goddess.)**

- **Baal is actually a title that can be ascribed to many male Canaanite gods. The biblical references to Baal refer to a young storm god and warrior. His weapons included the thunderbolt. Because storms were essential for agriculture, he is associated with fertility.**

- **Anat appears only in place names in the Bible, but she was a very important Canaanite goddess, known primarily for her warrior attributes.**

As Israelite culture became more urban, these cycles were written down. The writing process did not occur all at once. Instead, scribes wrote portions of these stories as new situations in Israel's history called for different elements to be highlighted. Scholars today recognize at least four distinct layers of writing in the Pentateuch. Three of these are seen in Genesis. The fourth is in the book of Deuteronomy.

These written traditions are called *sources*. They were used by the final author in composing the book of Genesis:

❯ The **Yahwist** (abbreviated "J") wrote in the south during the monarchy, when Israel was ruled by a king. This source provided a unified history for the twelve tribes. He's called the "Yahwist" because he has the patriarchs and matriarchs refer to God as Yahweh.

Source Criticism

If you read Genesis 12—22, you may begin to notice that rather than a continuous narrative, the Abraham cycle is episodic and disjointed. Some anomalies are rather glaring, such as these:

• There are three stories in which one of the patriarchs claims that his wife is his sister, placing her sexual purity at risk.
• In the story of the banishment of Hagar and Ishmael (Gen 21:15–16), the boy appears to be an infant or a toddler. However, according to the chronology of the text, he is well over fourteen years old.
• In Genesis 6:3 God limits human life to 120 years, but Abraham lives to 175 (Gen 25:17) and Sarah to 127 (Gen 23:1).

Source criticism is a method that provides a model for imagining the writing process that led to the Pentateuch and other biblical books as we now have them. Using source criticism, many theories and models have been developed for understanding the anomalies and discrepancies within Genesis.

One of the better scholarly theories imagines the author of the Pentateuch relying on multiple sources when compiling the books. Archaeological discoveries have provided evidence that it was common practice for authors to freely use and adapt earlier material. It was a way of showing respect for earlier scribes.

By the end of the nineteenth century, the four-source theory was well established. Julius Wellhausen published the most influential version of this model, using sociological theories of religious development in addition to literary cues. Here are some of Wellhausen's features of each of the sources:

	Yahwist	Elohist	Deuteronomist	Priestly Writer
Date	United Monarchy	Divided Monarchy	Reign of Josiah (Judah alone)	End of the Exile
Place	Southern Kingdom	Northern Kingdom	Northern Kingdom	Judah
Divine Name	Uses *Yahweh* throughout the Pentateuch.	*Elohim* used exclusively until the divine name is introduced in Exodus.	Not applicable	*Elohim* used exclusively until the divine name is introduced in Exodus.
Religious Features	Sacrifice is offered in different locations. Priests and heads of household offered sacrifices.	Sacrifice is offered in different locations. Priests and heads of household offered sacrifices.	Only the Levites can make sacrifices in the one place God chooses.	Only the offspring of Aaron can make sacrifices. A single place of sacrifice is presumed.
Literary Features	Lively narrative and anthropomorphic view of God.	Lively narrative and anthropomorphic view of God.	Sermonic, with characteristic phrases.	Preserves traditions, such as genealogies, precise locations, ages, and so on. Regal view of God.

Try to determine the source of a few passages in Genesis. Start with the examples of problematic passages listed above or with the story of Noah and the flood. Color-code each paragraph based on the divine name that it uses. Then read the paragraphs of like color in order. If you do any of these exercises, think about what this method of biblical interpretation is best used for. What questions about the text does it answer? What questions still remain?

▶ The **Elohist** (abbreviated "E") added material to J after the nation of Israel split in two. The Elohist wrote from the perspective of the northern kingdom. He is called the "Elohist" because the patriarchs and matriarchs usually call God "Elohim." Within the biblical texts it is sometimes impossible to distinguish between the Yahwist and the Elohist sources; this material is abbreviated "JE."

▶ The **Deuteronomist** (abbreviated "D") wrote toward the end of the monarchy. This source is called the "Deuteronomist" because it is found primarily in the book of Deuteronomy. It focuses on God's covenant mediated through Moses.

▶ The **Priestly Writer** (abbreviated "P") wrote at the end of the Babylonian Exile. The Priestly Writer preserves traditions that might have been lost during the exile, especially those associated with priestly groups

A *redactor*, or final editor, put all of these written sources together to form the Pentateuch. Sometimes it looks as if this redactor simply cut and pasted texts together; for instance, there are places where different stories contradict each other. Sometimes stories are repeated, and sometimes there are gaps that are hard to fill. When we look at the final form of the book, however, we can see that this final scribe had a plan in mind. If you read other ancient texts from the Fertile Crescent, you would see that repetition and gaps did not bother ancient readers as they do modern readers.

In summary, the book of Genesis was put together from various written sources and oral traditions. A final author wove them together around 400 BCE to create the book we now call Genesis.

Other Views of the Sources

Currently, Wellhausen's four-source model is being hotly debated. No, it is not because biblical scholars reject the idea that ancient authors used sources, but because they question whether "four" sources is overly simplistic. In addition, they wonder about the date and provenance of the sources.

In the past 110 years, the presence and identity of D and P have remained firm. These sources have very distinct language and literary style. They each have a consistent theology. They probably represent the work of schools of thought rather than the production of a single literary genius. Within each source there is use and development of earlier material.

One of the big questions for D is its extent and date. Is D limited to the book of Deuteronomy or can it be found in other parts of the Pentateuch? Did D redact the whole Pentateuch? What is the relationship between D and the history that follows in Joshua, Judges, Samuel, and Kings?

The date of P is also a major issue for source critics. Is it the presentation of an ideal Israel from the Restoration Period or of the laws of the priests of the monarchy? Is P the redactor of the Pentateuch or simply another source used by the final redactor?

The material outside of D and P does not show the same cohesion. Can this material be neatly divided up into two separate sources (J and E), or does it represent a much more complex accretion of various traditions over time? Was this material the early base which influenced D and P, or was it a series of late traditions added to a D and/or P base?

These questions are too complex to address in this course, but they do reiterate that source critics are trying to come up with the best model to understand the production of a complex text, such as the Pentateuch.

The World of Genesis 12–50

When we think about people in our past, such as the pilgrims, we have certain visual images already in place: the big buckle and tall black hats of the men, the plain dress and apron of the women. By the time my children were in kindergarten, they could recognize a pilgrim. If they watched a television special about the pilgrims, even if it was a cartoon, they expected a certain historical setting. The program would not have to describe or explain these elements.

The Israelites also had a traditional way to portray the background of the patriarchs and matriarchs. The "background" of these stories contains certain elements the writers could assume that readers would understand. Today, however, new readers often do not know much about the historical setting of the patriarchs and matriarchs. We need to explore that background in order to understand the accounts better.

The Family

The stories of the patriarchs and matriarchs are essentially the accounts of one family. But when they refer to the "family," they mean something different than we do. Many misunderstandings of Genesis can arise without a basic understanding of the Israelite family.

How Many Wives Did Abraham Have!?

One of the first things that strike students as odd is the fact that the patriarchs often had more than one wife at a time. This custom is called *polygamy*. Additionally, we hear about the patriarchs sleeping with slave women owned by their wives and keeping "concubines." The following chart illustrates the issue:

Patriarch	Wife/Wives	Concubines/Slaves
Abraham	Sarah	Hagar
		Keturah (Gen 25:1)
Isaac	Rebekah	
Jacob	Leah	Bilhah
	Rachel	Zilpah

Each of these women (except Keturah) is a matriarch, that is, the mother of a founding father, even the concubines.

Israelites accepted polygamy for men. They saw it as a just practice, given their economic system. Families dependent on agriculture needed to have many children, especially sons, in order for the family to survive. Children worked the land. In addition, only about one in every four children born would live to adulthood. Disease, accidents, plagues, and other such disasters claimed the rest. Moreover, many women died during pregnancy and childbirth. If a man hoped to have an adult son who would take over the family farm, he had to increase his chances with multiple wives.

Women were protected by this practice. Since women could not own property, and only landowners had full rights of citizenship, women living alone were unprotected members of society, vulnerable to violence, and with few rights under the law. The family unit protected women, and polygamy minimized the presence of unprotected women in ancient society.

There were two kinds of wives in ancient Israel, based on the economic standing of the woman's family: a full wife and a concubine. Let me describe each. If a young man came from a landowning family, his family would usually arrange for his marriage with the daughter of another landowning family. The future husband or his family would pay a "bride price" to the girl's father. The girl's father would provide her with a dowry that was hers if her husband ever divorced her. This exchange of "bride price" and dowry constituted a contractual agreement that served as a legally binding "betrothal" or engagement.

Girls were ideally married in early puberty, that is, around eleven or twelve years of age. If a female survived to age twenty, she would have been married for eight or nine years and would have had up to six children. If she had a son who survived to adulthood, he would be guaranteed to inherit the father's property. This son would also be the legal guardian of his mother, if his father died. Marriages were economic and social units that united families. They were not usually based on love or attraction, although certainly love could develop.

The second type of wife was a concubine. A concubine was *not* a prostitute. A concubine was a wife who came from a significantly lower status. Sometimes her status was lower because her father was not a landowner. However, lower status also defined a woman who had been divorced, sexually assaulted, or was an orphan. A prospective husband did not have to pay a bride price for a concubine. She had no dowry, and her sons were not automatically legal heirs of their father. However, a man could make her son an heir through adoption. Men married concubines for various reasons for example—to increase their chances to have sons or simply because they loved the woman.

POLITICS AND LAND OWNERSHIP

Landownership was the backbone of Israelite society, but only those men who could trace their ancestry back to one of the patriarchs could be landowners.

THOSE BORING "BEGATS"

If you picked up an older translation of the Bible, you would find long lists that followed the form "so-and-so begat so-and-so." Read Genesis 25:1–4 and 12–18, which comprise two lists of children. These lists of offspring are called genealogies, and at first glance they look like the most boring material in the Bible, filled with names that mean little to us today. While we may not be able to imagine people enjoying them, the genealogies carefully preserved the record of the core members of their society.

In Israel full citizenship was determined by landownership. Elders, that is, the oldest generation of landowners in the community, ran the cities. The eldest son in a family was usually the primary heir. Younger brothers could also inherit land, but the eldest son usually got the best land and the largest parcel. The genealogies are lists of primary landowners. Today when someone recreates his or her family tree, the goal is usually to list every relative. Israelite genealogies list primarily landowning offspring only. Notice first then that daughters were rarely listed, since they were not landowners. Daughters were only noted if they held some importance in their own right. Occasionally mothers were included, but usually only when their own families were so important that it enhanced the status of their sons. Sons of concubines were not listed unless they had been adopted into the list of heirs.

The genealogies from Genesis show the purpose of these lists. They record which families "belong" to Israel and which ones are considered "outsiders" or foreigners. Remember, Israelite tribes were not determined by geography, but by family line. If you were not born into one of the lines of the twelve tribes, you and your family were not full citizens of Israel unless someone adopted you or your family into their family tree.

Many diverse groups occupied the nation of Israel. It contained people who traced their ancestry back to Ishmael and Esau, as well as to Isaac and Jacob. The genealogies in Genesis make clear which families and clans were part of Israel. The descendants of Keturah were not full citizens, because their mother was a concubine whose sons Abraham did not adopt. The offspring of Ishmael were also not full citizens because their patriarch was a disinherited son of a concubine or surrogate mother.

Those "Mythic" Ancestors

The accounts in Genesis are not just some family's history, however. They define who and what the Israelites were as a people. It is hard for us to find a modern parallel because how we define what it means to be an American often comes from things like the news, movies, or the internet. However, I do think we have one thing in our own culture that helps us understand the stories of the patriarchs and matriarchs better, and that is Thanksgiving.

I bet most of you know something about the historical background of the celebration of Thanksgiving and the pilgrims. Why do we know this story of the pilgrims so well, as opposed to other events in U. S. history? Because of the way we celebrate Thanksgiving. Traditional foods are served to replicate the foods the pilgrims and Native Americans would have eaten. Certain virtues are associated with Thanksgiving, virtues such as hard work, perseverance, family unity, and the welcoming of the stranger, virtues that many would define as "typically American."

Our celebration of Thanksgiving has something to do with history: it's based on historical people and the celebration recalls certain historical details. But its purpose is not primarily historical. No one panics, for instance, if we use electricity that day. In fact, few people worry that pilgrims were not even technically "Americans," since there was no such thing at that time as the "United States of America."

The purpose of Thanksgiving is to affirm what it means to be an American. We use the holiday to define our cultural identity. For this reason, the celebration itself has a contemporary focus, even though it is presented as a celebration of the past. This contemporary dimension can be clearly seen in the stances of those who belong to a group that refuses to observe Thanksgiving, such as some Native American people for whom this historical story begins a long history of oppression.

Similarly, the stories of Genesis describe how the people of Israel came to be in the Levant, focusing on the accounts of their founders. Like Thanksgiving stories, these stories also had a historical element, but their real purpose was to affirm for the Israelites, during the monarchy and later, who they were as a people. When the biblical writers tell us about Jacob, whose name became Israel, they mean the story to be read not just as an account of an individual's history, but as a reminder of what it means to be his descendant.

Stories of founders, such as the patriarchs and the pilgrims, have "mythic" elements, meaning that the people in the accounts are portrayed as being "larger than life," figures that represent national and social values. They are founders not just of families, but of whole cultures. Certain elements in their lives can be exaggerated, others suppressed, in order to focus on this theme. For instance, some of the pilgrims may have been rude, loud, and obnoxious, but for the Thanksgiving celebration, the quirks of their individual personalities are not important. In the same way, the biblical writers picked stories that highlighted those socializing elements that were most important for their contemporary audience.

The Bible in the CHRISTIAN TRADITION

Inerrancy and Genre

One of the first questions that arises for my Christian students is the question of the historical reliability of the text. This question is often confused with the issue of the text's inerrancy, as if inerrancy and historical reliability are the same thing.

Many Christians believe that the Bible is inerrant, by which they mean that it contains no error. It is important for Christians that they can rely on the veracity of what Scripture says. But even evangelical Christians (sometimes called Fundamentalists), who have the most precise definition of inerrancy, recognize that the Bible contains texts of many different genres. To talk about the "inerrancy" of a poem is not the same thing as the inerrancy of a historical book.

Catholic theology attaches inerrancy to the truths that God intends to reveal in Scripture. The phrase most often used is "the truths necessary for salvation" (sometimes "for faith and salvation"). To put it in the language of Thomistic causality, if the text's primary intention is to convey something about God, then mistakes about the secondary elements of the text (not the primary purpose of the text), such as issues of science or medicine, can be in error. This tradition can be found even in the patristic period: Jerome, for example, does not hold to verbal inerrancy, but rather to inerrancy with respect to "meaning."

The importance of meaning and intent is why Catholic teaching on biblical interpretation stresses the importance of genre. Sometimes the genre of a biblical book is clear. For example, the Psalms are words for ancient songs. Sometimes a genre was used differently in the ancient world than it is today. Collections of ancient laws were not used as the primary basis of judicial decisions, but they were instead idealizations of the ruler's justice. Historical texts did relate events from the past, but ancient authors would alter facts, rearrange the chronology, and fill in details in order to convey the "lesson" from history, that is, what the historical events "meant."

The genre of a book like Genesis is not clear. Elements of the book, such as the genealogies, suggest that the genre was history. However, other elements, such as the elevated ages of the patriarchs and their interactions with divine beings, are close to ancient myth.

We Finally Get to Read Some Texts: Abraham and Sarah

Genesis 11:27–12:3: The Covenant with Abraham

In this section I will lead you through close readings of some biblical texts. Because I will first set the narrative context for these texts, you will probably want to read this section before reading the passage in the Bible.

The first reading begins the stories of the patriarchs and matriarchs. As I mentioned at the beginning of the chapter, this textbook covers the creation accounts of Genesis 1—11 in the chapter on wisdom literature. The genealogy of Terah, Abraham's father, serves as the bridge between the primeval history and the patriarchal narratives. It is all that we know of Abraham's life before he moves to the Levant. We start with a foundational text for both Jews and Christians: God's covenant with Abraham.

In Case You Were Wondering

In this section I will list things you may need to know to make sense of the story right away:

Abram. This was Abraham's original name. His name is changed to Abraham in Genesis 17:5. The two names mean the same thing. The lengthening of the name may simply be a more "exalted" form.

Sarai. This was Sarah's original name. Her name is changed in Genesis 17:15.

The old ages. The ages of the patriarchs and the matriarchs were added by the Priestly Writer and are part of the "mythic" quality of the stories. By having them travel great distances on foot at the age of seventy-five and become parents at the age of one hundred, the author is saying that these people belong to a mythic period.

Looking Closely at the Text

Read the passage carefully. Take time to notice the little details of the story. To help you notice some of the details that I will discuss, try to answer the questions in this section. Doing so will help you develop a proper habit of reading the Bible, since many of the questions in the early chapters of this textbook will focus on some significant details. As the textbook progresses I will shift the focus to more thought-provoking questions.

1. From where does Abram travel?

2. In Genesis 12:2 what does God promise Abram?

THE FIRST COVENANT WITH ABRAM

The verses cited do two things: they introduce us to Abram, and they tell us something about Abram's relationship with God. Notice what kind of information we get in this introduction. We find out who his family is, and we are introduced to his wife, Sarai. The passage also mentions that he has a nephew, Lot, and that his family is migrating.

Yet, there are many things about Abram that we are not told in this introduction. We don't know what kind of man he is. We don't know who his mother is, what kind of relationship he had with his father, or whether he loved his wife. Although we know that Abram moves from Haran because Yahweh commands him to, we do not know why God makes this command of Abram in particular. We may want to assume that it is because Abram is a very saintly man, but we will see in some other texts that Abram is not perfect.

We also see an example of a covenant. A covenant is a pact or an agreement between God and humans, often including a promise. There are several covenants in the Old Testament. In most of them, humans have a certain obligation for the blessings that God promises to bestow. This time, very little is required of Abram: he must simply move.

Notice that the first thing God promises is that he will make Abram into a great nation. This is ironic, because Abram's family is comprised of landless nomads. *Irony*, a literary device that is often used in the Old Testament, occurs when what is expected to happen does not happen or happens in an unexpected way. The irony is enhanced by the fact that Abram's wife is "barren," unable to have children. This man, who eventually becomes the "father" of a great nation, has trouble becoming a father at all.

Lastly, this covenant mentions blessings and curses. God blesses Abram, and promises that, in the future, other nations will be blessed or cursed through Abram and his nation. What does this mean? Israelites used this language to refer to countries, which are central in international politics. If a particular country has many allies that depend on it, then the fate of that country affects the fate of the dependent countries. Those dependent countries are "blessed" by the central country's good fortune, but "cursed" if that central country falls from power.

Here, then, God is saying that the nation that Abram will start will eventually become a world leader. This is also ironic, since the Yahwist relates this story during the monarchy when Israel is a tiny country. Moreover, it is retold again, as part of the larger book of Genesis, after this nation falls, at a time when the people knew that this promise had not been fulfilled.

Genesis 16:1–15: Sarah and Hagar

After God makes the first covenant with Abram, there is a drought in the land. Abram and Sarai immediately move to Egypt, an unexpected move, following as it does on God's promises to Abram. In Egypt Abram tells Sarai to lie about being his wife, because, he says, if other men know she is his wife, they will kill him so they can marry her, since she is so beautiful. Instead they claim she is Abram's sister. Sarai complies and enters Pharaoh's "house." Since Abram is paid well for this, we can assume that he received a bride price and Sarai is married off to the Pharaoh. Once the Pharaoh discovers that Sarai is Abram's wife, he banishes the couple, but Abram still leaves with the slaves and livestock he had gotten for Sarai's bride price. They re-enter Canaan far wealthier than when they had left.

This wealth leads to certain problems. First, we discover that Lot, Abram's nephew and apparent heir, has also become prosperous. Abram and Lot are both so wealthy that they must part ways; their livestock can no longer graze in the same land. Lot goes east toward the Dead Sea to the areas around the cities of Sodom and Gomorrah. When a coalition of four kings attacks the town of Sodom, Abram is able to muster a large enough army to save Lot and Sodom. It looks like Abram is well on his way to becoming a great nation, but in the very next chapter God appears again to Abram, telling him he needs an heir. We will look at this chapter soon, but first read the story of the birth of Abram's first child, Ishmael.

In Case You Were Wondering

Surrogate motherhood, not a modern invention, occurs when a woman cannot have children, so her husband impregnates another woman. That child becomes the legal son of the man and the barren wife. Ancient Israelite women could have surrogate children through their slaves. Hagar's child would have been Sarai's legal son.

<small>LOOKING CLOSELY AT THE TEXT</small>

1. Why does Sarai become angry with Hagar?

2. What does Sarai do to Hagar after Abram affirms that she is Sarai's slave?

3. Why does Hagar return to Abram and Sarai?

<small>THE ROLE OF THE MATRIARCHS</small>

God promised Abram that he would make him into a great nation. Eleven years have passed since God first called Abram and Sarai out of Mesopotamia, and yet Abram and Sarai do not have children. Notice that Sarai blames God for her barrenness. "You see that the LORD has prevented me from bearing children" (Gen 16:2).

Sarai offers her maidservant to Abram as a surrogate mother, an acceptable practice in the ancient world. Sarai's rivalry with Hagar stems in part from her own legal predicament. If Abram dies and Sarai has no son, she would become a "landless" person, having no access to the benefits of a landowning male.

The author of Genesis does not try to paint a "saintly" picture of Abram and Sarai. When she asserts her rights as master over Hagar, Sarai treats Hagar so badly that the pregnant maid chooses to survive alone in the desert, rather than live with Sarai.

Some scholars have wondered if Sarai's behavior might be motivated in part by racism; Hagar is, after all, an Egyptian, and her skin was probably a bit darker than that of Abram and Sarai. However, there is little indication that the Israelites discriminated on the basis of skin color. In fact, some biblical passages praise women for the darkness of their skin. This does not mean, however, that Israelites welcomed all people as their equals. Their sense of superiority was based on a person's family line, not on their appearance.

A further reason for Sarai's rivalry with Hagar may lie within the story itself. Notice that Hagar is an Egyptian slave. How did Sarai come to have an Egyptian slave? When her husband, Abram, married her off to the Pharaoh, her bride price included female slaves (Gen 12:16); Hagar is a constant reminder of what Abram had Sarai do.

Abram does not come off looking very good here either. He agrees to Sarai's plan to impregnate Hagar. He does not stick up for Hagar's rights, even though she is carrying his child. He returns her to the custody of Sarai, and he does not object to his wife's treatment of Hagar.

The only noble person in chapter 16 is Hagar. An angel of God appears to her, commanding her to return and submit to Sarai, which Hagar does, even though it means returning to an unjust existence. As a reward for her willingness to endure such suffering, God promises her that her son will become the founder of a great people. The little poem that the angel speaks denotes the character of this future people: wild like an ass or donkey, always fighting, never at peace.

Hagar names God "El-roi" meaning "God sees." The name connotes both the fact that she has been given the opportunity to see God herself, and that God has noticed her suffering. For this, God blesses her with a son who will be the founder of a great people. The irony of this text is that the people we expect to be righteous, Abram and Sarai, act in less than honorable ways, while Hagar, whom the text defines as outside of the covenant with Abram, is the most upright person in this story. She is rewarded by God with a vision and a promise.

Genesis 15:1–19; 17:1–27; 18:1–15; and 21:1–8: Isaac and the Covenant

Biblical authors used repetition to emphasize important things, but subtle changes in repeated stories are important to notice as well. There are three versions of God's covenant with Abraham. This is not mere repetition, but a further development of the plot. In between the stories, the text tells us about the birth of Ishmael, the story you read above. The other two passages relate the birth of Isaac.

In Case You Were Wondering

That weird covenant ceremony. Genesis 15:9–11 describes a ritual which validates the covenant. Five animals are sacrificed, and their carcasses are split. A similar ritual is found among the Hittites, a country north of Israel. The split bodies represented a curse that whoever would break this covenant would be cursed with being split open like these animals.

Circumcision. Genesis 17 requires the practice of circumcision, the act of removing the foreskin from the penis. Israelites were not the only ones who practiced circumcision; so did most of the people who lived around them (except the Philistines), including the Egyptians. We have Egyptian wall paintings of the ritual, although there it was performed at puberty.

Ancient hospitality. Abraham and Sarah greet their guests with abundant hospitality: cooking for them and serving them as honored visitors.

How old is old? Although Sarah and Abraham do have "mythic" ages, the account here wants us to realize they were past child-bearing years.

Looking Closely at the Text

1. In what ways are the specific things promised to Abraham in 12:1–3, 15:1–6, and 17:1–22 similar? How are they different?

2. What is the difference between what is promised to Ishmael and what is promised to Isaac?

3. The divine visitors tell Abraham that Sarah will have his son. How long until this son is to be born?

4. Why does Sarah laugh?

The Covenant Repeated

The covenant between God and Abraham is repeated two more times (15:1–6 and 17:1–22). Each time that the covenant is repeated, the account expands. Abraham, and later Sarah, is promised that their *biological* offspring will become founders of great nations. These founders will produce groups who will reside in the land of Canaan.

In the third version of the covenant (17:1–22), God makes clear that there is one obligation Abraham and his descendants must keep: the practice of circumcision. This is a fitting sign for this covenant for two reasons. First, this is a covenant that is passed on from father to son. Since ancient peoples did not know that women had ova, they thought that the material that became a child came from the man. Circumcision marks the body part that they thought was most responsible for creating this next generation. Second, the covenant is passed on like landownership. Abraham is promised an ancestral land, and this land will be handed down from generation to generation through the inheritance laws.

These passages are also important for other religious communities. Muslims, for instance, trace their ancestry from Ishmael. The twelve princes or patriarchs whom he fathered became the founders of the Arabic nations. Circumcision is still practiced by many Jews today as a religious obligation. Modern circumcision is referred to as a *bris*, the modern rendition of the ancient Hebrew word for *covenant*.

Within Christian tradition, Genesis 15:6 also became a central text. In this passage God deems Abraham as righteous. In the New Testament Paul notes that God declares Abraham as righteous, not because he is being obedient to certain laws, but simply because he believes. For Paul, and therefore for Christians, this means that salvation comes, not through obedience to the Jewish law, but through faith in God and God's promises, culminating in Jesus Christ.

These early Islamic, Jewish, and Christian interpretations show us how central the accounts of God's covenant with Abraham are for the biblical tradition.

The next passages describe the birth of Isaac. This story follows a popular pattern in Israelite stories: God blesses a righteous but barren couple with a son, who then grows up to be a hero. Because the pattern was familiar, variations give each story its own particular meaning.

The account also relieves some of the narrative tension in the book of Genesis. God has promised Abraham that he would father a great nation (chapter 12). The promise is repeated in chapter 15, assuring Abraham that this nation will come from his own offspring. In spite of the fact that Abraham succeeds in fathering a son in chapter 16, God returns again in chapter 17, telling Abraham that the founder of this nation will be his son born to Sarah.

The story of the birth of Isaac is such an uplifting story, that it might seem fitting to stop there. An old couple, who have been barren for many years, is blessed by God with the birth of a son. His very name resounds with the joy of this splendid occasion: Isaac, the son of laughter. But the birth of this child is set in narrative contrast with the fates of those outside of this covenant.

The story also contains a disturbing scene. After the angels who have announced Isaac's conception leave, there is another drought in the land. Abraham and Sarah move to Gerar, a city south of Canaan, and once again, Abraham has Sarah claim that she is his sister. Once again, she is sent to live with the king. This is incredibly odd behavior, considering that God has told them she will give birth to Abraham's son within a year; that will be impossible if she spends a few months living as another man's wife. God gets them out of this predicament by revealing to the king that he must not touch Sarah. They are banished from this land and paid well to leave. Why would the redactor place this story here? What does it suggest about the way he is portraying Abraham?

Genesis 18:16–19:38 and 21:9–21: The Fate of the Outsiders

In between the births of Ishmael and Isaac we read about the destruction of Sodom and Gomorrah. You may recall that this is the area where Lot settled when he split off from Abraham. These cities are located near the Dead Sea in an area so salty that mineral deposits have caused odd-looking formations around the sea.

In the biblical tradition, Sodom comes to represent the quintessential wicked city. But the story does not end with its destruction. The climax of the story takes place in a cave outside of Sodom. Take note whose ancestors are traced back to this scene.

The fulfillment of the promise to Abraham through Isaac also leaves Ishmael in a state of limbo. The second passage describes his fate.

In Case You Were Wondering

The Judge of all the earth (18:25). This is a title referring to God's role as insurer of justice.

Beersheba and Paran (21:14 and 21). These lands are both south of Judah. Beersheba is still within Israel, but Paran is in the Sinai Peninsula.

Looking Closely at the Text

1. What are the reasons that Sarah and Abraham banish Hagar and Ishmael after Isaac is born?

2. How do Hagar and Ishmael survive?

3. What is God's view of the actions of Sarah and Abraham?

Stories of Inclusion and Exclusion

The story of the destruction of Sodom and Gomorrah is easy enough to follow, troubling as it may be. The wickedness of the citizens is symbolized by their demand to sexually assault Lot's male guests. This act would have been seen as wicked on multiple levels to the original audience. Similarly, the righteousness of Lot is represented by his hospitality and protection of these strangers.

The women in this story remain more ambiguous. Lot's wife looks back at the destruction of the city and turns into a pillar of salt. Did this represent her desire to return? Or maybe it was her evil delight in their destruction? The text does not tell us why. Instead the focus seems to be on rock formations found near the Dead Sea.

Lot's daughters are also problematic. While they claim that they want to sleep with their father because there are no other men left on earth, the story tells us that they have just come from a smaller city that clearly survived the disaster. So while incest taboos would not have been in place if they had been the last people on earth, these girls are either stupid or have ulterior motives. In a word, this is not a flattering picture.

Notice who their sons are: the founders of the countries of Moab and Ammon, countries on the other side of the Jordan River from Israel. Nothing expresses the political theme of the book of Genesis more clearly for my students than this story. Think about it: what is the passage saying about the Moabites and Ammonites? Is this a story the Israelites would have told about themselves? Of course not. This is a story that relates Israel's recognition of cultural and kinship ties with the Moabites and Ammonites, while clearly distancing themselves from these two groups.

There are similar issues with the portrayal of Ishmael. Notice the pointed conversation between Abraham and God after God has told Abraham that Sarah will have a son. Abraham declares, "O that Ishmael might live in your sight!" (Gen 17:18). This is a request for God to keep Ishmael as part of the covenant. To this prayer, "God said, 'No'" (Gen 17:19). Ishmael and Hagar have been supplanted by Sarah and Isaac. Of course, what we learn here is not news to the reader. The text re-affirms that Hagar and Ishmael will survive, but not in the comfort of the only home Ishmael has ever known. Even Abraham is distressed by the situation.

Sad as these accounts are when read as the stories of individuals, these passages are best read as stories of later groups. They are poignant stories of inclusion and exclusion. We mentioned previously that Israelites were not racist regarding skin color. But theirs was a world that defined itself by national and family groups. Genesis is concerned with the establishment of genealogies which determine who is "in" and who is "out." The emotion in the text reveals that even during the monarchy these determinations caused heartache for those whose loved ones were excluded. They also show that status, a person's standing within the community, can change. Ishmael comes so close; he's "in" for a while, but then he and his mother are kicked out.

If Isaac represents the group that later becomes Israel, then Ishmael represents a group that the Israelites would see as closely related, but outside its social and national boundaries. This nation is described as one that often opposed Israel, struggled with it, a nation "wild" and "good with the bow." Ishmael is associated with drier, more nomadic areas than Israel. In other words, these stories could reflect Israel's relationship with people east of Israel, further east than Moab and Ammon.

GENESIS 22:1–14: THE NEAR-SACRIFICE OF ISAAC

The next story follows rather quickly on the notice of Isaac's birth. All that separates the two stories is a short account of a treaty that Abraham makes with another king. The following story is one of the most moving in the Old Testament, and, as with many stories from great literature, people have argued for centuries about its meaning. As you read it, take time to think about what each character is feeling and thinking.

In Case You Were Wondering

A **burnt offering** (22:2), also sometimes called a holocaust, is a type of animal sacrifice. In this sacrifice, the animal is slaughtered and totally burned on an altar as an offering to God.

Looking Closely at the Text

1. The first verse states why God asks Abraham to sacrifice his son. What does it say?

2. How would you tell this story from the perspective of Isaac or Sarah?

The Threat to the Promise

This text contains many graphic details that help the reader picture the scene. We are told that God commands the human sacrifice. The author uses repetition to say that the human to be sacrificed is Isaac, Abraham's only and beloved son. We know that the journey takes three days, that they gathered wood for the fire, and that Abraham brought along a knife. As we read the story, we can feel the pregnant pause as Isaac innocently asks, "Where is the sheep for the holocaust?" (Gen 22:7).

Historical research reveals that child sacrifice was practiced in the Levant throughout the period that Israel existed. The Phoenicians, in particular, practiced it. Recent archaeological discoveries in Phoenician settlements have made the practice clearer to us. These people believed that everything they had came as a gift from the gods. For example, a good harvest occurred because the gods had blessed them. In recognition of this belief, they offered a portion of the first things that they harvested to the gods, a ritual that symbolized thankfulness for their bounty. Similarly they were bound to offer the firstborn of every farm animal to the gods. The Israelites were bound by these same laws.

Some peoples of the countries in the Levant also believed that it was appropriate to sacrifice their firstborn human children as a sign that they recognized their children were a gift from the gods. However, most countries, Phoenicia included, sometimes used a practice called "substitution," whereby a lamb, goat, or ram was offered in place of the human child.

The Bible has laws about child sacrifice. In most (but not all) of these laws, however, it is clear that Israelites also practiced substitution, or "redemption" (see Exod 13:13; 22:29–30, and 34:19–20). In Israel the sacrifice that is owed to God may be redeemed by something else, such as another animal sacrifice, a monetary offering, or service to the temple. Some scholars believe that the story of Abraham's near-sacrifice of Isaac was originally told to explain why the Israelites practiced substitution. However, the story takes on a new meaning when told within the context of the Abraham cycle in the book of Genesis.

When we turn to the story as written, we realize that there are many other elements underlying the text that beg to be told. For instance, how does Sarah feel about this sacrifice? Did Abraham tell her about God's visit, or where he and Isaac were going? When Abraham returned did he ever tell her he had nearly slaughtered her only son? And what about Isaac? What was he doing as his father tied him up and laid him on the wood? Did he struggle? Did he think his father's actions were strange? We do not know.

We do not even know much about Abraham in this story. He carries out God's command, but what were his thoughts? We might know more if we knew how far it was from where he started to Mt. Moriah. The text tells us that it took three days, but what was the normal time it took? Was it a trip that normally took one day, so the three days shows his reluctance? Or maybe it normally took a week, so his three-day trip shows that he was eager to complete the task. We simply do not know. This question is complicated by the fact that the Bible does not tell us where Moriah is located, although 2 Chronicles 3:1 locates it in Jerusalem, at the spot where the temple was later built.

This story is tragically ironic. The narrative sequence up to this point has focused on the securing of the promise to Abraham and Sarah. Although Abraham does things that threaten that promise, from giving away his wife to other men, to abandoning the land whenever there was a drought, God had always stepped in to secure the fulfillment of the promise. The narrative tension surrounding Abraham's offspring builds up to the birth of Isaac. But just as the reader begins to relax, God appears and says, "Take your son Isaac, your only one, whom you love, and go to the land of Moriah. There you shall offer him up as a holocaust" (Gen 22:2). The God of the promise is the god demanding its brutal end. Part of what the text seems to say here is that, while human sin will not break this covenant with God, God can end it, but simply chooses not to.

Of all the gaps in the story, the one that gnaws at me most is this: what was Abraham's initial reaction to God's command? Although you might argue that he simply accepts it as a regular claim to perform child sacrifice, certainly Isaac is beyond eight days old, the normal age for child sacrifice. We are left with a picture of a nearly silent man, the same man who had once bargained with God over the destruction of Sodom and Gomorrah, cities notorious for their wickedness. So when God commands the sacrifice of Isaac, did he try to convince God that maybe this requirement wasn't such a good idea? Or did he see it as a just punishment for all the sins of his past, all the times he had turned his back on God's promises? The text never says.

I used to think that these gaps in the text were an example of poor story telling. I thought it showed how naïve and simplistic this literature was. But now I have come to realize that every single reader fills in those gaps. I find I have added different details through the years. At first I used to think that Abraham was noble; after all, he's a biblical hero. But now I find myself wondering about Sarah and Isaac; how would they tell the story?

If I were to ask you how Abraham reacted to God's message, I bet most of you would have an answer. This is not the same question as why did Abraham obey, but rather how did he feel about the job he had to do? Now where does your answer come from? It is not in the text. It comes from within you; you answer for Abraham. I have come to understand that the gaps are in the text for a reason. By withholding that information from the audience, the writer forces the reader to stand in the place of Abraham. Each reader or hearer of the text must respond to God. It is a masterful technique of story telling, and one reason why this story has remained so central for many different faith communities throughout the centuries.

Summary: Who Are Abraham and Sarah?

The stories of Abraham are told in a simple style. Details are few, and the stories are placed side-by-side with little connecting material. At first, Genesis looks more like a child's story than it does great literature. Moreover, much of the context of the stories is foreign to us. We may want to assume that these seemingly primitive stories have nothing to say to us today.

Yet, when we get past the cultural differences and appreciate the way the text is told, we find a surprisingly complex portrait of Abraham and Sarah. How much easier it would have been for the author to have only told the details of their lives that made them look good. (That's exactly what we find in a much later Jewish text titled "Jubilees.") Why, for instance, did the author include the stories of Hagar and Ishmael since the story of the covenant can still be understood without them?

This author is not interested in whitewashing Abraham and Sarah, because he wants the audience to know that Abraham and Sarah were like them. Although the original reader was the nation of Israel, the redactor has accomplished his task so artfully that, even thousands of years later, we can see the pair's humanness. The author draws us into the story through our ability to identify with the characters. By the end of the story, we are ready to answer for Abraham, Sarah, and even Isaac. In this way the author conveys his central message about God's covenant with a particular people.

THE PATRIARCHS, THE SEQUEL: ISAAC, JACOB, AND JOSEPH

GENESIS 24:1–67: THE BETROTHAL OF REBEKAH

After the story of Abraham's near-sacrifice of Isaac, Sarah dies and is buried. Genesis quickly moves on to the account of the engagement and marriage of Isaac to Rebekah. This is a charming story of how Abraham, through his trusted but unnamed servant, arranges the marriage of his son, Isaac, to a relative named Rebekah. It provides a glimpse into everyday life. Pay close attention to who speaks and what is said. Is Rebekah completely at the mercy of her family? How would you characterize Rebekah by the end of the story? What kind of a wife do you think she will make? It will be interesting to see if your initial assessment of her is borne out in the following chapters.

IN CASE YOU WERE WONDERING

Put your hand under my thigh (24:2). This text is maybe more accurately translated as under his genitalia. This probably symbolizes the importance of the oath.

Aram-naharim (24:10). This land is in northern Syria near the Euphrates.

Camels. Were you surprised by the camels in 24:10? You would have been if you realized that camels weren't domesticated until some time after this story takes place.

Bethuel. This is the name of Rebekah's father, who only appears in 24:50; otherwise, her oldest brother, Laban, acts as the head of household.

Looking Closely at the Text

1. Why does Abraham's servant have to travel so far to find Isaac a wife?

2. Where does the servant meet Rebekah?

3. How does Rebekah's family react to the servant's request to take Rebekah with him to marry Isaac?

4. How do Isaac and Rebekah react to each other?

5. What role does Rebekah play in the betrothal?

A Gracious Girl

Have you ever watched a movie where two characters meet in some fateful way and fall in love? This type of movie comes out of a human sentiment that some couples were simply "made for each other." This chapter in Genesis is an ancient version of the same theme. We are supposed to see God's hand in the events that brought the servant to Rebekah's house.

In ancient Israel, unmarried girls fetched the water for the family from the town well. There are several scenes in the Bible of men meeting young girls at the well. Rebekah, perhaps around twelve years old, is not yet betrothed, so her family was probably not the richest family in town. (Remember the richer you were, the earlier your marriage was arranged.) Her family is also quite willing, happy even, to arrange her marriage, so she probably had few, if any, prospects in her own hometown. If she had remained unmarried, her family would have had to take care of her. Extended families kept track of their lineage. The servant's long speech reveals who his master is, and Abraham's relationship to Laban, thus presenting Isaac as a suitable candidate for marriage to Rebekah.

Rebekah is portrayed as gracious and kind. She had a duty to be kind to a stranger, but, like Abraham, she goes beyond the normal expectations of hospitality by offering to water the man's camels. The servant has chosen this sign deliberately; he wants a generous woman for Isaac's wife. The text shows God's hand in this by revealing that Rebekah happens to be related to Abraham as well.

The personalities of Rebekah and her family show through here. Her brother and father are quick to arrange the marriage, a marriage that saves them the cost of housing and feeding her. They are paid well for the transaction (Gen 24:53); only after they receive these gifts does Laban wish the servant to stay a while longer. Rebekah, on the other hand, has a mind of her own, and a willingness to speak up. At the well, although she does not start the conversation, she takes the initiative to invite the man to her house. When her family and the servant disagree about when they should leave, Rebekah settles the matter. She travels unveiled and only dons her veil after she has seen her future husband. Rebekah is gracious, generous, and wise. No wonder Isaac finds "solace" with her (Gen 24:67).

Genesis 27:1–45: The Stolen Blessing

The genealogies of Abraham and Ishmael link Isaac's marriage to the birth of twin sons, Esau and Jacob. The birth scene depicts the two boys fighting within Rebekah's womb, a foreshadowing of troubled times ahead. Rebekah prays to God who answers her: "Two nations are in your womb, and two peoples born of you shall be divided; the one shall be stronger than the other, the elder shall serve the younger" (Gen 25:23). This response reminds the reader that stories of individual characters are really stories of Israel's national history.

As the two boys grow, they vie for their parents' attention. We are told that Isaac prefers Esau, the hairy hunter, while Rebekah prefers Jacob who stays home and cooks. The author does not paint a very flattering picture of Esau. He foolishly sells his birthright (his claim on a larger inheritance) because he's hungry (Gen 25).

In Genesis 26 God repeats the covenant promises to Isaac. Isaac also lives in a foreign land, telling people that Rebekah is his sister and never arranging for her to marry someone else. God saves them from any danger and repeats the covenant promises to Isaac. Readers are supposed to remember that this covenant is passed down from father to eldest son. Esau has already sold his birthright to Jacob, so we know that the heir of this covenant will be Jacob, not Esau. The point is confirmed at the end of the chapter when it tells us that Esau marries Canaanite girls.

In Case You Were Wondering

Deathbed speeches. Words spoken by a dying person were seen as being prophetic, bound to come true. Stories describing deathbed blessings and curses were a favorite literary type in ancient Israel. There is an irony in this text, however, because Isaac doesn't die until Genesis 36:28–29, approximately eighty years later.

A kid. This term (27:9) refers to a baby goat or sheep.

LOOKING CLOSELY AT THE TEXT

1. What is Rebekah's role in this story? Are her actions good or evil?

2. In a sentence, state what Isaac promises Jacob (as Esau) in his blessing in verses 28–29.

3. How do Esau and Isaac react when Esau returns and they discover Jacob's deception?

4. What is Esau promised in verses 39–40?

5. Why does Rebekah send Jacob away?

TRICKERY AND PROMISE

Sibling rivalry is a normal part of family life. The rivalry between Esau and Jacob, however, goes beyond the boundaries of normal behavior. Fueled by the preferences of their parents, these twins are never pictured as close. Jacob, the wily brother aided by his mother, repeatedly dupes Esau, the older and stronger brother.

Rebekah and Jacob together exemplify what scholars call the "trickster" motif. A *trickster* is a character who is apparently weak or powerless, yet who succeeds by fooling or duping the one(s) in power. Many cultures enjoy trickster stories. Bugs Bunny is a trickster, a powerless figure, who outwits the hunter and his gun. Although the trickster motif may look like lying and deception, to the original audience the story of how Isaac is duped by his wife and younger son was probably seen as clever and entertaining.

The humor can be better understood when we remember what Esau and Jacob represent: the nations of Edom and Israel. The identity of Esau as Edom is clarified in Genesis 25:30. Jacob's identity as Israel comes much later. This story expresses Israel's understanding of Edom's relationship to Israel, as well as its national character. Let's look at this briefly.

‣ Edom is Israel's brother. What would it mean to say that another country is our brother? Would you describe any country as a brother or sister to the United States? Many people of European descent may see Canada as being the country most like us. We have a similar history, culture, and heritage. This is probably what Israel meant by defining Edom as their brother.

‣ Historically, there were times when Edom did not support Israel in its fights against foreign invaders. In fact, when Babylon conquered Israel in 587 the

Edomites helped the Babylonians. The Israelites viewed this as a particularly painful betrayal.

▸ While Jacob is no saint, he is clearly the hero. Esau may be a sympathetic character, but he is not to be emulated. After all, who wants to be Elmer Fudd if you could be Bugs Bunny?

▸ The curse on Esau that Isaac must speak from his deathbed sums up the Israelites' view of the character of Esau. The land of Edom was in fact less fertile than Israel (26:39), and the Edomites had to fight for everything they got. Even the mention of Canaanite wives shows that, to the Israelites, the Edomites had added to their own ruin by intermarrying with the "locals."

The Edomites, then, were a people close to the Israelites culturally and probably ethnically, but whose interactions with Israel were contentious and problematic. These stories reflect Israel's view of Edom's moral and cultural inferiority.

Genesis 29:1–30: Laban Tricks the Trickster

Jacob leaves his home and moves in with his uncle, Laban in the city of Haran. On the way there, Jacob spends the night in the place that will become Bethel. There he has a dream of angels going up and down a ladder to heaven. In the midst of this dream, God repeats the promises of the covenant to Jacob. Jacob settles with Laban, his mother's oldest brother. There, Jacob falls in love with Laban's younger daughter, Rachel (yes, she is his first cousin), but he has met his match in Laban. What follows is a contest between trickster uncle and trickster nephew.

In Case You Were Wondering

The unknown partner. Oddly enough, it appears that in ancient Israel women were sometimes veiled during sexual intercourse. This is not the only biblical story where a man does not recognize a woman he knows quite well during an intimate act.

Working off a debt. Jacob is poor, so he works for Laban in trade for the bride price.

Weddings. Nuptial festivities lasted several days so that the community could serve as legal witnesses that the marriage had been consummated.

Looking Closely at the Text

1. Why is it surprising that Jacob moves the rock to water the flocks when Rachel arrives?

2. How does Laban get Jacob to marry Leah first?

Two Wives, Fourteen Years of Free Service

Laban, the brother who arranged for Rebekah's marriage, here arranges his own daughters' marriages to Rebekah's son. His character shines through. He not only succeeds in finding a husband for the girls, he also manages to get a wise and strong worker for his own flocks. Jacob's shepherding abilities were alluded to at the beginning of the chapter, in his conversation with the other shepherds. The text emphasizes his strength when he moves the rock off of the well for Rachel. Later we see his ability to increase Laban's flocks, an ability that translates into economic gain for Laban.

The trickster motif continues in this chapter. Laban tricks Jacob into marriage to both of his daughters. Why would Laban trick him like this? First, we can assume he had few, if any, other prospects for the girls. This suggests that Laban was not a rich man. Second, Laban has no sons, so he needs Jacob to work for him as cheaply as possible. Even more, he needs to have grandsons who can inherit his land. He wants to keep Jacob on his land for as long as possible to secure his own future. Third, from the perspective of the literary artistry of the text, both men are tricksters. Notice that Jacob does not cry out against the injustice of Laban's actions. He accepts them without comment, as if he recognizes that he might have done the same thing. Laban and Jacob deserve each other.

Did you notice, though, that we have no hint about what Laban's daughters think of all this? Neither girl speaks in the whole chapter. We may have romantic notions about their love for Jacob. We find out later in the book that Leah was hurt by the fact that Jacob loved Rachel more, but the fact remains that this story does not consider what these girls want regarding their father's choice of a husband.

Even more silent is God. No single character prays to God, nor does God intervene. I do not think God's absence in this chapter is accidental. It is not as if the author simply forgot to mention God. So what is the author trying to communicate? Are these marriages part of God's plan? Or are they a fitting punishment for Jacob's treatment of Isaac?

Genesis 32:22–33: Jacob Becomes Israel

A new contest ensues between Leah and Rachel to produce sons. Rachel is barren, so she gives Jacob her maidservant. Leah, not wanting to lose this race, also provides her maidservant to Jacob. While living with and serving Laban, Jacob fathers eleven sons and one daughter by four different women.

Jacob finally decides to strike out on his own. He demands payment from Laban for all of the work that he has provided. Laban tries to trick Jacob out of what is owed him, but Jacob gets the best of Laban. As the final act of trickery, Rachel manages to steal the household gods, the family's most sacred objects, hiding them from both Laban and Jacob. With this she proves herself the "best" mother, even though she has only one son, Joseph.

Although many years have passed, Jacob returns to Canaan, afraid of meeting Esau. First he sends envoys to Esau with gifts to appease him. Next, to protect his family from any act of revenge by his brother, Jacob sends his family, servants, and herds ahead without him. He himself beds down by the Jabbok River, a tributary to the Jordan, where he has another strange dream.

This story relates the events leading to Jacob's name change to "Israel." As such, the elements of Jacob's character told here are central to the way the author is defining the character of the nation.

In Case You Were Wondering

Peniel. This word means "face of God" (32:30).

Looking Closely at the Text

1. In verse 24, with whom does it say Jacob wrestles?

2. In verse 30, who does Jacob say he has seen?

3. What is the result of the wrestling match?

The Contender

For such a short text, there are many different things going on! First, the story has *three* etiologies. An *etiology* is a story of something that happened a long time ago that explains why things are as they are today. For instance, the Rudyard Kipling story "How the Elephant Got His Trunk" is an etiology. The story in Genesis 32 explains (1) how the city of Peniel got its name, (2) why Israelites do not eat a certain portion of a sacrificed animal, and (3) how Jacob's name was changed to Israel.

The first etiology, the naming of Peniel, reveals an important element of the story, that Jacob wrestles with God. The text emphasizes God's presence, most obviously by Jacob's statement in verse 30, "For I have seen God face to face."

Jacob's name is changed to *Israel*, which means "one who struggles with God." It is a fitting name for Jacob, who, while running scared from his brother Esau, wrestles a man whom he knows to be God. Even as he fights God, Jacob demands a blessing out of God. Jacob is a tenacious patriarch.

This struggle with God leaves Jacob lame, and the damage that he suffers is ritually memorialized in the taboo against eating part of a sacrificial animal. What does this injury add to the portrayal of Jacob? He is willing to wrestle with God for a blessing even if it results in permanent harm to himself.

This story is the etiology of the nation itself. The depiction of Jacob's character is Israel's depiction of its own national character. What does this story say about how Israel understands itself and its relationship with God? Notice that Jacob is not portrayed as submissive, pious, or particularly heroic. In fact, it appears that his greatest fault is also his greatest strength. He is a person who struggles to make things go his way, and God rewards him for his efforts. Jacob represents the nation. In other words, Israel depicts itself as tenacious in its demand for God's blessing. As a result of that tenacity, Israelites may be damaged, but they do get to see God face-to-face.

GENESIS 37:1–36; 39:1–41:57: JOSEPH ENSLAVED

The rivalry between Esau and Jacob was more perceived than real, as the next story shows. Jacob meets Esau, and Esau has no desire to kill him. The brothers make a pact, and each goes his separate way. Jacob settles in the central part of what later becomes Israel, living among the Canaanites. His interactions with the Canaanites, however, breed violence. A local man rapes Dinah, Jacob's daughter, and in revenge Dinah's brothers slaughter the people in the city where the man lives. Jacob and his family have to move south to avoid retaliation. Near the city of Bethel, where Jacob had earlier established an altar, God reappears to Jacob, confirms his name change to Israel, and repeats the covenant to him.

Jacob has one last son, Benjamin, born to the wife he loves most, Rachel. Rachel dies in childbirth, and Jacob's family is complete: twelve sons, and one daughter (that we know of) by four women. Isaac finally dies, and the genealogy of Esau's family forms the bridge to the story of Joseph. Notice how family violence leads Joseph to a long life of servitude. Is he saved by his own cunning or by God?

IN CASE YOU WERE WONDERING

Sources in the Joseph cycle. The story has some inconsistencies. For instance, the text says two different groups bought Joseph from his brothers.

The story's Egyptian setting. This story is set during a time period in Egyptian history when the Pharaohs were Asians. This would have made them closer in nationality to the Israelites. Joseph's rise to a high position in Pharaoh's court is more believable in this period of Egyptian history.

The Hyksos

Although we think of the ancient Israelites as contemporaries of the Egyptians, the fact is that by the time the nation of Israel came on the scene, the Egyptian kingdom had already experienced its most well-known eras. The famous pyramids at Giza, for example, were already around 1500 years old by the time David became king.

Egyptian history is divided into "kingdoms," eras when Egyptians maintained relatively smooth transitions between pharaohs. These kingdoms were separated by "Intermediate" periods, times of great national disruption. Although some of the dates of Egyptian history are currently in dispute, the following chart outlines the traditional divisions of Egyptian history:

Early Dynastic	2920–2572
Old Kingdom	2572–2134
First Intermediate	2134–2040
Middle Kingdom	2040–1640
Second Intermediate	1640–1532
New Kingdom	1532–1070
Third Intermediate	1070–712 (David becomes king in ca. 1000)
Late Period	712–343 (Jerusalem falls in 586)

As you see, most of Israel's national history corresponds to the periods after the New Kingdom era. The story of Joseph seems to be set in the Second Intermediate period. During this era, West Asian invaders had taken over the Egyptian throne. They were called the *Hyksos*. Archaeological evidence reveals that these people introduced the worship of West Semitic deities into Egypt, such as Baal and Anat. At this point in Egypt's history an Asian, such as Joseph, could have achieved a certain level of power.

When the Egyptians were able to regain control of the throne, they tried to erase the memory of this Asian rule. The statement at the beginning of Exodus ("Now a new king arose over Egypt who did not know Joseph" [Exod 1:8]) may signal to the reader this change in setting.

LOOKING CLOSELY AT THE TEXT

1. What is the relationship of Joseph to Benjamin? What is his relationship to his other brothers?

2. Why do the brothers dislike Joseph so much?

3. Is Joseph's fate part of God's plan?

CRIME AND PUNISHMENT

The story of Joseph and his brothers is universally recognized to be a great story. The style of the writing is typical of Israelite narrative. Details are sparse, and only the essential elements of the story are told. Yet even with this sparing style, the individual characters shine through. I find this portrait of family relationships, especially the rivalry among the brothers, to be sadly familiar to a modern ear. Violence within the family is not a new phenomenon.

Joseph's story opens with a group of brothers willing to kill one of their half-brothers because their father favors him. Joseph's bragging adds fuel to the fire. Even his most merciful brother is willing to sell him into permanent slavery and tell their father that he is dead.

The text focuses on the fate of Joseph. His life is hard. Enslaved, falsely accused of rape, and unjustly imprisoned, he manages to survive. He has little hope for justice, though. He has no one to advocate for him, no means to end his imprisonment, that is, until the story-teller reminds us of his ability to interpret dreams. Joseph interprets the dreams of his fellow prisoners, an idle entertainment, but one that proves fateful. When Joseph is finally brought before Pharaoh, he confesses that his power comes from God (Gen 41:16).

Joseph uses this opportunity wisely. When made a chief official in Pharaoh's court, he proves to be economically savvy, storing up provisions in time of plenty and selling them for profit at times of need. By the time Joseph's brothers re-appear in the text, the ironic shift is complete: Joseph controls all of the food stores in an economically prosperous country, while his brothers must travel to find something to eat.

GENESIS 42:1–45:28; AND 46:28–47:28: JOSEPH'S REVENGE

The second half of the story focuses on Joseph' reaction when his brothers appear before him, completely at his mercy. What will he do? Will he exact his revenge?

In Case You Were Wondering

An abomination. This is anything that is ritually taboo for a culture. Israel uses the term to refer to things that are ritually unclean. Here Genesis 43:32 says that the Egyptians have a taboo against eating with foreigners.

Divination (44:5). This is the art of determining the will of the gods by using some physical object or phenomenon.

Sheol (44:29). This is Israel's name for the place where the dead go.

Ramses (47:11). This is a name used by several pharaohs. The first one by that name ruled around 1400 BCE.

Goshen (47:27). This is a land in northern Egypt in the delta region.

Looking Closely at the Text

1. Why do Joseph's brothers come down to Egypt?

2. What things does Joseph hide in his brothers' baggage?

3. When does Joseph finally reveal his identity to his brothers?

4. Why does Joseph not tell his brothers who he is right away? Why does he "frame" them?

Revenge or Conversion?

Chapter 42 opens with Jacob sending his sons to Egypt in search of food, a search that lands them before their little brother, whom they do not recognize. Joseph does not immediately reveal his identity to them. Why the delay? Is he debating what to do with them? Or has he decided in advance to simply scare them a little? Joseph, it says, recalls his childhood dreams, and accuses them of being spies (Gen 42:6–11). He does not immediately forgive them. He then plants evidence of robbery in their packs. With this evidence he could have them imprisoned, if not killed. Instead, he uses this power to manipulate them into returning with Benjamin, an action he knows will grieve his father. Once Benjamin is in his power, he plants more evidence, this time in Benjamin's bag. His actions are cruel, leading his father and all of his brothers to fear for their lives. Joseph exacts revenge.

The text suggests that there was a limit to his wrath. At several key points in the text, Joseph weeps, overcome by his emotions (Gen 42:24; 43:30; 45:2). Would Joseph have been willing to hurt his full brother, Benjamin? The question hangs there unanswered until the final moment: Joseph's "conversion" in Genesis 45:1–3. At last he says, "I am Joseph," and he expresses some concern for Jacob, "Is my father still in good health?" What prompts this change of heart? Why does he not harm his half-brothers? The immediate answer seems to be Judah's noble offer to stand in place of Benjamin, out of concern for their father (Gen 44:30–34). If Joseph was testing his brothers, Judah's offer passes the test.

Where is God in all of this? God is not a prominent figure in the stories of Joseph and his brothers, but God is not entirely absent either. Whose side is God on? The reader is supposed to understand that God is with Joseph, protecting him in Egypt. But God is also with Jacob's family in Canaan; they survive because of Joseph. The covenant is preserved in and through this story. Abraham's family does not die of famine. It grows to a large number, even if it is not yet the great nation originally promised. Some people interpret the story of Joseph as a story of God's providence, a story that shows how God cares for the people through many trials.

However, we must not forget that the patriarchs and matriarchs do not end Genesis safely dwelling in the Promised Land. The book closes with them as economic refugees in a foreign land. To be sure, when they move there, they do so under a benevolent government, but their vulnerable position is made clear at the beginning of the next book of the Bible, Exodus. This book opens by telling us that many years have passed, and now Jacob's descendants are slaves in Egypt. The family violence has resulted in their location outside of the Promised Land, fated to years of servitude to a foreign power.

Read within the context of a political allegory, what does this cycle tell us about Israel's view of its own internal relations? Remember that we talked about the contrasts between Isaac and Ishmael, as well as Jacob and Esau, as reflecting Israel's expression of its relationship to the nations around them. The Joseph narrative deals with the relationships of the twelve tribes. The text suggests that internal rivalry and violence put the whole nation at risk. Internal dissent results in enslavement to a more powerful foreign power, loss of some of the tribes, and even annihilation. We will see this same theme played out in Israel's subsequent history.

Summary: God and the Founders

The stories of the patriarchs and matriarchs tell the earliest history of a group of people who can be identified as Israel. For Israelite society, based as it was on the family, this is the story of an extended family whose members are the founders of the tribes of Israel. The primary purpose of the stories, while rooted in history, is not to tell a factual history, but to narrate the stories by which Israel defined itself, and to express national values and the norms for inclusion in the nation. The biblical characters are more than just individuals; they are representatives of political/cultural groups.

The social and cultural background of these Old Testament stories is far removed historically and culturally from modern life and not every biblical book pictures God in the same way. In some books God is very distant; in others God is primarily angry. We shouldn't expect one biblical book to give a complete portrait of God. This God chooses sides (Abraham, not Lot; Isaac, not Ishmael; Jacob, not Esau), while still not abandoning the other side. God is patient, but not disinterested; merciful, but not placid; present, but also hidden; and certainly appreciative of life's ironies.

FOR REVIEW

1. What are the three sections of the book of Genesis?

2. Who were the patriarchs and matriarchs?

3. In what time period were the stories set?

4. When was the material written down?

5. What are the four sources of the Pentateuch?

6. What is the basic outline of the family?

7. Identify at least one story in the book of Genesis that displays the political purpose of the text.

8. How would you characterize Abraham, Isaac, Jacob, or Joseph?

FOR FURTHER READING

In this section I will list material that expands some of the topics we have looked at within the chapter. I have picked material aimed for a general audience rather than for scholars.

Although you can find a lot of excellent information in commentaries on biblical books, I will not list them here. There are many commentaries at various levels, aimed at different audiences. There are new ones published every year as well. Because of the variety of available sources, you would do well to ask your instructor to help you find appropriate commentaries, if you need them.

There are many good books that provide introductions to the use of sources in the Pentateuch. One that provides you with a reconstruction of each source is *Sources of the Pentateuch: Texts, Introductions,* "Annotations" by Antony F. Campbell and Mark A. O'Brien (Minneapolis, MN: Augsburg Fortress, 1993). Joseph Blenkinsopp is among those offering some revisions to Wellhausen's reconstruction in *The Pentateuch: An Introduction to the First Five Books of the Bible* (New York: Doubleday, 1992).

A classic reconstruction of Israel's early religious life is Frank M. Cross's *Canaanite Myth and Hebrew Epic: Essays in the History of the Religion of Israel* (Cambridge, MA: Harvard University Press, 1973). It spawned a whole host of other books in this area. For a readable translation of the Ugaritic myths, see Michael D. Coogan, *Stories from Ancient Canaan* (Philadelphia, PA: Westminster, 1978).

Two general surveys of the daily and domestic life of ancient Israel can be found in *Families in Ancient Israel*, edited by Leo G. Perdue et al. (The Family, Religion, and Culture; Louisville, KY: Westminster John Knox, 1997), and Philip J. King and Lawrence E. Stager, *Life in Biblical Israel* (Library of Ancient Israel; Louisville, KY: Westminster John Knox, 2001).

One of the great scholars on folklore in the Bible is Susan Niditch. She examines the trickster motif in *Underdogs and Tricksters: A Prelude to Biblical Folklore* (San Francisco, CA: Harper & Row, 1987).

3 THE EXODUS

The Israelites walked on dry ground through the sea, the waters forming
a wall for them on their right and on their left. Thus the LORD saved Israel
that day from the Egyptians.
(Ex 14:29–30)

CHAPTER OVERVIEW

This chapter presents one of the best-known narratives of the Old Testament, the story of the exodus. The stories cover material extending from the birth of Moses to the Israelites' delivery from slavery. This chapter will provide the following:

‣ An overview of the book of Exodus

‣ A discussion of the historical background of the story

‣ A consideration of how the text's details reflect its use in ancient Israel

‣ A brief presentation of the book's message of hope for the oppressed

This background will help you appreciate the details of the texts from Exodus that you will study.

The Bible and Film

Okay, I'll admit it. When I read about the exodus, I picture scenes from Cecil B. de Mille's *The Ten Commandments*. Maybe some of you do too, or maybe it's *The Prince of Egypt*. From Veggie Tales to Oscar winners, biblical texts make attractive subjects for movie makers.

Sometimes these film images help us to imagine the ancient world. When the film makers have done their homework, those images can be fairly accurate. For example, the depiction of the actual Ark of the Covenant in *Raiders of the Lost Ark* is quite true to some of the biblical texts.

However, often people forget that when they watch a movie based on the Bible, they are not getting the Bible itself. They are getting one person's interpretation of the Bible. I enjoy watching these movies and seeing their interpretations; sometimes they make me think about the Bible in ways that hadn't occurred to me. But I would never substitute watching movies for reading the Bible on my own.

Films can help us broaden our awareness of the interpretive process that takes place whenever anyone reads any text. Try this exercise. Imagine that you are hired to make a film of some biblical scene, such as the story of the near-sacrifice of Isaac in Genesis 22. Who would you cast in each role and why? How would the interpretation of the text be affected if you cast someone "against type"? How would you depict the mechanism of God's command to Abraham, and how would you deal with the question of Abraham's reaction to this command? Would Sarah be in the story? How will Isaac react when his father is tying him up? When you think about the text in this way, you can "see" how much interpretation these texts demand of the audience.

WHAT'S THE BOOK OF EXODUS?

The book of Exodus tells the story of the central theological event for the ancient Israelites: their deliverance from slavery in Egypt under the leadership of Moses and their formation as a people at Mt. Sinai. This account, more than any other, represented their understanding of God's concern for them. It also became a central theme in Christianity.

The term *exodus* can be confusing. It comes from a Latin word meaning "going out." On one level, it refers to the second book of the Bible, which describes God's deliverance of the Israelites from slavery in Egypt. On another level, it is used as shorthand for the event itself. In addition, "the exodus" is sometimes used to mean the whole sequence of events that led to the Israelites' deliverance from slavery. I will use *Exodus*, with a capital "E" to refer to the book of Exodus, and *exodus* with a lowercase "e" to refer to the event.

The book of Exodus can be divided into two parts. The first part focuses on the exodus. It opens some 400 years after the death of Joseph. The Israelites are called Hebrews in the book, a term probably referring both to their foreign origin (from the perspective of the Egyptians) as well as to their lower social status. They are slaves, who must endure Pharaoh's oppression. Chapters 1 and 2 of Exodus describe both this oppression and the birth of the person who will deliver them from it, Moses. As an infant, Moses is saved from certain death by a twist of fate. Instead of being killed by Pharaoh, he is raised by Pharaoh's own daughter!

The book quickly jumps to Moses' adult life: how he fled from Egypt, but was called by God to free the Hebrew people (Exodus 2:11—7:7). The central part of the first half of the book (Exodus 7:8—15:21) describes the "negotiations" between Moses and Pharaoh, resulting in a series of plagues. During the last plague, the Hebrew people slip out of the country.

The Habiru

Egyptian texts from the New Kingdom period mention a group of people called the "Habiru" (also spelled "Hapiru" and sometimes occurring without the "h"). These people were socially disruptive. The book of Exodus refers to the Israelites as "Hebrews" which has led some people to equate the two groups. The use of "Hebrew" to refer to the Israelites is rare in the Old Testament; the term usually refers to the language, not to the ethnic group. The identification of the biblical Hebrews and the Egyptian Habiru, however, is not so simple.

The Habiru are mentioned in a group of Egyptian texts called the "Amarna Letters." These letters, written sometime in the fourteenth century BCE, reflect life in Egypt about a hundred years before the narrative setting of the exodus. While the Habiru were among the workers for Ramses II, mention is made of them in texts scattered throughout the second millennium.

In these texts, they are not an ethnic group, but rather a social group. They were mercenary soldiers, slaves, fugitives, even outlaws. Perhaps the author of Exodus is depicting the Israelites' social status by calling them "Hebrews."

The Egyptian army pursues them, but God allows the Hebrews to escape. This is the heart of the exodus event.

The second half of the book of Exodus consists of the "wilderness narratives," so-called because the stories take place outside of Egypt, in the area the Israelites called "the wilderness." While the people wander in the wilderness, God leads them to a special mountain where God gives them many laws. This group of laws, which includes the Ten Commandments, form the basis of the *Mosaic covenant*, that is, the covenant God made with Israel through Moses. The final fifteen chapters of the book of Exodus deal primarily with the building of the *tabernacle*, the portable shrine that the Israelites used to worship God during this migratory period.

The book of Exodus, then, tells the history of Israel from the birth of Moses to the point at which the Israelites build the tabernacle in the wilderness. Embedded in this historical narrative are many of the laws that formed the basis of Israelite religion. This table summarizes the outline of the book of Exodus.

First Half of the Book	The Exodus
Chapters 1:1—2:10	The Birth of Moses
Chapters 2:11—7:7	Moses outside of Egypt
Chapters 7:8—15:21	Moses delivering the Israelites from oppression
Second Half of the Book	**The Wilderness**
Chapters 15:22—24:18	Laws given to the Israelites
Chapters 25:1—40:38	The building of the tabernacle

Sacred Landscapes: Cities, Mountains, and Wilderness

When I was a child, we had a globe that replicated the topography of the Earth. I used to love to run my fingers along the mountain ridges and deep valleys of the world. I would imagine going to far-off places, but I never thought that these natural formations were anything more than that.

Ancient peoples had a different experience of their world. Topographical features had cosmic significance. A mountain wasn't just raised earth; it was the home of a god. The sea wasn't just a body of salt water; it was the waters of death and chaos that threatened the world.

When you read biblical texts, remember that physical features aren't mentioned accidentally. Each feature means something. Take, for example, the use of the word *mountain* in the Bible. Mountains were homes of the deities, and so temples were built on "mountains," even if that "mountain" was only raised earth within a city. Sometimes what the Bible calls a mountain, we might call a hill or a rise in the earth. But if we spend our time worrying about whether or not a place is an actual mountain, we will not notice that the author is trying to convey the idea that an episode occurs at a sacred spot. Some other significant settings include the following:

- **The city** represented human culture and order. We will see when we study wisdom literature that this order and culture were evidence of God's creative activity. The ideological center of the city was the temple, so the city also represented God's presence with a particular people. The city included the cultivated fields that surrounded the city.
- **The wilderness,** which is sometimes translated as "the steppe," would have been the land beyond the cultivated fields. It was "wild" and uncultivated. Although the gods (and for the Israelites, Yahweh) cared for the wild animals of the steppe, it was also a territory inhabited by demons.
- **Springs** provided fresh water to an otherwise uninhabitable land. As such, they were a symbol of God's power over hostile forces.

HISTORICAL BACKGROUND FOR EXODUS

The book of Exodus, like the book of Genesis, was written much later than the events it describes and includes material from a variety of sources. To review, the first four books of the Bible rely upon at least three distinct sources, the Yahwist, the Elohist, and the Priestly Writer, from at least three different periods of Israel's history. Thus, the book of Exodus has elements probably written during the united monarchy (the date of the Yahwist), the divided monarchy (the Elohist), and the Restoration Period (the Priestly Writer).

Unlike most of Genesis, however, the story that is told in Exodus seems to be set in a specific time period. The book of Exodus tells us that a new pharaoh arose who "did not know Joseph" (Exod 1:8). This pharaoh and his son built the cities of Pithom and Ramses. These cities were constructed under the reigns of Seti I and Ramses II, who ruled during the New Kingdom period.

This date also matches some historical evidence after the exodus. The pharaoh immediately following Ramses II, Merneptah, mentions Israel, in a monument he wrote sometime in the twelfth century BCE, as a people settled in the Levant. This is the earliest mention of Israel outside the Bible. This means that any exodus had to have happened long enough before that date for the people to have settled in the Levant as an identifiable political group. Again, a date in the time of Seti I and Ramses II fits this information.

However, outside of this general information, there is no independent historical evidence for the exodus. Egyptian records mention no plagues. The inscriptions of Seti I, Ramses II, and Merneptah make no reference to a slave revolt or to the defeat of an Egyptian army at a "sea." Some people note that there could be many reasons for this. For instance, kings did not usually mention the battles that they lost. In addition, since the story is told for and by the Israelites, the events behind the narrative may have been much more modest in scale, exaggerated by Israelite storytellers over the course of a few hundred years to make certain theological points. This reminds us again that the main goal of the book of Exodus is not factual accuracy.

LITURGY AND ORAL TRADITION

What parts of the life of Jesus do most Christians know best? Is it the accounts of Jesus' birth? Or is it the events leading up to and following the crucifixion? Why is it that Christians know these stories better than other parts of his life? It is in large part because these accounts are "re-lived" every year in Christian worship services during important religious holidays.

This colossal black basalt statue of the head of Ramses II is located at the entrance to the Luxor Temple in Egypt. The Temple of Luxor was built by pharaohs Amenhotep III and Ramses II between 1293 and 1185 BCE.

Think about the Passion Narrative for a moment: these are the stories extending from Jesus' entrance into Jerusalem (Palm Sunday), through the Last Supper (Holy Thursday), the crucifixion (Good Friday), culminating in his resurrection (Easter Sunday). The narrative is a complex account containing many scenes, all of which are necessary to communicate the importance of the resurrection. This account is Christianity's "core narrative," the story that represents the essential elements of what Christians believe.

This complex of events is so central to Christianity that Christians use one element from the narrative to symbolize the essence of their religious belief: the cross. Catholics, in particular, display a crucifix at their gatherings. A crucifix is a cross with the body of Jesus displayed on it. When most people today walk into a room with a crucifix, even if they are not Catholic, they do not think, "How gross! They put a symbol of a dead guy in this room!" Instead they recognize that this crucifix, coming from one part of the Passion Narrative, summarizes and represents the whole cycle of Jesus' death and resurrection.

In the same way, the exodus was so central to the Israelites' history that later poets and prophets could refer to just one small part of the story and know that the audience would recall the whole span of events leading up to and following the exodus. I call this cycle of events "the exodus pattern." It includes three parts: slavery in Egypt, miraculous deliverance from that slavery, and laws given in the wilderness. The book of Exodus contains the fullest example of this pattern.

Christians know the Passion Narrative well because they hear it in church annually at their holiest time of year. The Israelites may have known the exodus accounts for the same reason, because they heard them on their high holy days. This was certainly true once Passover, the feast celebrating the exodus, became a regular part of Israelite ritual or liturgy. Liturgy was and remains an important way oral traditions are maintained.

Retelling a story in church is not the same as retelling a story for information. In recounting an event in a history book, the author wants to present an objective and fair account of what happened. A historical investigation of the crucifixion, for instance, might talk about the practice of crucifixion in the Roman era, the biological realities of such a death, the identification of a possible criminal named Barrabas, and so on. When the account is told in church, however, the focus is on God's salvation and the human response to that act of salvation. We see clear evidence of this approach in the way that the exodus story is told in the book of Exodus.

The book of Exodus has elements common to ancient folklore. For example, it does not give us specific names of pharaohs, the dates of their reigns, or even the exact location for the parting of the sea. Instead, it focuses on God's deliverance of the Israelites and on the reaction of Moses and the Hebrews to God's activity in their lives. The author uses mythic elements, such as we saw in Genesis, to heighten the importance of these events. These mythic elements include exaggeration (also called "hyperbole") and symbolism, elements that will be highlighted in the discussion of individual texts. These rhetorical devices remind the reader that these are "cosmic" events that changed the world.

Yahweh as Warrior

Because the story of the exodus is and has been so popular, we tend to expect it to be an uplifting story. Yet, whenever I teach this material, I find that there are a significant number of people for whom the biblical account of the exodus is troubling. We will see that the book of Exodus portrays God as violent and manipulative, especially in the treatment of the Egyptians. This description of

Focus on METHOD

Redaction Criticism

Source criticism seeks evidence of different written sources that were used in composing a text. It goes "behind" the text to investigate the history of its production. It arose as a way to explain such things as changes in style, vocabulary, and characterization, as well as repetitions and contradictions.

Like the author of the book of Genesis, the author of Exodus used sources in creating the text, including J, E, and P. Evidence of the sources can be found, for example, in the different explanations for the crossing of the sea in chapters 14 and 15. It is not surprising that each source has an account of the exodus, since this event was central to Israelite religion, just as all four gospels contain an account of the death of Jesus.

Source criticism aims to identify each separate strand of the text. Redaction criticism examines how and why these strands were put together. Source and redaction criticisms often go hand-in-hand; together they are tools for examining the history of the text's production.

Redaction criticism is most compelling when we have at least some of the sources that the redactor used. This is the case for the first three gospels in the New Testament (Matthew, Mark, and Luke), which exhibit interdependence; likewise, it is true for 1 and 2 Chronicles, which are dependent on several other biblical books. In these cases, a biblical scholar can see the additions, deletions, or rearrangements of material done by the redactor. These changes can reveal the particular interests or emphasis of an author.

These examples serve as a model when the earlier sources no longer exist. Such is the case for the Pentateuch. Clearly the redactor used different traditions Source criticism isolates these sources; redaction criticism asks why they have been put together in this particular way.

In this sense, redaction criticism highlights the literary artistry of the final author. Let me use a contemporary example. Many musical artists today produce "remixes" of earlier songs; similarly, many rap artists use bits of other people's music in their records. Their artistry comes from the way that they use these earlier musical sources.

The same is true for the redactor of Exodus. He used earlier versions of this event, but he is no mere copyist. He intertwines these sources so that elements of each play off against each other, highlighting some elements and pushing others into the background. Redaction criticism recognizes the sources because the artistry of the final text is the result of how these sources are used.

Try this exercise. Look at the three wife-sister stories in Genesis (12:10–20; 20:1–18; and 26:1–16). List the ways that the three versions are the same. Then note how the second and third versions differ from the first one. What issues do these changes address? Why has the redactor retained all three versions in the final version of Genesis?

God can offend modern sensibilities if readers do not take the time to understand why the Israelites found such a representation of God to be uplifting. We will deal with this issue more fully when we read specific texts, but I would like to introduce the problem here.

In the polytheistic cultures surrounding Israel, such as Babylon and Canaan, some of the most important and powerful deities were warrior gods and goddesses. These were divine beings that fought beside the human army in times of national crisis. Every nation in the ancient world had warrior gods, and ancient peoples did not venture into war without first being sure that their warrior gods were with them. Priests and prophets accompanied the armies to deliver oracles and perform ritual sacrifices. You may be familiar with certain

The Bible in the CHRISTIAN TRADITION

Liberation Theology

Liberation theology, which was developed in the second half of the twentieth century by Catholic theologians from Latin America, has spread to many different countries and religions. One of the central ideas of liberation theology is that God opposes all aspects of human oppression; it seeks to realize, here on earth, the belief that all people are created with equal dignity and worth.

Liberation theologians have many scriptural warrants to conclude that the God revealed in the Bible is a god who fights for the oppressed. One of the texts central to their conclusion is the exodus account.

When liberation theology first arose, it was a response to Christians who economically oppressed fellow Christians without recognizing the hypocrisy of such oppression. Some Latin American liberation theologians have pointed out the Catholic Church's complicity in this oppression. In addition, some liberation theologians also use Marxist economic theory. These elements led the Catholic Church at first to be wary of liberation theology. Now, however, the force of the argument that oppression is not compatible with the Christian message has led the Roman Catholic Church to accept liberation theology (as long is it avoids the reductionism of some Marxist theorists).

Recently, however, a new critique of certain uses of liberation theology has arisen, this from peoples displaced by invasion, colonization, or other acts of "conquest." These theologians point out that the exodus involved not just freedom from slavery but also possession of a land. This possession displaced the Canaanites. Similarly European Christians, for example, felt justified in displacing and annihilating people who were settled in a land that they believed was theirs by divine right. As the Native American theologian Robert Warrior points out, one group's liberation may be another group's oppression.

Greek or Roman myths in which the gods fight in heaven while the human army fights on earth.

The Israelites also believed that when their army went out to battle, Yahweh accompanied them. We will see this over and over again in the Bible. Parts of the book of Exodus, especially those from the Priestly source, portray God as a warrior defeating the army of Egypt.

Today we may be offended by the thought of God participating in the killing of human beings, especially if we concentrate on the graphic military images that the Bible uses. Yet, this idealization of God expresses a common theological hope that people have. Even today, when armies go off to battle, we pray for the safety of the troops and sometimes for the success of their mission. Some Christians believe that some wars are "justifiable," while other Christians are pacifists. Even pacifists, however, hope that God will reward the just and that a just peace will prevail.

Israel's language of a warrior God expresses this same human hope. The Hebrews in Exodus looked to God to relieve their oppression as slaves and to bring them to a land where they could live free and secure, a land where they would be able to worship their God. Their stories express this hope.

In addition, it is essential to remember that the Israelites never had a big and powerful army. Neither were they a country like the United States with weapons of mass destruction in their grasp. They were a weak nation during the monarchy. Their weapons tended to be inferior, and they had to buy military equipment from other, more powerful nations, such as Egypt. Because of this weakness, the Israelites had often experienced destruction at the hands of other more powerful nations, nations that were, from their perspective, evil and unjust. The poems and narratives that celebrate God's ability to kill the most powerful army in the world express the impossible hopes of a powerless nation, not the violent fantasies of a military machine. It is not surprising that as citizens of a powerful country, we may have trouble seeing a violent God as a comforting figure, while people in oppressed countries today may more easily see the God of Exodus as a liberating figure who saves people from injustice.

READING EXODUS

EXODUS 1:8–2:10: MOSES AND THE SILLY PHARAOH

The story of the birth of Moses is easy enough to follow, but the comic elements may be missed in a modern context.

IN CASE YOU WERE WONDERING

Midwives (1:15). Those who specialize in delivering babies, midwives, were prominent in the ancient world. In ancient Egypt, women in labor sat on a special chair called a "birth stool."

A nurse (2:7). Rich women, such as the pharaoh's daughter, as well as women who adopted babies, hired poor women who were still nursing their own children to breastfeed their babies as well.

LOOKING CLOSELY AT THE TEXT

1. Why did Pharaoh want to kill the Hebrew babies?

2. What roles do various women play in this account?

THE BIRTH OF MOSES

This is a very funny story. Weren't you laughing out loud when you were reading it? . . . Oh, you weren't? Well, that's the problem with humor, isn't it? Humor can often be lost, because it depends so much on an understanding of a particular context. The humor and irony in the birth story of Moses are like that: you have to know what is expected of kings or the pharaoh to see how comically he is portrayed here.

The ancient societies of the Fertile Crescent were *patriarchal*, meaning that they believed that men were more powerful, better, and had more rights than women. It was a man's job to care for and control the women who depended on him. This meant that a man "ruled over" his wife and his daughters.

Kings ruled over the whole country. One way to illustrate that a king was not strong enough to rule over a country was to show that he could not control women dependent on him. The Pharaoh in Exodus has no control over women; they repeatedly outsmart him. First, two midwives, that is, two lower-class women, dupe him. They are able to save the Hebrew babies simply by lying to the king. Next, he is undone by his own daughter, who finds a baby in the river, and, knowing that he is a Hebrew baby, brings him home to raise as her own. I would have liked to have been a fly on the wall when she came home and told her dad, "I found a Hebrew baby in the river. Can I keep him?" Lastly, he is outwitted by Moses' mother, even if he is unaware of it. Not only does the mother exhibit her wisdom by following Pharaoh's orders (she does put the baby in the river), but, with the help of her daughter, she manages to get paid by the pharaoh's daughter to nurse him herself. The great Pharaoh is manipulated by women.

Moreover, Pharaoh's original plan showed him to be unwise. The plan was based on his fears, which led him to make poor decisions. He fears two things. He fears that the Hebrews will become too numerous. However, the way to limit the population of mammals is to cut down on females, not males. He kills the wrong gender to cut down on the number of births, depriving Egypt of males who make up the bulk of his labor force. Also, he fears that the Hebrews will join a foreign army and fight against him. Do infants join armies? Of course not! In fact, by killing the sons of adult males, he gives the fathers of these boys more reason to revolt against him. The Pharaoh is not just weak; he is also stupid.

This portrayal of Pharaoh is a parody, ridiculing the character's self-perception. The Egyptians held that the Pharaoh was semi-divine, because they believed that while his mother was human, his father was the sun god. Israelites found this notion absurd and often parodied this Egyptian belief. They portrayed the Egyptians, especially Pharaoh, as overly proud. The same ridicule occurs in the text's portrayal of the boastful Pharaoh. This parody is part of the folkloric elements of the text.

This delightful story of the birth of Moses highlights some important elements of the book of Exodus. First, it vividly depicts the oppression and helplessness of the Hebrews. They had no control over their fate and were left to suffer at the hands of a stupid, paranoid king who thought he was a god. Second, it introduces Moses as the one chosen by God from birth to fulfill a special mission. When we see Moses and the Israelites express hesitancy at God's call later in the book, we are supposed to remember what God has already done for them.

Exodus 3:1–4:17: The Call of Moses

After the description of the birth of Moses, the text quickly jumps to his life as a young man. The Bible contains no descriptions of his life in the palace, or his relationship with the Pharaoh and his children. Instead, the text is clear that, even as a young man, Moses knows that he is a Hebrew. When he sees an Egyptian beating a Hebrew, he kills the Egyptian and must flee the country, because he is now a murderer.

Moses flees to "Midian," an area in the Sinai Peninsula. There he settles with a local priest, Jethro, and marries his daughter, Zipporah. They have a son, Gershom, and Moses seems content working for his father-in-law. Then God hears the cries of oppression from the Hebrews and decides to deliver them. This complex story of God's initial interactions with Moses reveals how little the Hebrews knew about God.

In Case You Were Wondering

Horeb. This is another name for Mount Sinai.

Bare feet. This reference signifies respect. Moses removes his dirty shoes (3:5), just as he would if he were entering a house or temple in the ancient world.

A sign (3:12). This was an event that would affirm that God's promises would come true.

Leprosy (4:6). This term refers to various skin diseases in the ancient world.

Aaron. He is Moses' brother, but we do not know where Aaron comes from (4:14). Was he older and, therefore, not killed when Pharaoh killed the other boys? Was he younger, at a time when Pharaoh had stopped trying to kill boys? The Bible never tells us.

Looking Closely at the Text

1. What was odd about the burning bush?

2. What four objections does Moses give God for not wanting to go to Egypt?

3. What does God say his name is?

4. What two signs does God give Moses that he will be successful?

5. How will Aaron help Moses?

THE CALL OF MOSES

This complex narrative tells the story of how Moses was first called by God to deliver the Israelites from slavery. Embedded in the call narrative are texts outlining the character of Moses as a reluctant leader, the revelation of God's name, and brief notices that link the exodus narratives with the stories of the patriarchs. Let's look at each of these in turn.

The portrayal of Moses seems to go out of its way to depict this biblical hero as an average person. He is not someone seeking power. He does not undertake the contest with Pharaoh to promote his own reputation and power. In fact, time after time, he raises objections to God's call, almost to the point of sinfulness. The objections help to focus attention on God's role in saving the Hebrews. They are saved, not because a great, powerful leader happened along at the right time. In fact, they are saved by a person with little natural talent for the job; therefore, their deliverance must be miraculous.

The call of Moses reflects the understanding of prophecy in ancient Israel. Today, we often think that a prophet is someone who predicts the future. However, this is not what the ancient Israelites thought. For them a prophet is an intermediary, a spokesperson for God, one who delivers God's messages to the people. This idea is highlighted in the passage concerning Aaron, in which God says that Aaron will be Moses' "mouth," and Moses will be Aaron's "god" (Exod 4:16). This means that just as Moses hears what God says and voices God's messages to the people, so too Aaron will hear what Moses has to say and will then deliver his message to the Pharaoh. This idea is reinforced in Exodus 7:1: "The LORD said to Moses, 'See, I have made you like God to Pharaoh, and your brother Aaron shall be your prophet.'"

One of the most surprising elements in this story is that the Hebrews, Moses among them, apparently have no idea who this god is that is going to deliver them. In Exodus 3:13–17, Moses notes that the Israelites would need to know who the god is who is sending Moses to deliver them. This suggests that either the Hebrews had forgotten the god that Abraham had worshipped or that the Hebrews were worshipping many gods and needed to know which of them was sending Moses. God answers by revealing the divine name. The Israelites can now call on God by this proper name, which signifies that they have a personal relationship with this god.

The name itself is a bit odd. It comes from the Hebrew verb "to be" and may mean any number of things. The pronunciation usually given the name Yahweh would suggest something like "the one who creates," inferring that this god was primarily the god who created the world. In other passages in the Bible, a longer version of the name, the LORD of hosts, could also be translated as "the one who created the heavenly armies." This would suggest that Yahweh was first and foremost a warrior God. The book of Exodus, however, first states that the name means "the one who is." The name itself was probably deliberately ambiguous so that all of these meanings would be conveyed.

After God reveals the divine name, Yahweh then proceeds to tell Moses, and therefore the Israelites, that this is the same god that the patriarchs and matriarchs had worshipped. This suggests that originally people thought of the god of Abraham and the god of Moses as two different gods. The author of this passage, however, is stating that they are the same god, the one God, known by different names at different times. This reminds us that the early Israelites believed in the existence of many gods, but that they worshipped only Yahweh.

The connection of the god of Abraham with the god of Moses also connects the two locations: Canaan and Egypt. Israel's delivery from slavery is not just delivery *from* somewhere: it is delivery *to* somewhere, that is, to the land where the

The History of the Name of God

Within the Bible, there are several names given to God, including *Elohim* (God), *El 'Abraham* (the God of Abraham), *Yhwh* (often transcribed as "Yahweh"), and *El shaddai* (God most high) to name a few. In addition, the revelation of the name of Yahweh occurs at two different points in the biblical text: Genesis 4:26 and Exodus 3:14–15.

The difficulty of this last name arises from a couple of different sources. First, in the biblical period, the Hebrew writing system had no way to indicate vowels. The system of indicating Hebrew vowels, called "pointing," developed much later.

By the time that pointing had developed, Jews were also following a tradition of not saying the divine name. In prepointed texts this tradition is indicated by writing the divine name in an ancient script, different from the rest of the scroll. In pointed texts, the scribes used the vowels from the Hebrew word for "lord" or "master"

(in Hebrew *'Adonai*) with the consonants for the divine name. In this way, when someone came across the divine name in a text, they would say "Lord" rather than "Yahweh." This is indicated in several modern translations that use "LORD" with small capital letters to indicate that the text has the divine name.

Many Jews today continue the tradition of not saying the divine name. Instead, a number of circumlocutions are used, such as G-d, *ha-shem* (Hebrew for "the name"), and even *ado-shem* (a combination of *'Adonai* and *ha-shem*).

For a long time, Christians were not aware of this tradition. This was especially true in the high Middle Ages when Christians began learning Hebrew. They simply thought that the vowels they found in the Hebrew text were correct. The name *Jehovah* is the result of this misunderstanding. It comes from the medieval transcription of the consonants for "Yahweh" with vowels of "'lord."

patriarchs had first settled. This passage recalls the covenant with the patriarchs and matriarchs, a covenant that promised them a particular homeland.

In sum, the call of Moses links the exodus to the stories of the patriarchs and matriarchs. First, it states that the god worshipped by the patriarchs and matriarchs is the same God who calls Moses. Second, it states that God will deliver them back to the land promised to Abraham and his descendants. This passage sums up the main theological framework of the story. Moses is God's human agent who will work wonders to deliver the Israelites. But the reader must remember that deliverance happens because of God's power alone, not because of Moses' power or the people's faithfulness. Salvation comes because God is merciful.

EXODUS 7:14–10:29: NINE PLAGUES

Immediately following his encounter with God, Moses sets off with his family for Egypt. On the way he meets up with his brother Aaron, whom God has sent to accompany him. God speaks again to Moses and Aaron, restating many of the things said to Moses alone. These speeches also connect the God of Abraham with Yahweh and repeat that the freed slaves will be led to the land promised to the patriarchs and matriarchs.

This speech also introduces the themes of Holy War. God describes the deliverance in military terms. For instance, the text talks about leading the people with an "outstretched arm," an image used by kings to depict their military strength. This speech comes from a different source than the speech at the burning bush (JE). This use of varying sources explains the repetition of similar ideas while using different images.

Whether the plagues are naturally occurring disasters or pure miracles, the text wants the reader to see the hand of God in them. Moses and Aaron meet with Pharaoh to request the release of the slaves. They perform "signs" and warn of the last plague, the slaying of the firstborn sons of the Egyptians. This material attempts to show that Pharaoh had plenty of chances to "do the right thing."

IN CASE YOU WERE WONDERING

Plague. Webster's dictionary defines *plague* as "a disastrous evil or affliction" or as "an epidemic disease causing a high rate of mortality." In the Old Testament it refers to a series of ten disasters sent by God to punish and persuade Pharaoh.

Miracles and magic. The Israelites believed that there were some miraculous acts that any holy person could perform. Yahweh proves the stronger god, however, by increasing the difficulty of the acts until Aaron and Moses alone can accomplish them.

Varying sources. Different sources probably provided different plague stories. For instance, some of the plague stories feature Aaron, while others have Moses alone. Some stories have the Israelites living in Goshen, an area in the northeast Delta region of the Nile, while others have them living among the Egyptians.

"Hardening of the heart." This phrase means that a person has become stubborn about a particular course of action.

Looking Closely at the Text

1. What exactly does Moses request from Pharaoh?

2. Why does God allow the plagues to go on so long?

Plagues as Miracles

Some people have tried to explain the nine plagues as a naturally occurring series of disasters. While such an explanation makes sense to our modern scientific way of thinking, it does little justice to the story itself. The plague narratives explicitly demonstrate to the reader that these were miraculous events, brought about by the power of God. Even if these disasters happened at other times, their occurrence at this particular time, in this particular order is divinely arranged. In addition, the number of plagues, their duration, and the fact that they only affect the Egyptians are all part of the mythic portrayal of this material.

I have found that some students have difficulty with the depiction of God in these stories. While the plagues begin with Pharaoh "hardening his own heart," they eventually talk about God hardening Pharaoh's heart. This seems particularly cruel for two reasons. First, in these cases, Pharaoh appears to have agreed to let the people go. God is manipulative and interrupts Pharaoh's exercise of free will. If we remember that this text is making fun of the Egyptian belief that Pharaoh was a god, then Yahweh's manipulation of Pharaoh is really showing Yahweh as the only true god. A second problem still remains, however. God's manipulation of Pharaoh results in suffering for both the Egyptians and the Hebrews. God is then unfair and cruel.

While I cannot explain away this dimension, a discussion of the use of this material can provide another way to think about the function of the story. We began the chapter by talking about Exodus as a version of the exodus event, probably retold within the context of a ritual reenactment. We paralleled the exodus to the Passion narratives, which are re-enacted during Holy Week. Let's return to that parallel for just a moment.

As the story of Jesus' death is retold on Palm Sunday and Good Friday the readings portray Judas in a particular way. He is depicted as evil, greedy, the worst kind of traitor. Neither the Bible nor the liturgy tries to understand his interior motivation. Judas's portrayal serves the function of moving the plot along, and he comes to represent those who turn their back on Christ. Certainly the historical Judas did have reasons for doing what he did that are unexplored in the liturgy. But when I participate in the Holy Week liturgies, I do not worry that we are not giving Judas a fair shake.

Pharaoh represents evil for the Israelites. He is proud, mean, a perfect "bad guy." He is a great foe for God, because he deems himself to be a god. The stories of the plagues are arranged to create dramatic tension. As the plagues progress, they intensify. By the time the Egyptian army drowns in the sea, the audience feels justified joy at their defeat. The biblical authors do not choose to explore the inner motivations of the Pharaoh. They do not choose to tell the story from his point of view, because the point of the narrative is for the audience to recognize the great power of God.

In some ways the book of Exodus is like a good action movie. It pits good against evil. It characterizes the villain as foolish, boastful, and deserving of his fate. It builds up the dramatic tension with increasingly spectacular plagues. It ends in the triumph of the "little guy." Moses is depicted as an unlikely hero, afraid and reluctant. The Hebrews that he saves are weak and oppressed. God is the ultimate hero, however, the one who does all this for a poor and lowly nation. God hears the cries of their oppression, and provides them with a spectacular defeat of their enemy.

Exodus 11:1–10; 12:21–36: The Death of the Firstborn

The tenth plague is so horrible that, at last, Pharaoh and the Egyptians not only allow the Hebrews to leave, they pay them to go. The plague that prompts their departure seems terribly cruel to a modern audience: the death of all the firstborn males of the Egyptians, even down to their animals. Yet, this gruesome tale becomes a central element in the life and identity of both Jews and Christians.

This story follows immediately on the previous ones. In the middle of it, however, the text gives specific regulations for how the Passover is to be celebrated annually. This ritual material does not fit the narrative context of the story, but it does show the true purpose of the narrative: to specify the proper observation of an annual festival.

In Case You Were Wondering

A lintel (12:7) is the cross beam over a door, and the doorposts are the sides of the door frame.

Looking Closely at the Text

1. What are the Hebrews supposed to ask from their neighbors?

2. How does the angel determine which house to spare?

3. How does this punishment mirror the oppression at the beginning of the book?

The Passover

Passover is a high holy day for Jews from biblical times to today. The celebration retains the spirit of the biblical text: this is a story of liberation, an account of God's miraculous delivery of the chosen people. It is so easy to get caught up in the "bloody" details of the story that we miss this point. Maybe it would help if we put it in a more contemporary context. What do you think twentieth-century Jews would have viewed as a just punishment for the Nazis? If God had freed the Jews from the concentration camps by slaying the Nazis, would this have been viewed as unjust on the part of God? The Egyptians here are not to be seen as innocent victims. Their whole culture enslaved and oppressed the Hebrews.

Passover is also a central theme for Christianity. In Luke's Gospel the Last Supper that Jesus has with the disciples is a Passover meal. New Testament writers concentrate on Passover as a ritual of liberation, not simply as a description of the death of some Egyptians long ago. Christians see salvation from sin as Jesus' ultimate act of liberation.

The legal material that brackets this story should remind us that the story first circulated to fit a liturgical or ritual setting. Just like the portrayal of Judas in the Passion Narrative, God's ability to take what is most precious to the evil Egyptians works within the symbolism of the Passover service. The biblical account of the Passover event retains the mythic elements that reflect this liturgical use throughout the story. Yahweh comes down to earth to mete out punishment. All of the firstborn males are killed, even of animals. The Hebrews flee with Egyptian silver and gold, freely given to them. The audience hears this account of the Passover as an event that changed history, an event whose effects continue to be felt throughout history.

The account of the death of sons forms an "inclusio" or closing parallel to the Egyptian slaughter of the Hebrew children in the first chapter. Where the "divine" Pharaoh's plan failed, Yahweh's plan cannot fail. As literature, this plague on the Egyptians retains a narrative justice: the Egyptians, following the orders of their Pharaoh-god by killing Hebrew children, now mourn the death of their own children at the hands of the Hebrew god. In this way, the Hebrews are freed by God's ironic punishment.

In addition, Israelite understanding of child sacrifice informs this story. Recall that child sacrifice was a ritual performed to thank the gods for the gift of children. Most ancient countries, including Israel, substituted the sacrifice of a lamb, ram, or goat for the child. God directs the Israelites to practice the substitution ritual; the blood of the lamb is evidence that the sacrifice has been made. The Egyptians have not performed the ritual, so the angel of death claims their children. The connection between the Passover and this redemption sacrifice is underscored in Exodus 13:11–16. These verses state that the redemption sacrifice reminds the Israelites that God redeemed their ancestors through the death of the Egyptians' first-born children.

We miss what this story is saying about God when we fail to recognize this ritual background. The people in the Levant believed that the god who provided children would be the one who would send a punishment on those who did not recognize the divine power. With the final plague, Yahweh is making a claim on all of Egypt. Yahweh claims all of Egypt by taking the firstborn of its children.

Exodus 13:17–15:21: The Crossing of the Sea

After another set of laws on how to observe Passover, this story follows immediately on the tenth plague. This part of the story completes the liberation of the Hebrews. Can you picture what the biblical writer is trying to describe?

In Case You Were Wondering

The Red Sea (13:18) should actually have been translated as the "Reed Sea." This was a much smaller body of water.

Place names in the narrative, although not all identifiable today, must have set a clear stage for the original audience.

Looking Closely at the Text

1. Note some of the military imagery used in these chapters.

2. How do the Hebrews survive?

3. How does Pharaoh's army die?

4. In what ways is the account of the Egyptians' defeat in the song similar to the prose accounts? How are they different?

A MIRACLE BY ALL ACCOUNTS

If you compare your answers to the above questions with other students, you may find that you disagree about the details of this story. While the general outline is clear enough, the details are unclear, due to the fact that the story of the crossing of the sea has been pieced together from several different sources. Not all source critics agree on which verses belong to which source, but they all agree that what we have here is a composite text.

The Yahwist version of the story depicts the event in more natural terms. A wind that comes in the night dries up a shallow lake bed. The Hebrews cross over safely, but the wheels of the Egyptian chariots get caught in the mud. As the wind subsides in the morning and the sea returns to its normal depth, the army is drowned. The Yahwist depicts this event as a miracle of timing. God sent the wind in answer to the cries of the Hebrews.

Another version of the story, by the Priestly writer, adds mythic elements, so that the reader does not miss the point. The writer has added military language throughout the material. The size of Pharaoh's army is recounted, and the unarmed Hebrews march in battle formation and set up a military camp. How is the victory achieved? Yahweh fights. This divine warrior will not be defeated even by Pharaoh and his whole army. The text makes clear that deliverance was not some lucky break for the Hebrews; it was a miracle! In order to stress this theme, P reinforces the miraculous elements. God orders Moses to lift his staff. When Moses does, the water splits, forming walls on each side of the fleeing slaves. As the Egyptian army enters this path, Moses lowers his staff and the waters come crashing down on them. The message in P is that, even if God would have had to firm up the waters like a wall, the Israelites would have been saved.

The earliest version of the story is actually found at the end. The poem in chapter 15 derives from a pre-Yahwistic source. Although the text has Moses singing the song, notice in verses 20–21 that his sister, Miriam, leads the women in this song. In Hebrew, a song's "title" was the first line of the song. The verses that credit Miriam with leading the song are probably more original, since women generally sang the victory song.

Yahweh is portrayed as a warrior in the poem, although the details of the victory are imprecise. Did the army sink (15:4), or was there a flood (v. 5); did the waters congeal (v. 8), or did the wind stir up a tidal wave (v. 10)? While these versions may disagree as to the mechanism of the event, they all agree it was a miracle. God saved the Israelites by getting them across that sea.

Summary: God, the Liberator

While the general outline of these stories from Exodus is probably familiar to many contemporary readers, the details of the text can be surprising and even troubling. Every time I teach this material, I have some students who love this material. They find the plot exciting and the power of God that it conveys uplifting. I also have other students who are upset by the way God is portrayed. However, no matter what your reaction is, the bottom line is that these texts were not meant for us. These were uplifting stories written by and for a people whose lives were very different from our own. The Israelites, who wrote and preserved this material, had experienced unjust oppression at the hands of their enemies for generations. They knew that the kind of slaves the book of Exodus is imagining are those whose lives were deemed not worth the bits of food it cost to feed them. They understood what it was to sit helplessly while an enemy slaughtered their children. Can you blame them for believing that God is powerful enough to remedy this unjust life? Sometimes I think that some of us live so comfortably that we identify too easily with the Egyptians in this story. After all, in the political arena today, the United States is far more like ancient Egypt than it is like the Hebrews.

People who hold these texts to be sacred need to remember a basic principle when reading the Bible. The Bible is divine revelation in human words. Humans experience God's presence imperfectly. Humans experience "bits" of God, really. The people who wrote these texts were trying to express their experience of their God. They were conveying something about God's power. They were saying that God can enter human history and shape its events, that God's power exceeds that of any great nation, any boastful leader, any person who would put themselves above God. They were also trying to express their experience of God's care for a people, a care that goes so deep that God would enter human history to remedy an unjust situation.

The text may lead us to think about God's justice. Is everything that God does just, or can God commit an unjust act? Can the experience of oppression be so great that God's power is justly expressed in terms of victory over human enemies? And is God any more just if the oppression is allowed to continue as a result of God's mercy on the oppressors?

In sum, the story of the exodus unfolds as a cosmic battle between the self-proclaimed god, Pharaoh, and the true god, Yahweh. Within this cosmic battle, an unlikely hero emerges, Moses, who saves a poor but righteous people. The story is filled with mythic elements, such as the miraculous survival of the infant Moses, the duration and variety of the plagues, the death of the firstborn, and the miraculous crossing of the sea. While these mythocosmic elements reflect the original liturgical setting of much of the material, the details also highlight the foundational nature of this account. It is not just about some slave revolt in the past. It is about God's gracious and powerful redemption of the nation. The mythic details keep the narrative focus on Yahweh. The narrative details prepare the reader to join the song of praise of the triumphant Hebrews that closes this material: "The LORD is a warrior; the LORD is his name!" (Exod 15:3).

FOR REVIEW

1. What is the difference between "Exodus" and "exodus"?

2. What is the general outline of the book of Exodus?

3. During what period of Egypt's history were the stories of the exodus set?

4. What are the three parts of the exodus pattern?

5. What is the purpose of mythic elements in a story?

6. What is a "warrior god"?

FOR FURTHER READING

On the history of ancient Egypt as it relates to Israel, see Donald B. Redford, *Egypt, Canaan and Israel in Ancient Times* (Princeton, NJ: Princeton University Press, 1992).

On the mythic elements of the exodus story, see Bernard F. Batto, *Slaying the Dragon: Mythmaking in the Biblical Tradition* (Louisville, KY: Westminster John Knox, 1992).

There are a set of articles that address the question whether the exodus narratives are stories of liberation or of oppression in *Voices from the Margin: Interpreting the Bible from the Third World*, edited by R. S. Sugirtharajah (Maryknoll, NY: Orbis, 1991); each one is written from a different cultural context.

4 · THE SINAI COVENANT

The Lord, our God, made a covenant with us at Horeb. Not with our ancestors did the Lord make this covenant, but with us, who are all of us here alive today.
(Deut 5:2-3)

CHAPTER OVERVIEW

In this chapter we will look at the laws found in the Old Testament. To help us do that, this chapter will provide the following material in the introduction:

❯ A description of the story-line within which we find the law

❯ A discussion of the distinction between the Ten Commandments and other laws found in the Pentateuch

❯ A treatment of the importance of the ritual laws in the Pentateuch

❯ A discussion of how the law is understood within Judaism and Christianity

By the end of this chapter I hope that you have a better appreciation for the legal material that has formed the central message of the Bible for modern Judaism.

READING THE LAW THROUGH A CONTEMPORARY LENS

AN OVERVIEW OF THE WILDERNESS PERIOD

Since this material covers so many books and is so complex, it will help you to have a general overview of the major events in the wilderness accounts. The Israelites first travel to a holy mountain, *Sinai* or *Horeb*. Often people mistakenly assume that Moses received only the Ten Commandments at Sinai, but in fact he received most of the laws that are in the Pentateuch.

This revelation takes a long time to occur; Moses is on Mount Sinai for forty days. The people, already characterized as ungrateful and complaining, presume he has died, and so they make Aaron their leader, and they fashion golden calves as representatives of their god.

God becomes angry and sends Moses down with a judgment against the people. Moses breaks the tablets engraved with the laws God has given him. He receives further laws, which include the laws for building the Tabernacle, for example. After two years the Israelites set out from Sinai. At first they try to enter the Promised Land directly from the south, but they grow fearful when they hear reports of the strength of the people who live there. God becomes angry at their lack of faith, and pronounces a judgment against the generation that came out of Egypt.

The Israelites continue their journey, first to Kadesh Barnea, then through Edom and Moab. According to Deuteronomy a journey that normally takes eleven days takes the Israelites forty years! Along the way they meet many challenges: kings who oppose them, rebellion within their own ranks, and the temptation to settle with the communities they were supposed to march past. At last the Israelites reach their destination, and they cross the Jordan River from the plains of Moab.

THE WILDERNESS AS A THRESHOLD

The Pentateuch portrays the wilderness period as a formative time in Israelite history. The number *40* is not to be read literally, but represents "a long time" and indicates that the wilderness was a significant part of Israel's history. Some of the prophets will refer to this as Israel's "honeymoon" period. The wilderness that separated Egypt and Israel served as the place where the contours of the later nation were formed.

Anthropologists would refer to this material as Israel's *liminal* period. The word *limen* means threshold in Latin, and something is "liminal" if it is between stages. For instance, a teenager is sometimes said to be at a liminal stage: the threshold of adulthood, when she or he is not really a child, but not yet an adult. In many premodern societies complex rituals marked the boundaries of a person's life, rituals that were believed to help the person cross the divide. For instance, in some Native American cultures, the Vision Quest is a ritual that marks a boy's transition to manhood.

Israel's wilderness wanderings mark its transition from a landless people called by God, to a settled society living in the Promised Land in accord with God's laws. This quest takes time and is fraught with danger and ambiguity. The narrative of the forty years makes clear that the biblical writers knew that the formation of a complex society cannot happen overnight.

Focus on METHOD

Tradition Criticism

Source criticism looks for evidence of written sources used by the redactor, while redaction criticism explores how the redactor put the sources together. However, the process of composition did not simply consist of cutting and pasting written sources together. Sometimes the text results from a complex development of various traditions.

Many biblical scholars view the giving of the law at Sinai as an originally separate tradition from the story of the exodus from Egypt. They note that, while many biblical texts outside of the Pentateuch make reference to one of the other events, only late biblical texts connect the two. Tradition criticism asks about the process by which separate traditions, such as the exodus and the events at Sinai, came to be linked.

An exercise with a more limited issue in tradition criticism may help you see what this method entails. Take a look at the following Passover laws: Exodus 12:13; Numbers 28:16–25; and Deuteronomy 16:1–8. Notice how they differ. The redactor of the Pentateuch probably found these laws in various written sources. However, the laws themselves give evidence of a changing tradition regarding how to celebrate Passover. A tradition such as this can have written and oral elements, and the changes can result from both formal changes made by authors or leaders, as well as from gradual changes that took place over the years as the festival was celebrated.

Tradition criticism considers these laws and proposes a model for how they developed over time. Where possible, it also looks at references to the Passover outside of the Pentateuch to help date the individual laws. Tradition criticism can be used to trace the history of a tradition behind a text, as well as how a tradition develops in written texts.

The core moment of the wilderness experience is the revelation of God's law to the community. Although some biblical texts suggest that this revelation took place at various stages throughout the years in the desert, the final form of the Pentateuch maintains that the core of the law was revealed at one particular time to Moses. The location for this revelation was a mountain in the wilderness, a mountain that the Elohist and Deuteronomist call Horeb, but that the Yahwist and Priestly Writer call by the more familiar name, Sinai.

You may recall that Horeb/Sinai was the place where Moses had encountered the burning bush. This mountain was experienced by the Israelites as especially holy to God, as sacred space, and we will see more than one divine appearance at this mountain in the Old Testament.

The wilderness narratives span four books in the Bible, each with its own narrative character.

Exodus. The book of Exodus, as you recall, tells the story of the exodus, but it also relates the key events at Sinai. At the end of the book, the Israelites build two special tents: a portable shrine, the Tabernacle, and a place for God to appear to them as they travel, the tent of meeting.

Leviticus. The book of Leviticus contains long lists of ritual laws revealed by God to Moses at the tent of meeting, while the Israelites are still encamped at Sinai.

Numbers. The book of Numbers describes the final years of the Israelites' sojourn in the wilderness. It begins by describing the order in which the tribes marched from Sinai, first to Kadesh Barnea, and eventually to the Jordan River. The narratives in the book describe the community's encounters with the people who will soon become Israel's neighbors.

Deuteronomy. The book of Deuteronomy opens with the Israelites encamped on the banks of the Jordan River. They are about to go into the Promised Land. The book is Moses' last speech before they set off. In this speech, he gives them the laws that they are to observe once they are settled in the land.

It's the Law!

Laws telling the Israelites how to live and worship are embedded within this narrative of Israel's travels to the Promised Land. It helps to know something about ancient legal texts before reading this part of the Bible.

The Code of Hammurabi is inscribed on an eight-foot-high black stela stone that was created around 1780 BCE. The laws are numbered to 282. At the top of the stone is this carved depiction of Hammurabi in front of the throne of a deity.

Law Codes in the Ancient Near East

Archaeologists have found several ancient law codes in the Fertile Crescent. Many of the codes have laws quite similar to those found in the Old Testament. It is not surprising that Israelite laws would be similar to law codes from countries that surrounded Israel. The authors were influenced by the cultures around them.

One of the most famous law codes comes from a Babylonian king named Hamurapi (sometimes spelled "Hammurabi"). This law code is written on a large stone, called a *stele*. The beginning of it talks about how the sun god, who is in charge of justice, revealed this law code to Hamurapi in order to reward him for his righteousness. At the top of the stone is a carving of the king receiving the law from the god.

The laws on the stele present an ideal society. While many of the laws are enforceable, several are not, carrying penalties that far exceed the crimes. Like the biblical laws outside of the Ten Commandments, the laws appear to be in random order. There has been no attempt to make sure that they are complete.

Law Codes in the Pentateuch

When we turn our focus to the laws in the Pentateuch, we find a complex collection of legal traditions. Source critics have demonstrated that what we now have in the Pentateuch is not a single law code, but several distinct law codes from various periods of Israel's history. How did these critics reach this conclusion? First, many topics are taken up several times in the Pentateuch, not always in the same way. Want to know what animals to sacrifice on Passover and where to perform the sacrifice? That answer will depend on which law about Passover you are using.

The various blocks of law reflect different social settings as well. One block seems to preserve the laws of an agricultural society, while another is more concerned with an urban society. Let me list the three most important law codes:

The Covenant Code. The Covenant Code in Exodus 21—23 contains laws stemming from a rural economy.

The Deuteronomic Code. The law code in Deuteronomy 12–26 reflects an urban-based monarchy. There is a law for the king here, as well as laws on how to conduct war and decide who is a true prophet.

The Holiness Code. The Holiness Code in Leviticus 17–26 was probably originally a law code for the priests. Here, however, it is presented as a law code for everybody.

God reveals these laws to Israel. They are not in any obvious order, nor are they complete, but they reflect a religious vision of a perfect society.

THE TEN COMMANDMENTS

The most familiar set of Israelite laws is probably the Ten Commandments. The *Ten Commandments* or *Decalogue* are ten short legal principles, inscribed by God onto two stone tablets and then given to Moses on Mount Sinai. They appear to summarize the many laws that follow, and these actually make up only a small percentage of the laws in the Pentateuch.

The Ten Commandments are different from the other laws in a couple of ways. First, they are physically set apart from the other laws, forming a complete unit by themselves. They appear in two places: Exodus 20:2–17 and Deuteronomy 5:6–21. In addition, they are arranged in a particular order. The first three or four (depending on which list you use) concern crimes against God, the last six or seven concern crimes against humans.

Second, the Ten Commandments are stated differently than most of the other laws. The majority of the other laws are expressed in a conditional sentence: if you do this, then that will happen to you. The Ten Commandments, on the other hand, are in the form of a negative command ("you shall not . . .").

This leads us to the most important difference between the two types of laws. Most of the other laws have a clear setting. These "if—then" statements arose from the setting of the court. (This does not mean that they were actually used in court cases, just that their language reflects that setting.) The description of the crime in the first part ("Whoever strikes father or mother . . .") is followed by the punishment (". . . shall be put to death" [Exod 21:15]). The Ten Commandments have no clear setting. In fact, they are not really *laws* in the strict sense of the term.

Let me give you an example. One of the commandments states, "You shall not murder" (Exod 20:13). This sounds like a very clear law, but think about its ambiguity. Does it say what you should do to someone who does kill? Does it mean that all forms of killing should have the same punishment? Should someone who carries out a premeditated murder be punished in the same manner as someone who kills accidentally? Did the Israelites punish their soldiers who killed an enemy in battle? The law codes make it clear that the Israelites understood these differences. There were laws for murder, but also specific ones for accidental death and what we would call manslaughter.

How were the Ten Commandments used, then? We're not sure. They seem to have been principles more than laws. They stem from a very old and important tradition in ancient Israel. The fact that they were reproduced in both Exodus and Deuteronomy is evidence of their significance.

RITUAL LAWS IN THE PENTATEUCH

When we think of laws today, we think of the rules that allow a society to run smoothly. Many Israelite laws have this same function. But in addition to laws on how to punish murderers, or what fine to impose on those who cheat others, many laws were religious in nature. They told the Israelites what holy days to observe and what kind of sacrifices to make. For the ancient Israelites, obeying religious regulations was just as vital for maintaining a healthy society as was preventing crime. I will refer to the religious laws as "ritual laws." The wording of the ritual laws presumes that you know something about Israelite worship. While I have discussed animal sacrifice in previous chapters, at this point I would like to say more about Israelite notions of sacred space, time, and people.

The Israelites did not experience the world as equitable. For them, certain things were "holier" than other things. They interpreted some things as closer to God than others. The concept of "sacred space" provides a concrete way to think about this notion.

Have you ever had the experience of being in a place so special that it seemed different from the rest of the world? Sometimes a place is special because it makes you feel closer to God. Native Americans have many such places where, as a community, they feel closer to the heavens.

Like Native Americans, the Israelites had certain places where they, as a community, felt closer to God, places which they agreed were holy. Mount Sinai was one such place, as was Bethel, where Jacob had set up an altar to God; eventually, their holiest place came to be Mount Zion in Jerusalem. They believed that these places were holy because God had picked them. The Israelites built altars at these places to mark them as holy.

The Israelites believed that God was greater than and superior to any creature. The way they expressed this idea was through their understanding of *holiness*. In Hebrew, the word for *holiness* also means "separation," and a thing's degree of holiness indicates its "place" in the world. Something was "holy" if it was good enough to be in God's presence. They believed that if something unholy tried to transgress or break through the boundary between heaven and earth, it would be destroyed. Recognizing that they could never attain the level of heavenly holiness, the Israelites feared contact with God because of their belief that such holiness could destroy them.

Purity or cleanness had nothing to do with hygiene. Rather it described something's capacity to attain holiness. If one was "pure" then one could attain a certain degree of holiness. God determined what made one "pure": something was pure if it corresponded to the way God created the world. When an element transgressed categories established by God, then it was impure.

Let me give you an example. The established place of blood is inside a body. Humans are not impure because they have blood. However, when blood comes out of the body, through a wound or menstruation, then it has transgressed its bounds, which renders the bleeder impure.

Impurity is not the same as sinfulness. Impurity imparts no guilt upon the one who is impure (although sin does result in impurity). It does limit, however, how close one can come to a holy place. Someone suffering impurity may not approach a holy place, such as a temple. If a person goes to a temple while impure, then she or he has sinned. So impurity limits your actions. Most impurities are temporary. When someone who is bleeding stops bleeding, then she or he can go through a ritual bath in order to become pure or clean again.

Some contemporary religions have retained some of these notions of holiness. For instance, Catholics are not supposed to eat for one hour before receiving Communion. If a Catholic has eaten within that time period, they have not sinned; their actions are simply restricted, in that they cannot receive communion. A Catholic does sin, however, if he or she ignores the prohibition and receives communion.

Let me use another example. Holy water is water that has been blessed; in other words, a ritual has been performed that renders it fit for certain religious uses, such as baptism. It is not supposed to be thrown away by pouring it down a regular sink drain, because then it would enter a sewer and come into contact with unblessed water. Instead, churches have special sinks that contain a pipe which leads directly into the ground. Holy water can go down this sink into the ground from which it came.

Temples, which represented a bit of heaven on earth, had clearly marked areas of holiness. Only certain people could enter certain parts of the temple. For example, in some temples only priests could enter the courtyard that surrounded the temple building.

Priests also kept careful watch over the calendar, which marked sacred time. The Israelites believed that God created the world in such a way that certain days were "holy" or sanctified. These were sacred times during which human activity was restricted. We will see that the Sabbath was one such day.

Lastly, the Israelites believed that not all people were able to attain the same degree of holiness, no matter what purification rituals they undertook. They believed that God had created certain families to be "holier" than others. This belief explains the hereditary priesthood. Most biblical texts agree that the tribe of Levi was holier than the other tribes. Moreover, within that tribe, according to some texts, the family of Aaron was the most holy. Therefore, since men were holier than women, the men of the family of Aaron were the priests who could make sacrifices at the holiest temple.

Holy Cow! Sacrifices in Ancient Israel

A common activity that took place at temples was sacrifice. Since this is a ritual that is not very common in the United States today, it is often misunderstood. Merriam-Webster dictionary defines a *sacrifice* as "an act of offering to a deity something precious; especially: the killing of a victim on an altar."

In the ancient Near East, sacrifices often resembled sumptuous meals. The daily sacrifices consisted of edible items: meat, grain (in the form of breads and cakes), produce (such as fruit and vegetables), oil, and wine. These were either placed on a table within the temple building or burned on an altar. Incense was also burned as an offering.

Many biblical texts focus on animal sacrifices. For the regular offerings, the animals were slaughtered, their blood was drained, and the blood was splashed on the outdoor altar. The carcass was then placed on the altar and burned completely; this was a whole-burnt offering (or holocaust). For other types of offerings, portions of cooked sacrificial meat might be eaten either by the priests and their families, and/or by the people making the sacrifice.

The most common animals used in sacrifice were oxen, sheep, goats, and birds. These sacrificial victims had to be "pure," meaning "without blemish or defect," and they had to undergo a ritual purification. There was a class of priests in charge of slaughtering and butchering the animals. Some biblical laws required that all butchering had to take place at a temple, an impractical law once the only legitimate temple was located in Jerusalem.

LAW AND GOSPEL: JEWISH AND CHRISTIAN ATTITUDES TOWARD THE LAW

Today, Jews and Christians have widely divergent attitudes toward the legal material in the Bible. For Jews, the law forms the center of the Bible. It is the holiest and most authoritative material.

Jewish tradition had many ways to deal with the repetitions and holes in the Bible's legal material. Much of the early post-biblical Jewish writing, such as the Mishnah and the Talmud, complete legal concepts and resolve apparent contradictions. Today different Jewish groups hold markedly different positions regarding biblical law; Reformed Jews, for example, differ radically from Hasidic Jews precisely on this question. But within broader Jewish tradition, the law informs Jewish identity as the people of God. Jews today strive to live in accord with these laws. They maintain the ancient notion that the primary purpose of the law is not to restrict human behavior, but rather to help people to live in accord with God's will. The law is God's most treasured gift to humanity.

Christian tradition has taken a much different position regarding Old Testament law. Although the issues are far too complex to explain fully here, Christians do not believe that Old Testament law still governs Christians. Rather, they believe that what is more important is what the law points to: the reality that there is a clear divide between God and humans and that human effort, on its own, can never secure one a place in heaven.

READING THE LAW

EXODUS 19:1–25 AND 20:18–21: THE SINAI THEOPHANY

After telling how the Israelites crossed the Sea and escaped the threat of the Egyptian army, the book of Exodus recounts how God aided them in their journey through the wilderness. As you recall, this was a people who had left with only the jewelry that they had taken from their neighbors. They now have to struggle to remain alive in a barren wasteland.

The people lament that they have no water, bread, or meat. God hears their pleas and sends each item to them in turn. These gifts prefigure the gift

The Bible in the CHRISTIAN TRADITION

Jesus and the Law

Christians have a particularly difficult time developing an appropriate attitude toward biblical law. New Testament texts, which reflect the debates of the early Christian communities about the law, reinforce a presumption that the law is irrelevant, if not downright bad. Yet, how can a Christian say both that the Old Testament is sacred Scripture and that the laws it contains are irrelevant?

It took a long time to get to where we are today. In the postexilic period, observation of the law became an increasingly important practice of Judaism. Concomitantly, Jewish groups differed on the way that they interpreted that law. As we see in this chapter, biblical law is not comprehensive or complete. Some Hellenistic Jewish groups, such as the Sadducees, believed that only those things explicitly forbidden in the law were binding. Other groups, such as the Pharisees, believed that the biblical precepts served as the basis for the development of parallel laws.

After the fall of Jerusalem to the Romans in 70 CE, the bases for modern Judaism, also known as "rabbinic Judaism," took shape. The dominant branch in this movement had roots in groups such as the Pharisees. Jews in the Diaspora had to decide how biblical law would apply in a world without a temple and in a wide variety of circumstances. A tradition of legal speculation led to the development of the Mishnah and, later, the Talmud, collections of post-biblical Jewish laws.

You can see some evidence of the Hellenistic debates about the law in New Testament texts. If you look carefully, for instance, at what Jesus says about the law in the four gospels, you will see different attitudes reflected. The Pauline epistles, however, have been the most influential texts for the development of Christian attitudes toward the law. In Galatians, Paul writes, "You who want to be justified by the law have cut yourselves off from Christ; you have fallen away from grace" (5:4).

From a contemporary Christian perspective, it can appear that Paul is saying that the law is bad. However, the New Testament texts are more complex than this. Paul assumes that the laws have a positive function, especially in what they demonstrate about the nature of God and, more significantly, the nature of humanity. "The law was our disciplinarian until Christ came, so that we might be justified by faith" (Gal 3:24). During the Reformation period, Martin Luther and other Reformers developed this statement into a theology of Law and Gospel: the Bible reveals both how people always fail to "earn" justification (the state of being in the right relationship with God), which is "Law," and how God's grace alone saves people, which is Gospel. Although Luther does not mean here that Law equals the Old Testament and Gospel equals the New (for example, he would view the epistle of James as "Law"), this is often how the passage is misunderstood.

An often overlooked text with respect to the New Testament understanding of Law is found in the Sermon on the Mount in Matthew 5—7. In this text, Jesus upholds the law, even "putting a fence around the Torah," that is, making the law stricter so that a person avoids breaking a command. In this speech, Jesus states that he has come to "fulfill" the law (Matt 5:17–18). What does that statement mean? It is one thing to talk about fulfilling a prophecy, but what does it mean to fulfill a law?

Careful reading shows that the author of Matthew's gospel and Paul reflect a similar assumption about the purpose of the Law. They both focus on what the law reveals about God and humanity, as well as how it functions to heal that relationship. Jesus fulfills the law in three ways, then. First, the nature of both God and humanity is clearer because of Jesus, especially God's desire for people to be saved. Second, Jesus functions in a variety of ways to heal the relationship between God and humanity, but especially through his death and resurrection. Third, both the Torah and the teachings of Jesus confess the belief that faith in this God requires a different way of living by those who enter into this covenant.

Christians need to read and understand the law because it is still revelatory of God and humanity. The message of the law has not been negated by the coming of Jesus. It has been fulfilled. Yet, we miss that revelation if we turn our backs on the law.

of law at Sinai: they are given to the people through Moses. It takes the Israelites three months to travel to the "wilderness of Sinai." There they experience God's presence on the mountain.

In Case You Were Wondering

Sinai is holy. This passage treats Sinai as sacred space. The people must avoid anything that would make them impure or unclean, such as menstrual blood (Exod 19:15), and they must undergo ritual purifications, such as cleaning their clothes (Exod 19:10).

Boundaries. This sacred space has clear boundaries. The text plays on this notion of boundaries in Exodus 19:24: if the people "break through" the boundary set for them, God will "break through" to attack them.

Looking Closely at the Text

1. In Exodus 19:6, what does God say the people will be? What does this mean?

2. According to Exodus 19:16–17 and 20:18, what else happens as God comes down to the mountain?

3. Why don't the people go up the mountain? Is this due to piety or is it a lack of trust in God?

Fear and Trembling

The Israelites, on the road for three months now, have known hunger and thirst, but they have also experienced God's blessing. Moses has led them to the base of a mountain and told them to prepare to meet God. The passage combines several different sources about this divine-human encounter; notice how many times Moses travels up and down the mountain. What comes through clearly, however, is that this encounter with Yahweh is not to be taken lightly.

Sinai replicates God's home in heaven. To enter God's home required great respect, humility, and ritual purity. It also required an invitation, which God extends. Along with the invitation came instructions to make this crossing safe.

God promises to appear to the people once they are ready. What follows is a *theophany*, that is, "a visible appearance of a god." There are several theophanies of Yahweh in the Old Testament. Most are accompanied by a storm, earthquake, or volcanic imagery. The Sinai theophany has all three.

The reaction of the people to the theophany is such a great fear that they turn down any further direct experience of God. In their place God invites Aaron and the priests to come up the mountain. The text is telling us something about the function of priests. In Exodus 19:6 God states that all of Israel will be "a priestly kingdom and a holy nation." This passage suggests that God had intended for all people within the covenant to be able to enter into God's abode, to step over into holy territory. The people choose not to go but to send others who then have the permanent job of mediating God's holy presence to the people. This story is an etiology for a designated priesthood, but it also seems to suggest that the priesthood is a concession by God, who had originally desired that all Israelites have direct experience of the divine presence.

In summary, the text continually reinforces images of sacred space in its depiction of Sinai. The people must be purified, as if entering a temple. They are preceded by Moses and then by the priests, who would go before them in any procession to a temple. Even the trumpet blast recalls temple worship: Israelites were called to worship by the blowing of a horn called a *shofar*. The narrative's description of the theophany also explains the reality behind temple rituals.

Exodus 20:1–17: The Ten Commandments

The Ten Commandments are at the heart of the law for both Jews and Christians. This passage is inserted in the middle of the previous material. Only Moses and Aaron have gone up the mountain, but the people can hear what happens. God reveals the Ten Commandments, a revelation accompanied by thunder, smoke, and trumpet blasts.

In Case You Were Wondering

Sabbath. Israelites began their day at sunset, not midnight, nor sunrise. The Sabbath was the last day of the week, that is, Saturday. Sabbath begins at sunset on Friday and lasts until sunset on Saturday.

An outstretched arm. When we talk about a "hand-out" we mean someone is helping us. In the ancient Near East, the outstretched arm was a symbol of strength and violence, like a clenched fist today.

Looking Closely at the Text

1. Why should Israelites keep the Sabbath holy?

2. Why should Israelites honor their fathers and mothers?

3. Do Christians keep the Ten Commandments?

The Decalogue

We are used to thinking of the Ten Commandments as a kind of universal law, so it is easy to forget that they were addressed to a people who lived in a culture different from ours. Therefore, I would like to treat each commandment individually, so that I can explain what it meant for the Israelites. The contemporary meaning for Jews and Christians is more appropriately explored in a course on moral theology.

There shall be no other gods before me. The ancient Israelites were not monotheistic; they believed that other gods existed. This commandment notes that they owed strict allegiance to the god that had chosen them. They were not to worship the sun god of Egypt nor the fertility god of Canaan. Yahweh alone was the god they should worship.

You shall not make an idol. An idol was a symbol of a god's presence within a temple. The people in the ancient Near East believed that a temple was the home of the god. To symbolize the god's real presence in that temple they would place an object, such as a statue, that "pictured" that god within the innermost room of the temple. Worship of the god consisted in treating this symbol as if it were the actual god. Daily sacrifices were the god's food, and priests were the god's servants.

The Israelites did not use a statue in the form of a person or an animal to represent God's presence in the temple. Instead they had the Ark of the Covenant and the cherubim that were God's throne. For the Israelites, God dwelled invisibly above the ark and the cherubim. This commandment shows that this was considered a fundamental element of Israelite worship of God.

You shall not misuse the name of God. In the ancient Near East people swore solemn oaths by invoking the name of the gods. They swore in court proceedings. They made treaties and business deals by calling on the gods. They took vows by calling the gods to witness their solemn statements. They believed that the divine realm would "back them up," that is, carry out any punishment associated with violating solemn statements. Here Yahweh reminds them to invoke this divine partner carefully. They must not swear in the name of God if they have no intention of carrying out what they vow. They must not ask God to witness a treaty that they intend to break.

Remember to keep the Sabbath. This commandment may show the most differences in its observance between ancient Israelites and contemporary Christians. This law demarcates sacred time: one day a week is "holy" to God.

For Jews this day is the Sabbath, the last day of the week. In Gen 2:2–3 God rests on this day, sanctifying it (that is, making it holy). It signifies that God's creation of the cosmos is complete and that there is nothing left for God to "touch up." According to Exodus, humans rest on this day in imitation of God. Deuteronomy 5:15, however, provides a different motivation for keeping the Sabbath. In Deuteronomy the Sabbath is a labor law, legislating a day of rest for every worker, including slaves. In Deuteronomy, God is primarily known for delivering the Israelites from slavery in Egypt. Thus, the Israelites honor God by recalling this deliverance each week.

Christians believe that they are heirs to God's work as creator and deliverer. But they also believe that God is most fully seen in Jesus. Jesus' resurrection, which is celebrated on Easter Sunday, marks a new era for Christians, in sum, a new creation. Christians recognize God in their lives by observing this new day, Sunday, the Lord's day, in place of the Sabbath. To symbolize that Christ's resurrection does in fact signal a new creation, the Lord's day coincides with the first day of creation, Sunday, rather than with the last day, Saturday.

Honor your father and your mother. I remember being threatened with this commandment during my childhood! How easily it was translated into the more benign, "Obey your parents!" Originally, this law had little to do with childhood misbehavior. This commandment expressed the Israelites' respect for the elders in their community, stating how they should be treated by the adults of the next generation. Israelites lived and worked together as multigenerational families. In this setting, the eldest generation had the final authority and was given the most honors. They made the decisions about personal and economic matters, including marriages; they determined how much to give to the temple, what gods the family would worship, and so on. Even if their mental faculties were not sharp, they were to be honored for their wisdom and experience.

This honor was a serious matter because it formed the very fabric of Israelite society. Offspring, that is, adult offspring, could be "divorced" from the family, by being disinherited and, in some cases, stoned to death. The term "parent" referred to any elder who exercised authority in the family. Sometimes this was not a biological parent, since many women died in childbirth. Yet, this commandment requires the same intergenerational honor, no matter what the family structure. The commandment suggests that its observation is crucial to Israel's social stability, when it says, "so that your days may be long in the land" (Exod 20:12).

You shall not murder. The original Hebrew word can be translated as either "kill" or "murder." Since we discussed this commandment previously in the introduction, let me simply summarize that discussion here. This commandment provides a basic principle that all human societies adhere to. Unjust killing of another member of one's society is destructive to that society. We know that this commandment does not forbid justified killing. For instance, it does not forbid killing on a battlefield nor killing someone who attacks you. It does not even forbid the use of capital punishment. Whether the Israelites believed this commandment included all acts of unjust violence against another person is unclear.

You shall not commit adultery. For the ancient Israelites this commandment restricted female behavior more than male behavior. Adultery was defined as sexual intercourse with a woman who was married or betrothed to another man. It is a violation of a man's right to exclusive ownership of a woman's reproductive capacity. When such intercourse occurred, assuming both partners were willing participants, both the man and the woman violated the husband's rights. If a man who was married or betrothed, however, had intercourse with an unmarried, unbetrothed woman or a prostitute, then he was not guilty of adultery, since a wife could not expect that she was her husband's only sexual partner.

You shall not steal. This is a very straightforward commandment. The Israelites believed in private ownership of goods. Taking someone's private possession, either by stealth or trickery, was an offense against God. This commandment applied even to kings; when King Ahab takes a field owned by a neighbor, God condemns him.

You shall not bear false witness against your neighbor. The wording of this commandment reflects a courtroom setting. This commandment forbids lying in court against a fellow citizen. This must have been a serious problem in ancient Israel. We saw above that a person was forbidden from swearing falsely in God's name. Here again we see that perjury was a grave matter. It reminds us that modern criteria for guilt, which require corroborating physical evidence and eyewitness testimony, were not the rule in the ancient world. All that was needed to convict someone was testimony from one or more citizens, depending on the crime; we see examples of unjust imprisonment based on such testimony within the Old Testament.

This commandment is the first that uses the term *neighbor*. This was a technical term that demonstrates that the Israelites did not believe in identical treatment of all people. In the gospels, written much later, someone asks Jesus for a definition of the term *neighbor*, and he answers the question with the story of the Good Samaritan (Luke 10:29–37), in which he extends the term far beyond its original meaning. In Israel a *neighbor* often meant a land-owning male or a social equal. In some texts it may not include women, slaves, resident aliens, or foreigners. This commandment probably envisions a broader definition, but it is striking that the text focuses on perjury only against those in your community.

You shall not covet your neighbor's goods or his wife.   These two commandments, which the book of Exodus combines into one prohibition, seem to want to limit emotions, things that today we believe we cannot limit. Scholars debate this very point. We don't really know what was meant by the word translated as "covet." It does mean "want" or "lust after," but the degree to which it included planning or concrete action, such as stalking, is ambiguous.

In summary, the Ten Commandments were addressed to and preserved within a particular ancient near-eastern culture. Their unique wording reflects that setting, but the principles of justice and respect remain universally valid.

Exodus 21:22–22:15: The Covenant Code and Laws for a Just Society

Many Christians who read only the Ten Commandments believe they have a good idea of Israelite law, but the Decalogue only scratches the surface of how legal principles played out in Israelite society. Some students think it is funny that I enjoy reading the other laws, but they help me to imagine how people lived then. They give me a sense of what was important to the Israelites and how different elements within their society interacted. To help you better understand Israelite society, we will look here at a small sampling of their social laws, that is, laws that governed how they interacted as a society. If you had to reconstruct Israelite society based only on what you know through your reading of the laws, what would their society look like? Where would there be potential conflicts and problems?

The text in this section is part of the Covenant Code, one of the law codes found in the Pentateuch. Source critics believe that this law code is one of the earliest preserved in the Pentateuch, that it is a law code from either the early monarchy or just before the monarchy. The final redactor of the Pentateuch inserted it right after the people state that they do not wish to go up the mountain. It is separated from the Ten Commandments.

The law code seems to have no clear order; it does not differentiate between ritual and social laws. We may not have the whole law code. In fact, presumably, when it was originally promulgated, it had its own introduction. This material starts with laws on slave trade, and then it moves on to several examples of assault. The material you will read is followed by laws dealing primarily with sexual and religious crimes, ending with an exhortation to keep the law.

In Case You Were Wondering

Slaves. Israelites owned slaves. Slaves were of two types. There were permanent slaves, usually acquired as prisoners of war, and debt slaves, that is, fellow Israelites who agreed to serve a master to work off a debt. The Covenant Code notes that a man can sell his daughter into slavery to pay off his debts.

Stoning. The most common way to carry out the death penalty was by a communal stoning of the criminal. Hanging was rare, as was drowning.

Shekels. A shekel was a form of Israelite money. Shekels were made out of silver. This code reflects enough centralization that money did exist, although probably most transactions involved bartering for goods or services.

Looking Closely at the Text

1. In Exodus 21:22–27, how is the principle "an eye for an eye" applied to the slave who loses an eye?

2. In Exodus 21:28–36, when is the owner of an ox personally liable for the actions of the ox?

3. In Exodus 22:8–12, how are cases with no witnesses resolved?

An Eye for an Eye

Today when people believe that crimes should be strictly punished they often cite the biblical warrant, "an eye for an eye." But the reality is that in the ancient Near East, this phrase meant something quite different. We first find this phrase in Mesopotamian law codes. Both there and in the Bible the intent of this law was to limit the punishment that could be carried out. If someone poked out your eye, you could not kill that person in return. You could only punish them to the same degree that they caused you harm. In the laws in this section, the phrase is also used to justify compensating a slave for loss of an eye or a tooth. Even a slave deserves just application of the law.

These laws reflect a rural society. For instance, there is no distinction between city dwellers and farmers. The society seems locally based, not centralized like you would find in a strong monarchy. Several of the laws deal with domestic animals. We see that Israelite farmers had oxen, meaning any kind of

Crime and Punishment

An eye for an eye! Stoning people for bestiality! Putting a woman who was only suspected of adultery through an ordeal! What's going on here?

To our eyes, the biblical laws may seem unduly harsh. Once again, examining the historical context can help us. There were no prisons in the ancient world. People could be locked up in a room or put into stocks, but these were usually only temporary measures. Think about the expense on a city to maintain a jail system: food and lodging for the prisoners, money to build the facilities, and the "man power" needed to guard, cook for, and care for the inmates. In a society barely over the subsistence level, it's no wonder ancient Israel used other means to punish crimes. The lack of a prison system meant that there had to be other means for protecting society from criminal behavior. The prevalence of capital punishment was one such means.

The court system in ancient Israel was also different from today's judicial system. Most legal decisions took place at the city level. Elders in the community would sit in the city gates (these were large structures with rooms on the sides), and other male landowners could bring cases to them to decide. There were no lawyers, police force, or jury. The person bringing the charges had to provide the evidence as well, including two witnesses for any capital offense. Women had access to the judicial system through their husbands, sons, or fathers. Non-landowners had no access to the judicial system prior to the monarchy.

Sometimes the judicial system failed. For example, when King David's son rapes his daughter, David does not bring him up for trial. In cases such as these, the next male in the family hierarchy could carry out a punishment against the criminal without a trial. This is called "vigilante justice." In the above story, David's next oldest son kills the brother who has raped his sister.

Obviously vigilante justice can quickly escalate. Let's say my brother dies in a fight, but my father does not take it to the elders. I proceed to kill the man who killed my brother (an eye for an eye), but his family claims that someone else had killed my brother. Now they set out to kill me in retaliation. This retribution could go on and on.

The law codes describe a system of "cities of refuge." These were cities where people who had either carried out vigilante justice or who were afraid of being its victims could live safely. We do not know if there was a way to determine whether these people were justified or not, but perhaps it didn't matter. Since they could not leave the city without risking their lives, these cities would have functioned as *de facto* prisons.

People being pursued for punishment could also enter a temple precinct and "grasp the horns of the altar." Some altars had projections on the corners called "horns" in Hebrew. Because the altar was in a sacred site, and a bleeding wound would defile that site, a person was pretty sure that their pursuer would not kill them in the temple. In these cases, the priests would decide who could have "sanctuary" in the temple.

bull or cow, and sheep, a term that can also be translated as "goats." These animals were used primarily to provide dairy products, although they could be slaughtered for meat as well. Donkeys were more common than horses as beasts of burden and transportation.

People were responsible for their animals. Notice that if an ox gets out and injures someone with its horns (Exod 21:28), then the animal is destroyed; but if the owner is known for negligence, then the owner becomes liable for the injury caused by the ox. Although this law code does not cover every instance of negligence, enough examples are provided so that citizens would understand their responsibility. The material that this passage covers deals with the economic livelihood of the nation and the basic social issues that every community must solve. The ancient Israelites were no different.

One way that the Israelite judicial system differed greatly from ours, however, was the way in which it dealt with cases where guilt was difficult to determine. In those cases, suspects were "brought before God" to determine their guilt. We do not know precisely what this means, but there are a few clues in the Old Testament and other ancient material. The phrase "before God" means the accused was brought to a temple. Priests, acting as judges, had means other than physical evidence to determine guilt.

First, they could require a person to undergo an "ordeal," that is, go through something that could kill or harm them in order to determine their guilt or innocence. In Num 5:11–31, a woman accused of adultery was required to drink something that could cause her to have uterine problems. If she did not experience these problems, then she was innocent.

Second, a priest could also consult oracles or other omens that would relay a divine message of guilt or innocence. Israelite priests could use sacred lots to determine guilt. They believed that God would control the process so that the guilty person was punished. In biblical stories that involve the use of lots, the lot never falls the wrong way.

Lastly, people could swear a solemn oath of innocence in God's name before the priest. This is the case in Exodus 22:10–11. Israelites believed that if someone lied during this process, then they and their family would incur punishment from God. The commandments against swearing falsely and bearing false witness become clearer in this light.

LEVITICUS 11:1–47 AND 23:1–44: SACRED FOOD AND SACRED OFFERINGS

The laws in Leviticus are revealed to Moses at the tent of meeting, while the Israelites are still encamped at Mount Sinai. Most of the book deals with ritual laws, including laws regarding who can make a sacrifice, what types of animals can be sacrificed, how many animals to sacrifice on which days, and how a person who has experienced an impurity can become ritually clean again.

Much of this material defines the boundaries between sacred and profane items. We will look at the material that has become the basis for later kosher laws and at the sacred calendar, which describes the primary feast days for the ancient Israelites. However, the principles we see at work in this material can be used to clarify similar passages.

In Case You Were Wondering

Weights and measures. Some of the sacrificial laws use terms for the standard weights and measures used in ancient Israel. An *ephah* is a measure for dry goods, and a *hin* measures liquids. A *sheaf* is a bundle of grain.

Looking Closely at the Text

Make a list of the holy days that Leviticus 23 describes.

Purity

I find these laws frustrating. Some of them, such as the list of clean and unclean meat, give too many details, while others give too few. I often turn to these ritual laws expecting that they will describe what exactly happens in a ritual, but these laws presume that you know how the rituals are performed. Because of the complexity of the lists, and the presumption of previous knowledge, these lists may have been designed for priests.

Let's turn first to the list of clean and unclean meat. Besides wondering who in the world would eat a gecko, what do you notice about this list? Scholars have noticed that it divides animals up according to the categories of creation: land animals, creeping things (bugs, insects, lizards, and so on), animals that inhabit the sky, and water animals. This classification is different from our modern classification of mammals, fish, reptiles, and so on. Animals that cross the boundaries of this ancient classification are unclean. For instance, a bat, which appears to be a land animal that can fly, is ritually unclean. This shows us that this list has nothing to do with hygiene, nor is it based on Israelite experience of food poisoning or other meat-borne diseases. Animals that most fully exemplify God's plan for the world are "clean." Originally this probably meant that they were suitable to offer as sacrifices to God. "Clean" animals are the most perfect animals.

The list here is "democratized," that is, extended to apply not just to what one may sacrifice, but to what any person who wishes to maintain a state of ritual purity may eat. That which is clean is called *kosher*, and contemporary Jewish kosher laws are those that tell Jews what they may or may not eat. Not all the kosher laws are here in Leviticus 11, but this is a convenient place to see some of them. Jews today who keep kosher see the practice as a way to give reverence to God in their daily lives.

There are several lists of holy days in the Pentateuch. Often these lists are in disagreement. Every list includes the Sabbath, but most calendars also list a monthly festival on the day of the new moon. Beyond these were more important holy days. They include the New Year's festival plus three pilgrimage feasts, so named because Israelite males were required to travel to Jerusalem for one of them each year.

Most of the festivals derived from Israel's life in the land, rather than from commemorations of historical events. Since the festivals were tied to the natural cycle of the year, the timing of the festivals was crucial to their proper observation. The Israelite calendar was a lunar calendar. It required specialists in astronomical observation to determine the precise dates of high holy days. Some of the priests were trained in this science.

When we try to reconstruct the calendar of ancient Israel, two festivals are especially problematic: Passover and the New Year's festival. Not all calendars include Passover on their list, and some that do list it as only one part of the more important festival of unleavened bread. The date of New Year seemed to change throughout Israel's history. Sometimes it was celebrated in the fall, at the time of the harvest. Other times it was celebrated in the spring, at the end of winter. Usually the New Year is associated with the Day of Atonement. This reading has a festival before the Day of Atonement, but places these festivals in the seventh month rather than the first month. The following chart represents the most common dates for the festivals:

Festival Name	Other Names for the Festival	Date	Associated Festival
New Year's Festival		Spring or fall equinox	Day of Atonement
Unleavened Bread		Beginning of the barley harvest	Passover
Weeks	Pentecost	End of the wheat harvest	
Booths	Tents, Tabernacles, Ingathering	Harvest of all other produce	

EXODUS 15:22–16:15; NUMBERS 13:2–14:38 AND 20:1–13: COMPLAINT AND CONDEMNATION

The first passage comes right after the Israelites have crossed the sea. It shows their adjustment to life in the wilderness. These stories of prayer are scattered throughout Exodus and Numbers, in particular. In most of the stories, God grants their request, but in a few of them God becomes angry. It is not always clear why God reacts differently.

The next two texts explain why neither the first generation of Israelites nor Moses was allowed to enter the Promised Land. Both stories occur after the Israelites have left the region around Mount Sinai. The first happens soon after they had set out, and it shows that their long sojourn in the wilderness came as a result of their own mistrust. The second passage occurs no more than a few years later. Notice that both stories use the language of complaint, but in these stories there is a negative outcome. Can you figure out why God condemns the people and Moses?

In Case You Were Wondering

Manna. Later in the chapter we find out that the bread, which God rains down on the Israelites, is called *manna*. In Hebrew the word we translate as "bread" also means simply "food." So manna is probably not what we would think of when we hear the word "bread." It is some kind of starchy food.

The Negeb. The Negeb is an arid area that separates Israel from the Sinai Peninsula. The book of Numbers states that the Israelites first tried to enter the land from the south, the closest route.

A land flowing with milk and honey. This phrase is not to be taken literally. It simply connotes the bounty of the land. The abundance of milk means that it is a land good for raising dairy animals, while abundant honey suggests plentiful plant life.

The Nephilim. Do you remember the Nephilim from Gen 6:1–4? They were the giants that came from human women and the "sons of god." When the spies say that the land is full of "Nephilim" (Num 13:33), they mean that the people are large, gigantic even.

The "-ites." Amalekites, Canaanites, Anakites, Hittites! Who are all these people? First, don't worry about it; you won't need to remember who all these people were, in part because we're still not sure today who some of them were! Israelites used that ending "-ite" to mean someone who lives in that country: an Israelite lives in Israel, a Canaanite lives in Canaan, and so on. Many different people who did not organize to form a larger nation inhabited the Promised Land. Each city, or group of cities and towns, had its own king; we call this type of organization a *city-state*. The whole area was called "Canaan," so sometimes the Bible simply refers to Canaanites, but at other times it lists some of the groups that comprised the Canaanites, such as the Amalekites, the Jebusites, the Hittites, and so on.

Looking Closely at the Text

1. Are the people's requests for food justified or do they lack faith by complaining?

2. Is it fair for God to keep them out of the Promised Land because they were afraid?

3. What does Moses do wrong? Does he deserve the punishment that God gives him?

Complaints or Prayer?

The Pentateuch's portrayal of the Israelites in the wilderness is less than flattering. Their character is complicated by our translation of a particular Hebrew word as "complain." The Israelites bring their physical needs to God as they travel. When they are thirsty, they communicate their thirst to God, as they do when they are hungry. In their tradition it was perfectly acceptable to "complain" to God in this way. Our translation of this word shows a bit of our own reservations of the acceptability of such prayer.

The Pentateuch portrays God answering the cries of the Israelites. The stories, and others like them throughout the Pentateuch, show that the author was aware how difficult a migration like this would have been. It would be hard enough for a single person or family to travel through that desert carrying none of their own food or water. The Pentateuch states that Moses is leading thousands of people. Sometimes God responds to the physical needs of this large group.

At other times, however, God becomes angry with their requests. When the people despair, God's anger boils. In Numbers 14:12 God is ready to wipe them all out and create a new people for Moses to lead: "I will strike them with pestilence and disinherit them, and I will make of you a nation greater and mightier than they." Moses has to remind God of the divine promise to be patient.

> The LORD is slow to anger,
> and abounding in steadfast love,
> forgiving iniquity and transgression,
> but by no means clearing the guilty,
> visiting the iniquity of the parents upon the children
> to the third and the fourth generation. (Num 14:18)

Only upon hearing this does God agree to lessen the punishment, allowing the adults to live, but not allowing them to see the Promised Land.

This passage depicts Moses as a prophet. The job of the prophet was not just to deliver God's messages to the people but also to intercede on their behalf when God wanted to punish them. Throughout the Pentateuch the redactor stresses Moses' prophetic abilities. The book of Deuteronomy calls him the greatest prophet who ever lived.

So why does God punish Moses so harshly in Numbers 20? This passage is quite difficult to understand. One of the problems is that it is unclear exactly what Moses has done to deserve such a punishment. Let's look at the details of the story. The people complain that they need water; this is not surprising, because they have moved to a place which has no natural spring. Moses and Aaron bring their complaint to God, and God agrees to send them water. Moses is commanded to strike a rock, which will then provide water for the group. Moses does this, although he first says, "Listen, you rebels, shall we bring water for you out of this rock?" (Num 20:10). Then Moses strikes the rock twice, an odd detail within a narrative that is usually so sparse. God says to Moses and Aaron, "Because you did not trust in me, to show my holiness before the eyes of the Israelites, therefore you shall not bring this assembly into the land that I have given them" (Num 20:12).

But what had Moses done? Was it because he called them rebellious, although God had not condemned them? Was it because he did not say specifically that God had sent the water? (This depends on how you interpret the use of "we"; did Moses mean himself and Aaron, himself and God, or all three?) Was it because Moses struck the rock two times instead of once? The text simply does not say.

No matter what Moses' crime, his punishment has always struck me as unduly harsh. After all, he has done everything God has told him to do. Even when he did bad things, such as murder an Egyptian guard, God stuck by him, so why condemn him now? The punishment makes God's anger appear arbitrary and unpredictable. Is that the message of this story? It could be.

An Israelite might argue that, since Moses was a prophet and talked to God, he clearly knew what God wanted. We will see that God does hold certain people to a higher standard than others, for just this reason. But it could be a simple reminder to the ancient audience that God can choose to punish actions as they deserve and that God's mercy is not something to be taken for granted or expected.

EXODUS 32:1–29 AND 40:16–38: GOD WITH THE ISRAELITES

These two passages deal with the question of how the Israelites were supposed to represent God's presence. We noticed that the commandments state that they were not supposed to make an "idol," that is, a statue that replicated what God looks like. That commandment does not mean, however, that they were not supposed to have any symbol for God. For ancient people the choice of symbol was not arbitrary; the deity chose it. These stories provide two examples of how the Israelites tried to make something to represent God: one does not work, but the other does.

The first story is set during the time that Moses is on Mount Sinai receiving the laws. The text states that he had been up on the mountain a long time. As you recall, the people below saw that the mountain was consumed by fire and earthquake; it is not a leap to assume that he was dead. So they turned to Aaron to lead them, and they asked him to fashion a religious symbol.

The second story closes the book of Exodus. Before the events with the Golden Calf, God had revealed to Moses the laws on how to worship God in the desert. After the Golden Calf story, we see Moses and the Israelites carrying out these commands. The laws on how to build the Ark of the Covenant are part of

This stone carving of the Ark of the Covenant is one of many reliefs found in the remains of the Capernaum Synagogue. Dating of the synagogue is debated, but it likely stood in the second to fourth centuries CE.

these commandments. The *Ark of the Covenant* was a gold-covered box, which represented God's presence to the Israelites up until the late monarchy. Its exact measurements and materials are described in Exodus 25:10–22 and 37:1–9. In the closing chapter of Exodus, God's appearance as a cloud above the ark signifies divine approval.

In Case You Were Wondering

Drinking powdered gold. Moses making the Israelites drink the gold powder is an example of an ordeal. Whoever is guilty is supposed to become sick from drinking the water.

Setting up the tabernacle. The second passage briefly summarizes everything related to the tabernacle. Try to get a general sense of the actions in the passage.

The Covenant. "The covenant" that Moses puts in the ark is the stone tablets with the laws written on them.

Looking Closely at the Text

1. Did the calf represent Yahweh, or did it represent other gods?

2. After Moses finishes his work of setting up the tabernacle, what happens?

Symbols of God's Presence

The story about the golden calf and the one describing the establishment of the Ark of the Covenant concern the same thing: the proper way for the Israelites to symbolize God's presence in their midst. Ancient people, including the Israelites, believed that their gods were tangibly present to them. Does this mean that they felt that God was somehow a limited creature who appeared and disappeared? Not at all! When they talk about God being with them they did not deny that God is primarily in heaven, nor were they asserting that God is only in the temple or tabernacle. But they believed that there were times and places when God's presence was more accessible.

The use of statues, either in human or animal form, was the most common way people in the ancient Near East symbolized a divine presence, but not the only way. A few of the countries in the Levant used what archaeologists call an "empty throne." Instead of putting up a statue of the deity in their temples, people in Syria and elsewhere set up a throne, chair, or pedestal over which the god's presence was to hover invisibly. The Israelites used this method of representing God's presence. The ark and the cherubim formed a throne and footstool over which God would be present.

Cherubim were not depicted in the form of babies, as we think of them; they were composite beings, part human, part animal, always winged, which guarded entrances, kings, and temples. Depictions of cherubim were common features on the thrones of human kings in the Levant. In the desert, the ark and cherubim go hand-in-hand. The Israelites carved the cherubim right onto the lid of the ark. In the temple of Jerusalem, the two are separate pieces.

While using a chair was one way to depict an empty throne, another way was to use bull icons. Although it first looks as if the bulls symbolized the god in animal form, the fact is that the god is understood as standing on the backs of bulls. We know this from archaeological artifacts showing a god on the back of two bulls. During the Divided Monarchy, the Israelites in the northern kingdom used bull icons to represent Yahweh's presence. Whoever wrote this story, however, did not think that what the northerners did was right.

In fact, the story provides several elements that give away the author's point of view. First, notice that Aaron and the people decide on their own to construct the calves, not on God's command. This does not fit the proper procedure for fashioning an empty throne. Second, the author calls these animals "calves," not "bulls," thus lessening their importance. Most telling of all, however, is that in Exodus 32:4, Aaron proclaims that the calves did, in fact, represent Yahweh. For the person who preserved this text, bull icons are not good because they can be too easily mistaken for an idol. A throne, whose main element is a simple box, can never be mistaken for an idol.

The final redactor of the Pentateuch contrasts the legitimacy of the ark with that of the golden calves. In the account of the ark, God commands the construction of the ark, down to the last detail. Moreover, the ark contains sacred objects. Here it is the law codes, but in other texts, the ark holds various items. Most importantly, God is active in the process. After the tabernacle has been set up with the ark inside, "Then the cloud covered the tent of meeting, and the glory of the LORD filled the tabernacle" (Exod 40:34). This is a sign that God has approved this object.

DEUTERONOMY 4:1–6:25: MOSES' LAST SPEECH

Deuteronomy is the last book of the Pentateuch. It contains Moses' last speech before he dies. As part of the speech, he summarizes the main elements of Israel's life in the wilderness, and he predicts some of the troubles that the Israelites will face once they enter the Promised Land. This short passage summarizes some of the most important features of the theology of the book of Deuteronomy.

In Case You Were Wondering

Baal of Peor. In the ancient world, different places, such as the city of Peor, could be associated with different manifestations of a particular deity, such as Baal.

The Land of Og. The verses in Deuteronomy 4:44–49 list the lands already controlled by the Israelites. These are all beyond the Jordan River.

Massah. This was one place where the Israelites complained to God about their condition.

Looking Closely at the Text

1. According to Deuteronomy 4:5, when should the Israelites observe the laws that Moses will now give to them?

2. According to Deuteronomy 4:40, why should the Israelites keep God's commandments?

3. How does this passage relate to texts that we have read earlier in this chapter?

4. According to Deuteronomy 6:5, how should we love God?

Love God with All Your Heart

As the book of Deuteronomy begins, the Israelites are encamped on the banks of the Jordan River, ready to cross over on the next day. Moses, knowing that he is about to die, turns to the Israelites to deliver his dying words. As you may recall from the story of Isaac, the Israelites believed that what a person said at this time would come true. Moses' repetition of the laws from Sinai and his announcement of punishment if the Israelites failed to observe the law placed a curse upon them.

Moses presents these laws as the ones that the Israelites must obey after they enter the land. If we were to look at the individual laws in Deuteronomy, we would see laws suited to a settled life, such as laws pertaining to government officials, which are typical of a monarchy and reflect a more urban society. This detail suggests that the Deuteronomist wrote during the period of the monarchy.

Furthermore, if we made an outline of Moses' speech, we would see that it follows the basic outline for making a treaty in the ancient world. Using this structure is a way of claiming that God's relationship with Israel has the weight of an international treaty. This approach fits the theology of Deuteronomy well, because in a treaty, when the lesser party violates its conditions, the stronger party can nullify it and even attack the lesser party. The Deuteronomist believed that Israel's covenant with Yahweh was conditional. It was only in effect as long as the Israelites, the lesser party, followed the stipulations of the agreement. We see this notion repeated in our passage: if they obey the statutes, then they will live long in the land. If they break the statutes, they will be punished and exiled.

For the Deuteronomist, the worst sin Israel could commit was worshipping other gods. Our passage has a long warning against this conduct, while there is relatively little focus on caring for the poor, avoiding violence, or even transgressing purity boundaries. In other words, the Israelites' worst sins would be religious sins. Perhaps you are beginning to see that the main concerns of the Covenant Code (social order), the Holiness Code (sacred boundaries), and the Deuteronomic Code (religious concerns) are distinct.

Deuteronomy and Treaty Outlines

The redactor of Deuteronomy uses a couple of structuring devices for the book. On the one hand, the book is the last will and testament of Moses. On the other hand, the speech that Moses delivers follows the outline of international treaties between vassal states and ruling powers, such as we find in some Hittite treaties. See the following chart for a comparison:

Hittite Treaty	Deuteronomy
Preamble: The great king gives his name and titles.	Deuteronomy 1:1
Historical prologue: The stronger king recites the historical basis for the treaty.	Deuteronomy 1:2—11:32
Stipulations are imposed on the smaller kingdom.	Deuteronomy 12—26
Preservation and public proclamation of the treaty are outlined.	Deuteronomy 27:1–8 and 31:9–13
Witnesses to the treaty are listed.	None (perhaps 32:1)
Blessings and curses are pronounced if the treaty is not kept.	Deuteronomy 27:1—28:68

The ideology behind Deuteronomy also matches the ideology underlying secular treaties of the time, which are not treaties made by equal nations, but by a smaller nation and a great nation which dictates the terms of the treaty. In Deuteronomy God takes the part of the great nation, setting the parameters of the treaty. Israel is the lesser nation, agreeing to these terms.

Covenant loyalty depends on the lesser party's compliance with the terms. The greater party swears to maintain a positive relationship with the lesser party as long as the lesser remains compliant. So too Israel's activities are more defined by this covenant than are God's.

Deuteronomy 5 portrays fear of God as the proper response to God's covenant. God declares, "If only they had such a mind as this, to fear me and to keep all my commandments always!" (5:29). We tend to think of fear as a bad thing, but is it ever appropriate to fear something or someone? Would you have any fear if you were to meet God? I know I would!

But Deuteronomy is not simply about fear; its passages also speak of the love and fidelity that should exist between God and the people. One characteristic term that the Deuteronomist uses is the Hebrew term *hesed*. *Hesed* is often mistranslated as "steadfast love," which suggests that it is an emotion. A better translation might be "loyalty." It is the term used to describe the relationship between a husband and a wife. While Israelite spouses may have loved each other, Israelite marriages were not based on love. Instead they were based on loyalty to the contract made between the spouses and their families. God promises loyalty to Israel, and, in return, expects loyalty.

In Deuteronomy 6:4 we find one of the most fundamental passages for Judaism. This passage is the base for a common prayer and declaration of faith for Jews, the *shema*: "Hear, O Israel: The Lord is our God, the Lord alone." The next verse proclaims, "You shall love the LORD your God with all your heart, and with all your soul, and with all your might" (Deut 6:5). Here the actual word for *love* is found. This passage seeks more than a passing emotive response to God. The Deuteronomist calls the people to a way of life that cannot be lived apart from God. The further command to bind this prayer onto their bodies and place it on their doorposts has been taken literally by many Jews throughout the centuries. Jesus' inclusion of this command as one of the two great commandments reflects his own Jewish context (Mark 12:29–30, Matt 22:37, and Luke 10:27).

The book of Deuteronomy is a literary masterpiece. Did you notice how many times this short passage reminds the audience to teach these laws and this history to their children? Think about the didactic purpose for the book. Who is Moses talking to? Remember that from the generation who had been adults at Sinai, only Joshua and Caleb entered the land. This means that the majority of people that Moses is addressing had not even been born when he received the law.

Yet, Moses is constantly telling his audience that they had been there when God spoke to Israel. Were they at Sinai when God spoke? According to the book of Deuteronomy, yes, they were: "The LORD spoke with you face to face on the mountain, out of the fire" (Deut 5:4). The literary effect of this text is that every reader understands that he or she is the one whom Moses is addressing. Each member of the audience "was there" and must continue to pass on "what they heard" to the next generation.

The author stresses the marvel of this:

> For ask now about former ages, long before your own, ever since the day that God created human beings on the earth; ask from one end of heaven to the other: has anything so great as this ever happened or has its like ever been heard of? Has any people ever heard the voice of a god speaking out of a fire, as you have heard, and lived? Or has any god ever attempted to go and take a nation for himself from the midst of another nation, by trials, by signs and wonders, by war, by a mighty hand and an outstretched arm, and by terrifying displays of power, as the Lord your God did for you in Egypt before your very eyes? (Deut 4:32–34)

SUMMARY: HOLINESS, LOYALTY, AND LOVE

By placing Deuteronomy at the end of the final redaction of the Pentateuch, the author helps his audience to understand an important concept. In order for the Israelites to pass from their liminal stage in the wilderness into the next stage, as a permanent nation living under God, they had to recognize that this story was not only about their ancestors' travels, but it was also about their own journey. The journey through the wilderness transformed the people from a community who was not sure that Yahweh could answer their basic needs to one whose very essence had been transformed by Yahweh's law and the covenant.

No matter who the audience is, the legal texts remind them of one very important thing: a relationship with God is life-changing. Whether the Pentateuch uses the language of purity or the language of *hesed*, it seeks to remind readers that it is not enough to hear God's voice or to study God's word; encounters with God must result in fundamental decisions regarding how a person leads her or his life. These decisions cover everything from politics to religion, from social interaction to individual intimate acts, even down to the food one eats. No wonder the law became so important in defining what it meant to be a Jew.

The Israelite law codes help us understand Israelite society at different stages in its history. But the codes have been combined to present a broader reflection on both what this period of Israelite history represented and why the law in general was so important.

FOR REVIEW

1. What does it mean to say that the wilderness period reflects Israel in a "liminal" period?

2. How are the Israelite laws like other ancient near-eastern laws?

3. What are three law codes in the Pentateuch?

4. How do the Ten Commandments differ from most of the other laws in the Pentateuch?

5. How did the Israelites decide where to build a temple?

6. What is "holiness"?

7. Why were Israelites afraid to come into contact with God?

8. In addition to space, what other elements have different degrees of holiness?

FOR FURTHER READING

For a collection of ancient near-eastern law codes, see Martha T. Roth, *Law Collections from Mesopotamia and Asia Minor* (SBLWAW 6; Atlanta: SBL, 1997).

There are several good studies of holiness and purity in ancient Israel. Three that I find present a readable overview of the topics are John G. Gammie, *Holiness in Israel* (Overtures to Biblical Theology; Minneapolis, MN: Fortress, 1989); Philip P. Jenson, *Graded Holiness: A Key to the Priestly Conception of the World* (JSOTSup 106; Sheffield: JSOT, 1992), and Saul M. Olyan, *Rites and Rank: Hierarchy in Biblical Representations of Cult* (Princeton, NJ: Princeton University Press, 2000).

Jon Levenson provides a good overview of the significance of Sinai traditions as they relate to the official temple worship in Jerusalem in his book, *Sinai and Zion: An Entry into the Jewish Bible* (San Francisco: Harper and Row, 1987).

OVERVIEW

A VEIL OF TEARS: READING ISRAEL'S HISTORY THROUGH THE LENS OF THE EXILE

I am one who has seen affliction under the rod of God's wrath. (Lam 3:1)

ONE ERA ENDS, ANOTHER BEGINS

As the Pentateuch comes to a close, the Israelites are encamped on the eastern banks of the Jordan River, awaiting their moment to take possession of the Promised Land. They have a new leader in Joshua, Moses' successor. The laws revealed to them at Mt. Sinai provide the blueprint for a new society. And they have the words of Moses still ringing in their ears: "Choose life so that you and your descendants may live . . . in the land that the LORD swore to give to your ancestors, to Abraham, to Isaac, and to Jacob" (Deut 30:19–20). The Pentateuch ends before the story is finished. Will the Israelites follow the law so that they will prosper in the land? Will they live a life in covenant with Yahweh, their God?

As we read the narrative account of Israel's history, we in some way become part of the nation of Israel: their story becomes our story, and we are ready to go with them into their land. But we also remember that there was another time when Israel stood outside of the land, forced to ponder what kind of a life they should lead if they ever (or never) came to live in the land again.

WHAT IS THE BABYLONIAN EXILE?

As you may recall, after the Israelites took possession of the land, they organized into a coalition of separate tribes, under the guidance of tribal leaders. As the need to unify grew stronger, however, they eventually merged into a single nation ruled by a king. Although the nation later split into two kingdoms, each kingdom was ruled by kings throughout this period.

One of the central symbols for the monarchy, especially in the south, was the city of Jerusalem. This city was founded by King David, and it became the nation's capital. David's son, Solomon, increased the city's importance by building a great temple to Yahweh there. These twin institutions, monarchy and temple, solidified Jerusalem's place as the most important city in Israel.

One of the reasons that Jerusalem was so important to the Israelites was that they believed that God would defend the city against foreign invasion. While some people believed that God would do this only if the Israelites remained faithful, others believed that God would defend the city no matter what.

We know that this belief was ill-founded. In 596 BCE the Babylonians took control of the city. Ten years later, after rebellion by the people of Jerusalem, the Babylonian king destroyed the city, tearing down the temple to its foundations. The nation of Israel was gone. God had not saved the city, the temple, or the nation.

Many of the people who survived were taken into exile in Babylon. There they were settled in various towns throughout Mesopotamia. The exiles were primarily from the upper classes. The second book of Kings 25:12 states that the poorest people were allowed to stay in the land, as long they worked the land for the Babylonian government. This means that the exiles had been the leaders of the nation before the fall of Jerusalem.

EXILE: THE IRONY OF HISTORY

Let me take you on an imaginative journey. Have you ever been to summer camp? My daughter goes to a camp every summer with girls who come from many different states. Yet, every year she makes new friends. What do they talk about? Well, they probably talk about music that they like, movies that they've seen, who they think is "hot," how to do their hair, and so on. In other words, they share a common culture, a common "language," and common interests that unite them.

Now, let's take this same group of girls and put them together in a camp again, but this time it is a camp for prisoners of war. Imagine that the United

States has been destroyed. Washington, DC, has burned to the ground, and the nation has fallen brutally.

First, the enemy had starved the people, cutting off food supplies for a year and a half. This group of girls had to watch members of their family die. They may have had to eat their family pets to stay alive. They may even have known people who ate their dead relatives to keep from starving.

Once the nation had been weakened with hunger and disease, the enemy made its final push, destroying every major city in the land, until at last it reached the nation's capital. As its program of destruction unfolded, each city was looted and burned. People died defending their homeland, but the enemy laughed as it gained the upper hand.

The survivors were ghosts of themselves as the enemy led them off to a P.O.W. camp. They got new homes, but they were in the enemy's homeland. They got new jobs, too, working for the enemy. They could even eat again; but it was the food of the enemy.

Now imagine the conversations of those girls in their "new" camp. What would they talk about? I suspect that many of them would talk about what life had been like before the fall of the nation, back in the "good old days." They would tell stories of former heroes and heroines, sing songs of people they used to listen to, and describe how life is "supposed" to be.

They would also probably try to make sense of the disaster. "Why did this happen to us?" they might ask. Some of them might look back on the way they used to live, and they might point out how their old lifestyle had led to the fall of the nation. Maybe some would claim that they used to worry about their looks but that they had failed to stay morally strong. Someone else might tell the history of the United States, with the purpose of explaining how its people ended up being so weak and pointing out every time the people did something that weakened the nation as a whole.

Others might try to preserve their old lifestyle, gathering the words to old songs from anybody who could remember them, collecting famous American folktales, or cataloguing old sayings and proverbs that were part of the common language as they grew up.

Of course, some people would produce new poems and new songs that expressed their fear and sorrow in this time of tragedy. They would give voice to emotions that ran deep in a group so bitterly scarred.

Maybe a few brave souls would prepare for the future. Armed with an illogical hope, they would imagine a day of return. What if there would be an opportunity to rebuild the world. What would it look like?

And they would write. Without access to the Internet or television, they would communicate through texts. They would write to those in other settlements. They would write to old friends left behind. They would write to refugee camps where other friends had found safety. As the years passed and they started families with others in their camp, they would eventually write for their children and their children's children, for the newly born and those yet to be born. They would write so that these children would know who they were, where they came from, and what they stood for. They would write in order that the nation would not die.

The single, most important event that led to the formation of the Bible was the Exile. Why is that? Because the collapse of the nation and the experience of the Exile gave the Israelites a reason to write accounts of their history, their traditions, their laws, their songs, and so on. Let's explore this assertion a bit.

Let's imagine that I lived in Judah before the exile and that I knew special songs that were sung at the temple. My children learned these songs easily, because every year we heard them when we went to the temple. Now, let's also imagine that the exile occurred when my youngest child was just a baby. We can no longer go to the temple, and some of these songs cannot be sung outside of the temple. So how will my child learn them? Someone will have to write them down, just in case, God willing, we can someday return to the land.

READING AHEAD

I cannot stress enough how important it is to enter into this world of destruction as we read about the history of Israel. This history was not primarily written for us. It was written for the Israelites who knew the reality of exile. As you read the text, you are invited to join Israel in exile.

Taking this perspective will help you understand why Israelite history is written in the way that it is. The material that we will next examine comes from a history of Israel that was finalized in the time of the exile. As with any history, the writers had to decide what events and details they would include in writing their history. Part of the process of writing a history is choosing what information to include and what material to set aside. These choices are based in part on what the historian thinks is important within the nation's history.

We will see that many of the details that this particular historian relates serve his larger purpose, which is to explain why the nation of Israel did not last. Israel's history is a tragic history. It is not designed to glorify a strong nation; it is meant to lament one that has been lost. Try to read this history from the perspective of an exile in Babylon.

We will also be looking at other kinds of material besides the history, namely the psalms, the prophets, and the wisdom materials. These collections were also probably completed after the fall of Jerusalem. While not every text will have been rewritten to reflect this tragedy, the fact that these materials were collected reflects the desperate efforts at preservation that marked many of those touched by disaster. These collections should be read as traditions that the Israelites deemed most essential to defining who they were and what they stood for.

LOOKING BACK

The Pentateuch also took its final form after the city of Jerusalem had fallen. Some scholars have suggested that the Pentateuch ends with the Israelites outside of the Promised Land because the original audience also stood outside the land. If this is the case, then both the Israelites at the time of Moses and the Israelites at the time of exile were asking themselves, what must we do to survive in this land?

The Pentateuch has two main elements: the account of the history of Israel, from the beginning of the world until the death of Moses, and the legal texts meant to be permanently binding on Israel, imbedded within that historical framework. Let's look again briefly at these two elements from the perspective of those who experienced exile.

The historical narratives can seem rather hopeful at first glance. They include the great figures of Israel's beginning: Abraham and Jacob, Sarah and Rebekah, Moses and Aaron. Yet, we saw on a closer reading of the texts that these figures displayed human failures. Abraham did not always act in ethical ways. Jacob was a trickster. Moses tried to refuse God's call. While the nation had a glorious beginning, it was certainly not a perfect one.

The Israelites, especially in the narratives from Exodus to Deuteronomy, were portrayed rather negatively. They did not know who God was; they asked God to stop speak-

This is a view of Mount Sinai (Mount Moses), in central Sinai, where the Lord spoke with Moses (Num 3:1).

ing to them directly on Mt. Sinai; they grumbled about the hardships in the wilderness; and they even worshipped a golden calf. This emphasis in the account made sense to a people living in Exile, who were wondering what went wrong. Hearing the historical accounts, they may have asked, did it ever go right? The beginning of the history hints of its end.

The legal texts also have something to say to people living in the period of the exile. First, the collection of legal texts was an attempt to preserve the old legal traditions, even if the process of collection resulted in some contradictions. Moreover, the laws were gathered both to condemn those who had failed and to offer hope for the future.

The laws condemned the failed generations, insofar as they provided the historian with the basis for asserting that the Israelites knew what they should have done and did not do it. We will see that this is especially true for the Deuteronomistic history that follows, which is told through the lens of laws in the book of Deuteronomy. To paraphrase Deuteronomy, they chose death, not life.

REVIEW AND PREVIEW

You have just finished reading the Pentateuch, the account of Israel's history from the beginning of the world until the death of Moses. You began with Abraham and Sarah, that is, with the start of Israel's history. You have learned about Israelite families and about the way they told stories. You have met Moses, and you have followed the great epic of Israel's escape from slavery in Egypt. You have learned about the function of law in Israel.

You will now enter the land with these Israelites, and you will find a land fraught with many dangers. The Israelites must face enemies who want to kill them; and, once security sets in, they must resist the temptations of the rich life. You'll read the history of Israel, mainly told through the lives of its leaders. You'll be "taught" how to be a good Israelite through an invitation to pursue wisdom. You'll look at Israel's songs and prayers, and you'll hear the words of the prophets who tried to save the people. Remember that you are entering *their* world. The texts that have been so carefully preserved ask us, first and foremost, to listen to what they have to tell us.

5 CONQUEST AND CONFUSION: JOSHUA AND JUDGES

In those days there was no king in Israel; all the people
did what was right in their own eyes.
(Judg 21:25)

CHAPTER OVERVIEW

This chapter deals with the Israelites' struggle for survival once they enter the Levant. The time frame of this history extends from their first entry into the land until the end of the period of tribal rule. We will look at how this history characterizes Israel's settlement in the Levant and the eventual establishment of a monarchy. The chapter will provide the following:

› An explanation of Deuteronomistic History

› An examination of Israel's struggle for survival as a nation

› A consideration of how Israel's failures address the theological concerns of the book's audiences

The texts, which we will consider in some detail, come from two biblical books: Joshua and Judges. The period covered in these books was a very turbulent time for Israel, and this turbulence resulted in social instability.

A Doomed History

What Is the Deuteronomistic History?

Most of what we know about Israel's life as a nation comes from the Old Testament's historical books. These include Joshua, Judges, First and Second Samuel, and First and Second Kings. The same person or group probably wrote all these books. The writers use the law code in the book of Deuteronomy as the basis for their evaluation of this history. We call these books, along with the book of Deuteronomy, the *Deuteronomistic History.* A brief description of the content of each book will help to give you an overview of its outline:

The Deuteronomistic History starts with the last speech of Moses in the book of Deuteronomy. At the end of the book Moses selects Joshua to lead the Israelites after he dies.

The book of Joshua describes Israel's entry into the land and the battles they fought to secure their place there. This entry and the battles that follow are called the *Conquest.*

The book of Judges presents a picture of what life was like for the Israelites once they were in the land, but before a king unified them. During this time they functioned as separate tribes. One form of leadership at this time involved a figure called the judge. The book of Judges depicts this time as one of great uncertainty, when the Israelites needed stronger centralized leadership if they were to survive.

First and Second Samuel are two parts of one long book that describes how Israel became a monarchy. It depicts the first king, Saul, as unfit for the job, while the second king, David, is shown to be a brilliant leader who secures Israel's future. The books of Samuel stress that God established the monarchy through prophets. Israel's "real" king is always Yahweh; the human king simply represents Yahweh on earth.

First and Second Kings, also one book, tells the history of the nation of Israel, beginning with the death of David. The monarchy was not particularly stable. After the reign of David's son, Solomon, the nation splits in two. The book of Kings describes the rise and fall of both nations. Because the last thing that the history describes is the fall of Jerusalem with the final king living in Exile, we know that the history did not reach its final form until after 587 BCE.

In summary, the Deuteronomistic History develops over a long period of time and is completed after 587 BCE. It tells the history of Israel from the death of Moses (ca. 1250) to the fall of Jerusalem in 587 BCE. It is divided in the following manner:

Book	Events	Approximate Dates
Deuteronomy	Death of Moses	1250 BCE
Joshua	Conquest of the Promised Land	1250–1200 BCE
Judges	Leadership under a judge	1200–1020 BCE
First and Second Samuel	Reigns of Saul and David	1020–960 BCE
First and Second Kings	Reigns of all other kings, starting with Solomon, and ending with the fall of Jerusalem	960–587 BCE

Redaction of the Deuteronomistic History

This textbook focuses on the final form of the Deuteronomistic History which was completed after the last event that it describes, placing its composition during the Exile. However, we will see that this history is not all of one piece. Not only were earlier sources used in its composition, but the production of the final form of the text may have taken place in stages over a couple of hundred years. Some scholars hold to a double, and even a triple, redaction of the Deuteronomistic History. This is why I refer to redactors of the texts. Where you think the most formative layer of the text lies affects what you think are the general purpose and mood of the text.

Two kings in the history are singled out for favorable comparison with David: Hezekiah (2 Kgs 18:3-5) and Josiah (2 Kgs 22:2). This suggests that the descriptions of their reigns purposefully parallel the description of David's, forming an "inclusio" in the account of the monarchy. Furthermore, the accounts of both kings have parallels in Deuteronomy. Hezekiah is compared to Moses, and the description of Josiah's religious reform has almost verbatim parallels with Deuteronomy (compare, for example, Deut 6:5 and 2 Kgs 23:3). Again, these parallels suggest a deliberate compositional strategy to tie the long history together.

If either of these reigns formed the original ending of the history, then one of its purposes may have been to exalt one or both of these kings. We could imagine a royal historian working during the reign of Josiah, for example, praising his royal patron by comparing him to two great paragons in Israel's history: David and Moses. This would explain elements of the history that are supportive of monarchic authority. If the text was written during a successful nationwide religious reform, the text would also convey the hope and zeal of those supporting the reforms. The political exaltation would be part of the exaltation of Yahweh, the god of the nation.

However, even if the description of these reigns formed the original ending(s) of the book, the fact remains that this is not the form of the book that has come down to us. The preserved text clearly moves beyond the hope of the supporters of Josiah to the theological scandal following the events that occurred after his early death. We will read more about these details in future chapters. The additional material raises a methodological question: if there was an early edition of the history, did whoever added the account of the fall of the nation edit the whole history or only add the last chapters? Scholars disagree as to the amount of editing this final redactor did to the whole history, and, therefore, they disagree about the main purposes of the text. While I think there were over-arching redactional changes, you may find others with a different view. As you read the whole history, think about which purpose makes the most sense of the variety of details the text provides.

In the next three chapters I will present this history of the nation of Israel. Oftentimes students conclude that, since these books are historical, they present an objective view of Israel's history. However, accurate historical accounting is not the aim of ancient histories, so it is unfair and inaccurate to expect it from the biblical authors. Instead, we will focus on the ways in which the texts provide not just a record of events, but rather a theological interpretation of that record. My aim is to move readers beyond basic content to the underlying theology of the writers. In learning how to do this, you will develop better skills for reading ancient histories.

FROM CONQUEST TO TRIBE: HISTORY AND SOCIETY

[handwritten marginal note: small? not according to Exodus]

The stories that describe Israel's conquest and settlement of the land depict it as an amazing tale of survival. Moreover, these texts lead us to ask how a small group of slaves who had been wandering around the desert for forty years came to take over cities with kings and armies, eventually controlling most of the southern Levant.

A WORLD IN TRANSITION: FROM THE BRONZE AGE TO THE IRON AGE

The years 1550 to 1000 BCE were ones of great cultural and material transition for the Levant. Evidence for the emergence of the people of Israel occurs at the same time that civilization was moving from the Bronze Age to the Iron Age. (The beginning of the Iron Age is usually dated to around 1200 BCE.) This technological advance changed the conduct of war and agricultural productivity. These changes, in turn, affected economics, trade, and national organizations. Soon after the development of iron technologies, the first empires pop up in the historical record.

These years also brought significant shifts in the interactions of the people of the Levant with other world powers. The Levant of the late Bronze Age was heavily influenced by Egypt. Some of its areas were under direct Egyptian control. Other areas show the impact of Egyptian cultural influence in things such as burial customs and iconography.

Toward the end of this period, Sea Peoples invaded the Levantine coastland. We do not know exactly where they came from or why they migrated, but Egyptian paintings reveal that they came with whole families, suggesting that their migrations were the result of economic or military collapse in their homeland. Archaeological evidence suggests that they most likely came from somewhere in the Aegean, probably by way of Cyprus. Among the Sea Peoples were the Philistines and perhaps the Israelite tribe of Dan.

[handwritten marginal note: Dan are not descendants of Jacob? Not according to Genesis]

There were also new settlements in the Central Highlands of the southern Levant. We do not know who was responsible for these settlements, but evidence suggests that they pushed west at the same time as the Sea Peoples pushed east.

Egyptian influence dwindled in the Early Iron Age; it was a time of political upheaval in Egypt. Similarly, the nations of Mesopotamia declined. The Bible tells us that the Levant was occupied by a variety of peoples: Canaanites, Philistines, Moabites, Phoenicians, Jebusites, Ammonites, and so on. Outside

Biblical Archaeology

Modern *archaeology* is often dated to the excavations of the ancient city of Troy by Heinrich Schlieman between 1870 and 1890 CE. This event marked a transition from the looting of ancient sites to the systematic excavations of sites in order to trace a site's history. Although this example of early archaeology sought to "prove" the historicity of Homer's *Iliad*, it was not long before archaeologists turned to biblical history. As you can imagine, there were many donors willing to fund efforts to "prove" that the biblical account is historically accurate.

Luckily for historians, archaeological methods have drastically improved since those early tendentious days. Today archaeologists try to provide an accurate account of the history of a site, without trying to fit the evidence into a preconceived picture of what they may find.

Modern archaeologists first delineate the layers of occupation of a given site. This approach is aided by the fact that the ancient peoples of the Levant built on top of the ruins of earlier sites, forming a *tel* or mound of occupation. In the early days of biblical archaeology, archaeologists would strip the tel, taking one layer of occupation off after another. However, this destroys the site for future research, which is better equipped with new scientific tools to analyze the finds. Today, archaeologists do "soundings," digging shafts into various parts of the tel to get a kind of vertical timeline of occupation. These layers can tell us whether a city was destroyed by fire, military conquest, or gradual development, for instance.

Analysis of pottery is especially important for archaeologists, because experts have catalogued enough pottery to enable them to reliably date a site based on the type of pottery found there. I tell my students that it's a little like examining layers containing different styles of Tupperware; if you can reconstruct a Tupperware catalogue, you can figure out the date of a site.

The impact of modern archaeology on biblical studies cannot be overestimated. First, it has provided us with a great deal of insight into the life and times of the ancient world. Modern researchers focus less on monumental buildings, and more on reconstructing the everyday life of the average person. Doing so fills in the gaps in the biblical texts, which come primarily from the elite classes of ancient Israel.

Second, archaeology has provided us with some written texts. Of course, the majority of these come from lands outside of Israel and are inscribed on clay tablets. But, even so, some monuments, ostraca (pottery shards with writing on them), and other items have been discovered in the Levant. These discoveries help us reconstruct the history of the Hebrew language, fill out details behind the text that the writer assumes the audience knows, and tell us about Israel's neighbors from their own perspective.

Third, quite frankly, archaeology helps us get a more accurate account of Israel's history. Sometimes that history matches what is in the Bible, but sometimes it does not. When it does not, archaeological research helps those of us who focus on texts to see what other purposes these texts may be serving rather than just reporting a series of events in ancient Israel. Doing so helps us realize that the meaning of these texts lies more in their interpretation of their history than it does in the events themselves.

of the Philistines, however, the archaeological remains usually cannot be used to distinguish one group from another.

Conquest or Settlement

The books of Joshua and Judges offer two different accounts of how the Israelites came to possess the Levant. Joshua describes a series of quick attacks that led to a swift conquest of the area. Judges describes a gradual settlement of the land starting first in the eastern hill country, then spreading west, south, and north. The archaeological record fits neither schema completely.

Archaeological digs support the account in Judges more than the account in Joshua. We know that this was a period of social unrest. Some Canaanite cities were burned, and there were many new settlements in the dry, eastern high country. Whoever settled in the hill country was not culturally distinct from the people in the Canaanite cities: they built the same types of houses, used the same pottery, had similar weapons, and so on. The similarities suggest that these settlements had a large percentage of people who were from Canaan. These Canaanites most likely were either poor people trying to find a better life, away from rich landowners who controlled the fertile valleys in the center of the land, or peoples displaced by invading groups.

an interesting but implausible theory

Biblical historians now believe that a good portion of the citizens who later become Israelites had once been Canaanite peasants. These Canaanites may have joined a smaller group of refugees who had settled in the highlands after they had escaped from slavery in Egypt. As this group in the highlands moved west, they were joined by other tribes and groups also settled in Canaan. We will see that until Israel had a monarchy, the tribes had difficulty uniting to fight for a common cause. The fact that these tribes were comprised of very diverse groups makes this inability to unify understandable.

This mixture of peoples is important for understanding Israel's religious history as well. What connected these people was worship of one particular god, Yahweh. Who was this Yahweh that they worshipped? Yahweh was known as the God of the poor, the God of the enslaved, the God who fought injustice.

The Period of the Judges

The period of the conquest is followed by a period of tribal rule. The book of Judges delineates the territories controlled by each tribe as a way to bridge the two eras. Such an opening, however, belies the fact that control of the area came gradually.

Three Theories of the Conquest

Reconstructing the history of the *Conquest* has always been a fascinating subject for biblical historians. Early archaeologists eagerly excavated sites associated with the Conquest, confident that they could find the tumbled-down walls of Jericho or the burn layer of a defeated Ai.

What they found, however, did not fit the biblical records. Nor did the biblical record present a univocal view of the Conquest. This discrepancy of evidence has led to three predominant theories of the Conquest that underlie the text.

The Conquest Theory. This view sees a historical core in the tales of swift attacks on Canaanite cities. It favors the evidence in the book of Joshua, and interprets the destruction layers of various cities at this time as evidence of some attack by an invading group. Proponents of this model hold that the stories in Joshua get the names of specific cities wrong, but correctly create a general picture of some aggressive strikes which provided the invading Israelites with a foothold in the Land.

The Peaceful Infiltration Theory. This model reconstructs a more gradual takeover of land by a group invading from the east. New settlements would have been established first in the sparsely populated central highlands and then later, in the western fertile valleys. This theory favors the evidence in the book of Judges.

The Peasant Revolt Theory. In this theory, the archaeological evidence takes precedence. It also holds that "proto-Israel" (that is, the group that later came to be known as "Israel") can be found in the central highlands, but, more importantly, that the material culture of these settlements gives no indication that it stemmed from a group coming out of Egypt. Although some architectural differences are apparent from Canaanite cities in the valleys, these differences stem from adaptations to a harsher climate. This theory holds that early Israelites were actually Canaanite peasants looking for relief from economic oppression.

Each of these theories has something to offer, but each also has weaknesses. The Conquest and Peaceful Infiltration theories have difficulty explaining the complete archaeological picture. The Peasant Revolt theory has difficulty explaining the prominence of a Conquest by an invading group in the biblical record. These theories demonstrate the complexity of balancing textual evidence about Israel's history with the archaeological evidence and raise some interesting questions:

- **Which evidence should take precedence when reconstructing history?**

- **How does that reconstructed history impact the text's theological meaning?**

- **How do the different theories affect the way one views the stories in the Pentateuch?**

Pre-monarchic society was based on kinship ties. Each kinship group would have had a group of "elders" who ran the local communities. But there was probably still a need for some sort of centralized leadership of the coalition of clans at the tribal level. This leadership did not collect taxes or institute national policies. They did not claim dynastic rule, such as a king would, nor did they engage in large building projects at the public's expense. But they were needed to lead an army, both for defense and the execution of justice.

The Israelites referred to these leaders as judges, although the term might be better translated as "bringers of justice" or "rulers." The book of Judges does not define what a judge was; in fact, Scripture's presentation of the judges is ambiguous as to their function. Most of them are military leaders who achieve their authority once the "spirit of God" descends on them. Indeed, most of them appear to be military heroes who arise in times of crisis and rule by virtue of this "charism" or spirit. However, many of them "judge" for long periods of time, and some are never military leaders.

It is clear that the book of Judges does not provide a complete presentation of all of the judges. The historian has chosen certain stories to tell. It is more likely that the emphasis on military prowess is the result of the stories that the writer picks rather than a balanced account of what a judge was.

SOURCES IN JOSHUA AND JUDGES

The Deuteronomistic Historian used sources in creating the history. At times he names these sources (for example, Josh 10:13, and 1 Kgs 14:19 and 29). At other times, the sources are evident from changes in literary style and ideology within the text. This is especially true for the books of Joshua and Judges.

When you read parts of Joshua closely, you will see ritual features scattered throughout the book. Early source critics conjectured that the Priestly source in the Pentateuch extended into the book of Joshua. The ritual elements in Joshua are not identical to those of P, however. Today, it is more reasonable to suggest that the Deuteronomistic Historian used sources other than P.

The sources are even more obvious in the book of Judges. Many of the stories about the judges lack the characteristics of the Deuteronomistic Historian. In chapters 1—18, evidence of the Deuteronomistic Historian is found in the material that connects these stories. He depicts this time period as one in which the people get caught up in an ever-descending circle of sin, linking the stories of individual judges by a common pattern:

➤ Israel is secure in the land.

➤ Israel sins (usually by worshipping other gods).

➤ Israel is oppressed by a foreign enemy.

➤ Israel cries out to God.

➤ God sends a deliverer in the form of a judge.

➤ Israel is secure in the land, and so on.

The cycle becomes a downward spiral, however, because Israel's sins become increasingly atrocious, and the judges themselves become ever more part of that sin.

When I think of the redaction of the book of Judges, I imagine a string of pearls, in which the individual pearls are the older chunks of stories, and the string that binds them together is material provided by the Deuteronomistic Historian.

STORIES OF VICTORY AND FAILURE

JOSHUA 6:1–27 AND DEUTERONOMY 20:1–18: HOLY WAR AND CONQUEST

The book of Deuteronomy ends with the death of Moses. Just before he dies, he commissions Joshua, one of the two righteous spies, to lead the Israelites into the Promised Land. The book of Joshua begins with a description of how the Israelites cross the Jordan River and enter the land. The description resounds with religious undertones. For instance, the Jordan splits in two when the priests carrying the Ark of the Covenant enter it; the Israelites cross through on dry land. Once on the other side, they set up twelve stones as a memorial to the twelve tribes that entered the land on that day. Joshua circumcises all of the Israelite males, after which they observe Passover. Joshua 5 ends with the appearance of a divine general to Joshua, a sign that God is now ready for the battles for the "Promised Land" to begin.

Joshua 6 is the best representation of the kind of wars that the book of Joshua describes. The religious elements are prominent. The law of war in Deuteronomy provides the background for the story.

IN CASE YOU WERE WONDERING

The number seven. The number seven was considered a perfect number. Here it represents the days of the week, a perfect and complete period of time.

The ram's horn. The ram's horn that is blown at the end of seven days is the *shofar*, a horn used to call Israelites to worship.

Rahab the harlot. Before the Israelites attack Jericho, they send in spies to look over the city's defenses. A Canaanite harlot named Rahab hides these spies. Her whole family is rewarded for her kindness.

The treasury of the house of the LORD. This reference is unclear. There is no "house" of Yahweh yet; the ark is kept in a moveable tent. This reference is probably an anachronism.

LOOKING CLOSELY AT THE TEXT

1. Look carefully at Deuteronomy 20:10–14 and 15–18; how do the two types of war differ?

2. How do these laws explain what the Israelites do when Jericho falls?

3. How many ritual elements can you find in the description of the battle against Jericho?

4. Does the Bible assert that God desires war?

VICTORY FOR THE LORD

This text presents a vivid depiction of the fall of Jericho. Tension builds until the final moment, when the walls miraculously come tumbling down. Although early archaeologists thought that they could find the biblical Jericho, many scholars today recognize that this story is not intended to be an accurate account of the fall of a particular city.

First, the text describes the event in rather unrealistic terms. It does not say how the inhabitants of the city reacted to the motley crew of invaders marching around their city. The description presumes that the Israelites had besieged the town. A *siege* is when an army surrounds a city and cuts off its food and water supplies, hoping the citizens will surrender once they are starving. The large equipment needed for a siege, such as a battering ram, siege engines, and military gear, makes such an attack by the Israelites unlikely.

Second, archaeological excavations in Jericho have revealed that it was not a walled city at this time. Although the account may refer to another city destroyed by the Israelites, the book of Judges suggests that swift military attacks were not the most common way the Israelites settled into the land.

Third, many Jews and Christians have difficulty imagining that God ordered and carried out the annihilation of the citizens of Jericho. If the fall of Jericho happened in this miraculous manner, then God is directly responsible for the deaths of "both men and women, young and old" (Josh 6:21). So while the miracle was certainly possible, it presents greater theological problems than it solves.

The story probably represents a setting in which the polarized language of good versus evil makes sense. When we studied Exodus, we saw that one place where this dichotomy made sense was ritual. The book of Joshua begins with the setting up of ritual stones, circumcision, and Passover; it ends with a covenant renewal ceremony. Sandwiched between these rituals are the stories of the Conquest of the land, a battle of good versus evil, accomplished with the help of priests, the ark, and the *shofar*. The book of Joshua places the defeat of Jericho squarely within a ritual setting.

We must turn to the laws of war in Deuteronomy to understand this religious context more fully. We see two types of war in Deuteronomy 20. In the first type the leader negotiates with the enemy, but, if that fails, the army tries to avoid harming anyone who is not a soldier. According to Deuteronomy 20:15, this law applied to wars waged outside of the southern Levant. Verses 16–18, however, describe how the Israelites should fight "the towns of these peoples that the LORD your God is giving you as an inheritance" (20:16). In this type of war, the Israelites were commanded to kill *all* living things, from humans to animals. This law is applied to the city of Jericho.

How are people today, who hold this text as sacred, supposed to understand such a law? This is a difficult question to answer, but let me point to six issues that put this law in its historical context.

The war ban is about the spoils of war. The Israelites believed that wars were fought with the help of God. Before the Israelites went into battle, they would offer sacrifices, so that God would go out with them to fight. It was this divine aid that was the real reason they would win. As a symbol of that belief, when a battle was won, a significant portion of the spoils of war were offered to Yahweh.

The laws of war in Deuteronomy dictate the distribution of the spoils of war. The first law reflects common practice. A significant portion was set aside for God, while the rest of the spoils went to the army. In the ban, Yahweh commands that everything within a city belongs to God. The soldiers can take none of the spoils. When the book of Joshua says that these things are "devoted to the LORD for destruction" (Josh 6:17), this means that they must be turned over to Yahweh. Living things were burned as a sacrifice, while the spoils were stored in the temple.

This law was not unique to Israel. Other countries also had a similar ban law used for certain types of battles. For instance, archeologists have discovered a monument from Moab, the Mesha Inscription, in which the king states that he placed an enemy city "under the ban." Israel was reflecting the standard methods of warfare in its day.

The ban is a religious law. The Hebrew word for the "ban" (*herem*) is used in a variety of Old Testament texts in slightly different ways. In Leviticus 27:28, it refers to a certain class of things "devoted" to God. What these uses have in common is the belief that something devoted to God belongs exclusively and irrevocably to Yahweh.

The ban can function as a purification ritual. The law in Deuteronomy tells us the law is observed in order to purify the city. By placing a city under the ban, the Israelite army purifies it of all "foreign" or impure elements. The Israelites believed that the land of Israel was actually *God's* land. The purification of the land was needed to make it fit for God's ownership. Just as a temple was purified before a symbol of God resided there, so too the land was purified to prepare it for God.

The ban addresses the problem of religious identity. We saw previously that the Israelites were not culturally distinct from the Canaanites. In the story of Jericho, Rahab and her Canaanite family are not just spared but welcomed into the community. Joshua 6:25 tells us that "her family has lived in Israel ever since." The ban was not intended to represent an attack on people based solely on ethnic or racial identity. It was directed against those who opposed Yahweh and Israel. Remember that in the Golden Calf story in Exodus 32:25–28, the Israelites who would not turn back to Yahweh were similarly killed. The ban is directed against those who opposed Israel's identity as a people dedicated to Yahweh.

The ban is not a "real" law; it represents an ideal. This brings me to my last point about the ban. In the last chapter on the laws, I mentioned that the law codes that we have were idealizations. They described the "perfect world." The book of Deuteronomy clearly has ideal laws. The history itself tells us that the laws were only in effect during the reign of Josiah (640–609 BCE). The ban was one such "ideal." What it expresses is not the reality of how war was conducted, but the projection of an Israelite ideal that, if the people had really been faithful to Yahweh, the Conquest would have been "ideal," that is, swift and miraculously successful. It would have rid the land of all things that drew the people away from the worship of Yahweh.

We will see many other texts in the Old Testament that command the Israelites to treat the "foreigners" in their midst with respect, justice, and even kindness. The stories in Joshua are not stories that support harming people who are nationally, racially, or ethnically different. These are stories about religious temptation. In the ban, the "foreigners" are those who tempt the Israelites to worship other gods and thus lose their identity. God commands that they sacrifice anything that might lead them astray.

JUDGES 3:12–30: A LEFT-HANDED WARRIOR

According to the book of Joshua, the Israelites gained a foothold in the land after several swift attacks on the Canaanites. Throughout the book the author describes the land-holdings of each tribe. The book ends with a celebration of their victory and the renewal of their covenant with God.

The book of Judges opens with a list of cities and areas that the Israelites do *not* control. Chapter 2 recounts the death of Joshua, and it begins the tale of Israel's sinfulness in the land that God has given them.

The book of Judges tells the stories of a few of the judges who ruled the Israelite tribes before there was a king. The early judges in the book are upright figures. The first narrative about a judge is the story of Ehud, the left-handed warrior. He arises during a time that the Israelites are being oppressed by Eglon, a king from Moab. This simple narrative illustrates the storytelling

The Bible in the CHRISTIAN TRADITION

Just War Theory

In 1983, the U.S. Conference of Roman Catholic Bishops issued a statement on the practice of *just war*. In the document, they outlined six conditions that must be met for a war to be considered just:

1. There must be a just cause.
2. The war must be undertaken with the right intention.
3. It must be publicly declared by a proper authority.
4. It must be the last resort.
5. There must be a probability of success.
6. The evil that comes from the war must be in proportion to the good that it is trying to achieve.

Today some Catholics, noting that these conditions can rarely be met, have become pacifists, viewing all kinds of communal aggression as contrary to the will of God. They join many Protestant denominations that have long been pacifists, such as the Seventh Day Adventists and the Mennonites, as well as global religious movements advocating nonviolent resistance, such as those led by Gandhi and Martin Luther King, Jr.

Christian movements have taken their lead from the teachings of Jesus, but they do not always deal directly with the Old Testament witness to a God who commands war. Biblical theologians struggle with these problems: a biblical text that repeatedly depicts God's participation in and support of some forms of human aggression and a realization of the harm that has been done "in God's name" on people that Christian societies have attacked. To give just two examples, both the Crusades and the wars on indigenous peoples in the Americas were justified in part by viewing these wars as a new Conquest commanded by God.

Is it possible for a community to both view these texts as sacred and denounce military attacks on those of a different religion? Does God command war? Are there conditions by which a war is justified? Or are all forms of communal violence wrong? Texts such as Deuteronomy 20 give us evidence that the ancient Israelites struggled with similar questions, although in a way that reflects their cultural context.

brilliance of the Deuteronomistic Historian. Notice how every element in the account is essential to the plotline.

IN CASE YOU WERE WONDERING

The Amalekites. Amalek was to the south of Judah.

Seirah. It is unclear where this is located.

LOOKING CLOSELY AT THE TEXT

I usually ask you about certain details of the text here, but this time I want you to read along with me. I will point out some of the details and explain how they fit into the story.

COMEDY, IRONY, AND VICTORY

The story of Ehud is an example of Israelite story telling at its best. The story opens with the notice that Israel has once again fallen into a cycle of sin. As a result God has allowed them to be ruled over by the Moabites. The Israelites cry out to God, and a deliverer is sent. These first few verses set the background for the rest of the story.

In Judges 3:15 we are told that Ehud, the Israelites' deliverer is (1) from the tribe of Benjamin and (2) left-handed. These two details fit literally hand-in-hand. The name *Benjamin* means "one of the right," or a right-handed person. The irony is that this "righty," is left-handed. In the ancient world, few people were left-handed, since children were trained to use their right hands. Next we are told about Ehud's small sword or dagger. It is a cubit in length, which is the length of a forearm. Why are these details important? They explain how Ehud was able to sneak a dagger into the king's room. He sneaks it in because (1) it is short enough to remain hidden under his clothes, and (2) it is tied to the opposite side from where the guards would look, since they thought he was right-handed.

We are told that Ehud is delivering "tribute" to Eglon, king of Moab. Tribute is a form of heavy taxation imposed by a larger nation on a smaller one. By paying the tribute, the people of Benjamin buy their peace. Ehud tells Eglon that he has a secret message for him (3:19), a message from God (3:20), a comic piece of irony. The reader knows that the "message" is the sword Ehud carries, but foolish Eglon presumes that Ehud means him no harm, since he has just paid the tribute.

Judges 3:17 tells us Eglon was very fat. This is an odd detail. Do we know about the physical appearance of many other biblical figures? Only rarely does the Bible give us a physical detail, and when it does, it is because it is important to the story line. We will see that Eglon's size is one such detail.

These dagger and sword heads were found in Kadum, Sumeria, and date to the fifteenth century BCE.

Judges 3:21–22 describes Ehud's attack on Eglon. He stabs him with such force that the whole dagger goes inside of Eglon, and Ehud leaves it there. The Bible even notes that "the hilt also went in after the blade, and the fat closed over the blade." Next the Bible states, "The dirt came out." Why all this detail?

The "dirt" is fecal matter; Ehud's dagger had pierced Eglon's bowel area. Does the writer simply enjoy being "gross"? To answer that, look at what happens next. The guards do not go into the king's room after Ehud leaves; they wait, assuming that he is "relieving himself." Why would they assume this? Because they can smell the feces that result from Eglon's mortal wound. They do not know this smell is the result of injury; they simply think the king is doing what we all do.

I have long been amused by this story. I've wondered how long those guards stood out there before they checked on the king. I can hear their conversation: "The king's sure been in there a long time; do you think we should check on him?" "I'm not going to check on him; you go." "Maybe we should wait a while longer." And so it would go. In the meantime, what's Ehud doing? Why, he's escaping, of course!

The escape is further aided by the fact that the dagger is not visible. Once the guards enter the room, are they going to know that the king died from a stab wound? No! Since there is no dagger to be seen, they would not at first realize that Ehud had stabbed the king. As the text succinctly puts it, "Ehud escaped while they delayed" (Judg 3:26).

The text finishes by recounting the victory that the Benjaminites won against the Moabites as a result of Ehud's heroic and clever act. This story has many memorable elements. It has violence, humor, and irony, and it is exciting. It is told in a very concise manner, and each detail adds to the plot. Yet within this compact story, the details pique the reader's imagination.

THE PORTRAYAL OF WOMEN IN THE BOOK OF JUDGES

Rather than pick some episodes described in the book of Judges, I will turn to the various stories about women that have been included in this book. Read the passages assigned to get a general impression of these women. Notice who talks and who is given a name; observe which ones are positive figures and which ones are "evil women." We will see that this focus on the fate of women illustrates the theme of social disintegration.

JUDGES 4 AND 5: THE HEROINES, DEBORAH AND JAEL

The first prominent women in Judges are Deborah and Jael. Deborah is not a warrior. She is a prophetess whose job it is to tell the army whether or not Yahweh is going to fight for them. Deborah tells the warrior, Barak, that God "commands" him to engage in battle and has promised him victory. When Barak insists that she come with him, he reveals his lack of faith in God's prophet. The judgment is swift: Barak will be shamed, because the head of the enemy will fall by the hand of a woman. At this point in the story, the reader expects that this woman will be Deborah.

The battle ensues, and Barak quickly routs the forces of Sisera. Sisera flees on foot, an act of cowardice. As he escapes, he comes upon the tent of Heber and his wife, Jael. Heber is an ally of Sisera; the Kenites were a nomadic people, "tent-dwellers." This explains why Jael would be in a tent within running distance of the battleground.

Jael invites Sisera in, which appears at first to be an act of hospitality. However, women who were alone were not supposed to invite men into their tent. In fact, "opening your tent" for a man was a euphemism for sexual contact. We are not sure where Heber is at this point, but clearly Jael is alone. She also goes beyond the norms of hospitality. He asks for water but she gives him milk, something a guest would not have expected. When he sleeps, she "covers" him, another euphemism for sexual contact. This also indicates greater hospitality than he deserved: a fleeing general may have expected a horse and a little water, but he gets a bed and something of substance.

Feminist Hermeneutics

In the last few chapters I have described methods of biblical interpretation that focus on uncovering the historical setting of the production of the text. Yet, most people today read the Bible for what it means to them now.

How does the meaning that the text had in the past relate to the meaning that it has for communities of faith today? Should a religious group simply assume that what the text said in its original context should be binding on them today? What about the law of the ban? Or capital punishment for those caught in adultery? Or polygamy? These examples demonstrate the difficulty of bridging the gap between what a text originally meant and what it means today.

The theory concerning how one bridges that gap is called *hermeneutics*. Hermeneutics is a complex issue, involving issues of meaning and interpretation. For our purposes, we will focus on the basic question: what is the relationship between what a text meant and what it means. Hermeneutics surrounds us, even if we are unaware of it. Whenever you hear a claim that something is "wrong" because the Bible says so, that's a hermeneutical claim.

It is important to think about this issue for two reasons. First, a claim based on the Bible has a certain amount of authority for many people. This authority requires that we not treat such claims casually. Second, oftentimes when people make these claims, the assumptions underlying these statements are invisible, even to those making them. The best way to explore this second proposition is through a specific example.

Although hermeneutics has always been an important part of biblical interpretation, from the 1960s onward, it has taken on new life as academic study of the Bible has become increasingly available to more diverse groups. The rise in the number of women and ethnic minorities in American theological graduate schools, for example, has led to awareness that some of what was formerly taken as objectively "true" in biblical scholarship was really the interpretation of a particular, dominant social class.

The emergence of *feminist hermeneutics* is one example of how this change in the demographics of scholarship has filled out research on biblical history and broadened awareness of the impact of interpretation on the contemporary world. Like any interpretation from a cultural perspective, feminist hermeneutics does not take a single position. Not all feminists think the same thing, just as not all white males have the same perspective. But there are three major branches that one finds in feminist interpretations of the text:

Historical and literary recovery. Some feminist interpretations seek to recover the important role women play in the Bible. Sometimes this recovery focuses on historical questions: what role did women play in the royal court? In the family? In religion? Sometimes scholars focus on the literary characters often overlooked in traditional interpretations; this sometimes means reading from the perspective of unnamed and silent characters. This work of recovery has led to a fuller and more accurate picture of the world of the biblical text.

De-centering the question of meaning. An older model of biblical interpretation sought to articulate the meaning of the biblical text. But often what was accepted as that meaning came out of a set of assumptions shared by the dominant academic group. The increasing diversity of biblical scholars has led to awareness that interpretation always comes out of a cultural context. This does not mean that it necessarily stays there, but rather that each community of scholars provides a unique and important voice to interpretation. Feminists challenge claims of a text's "objective" meaning.

The danger of interpretation. Feminists have also made us all more aware of the impact of biblical interpretation on the lives of women, especially in societies dominated by Christianity. Some feminist scholars trace the impact of a particular interpretation on women. The interpretation of Genesis 3:16, "Your desire shall be for your husband, and he shall rule over you," as a universal command rather than a curse within a particular piece of literature, for example, has reinforced women's legal subordination to men throughout much of Christian history.

Sometimes people blame feminism for the discomfort that comes when the world is more complicated. However, movements such as feminist hermeneutics simply remind us of things that Christian interpreters have known since the church began: that interpretation is always a complex process; that "meaning" in a text always encompasses a range of possibilities (what is traditionally called "layers of meaning"); that interpretation should always be a communal process; and that a lot is at stake whenever anyone interprets the Bible, because of its authority for many communities of faith.

And then she kills him. The force with which she kills him suggests extraordinary strength, since she drove the tent peg through him and into the ground in one fell swoop. We never know why she does this, and we have no idea what happens to her after this event. Since her husband had been an ally of Sisera, surely her fate would not have been good. Deborah, on the other hand, sings a victory song, which in part praises Jael.

The only other woman we hear from is Sisera's mother at the end of the poem in chapter 5. She poignantly waits by a window for her son to return. Once again the poem leaves us to imagine the scene, as the messenger tells her that her son lies pinned to the ground in the tent of Jael. The poetic irony is subtle: Sisera's mother has made it clear that women were part of the "prize" male soldiers got when they won a battle. But instead of a virtual "trophy" girlfriend, Sisera is killed by a woman's hand.

The story sounds glorious. Israel wins, exacting an ironic defeat on its enemy. In addition, both Deborah and Jael are positive characters who act independently, speak their own words, and have names.

But even here there are little hints that the story has begun its slow decline. Notice in the poem that several of Israel's tribes, although called to join in the fight, refuse to come. Since the Israelites believed that the war was fought at God's command, absence indicates a refusal to obey God. A tiny footnote in the story will fester and by the end of the book grow into a problem that cannot be ignored.

JUDGES 11: JEPHTHAH'S TRAGIC DAUGHTER

Between the death of Sisera and the story of Jephthah, the book of Judges preserves stories about several other judges. Featured in these are Gideon, who leads the Israelites to victory over the Midianites (chapters 6—8), and Abimelech, who tries to become a king (chapter 9). The next prominent female character in Judges, Jephthah's daughter, does not get a name, a fact that matches her status as a victim of her father's rash vow.

The story begins inauspiciously. Jephthah is the son of a prostitute, whose half brothers kick him out of the family. This is hardly the birth story of a hero, and the audience should not expect a good outcome from Jephthah.

He is brought back by his half brothers when they are attacked by a foreign enemy. Jephthah makes a vow to God that he will sacrifice the first thing that comes out of his house to meet him if he returns victorious. What did he expect it would be? Many rural homes at this time housed the farm animals

This is a model of a typical Israelite farmhouse circa eighth to sixth century BCE.

on the ground floor, while the family slept above. Perhaps he thought that an animal would come out first.

However, we have seen that women sang the victory song when men returned from battle. When Jephthah returns, his daughter comes out singing his praises. The text notes that he did not expect her, although perhaps he should have. His vow was rash and impulsive. This motif of the "rash vow" is seen in other ancient literature. Recall that among the Ten Commandments there was an injunction not to break a vow to God. In some of the law codes in the Pentateuch, women could not make a vow unless it was approved by their father or husband; a horrible fate would befall her if she vowed something that could not be fulfilled.

Jephthah's daughter is a passive but noble character. She knows that her father must keep his vow, and she convinces him of his duty. She requests time to "mourn her virginity," that is, the fact that she has no children to carry on her memory. The Bible tells us that this mourning time turns into an annual ritual for young girls. (It is not surprising that there is no mention of this ritual in the Pentateuch, since it would not have been a ritual associated with the temple or with the male leaders who wrote the legal texts.) Notice the ritual that involves young women later in the book.

Judges 13–16: Samson's Love of Philistine Women

In popular culture Samson is portrayed as a tragic hero tricked into his defeat by the evil Delilah. A look at the whole Samson cycle, however, reveals his pattern of complex relationships with women.

The account begins with Samson's birth. This birth story follows a pattern commonly used in the Bible whenever an author wants to relate the birth of a hero. In this pattern, there is usually a barren woman who is especially loved by her husband. A divine messenger appears to one or both of the spouses and tells them that they shall have a son. Sometimes the messenger also gives special instructions for raising the child; Samson, for example, is to be brought up according to the laws of the nazirite. (A nazirite was someone who took a vow to remain "ultra pure" for a particular period of time.) Then the messenger tells the couple what to name their son. When you encounter a story like this, you can be sure that the boy will grow up to be an important Israelite leader. By the end of chapter 13, we know that Samson will grow up to be a great leader as long as he does three things: keeps away from anything made of grapes, avoids ritual impurity, and does not cut his hair.

The story of Samson occurs a little more than halfway into the book of Judges, and it represents part of the downward spiral of the Israelites. Samson's mother is featured in this story. The angel appears twice to her alone, although the second time she fetches her husband. Notice, however, that her husband does not believe what she has told him. This is not the depiction of a loving couple, and it foreshadows problems in Samson's life.

Samson's blatant disregard for others is apparent. At his wedding he "sets ups" his thirty companions by giving them a riddle that they cannot possibly solve, and he pays off his debt by killing thirty men and stealing their clothes. He disregards his nazirite obligations. He eats something ritually impure: the honey from the dead lion. He sins further by giving some to his parents without telling them where it came from (14:9), which makes them impure.

Samson's foolishness is most clearly shown, though, in his choice of women. He lives during a time when Israel's greatest enemy was Philistia. God chooses him to be a judge because of the oppression that the Israelites are suffering at the hands of the Philistines. But what kind of women is Samson always seeking out? Philistine women! In the first story of the adult Samson, he has fallen in love with a Philistine woman. He rudely demands of his mother and father that they "get her" for him. He sleeps with a Philistine prostitute in Gaza (16:1), and

The Philistines

From about 1400 to 1200 BCE there was a movement of people whom the Egyptians called "the Sea Peoples." These were probably groups of refugees from the Greek islands, forced to flee for some unknown reason. Groups of these Sea Peoples attacked Egypt, but they lost. Around 1200 BCE, the Egyptians settled one of the groups on the coast of the Levant, the Philistines.

The *Philistines* organized themselves as a coalition which included five major cities (Ashdod, Ashkelon, Ekron, Gath, and Gaza). They were settled in the Levant during a period when Egypt, Assyria, and Babylonia were all relatively weak. The Philistines flourished from about 1200 to 1000 BCE, and their expansion during this time put them in conflict with the growing nation of Israel. King David (ca. 1000-960) ended this expansion. Philistia eventually suffered the same setbacks and defeats at the hands of Assyria and Babylon as Israel did from about 750 to 500 BCE.

During the early period of Philistine settlement, the Philistines maintained their own distinct culture. Their pottery provides perhaps the clearest indication of this fact. Philistine pottery blended the styles of the Greek islands with those of the Levant. Pictures of Philistines in Egyptian carvings depict their unique weapons and dress. Archaeological digs have confirmed that the Philistines were also expert metalworkers, being one of the first nations able to work in both iron and bronze.

We do not know much about the religion or literature of the Philistines because we do not have any of their texts. Apparently they worshipped a Greek earth goddess, but eventually their main god became a local grain god named Dagon.

After their defeat by David, Philistine culture became more and more assimilated to the local culture, and distinct Philistine names, pottery or architecture faded. By the Babylonian period (ca. 550 BCE), Philistine culture is not distinct from other groups in the Levant.

Delilah comes from a Philistine city. Samson's affairs have political implications. To give you a modern parallel, would Franklin Roosevelt have had a Nazi mistress during World War II? Samson's choices are not just matters of personal preference; he puts Israel's security at risk with these women.

In addition to his poor choice of women is his incredible stupidity! Each time he tells Delilah the "secret" of his strength, she tries to have him captured. What did he think would happen when he told Delilah his strength was in his hair (16:17)? Again, notice the political implications. He not only has Philistine mistresses, but he is willing to tell them secrets that could help the Philistines defeat the Israelites.

The women in these stories are not positive figures. Both the first unnamed wife and Delilah, in collusion with Philistine men, betray Samson. The unnamed woman agrees to get the secret because the men of the town threaten to burn her and her family, a fate that comes to pass after Samson burns the fields. The audience has little sympathy for these Philistine women because the book of Judges has portrayed them as foreign temptresses. They "get what they deserve."

Judges 19–21: Nameless Victims

After the death of Samson, the book of Judges relates the story of a judge named Micah who steals money from his mother, builds his own temple, and hires his own levitical priest. An idol is stolen by the tribe of Dan, which has been forced to migrate to the northern part of Israel. Chapter 18 ends by stating that there are rival cults of Yahweh: one at Shiloh and one at Dan. This story highlights the religious deterioration of the nation.

At this point the historian has reached the climax of his story. There is nothing good that happens to women in the final three chapters of the book. The story of the concubine serves to highlight the depravity of the men of Israel at this point in the historical narrative. The Levite is not a positive figure: he allows his wife to leave him. Then he decides, some three months later, to "speak tenderly" to her. Yet, when he arrives at his father-in-law's, the two men spend the whole time eating and drinking.

Notice that the concubine never says a single word in the whole account. She is cast out by her husband to a gang of men intent on rape. She dies with her hands on the threshold of the house where her husband has apparently spent a restful night. When the Levite sees his concubine the morning after the gang rape, he finally speaks to her these tender words, "Get up. We're going!" Then, realizing that she is dead (or so we are led to assume), he is suddenly outraged at this insult to him. He rallies the Israelites for war against one of their own tribes. Ironically, it is the only time in the whole book where most of Israel shows up for a battle. They place Benjamin under the ban, putting to the sword "the city, the people, the animals, and all that remained" (Judg 20:48).

At the end of months of slaughter that have led to the extermination of all Benjaminite females, the men of Israel finally realize that a tribe is going to be wiped out. They need to find wives for the remaining men, even though they have sworn not to let their daughters marry Benjaminites. First, they attack the Israelite city of Jabesh-Gilead to get four hundred virgins as part of the spoils. Then they authorize the Benjaminites to "take wives" for themselves from a group of virgins celebrating a ritual at Shiloh. How did you "take a wife" in the ancient world? You raped her: the law of rape in Exodus 22:16–17 states that the punishment for the rape of an unbetrothed virgin is that the rapist must marry her. (He pays twice the bride price, cannot divorce her, and must impregnate her if she wants, thus making him financially responsible for her for the duration of her life.) The book of Judges with its heroines, such as

Deborah and Jael, ends with the gang-rape of two hundred unnamed Israelite virgins. The story closes with the repetition of a phrase found at the beginning of this section (17:6): "In those days there was no king in Israel; all the people did what was right in their own eyes" (Judg 21:25).

At this point, the political purpose of the narrative sequence comes into sharp focus. The book has painted a wrenching tale of social disintegration. The Deuteronomistic Historian is suggesting that Israel needed a king, not because the monarchy was a divinely ordained institution, but because those most vulnerable in Israelite society were victimized by those in power when they were left to their own devices.

SUMMARY: THE RHETORICAL FORCE OF THE DEUTERONOMISTIC HISTORY

The Deuteronomistic Historian was a brilliant author. He painted a convincing picture of Israel's settlement and moral decay. Whenever I teach these texts, students want to know why Israel had been so sinful. They are convinced that the historical books present a literal description of Israelite history. But this view does not do justice to the literary quality of these texts.

The historical accuracy of the material is hard to maintain for several reasons:

› The archaeological record does not match the history.

› The historical account was completed some 500–600 years after the events it describes.

› There are several anachronisms.

› Early Israelites were not as distinct from Canaanites and Philistines as the history maintains.

It is important to recognize that these books do not contain historical writing in the sense that we think of it. Ancient histories, such as those produced by Herodotus and Thucydides, were more interested in interpretation than facts, as were those produced by the ancient Israelites. The Deuteronomistic Historian portrays the Israelites—his people—as sinful because it fits his overall theme for the material. We will examine this theme more thoroughly over the course of the next two chapters.

FOR REVIEW

1. What books make up the Deuteronomistic History?

2. Why are these books called the Deuteronomistic History?

3. What events in Israel's history are covered in this history?

4. Joshua and Judges give different pictures of how Israel came to possess the land. State what that difference is.

5. Why do biblical historians assert that the later citizens of Israel probably had originally been inhabitants of Canaan?

6. If the Israelites came from different places, what united them?

7. How does the portrayal of women in the book of Judges illustrate a major theme of the book?

FOR FURTHER READING

This chapter introduces you to the Deuteronomistic History. If you want to explore this further, you might start with Richard D. Nelson's *The Historical Books* (Interpreting Biblical Texts; Nashville, TN: Abingdon, 1998), or Anthony F. Campbell and Mark A. O'Brien, *Unfolding the Deuteronomistic History: Origins, Upgrades, Present Text* (Minneapolis, MN: Fortress, 2000).

There are several good monographs that deal with the theology of the Bible's laws on war. From a Roman Catholic perspective, see T. R. Hobbs, *A Time for War: A Study of Warfare in the Old Testament* (Old Testament Studies 3; Wilmington, DE: Michael Glazier, 1989). From a Jewish perspective, see Susan Niditch, *War in the Hebrew Bible: A Study in the Ethics of Violence* (New York: Oxford University Press, 1993), and from a Mennonite tradition, see Millard C. Lind, *Yahweh Is a Warrior: The Theology of Warfare in Ancient Israel* (A Christian Peace Shelf Selection; Scottdale, PA: Herald, 1980). For the ancient near-eastern context, see Lori L. Rowlett, *Joshua and the Rhetoric of Violence: A New Historicist Analysis* (JSOTSup 226; Sheffield, UK: Sheffield Academic, 1996).

Unfortunately, for people who are not biblical scholars, most of the works that lay out the different understandings of the Conquest are very detailed and provide technical analyses of the archaeological and textual records. However, my students have found the following helpful in laying out the options or covering some of the issues that are at stake in any reconstruction: Hershel Shanks, et al., *The Rise of Ancient Israel* (Washington, DC: Biblical Archaeology Society, 1992), B. S. J. Isserlin, *The Israelites* (London: Thames and Hudson, 1998) and

The Bible Unearthed: Archaeology's New Vision of Ancient Israel and the Origin of Its Sacred Texts (New York, NY: Free Press, 2001) and William G. Dever, *What Did the Biblical Writers Know, and When Did They Know It?: What Archaeology Can Tell Us about the Reality of Ancient Israel* (Grand Rapids, MI: Eerdmans, 2001).

This chapter has used a form of narrative analysis on the text of Judges. For a readable introduction to narrative analysis, see Robert Alter, *The Art of Biblical Narrative* (New York: Basic Books, 1981). The analysis of the Ehud pericope is heavily dependent on Baruch Halpern's *The First Historians: The Hebrew Bible and History* (University Park, PA: Pennsylvania State University Press, 1996).

A book that looks at the impact of newer methods of biblical interpretation on the understanding of the book of Judges is *Judges and Method: New Approaches in Biblical Studies*, edited by Gale A. Yee (Minneapolis, MN: Fortress, 1995).

6 The Rise of the Monarchy: 1 and 2 Samuel

I will establish the throne of his kingdom forever.
I will be a father to him, and he shall be a son to me.
(2 Sam 7:13a–14b)

CHAPTER OVERVIEW

The books of Samuel depict Israel's transition from a tribal society to a united monarchy. Although these texts were written centuries after the events they describe, they convey the author's assessment of the kinds of power struggles and ambiguous moral situations that such a transition may have entailed.

This chapter will provide the following:

› An overview of the contents of this biblical book

› A discussion of the sources that the final redactors used in composing this material

› A summary of the historical background of this period in Israel's history

› A survey of the ethics of leadership that the text assumes

The texts that I have chosen for close readings focus on the triumphs and failures of Israel's leaders. As you read the individual pericopes, remember to ask yourself, why did historians include this material in their account of Israel's history?

To Have a King or Not to Have a King: That Is the Question

The Plot Line of 1 and 2 Samuel

First and Second Samuel comprise a single literary unit; their division stems from the length of the text which had to be transmitted on two different scrolls.

These books narrate the processes leading to the monarchy. First Samuel opens with the birth and childhood of the prophet Samuel (1 Sam 1—3), who will anoint both Saul and David as kings. By starting with the figure of the prophet, the text implies that the monarch is subordinate to the prophet.

Before Saul is introduced, the author also tells about the fate of the Ark of the Covenant (1 Sam 4—7). Its capture by the Philistines and eventual return to the Israelites reminds the audience further that the monarchy should be in service to God, and not vice versa.

The stories of Saul, the first king of Israel, are surprisingly complex. He is portrayed in turn as a sympathetic figure and as a doubting ineffectual leader. The result, whether intended by the author or not, is that he is a somewhat tragic figure, caught up in momentous events that he had neither the skill nor the confidence to negotiate. As Saul's reign deteriorates, David's rise to power begins. The bulk of 1 Samuel 8—31 braids together the narratives of these two men. It ends with the death of Saul in 1 Samuel 31.

The second book of Samuel tells the story of David's reign as king, but, again, it is not the story that we might expect. Instead of reporting his battles, economic policies, building projects, and so on, it focuses on his personal life: his marriages, his intrigues, and his family. It is not a pretty picture, either. Yet, about a third of the way into it, the redactors imbed an eternal promise that David and his offspring will always be kings over Israel.

In summary, the book has three main sections: the period right before the monarchy, the reign of Saul with the rise of David, and the story of David's reign.

Stories of Samuel and the Ark	1 Samuel 1—7
Saul's reign and David's rise	1 Samuel 8—31
David's reign	2 Samuel 1—24

At the end of this section, the audience is left to wonder: does the Deuteronomistic Historian like the monarchy or not?

Sources Used by the Deuteronomistic Historian

Although the final form of the Deuteronomistic History was written about four to five hundred years after the events that it describes, it is clear that it incorporates a number of sources, resulting in a very complex text.

Like the book of Judges, there are whole blocks of material that do not fit the traditional style or characteristic phrasings of the Deuteronomist. Let me give you three of the most glaring examples:

> ‣ The stories about the Ark of the Covenant scattered throughout 1 and 2 Samuel seem independent of the material surrounding it. For example, the chapters about the ark imbedded in the Samuel material make no mention of Samuel.

> ‣ The depiction of Saul is varied. In some texts he is a positive figure, suggesting the use of an independent pro-Saul source.

> ‣ The second book of Samuel 9—20 has very few Deuteronomistic elements. For example, God is only mentioned three times in these chapters, and those verses could be removed without hurting the overall integrity of the material. These chapters depict David's sinfulness and the deterioration of his family, in contrast to the positive portrayal of him in other Deuteronomistic texts.

The presence of earlier sources does not mean that they are automatically historically reliable. Each section must be judged independently. But their presence does offer some explanation for the variety of perspectives in the final text.

Historical Background for the Books of Samuel

So are the books of Samuel historically reliable? There is only scant evidence for this period of Israel's history. Excavations in the city of Jerusalem are sparse. They have yielded remains of a few buildings, but no evidence of who built them. An inscription from the period of the Divided Monarchy, found in northern Israel at Tel Dan, probably mentions "the house of David," but this does not "prove" the details of the biblical narratives about David.

At most, biblical historians can provide a general picture of the world into which David and Saul entered. This general picture supports the fact that conditions were ripe for some group to consolidate power in the Levant.

A Power Vacuum in the Levant

Throughout most of ancient history, the Levant was controlled by large powers, such as Egypt, Assyria, and Babylon. Israel arose during a brief span of time in which these superpowers were unable to control this area. Egypt was busy fighting invasions from its south and west, while Assyria and Babylon were in a bitter struggle to control Mesopotamia.

The Canaanite city-states did not take advantage of this situation by unifying into a single nation. Instead, they became vulnerable to outside invasion. Two groups that invaded Canaan at this time were the Philistines, who entered from the southwest, and a group in the central highlands, from whom Israel would emerge. As the two invading groups grew, they came into conflict, since both groups wanted to control the fertile center of the land. The biblical text and archeological evidence tell us that the Philistines were technologically more advanced than the Israelites, especially with respect to metal working. The Philistines also had more horses and chariots, the equivalent of tanks in the ancient world. Israel's only hope of surviving the Philistine advance was founded on one asset: the Israelites outnumbered the Philistines.

It is likely that the first "kingdoms" of Israel were probably little more than local chiefdoms, similar to previous Canaanite city-states. There is no archaeological evidence of an expanding empire during the early United Monarchy. Moreover, it is likely that the transition from a political system based on judges to that based on a king would happen incrementally.

The narratives in 1 Samuel are set within this particular historical period. I would assume, all things being equal, that the redactors would want to depict the setting as accurately as possible. To do so, they used the sources at their disposal, even if these came from a variety of different genre, such as legendary texts, oral traditions, family histories, and so on. This mixing of genre did not bother them, since it was the lessons from this history that motivated their work.

According to the literary record in both Judges and Samuel, the Israelite judges had trouble uniting the different tribes. When one tribe was attacked, the others were supposed to come to their aid, but too often they were reluctant to do so. Israel's move to a monarchy is presented as an attempt to build a better army

The Assyrian war chariot shown here is from Sennacharib's palace at Nineveh and dates to 700 BCE.

and find a more effective way to unify the different tribes. The archaeological record also supports the theory that the monarchy arose as a strategy to ward off the Philistine threat and secure the Israelites' hold on the land.

In addition to showing the military threat that the Israelites faced, the history focused on a bigger hurdle. The book of Judges depicted the social instability of Israel without strong leadership. Social norms disintegrated so completely that, by the end of the book of Judges, the Israelites had turned on each other. The Deuteronomistic Historian depicts the monarchy as a response to sin and moral failure; it was a necessary evil if Israel was going to survive socially, morally, and religiously.

LIFE IN A MONARCHY

The setting for the accounts of Saul and David also depicts a major change in social organization, one which affected many areas of Israelite life. However, some of what has been previously described does not change in the monarchy. Families still formed the basis of society, and agriculture remained an important element in the economy. Men owned the land, women married young, and many children still died from childhood disease. But the creation of a monarchy did affect the daily lives of many Israelites, and not all of those changes were for the better.

Focus on METHOD

Sociological Analysis

Much of what we have been doing in this textbook involves sociological analysis. This method of biblical interpretation seeks to uncover how different sociological phenomena functioned and interacted in the ancient world. Sociological analysis can have three different aims. It can provide a social description of how different groups interacted. It can seek to reconstruct a social history of how different social relationships changed. It can use social theory to reconstruct gaps in the record.

While there are many different social theories utilized by biblical scholars, all of them employ some form of comparative analysis. That comparative analysis can be localized, meaning that the scholar looks for parallels in cultures closest in date and region to the biblical texts. Or it can be based on cultures, ancient or modern, with social structures resembling those of ancient Israel. For example, parallels with other preindustrial, agrarian-based cultures may provide models for analyzing social phenomena evident in the biblical text.

Some theories of social construction are based on economic factors. Marxist analysis, for example, focuses on the way the means of production affect social rank, interaction of social tiers, social flexibility, and so on. Others are based on political factors, for instance, the difference between a society based on a monarchy versus one based on tribal organization. There have even been some attempts to use religion as the organizing feature, resulting in the examination of a monotheistic society versus a polytheistic one.

Sociological analysis has been criticized both for its speculative nature and for the excesses of those who reduce all phenomena to a single model. But these abuses of the method are not unique to sociological approaches. Sociological analysis asks a different set of questions than other methods, questions aimed at leading us to notice a broader range of things in the text.

Sociological method asks what general structures in Israelite society shaped the way different groups acted. Are there things that are "typical" of a particular group? How do social concepts, such as honor and shame, affect behavior? How do structures of power and prestige within a group play out? Are there actions that people within that society would understand that seem bizarre or foreign to us today?

In this chapter, we focus on the interactions of fathers and sons in the text. If we presume that the ancient Israelites had the same view of children that moderns do, we may misinterpret the text. How would you go about understanding what it meant to be a "father" in ancient Israel? This is, in part, a sociological question. To answer it, you would first want to look at other biblical texts about fathers. You would find that there are issues of "honor" or prestige associated with being a good father. A father's primary duty was control of his children, not love or affection. The father was responsible for maintaining the hierarchical relationship on which society was based.

You could also look at fathers in other ancient near-eastern societies. Perhaps there is more direct discussion of the "good father" in other Semitic texts. You could trace whether the view of the "good father" changed throughout Israelite history. You could also look at fatherhood in similarly organized cultures today, whether you base that similarity on economic structures, political organization, or some other integrating principle.

Such sociological analysis would fill out why the Deuteronomistic History focuses so much on stories of fathers and sons in its narration of the rise of the monarchy. We can only understand the parallel it is trying to make between fathers and kings if we understand the thing to which the monarchy is being compared.

As a rule, monarchies arose in conjunction with increased urbanization. As cities became larger, the crops that farmers grew had to feed city dwellers. When farmers could sell their crops for a profit, urbanization was good, but when the farmers had to sell at a loss, the cities became a drain on the farmers.

The monarchy increased the number of city dwellers. Kings and "big" governments needed more than just crops to run a country; they needed soldiers, scribes, sages, officials, architects, musicians, weavers, and so on. These people usually lived in cities; they did not till the land. As a result, the monarchy gave people more choices regarding how they earned a living, but it also guaranteed that the old system of town elders and local governing communities gradually lost much of their authority.

On the positive side, the monarchy helped to "stimulate" the economy. Let me give you three examples of this benefit.

New employment opportunities! People who had trouble working when the economy was based primarily on owning land could now find work at skilled professions. For instance, the eighth son of a small landowner, such as David, could still earn a name for himself in the army.

Booming sales in luxury items! Kings paid for technical skill. Rich people bought luxury items, and sponsored artists, jewelry makers, and so on. Demand for luxury items put more people to work.

International trade! Third, monarchies could establish trade agreements with other nations. Not only did these trade agreements bring in products that Israelites might have found rare prior to the monarchy, they also created markets for Israelite products.

On the negative side, however, was the reality of economics in the monarchy. Economic prosperity did not "trickle down." In fact, as Israelite kings tried to compete with bigger countries, they heavily taxed the people to pay for their large armies, their grand palaces, and their luxurious lifestyles. King Solomon, for instance, was reported to have had seven hundred wives and three hundred concubines. How do you think he paid to feed them all (and all of their children, and all of their servants, houses, clothes, and so on)? He did it in large part with tax dollars. This economic burden meant that average landowners went deeper into debt, until they eventually lost their ancestral land in bankruptcy. And who bought their land? Those who had become rich because of the monarchy.

Finally, Solomon quite deliberately undercut Israelite society. He arranged that the nation would not be divided according to tribal holdings. Instead, he made new districts that disregarded tribal boundaries, in order to break the power of the older tribes, thereby undercutting the larger components of family social structure.

So, was the monarchy a good or a bad thing for the people of Israel? The fact is that it had the potential to be a very good thing for the people, but the books of Samuel depict it as easily abused by sinful kings.

THE ETHICS OF LEADERSHIP

Urbanization typically resulted in power being consolidated in a small number of persons or groups. In a monarchy, these groups often set up dynastic successions so that power remained within a particular family or clan. This system is never questioned in the Bible, but the abuses of the system were clearly apparent.

The book of Deuteronomy includes the laws governing different types of leaders in ancient Israel. The Deuteronomistic History always has these laws in mind. Leaders were held to a higher standard of moral behavior, because their actions affected thousands of people.

The king. Israelites believed that the king ruled because he and his family were chosen by Yahweh to do so. But Yahweh remained their true king; the human king only ruled as Yahweh's substitute. The Deuteronomist stresses this theological context for the monarchy and judges kings if they do not accept religious limits on their royal power.

The prophet. In the history of the monarchy, the Deuteronomistic Historian places the prophet above the king. Kings were chosen and crowned by a prophet. Prophets, as the voice of Yahweh, also judged the king, enforcing the limits placed on a king's power.

The priest. This figure is not as important in the books of Samuel as it will be in the books of Kings. However, the history contained in the books of Chronicles highlights the importance of the relationship between the priestly family and that of the king. We will see in the next chapter that kings chose which family would control the national temple, and the priests helped legitimate the king's claim to the throne. The book of Deuteronomy, however, supported a levitical priesthood that lived throughout Israel in special towns. Any of these levitical priests should be able to serve in the temple of God (Deut 18:1–8).

Judges and other officials. Deuteronomy also describes judicial systems for the monarchy. One appears to be comprised of tribal leaders (Deut 16:18–20) and the other uses levitical priests serving at the temple of Yahweh (Deut 17:8–13). The first passage warns leaders to avoid corruption, and the second passage urges people to obey the rulings of these priestly judges.

The books of Samuel depict the establishment of monarchic society. By the time the final edition of this history had been written, that monarchy had been destroyed. We expect that the Deuteronomistic Historian has planted the seeds of that failure in the founding of the monarchy. For the historian, the failure was not God's but that of the people, and especially of their leaders.

STORIES OF THE UNITED MONARCHY

1 SAMUEL 1:1–2:11: THE BIRTH OF SAMUEL

This story tells of the birth of one of Israel's greatest prophets, Samuel. As you read it, notice the similarities between Samuel's birth and the birth of Samson.

IN CASE YOU WERE WONDERING

The book of Ruth interrupts the history. In Christian Bibles, the book of Ruth immediately follows the book of Judges. This was not its original place; the book of Ruth is not part of the Deuteronomistic History. In the Jewish arrangement of the Bible, Ruth appears much later, among the writings. In the Septuagint, or Greek version of the Bible, Ruth was placed here for two reasons: (1) it is a historical narrative, so it is placed among the histories, and (2) the story takes place during the time of the Judges. We will look at Ruth later in this book.

The temple at Shiloh. The temple at Shiloh was a main center of worship for Israel at this time. In later chapters we learn that the Ark of the Covenant was housed there.

Weaning a child. This term refers to the process of having children cease breast-feeding. In the ancient world, this would have occurred well after the child was a toddler.

LOOKING CLOSELY AT THE TEXT

1. Find the similarities and differences between the births of Samson and Samuel.

2. Why would Hannah give up Samuel after he is weaned?

3. What does Hannah do in 1 Sam 2:1–10?

THE BIRTH OF SAMUEL

The books of Samuel open with another heroic birth story. This one tells us about Samuel, one of the greatest prophets in Israelite tradition. He is the one who will coronate the first two kings of Israel: Saul and David. So central is he to this task that the books about the founding of the monarchy are named after him.

The central character in the birth story is Samuel's mother, Hannah. Although the texts about her are brief, the author succeeds in painting a clear portrait of her. Within a few short verses we know that she is beloved by her husband, Elkanah, and that she is "provoked" or teased by her husband's other wife, Peninah. We empathize with Hannah because Peninah teases her about something over which she has no control: her barrenness.

We also know that Hannah is a pious woman. Notice that the majority of the action is set around the temple at Shiloh and the annual sacrifice that the family makes there. Hannah turns to God as her only hope to escape her suffering. Her prayer expresses her trust that God will grant her request. Furthermore, she vows to bring up this child a nazirite if her prayer is answered.

The text further highlights the depth of Hannah's piety when Eli, the priest of Shiloh, does not recognize that she is praying. Seeing her presumably talking to herself, he assumes that she is drunk, and he demands that she sober up. It is Hannah who must instruct the priest about prayer. Hannah's piety is not hypocritical, soon forgotten once her son is born. She keeps her vow to bring up Samuel as a nazirite, and she goes one step further by sending him to live with Eli, that he might serve God for the rest of his life.

The text reaches its high point with Hannah's prayer in chapter 2. This prayer of thanksgiving was probably sung. Although it does mention a barren woman who gives birth to seven children (2:5), most of the poem has nothing to do with the birth of Samuel. Instead, it is a prayer about God's aid to the oppressed. The poem uses ironic contrasts to depict God's salvation: the feeble become strong (2:4); the hungry grow fat (2:5); and the poor inherit seats of honor (2:8). The poem fits Hannah, because she sees herself as a righteous person who was oppressed, but who was saved by God through the birth of her son. We learn later in the chapter that God rewards Hannah's piety with three more sons and two daughters (1 Sam 2:21). In the New Testament, Hannah's prayer becomes the model for Mary's prayer of thanksgiving about her pregnancy in Luke 1:46–55.

1 Samuel 8:1–22 and Deuteronomy 17:14–20: Israel Gets a King

While Samuel is still a child, God makes him a prophet. The first prophecies that Samuel delivers concern God's rejection of the priesthood of Eli and the prediction that the Philistines are going to capture the Ark of the Covenant. The first book of Samuel recounts how these prophecies came true.

The Deuteronomistic Historian depicts Eli's whole house as corrupt; his sons take the best of the sacrifices, violating the law (1 Sam 2:12–17).

The battles show how dire things are for Israel. Its national symbol is temporarily lost, and one of its major cities destroyed. Although the Philistines eventually return the ark, Israel remains in constant war with the Philistines.

1 Samuel 7:15–17 tells us that Samuel became a judge over Israel, serving primarily in and around the tribe of Benjamin. It is at this point that the people request the establishment of the monarchy.

These two passages best portray what the Deuteronomistic Historian thinks of the monarchy. When you read these passages, you will see that, although the historian does regard the king as better than the judge, the historian believes that there should be limitations placed on the amount of power a king can have.

In Case You Were Wondering

Ramah. Ramah was a city in Benjamin where Samuel spent most of his time.

Egyptian horses. Egypt was known for its horses, an essential part of a well-equipped army. The law of the king in Deuteronomy warns against the dependency that comes from trading with Egypt for horses.

Looking Closely at the Text

1. Why does 1 Samuel 8 tell us about Samuel's sons?

2. Why does God grant the people's request?

3. Compare and contrast the law of the king in Deuteronomy 17:14–20 and the warning about the king in 1 Samuel 8:11–18.

A Law and a Warning

As the Philistine threat grows, and the Israelites fail to unite to fight, they conclude that they need a king "like the other nations" (1 Sam 8:5). In order to understand this request, it is helpful to examine what it was that kings in other countries did.

First, a king differed from a judge in that a king had dynastic rule, meaning that not only is an individual person chosen by God to be king, but also all of his family. The judge, on the other hand, ruled as an individual, when the "spirit of God" came on him or her. However, in 1 Sam 8:1, it looks as if Samuel is moving toward a dynasty by appointing his own sons to rule after him.

Second, the king insured justice in the land. He did this in a number of ways. First, kings usually produced law codes. Second, they set up a system of courts so that laws could be enforced. Third, they made sure that justice was rendered for those who were particularly vulnerable. The biblical phrase that captures this idea is the king's care for "the widow, the orphan, and the resident alien," those people who had no access to justice through the courts of the land-owners. The rejection of Samuel's sons, because they "pervert justice," should be seen in this context.

Third, kings built temples and established priestly families to administer those temples. In Mesopotamia, kings were not themselves priests. However, Mesopotamian kings did perform certain national sacrifices. In Israel, sacrifice was usually limited to the priests. In fact, we will see that Saul gets in trouble for trying to take on religious duties that the Israelites reserved for the priests.

Fourth, a king was the head of the army. Sometimes this was literally true; young kings did go into battle. Kings also had generals who fought beside them, or who could fight on their behalf. Kings hired a permanent professional army. While this insured a core of professional soldiers who would understand the strategies of warfare, this army also gave the king the power to "take care of" any opposition. The Israelites wanted a king because they needed a professional army.

A portion of a king's wealth came through taxation. This taxation could be paid in goods or in money. It came on top of a tax levied by the temples. Israelites could have spent twenty percent or more of their income paying royal and temple taxes. The king could also establish a tax in the form of forced labor. This was a type of draft in which citizens were required to work for the crown. Sometimes this service included military duty, but it could also consist of hard labor, such as the construction of public buildings.

The law of the king in Deuteronomy set limits on some of the powers that kings had in the ancient Near East. First, the law stipulated that the king could not be a foreigner; this is not surprising. The king also had to limit the size of his army: he could not own many horses himself, nor could he sell the people's services to Egypt in return for horses. This, in effect, controlled military spending and limited the king's personal army, making him answerable to the people.

Deuteronomy 17:17 also severely limited the king's wealth. First, it limited the number of wives a king could have, a sign of a man's wealth in the ancient world. In addition, it stated that he could not own a lot of gold, limiting his personal assets. Again, this makes the king more answerable to the people, because he does not have the personal wealth to do whatever he chooses.

Deuteronomy 17 ends with a command that the king read this law every day. Notice that the priests write out the law for him (Deut 17:18); this is not a law promulgated by the king. The king's duty is to meditate on the law and follow it exactly. Again, this parameter limits the power of the king. He is subject to the law; he is not the maker of the law.

1 Samuel 8 articulates the effects of the monarchy on the people. It warns the people of the reality of a monarchy: although the monarchy may help them in their present crisis, it comes at a significant cost to them and their children. Samuel's speech recapitulates the warnings in the law of the king in Deuteronomy 17. He tells the people that the males in the population will be forced to serve in the army and to labor like servants in the fields of the king. The female citizens will be made into domestic servants. Their income will be so greatly taxed that they will eventually cry out to God to deliver them from the oppression of their own king.

Notice that when the people respond to this warning in 1 Samuel 8:19, they do not argue with Samuel. Instead, they simply insist that they need a king because of the military threats to the nation. On some level God agrees, telling Samuel to help them set up a monarchy.

1 Samuel 9:1–10:16: Saul, the Pious Son

This story presents a very positive portrayal of young Saul, the boy who will grow up to be the first king of Israel.

In Case You Were Wondering

A man of God; a seer. These are two different terms used for prophets in ancient Israel. The boys hope that the prophet Samuel will tell them where they can find their donkeys, but notice that they presume they will have to pay him before he will prophesy for them.

A place at the head of the table. When Saul and his servant eat with Samuel, they are given the place of honor.

Sleeping on the roof. Saul and Samuel sleep on a roof, a place where they can feel some cool night breezes.

A prophetic frenzy. Apparently when people prophesied, they acted differently than normal people. We don't know if every prophet went into a frenzy, or if it just happened sometimes. We also don't know what the frenzy looked like. It might have included dancing, singing, acting out in certain ways, or speaking in a different voice. Whatever it was, it must have been quite noticeable.

Speeches in the Deuteronomistic History

When I studied ancient Greek literature, my instructor said to us, "If you want to know what the historian thinks, look at the speeches of his heroes." He was pointing out that Thucydides' view of his history was most clearly contained in the speech of Pericles.

The same is true of Israelite historians. On the one hand, the perspective of the Deuteronomistic Historian is found in the material that connects scenes and summarizes sections. But the historian's view is also found in various speeches that pepper the history, some of which mark transition points. Below are some key speeches in the history.

Speech	Transition
Moses' summary speech: Deuteronomy 29:2—31:6	The end of the wilderness period
God and Joshua speak to the Israelites: Joshua 1	The beginning of the conquest
Joshua's last speech: Joshua 23—24	The end of the conquest
Samuel's speech to Israel: 1 Samuel 12	The beginning of the monarchic period
Nathan's oracle to David: 2 Samuel 7	The beginning of the Davidic dynasty
Solomon's prayer at the dedication of the temple: 1 Kings 8	The beginning of the temple era
The prophetess's message to Josiah: 2 Kings 22:15–20	The last glory of the kingdom

Take a look at three or more of these speeches. What are some of the common literary features of these texts? Is there a common vocabulary? What issues are uppermost for the Deuteronomistic Historian?

By considering these questions, you will begin to get a better overview of the major themes of the Deuteronomistic History. As an added bonus, you will be able to recognize non-Deuteronomistic material more easily.

LOOKING CLOSELY AT THE TEXT

1. What does Saul look like?

2. According to 1 Samuel 9:5, why does Saul decide he must return home?

3. How does Samuel know that Saul is the one he is supposed to anoint as king?

4. Who was with them when Samuel anoints Saul as king?

5. What are the three signs that Samuel gives to Saul that assure Saul he will be king?

6. When Saul returns home, does he tell anyone that Samuel has anointed him to be king?

SAUL, THE PIOUS SON

This story introduces the audience to Saul. Unlike later texts about him, this account is very positive, probably stemming from a source used by the Deutereonomistic Historian. Saul is a pious son (in stark contrast to the rude Samson). He puts in every effort to find his father's donkeys, and he wishes to break off the search only because he's concerned that his father might be worrying about him.

Embedded in this story is the account of Saul's secret anointing as king by the prophet Samuel. The essential part of the coronation ritual in ancient Israel was *anointing*, pouring olive oil on the head of the one assuming the office of king. The Hebrew word for "anointed one" is *messiah*. A messiah, therefore, is any current or future king.

Samuel treats Saul and his servant like honored guests. He seats them at the most prestigious places at the table, serves them the choicest parts of the sacrifice, and has them share his sleeping area. I can imagine the look on the faces of the elders of the town as this famous seer so honors a young boy looking for lost donkeys!

Even so, notice that the anointing is a completely private affair. Even Saul's servant has been sent away. Later in 1 Samuel we read about the death of Samuel. Who would have been around, then, to tell the story of this secret anointing of Saul as a young boy? Clearly, only Saul. This story probably stemmed from some ancient source that favored Saul and viewed his monarchy as legitimate, because it depicts Saul's reign as divinely arranged.

The tale ends with Samuel telling Saul about three successive events that will confirm that the prophecy will come true. This is a very complex symbol, conveying the gravity of what is being promised. One of these signs, the prophetic frenzy, happens twice to Saul. Here it has a positive spin, but in its repetition (1 Sam 9:23–24) it is an example of Saul's increasing madness. The command to wait seven days for the sacrifice (1 Sam 10:8) will reappear later in the account.

The chapter ends with a bit of foreshadowing. Saul, the beloved son, is asked about his encounter with Samuel. This formerly pious son becomes suddenly silent. "But about the matter of the kingship, of which Samuel had spoken, he did not tell him anything" (1 Sam 10:16). We will see that this silence introduces us to a prominent theme in the portrayal of Saul: his own lack of faith in the prophetic word.

1 Samuel 10:17–24: The Choice of Saul as King

This short passage presents a different account of how Saul was chosen as the first king of Israel. As you read it, think about Saul's reactions in this account.

Looking Closely at the Text

1. In his speech in verses 17–19, whom does Samuel say that the Israelites are rejecting by asking for a king?

2. Where is Saul while the lots are being picked?

3. How do the people react when Samuel presents Saul to them?

A Big Man Who Wants to Hide

This passage probably comes from a different source than the last story. The two passages have very different views of Saul: they use different writing styles, and, most importantly, they give two very different accounts of how Saul came to be king.

In this account, Saul is part of a large assembly that includes representatives from all of the tribes of Israel. Samuel casts lots, which determine whom God has chosen to be the first king of Israel. The Pentateuch tells us that God had given the lots to the priests, so that they could determine what God wanted (Exod 28:30; Lev 8:8; see also Num 27:18–21). While to us the idea of casting lots to determine God's will sounds superstitious, it did not seem so to the Israelites. For them casting lots was a legitimate vehicle for divine revelation.

When we read 1 Samuel as a whole, that is, when we read the *two* stories of how Saul became king one after the other, we see that the redactors have put these stories together on purpose. We are aware that only two people in the second story know how the casting of lots will turn out: Samuel and Saul. As the names of the tribe, clan, and family are read, we can imagine Saul's joy, and maybe his excitement, that finally everyone will know that he has been chosen as king. So it comes as a surprise that tall Saul is actually hiding among the baggage! Picture the scene, if you can. I always imagine a large man, cowering like a scared child at the back of the crowd.

This story presents another negative view of Saul, introducing a theme that will remain throughout the account of his reign. Saul does not believe in his own ability to rule. Of all the people in that room, only Saul does not believe that God has chosen the right man. As Samuel will point out later, such a lack of faith in one's own ability is the same as a lack of faith in God.

1 Samuel 13:2–14 and 15:1-35: Saul's Dynasty Rejected by God

After Saul is chosen by lot to be king, we see him win a major battle against the Ammonites. At the end of this story he is declared king again. This was probably a third account of how he came to be king. A long speech by Samuel follows, in which he again scolds the people for their choice of a monarchy and warns them of what may happen if they turn from the law. Chapter 13 of 1 Samuel opens with a brief notice about the length of Saul's reign. However, the numbers were not preserved, a rather common practice in the ancient world; it is an attempt to erase the memory of a bad king by not preserving details of his reign.

In between these two stories there is a narrative about a great battle that Jonathan, Saul's son, wins for Israel. The story presents a very positive view of Jonathan, which might suggest that Saul's dynasty is in safe hands. However, the story is sandwiched between two stories in which God clearly rejects Saul and his dynasty.

In Case You Were Wondering

Jonathan. Jonathan is never formally introduced to the reader, nor do we know about his mother. This is probably another instance in which the historian is trying to wipe out the memory of Saul.

Sacrifices before battle. If you remember, the laws of holy war require that a sacrifice must be made before a battle, and a prophet or priest must determine whether God wants the army to fight. Saul cannot go to the battlefield until this occurs.

LOOKING CLOSELY AT THE TEXT

1. Why did Saul make the sacrifice in 1 Samuel 13:8?

2. According to 1 Samuel 13:11–14, what is Saul's punishment for not waiting longer?

3. According to 1 Samuel 15:3, what was Saul supposed to do when he attacked the Amalekites?

4. In chapter 15, how does Saul sin?

5. What is Saul's punishment this time?

6. According to 1 Samuel 15:29, why doesn't God forgive Saul when he repents?

GOD REJECTS SAUL

These stories give two different accounts of why Saul was unable to establish a dynasty. It helps us understand the text better when we notice how the Deuteronomistic Historian uses these stories. First, he places one of them right at the beginning of Saul's reign as king, so that no matter what else we read about Saul's reign, we know that he will ultimately be a failure.

Second, the Deuteronomistic Historian has been quite selective in the stories he chooses to tell. We do not hear about Saul's wives and family. We do not read about his establishment of a central government, his choice of capital cities, whether he taxes the people, and what kind of religious institutions he founded, and so on. We do not even get to read about the successes he must have had in order to establish the monarchy. This lack tells us immediately that the story was not designed to convey history. This historian is interested in something quite different.

The Deuteronomistic Historian wants the reader to focus on the limitations on the king, especially with respect to religious matters. Notice that in both of these accounts Saul is punished because he tries to take religious matters into his own hands. In the first story, he decides to make a sacrifice because he is afraid that he is losing the support of the army. The decision that as king he could make a sacrifice before a battle is not absurd; after all, in other near eastern countries, kings did participate in these sacrifices. The Deuteronomists, however, limited the kind of sacrifices kings could make. The only example of a king making a sacrifice that is not judged as bad is Solomon's sacrifices when he builds the temple in Jerusalem. In both the historical books and the laws in the Pentateuch, priests made sacrifices, not kings.

He also did not wait the full "seven days" for Samuel to arrive. The audience must presume that this refers back to Samuel's speech in 1 Samuel 10:8, although it certainly seems as if a lot more time than seven days has gone by. While this condemnation might seem unfair, it highlights the king's subordination to the prophet.

In the second story, Samuel declares that the war against Agag is to be conducted under the ban; the army is supposed to "devote" all living things to Yahweh. Once again, Saul chooses to ignore this prophetic command. Perhaps he feels that, as king, he does not need to listen to prophets. What the text tells us is that Saul claims that the *people* were the ones who sinned by keeping the spoils. Such a statement shows Saul's inability to control the people, not a good quality in a king.

The account again manifests Saul's fatal flaw. Samuel asks, "Though you are little in your own eyes, are you not the head of the tribes of Israel?" (1 Sam 15:17). This big, strong man, picked twice by God, is "little in his own eyes." He does not trust God's ability to work through him. He is afraid of the people, often letting them do things he knows are wrong, because he fears their disdain.

The punishment of Saul is borne by his son, Jonathan. Although the text states that God rejects Saul, we see him rule for many years. God's rejection of Saul comes seven years after Saul's death when his son, Ishbaal, fails to hold onto the throne of Israel. In place of Saul, God chooses David, whose dynasty will last for nearly 450 years.

But why doesn't God forgive Saul when he repents in chapter 15? Why does Samuel say that God's mind does not change, even though God has just reversed the choice of Saul as king? The story depicts Saul's military and political failures as a punishment for sin. Even so, this is a troubling passage, especially when we realize that the Bible often depicts God forgivingpeople who repent of their sins. It's important to remember, however, that the book's final audience knows the reality of a nation that has fallen; they have seen God not "recant or change his mind." Their experience tells them that sometimes God lets the punishment stand. Saul's rejection prefigures their own rejection by God, and Saul's punishment, visited on his sons, parallels their own punishment, which bears down hardest on their own children.

1 Samuel 17:1–58: David and Goliath

We ended the last chapter with the condemnation of Saul as king. We know that his family will not keep control of the throne of Israel and that God has already "given it" to another (1 Sam 15:28). The audience is ready to meet David.

In between the story of Saul's rejection and David's victory over Goliath, Samuel secretly anoints David as the next king of Israel. David is the eighth son of Jesse, a landowner in the city of Bethlehem. David is young, and he tends the flocks for his father.

The story of David and Goliath is probably the best-known story about David. David is not yet king, but he clearly has the courage needed by a great leader.

In Case You Were Wondering

Socoh and Azekah. The confrontation between David and Goliath takes place in the territory of Judah, near the Philistine border.

What's a wadi? A wadi is a dry riverbed. In dry climates the rivers only run for part of the year. A wadi would be a ditch or small valley made by a river, at the bottom of which would be stones worn smooth by the flow of water during the rainy season.

Six cubits and a span. A *cubit* is the length of a man's forearm, about twelve inches. This means that Goliath was well over six feet tall, a huge height in ancient times. This is why Goliath is often portrayed as a giant.

What's a weaver's beam? The *shaft* of a spear is the wooden part; it would have a sharp metal tip that formed the spear. A "weaver's beam" is a large piece of wood in a machine for weaving.

Ekron and Gath. Ekron and Gath were near the border separating Judah from Philistia.

Abner was Saul's general. He was also his uncle.

Looking Closely at the Text

1. What is the challenge Goliath poses for the Israelites?

2. According to his speech in 1 Samuel 17:34–36, how does David convince Saul that he will be able to defeat Goliath?

3. Why doesn't David wear Saul's armor?

4. According to 1 Samuel 17:50–51, David kills Goliah twice. What are the two ways Goliath dies?

SMALL FRY AND BIG POTATO

What an entertaining story! The details are clear, the action swift, and the conflict exciting. A great but evil Philistine warrior challenges the Israelite army to find someone to fight him in one-on-one combat. The Israelites cower in fear before him, until an unexpected hero appears: David. The text goes out of its way to tell us how young and unexpected he is. He is the youngest son of a large family, a mere boy, according to the words of Saul.

As the eighth son, he has little hope for a glorious future. His elder brothers stand to inherit the bulk of his father's land. The text hints that Jesse was probably not a rich man, either, since his flocks were small (1 Sam 17:28). A boy like David needed to find another way to make something of himself. In the ancient world, the best way for poorer men to succeed was in the army. By proving themselves good fighters and capable leaders, poor men could literally move up in the ranks under the watchful eye of the king. David has little to lose and much to gain by fighting Goliath.

Notice all the ways that the text plays with images of size. It depicts the large bulk of Goliath. It lingers over the boy, David, struggling to put on the armor of his gigantic king. Why such a focus? How does the rhetoric of size convey the meaning of the story?

The theme of "big versus little" functions on at least three levels in the story. First, it works as a symbol for the odds that Israel as a people faced in confronting the Philistine threat. The text connotes that Goliath represents, and therefore embodies, the size of the threat that Philistia posed at this time. Israel, embodied by David, is the small, unarmed country with an impossible task.

Second, the smallness of David—on the physical (he's small), chronological (he's young), and social (he's the eighth son who must work tending sheep) levels—serves as a condemnation of the larger, older, and more prestigious Saul, who is too cowardly to fight. The story becomes another lynchpin in Saul's moral coffin.

Third, by focusing on the impossibility of David's task, the reader concludes that the victory is really Yahweh's. Of course, the text foreshadows this conclusion when David says, "The LORD does not save by sword and spear" (17:47). At this point, the reader knows that David will win.

Goliath's death is also fitting, given this metaphorical contrast: the giant falls. You can almost feel the ground shake as he lands with a thud. The text even practices a bit of "overkill" by having David "kill" him twice. The fact that by "getting rid" of Goliath, David also "gets rid" of the Philistine army, which flees at the end of the pericope, reinforces the message that this victory was not for David's personal glory. Instead, he is a hero who *saves Israel*.

The account of David and Goliath attributes four very important characteristics to David. First, it tells us that he enters Saul's court, not as a rival to the

David and Goliath/Israel and Philistia

Throughout most of the Bible, the Philistines are portrayed as "foreigners," and, like other foreigners, worthy of God's wrath. But they are not singled out as uniquely evil. This is not so for the books of Judges and Samuel. In these books, the biblical historian characterizes the Philistines as wholly foreign, in order to enhance the theological significance of Israel's rise to nationhood. This literary purpose is seen most clearly in the stories of Samson, Saul, and David. For all three men, their victories over this powerful foreign enemy signified that God's spirit was with them. The foreignness or "otherness" of the Philistines is an important element of this theme.

The stories of Samson contrasted the urban lifestyle of the Philistines with the more agrarian Israelites. The weapons that Samson used were those of rural people: fire, bones, and hand to hand combat. Samson destroyed elements of Philistine urban culture: he burned their cultivated fields, tore up their city gates, and brought down their temple. Nature triumphed over culture.

In 1 Samuel 4–6 the Philistines capture the Ark of the Covenant. The account of the capture of the ark focuses attention on the religious "otherness" of the Philistines. The fact that the statue of the Philistine god, Dagon, falls, breaking off both its head and hands, shows the invalidity of Philistine religion.

David's rise to power reinforces the characterization of the Philistines as violent urban aggressors who are sexually and religiously impure. David's defeat of Goliath (1 Sam 17:19–54) pits the crude but effective weapon of a rural shepherd against the military equipment of the warrior. The young, small, pious David, symbolizing the young, small but faithful nation of Israel, defeats the older, larger, and better equipped uncircumcised warrior, symbolizing the more established, larger but arrogant pagan Philistines.

In the account of David's marriage to Saul's daughter, Michal (1 Sam 18:20–29), David must pay an unusual bride price for the girl: one hundred Philistine foreskins. The request for this body part focuses attention on the fact that the Philistines did not practice circumcision, another mark of their "difference" from the Israelites. David's acquisition of double the bride price foreshadows his eventual subjugation of Philistia.

For the authors of the Deuteronomistic History, the Philistines represented the "Other," a group whose very existence stood as an affront to everything the Israelites held dear. The texts express Israelite fear of annihilation at the hands of foreign powers. Recalling that the final version of these texts were written during the Babylonian exile, a time when Israel had been annihilated by urban foreigners who also did not practice circumcision, invites us to rethink the literary function of this depiction of an archenemy of Israel at the very beginning of its national history.

Who can be successful against such foreigners? Only someone like faithful David, who declares, "The LORD does not save by sword and spear" (1 Sam 17:47). If we read the history as an attempt to explain why Israel fell, the historian provides part of the answer. The Israelites did not lose to the Babylonians because the Babylonians had a larger, better-equipped army, nor because they were an older civilization, more urban and culturally advanced. They lost because their leaders at the time did not have the faith of David. They were seduced into believing that cultural and military superiority were the deciding factors in conflicts with a foreign power. They were Saul, looking for someone else to fight this challenger, rather than David with his five smooth stones.

This depiction of a person shooting a sling was discovered at Tel Halaf, in Northern Mesopotamia, and dates to the ninth century BCE.

throne, but in service to the king and Israel. Second, he is not rich or powerful, so anything he accomplishes he does with the help of God. Third, David is heroic. In a truly noble act, he ignores his own personal safety, and steps into that wadi, with only five smooth stones in his pouch. His success leads to Israel's victory. Lastly, and most importantly, we learn that David is characterized by his faith in Yahweh, a devotion that will play itself out in subsequent chapters.

1 Samuel 14:1–46; 18:1–5; 20:1–42; and 2 Samuel 1:17–27: David and Jonathan

This group of texts describes the relationship between David and Saul's son, Jonathan. The first text introduces the audience to Jonathan. The second text describes Jonathan's reaction to David's defeat of Goliath. The third text relates the covenant that the two make with each other, and the last text is a dirge that David sings after Saul and Jonathan have been killed on the battlefield fighting the Philistines. These texts occur after the condemnation of Saul's dynasty, so the audience never expects Jonathan to succeed as king. The depiction of the relationship between Jonathan and David legitimizes David's claim to the throne, since even the heir apparent recognizes that David will be the next king.

In Case You Were Wondering

The armor-bearer. Military leaders were accompanied by armor-bearers. A little like caddies in golf, they not only would carry the warrior's equipment, but they could also be advisors. In Hebrew they are called "young men" (sometimes translated as "boy" or "lad"), which does not denote youth, but rather a subservient position.

The ark and a priest. The presence of the ark and a priest in Saul's military camp illustrates the sacred setting of ancient war.

Saul's altar to the LORD. After the soldiers defile themselves by eating meat improperly slaughtered (1 Sam 14:31–32), Saul provides an altar for them so that the animals can be sacrificed and the blood drained instead. This would make the meat ritually clean.

Jonathan's robe. When Jonathan gives David his robe, armor, sword, bow, and belt (1 Sam 18:4), he gives David the symbols of his rank.

"The LORD do so to Jonathan, and more also" (**1 Sam 20:13**). This is a common phrase in the Hebrew Bible. The speaker is uttering a curse, but the curse is not spelled out, so that it does not come true.

LOOKING CLOSELY AT THE TEXT

1. What does Saul vow in 1 Samuel 14:24?

2. Who convinces Saul not to kill his son for breaking the vow?

3. When Jonathan eats honey, what do the people eat?

4. In 1 Samuel 18, how does the text describe Jonathan's feelings for David?

5. In 1 Samuel 20:13b, what does Jonathan wish for David? In verses 14–15, what does he request of David?

6. Who does Saul try to kill in 1 Samuel 20:30–33?

7. In 2 Samuel 1:26, how does David describe his feelings for Jonathan?

JONATHAN, BELOVED AND LOVELY

The depiction of the relationship between Jonathan and David helps the audience accept the substitution of David for Jonathan as the successor of Saul. The text goes out of its way to show that Jonathan viewed David as his superior. First, he gives him his clothes, outward symbols of his rank. Second, he wishes that David will have the same divine favor as his father. But most significantly, as the text describes, he expresses the strong love that he feels for David.

Love between male equals is a common motif in ancient near-eastern literature. Probably the best-known example is in an ancient poem called *Gilgamesh*, whose plot hinges on the love between king Gilgamesh and his friend, Enkidu. In the contemporary world we have trouble understanding this motif, since in our culture we reserve such language for sexual and romantic love. In the ancient world, however, men did not have just two categories of relationships (friends or lovers), but at least three: associates or comrades (friends); sexual partners (usually wives and slaves, so love was not the defining feature); and what we see here. I do not even have an adequate English word for this relationship, except perhaps the sophomoric "best friends." Did these relationships presume sexual encounters as well? That's a question for debate.

As a character in this text, Jonathan mediates the tensions between Saul and David. As David's popularity grows, Saul's opposition to David increases. The texts that link the passages that you have just read depict Saul's attempts to kill David.

In spite of that, the text does not depict David as someone who led a revolution against the Saulide dynasty. David flees rather than defend himself. He has several opportunities to kill Saul, but he refuses to raise a hand against "the LORD's anointed." Two of Saul's children, Jonathan and Michal, help David escape their father's violence. Saul's opposition to David looks more like paranoia than a clear assessment of the threat that David poses.

Jonathan is portrayed as a rebellious son. He consistently thwarts his father's attempts to deal with David. On the battlefield, he acts independently of his father, attacking the Philistines without informing Saul of his plans. He opposes his father's vow on the battlefield. Although the NRSV translates the vow as "rash" (1 Sam 14:24), the Hebrew text omits this assessment. The result of Jonathan's critique of his father's vow is disastrous. The soldiers not only follow Jonathan's lead by eating, they do so uncontrollably. Although Jonathan appears to be favored by God, pious, brave, and self-sacrificing, he is also a rebellious son who displays poor judgment as a leader.

I am stressing the narrative purpose here, because it doesn't take much to read between the lines. Think about it. How does Jonathan die? He dies on the battlefield fighting alongside his father; that is, he does not abandon his father. He never acts in a public way that would suggest that he favored David over his father. Even the "covenant" between David and Jonathan was spoken with no witnesses present. And who survived to tell us that Jonathan had made a covenant with David? Well, I guess that would be David. Did the historical Jonathan favor David? Who knows? What we do know is that the redactors use the character of Jonathan to smooth the transition of the monarchy to David.

2 SAMUEL 5:1–12 AND 6:1–23: DAVID AND JERUSALEM

THE TIES THAT BIND

The second half of 1 Samuel describes Saul's pursuit of David. It is a game of cat and mouse. As part of his opposition to David, Saul arranges for Michal to remarry.

In his banishment, David forms a personal army of devoted soldiers and becomes a mercenary soldier for the Philistines. However, the text goes out of its way to assert that he never attacked Israelite cities. Instead, he ran a protection racket for the cities in Judah, which allowed him to build up allegiance with these citizens. The text also maintains that David refuses to kill Saul, even though David has ample opportunity to do so. This suggests David's faith in God's control of history.

In the meantime, the Philistines continue to grow in strength. They defeat Israel on the battlefield, and both Saul and Jonathan are killed. The nation of Israel splits for a while. In the north, another of Saul's sons, Ishbaal, is made king, while the people of Judah in the south declare David king. His capital is in the southern city of Hebron; Jerusalem was not yet part of the kingdom.

This split lasts seven years, until Ishbaal is assassinated. Then the northerners accept David as their king. David needs a new capital, one in between the north and the south, as a symbol of the reunification of the twelve tribes of Israel. The first story tells of David's capture of Jerusalem. The second one relates how Jerusalem became a holy city.

Throughout all of these texts we learn about several of David's marriages, and we get lists of some of David's sons. The Deuteronomistic Historian also tells about David's "remarriage" to Michal, as part of a treaty between Ishbaal and David. The story is a sad one, depicting Michal's second husband following in tears as his wife is taken from him. No wonder Michal no longer "loves" David.

IN CASE YOU WERE WONDERING

Jebus. Jerusalem was originally a Canaanite city named Jebus.

Zion. Jerusalem is hilly. For the Bible, the most important hill is Zion, because eventually the temple will be built on it. When you hear the word Zion, you should think "Jerusalem."

What is a water shaft? A water shaft is a vertical tunnel that leads to an underground spring. The hills under Jerusalem are full of caves, and David is able to invade the city by going through caves and shafts into the interior of the city.

King Hiram of Tyre. Tyre was the most important city in Phoenicia. Since Phoenicia was a very strong country, the king of Tyre was a prominent political figure. When King Hiram sends David gifts to help him build his capital, David realizes he has a very important ally.

Where was the ark? After Shiloh was destroyed, the ark was kept in a shrine run by Abinadab. David moves the ark from that shrine to Jerusalem.

Wasn't Uzzah just trying to help? Yes, Uzzah was trying to keep the ark from falling to the ground, but because he was not a priest and because the ark contained God's holy presence, he dies when he comes into contact with this holy object. Here is an example of why the Israelites were afraid to be in God's presence.

Ephods and dancing. David acts as a priest in the second half of chapter 6, wearing a priestly garment called the "ephod." He also dances a sacred dance before the ark, one that priests or other sacred persons usually performed.

Looking Closely at the Text

1. In what ways does the text stress the holiness and power of the ark?

2. How would you characterize the relationship between Michal and David?

3. Why is it important for David to move the ark to Jerusalem?

Jerusalem: Washington, DC, and Vatican City, All Rolled into One

Do you know how Washington, DC, became the nation's capital? The land upon which the city was built was located where the north and south met. As such, it was a symbol of the unity of the states. Jerusalem was similarly chosen. As a Canaanite city, it was not originally part of any tribal territory. There were no ancient Israelite families living there, no Israelite elders with whom David had to interact. Instead, it was a new territory between the north and the south.

David made quite a statement with his choice of capital. He saw this decision as a necessary step to secure his claim to rule over the north. By capturing the city with his personal army, the capital served no other function than the needs of the royal family. As the text says, this truly was "the city of David" (2 Sam 5:7). When the king of Phoenicia, the most powerful kingdom to the north of Israel, recognized David as the legitimate king of both Israel and Judah, David knew that he was secure. If the north rebelled against him, he could count on Phoenicia to support him. In other words, the northern tribes were surrounded.

The text concludes by stating that David perceived that his own exaltation was done for the sake of the people. David recognized that the unification of Israel and Judah, symbolized by the new capital, Jerusalem, made the nation stronger, and more able to withstand external threats.

David wanted Jerusalem to represent more than just the political center of his power. He wanted it to symbolize the source of his own support: Yahweh.

David had many faults, which the final text will not refrain from showing, but what saved him was his undying devotion to Yahweh. Not once do we see him worship other gods. David's reign established the main values of this new kingdom, and David's prime value was his affirmation of Yahweh, and Yahweh alone, as the god of Israel.

When David moved the Ark of the Covenant to Jerusalem, he established the city as the religious center of the nation. For the Deuteronomistic Historian, his choice of the ark was important. It was the ark that had led the Hebrews from Sinai to the Promised Land, the ark that represented Yahweh of hosts at Shiloh, and the ark that best symbolized Israel's religious unity.

Moving a sacred object, such as the Ark of the Covenant, required proper rituals throughout the whole process. Music, dancing, and sacrifices were part of the trip. Although we can understand why Michal hated David, she was wrong to scold him for dancing in front of the ark.

The story of the death of Uzzah, preserved in both Samuel and Chronicles, mars the celebrations. Although I sometimes like to think that maybe his death was just a coincidence, that God didn't really kill him for steadying the ark, I also realize that the Bible states that God struck him down. In part, Uzzah dies because David had not moved the ark properly. It should have been carried by priests, not transported on a cart. When David brings the ark from Obed-Edom's house, he makes sure that the ark is carried properly.

But this account is about more than ritual law. What other point is the text trying to make? It shows that the ark represented Yahweh's real presence. David himself recognized that he could not simply use the ark for his own purposes. God cannot be manipulated. In addition, think about how this affects the end of the account. God did not kill David for bringing the ark to Jerusalem. This story implies that God supported David's decision to move the ark to Jerusalem. In a subtle way, this chapter depicts God's tacit approval of Jerusalem as a sacred center.

2 SAMUEL 7:1–29: GOD'S COVENANT WITH DAVID

The next passage puts into words what the last text implies: God approves of David and Jerusalem. This text is the basis for the Davidic Covenant.

IN CASE YOU WERE WONDERING

The metaphor of the shepherd. In the ancient Near East, kings were often called the "shepherds" of the people. Their job was similar to that of a shepherd: to protect the "flock," the people, from harmful enemies, to keep them together, and to guide them so they did not become lost.

LOOKING CLOSELY AT THE TEXT

1. What are the different meanings of the word *house* in this passage?

2. According to the oracle, how long will there be descendants of David on the throne in Jerusalem?

3. Who will build God's house?

4. What will God's relationship be with David's son?

BUILDING A HOUSE

This is one of the most important passages in the Old Testament for both Jews and Christians. The heart of this text is the prophetic oracle that Nathan delivers to David in verses 5–16. Notice that just prior to the oracle, Nathan had told David that it was fine for David to build a temple to Yahweh. But then God appeared to Nathan that night, to let Nathan know that he had misled David.

Notice what God promises in this passage. First, and most clearly, God promises an eternal reign to David's offspring. The text recognizes that not all of David's offspring are going to be moral men, but it says that, while God will punish them, the covenant with David will not be revoked, as it had with Saul.

The second element promised is less obvious. God makes a covenant with David because David wants to build a temple to Yahweh in Jerusalem. Since David's offspring will always remain in power, and since they will maintain the temple in Jerusalem, the text is suggesting that God will always reside in Jerusalem.

Yet we know that these two promises do not last forever. The city of Jerusalem fell to the Babylonians in 587 BCE. The temple was utterly destroyed, and the offspring of David never again ruled over the nation. So why do we have this oracle in the Bible? Perhaps, because it was a source of hope. David expresses this hope in 2 Samuel 7:25 and 29, when he prays that God's promises will come to pass. By including David's prayer, the Deuteronomistic Historian reinforces the significance of the oracle: even in Israel's darkest hour, this oracle stands as God's word.

If the Deuteronomistic History was first edited in the reign of Josiah, this passage expressed the ideology of Josiah's monarchy. The promise to David was eternal, and Josiah was living proof of the realization of the promise. However, the book was reedited in the early exile. Israel's only hope was that God would remember this covenant and would reestablish the monarchy and the

The Bible in the CHRISTIAN TRADITION

Messianism and Zionism

Hope in the Davidic Covenant extends beyond the Deuteronomistic History. We will see in some prophetic texts that David's kingdom remains the model for visions of an ideal Israel. Their oracles of hope envision a new Israel with all twelve tribes reunited under one king. The Israelites would refer to this future king as the *messiah*. Hope in the return of the monarchy is called *messianism*.

Other visions rest their hope in the rebuilt temple; the twelve tribes will be united in their worship of Yahweh in and around the temple in Jerusalem. This hope picks up on the second element promised in God's covenant with David: God's eternal presence in the temple. Because the temple was built on Mount Zion, such hope is called *Zionism*.

New Testament texts pick up much more on the theme of messianism than they do on that of Zionism. This could be, in part, because the second temple had been destroyed by the Romans before most of the New Testament texts were written, and so salvation through Jesus was interpreted by early Christians as a replacement of (and improvement on) the ritual system of the temple. Jesus' death was the final sacrifice, after which animal sacrifices were no longer needed. Jesus was the high priest serving God in heaven in the book of Hebrews. To replace the temple would be to return to a system that the followers of Jesus believed God had replaced.

The gospel writers, however, do describe Jesus as the "messiah" or "anointed one." Because of this title for Jesus, many Christians mistakenly think that "messiah" means that he is divine. This is not accurate. The gospel writers are connecting Jesus to the promises made to David. The accounts of the birth of Jesus in Matthew and Luke explicitly link him to the Davidic line. His birth in Bethlehem in Luke's gospel makes the connection especially clear. What were the gospel writers trying to express by calling Jesus the "messiah," that is, the one who fulfills the promises made to the earthly king, David?

This is a very complex question, and we can only touch on a couple of main points. There is a noticeable irony here; Jesus is a poor man who is executed by the Roman government for claiming that he is "king of the Jews." It would seem, then, that his life proved he was most assuredly *not* the messiah. The gospel writers play with the expectations of the messiah, however, in their portrait of Jesus. He is not a political powerhouse, but a man who identifies with the poor and disenfranchised. He is not born into the lap of luxury, but rather his first cradle is a feeding trough for farm animals. He does not have a big army, many wives, or a royal court. He has poor disciples with whom he travels about, preaching of the true kingdom: the kingdom of God. In this sense Jesus returns to the heart of the message of Samuel, that it is God who is king, God who has the true power and right to rule.

It is only when we take seriously the Old Testament background of the language of the messiah that we can begin to appreciate how later Christian writers are using these earlier images. As you read the Bible, notice who else is called a messiah. What did a messiah look like for ancient Israelites?

temple. In fact, 2 Kings ends by telling us that the last king of this line was still alive, even though he was living in Babylon. It is a passage that both recognizes the disaster and yet offers a glimmer of hope. Similarly, the account of God's covenant with David is included because it expressed a hope in Israel's future.

2 Samuel 11:1–12:25: David and Bathsheba

After the story of God's covenant with David, 2 Samuel presents information about some of the wars that David fights. First, he finally "subdues" the Philistines. Never again do we read about the Philistines as a real threat to Israel's existence. Second, we see David move the sole descendant of Saul to his palace. On the one hand, this action shows David's respect for Saul's family, but it also insures that Saul's family cannot rebel. Third, the Ammonites mount an attack on Israel. The events with Bathsheba occur during this war.

This passage is near the beginning of a section that scholars have named the *Court History*. (It is also called the "Throne Succession Narrative.") The material in 2 Samuel 9—20 comes from a source used by the Deuteronomistic Historian. Its literary style and portrait of David contrast with the typical Deuteronomistic accounts of his reign. Scholars have debated the date and original purpose of this material, but the debate has yielded little consensus. The most important question for our purposes is why the historian would include this material in his account of David's reign.

While the account of David and Goliath might be the most famous positive story about David, his interactions with Bathsheba are perhaps the most famous negative stories about him. Try to decide who you think is the guilty party as you read this material.

In Case You Were Wondering

Ammon and Rabbah. Ammon is a country east of the Jordan River. Rabbah is an Ammonite city, located about forty miles from Jerusalem, which the Israelites besieged.

Why is she bathing on the roof? This is the most common misunderstanding of 2 Samuel 11. Bathsheba is *not* on the roof. David is on his roof, while Bathsheba is in an inner courtyard of her house.

Uriah is a Hittite. This means that he is not part of the Israelite tribal lineages but from a Canaanite family. Notice his devotion to Yahweh.

"Booth" is another word for tent.

"**Who killed Abimelech?**" Here we have a reference to an event during the time of the Judges. While a city was under siege, a woman on the city wall dropped a large stone used to grind grain (a millstone) on Abimelech's head, killing him.

Looking Closely at the Text

1. Why does David sleep with Bathsheba?

2. What various things does David do when he finds out she is pregnant?

3. According to 2 Samuel 12:11, what will be David's punishment? In light of God's rejection of Saul, is David's punishment just or fair?

David's Sins

David's behavior is shocking. He sleeps with the married woman next door, and then, when he can't cover it up, he has her husband killed. David does not get off the hook here; these are very bad acts.

People are often uncomfortable recognizing that this great leader did such horrible things. One common way to deny his guilt is to blame Bathsheba. She is seen as the "temptress," bathing in the open so she can seduce the king. Notice that the text says, "the woman was very beautiful" (2 Sam 11:2b). Some in the audience might conjure up the picture of a beautiful, naked woman. A male audience might empathize with David's reaction.

Look carefully again at the story. Does the text say that she tempts him? No. In fact, check how often Bathsheba speaks in these two chapters. That's right: *never* ! She does "send word" to David when she finds out that she is pregnant, but she is never shown actually saying anything.

Maybe you assume that if Bathsheba is bathing in the open that she must be trying to seduce David, but this interpretation presumes the existence of private bathrooms such as we have. The facts are that (1) the Israelites did not have indoor plumbing and (2) houses had inner courtyards, sealed off from the streets, where people bathed. It was a perfectly private spot since it was walled off by rooms. The only reason David can see Bathsheba is because he's on his roof.

Moreover, she is bathing in the afternoon, when men would be away from their homes working, or, if you're a king, away at war, as her husband was. What reason would she have to think that David would be up there looking at her?

Finally, let me point out that if you happen to be walking down the street, and you glance at a neighbor undressed within his or her house, not realizing they can be seen, the perfectly decent thing to do is to avert your eyes and walk on. We call people who stop and stare "peeping Toms," an illegal act in many states. David not only stops and watches, but he takes time while he's doing so to find out who she is.

David sends his messengers to "get" her. The text is better translated as "David sent messengers to take her" (2 Sam 11:4). The verb is the same as one used in other biblical rape scenes. Did Bathsheba object? We do not know. How much could a woman back then have refused the king? Again, this is unclear. Nor do we know if there was overt force, subtle coercion, or if she jumped at the chance to sleep with the king. Just understand that any answer you provide is something you have read into the text, not something that the text itself states.

Bathsheba's silence is meant to make the reader focus on David's acts. The writer is trying to convey the fact that it is David who holds all the power in these episodes, and that no matter what Bathsheba may have said or done, he is ultimately the one responsible. The text says that he knew she was married, so he knows he is committing adultery. And in case you still hope that he can slide off that guilty hook, there's always the matter of Uriah's death.

Frankly, chapter 11 spends more time on David and Uriah than it does on David and Bathsheba. The text suggests that David and Bathsheba had only one encounter: she was impregnated the first time, because we know she was at the fertile part of her monthly cycle (after the ritual purification). Bathsheba also must send word to David when she concludes that she is pregnant, which suggests that they were not in regular contact.

Notice that David does not answer her, but immediately sends to Joab for Uriah. He knows what he's going to do: cover up the deed. He is not going to take responsibility for his sin of adultery. He's going to try to get Uriah to sleep with Bathsheba so that Uriah will think that the baby is his. His plan is foiled by Uriah's piety! Remember that army camps were treated like sacred space, because God was present with the army. If Uriah sleeps with Bathsheba, he will become ritually impure and unable to fight with the army for a while. His devotion to the army and to Yahweh prevents him from sleeping with Bathsheba, even after David gets him drunk. In a moment of biting irony, Uriah unknowingly details David's sins. "The ark and Israel and Judah remain in booths; and my lord Joab and the servants of my lord are camping in the open field; shall I then go to my house, to eat and to drink, and to lie with my wife?" (2 Sam 11:11). Uriah has described what David has done.

Still not admitting his sin, David concludes that he has to get rid of Uriah and marry Bathsheba quickly, so that people will think that the child is David's legitimate offspring. Publicly, Uriah's death simply looks like a casualty of war; only the audience and Joab know differently. As for Bathsheba, once again, the audience is left in the dark. We do not know if she wanted to marry David, nor do we know if she ever learns the real cause of her husband's death. All we know is that she mourns her husband's death.

If the reader is still unclear about David's guilt, the account includes Nathan's oracle against David. Yahweh sends Nathan with an oracle that forces the king to admit his guilt. Nathan tells a parable, although David thinks that it is a real case. Nathan asks David to act as judge on behalf of a poor man. Remember that kings ran the courts that protected the rights of people who could not own land. The parable is a fitting one because Uriah, who was not an Israelite, would have had to use the royal court system. David is outraged that a man who has his own large herds would take the poor man's one lamb for his own. The parable is a reference to David who has many wives, taking Uriah's one dear wife for his own.

David declares a harsh sentence against the rich man, stating that he "deserves to die." Nathan reveals the trick: "You are the man!" David has pronounced his own guilt. When the child becomes ill, David believes that the illness is his punishment from God. He repents by fasting and lying on the ground; these are actions that people who are mourning also do. David's servants assume that he is mourning, but the audience (and Nathan) realizes that he is repenting. When the child dies anyway, repentance becomes pointless; the punishment has been enacted. David does not mourn the death of the child.

David "comforts" Bathsheba, who becomes pregnant again, giving birth to the next king of Israel, Solomon. The final verses of chapter 12 suggest that everything is fine once again. Yahweh loves Solomon, and even sends Nathan with a special name for the boy to symbolize this divine favor: Jedidiah, which means "Beloved of Yahweh."

But there is no rest for the wicked. The words of the oracle still remain unfulfilled. "I will raise up trouble against you from within your own house." David's real punishment is yet to come.

2 SAMUEL 13:1–38: TROUBLE IN DAVID'S HOUSE

The only thing that intervenes between the birth of Solomon and this story is the account of the defeat of the Ammonites. This passage begins a long account of increasing troubles within David's household. Eventually the events described

The Chronicler's History

This textbook focuses on the Deuteronomistic History. However, there is another history of the same period preserved in 1 and 2 Chronicles. This history uses large sections of Samuel and Kings in its retelling of Israel's history. As I mentioned in the section on redaction criticism, this re-use helps us to see the intentions of the Chronicler more clearly. Because this history was written during the Persian period when the nation of Israel was rebuilding, it is a much more hopeful history. It only reports on the history of the southern kingdom, however, so it is not the primary focus in this textbook.

An analysis of the changes that the Chronicler makes to his sources reveals some interesting things, not just about Chronicles, but about the books of Samuel and Kings as well. The majority of changes that the Chronicler makes are in the portrayal of the reigns of David and Solomon. First, these changes depict the building of the temple as the most important action for either of these two kings. The account greatly increases David's initiation of the temple building project. He receives a divinely revealed temple plan. He decides on the priestly personnel who will serve at the temple, and he establishes singers and other groups who will eventually lead services at the temple.

Second, the Chronicler removes most of the negative material about David. There is no Court History in the Chronicler's account of David. That means that there is no story of Bathsheba or of the deterioration of David's family.

This fact indicates that ancient authors were not slaves to earlier accounts. They could pick and choose what material to include in their histories. The author of the account in Chronicles is aware of David's sins but does not choose to include them. Why, then, did the Deuteronomistic Historian include them? The account in Chronicles suggests that this is a legitimate question to ask. The sins of David could have been ignored by the redactor. Instead, the books of Samuel make them central to their account.

lead to a civil war that is led by one of David's own sons. Notice the role that another "cover-up" plays in the story. This chapter begins by stating that several years have gone by between the birth of Solomon and the fulfillment of the oracle against David.

In Case You Were Wondering

A complicated family tree. Absalom and Tamar are full brother and sister, meaning they have the same mother and father. Amnon is their half-brother: David is the father of all three of them, but Amnon has a different mother.

Escaping punishment. At the end of the passage, Absalom flees to Geshur, a country east of the Sea of Galilee, and north of Ammon.

Looking Closely at the Text

1. How are Amnon's actions like his father's? How are they different?

2. Who knows about the sins within David's house, and when do they know it?

3. What should have been David's responsibilities in these stories, either as king or as father?

4. Is Absalom justified in killing his brother and revolting against his father?

What Goes Around, Comes Around

There is no ambiguity in this story. In the account of David's encounter with Bathsheba we were never told what she thought, if she objected, or if David coerced her into having sex with him. In this story, however we clearly have a rape. The text records Tamar's pleas to her brother not to "lie with" her. We see her devastation after the assault. Although she is never mentioned again after this chapter, we can easily imagine her desolate life. Remember that this rape would have ruined her life economically as well as psychologically. As a rape victim, she would not have been a desirable wife; she could look forward to remaining unmarried, without children, and without a future.

We also know something of Amnon's sick mind. Notice the use of the words *love* and *loathing* in this chapter. Before the rape, Amnon "loves" Tamara so much he makes himself ill. After the rape, he "loathes" her, kicking her out, although she begs him to help her. In Hebrew there is no word for *lust*. By playing with the words *love* and *loathe*, the author effectively conveys the fact that this was not really "love."

David does nothing to protect his daughter. When he sends her to cook for Amnon, he is sending her into a trap. Should he have recognized what danger she was in? That is unclear, but I would suspect that, after he realized what had happened, he would have felt some guilt for his unwitting role in the assault.

After he learns of the rape, David does nothing to punish Amnon. Remember that one of the primary duties of a king was to maintain justice in the land by punishing crime. This was another cover-up. Amnon is David's firstborn, which means Amnon was the obvious choice to be the next king of Israel. It would have been a huge scandal if the rape had been made public. In 1 Samuel the people had rejected Samuel as their ruler because his sons were evil; in addition, God had rejected Eli as his priest, because Eli had evil sons. If people had known about Amnon's rape of Tamar, they may have concluded that (1) David should be rejected as king, because his sons were evil, and/or (2) David was unfit to rule a whole country, since he could not keep rule over his own children. Therefore, David chooses to do nothing, to pretend the rape never happened.

Absalom, as Tamar's full brother, has the legal right to take revenge if the court system fails to render justice. Why he waits two years to avenge his sister's rape is not clear, but it suggests that he is calculating and patient. Since David had covered up the rape, the death of Amnon appears to be cold-blooded murder to everyone but David. Once Absalom has Amnon killed, David has only two choices: (1) he can save Absalom by admitting he had covered-up the rape in the first place, or (2) he can convict Absalom for "murdering" Amnon, a conviction whose punishment is death. Clearly, Absalom expects David to pick the second option, so he immediately flees the country.

To me, the most intriguing character in the chapter is Jonadab. The text says that he is "very crafty," the same phrase that is used to describe the serpent in the Garden of Eden, who convinces Eve to eat the fruit. This phrase tells us that Jonadab is smart, clever, and scheming. He can get other people in trouble by convincing them to do things they would not do on their own. It is he that puts the idea in Amnon's head that he can satisfy his "love." Why would Jonadab do that?

Notice that Jonadab shows up again at the end of the chapter. Absalom has had Amnon killed, but David thinks that Absalom has killed all of his sons. It is Jonadab who tells him Amnon alone was killed. How does he know this? The text makes it clear that he hadn't been at the feast. Jonadab must have known about Absalom's plan in advance. In 2 Sam 13:32, Jonadab states that Absalom had been planning the murder ever since Tamar's rape. It leaves the reader wondering about Jonadab's role in the plan, and his failure to warn Amnon.

By the end of the story, four people remain alive who know about the rape and the cover-up: Tamar, Jonadab, Absalom and David. The first two are never heard from again. The next seven chapters detail Absalom's return to Israel, and his eventual rebellion against his father. During the rebellion, Absalom sets up a tent on the roof of the palace and sleeps with the concubines that David had left behind, thus fulfilling the prophecy, "I will take your wives before your eyes, and give them to your neighbor, and he shall lie with your wives in the sight of this very sun. For you did it secretly; but I will do this thing before all Israel, and before the sun" (2 Sam 12:11–12). Absalom is eventually killed in the rebellion by Joab, David's general. Absalom's rebellion ends in the deaths of David's oldest sons, the unraveling of family unity, and the near destruction of David's dynasty.

Parallels between the accounts of David and Bathsheba and Amnon's rape of Tamar link the two stories. David lusts for a beautiful woman whom he could not marry, sleeps with her, has her husband killed, and tries to cover up the whole incident. Amnon lusts for a beautiful woman whom he could not marry, rapes her, and is killed in revenge, while his father tries to cover up the crime. David's punishment mirrors his crime, and "trouble" fills his "house."

SUMMARY: THE KING AS THE FATHER OF THE NATION

The story of the rise of the monarchy in Israel ends with the tragic unraveling of the royal family. In fact, this theme of broken fathers and sons runs throughout the book of Samuel. In each case the faults of the fathers are magnified in their sons:

> ‣ Eli does not recognize prayer when he sees it; his sons abuse the sacrifices, taking the best for themselves.

➤ Samuel resists God's granting of a king; his sons pervert justice.

➤ David "takes" Bathsheba; Amnon rapes his half-sister.

About the only father and son who do not seem to fit this pattern are Saul and Jonathan. However, even with them, Jonathan often acts contrary to his father's wishes and is a poor leader.

Why would the Deuteronomistic Historian include these stories of family relationships in a book primarily about the rise of the monarchy? Perhaps he wants the audience to view the relationship between the king and the people as similar to that between a father and a son. A father/king should realize that any imperfection he may exhibit will only be magnified in those who look up to him. It contributes to the historian's portrayal of the ethics of leadership: a king leads as much by example and fidelity to God's law as he does by running the government.

FOR REVIEW

1. Why was Israel able to gain a foothold in the Levant?

2. What other group was trying to control the Levant at this time?

3. What was Israel's strength in meeting this threat?

4. How is the monarchy a response to this historical situation?

5. How are judges and kings different? How are they similar?

6. What is the relationship between God and the king?

7. According to the Deuteronomistic Historian, what was the relationship between prophets and kings?

8. Why is it important to remember that this history was written after 587 BCE?

9. Describe the audience of the Deuteronomistic Historian.

10. Why does the historian focus on personal and family relationships in the accounts of the reigns of Saul and David?

FOR FURTHER READING

The biblical material in this chapter involves a change in Israelite society from an agrarian, tribal-based society to a more urban, centralized monarchy. There have been many good studies of the social structure of the monarchy. Two very accessible studies are Victor H. Matthews and Don C. Benjamin, *Social World of Ancient Israel 1250–587 BCE* (Peabody, MA: Hendrickson, 1993) and Paula McNutt, *Reconstructing the Society of Ancient Israel* (Library of Ancient Israel; Louisville, KY: Westminster John Knox, 1999).

My analysis of the rise of David and the portrayal of the Philistines is heavily dependent on David Jobling's commentary, *1 Samuel* in the Berit Olam series (Collegeville, MN: Liturgical Press, 1998). A book that looks at the historical evidence for David is by Steven L. McKenzie, *King David: A Biography* (New York, NY: Oxford University Press, 2000).

For a recent study of the ideological importance of Jerusalem, see Leslie Hoppe, *The Holy City: Jerusalem in the Theology of the Old Testament* (Collegeville, MN: Liturgical Press, 2000). From a Jewish perspective, see Jon D. Levenson, *Sinai and Zion: An Entry into the Jewish Bible* (New Voices in Biblical Studies; Minneapolis, MN: Winston, 1985). For a look at the influence 2 Samuel 7 has had on the Bible and within early Christianity, see William M. Schniedewind, *Society and the Promise to David: The Reception History of 2 Samuel 7:1–17* (New York, NY: Oxford University Press, 1999)

Many of the discussions of the Court History or Throne Succession Narrative are addressed to biblical scholars. Nelson's book, *The Historical Books*, summarizes the redactional issues. (See the bibliography in the last chapter.)

There have also been many excellent studies of the figure of Bathsheba. One that helps my students to think about whether she would have been free to resist David is by Archie C. C. Lee, "The David-Bathsheba Story and the Parable of Nathan," in *Voices from the Margin: Interpreting the Bible in the Third World* (Maryknoll, NY: Orbis, 1991) pages 189-204 (previously published in *East Asia Journal of Theology* 3 [1985]).

7 THE POLITICS OF THE MONARCHY

Indeed, Jerusalem and Judah so angered the LORD that he
expelled them from his presence.
(2 Kgs 24:20)

CHAPTER OVERVIEW

In this chapter we will focus on the literary pattern of 1 and 2 Kings, the final books of the Deuteronomistic History. We will pay particular attention to what the kings did and how their actions affected the fate of the nation.

In the introductory material you will learn about the historical background of the time period and how the historian judges the kings of Israel. This information will help you understand the nonhistorical texts that we will examine in the next chapters.

We will concentrate on some representative "good" and "evil" kings. The narratives highlight the main ideological points of the Deuteronomistic Historian. Other important texts from Kings will be assigned in future chapters, where they will be used as background for nonhistorical texts. This chapter is designed to give you an overview of the themes, outline, and literary style of this material, without being exhaustive of the contents.

The Nation of Israel

A Basic Outline

The period of the monarchy can be divided into three general periods: the United Monarchy (ca. 1020–920 BCE), when all of the tribes were unified under the rule of one king; the Divided Monarchy (920–722 BCE), when there were two kings, one in the north and one in the south; and the period of Judah alone (722–587 BCE), a period of time after the northern kingdom had fallen and only the southern kingdom remained.

The account of the United Monarchy is contained mostly in the books of Samuel, while the books of Kings tell us about the Divided Monarchy and Judah alone.

1 Samuel 13—31	Reign of Saul
2 Samuel 1:1—1 Kings 2:11	Reign of David
1 Kings 2:12—11:43	Reign of Solomon
1 Kings 12—2 Kings 17	Divided Monarchy
2 Kings 18–25	Judah alone

Certainly the most confusing part of this history is the period of the Divided Monarchy. At any given moment you will have two different kings, one reigning in the north and one in the south. Some of these kings have very long reigns, while others last only a few months. In addition, while one king rules one region, there may be four or more kings in the other.

Also, the way the Deuteronomistic History recounts the history of the Divided Monarchy is confusing. The history starts with the southern kingdom and speaks of the reign of its first king, Rehoboam. Next, it turns its attention to the north and tells of the king(s) who reigned at the same time. The account will stay focused on the north until the time of the death of the southern king; then it will switch to the south and tell about the southern king; then it will refocus on the north, and so on.

One of the reasons it jumps around such as this is because the redactors can assume that their Israelite audience is familiar with the history. The audience knows the difference between Samaria and Jerusalem, just as we know the difference between New York and Los Angeles. No one would have confused Ahab and Jehoshaphat, just as we would not confuse Abraham Lincoln and Robert E. Lee.

Kings and Prophets of the United Monarchy

Kings	Prophets
Saul 1020–1000	Samuel
David 1000–960	Nathan
Solomon 960–922	

Kings and Prophets of the Divided Monarchy

Kings of Judah	Kings of Israel	Prophets	Ancient Near East
Rehoboam 922–915	Jeroboam I 922–901		**Egypt:** Shishak Invades Judah 918
Abijah 915–913			
Asa 913–873	Nadab 901–900		
	Baasha 900–877		
	Elah 877–876		**Syria:** Benhadad I 880–842
	Zimri 876		
	Tibni 876–?		
Jehoshaphat 873–849	Omri 876–869		
	Ahab 869–850	Elijah	
	Ahaziah 850–849	Elisha	
Jehoram/Joram 849–842	Jehoram 849–842		Hazael 842–806
Ahaziah 842			
Athaliah 842–837			
Joash/Jehoash 837–800	Jehu 842–815		
Amaziah 800–783	Jehoahaz 815–801		Rezon 740–732
	Joash 801–786		
Uzziah 783–742			
Jotham 750–735	Jeroboam II 786–746	Amos (ca. 750)	**Assyria:** Tiglath-Pileser 745–727
	Zechariah 746–745	Hosea (ca. 745)	
Ahaz 735–715	Shallum 745		
	Menahem 745–736	Isaiah (ca. 740)	
Syro-Ephraimitic War 734	Pekahiah 736–735		
	Pekah 735–732		
	Hoshea 732–722	Micah (ca. 730)	Damascus Falls to Assyrians in 732
	Samaria		Shalmaneser V 727–722
	Falls to Assyrians 722		Sargon II 722–705

Kings and Prophets of Judah Alone

Kings of Judah	Prophets	Ancient Near East
Ahaz 735–715	Isaiah	**Assyria:**
Hezekiah 715–687	Isaiah	Sennacherib 705–681
		Siege of Jerusaem 701
Manasseh 687–642	Jeremiah	Esarhaddon 681–669
Amon 642–640	Zephaniah	Ashurbanipal 669–633?
Josiah 640–609	Habakkuk?	Ashuretililani 633–629?
		Sinsharishkun 629–612
		Fall of Nineveth to Babylon 612
Battle of Megiddo 609	Nahum	**Egypt:** Necho 609–593
Jehoahaz 609		
Jehoiakim 609–598	Jeremiah	**Babylon:** Nebuchadnezzar
Jehoiakin 598–597		605–562
(in Jerusalem)		
First Deportation 597	Ezekiel	Battle of Carchemish 605
Zedekiah 597–587		
Fall of Jerusalem to		
Babylon 587		

We will see, however, that in the history, as well as in the psalms and the prophets, certain elements of the two kingdoms are referred to more often than others. This chart provides the bare bones of the Divided Monarchy.

CHART OF THE TWO NATIONS

	South	North
Name of the country	Judah	Israel
Number of tribes	2	10
Capital city	Jerusalem	Samaria (most often)
Location(s) of the national temple(s)	Jerusalem (also referred to as "Zion")	Dan and Bethel
Royal family	Davidides	Various families; the most prominent were the Omrides
Year the nation fell	587	722
To whom did it fall	Babylonians	Assyrians

Notice that the word *Israel* is ambiguous. On the one hand, *Israel* means the whole nation, including all twelve tribes. On the other hand, *Israel* can also refer solely to the northern kingdom. In addition, there were temples to Yahweh at various Israelite cities throughout the period of the Divided Monarchy.

The final thing to notice is that Israel, the northern kingdom, was the larger and more prosperous nation, because it was so fertile. Although you might conclude that it should have lasted longer, you can see that it fell almost 250 years before the south. Part of the north's problem was that it was more unstable than the south. It suffered many internal wars, as its throne passed from one family to another. It had no fixed capital and no single national shrine. Therefore, remaining unified was more difficult for Israel. In addition, the fertility of the land and the presence of good roads made this area attractive to foreign conquerors.

SIGNPOSTS OF THE DEUTERONOMIST

You know that the Deuteronomistic redactors used sources in composing this history. These sources included lists of tribal holdings, stories of individual judges, and David's Court History. In the book of Kings, the redactors state that they used royal annals (none of which have survived). They also probably used some prophetic tales, especially those about Elijah.

But even with these sources, the historian's hand is seen most clearly in the book of Kings. The Deuteronomistic redactors begin and end the account of each king in a similar way. Each account starts with how old the king was when he came to the throne, what year he came to the throne, and often who his mother was. Each account ends with how long he reigned and whether he was a good or a bad king.

These assessments of each monarch utilize a consistent set of criteria. Those kings who are evil do a number of similar things:

› They worship other gods.

› They allow for temples to Yahweh outside of Jerusalem.

› They maintain certain religious objects in the temple of Jerusalem that the Deuteronomists do not like.

› They do not listen to the prophets of Yahweh.

› They participate in religious rituals that the Deuteronomists consider illegitimate.

Notice that the kings are judged solely on their religious policies.

It is not hard to read between the lines: most of the kings of Judah and all of the kings of Israel do not meet the Deuteronomists' standards. And yet there were not religious revolts against this *status quo*. What should this tell you? While the Deuteronomists might say that it means that Israel was always evil, a contemporary historian would say that the Deuteronomists' view of Israelite religion was a minority position; it was not the official religion of Israel or Judah throughout most of their histories.

The deuteronomic portrayal of the consistent religious failures of the two kingdoms helps the audience accept the fall of the two nations as God's just judgment on a sinful people.

General History of the Fertile Crescent

Don't worry; I won't flood you with dates and names. While this is a very complex time in Israel's history, I want to present those elements of its history that had the greatest impact on the nation of Israel. There is a fair amount of archaeological evidence for this period of Israel's history, since much of the relevant data comes from outside of Jerusalem. This evidence includes architectural, inscriptional, and religious remains.

A Power Vacuum

Within the Fertile Crescent, two areas had enough fresh water to support larger kingdoms: the Nile River Valley in northern Africa and Mesopotamia in the east. Israel arose as a nation when the countries that controlled these areas were busy fighting wars elsewhere. In fact, the nation of Israel was at its height under David, when there was a significant power vacuum in the Levant.

Assyrian Advance

The situation was quite different two hundred years later. By then, the Egyptians were no longer at the peak of their power, although they had attained some stability in their royal succession. Assyria, located in the upper part of Mesopotamia, was a rising power; its two main cities were Ashur and Nineveh. After defeating the Babylonians to the southeast, the Assyrians gained control over all of Mesopotamia. Knowing that Egypt was not as powerful as it had once been, and that Egypt was a rich and fertile country, the Assyrians set their sights to their west and south. In between Assyria and Egypt lay the smaller countries of the Levant, countries such as Phoenicia, Syria,

Focus on METHOD

Historical Criticism and New Historicism

The phrase "historical criticism" can be confusing. On the one hand, it refers to all methods focused on the ancient meaning and context of the text, including source criticism, redaction criticism, text criticism, and so on. On the other hand, it is sometimes used to refer to the effort to reconstruct the history of ancient Israel. In this more narrow sense, the text is used as evidence for the historical reconstruction.

Historians use all evidence available to them. This includes archaeological evidence, texts found outside of the Bible, music, art, and so on. Historians know that their reconstructions are imperfect, but their goal is to account for the widest variety of evidence.

The use of biblical texts in historical reconstructions has always been a tricky matter. For some people, the Bible's sacred character makes it *de facto* a reliable source for Israelite history. For them, the account of the reign of Ahab, for instance, is a direct window into that history. For others, the fact that this material has an obvious point of view or ideology makes it worthless for deriving an accurate view of history. Sometimes people who assume the general reliability of the biblical text are called "maximalists," while those who are skeptical about its historical value are called "minimalists." Most historians of the biblical period fall between these two extremes.

One question that arises with reference to the biblical text is what are these texts evidence for? Given that they were written sometime in the ancient period, they do provide some evidence for the issues facing Israelites in the period in which they were written. Let me give you a modern example. If you were writing a paper for your U.S. history class about the lives of women in the South during the Civil War, you would probably get a very bad grade if your only source was Margaret Mitchell's *Gone with the Wind*. However, if you were writing a paper about southern women in the early 1930s, you could use the novel as evidence of the issues and struggles that appealed to women of that era. The biblical texts *do* provide evidence of ancient history; the question is, what aspects of that history are they evidence for?

Historians of ancient Israel use the biblical texts more as evidence for issues facing the community at the time they were written than they do as direct evidence of the contents of that history. In addition, if we can isolate earlier sources that a redactor used, we can also use these sources as evidence for issues in the period of their composition. This is why biblical scholars invest so much effort in debating the date of various biblical texts. The Deuteronomistic History tells us more about Israelites in the late monarchy and early exile than it does about the historical David.

The latest development in historical criticism is called New Historicism. *New Historicism* is a term used for approaches that are more consciously aware of the literary and ideological nature of textual evidence. Rather than searching for nonbiased sources, it notes that all evidence has an ideology. Even an annal that records events is the result of someone deciding which events warrant recording. The solution for historical reconstruction is to embrace and explore the ideology rather than try to neutralize it.

New Historicism applies this approach to all historical evidence: iconography inscribes its ideology in its pictorial record. Architecture embodies spatial hierarchy. Art serves the interests of some patron. New historicism asks whose interests are served by each piece of historical evidence.

New Historicism also focuses on the ideology of the historian. There is no neutral historical reconstruction. It is always undertaken to serve some purpose. Again new historicism does not seek to neutralize the historian's bias; objectivity cannot be a goal because it does not exist. Instead, new historians advocate making the purpose for historical research explicit.

Philistia, and Israel. In the 700s BCE, the Assyrians waged an assault on the Levant. Egypt, wishing to keep war away from its own country, sent troops to the area in an effort to stop the Assyrian advance.

THE BRUTALITY OF ASSYRIAN WARFARE

The Assyrians were known throughout the Fertile Crescent for their brutality. In fact, the Assyrian kings loved to display their violent victories on large monuments. Israelite texts reflect their fear and hatred of the Assyrians.

One of the most common techniques for warfare in ancient times was siege warfare. Understanding what it involved can help to clarify some biblical texts, and even some biblical poetry and prophecies that we will later consider. To review, siege warfare refers to the process by which an invading army surrounds a *fortified city* (that is, a city that has high walls around it) for the purpose of cutting off the city's food and water supplies. The invading army hopes to "starve out" the people inside. They also try to break down the gates of the city or make holes in the walls. In addition, they try to convince the people inside to surrender. Siege warfare was a practice often used by the Assyrians.

The Israelites knew this, and so they prepared their cities in advance. They stored up enough food to last at least a year. They stored up water and wine. In Jerusalem, one of the kings built a tunnel to an underground spring so that the city would have a fresh water supply.

The reality of a siege is pretty grim. Imagine a city of several thousand people slowly starving to death. As starvation grips the population, the very old and the very young are among the first to die. People become more susceptible to disease; even a common cold or flu bug could wipe out a large segment of the population. Food and water supplies eventually become contaminated. The grain starts to mold, making already weak people susceptible to food poisoning. Ancient near-eastern texts describe people drinking their own urine to keep from dying of thirst and eating the newly dead to keep from starving.

The people within the city would try to hold out as long as they could, hoping that something would happen to their enemies to cause them to give up. For instance, the enemy army might run out of money, or they might be attacked by one of the city's allies. Or there might be a revolution back at the enemy's capital, or a disease might strike the enemy camp. Again, there is ancient evidence that all of these things could happen.

When an army, such as the Assyrians, actually managed to conquer a city, they would loot the city, taking anything of value, raiding businesses, temples, private homes, and the palace. They would kill those who fought against them, imprison important citizens, and sexually assault their captives. The Assyrians would "depopulate" the cities that they conquered, forcing the elite classes to move to some other location within the Assyrian empire, usually quite far away. They would scatter these powerful citizens in different cities so that they could not band together and fight.

When the Assyrians conquered Samaria in 722 BCE, they dispersed the upper classes of the ten tribes of Israel all over the ancient Near East. Sometimes you hear references to the "lost tribes of Israel." That phrase refers to this event. The practice of depopulation is more commonly called *exile*. As the Assyrians conquered and exiled other nations, they would settle some of those foreign groups in Samaria and Israel.

THE ATTACK ON JERUSALEM

The Assyrians did not stop at Samaria. They advanced into Judah, attacking cities such as Lachish and Jerusalem. The Assyrian reliefs depicting the attack on Lachish have survived, providing historians with a unique glimpse into ancient war propaganda.

In addition to reliefs, we also have scattered annals and inscriptions from Assyria and Babylon that cover these final centuries of Israel and Judah's existence. In many ways, these annals fill out the biblical picture, although at times they contradict the biblical account. While modern scholars refer to these documents as "annals," the fact remains that they are no less ideological than any other ancient texts.

The biblical record and the Assyrian annals all attest to a siege of Jerusalem and a subjugation of its king, Hezekiah. They also agree that the city of Jerusalem did not fall in the siege, although they disagree as to the reason why the city was spared. For our purposes, the reason is irrelevant.

What is relevant is the fact that the people of Judah interpreted their survival as a great miracle. The city was saved by Yahweh, the divine warrior, and this belief affected the way some Judean leaders approached the Babylonian siege, more than a century later.

THE REVENGE OF THE BABYLONIANS

Babylonia was located south and east of Assyria, and remained Assyria's bitter enemy. Although the two countries worshipped the same gods and had similar ethnic backgrounds, the Babylonians hated the Assyrians for destroying their city and taking the symbols of their gods back to Assyria. As the Assyrian empire expanded, its home rule became increasingly unstable. Civil wars became more common, until eventually Babylonia was able to defeat Assyria (614–612).

Annals, Inscriptions, and Other Political Propaganda

There is a large quantity of written evidence from Mesopotamia during the Iron Age period. Some of it is in the form of contracts, letters, and other material not meant to render a lasting legacy. This evidence is invaluable for reconstructing daily life because it is not focused on influencing a public audience. Historians would judge the bias of this material as "neutral."

On the flip side, texts meant to glorify a particular king or temple have an obvious point of view. This material helps historians explore the ideology of various ancient social institutions.

In Mesopotamia these public documents came in a variety of forms, including the following:

Annals. These records provided a chronological listing of a king's achievements. Although many modern annals attempt to be free of bias, merely recording events, ancient annals were not as historically reliable. They tended to record only successes and downplay defeat.

Inscriptions. These came in many forms. Sometimes they were very public, such as victory stele celebrating a king's military campaigns. Sometimes they were literally buried, such as the inscribed foundation stones of public buildings. These burials were public events, however, which probably included a public declaration of the building inscription.

Iconography. This term refers to the visual elements of public works. The Assyrian reliefs depicting the siege of Lachish are examples of iconography.

Prophetic records. We will read more about prophecy in future chapters. We do have records of prophetic oracles and dream visions from Mesopotamia. The ones from the Iron Age, such as the "Marduk Prophecy," provided explanations for turning points in Mesopotamian national history.

These materials are important for historians, because they present the view of the monarchy and its relationship to the divine world that was operative in this society.

Babylonian power, however, did not differ much from Assyrian power. The Babylonians also wanted an empire, and they saw the defeat of Egypt as an important step. Once again war came to the Levant, as the Babylonians and Egypt went head to head. Although they also practiced siege warfare, at least their memorials did not glorify their violence. The Babylonians tried to control the peoples they conquered by setting up native-born kings who were sympathetic to them, or they would exile the elite classes to Babylon, stripping an area of its population. The Babylonians, however, kept national groups together.

The fate of Judah was linked to the whims of the Babylonians and the Egyptians. After 609 BCE, every king of Judah was put on the throne by either Egypt or Babylon. Judah may have looked like an independent nation throughout this time, but in reality it could do nothing without the support of one or the other of these superpowers.

When at last Judah tried to rebel against Babylonian control, the Babylonian king, Nebuchadnezzar, ordered the destruction of the city. This destruction came at the end of an eighteen-month siege, which was notable for the vast destruction that resulted. The city was burned, the temple torn down to its very foundations, and anyone with power was exiled to Babylon. Judah was not "lost," however, because these exiles lived together and maintained a sense of national and religious identity.

Summary

To recap, the history of the nation of Israel was linked to the history of the Fertile Crescent. When Egypt, Assyria, and Babylon were waging war elsewhere, Israel could thrive. When any of these nations turned their sights on Israel, however, this small nation did not have the military power necessary to resist them. Israel's rise and fall depended on the fortunes of these three nations.

THE IMPORTANCE OF THE TEMPLE

One of the most important social institutions in the monarchy was the national temple at Jerusalem. Solomon, the son of David, built the temple of Jerusalem. As you may remember from the chapter on Israelite law, the Israelites marked places that they felt were "holy" by building a temple. For the Israelites, a location was holy because it was chosen by God as a place where people could feel closer to God. The most common way for the Israelites to express this idea was to call the temple the "house" of Yahweh. In fact, there is no separate word for *temple* in Hebrew; the word we translate as *temple* is the word for *house* in Hebrew.

A temple, was literally God's house. Although Christians sometimes also refer to a church as God's house, the Israelites expressed this metaphor in a broad variety of ways. For example, the architecture of the temple mirrored the architecture of rich palaces, with the main building representing the residence itself, surrounded by courtyards, areas for cooking, storerooms, and so on. The priests who served at the temple were sometimes called God's servants, and their jobs paralleled the duties servants had in rich houses. Some were cooks; some were guards, musicians, butchers, tailors, and so on. The sacrifices that took place at the temple often mirrored lavish banquets, with large quantities of meat, breads, fruits, vegetables, wine, and oil offered to the divine resident. When a community gathered around the temple, they gathered around the house of the divine resident.

Israelite Temples outside of Jerusalem

The Deuteronomistic Historian is so rhetorically effective that readers of the Bible even today are often convinced that his record of Israelite history is accurate. One example of this is the myth of the single temple.

Since the historian advocates having a single legitimate temple to Yahweh, many people assume that there was only one. However, it does not take much reading between the lines to realize that throughout most (if not all) of the monarchy there were temples to Yahweh outside of Jerusalem. After all, if there hadn't been, why would Josiah have been praised for closing them?

Obviously, there were Yahweh temples in the northern kingdom while it existed. But even in Judah, there were temples outside of Jerusalem. The most obvious example is one found in the southern border fortress of Arad. This would have been a government-sponsored temple. The altar found there corresponds to the law of the altar found in Exodus.

Some historians claim that Josiah successfully consolidated the worship of Yahweh in a single temple. However, there is a wide variety of evidence of the existence of other temples after this time frame. The most famous of these is a temple in southern Egypt (Elephantine) where Jews had lived for centuries. Thus, archaeological remains of temples outside of Jerusalem are widespread both in terms of chronology and geography.

The focal point of the temple liturgies was within the interior of the temple complex, even if the liturgies could not be seen because of the courtyard walls. People prayed facing toward the temple, as if speaking to God there, just as many Christians pray facing the altar in a church, and Muslims pray facing the holy city of Mecca. Worship services used music as a central feature, just as ancient banquets featured music.

It may sound "primitive" or naive to say that the Israelites believed God lived in the temple, but the idea is common in the ancient Near East. Israelites did not believe that the temple contained God fully. Instead, they talked about the temple housing one aspect of God. Most often this aspect was called "God's glory," although other texts call it "God's name." This idea is meant to convey the theological notion that God was really present in the temple, even though God is not fully contained there. God still resides in heaven, even while in the temple.

THE LAYOUT OF THE TEMPLE

There are several texts in the Bible that strive to provide a description of the layout of the temple. These temple descriptions are not archives of actual plans, but rather ideal plans for the perfect temple. The temple descriptions do not completely agree with each other.

This genre of temple description is foreign to us; we do not usually think of church plans as theological revelations, so it is difficult for us to appreciate these kinds of texts. There are two major theological issues addressed in these plans: the presence of God and the proper order of human society. Let me consider each in turn.

The Bible in the CHRISTIAN TRADITION

Jesus' Presence in the Eucharist

Don't worry; I'm not going to rehash the arguments concerning consubstantiation and transubstantiation. However, the Christian belief that Christ is present in the Eucharist can give some Christians a way to think about the ancient view that God was present in the temple.

Many Christian denominations, including Catholics, believe that Christ is really and actually present in consecrated hosts. For them, the words, "This is my body; this is my blood" are not just metaphors. There is a real change of the bread and wine into the body and blood of Christ. These Christians do not believe that Christ is fully contained in the hosts, but rather that some aspect of Christ is contained there.

In Catholicism, this belief is manifested in a variety of rituals and practices. For instance, consecrated hosts are stored in something called a "tabernacle" (notice that it is named for the portable "temple" or tent shrine used by the Israelites in the wilderness). A special candle is lit in the church to indicate that consecrated hosts (and, therefore, Christ) are present. Catholics cannot just put the host in their pocket to eat later. Leftover wine cannot be poured down a sink, where the liquids end up in a sewer; it must be drunk. (Similarly, holy water and water used to wash dishes used in Mass have to be poured down a special sink that goes directly into the ground, rather than one attached to the sewer system.)

These brief examples show that some Christian denominations, just like ancient Israelites, viewed the real presence of their god as so central to their worship that many aspects of their rituals reflect this theological tenet.

Because the temple housed the real presence of a god, ancient near-eastern texts reflecting on divine absence in times of national disaster sometimes portray this situation as the god's abandonment of the temple. We will see that Israelite texts do the same thing.

Temple plans also had clearly marked spheres of holiness. Whatever was closest to the place where the divinity resided was holiest. Access to different spheres was increasingly limited, then, and these gradations of access demonstrated the Israelites' view of social organization. This aspect of the temple changes in Israelite texts. For example, some plans allow foreigners who worship Yahweh to be in the same area as Israelites, but others exclude them. The separation of men and women is a very late development, not reflected in the texts of the Hebrew Bible.

THE POLITICS OF THE MONARCHY: READING THE BOOKS OF KINGS

1 KINGS 3:3–28: A WISE KING

As 1 Kings opens, David, on his deathbed, must decide which of his remaining sons will rule after him. He picks Solomon, although Solomon is neither the oldest son nor the son of an important wife. He is crowned king before David dies. After David dies, Solomon kills or banishes his opponents. At the beginning of chapter 3, the text notes that he marries the Pharaoh's daughter, a sign of how powerful Solomon has become.

One of the most important attributes that a king needed in the ancient world was wisdom. This was because the king's primary duty was to maintain justice in his realm, and the ability to judge what was just was part of being wise. This text tells us how Solomon acquired his great wisdom.

IN CASE YOU WERE WONDERING

Gibeon. A city that was north of Jerusalem in the territory belonging to Benjamin. It is not clear why this was the main shrine at the time, since the Ark of the Covenant was in Jerusalem. Perhaps the altar associated with the ark was too small for the "1000 burnt offerings" made at Gibeon.

A dream vision. Israelites believed that God could speak to prophets (and others) through dream visions.

"I do not know how to go out or come in." This phrase means that the person does not know right from wrong.

Looking Closely at the Text

1. This text describes the source of Solomon's wisdom. Why does God grant it to him? What else is he given?

2. How is the story of the two mothers related to the account of Solomon's wisdom?

Solomon, the Wise

Here's a story that would have made perfect sense to an ancient audience, but that strikes us as a bit odd today. The story presumes that you know that the most important thing a king needs to be great is wisdom. There are many tales from Mesopotamia and the Levant of wise kings. The kings were the "Chief Justices" of their day, the final court of appeal. You will recall that the court system of the elders, which was in place before the monarchy, only served landowners. Royal courts also served the poor.

A judge needed "wisdom" to make just decisions. While this is still true today, it was even truer in an era that had no DNA testing and no access to fingerprints or other scientific methods of investigation. In cases where people were lying, it was the judge's responsibility to "discern" who was telling the truth. Wisdom, kingship, and justice are so closely intertwined, that even texts that praise Yahweh as king note God's wisdom and justice.

This text relates how Solomon attained his wisdom. He is depicted as a pious man, making many sacrifices to Yahweh. There are a few "irregularities" in this text. First, he acts like a priest, making sacrifices, and sleeping in the temple. While Saul was punished for making sacrifices, Solomon seems to be rewarded. Second, he acts like a prophet when God appears to him in a dream. He is the only king who receives such a prophetic revelation.

We do not know what motivates God to offer Solomon anything that he wants. Instead, the text focuses on Solomon: what will he do with this opportunity? The text suggests that it was a test. Will Solomon ask for something selfish or foolish? He passes the test by asking for wisdom.

Solomon's speech is marked by its elevated rhetoric. He speaks as a humble servant. When he states that he is only a child, we are supposed to understand this as a metaphor. He's an adult, who has already married the Pharaoh's daughter, and has "taken care of" his opposition. The metaphor of a child matches Solomon's request. A child is someone who not is able to make his or her own decisions, someone an adult must speak for. Solomon uses the metaphor to suggest his assessment of his faults: his inability to discern what is right and wrong.

The second half of the chapter follows the first quite naturally. The account of the two women illustrates Solomon's great wisdom. He must judge a case between two poor people. There is no evidence that he can rely on to make a judgment: there are no witnesses to the alleged crime and no physical evidence available in ancient times to determine the real mother. Solomon must discern who is telling the truth; that is, he must reach a decision on the basis of his wisdom. While we might be horrified that he first proposes to cut the surviving child in half, we soon realize that he never intended to carry through his proposition. Solomon realized that the real mother would not allow him to do this. That is how he decides the truth in this case.

The text ends with the public acknowledgement of Solomon's wisdom. The people realize that he has "God's wisdom," and so they know that he can make just judgments and rule as a great king.

1 KINGS 6:1–38: SOLOMON BUILDS THE TEMPLE

According to the account in Kings, Solomon's greatest achievement was building the temple to Yahweh in Jerusalem. This passage describes the construction of the main part of the temple, the divine residence.

IN CASE YOU WERE WONDERING

The main parts of the temple. Another name for *vestibule* is "porch." The *nave* was the central room in the building. The *inner sanctuary* was also called the "Holy of Holies." It was the place where the ark was located. Because the ark was there, God's presence was there as well.

Cherubim. These were composite beings who served God in heaven. The Israelites pictured a cherub with a human body, multiple wings, and a head with two or more faces. One of the faces was human, but the others were usually animals.

LOOKING CLOSELY AT THE TEXT

1. Why does the text provide so much detail about the materials used to build the temple?

2. How are the cherubim similar to and different from the cherubim described in Exodus 25:17–22?

The Glory of the Temple

This text shows the importance of every element of the temple for the ancient Israelites. This chapter carefully describes the sanctuary building, which would have corresponded to a king's personal living quarters in a royal palace. A courtyard, where the animal sacrifices were burned, surrounds this "house," just as a palace had courtyards. The following chapter describes the parts of the courtyard, as well as some of the items used inside the sanctuary.

The descriptions are so detailed that people today can make models of the temple from them. When the descriptions are precisely followed, it is clear that the materials used reflect the holiness of different areas of the temple. The closer to the center or Holy of Holies, the more expensive are the materials used. The details about the building materials express this belief in spheres of increasing holiness.

We presume that the temple rituals generally follow the descriptions of the ritual calendars in the Pentateuch. According to the descriptions, there were a variety of sacrifices conducted by the priests on behalf of the people. These would include daily offerings, offerings on the Sabbath, New Moons, and high holy days, sin offerings, thank offerings, peace offerings, and so on. These offerings were accompanied by prayers, music, and processions. We will look at the temple music, known now as "the psalms," in a later chapter. At some point in Israel's history, access to the inner court of the temple was strictly limited to the priests; it is debated when this practice developed.

The Babylonians destroyed this temple in 587 BCE, when they destroyed Jerusalem. A second temple was built at the same spot after the Jews returned from the Babylonian exile, and this temple lasted until the destruction of Jerusalem by the Romans in 70 CE. Both temples started out modestly but were expanded by later rulers. Judean kings added courtyards to the first temple. King Herod sponsored a massive expansion of the second temple in the years just prior to Jesus' birth. All that stands of the temple today is a retaining wall Herod had built to increase the size of the courts around the sanctuary. Today this wall is called the "Wailing Wall" or "Western Wall" where Jews gather to both pray and mourn the loss of the temple.

1 Kings 8:1–11 and 22–30: Praying toward God

After the description of the temple, the story in Kings speaks of the dedication of the temple. The main part of this ritual was the procession and placement of the ark into the sanctuary, marking God's entrance into the house. Solomon then offers a long prayer on behalf of the nation.

The first passage describes the entrance of the ark into the temple, which represents God's entrance into the sanctuary. The second passage is part of Solomon's prayer after the ark was installed, in which he talks about the temple's connection to prayer.

In Case You Were Wondering

Horeb. This is the Deuteronomist's name for Sinai.

God's glory. One way of describing God's presence is to speak of "God's glory." This "glory" is sometimes described as a light, other times as a cloud. While we think of these as two different things, the Israelites probably meant something that obscured the view of all else, such as glare in fog. The Deuteronomist usually refers to God's presence, however, as "God's name."

Looking Closely at the Text

1. When does God's glory appear to the crowd?

2. In 1 Kings 8:24, what covenant does Solomon mention?

The Temple and Prayer

The first part of the reading describes the entrance of the ark into the temple. Notice the solemnity that surrounds this procession: Levites carry the ark, while Solomon makes a huge number of sacrifices. While the passage connects the ark to the days of Moses, what is really important is that it symbolized God's presence in the temple. That presence is manifested in the glorious cloud that shines from the building after the Levites exit.

The second passage comes from a very long prayer that Solomon utters after the ark is installed. The part that I had you read describes the theology of God's presence. The first thing to notice is the connection between the temple and the Davidic monarchy, made explicit by the reference to the covenant with David in 1 Kings 8:24. The temple symbolizes God's approval of this dynasty. The temple and the monarchy go hand in hand.

The prayer of Solomon makes clear that the Israelites did not believe that God was actually "contained" in the temple or physically located there. As Solomon states, "Even heaven and the highest heaven cannot contain you, much less this house that I have built!" (1 Kgs 8:27). Solomon is not denying that some real aspect of God's presence is in the temple. He expresses this a bit further on when he quotes God saying, "My name shall be there" (1 Kgs 8:29).

These two lines recognize that God is present everywhere yet experienced as more present in certain holy places.

What is most interesting about Solomon's prayer is the connection that it makes between the temple and prayer. In reality, most of the rituals that took place in the temple were unobserved by the outside world. The priests alone made the daily sacrifices in the courtyard. Later temple plans forbade Israelites from entering this inner courtyard where animal sacrifice was carried out. This seems to leave no place for most Israelites to worship Yahweh. Yet, we know that people did gather on holy days in the outer courts of the temple to pray as the sacrifices were carried out. They also gathered at times of national crisis to pray to God to come to their aid.

Solomon's prayer states that prayer directed toward any aspect of God's presence is heard by the one whose "eyes (are) open night and day" (1 Kgs 8:29). Remember that the Deuteronomistic History, of which this is a part, was completed after the Babylonians had destroyed the temple. This text confirmed to the audience of kings living in exile, who had seen the temple destroyed, that prayer to God was still effective. God's presence in the temple was not what was most important, since the temple could not contain God anyway; people can pray to God anywhere.

1 Kings 21:1–29: The Evil that Kings Do

Following the narratives that concern the temple, the accounts turn to all the evil things that Solomon was doing: he had too many wives, overtaxed the people, ignored tribal boundaries, and built temples to gods other than Yahweh. After his reign, the kingdom of Israel split into two separate countries: Judah and Israel. The Deuteronomist depicts this split as a result of the sinful economic policies of Solomon's son, Rehoboam.

At this point, the history jumps back and forth, telling us about every king of these two countries. As part of that description, the redactors judge whether the king is good or evil. The remaining texts will examine some examples of each of these types.

We start with a northern king, Ahab, from around 873–853 BCE, who is greedy and misuses royal power. He was from a very powerful family, and reigned during a time when Israel was a prominent nation. One sign of his position is the fact that he married a princess from Phoenicia named Jezebel. There are several stories about Ahab in Kings, none of them good; we will read a few more when we study the prophet Elijah. In this story

This cast of a royal seal is inscribed "Shema, servant of Jeroboam." The seal was found in Megiddo, and likely refers to Jeroboam II, King of Israel in the ninth century BCE.

you will see that all of his wealth and position did not satisfy his personal greed.

In Case You Were Wondering

Jezreel. This is a very fertile valley in Israel.

Ancestral land. The Israelites believed that most of the land was given by God to certain tribes and families. Their inheritance laws were strict because the land needed to stay within that family.

The royal seal. This was an official stamp put on documents, which was supposed to be used only by the king. It guaranteed the authenticity of a given document.

Elijah the Tishbite. He was the most famous prophet of his day. We will read more about Elijah when we look at prophecy.

A bad death. Certain types of death were considered more shameful than others. For the Israelites, burial of the body was important, so it was bad to die in such a way that dogs ultimately ate your body.

Torn clothes, sackcloth, and ashes. These are all signs of repentance, as well as mourning. In this case, Ahab is repenting.

1. Why does Ahab want Naboth's land? How does Ahab eventually come to own it?

2. What will be the four punishments for Ahab?

3. How is the oracle modified in response to Ahab's repentance?

Ahab and Jezebel

Compared to Ahab, the sins of David and Solomon look mild. Ahab has no redeeming qualities and is rarely shown in a positive light. His biggest problem seems to be his wife. Ahab is a weak pawn in the hands of wicked Jezebel. In this story, Ahab acts like a spoiled child. He offers to buy Naboth's vineyard for a fair price, but when Naboth refuses, Ahab goes home and sulks. At this point, he seems petty but not dangerous. When Jezebel offers to get the vineyard for him, he does not ask her how she'll do it.

Like David plotting to kill Uriah, Jezebel conceives a plan to get rid of Naboth without being accused of murder. By sending word in the name of Ahab, the elders of the city assume that the plan is a command from the king himself. At the feast, the two men sitting on either side of Naboth are the only ones who can hear him. Israelite law stated that two witnesses were needed to convict someone of a capital offense. The two men can claim they heard him blaspheme God ("curse God") and speak treason ("curse the king"), even though he did no such thing. There are no other witnesses, so Naboth has no way to refute the charge. He is immediately stoned to death.

Why Ahab is then able to take possession of Naboth's land is unclear. We would have expected it to go to the oldest living male relative. Perhaps the text assumes that we know that Naboth was the last male in his line. Or perhaps land belonging to executed criminals was confiscated by the crown. What is clear is that taking Naboth's land was an act of pure indulgence. Ahab had no need for the vineyard; he simply wanted a vegetable garden near his house. Jezebel had no compelling reason to send the message, except she wanted to indulge her sulking husband. Naboth dies for no good reason.

While the crime is hidden from the people, God reveals it to Elijah. Notice that in the text Ahab is ultimately held responsible for Naboth's murder, even though he had no knowledge of Jezebel's actions. For the author, a good king should have known what was happening.

The oracle against Ahab represents a typical cursing formula. It starts out bad enough (dogs will lick your blood), and then escalates at every step in the curse: you'll have no dynasty; dogs will devour wife's body; in fact, dogs will eat your whole family. And, by the way, in case that's not enough, even if your family dies away from the city, birds will eat their carcasses. This oracle is typical cursing "overkill." It suggests that what Ahab has done is completely unacceptable.

Ahab, however, does one redeeming thing: he repents. God responds to his repentance, but it is small comfort. Okay, God says, I won't do this to you. I'll do it to your son! If you read further into the book of Kings you will see some of these prophecies fulfilled. Ahab dies on the battlefield in the Jezreel valley, and dogs lick his blood (1 Kgs 22:29–38). The widowed Jezebel is thrown from a window, and no one buries her. Instead, dogs eat her body, so that all that is left are her skull, hands, and feet (2 Kgs 9:30–37).

2 Kings 22:3–23:3: Josiah, the Pious King

The northern kingdom falls to the Assyrians in 722 BCE, but the south is saved when good king Hezekiah prays to God. We will read about Hezekiah in connection with the prophet Isaiah. The next two kings we will consider reigned over Judah alone. Manasseh, whom we will look at last, reigned from 698 to 643, and Josiah from 640 to 609. They are the last two kings under whom there was some political stability. In Josiah we have an account of a good king. In fact, the Deuteronomistic Historian says he was the best king ever. Notice the role religion plays in this account. After the death of Josiah, the reigns of the kings are short-lived and are all determined by outside forces. The southern kingdom falls less than twenty-five years after the death of Josiah.

In Case You Were Wondering

Not another batch of names! Don't worry about all these names and positions. Just remember Josiah. These other names show how complex ancient government was.

"Inquire of the Lord." This means that Josiah wants them to consult a prophet so Josiah will know what he needs to do.

"The king stood by the pillar." There were two large pillars in the Jerusalem temple. The king read the law to the people while he stood by one of these pillars in the temple courtyard.

Looking Closely at the Text

1. In verses 4–7, what has Josiah commanded his workers to do?

2. What does the high priest find?

3. How does the king react when the law is read to him?

4. Who tells the king what the law means?

5. What does the oracle say?

6. What does Josiah do after hearing the oracle?

The Book of the Law

Although this passage is very repetitive, it shows what the redactors liked in a king. They wanted him to be pious, faithful to Yahweh, and willing to repent when confronted with his own or his people's sins. When Josiah dies, the text says, "Before him there was no king like him, who turned to the LORD with all his heart, with all his soul, and with all his might, according to all the law of Moses; nor did any like him arise after him" (2 Kgs 23:25). Notice how similar this verse is to the material we read in Deuteronomy 6:5. This may have marked the original ending of the earlier version of this history; it glorifies Josiah as the pious king, forming an *inclusio* with the first book of the Deuteronomistic History.

Josiah serves as the model of the perfect king for the Deuteronomistic Historian. Unlike even David, he remains upright and faithful throughout his life. When he realizes that his country has not been following God's law properly, he immediately responds: first by repenting and then by implementing nation-wide reforms to bring his country into conformity with the law.

Biblical scholars have wondered what this "book of the law" was that Josiah found. After the book is found, 2 Kings 23 describes a series of religious reforms that Josiah implemented in response to the law. When we look at the reforms that Josiah enacted, and we look at the legal texts in the Bible, it becomes clear that Josiah is observing the laws set out in the book of Deuteronomy. Some scholars conclude that "the book of law" that Josiah found was the law that is now contained in the book of Deuteronomy.

A large part of this law included shutting down all temples, shrines, and altars to Yahweh outside of Jerusalem. Remember that Solomon had built the temple to Yahweh, but he had not made it the only temple. There were still temples to Yahweh throughout Israel, and there were even temples to other gods built by kings such as Solomon.

This multiplicity of temples did not sit well with Josiah, for under him Jerusalem would reach its zenith. First, Josiah shut down all the temples to other gods throughout the land. Second, and equally significant, he made Jerusalem the only city where sacrifices to Yahweh could be offered, the only place where God "dwelled." Third, he cleared the temple of items that the authors of the text did not like, such as the "image of Asherah" (23:6) and "the chariots of the sun" (23:11). For the Deuteronomistic Historian, Josiah's insistence on only one temple was correct theology. Yahweh alone was Israel's God. Yahweh alone chose where to dwell. Jerusalem alone was the place for this temple.

The reign of Josiah, however, posed a small problem for this history. According to Deuteronomy, God rewards good actions, and punishes evil actions. We have seen this principle at work in the oracles against David and Ahab. Josiah, as the most pious king, should have lived a long and blessed life. However, he dies on the battlefield at a relatively young age, around thirty-nine or forty. Furthermore, as I noted earlier, Jerusalem, the temple, and the whole nation are completely destroyed by the Babylonians less than twenty-five years later, in fulfillment of the oracle that the prophet speaks when she reads the law. How can this be? Why was God so cruel to Josiah?

2 Kings 21:1–18: The Sins of Manasseh

The Deuteronomistic Historian believed that Josiah and the nation suffered as punishment for the many sins of Manasseh. While the previous text told us what the best king was like, this one shows us the most evil one.

This story actually comes before the last one. We are reading it last because, more than any other story, it demonstrates that the whole point of Deuteronomistic History is to explain why the nation fell and why not even the glory of David nor the piety of Josiah could save it.

In Case You Were Wondering

Worship of other gods. In describing the sins of Manasseh, the history focuses on his worship of other gods. Baal and Asherah were gods of the Canaanites, and the "host of heaven" referred to the pantheon of polytheistic nations such as Assyria.

"He made his son pass through the fire." This means he performed child sacrifice.

Your ears will tingle. This biblical expression means you have heard something shocking.

A measuring line and a plummet. These were builders' tools, which gauged whether a structure was sound. If not, it was destroyed. God is going to "measure up" Judah. The presumption is that it will not be "straight" and God will have to destroy it.

The Book of the Annals of the Kings of Judah. This is one of the sources that the Deuteronomistic Historian used to write this history. It did not survive; all we know about it is its title.

Looking Closely at the Text

1. Name at least three evil things that Manasseh did, according to 2 Kings 21:3–7.

2. What will be the punishment for all of this evil?

The Sins of the Fathers

The text is clear: Manasseh is evil, and because of him Judah and Jerusalem will be destroyed. Notice the religious focus of this account. He is not accused of greed, oppressing the poor, or sexual misconduct. Manasseh's sins are religious sins. Except for verse 16, which states that he killed many innocent people, all his sins had to do with religion: the worship of other gods and the improper worship of Yahweh. In fact, it is significant that the oracle of punishment comes before verse 16; Manasseh and Judah are condemned for religious violations, not because of violence and bloodshed.

The burning indictment against Manasseh reminds us that this is not a purely political history. Politically and economically, Manasseh was quite successful. He had a long reign (fifty-five years) and lived a long life, dying at the ripe age of sixty-six. Judah was at peace throughout his whole reign, and, in fact, grew under his leadership. Other biblical texts do not judge Manasseh so harshly, and there is even a whole separate text entitled, "The Prayer of Manasseh" which is considered canonical by Eastern Orthodox Christians.

For the Deuteronomistic Historian, Manasseh's reign leads to Judah's death sentence. Although the enactment of this punishment does not occur until three generations later, not even the piety of Josiah can turn it back. The Deuteronomists believed that God could and did punish sin up to three generations after the sin had been committed. Many biblical texts disagree with the history on this point. Jeremiah, Ezekiel, and Chronicles, for instance, all insist that God does not mete out punishment on succeeding generations. Here, however, the end of this history shows the principle of intergenerational punishment at work. Judah falls because of the sins of Manasseh.

The Third Generation after Manasseh

It may be hard to follow how the Deuteronomist determines that the sin of Manasseh is punished within three generations, since there are six kings that follow him. However, this chart shows you how each king is related to Manasseh:

Manasseh	Sinful king responsible for the fall of Jerusalem	Generation 0
Amon	Son of Manasseh	First subsequent generation
Josiah	Son of Amon, grandson of Manasseh	Second generation
Jehoahaz	Son of Josiah, great-grandson of Manasseh	Third generation
Eliakim/Jehoiakim	Son of Josiah, great-grandson of Manasseh	Third generation
Jehoiachin	Son of Jehoiakim, great-great-grandson of Manasseh; exiled to Babylon	Fourth generation
Zedekiah/Mattaniah	Uncle of Jehoiachin, therefore a great-grandson of Manasseh; the city falls during his reign	Third generation

You see, then, that Zedekiah is part of the third generation after Manasseh; punishment for Manasseh's sins occurs within that generation.

What about Jehoiachin? Isn't he also punished, even though he's part of the fourth generation? Look at the end of the history, 2 Kings 25:27–30. The book ends with a notice of the release of Jehoiachin. Scholars debate the meaning of this ending for understanding the purpose of the Deuteronomistic History as a whole. Some people see this as a late, secondary addition. Others view it as a note of hope, and some even say that the whole history leads to an exaltation of Jehoiachin. I think the answer is much simpler. I think it merely cleans up the Deuteronomist's historical schema. By including these lines, he can maintain that the fall of the city was the result of the sins of Manasseh, while still holding that God's punishment only lasts three generations.

We are meant to read the final edition of the Deuteronomistic History through this lens. As we read about Israel's corruption under the judges, David's sins with Bathsheba, and Ahab's childish greed, we read an explanation. It is an explanation why the glorious temple of Yahweh, God's own and only dwelling place, was looted, burned, and torn down by the defiling hands of the Babylonians. How could this happen? How could God have stood by and watched as the evil ones celebrated on the rubble of the house of the LORD? For the Deuteronomist, it was Israel's just punishment for a history of sin, greed, and corruption.

SUMMARY: A FAILED HISTORY REVISITED

Unless we understand the primary purpose of this history, we can easily forget that it is calling the audience to examine its own sin and guilt. It is so easy to read this history and think, "Why were *they* always sinning? Why didn't *they* just do what they were supposed to do?" But this is not about some other evil "them." This was written by Israelites for Israelites.

The accounts of the kings of Israel and Judah ask the audience to look at themselves in this history of sin and failure. The Deuteronomistic Historian is a skilled author. The questions the history poses still resonate in the modern world. What is the relationship between power and responsibility? Are there limits to human authority? Does an individual's power render her or him above the law? What motivates people who have power, money, and prestige to continue to take what is not theirs? And, finally, if a person is blessed with success, does that mean that they are a moral person and in God's graces?

FOR REVIEW

1. What are the three periods of the Monarchy?

2. Why is the word *Israel* ambiguous?

3. During the Divided Monarchy, which country was larger and more prosperous, although less stable?

4. What is siege warfare?

5. How did the policies of exile differ between Assyria and Babylon?

6. What is the general layout of the temple, and what two issues do temple plans address?

FOR FURTHER READING

This is a good place to delve into the question of the double redaction of the Deuteronomistic History. One of the most influential books on this topic is the work of Frank Moore Cross, *Canaanite Myth and Hebrew Epic: Essays in the History of the Religion of Israel* (Cambridge, MA: Harvard University Press, 1973). For contemporary discussions of the issue, see *Reconsidering Israel and Judah: Recent Studies in the Deuteronomistic History*, edited by Gary N. Knoppers and J. Gordon McConville (Sources for Biblical and Theological Study 8; Winona Lake: Eisenbrauns, 2000) and *Israel Constructs Its History: Deuteronomistic Historiography in Recent Research*, edited by Albert de Pury, Thomas Römer, and Jean-Daniel Macchi (JSOTSup 306; Sheffield: Sheffield Academic, 2000).

For an interesting study of the narratives concerning Jezebel, see Patricia Dutcher-Walls, *Jezebel: Portraits of a Queen* (Interfaces; Collegeville, MN: Liturgical Press, 2004)

There have been several good discussions of the ideology of Solomon's temple. From the perspective of archaeology, see Elizabeth Bloch Smith's essays, " 'Who Is the King of Glory?' Solomon's Temple and Its Symbolism," in *Scripture and Other Artifacts: Essays on the Bible and Archaeology in Honor of Philip J. King*, edited by Michael D. Coogan, et al. (Louisville, KY: Westminster John Knox, 1994) pages 18–31, and "Solomon's Temple: The Politics of Ritual Space," in *Sacred Time, Sacred Place: Archaeology and the Religion of Israel*, edited by Barry M. Gittlen (Winona Lake: Eisenbrauns, 2002) pages 83–94. For the royal ideology behind the account in 1 Kings, see Victor Hurowitz, *I Have Built You an Exalted House: Temple Building in the Bible in Light of Mesopotamian and Northwest Semitic Writings* (JSOTSup 115; JSOT/ ASOR monograph 5; Sheffield: JSOT, 1992).

There have also been a variety of studies of Israelite religion during the period of the monarchy that have challenged the Deuteronomistic depiction of the period. Many of these are written for specialists in the field.

8 ISRAELITE POETRY: PSALMS AND SONG OF SONGS

Hear the plea of your servant and of your people Israel when they pray toward this place; O hear in heaven your dwelling place; heed and forgive.
(1 Kngs 8:30)

CHAPTER OVERVIEW

This chapter focuses on Israelite poetry. I have placed this chapter here in part because the psalms are associated with David and the temple. In addition, most of the prophetic and proverbial literature that we will study subsequently utilizes the features of Israelite poetry. You may be asked to read all or parts of this chapter at another point in the course. It is written to accommodate such flexibility.

This chapter will cover a number of poetic elements:

› The main features of Israelite poetry, such as parallelism, symbolism, and metaphor

› The characteristic features of the Psalms, including the psalm titles and musical notations

› The ancient near-eastern context for both the psalms and the poems in the Song of Songs

When we turn to specific texts from the Psalms and Song of Songs, we will illustrate their major themes, and how these relate to contemporary audiences.

Israelite Poetry

Features of Israelite Poetry; The Style of the Poems of Israel

Israelite poetry is not like English poetry. For example, it does not use the elements we usually associate with poetry, such as rhyme or strict meter. While there have been several attempts to find a metrical system, no reconstruction works in all cases. This lack of specific poetic markers has led some scholars to conjecture that there is no such thing as a distinct poetic genre in biblical Hebrew.

This does not mean that Hebrew poetry is just like Hebrew prose material such as the Deuteronomistic History. There are specific stylistic elements found in Hebrew poetry. The most prominent of these are parallelism, terse language, and fluidity in grammatical forms. This last element is not obvious when reading the poetry in translation, but it explains why different translations of Hebrew poetry will vary more than translations of Hebrew prose material.

One of the most obvious features of Israelite poetry is "parallelism." *Parallelism* is a literary device in which an author repeats an idea twice in paired lines. Look at the title of this section: I used parallelism to convey my idea. Poetry in the ancient Near East was full of parallelism. The best way to understand parallelism is to consider a few examples.

Sometimes the parallel lines say the same thing using slightly different words, as in the following:

Give ear to my words, O LORD;
give heed to my sighing. (Ps 5:1)

Sometimes the same idea is presented with contrasting images:

For the LORD watches over the way of the righteous,
but the way of the wicked will perish. (Ps 1:6)

Sometimes the second line completes the actions or ideas of the first line:

I lie down and sleep;
I wake again, for the LORD sustains me. (Ps 3:5)

Lastly, when numbers appear in Hebrew poetry, the second line will increase the number in the first line:

Once God has spoken;
Twice have I heard this. (Ps 62:11)

Parallelism is used in psalms, proverbs, and many prophetic texts.

This *Is* Poetry, After All

Those of you who love poetry will welcome this change from the prose material that we have been covering so far. We are now considering poetry, and with it come all those lovely poetic features: the use of symbols and metaphors, inexact language, cryptic wording, fancy expressions, and so on.

Note, however, that Israelite poets tried to say as much as they could with as few words as possible. In one type of lament psalm, the dirge for instance, one line would have three words, while the second line would have only two! (We need many more words in English to translate these five words, so it is hard to detect this sparseness in translation.) This drive toward brevity means that each word is packed with significance and nuance. Many times these words create symbolic images that stimulate the audience's imagination.

Some of these images are pretty obvious: there are lots of royal images in the psalms, plus images taken from farming, nature, and war. The more you know about everyday life in ancient Israel, the more these images and metaphors make sense. A *metaphor* is a figure of speech in which a word or phrase literally denoting one kind of thing, such as a snake, is used in place of another, such as a person who is sneaky, to suggest a likeness or analogy between them. Unfortunately, we often miss what Israelite images are trying to communicate because we didn't live back then. Let me give you some examples of common images.

First, royal images are used for both the human king and for God. The human king is often pictured as a new David, because David was the first of the royal family who ruled in Jerusalem. The psalms will refer to justice, another royal image, because the king insured justice within the kingdom. God's royal rule is sometimes connected to acts of creation: since the creator god rules over the earth as a king. Kings were also called the "shepherds" of the people, because they protected the people/flock from danger. Conversely, wild animals and thieves represented the enemies of the nation.

The nation of Israel was not just David's "flock"; it was also a vine or plant that God planted in the soil of the land. In plant imagery, the king is the "branch," that is, an offshoot of the nation. The nation is also sometimes called "Jacob," a reference to the patriarch whose name was changed to Israel and who was the father of the founders of the twelve tribes of Israel.

The temple was symbolized as God's royal residence. Sometimes the psalms refer to the hill on which the temple of Jerusalem was built: Zion. Other psalms praise the temple as God's "tent," a reference to the days when the Ark of the Covenant was kept in a tent.

A common image in the psalms is that of "enemies." Sometimes these are personal enemies. Other times these refer to national enemies, such as the Assyrians or the Edomites. The strong language used in the psalms about the enemies can be quite shocking. They are despised, and the psalmist prays for revenge.

When psalms refer to national crises, the image often used of God is that of the Divine Warrior. The psalmist beseeches God to deliver Israel on the battlefield or praises God for destroying the armies of the enemies. This violent imagery can be disconcerting to a modern reader, but it expressed the Israelite belief that God helped the oppressed in times of crisis.

I recommend that you read the poetic texts with your poetic mind, not your literal mind. Don't analyze the poems as if they are communicating data, facts, or information. Instead, let the language stimulate your imagination. Approach Israelite poetic material with an openness to the play of its language.

The Psalms

The main part of this chapter is devoted to the book of Psalms. This book has had a profound impact on Christian spirituality, remaining a vibrant source of prayer for contemporary readers of the Bible. Yet, these ancient poems reflect the liturgical and musical conventions of their day. We can appreciate the language of these poems better when we know more about their form and function.

Focus on METHOD

History of Biblical Interpretation

One new movement within the field of biblical interpretation is an increased interest in the history of the interpretation of a particular text. There are many reasons for this renewed interest, and each of these reasons affects both the material that is reviewed and the treatment of that material. Because this is such a new field, however, many scholars are unaware of the variety of purposes that it can serve.

Some of the most prominent approaches to the history of interpretation focus on the work of "recovery." This approach can sometimes be coupled with a negative attitude toward contemporary methods of biblical interpretation. Pre-critical interpretations, meaning those dating before the Enlightenment, are usually privileged, and within those, the goal is usually to uncover the dominant interpretations, especially those that have the most influence on denominational teachings, as a kind of normative project. This approach tends to privilege interpretation within larger theological treatises or sermons.

This, however, is only one of the reasons why the history of interpretation is important. Alternatively, some biblical scholars have used the interpretation of the text as a way to reveal where persistent difficulties in the text lie. By looking at sticking points in interpretation across a wide variety of time periods, the problematic or ambiguous nature of the text becomes more apparent. This approach uses history as a way to see the biblical text better. This approach often focuses on formal treatises of biblical interpretation, such as commentaries, since that is where scholars usually delve deeper into the technical aspects of the text.

Others have looked at the text's interpretive history in order to uncover the cultural context of contemporary interpretation. For example, most Christians assume that the story of Adam and Eve is about the Fall and original sin, even though those terms do not appear in the account. Many of my students are surprised to learn that Jews do not have the same interpretation as Christians. They had not been aware that their assumptions about the text are the result of a long history of Christian interpretation of this material.

Some scholars using this last approach want to find ways to resist a given interpretation. The first step to resisting an interpretation, or at least relativizing it, is to set it as one option among several. Scholars explore the way that the historical context of the interpreter affects interpretation. These scholars often use nontraditional material to demonstrate an interpretation's influence. In particular, works of art and literature which have a greater impact on a wider variety of people are explored as vehicles for interpretive traditions.

The sidebars in this chapter will explore some of the more prominent interpretations of biblical poetry. Psalms, in particular, have always had a special place in the life of Christians. These forays into the interpretive tradition may give you some insight into why such an approach may be fruitful for a contemporary reader.

WHAT ARE "THE PSALMS"?

The simplest answer to this question is this: a *psalm* is an ancient musical prayer. Many psalms were probably first used in the worship services at the temple, although individuals could have also used them in private prayer.

The book of Psalms is a collection of songs that had been written and used at various times in Israel's history. Since most of them had probably been used at the temple, the book of Psalms is sometimes referred to as "the hymnbook of the temple." When you think about hymnbooks today, you'll find many parallels with the book of Psalms. Church hymnbooks have songs from different time periods, and

The Canonical Shape of the Psalms

The present book of Psalms is divided into five parts, each one separated by a doxology or short hymn of praise. The Jewish Talmud claims that this is a deliberate division so that the book corresponds to the five divisions of the Torah or Pentateuch. For a long time, scholars have wondered about the present arrangement of the psalms.

When we look at the Psalms scrolls found at Qumran, we find that the book of Psalms did not reach its final form until late in the Hellenistic period. In all of the manuscripts, the first three sections of the psalms are identical in number and order to that found in modern Bibles. However, the earliest scrolls differ in the fourth and fifth sections, while the latest scrolls are identical throughout. Scholars conclude that this is evidence that the book of Psalms was reaching its final version during the Roman Period.

Some contemporary biblical scholars continue their attempt to account for the present arrangement of the Psalms, but no reconstruction has gained general consensus. However, their efforts have highlighted some "mini-collections" within the book as a whole. For example, there are a group of Elohistic psalms in 42–83, so called because they use the divine name Elohim throughout. Notice, for instance, how Psalms 14 and 53 are nearly identical, except for the use of the divine name. Psalms 120–134 have the title "A psalm of ascent," which may stem from their use at pilgrimage festivals. The book opens with two psalms urging meditation and ends with five psalms calling on the community to praise God.

In general terms, the following table demonstrates the overall arrangement of the psalms.

	Psalms	Predominant Element
Book I	1–41	Psalms of David
Book II	42–72	Psalms of Korah (a priestly group)
Book III	73–89	Psalms of Asaph (another priestly group) and communal laments
Book IV	90–106	Yahweh's kingship
Book V	107–150	Ends with five Hallelujah Psalms

In the Christian era, the arrangement of the psalms continued to show some slight variations. For example, some manuscripts divide up the individual psalms differently. When verse numbers were added in the Middle Ages and later, some traditions gave the Psalm titles verse numbers, while others did not. The result is that when you are reading an article about the Psalms, and it mentions something by chapter and verse number which you cannot find, then check first the verse above or the verse below. If that doesn't work, check the psalm before the one in your Bible or the psalm after it.

the style of the music varies from song to song. They are not all written by the same person. Some can be used in many ways, while others are designed for use at specific points in the liturgy. While most add to the enjoyment of the liturgy itself, some, such as a sung Eucharistic prayer in a Roman Catholic mass, are an essential part of the liturgy. The psalms were similar: representing different time periods, different styles, and written by different people for different reasons. Unfortunately, we usually do not know exactly how they were used in the liturgy.

The book of Psalms contains some indications that it was assembled over a long period of time. The book is divided into five sections, each of which may comprise an addition to an original collection. But just because a psalm is contained in the latter half of the book does not necessarily mean it was *written* later than psalms in the first part of the book. It simply means that it was added to the collection later.

MUSIC IN ANCIENT NEAR-EASTERN TEMPLE RITUALS

One of the problems with thinking about the psalms as hymns is that we might think they were "just music," something to make the service "prettier." We will really miss the point if we think that's all they were! In the ancient world, sung prayers were vital parts of the ritual. Some texts tell us that they were as important to the liturgy as the sacrifices. The psalms were first and foremost *prayers* that called on God for help or thanked God for divine aid. The Israelites sang them as a way to speak to God directly: God would hear these sung prayers and respond.

Israelite texts also view these sung prayers as something that *God* wants, not just something that humans enjoy. Sung prayers were so important to God that later Israelite texts depicted angels singing to God on the Sabbath. A liturgy without psalms simply did not work.

Like a modern hymnbook, the book of Psalms does not tell its audience how to use the songs. It assumes that there is a leader of music who would have that information. Sometimes biblical narratives will depict a character voicing a psalm, but we do not have enough examples to trust that we understand the full range of use available.

We have more information concerning prayer-songs from Mesopotamia. For example, a text that describes the rituals that needed to be performed when a temple wall was repaired suggests that music was an essential part of the ritual. In fact, the text indicates that specific types of music played on the proper instruments by the required musicians were important elements of the ritual. Moreover, collections of ritual poems, such as a certain type of lament, have been preserved.

PSALM TITLES AND OTHER DISTRACTIONS

Think for a moment about the significance of the fact that the psalms were words to songs. When you simply read the words of a song, don't you find the experience incomplete without hearing the music? Since we know very little about ancient music, it is impossible to re-create that musical context.

This relief, dated to circa 700 BCE, shows prisoner musicians singing and playing the lyre.

However, we know that the psalms were certainly set to music, because there are notes to the musicians preserved with the words of the psalms. Most of these notes are in what are called the psalm "titles," those brief comments that occur in many psalms right after the psalm number. Unfortunately, we do not know what most of these notations mean: the music itself cannot be recovered. But the titles do tell us that these poems were sung.

Look, for example, at Psalm 88. First, the title tells you what kind of musical piece this psalm is: it is a "song," whatever that meant to the Israelites. Second, it tells you it was written, or perhaps performed, by a particular priestly group called the Korahites. Next, there's a note to "the leader," presumably whoever directed the musicians, sang solo, or led the congregation. That note tells him what tune to use: Psalm 88 was to be sung according to the tune of a different song type (*maskil*) titled, "Heman the Ezrahite." Now doesn't that tell you something!

Another common musical notation occurs in the body of the psalms: the word *Selah*. You see it at the end of Psalm 88:7. Again, we do not know what this word means, although it may note the end of a section, a change in music, or a repetition of a refrain. My advice concerning the obscure references in the titles and the note "Selah" is to ignore them.

One common notation in the psalm titles is the statement that a particular psalm is "of David." Again, what this means is unclear. It could mean that

David wrote the psalm. There are biblical texts that describe the young David's musical abilities. However, it is unlikely that as king he would have had the time to compose the number of psalms attributed to him. The Hebrew word translated as "of" more often means "to" or "for." The phrase could mean a psalm was written for him, such as a tribute to the king. More likely, the phrase means that people who worked for David, or one of his descendants, wrote the psalm. In other words, a psalm "of David" probably was a psalm written by someone who worked for the royal family in Jerusalem.

Lastly, a few psalms have historical annotations. Look at Psalm 51. Here the title makes reference to Nathan's condemnation of David's affair with Bathsheba. Did David write the psalm at that time? While that is possible, it is unlikely. We have a lot of ancient scrolls of the Psalms, especially among the Dead Sea Scrolls. The notes in these manuscripts differ from scroll to scroll: some have no references to historical events, some have historical references for every single psalm, and some have just a few. This suggests that scribes added these elements in the psalm titles at a later time, in order to give users a context for individual psalms.

Praise and Lament

Even though we do not know about the detailed intricacies of Israelite music, we can still recognize some general patterns in the psalms. First, some psalms are written as if an individual is singing them alone, while others are clearly sung by a group. Second, biblical psalms are generally one of two types. Either they are psalms of praise, or they are psalms of complaint or lament.

In a psalm of praise, the singer can praise God for any number of things, such as the beauty of creation, or God's aid in time of war. The most common type of praise is one in which God is praised as king, who rules over Israel, protects it, and enacts justice within it. Sometimes the praise of God as king includes praise of the human king, who rules on behalf of God. Another very common type of psalm praises God in the temple. The word *hallelujah* is a Hebrew sentence meaning "Praise Yah(weh)."

A *lament* psalm is one in which the psalmist prays to God with a request or petition, and these are often written as if an individual sings them. These requests cover the gamut of human problems. Some lament psalms look for relief from illness, others from the loss of prestige or reputation. Some psalms lament a national disaster, others a natural disaster. The strong images of anger in the lament psalms are striking. The singer expects God to deliver him or her, and the psalmist sometimes even accuses God of acting unjustly by delaying deliverance. In very few of the psalms does the psalmist confess that the suffering is punishment for sin.

Often students assume that the book of Psalms contains more psalms of praise than it does of lament, but this is incorrect. By far the most common type of psalm in the Bible is the lament sung by an individual. This is an important point to notice because it expresses an important element of both Judaism and Christianity: that God cares about those who suffer and expects prayers which give voice to their experience of anguish.

PSALMS 15, 24, AND 84: IN PRAISE OF THE TEMPLE

The first group of psalms praises the temple as God's dwelling place. Read each psalm as an individual poem, but also notice that there are similar images or themes in this group of psalms.

IN CASE YOU WERE WONDERING

The "valley of Baca" in Psalm 84:6 is an unknown place.

LOOKING CLOSELY AT THE TEXT

Instead of asking you questions as you look at the psalms, I would like you to try to summarize in one sentence the main theme or images in each psalm.

IN PRAISE OF GOD'S DWELLING-PLACE

I've always hated trying to explain a poem: it's like having to explain a joke. Of course, the best way to "experience" a poem is to enter into its beauty, the logic of its images, and the interplay of its metaphors. But I also have learned that this is hard to do if you don't understand what is going on in the poem. As I go through these psalms, I will not try to explain every image. Instead, I want to point out some of the main features of each type of psalm.

The psalms in this group praise the temple, and they give you insight into how the Israelites *felt* about the temple. The first thing you might notice is that all three psalms are concerned with the status of the person who can enter the temple. Psalm 15 states that only those free from sins against their neighbor can "abide" in God's "tent." Psalm 24 says the "pure of heart" can approach the temple, while Psalm 84 ends by stating that God "bestows favor" on "those who walk uprightly." Although the ritual laws in Leviticus were concerned with the ritual purity of the person who comes to the temple, these psalms focus on ethical behavior, demonstrating that the two categories are intertwined.

The view of God in all of these psalms is very exalted. God is pictured as judge, king, or warrior. Psalm 15 presumes that God can judge the sins of those who enter the divine residence. Psalm 24 praises God as the "King of glory" in verses 7–10. This king is returning triumphant from the battlefield, "strong and mighty . . . mighty in battle" (Ps 24:8). Psalm 84 also combines royal and warrior imagery, although emphasizing the latter. While Yahweh is called "king" in verse 3, five times the psalmist calls God, "LORD of hosts," a reference to Yahweh as leader of a divine army.

In all of these, the temple is a refuge for "pure hearts" (Ps 24:5). The psalmist is safe there from any further harm (Ps 24:5), not having to seek another place (Ps 15:5). Psalm 84 resounds with this experience of God's dwelling place. The poet can barely find words to describe the joy of being in the temple. "For a day in your courts is better than a thousand elsewhere" (Ps 84:10).

Psalms 23, 96, 103, and 104: In Praise of God

These psalms praise God as king and creator. Again, try to let the language of the poems draw you in.

In Case You Were Wondering

The metaphor of the shepherd. Remember that a common metaphor for king is "shepherd." With this in mind, think about the specific images of Psalm 23.

Bless the Lord, O My Soul

Here the psalms praise God. The outline of communal psalms of praise, also called *hymns*, is fairly simple. They begin with a call to praise, followed by the body of the poem and a concluding statement. See if you can identify these parts in Psalm 103.

Each of these four psalms focuses on a different aspect of God's "mighty deeds." In fact, the first psalm, Psalm 23, is quite personal: God's "mighty deed" is the care of the individual psalmist in a time of great trial. Although many people think of Psalm 23 as a poem about death, the fact is, it is a prayer by the king to God as king. God is the king's "shepherd" who protects him "in the presence of" his "enemies" (verse 5). It is God who *anoints* the psalmist, revealing the psalmist's identity as the human king. Notice once again the connection between royal and temple imagery: the psalm ends with the royal psalmist declaring that he "shall dwell in the house of the LORD my whole life long," meaning that his reign is secured by God's presence in the temple.

Psalms 96, 103, and 104 praise God in more universal terms. Psalm 103 praises God as king, especially over the chosen people. God's covenant with Israel is eternal, and the people are called to trust in God's care. The psalm stresses God's mercy for people who are sinful and weak, and it begins and ends with a call to the people to praise, or "bless," God's mercy and love. Psalm 96, on the other hand, views God as the Lord of all peoples and nations. God's rule is not over only one particular nation, but over the whole earth. This reign is also marked by God's just rule.

Psalm 104 praises God's creative powers. Through the description of God's acts of creation, the poem depicts the Israelite view of the natural world. Each realm of the created order is described, from the heavens above to the foundations of the earth below; from the vegetation in the wilderness to the sea monster, Leviathan, who inhabits the sea.

Notice how these four psalms move out in ever-widening circles. One praises the personal relationship between God and the psalmist. Another praises God for the Lord's actions on behalf of Israel. Still another praises God as the only god, king of all nations. Finally, Psalm 104 praises what God does, not just for humans but for all of creation.

PSALMS 112 AND 113: THE RIGHTEOUS AND THE POOR

These two psalms express a common theme in the psalms: that God exalts the righteous, whether rich or poor.

IN CASE YOU WERE WONDERING

The ash heap (Ps 113:7) is similar to the city dump. People who were ostracized or suffered from a defiling illness, such as oozing sores, were confined to the "ash heap" where they would contaminate no one else.

CARE OF THE POOR

These two psalms describe two groups for whom God had particular compassion: the righteous and the poor. The first psalm, Psalm 112, describes those who deserve what wealth they have. This psalm makes clear that the Israelites believed God blessed the righteous with riches. While Old Testament texts recognize that unjust people could also succeed, this psalm addresses people who deserve their wealth because they are generous to those less fortunate. "They have distributed freely, they have given to the poor" (Ps 112:9).

The second psalm describes God's care of the poor. When these two psalms are read back-to-back, they reveal that the rich person's care of the poor is related to God's concern for the poor. Psalm 113 shows that the Israelites did not believe that everyone who was poor was necessarily sinful. While God could punish the wicked by taking away their wealth, some people suffered poverty through no fault of their own.

We have previously noted that Israelite authors loved to use irony. Here we see irony being used in the psalms: the poor person, who had been ostracized to the ash heap, now sits with royalty, and the barren woman becomes a mother.

Because the Israelites had faith that God would save the righteous and punish the wicked, they confidently prayed to God to relieve their suffering, especially when they felt that they did not deserve what they were suffering.

Psalms 3, 5–7, 38, and 55–60: Israel Cries Out to God

Now we turn to the psalms of lament, the prayers in which Israel asks for God's help. While you have several psalms of lament to look at here, remember that lament psalms are by far the most common type of psalm in the book of Psalms.

In Case You Were Wondering

Sheol. This is the Hebrew name for the land of the dead. It is not exactly like heaven or hell. It was a dark place, cut off from God, where most people went when they died. In some psalms, such as Psalms 6 and 55, we see the Israelites' fear of death.

Animals in the psalms. Animals often symbolize enemies. Here they are called "lions" (Ps 57:4).

To "hold someone in derision" (Ps 59:8). This phrase is a way of saying that you think someone is a fool, that you have no respect for that person.

A cup of reeling. When people are exhausted or wounded, they lose their balance, stumble, and can be incoherent; in other words, they act like they are drunk. In Ps 60:3 Israel acts like drunkards, presumably from their wounds and exhaustion.

All those place names. Psalm 60:6–8 contains many place names. Most of them should be familiar, such as Moab, Edom, and Philistia (verse 8). Four of the names refer to Israelite tribes (Gilead, Manasseh, Ephraim, and Judah). Shechem was an important city in the northern kingdom, and the Vale of Succoth was near the Jordan River.

CRYING OUT TO GOD

You may wonder why these are called psalms of lament when so many talk about praising God. Praise is a common element in the psalms of lament. Biblical laments have a fairly standard form, which may stem from how they were used at the temple. There are generally five parts to a psalm of lament:

A cry to God. The poems often begin with a direct cry to Yahweh.

The complaint. This is a vivid description of what the psalmist is suffering.

Expression of trust. The psalmist expresses confidence in God's aid, sometimes by reminding God why there should be a response.

The petition. Here the psalmist explicitly asks for something.

A vow of praise. The psalms often end with the psalmist vowing to praise God in some way, sometimes by returning to the temple and making known God's saving works to the people.

Look at Psalm 3. It has these five parts:

> ‣ The first half of verse 1 has the direct cry to God ("O LORD, how many are my foes!").

> ‣ The second half of verse 1 through verse 2 contains the complaint ("Many are rising against me . . .").

> ‣ Verses 3–6 express the psalmist's trust in God ("But you, O LORD, are a shield around me . . .").

> ‣ Verse 7 has the petition itself ("Rise up, O LORD!).

> ‣ Verse 8 is the vow of praise (". . . May your blessings be on your people!").

I want to start with the vow of praise, because it links up with the last two psalms we read. In those psalms we saw Israel express its view that God does indeed save the poor and the righteous. In these psalms, the singer turns to God in confidence that God will respond; the praise expresses in advance the confidence that the prayer will be heard. At the heart of the laments, then, is the firm belief that God cares.

But don't let the praise distract you. These psalms contain strongly worded complaints about a variety of bad things. In most of them, the speaker asserts or implies that what they are suffering is unjust. Psalm 5, for instance, appeals to God as judge; doing so implies that the psalmist assumes that God will find no reason to punish him or her, and will redirect the punishment to the wicked. While Psalm 7 affirms that God has every right to afflict the wicked, it does so after the psalmist has vowed that *this* suffering is not deserved.

The one exception to the theme of unjust suffering in this group of psalms is Psalm 38. Here the psalmist confesses sin: "I confess my iniquity; I am sorry for my sin" (Ps 38:18). Clearly the singer does so expecting God's forgiveness. While we might think that this confession of sin was common in the psalms, there are only about five such psalms in the whole book.

The psalms of lament show the petitioner praying about many different problems. Sometimes the person suffers illness and fears death, as expressed in Psalms 6 and 38. One of the psalms, Psalm 60, is sung by the whole community during a time of war. It asks God to fight for them: "Give victory with your right hand, and answer us" (Ps 60:5). One of the psalms, Psalm 55, expresses frustration and anger at a friend's betrayal: "It is not enemies who taunt me— I could bear that . . . But it is you, my equal, my companion, my familiar friend" (Ps 55:12-13). Even over the span of 2500 years, we can still identify with the pain of being betrayed by a friend.

One of the most common themes in these lament psalms (and even in some of the psalms of praise) is the complaint about the "enemy," the "wicked," the "foe." As you have seen, rarely does this mean a national enemy; in this group of psalms, only Psalm 60 refers to a national enemy. The enemies oppose the psalmist, set traps for him or her, and taunt or mock him or her. Most of the time the term seems to imply someone within the psalmist's own community, such as a rival. The psalm also reflects a common human experience: that some people who undeservedly succeed enjoy the failure of their rivals. More than anything, the psalmist prays for vindication, that is, that God will both reward the one praying and punish his or her enemies.

Psalm 58 contains a particularly colorful description of what the psalmist wishes on the enemies:

> O God, break the teeth in their mouths;
> tear out the fangs of the young lions, O LORD!
> Let them vanish like water that runs away;
> like grass let them be trodden down and wither.
> Let them be like the snail that dissolves into slime;
> like the untimely birth that never sees the sun. (Ps 58:6–8)

This psalm vividly expresses the psalmist's anger.

The Use of the Psalms in the New Testament

The Psalms were very popular among Jewish communities of the Roman period. For example, they are one of the best-attested Old Testament books among the Dead Sea Scrolls. Similarly, they are one of the most quoted Scriptural texts in the New Testament.

One compelling example of the use of earlier poetry is the parallel between Hannah's song praising God for removing her barrenness in 1 Samuel 2:1–10, and Mary's song of praise for conceiving Jesus in Luke 1:46–55 (sometimes called the *Magnificat*). Both poems use ironic imagery of the weak prevailing over the strong. As part of that imagery, both include references to military might, and neither talks much about pregnancy, childbirth, children, fertility or other expected topics. The parallels are so acute that most scholars would assert that the author of the Lukan text used Hannah's prayer as a model. What makes the parallel so interesting is the irony of Luke's gospel. The problem for Hannah was that she was barren; her conception is a miracle. In one sense, Mary's problem is that she shouldn't be pregnant (she has not yet known a man), and yet, by using words that echo Hannah's, the author signals that this conception is also miraculous.

Another use of Psalms prominent in both Matthew 27:46 and Mark 15:34, depicts Jesus praying Psalm 22 from the cross. In the gospel texts it says, "At three o'clock Jesus cried out with a loud voice . . . 'My God, my God, why have you forsaken me?'" (Mark 15:34). In the Bible, the first line of a psalm is its title. This means that the gospel writer wants us to think about the meaning of the whole psalm at the point of Jesus' death on the cross.

You can probably see many elements in the psalm which have parallels in the life of Jesus: his unjust suffering, the taunting by the enemies, and the division of his clothes. The psalm was not written as a prophecy of Christ (in fact some elements of the psalm contrast with the life of Jesus), but this reuse of the psalm shows that a psalm's meaning is not just limited to its original setting. Those who continued to use the psalms did so because they saw their own lives reflected there.

When Jesus prays the psalm, however, it is more than a musical interlude in the midst of his death scene. The New Testament text is saying something theologically. It may strike Christians as odd that Jesus, who is God after all, would pray a lament that accuses God of abandoning him. While there is not space here to explain how this conveys the fully human nature of Jesus, I want to note that on the cross, Jesus himself takes up the prayer of lament. At that moment, which for Christians marks the transition from the Old Covenant before Christ to the New Covenant after Christ, Jesus prays an individual lament. What the text asserts by recounting this is that it is still appropriate, in fact God-given and Christ-confirmed, to pray laments.

This particular lament ends with an expanded vow of praise. This turning notes that God's salvation reaches to the "ends of the earth" (Ps 22.27) and to all ages (Ps 22:30-31). The praise of God is linked here, not just to God as creator, as we saw earlier in Psalm 104, but more specifically to God who hears the cry of the poor, the afflicted, and the suffering, and saves them.

PSALMS 137 AND 126: TO MORDOR AND BACK AGAIN

Have you read or seen *The Lord of the Rings*? In this trilogy, the good hobbits must go into the very heart of the kingdom of an evil power in order to destroy a powerful ring.

Psalm 137 was written by an exile in Babylon. He has been forced to live in the company of his bitter enemies. The poem asks what kind of prayer is fitting when you're exiled from Jerusalem and the temple no longer stands.

Psalm 126 expresses the incredible joy of those who finally get to leave this land. It reminds me of the songs sung in the *Wizard of Oz* when the two bad witches are killed.

In Case You Were Wondering

The Edomites, neighbors of Judah, rejoiced when Jerusalem fell. Israelites were especially upset by the reaction of the Edomites.

The Negeb is a dry desert south of Jerusalem. It has some springs or "watercourses" in the midst of the dry land.

Sheaves are bundles of grain brought in at harvest time.

From Sorrow to Joy

The first psalm is one of my favorites. I can hear the voice of this ancient poet struggling with the question, "How do I live in this land?" He has been asked to perform one of the temple songs for a Babylonian audience while living in Exile, but he queries, "How could I sing the LORD's song in a foreign land?" Remember, these were songs sung in temple liturgies in Jerusalem. Is it right to sing them in a foreign land? Are these songs merely forms of entertainment that can be sung anywhere, as if nothing had happened?

His sweet memory of Zion is mixed with anger. The final three verses of the poem express his raw emotion.

Happy shall they be who take your little ones
and dash them against the rock! (Ps 137:9).

While the image of revenge that he paints is abhorrent, we hear his anger and frustration. He expresses his desire for a just judgment on those who have killed the children of Jerusalem.

I think it is important to recognize the experience behind Psalm 137 before turning to Psalm 126. Unless we understand what was lost, we might think that Psalm 126 was written by some overly pious person. As you will see in a later chapter, the rebuilding of the temple in Jerusalem was the fulfillment of a dream to the exiles. It was all they had hoped for since the day of its destruction. It was a hope that seemed impossible because of the strength of Babylon. In this psalm you can hear the joy of those who had once "sowed in tears" and "gone out weeping" (Ps 126: 5 and 6). For them, the return was a dream come true.

The Bible in the CHRISTIAN TRADITION

Psalms in the Life of the Church

Psalms have always been an important part of the prayer life of Christians. Early prayer books included the psalms. One important prayer tradition within the Church has been a book of prayers called the Liturgy of the Hours or the Divine Office. This is a cycle of prayers, which, in its fullest form, fills the whole day. It was developed in the early Church and became part of the devotional life in monasteries. The Psalms are at the core of the Divine Office, and many people today observe a shortened form of the Office, which includes the psalms, as part of their personal spirituality.

Today many Christians hear the Psalms in the context of a Sunday liturgy. Some Christian churches use a lectionary. The *lectionary* is a schedule of readings shared by various churches and denominations. In the Catholic version of the lectionary, for instance, parts of psalms are proclaimed between the first and second readings.

One of the problems today, however, is that many people do not read or pray the psalms outside of Mass. If you look at the readings in a Catholic lectionary for a given Sunday, you will notice that usually it does not include whole psalms. Instead, verses have been chosen to highlight the theme for that particular liturgy. As a result, often the verses that are left out are those that contain some of the strong lament language, thus giving the impression that the psalms are primarily hymns of praise.

The lectionary assumes that people read the Bible outside of the context of liturgy. If Christians rely only on the liturgy for their knowledge of the psalms, they miss a fruitful source for a variety of prayers. But if the psalms are read and prayed outside of Mass, then, when they are sung or chanted in the Liturgy of the Word, they mean even more.

SONG OF SONGS

There are two other books of poetry in the Old Testament: the Song of Songs (also known as the Song of Solomon) and Lamentations. Lamentations contains five poems mourning the fall of Jerusalem. We will look at those in the chapter on responses to the Exile. Song of Songs, one of the most interesting books in the Old Testament, contains love poetry.

Long a subject of debate, scholars today still do not agree as to its exact purpose or structure. The book itself is about love and sexuality. There are a variety of speakers in the book, most prominently a female, a male, and a chorus of female voices. But it is not clear if the book is a unified whole or simply a collection of discrete poems whose divisions are not obvious. Some of you may have Bibles whose translations designate which of these options is used. It does make a difference on how one reads the text.

If the book is a unified whole (the NAB translates it as a drama), then you can read all of the poems by the female speaker together to arrive at a composite

Traditional Authors of Biblical Material

Within both Jewish and Christian traditions, people associated certain texts with certain authors. For example, because later biblical texts refer to the Pentateuch as "the books of Moses," Moses was attributed as the author of the Pentateuch. In a similar way, David became the author of the psalms by virtue of the notice "A Psalm of (for, to, or by) David."

Wisdom traditions developed around Solomon. In 1 Kings, God tells him to ask for anything, at which point Solomon says that he wants wisdom. This text associates Solomon with wisdom traditions. The association is picked up in Proverbs (1:1; 10:1; and 25:1), Song of Songs (especially 1:1, but see references to Solomon in 1:5; 3:7; 3:9; 3:11; 8:11; and 8:12), as well as Qoheleth who, in 1:1, is supposed to be a son of David who became king (thus, Solomon). Most scholars view these titles to be as late as the ones ascribing psalms to David. The historical notes relating some of the psalms to events in the life of David are an early example of this form of interpretation.

From these biblical texts the following tradition arose: Solomon, it is said, wrote Song of Songs when he was a young man (remember his multiple wives). He wrote Proverbs as a mature man, and Ecclesiastes as an old man, reflecting back on his life.

Although there are some Christian and Jewish groups today who still hold that these traditions are true, the fact is that our earliest copies of these texts list no authors. These are probably later traditions, reflecting later interpretive traditions.

whole. When you do this, she is an unmarried girl, still living in her parent's home. She is searching for opportunities to meet her lover clandestinely, and she describes, in language more graphic than perhaps your translations let on, some of their intimate encounters. In other words, it's a book celebrating unmarried sexuality.

As you can imagine, early Jews and Christians had trouble with this plain meaning of the text. Even today some of you may be surprised that there might be such literature in the Bible. We will look briefly at both the attitude toward sexual intimacy in Israel's immediate environment and also at some classic interpretive traditions of this material.

Erotic Poetry in the Ancient Near East

In a word, there is a lot of sexually explicit poetry found throughout the ancient Near East. Most of it describes the sexual encounters of the divinities, and, as such, does so with a stress on the grandiosity of these episodes. Therefore, when it describes a male god's body parts, you can correctly imagine that the texts emphasize size, potency, and endurance. They are also quite blunt in talking about goddess genitalia in intimate detail. In addition to divine love, Egyptian literature includes poems describing human love. These are closest in form to the material in the Song of Songs.

Remember that these cultures were not ones that believed celibacy was anything to be proud of. They were certainly concerned about limiting female sexual behavior, so that they could control issues of paternity. But the goal of every person was to be married, and the assumption was that marriage is defined by sexual activity. The fact that Jeremiah, for example, was unmarried was a way the author marked him as odd.

There is also nothing in the Hebrew Bible against birth control or noncoital sexual acts between males and females. Onan, the son of Judah, is killed after spilling his seed on the ground in Genesis 38, but that is because it was his legal duty to impregnate Tamar. There are texts scattered throughout the Old Testament that presume sexual pleasure is a good thing, a gift from God. In light of these presumptions about sexuality, a collection of poems in praise of human sexuality is not so surprising.

The Song of Songs as an Allegory

One of the effects of Israel's interaction with Greek culture was Israel's development of a more dualistic worldview. Part of that dualism was the assumption that spiritual things are "better" or "higher" than physical things. By the Roman period, when both rabbinic Judaism and early Christianity arose, celibacy and other forms of asceticism were a spiritual practice of many different religious and philosophical movements.

As part of this shift, Jews, Christians, and even "pagans" found it necessary to interpret their earlier traditions in light of their later worldview. For example, Greek and Roman philosophers read the works of Hesiod and Homer, which contained narratives of the gods, not as literal descriptions of events, but rather as allegories of philosophical principles. Using this approach, a god of love, such as Aphrodite, became a symbol for human passions, while a god of war, such as Athena, represented anger. Fights among the gods were a symbolic way to describe battles within the human psyche.

Allegorical interpretation of biblical material can be found among both Jews and Christians of this period. For example, Augustine's allegorical interpretation of Genesis reads the seven days of creation as an allegory for the order of nature. Thus, scholars were able to deal with the "scandalous" behavior of biblical characters by viewing them as symbols for human nature or other such things.

Interpretations of the Song of Songs from the Roman period often used this same technique. The book was read as an extended allegory. For Jews it was an allegory of God's love for Israel, while for Christians it could be seen as a symbol of God's love for the Church. There are a variety of allegorical interpretations of the Song of Songs, but each proceeds from this general approach toward reading.

The allegorical interpretations for the Song of Songs have had a more lasting impact than other instances of allegory, probably because the sexually explicit material remained problematic for some people. Knowing this history of the text's interpretation is important, but it does not mean that today we cannot go back to appreciating what was probably the original intention of the material: to explore the human experience of sexuality.

Read the whole book, and don't sweat the details. As the prologue has pointed out, people have spent their lives trying to unravel the structure of the book. In addition, it deals with topics for which every culture has pet phrases and colloquialisms: love and sex. So instead of worrying about the details, let the mood of the poetry sweep you up.

SONG OF SONGS: IN PRAISE OF LOVE

The poetry in the Song of Songs is moving. It moves audiences today, just as it did in the Middle Ages, in the Patristic Period, and in the time of its composition. In fact, to me, one of the best testimonies to its effectiveness is the fact that people throughout the ages have worried about people reading this book and "getting the wrong idea." If the poetry weren't so good, no one would be worried. I think every human person can relate to the desire that the book attests to, even the forbidden desire. Most of us can imagine trying to describe to someone else why this other person is so attractive. We can even relate to the knowledge that a passion we feel might be dangerous. How wonderful, then, that this book is among the collection of sacred texts; it is an affirmation that something so powerful in human experience comes from God.

The text is full of double *entendres*: words or phrases that mean one thing on the surface, but mean something else within a particular setting. For example, the phrase "a bun in the oven" can simply refer to part of dinner, but it can also mean that someone is pregnant. Because double *entendres* are so culturally defined, they can be hard to catch. For example, the palm tree is associated with the fertility goddess Ishtar who is the subject of many erotic texts. References to honey are found in other ancient near-eastern erotic poetry as a reference to female bodily fluids that increase during arousal. Even the locked door into which the lover puts his hand may be more than a lock.

One prominent feature in the poems that we have trouble appreciating today are the descriptions of the lovers' beauty in 4:1–11; 5:10–16; 6:4–7; and 7:2–6. I don't know about you, but if someone I loved told me I had a nose like a tower in Lebanon, I'm not sure I'd take that as a compliment.

There are a couple of things to remember as we read these texts. First, beauty has always been culturally defined. At one time in Europe, thin women were considered sickly and undesirable. Men wore makeup and wigs. In some parts of Africa in traditional societies, women scar their faces to make themselves more beautiful. There is no universal standard for beauty or modesty or charm or any other attribute that can be applied across cultures.

Second, notice the grandiosity of some of the elements to which the lovers are compared: towers, battlements, animals, columns, and so on. Such grandiose imagery fits nicely with the poems praising divine love. This may be typical language that appears in this genre of poetry.

The poems also have a fair degree of ambiguity. On the one hand, they do not chastise the lovers for trying to be together. In fact, they seem to look forward to that moment of consummation. On the other hand, there is also the fear in 8:8–9 that the girl is too young for marriage, probably something many a brother, father, or cousin felt watching their eleven- or twelve-year-old sister/daughter/cousin marry. There are also warnings throughout the text against stirring up love.

> I adjure you, O daughters of Jerusalem, by the gazelles or the wild does: do not stir up or awaken love until it is ready! (2:7; see also 3:5 and 8:4)

This warning is not as clear in the Hebrew as it is in the English translations. In Hebrew the text merely reads, "Do not stir up or awaken love until . . . ," leaving the point of proper time unexpressed.

Rather than read these warnings as some sort of taboo against premarital sex, it is probably better to see them as an awareness of the power that sexual love has. Anyone who has ever felt such passion could attest to that power. We all know people who have done things they never would have done because they were doing it "for love." There is also a vulnerability and intimacy in this kind of love, even today. Imagine how much more that would have been true in a culture where women were veiled and kept from interacting with males.

This sentiment is expressed best in 8:6:

> Set me as a seal upon your heart, as a seal upon your arm; for love is strong as death, passion fierce as the grave. Its flashes are flashes of fire, a raging flame. (Song 8:6)

This verse probably sums up the warning about passion. It is dangerous, not just to the young or the unmarried, but to everyone. In one way, this danger is very real, especially for women. The curse on Eve in Genesis 3:16 expresses a similar view. It talks about the fact that women will have "pain" in childbirth, and yet they will still desire their husbands. In other words, even though women know they can die in pregnancy and childbirth, they still desire sexual contact.

This poem is not just about passion, however. It moves beyond the physical dangers of intercourse to the emotional vulnerability it brings. Isn't it amazing that, even though sexual standards and cultural expressions have changed over the years, this biblical message about a universal human experience still rings loud and clear!

CONCLUSION: GOD IS PRESENT IN JOY AND SUFFERING

The Israelites believed that God was present in their midst in a very real way. This core belief was represented first and foremost by the national temple. But when that temple was destroyed, the theology of God's presence was maintained through the Israelites' use of psalms.

The Psalms were sung prayers that asserted that God is truly present to those who pray. God cares for and responds to the prayers of those who suffer unjustly, as well as those who seek forgiveness. In addition, God invites the people to bring all of their emotions to their prayer, from joy to anger, from praise to fear, from happiness to despair.

The Song of Solomon is an example of another type of poem: those celebrating sexuality. It shares the Psalms' view that all human experience has its origin in God. It reminds the audience that all aspects of human existence, even sexuality, matter to Yahweh.

FOR REVIEW

1. What is parallelism?

2. What are some common metaphors used in Israelite poetry?

3. What is the book of Psalms?

4. What is a psalm?

5. What are the two basic types of psalms?

6. What is the book of the Song of Solomon?

FOR FURTHER READING

There have been some interesting readings of the psalms that address their importance for contemporary audiences. J. Clinton McCann, *A Theological Introduction to the Book of Psalms: The Psalms as Torah* (Nashville, TN: Abingdon, 1993) introduces the psalms with an eye for how they shape a community of faith. Stephen Breck Reid has written *Listening In: A Multicultural Reading of the Psalms* (Nashville, TN: Abingdon, 1997), and he has edited *Psalms and Practice: Worship, Virtue, and Authority* (Collegeville, MN: Liturgical/Michael Glazier, 2001).

Readable discussions of biblical poetry can be found in James Kugel, *The Idea of Biblical Poetry: Parallelism and Its History* (New Haven, CT: Yale University Press, 1981) and Robert Alter, *The Art of Biblical Poetry* (New York: Basic Books, 1985).

We talked about the psalms as sung prayer. Patrick D. Miller provides a study of biblical prayer within its ancient near-eastern context in *They Cried to the Lord: The Form and Theology of Biblical Prayer* (Minneapolis, MN: Fortress, 1994). William L. Holladay surveys the use of the psalms within Christianity in his book *The Psalms through Three Thousand Years: Prayerbook of a Cloud of Witnesses* (Minneapolis, MN: Fortress, 1993). A collection of essays that deal with their interpretation is *Psalms in Community: Jewish and Christian Textual, Liturgical, and Artistic Traditions,* edited by Harold W. Attridge and Margot E. Fassler (Society of Biblical Symposium series 25; Atlanta, GA: Society of Biblical Literature, 2003). A detailed study of the order of the psalms can be found in Gerald H. Wilson, *The Editing of the Hebrew Psalter* (SBLDS 76; Chico, CA: Scholars Press, 1985).

A book that places the language of the Song of Songs within the context of the Old Testament view of sexuality and love is by Carey Ellen Walsh, *Exquisite Desire: Religion, the Erotic, and the Song of Songs* (Minneapolis, MN: Fortress, 2000). Michael V. Fox compares it to Egyptian love poems in his book *The Song of Songs and the Ancient Egyptian Love Songs* (Madison, WI: University of Wisconsin Press, 1985). For a quick survey of the interpretation of the book, see the entry on the text by E. Ann Matter in *Dictionary of Biblical Interpretation*, edited by John H. Hayes (Nashville, TN: Abingdon, 1999); this two-volume book provides quick surveys to the history of interpretation of every biblical book.

9 THE PROPHETS OF THE DIVIDED MONARCHY

I will put my words in the mouth of the prophet, who shall speak
to them everything that I command.
(Deut 18:18)

CHAPTER OVERVIEW

The aim of this chapter is to help you read the prophets. In order to do this, the chapter will provide the following:

› An explanation of how the Israelites viewed the prophets

› A discussion of what prophets actually did and how they acted

› An examination of the kinds of language the prophets used when they delivered an oracle

› An analysis of a prophetic oracle through a series of questions

In this chapter we will consider two different kinds of materials in the Bible. We will read about the prophet Elijah, which will explain what a prophet is. Then we will look at prophetic oracles, which will demonstrate how prophets spoke.

By the end of this chapter you will not be an expert in the prophets. Frankly, the texts in the books of the prophets are the most difficult material in the Old Testament. My goal is to help you to simply appreciate the prophets and have a better understanding of their main goals.

Defining the Prophets

What Is a Prophet?

You might think that the answer to this question is simple: a prophet is someone who predicts the future. But this is not the biblical understanding of what a prophet is. The Bible defines a *prophet* as a spokesperson for God. As the quote at the beginning of this chapter states, the prophet reports to the community what God speaks to him or her.

Usually the prophets' messages warn the people when they are sinning and tell them how God will punish them if they continue to sin. Sometimes the reports from the prophets describe how God will save the people from present oppression and outline how they should respond to God. It can appear that prophets are predicting the future, because what they warn often comes to pass. But we must always remember that the words of the prophet are God's speech.

We call prophets' speeches *oracles*. An *oracle* is a message from God delivered to the people by a prophet. Prophets can deliver these oracles in many different ways. They can speak them, sing them, or even act them out. We will look at these various ways in more detail later.

Prophets were not necessarily passive mouthpieces. Some prophets argued with God; the Bible says that a few even changed God's mind. Prophets also delivered God's message in ways that their community would best understand. We see prophets adding to their oracles to make God's message clear.

Facing Our Own Problems with the Prophets

It is hard for us today to imagine prophets of old, because we live in a world where prophets are viewed with suspicion. Some might picture them as people who were always ranting and raving, as if they were a little "nuts."

Part of the problem is that we live in a society where people tend to put down those who claim to be prophets. Think about what the most common reactions to the following scenarios might be.

›	Imagine that during a presidential election one of the candidates states that he developed his platform based on conversations he had had with God? How much chance would he have of being elected?

›	Imagine that you are watching a popular courtroom drama on TV. Faced with a difficult case, the judge decides to determine the accused person's guilt by tying her up and throwing her in a river to see if God will save her. How would the television show depict this judge?

▶ Imagine that you are walking down a busy city street, and you see a person with unkempt hair and clothes shouting that he or she talks to Jesus. Do you stop and listen for the word of the prophet? Or do you assume that this person is probably mentally ill (and may even be dangerous)?

▶ Imagine that you meet someone at a party, and there's instant chemistry. You are talking in a quiet corner of the room when this person says, "I talk to God . . ." Do you make a date for the following day?

Even if you personally believe that there are prophets among us today, we live in a culture where those who feel that way are in the minority.

When we read stories about the prophets, we bring our current attitudes with us. We read biblical texts as twenty-first-century Americans, not as sixth-century BCE Israelites, which makes it hard to take the prophets seriously. I can't tell you how many times students have asked me, "Did the prophets *really* talk to God?" We know that many people today doubt this claim of the biblical prophets.

Israel's View of Prophets

In contrast to our culture, the Israelites were very accepting of prophets. They believed that God communicated to the people through the words of a prophet. This attitude toward the prophets was especially strong during the monarchy, when Israelite and Judean kings had prophets as part of their royal administration. What do we know about the Israelite prophets?

Prophetic activity was a social phenomenon. Today when we think about the prophets, we tend to imagine solitary, holy individuals, similar to saints and hermits. We might conclude that what is important for making someone a prophet is their piety. But prophets are not prophets unless they deliver God's message to the people. Having an individual experience of God does not make someone a prophet.

Conversely, prophets are not prophets unless some group recognizes them as prophets. The Israelites knew that people could *think* that they were hearing God's voice but could be mistaken or delusional. They had a couple of ways to explain this phenomenon. First, they might say a god other than Yahweh could be talking to the prophet (remember they did not yet believe that

Yahweh was the only God). Second, they might say someone was possessed by a demon or a "lying spirit." So it was not enough for persons to claim that they had talked to God. The community played a role in determining whether such a claim was true.

Israel had hundreds of prophets. People often think that the only prophets who were around in ancient Israel were the ones named in the Bible. We might imagine a famous prophet, such as Elijah, as a solitary prophet in his day. That is far from the truth. The Bible tells us that there were hundreds of other prophets when Elijah lived, just in the small area around the city of Samaria. So the answer to the question, why didn't the people listen to the prophet? is that they probably did. It just may have been the wrong prophet.

There were many different kinds of prophets. We tend to think that all prophets were alike: they heard God's voice, and they spoke it back to the people. Again, the Bible tells us something quite different. There were different types of prophets. Some worked for the king. Some worked in groups. Some worked at temples. Others were solitary, roaming the country and living off donations. Some were prophets their whole lives, while others were prophets for only a while. Some heard a voice. Others had visions, while still others were "possessed" by a spirit sent from God.

Prophets did more than speak. Because the most common place to hear these oracles today is in church or synagogue services, we tend to think that prophets gave speeches. The Bible, however, describes prophets going into a "frenzy." The texts do not describe this frenzy because they assume that everyone knows what it is. Prophets also acted out oracles in strange and sometimes shocking ways. For example, Ezekiel lies on his side for 430 days to act out the siege of Jerusalem (Ezek 4:5–6), while Isaiah walks around the city naked to demonstrate the coming defeat of Egypt and Ethiopia (Isa 20:1–6). At least some of the oracles were sung.

Other cultures also had prophets. To think that only Israel had prophets is far from the truth. All ancient near-eastern countries had prophets. Often these prophets acted in much the same way as Israelite prophets. Prophets are a common part of many cultures even today. For instance, Southeast Asian communities often have a prophetic figure called a *shaman*. We see the same figure among tribal groups in Africa and among some Native American groups. When we consider the prophetic figures in these cultures, we find that Israel's prophets shared many things in common (their role in society, group approval, problems determining who is a true prophet) with other cultures even today.

Prophecy in the Ancient Near East

The law of the prophet in Deuteronomy 18:9–22 contrasts the legitimate prophet with other types of intermediaries. However, other biblical texts have a wider definition of prophetic activity than is found in Deuteronomy. The debate about how one defines a "prophet" extends to today. Biblical scholars do not agree on how to distinguish prophets from other intermediaries and religious functionaries.

In both Israel and Mesopotamia there were groups of people who received visions and delivered messages from the divine realm. The evidence for prophets in the ancient Near East is sporadic, but widespread. For example, there are letters from the city of Mari in Mesopotamia, dating to the eighteenth century BCE, which contain some prophetic oracles. There are a few neo-Assyrian collections of oracles. Everyone agrees that these were prophets.

There were also religious personnel in both areas who practiced forms of divination. Divination involves the use of objects and/or natural signs to determine the divine will. In Mesopotamia this included "reading" the livers of sacrificial animals, observing the arrangement of the stars, consulting the dead, and even shaking arrows, presumably because their configuration revealed a communication from the gods. The book of Deuteronomy condemns divination of this sort, but many other cultures accept it as part of prophecy.

Even so, Israelite priests used the sacred lots, the Urim and the Thumim, in a similar way. Often ancient near-eastern diviners were part of the official religious system of their nation. In some Israelite texts, the Urim and Thumim were wielded by the high priest; in Babylon, liver omens were deciphered in the context of sacrificial ritual.

This raises the question about the location of Israelite prophets. Certainly many of them worked outside the temple system. But did temple personnel include some prophets? While many biblical scholars would answer with a firm no, others point out the ritual setting of a variety of biblical prophets. Samuel was part of the temple at Shiloh. Elijah makes a sacrifice when he wins the contest with the prophets of Baal. Isaiah seems to be in the temple when he is called by God.

There were both male and female prophets. Although the collections of prophetic oracles were all from men, other biblical texts talk about female prophets, such as Miriam, Deborah, and Huldah.

Some prophets performed miracles. This is especially true for Elijah and Elisha. We see this same thing in the prophets of other countries as well. In fact, one biblical scholar renames these miracles, "prophetic acts of power." These miracles pop up especially in times of crisis, when a prophet is being ignored. The miracle demonstrates to the community that the person is a true prophet, with a reliable connection to the divine realm.

Prophets Spoke to a Nation

If there is only one thing that you learn in this chapter, let it be this: the prophets spoke to their own community about issues facing them in their own day. To be sure, sometimes these oracles had elements that looked to the future, often to a happier future, but, even then, the first audience for these oracles was ancient Israel.

This clay model of a liver from Babylon, circa 1830–1530 BCE, is inscribed with omens and magic formulas used by diviners.

Prophecy flourished during the monarchy. These men and women were the ones most able to critique kings and other powerful members of Israelite society. They sometimes were the voice of the poor and oppressed. They could tell a king when he sinned, or they could advise him that his public policies were not in accord with God's will.

I do not doubt that there were prophets who delivered oracles to common people about common things, such as their crops, their children, their business, and so on. But the oracles that have been preserved are those dealing with issues facing the nation as a whole. Why? Because these were the oracles delivered to people who knew how to write and who had the means to pass on written collections of oracles. These oracles also had a wider significance.

Overwhelmingly, then, the audience of the biblical prophets were the kings, priests, and other elites within Israel and Judah. Their topics dealt with such things as national security, economic policies, government stability, military decisions, and so on. Reading the prophets can be more like reading the editorial page of a major newspaper than reading the meditations of the saints.

Because these prophets were some of the most important, learned, and respected people of their day, their words were valued. Some of their oracles were understood as having a lasting meaning: that is, while they addressed events in their own day, they also hinted at events in days far beyond their own. We see this in a book such as Isaiah: the first part has oracles from Isaiah, but the second part has oracles from a much later time, written as if Isaiah were still alive.

The oracles that most often were understood as having a lasting meaning were the oracles of hope. We will see that the prophets described a glorious future for Israel. We also know that this future never came to pass. Instead, they were preserved as visions of a blessed future God held out for the people.

READING ABOUT THE PROPHETS: THE ELIJAH STORIES

The first four passages relate stories about the prophet Elijah. Israelites considered Elijah to be one of the greatest prophets who ever lived. The Bible does not contain a collection of his oracles, however. Instead, we have stories about Elijah imbedded in 1 and 2 Kings, as well as 2 Chronicles. It is wise to start an investigation into prophecy with these stories, because they can help us understand what prophets did, how they lived, and how they interacted with both royalty and the common people.

Elijah prophesied in the northern kingdom of Israel during the reign of King Ahab, whom we read about in the previous chapter. One of the strongest kings in Israel's history, Ahab had married a Phoenician princess, Jezebel. Jezebel wanted to make the worship of her gods, Baal and Asherah, the national religion of Israel, and so she and Ahab outlawed the worship of Yahweh. Elijah was a prophet of Yahweh during this time. These four stories reflect the religious conflict of his day.

I KINGS 17:1–24: ELIJAH IS INTRODUCED

The first story introduces Elijah. From its abrupt beginning, it is clear that the author presumes that the audience knows who Elijah is.

IN CASE YOU WERE WONDERING

Sidon is a major city in Phoenicia.

A cake was not a dessert. It was small bread, such as a biscuit.

Meal is another word for "flour."

Looking Closely at the Text

1. After God commands Elijah to leave Israel, how does Elijah find food?

2. What do we know about the woman in Zarephath?

3. Why does she feed Elijah?

4. Why does he demand to be fed?

Elijah Performs Miracles

This story seems to start in midstream. Although it briefly mentions where Elijah is from, we know nothing else about him. It presumes that the audience knows who he is. What is clear from the beginning of the chapter is that Elijah opposes King Ahab, and that there is a severe and widespread drought in the Levant.

The account calls Elijah a "man of God" (17:24), another term for a prophet. But notice he is not a prophet because he delivers oracles to people. We do not see him telling the widow how to live, when to plant crops, or even what God's will is. He is also not known as a "man of God" because he goes to the temple a lot or performs other acts of piety. He is recognized as a prophet because of the way that God acts for him (feeding him with the help of ravens) and through him (saving the widow and her son). In other words, he is a man of God because of his connection to God.

The miracles highlight this connection. Elijah performs no miracles until God first performs one for him. The account of God feeding Elijah is the backdrop for the account of Elijah and the widow. Just as God feeds the prophet, so too does God feed the widow through the prophet.

The aim of these miracles is to build people's faith in the prophet and his or her god. The woman, who is not Israelite, believes in Elijah, and therefore in his god, because of the miracles he performs.

1 Kings 18:1–46: The Contest with the Prophets of Baal

In Case You Were Wondering

Mount Carmel. A site located close to the northern coast of Israel. It was a very fertile area, heavily dependent on rainfall, and so gravely affected by the drought.

These jars and pots date from the tenth to eighth century BCE. They were excavated from "Area G" in the City of David, southeast of Jerusalem.

A prophetic frenzy. Limping or dancing, crying out, and cutting oneself could all be elements in a prophetic frenzy, especially in Phoenicia.

Jars of water. The jars of water would have been large storage jars, each capable of holding several gallons of water.

Jezreel. This rich Israelite city was located north of Samaria.

Looking Closely at the Text

Note the references to water, rain, and drought in the chapter. Why are these references so prominent in a story featuring Elijah and the prophets of Baal?

A Prophetic Contest, or, Who Will God Vote Off the Show?

Have you ever watched a "reality" show, where groups of people are placed in bizarre situations and compete to see who will survive the ordeal? Well, think of this story as the original "Survivor." There is a contest between two sides. One side has 450 people, and the other side has one; but the only one voting is the God of Israel. And the losers don't just have to leave the set; they are killed. Now that's excitement!

The contest has impossible terms: calling down fire from heaven in the middle of a drought. The most probable source for this heavenly fire would be lightning, which is a rare occurrence during a drought. But Elijah ups the ante by pouring gallons and gallons of stored up, precious water over his altar. If he loses, he has just wasted a significant part of the city's water supply.

But, of course, Elijah is not going to lose, because, although this looks like a contest between prophets, this contest is really between gods: Baal and Yahweh. The irony in this contest is that Baal is a storm god. He's called the "Rider of the Clouds," and throws thunderbolts as his weapons. It looks as if he'd have this contest locked up—except for one thing: he doesn't show up. Elijah taunts the other prophets: maybe Baal's sleeping, maybe he's on vacation. In other words, maybe he's not worth worshipping.

This chapter shows the effect of royal sponsorship on the prophets. Kings and queens could decide which prophets could work in their land and which could not. The people of Israel are the target audience: who will they believe? Who will they follow? The miracle is designed to convince them what to believe. The end of the drought at the close of the story makes the people the real winners, as the glimpse into the life of the poor during the drought in chapter 17 made so clear.

Elijah kills the 450 prophets of Baal. I am not able to picture that part of the story. First, quite simply, the feat would be impossible. Did they all just line up and let him kill them? In other words, it was another miracle. It would be nice to read this metaphorically: they "died" in the sense that they now worshipped Yahweh and "died" to their old way of life. But I don't think that's what the author meant. These prophets, and their queen, were enemies of the nation of Israel and enemies of Yahweh. In the ancient view, they deserved to be killed in order to preserve the nation.

Explaining False Prophecy

Every society that accepts the legitimacy of prophetic claims still must deal with the issue of false prophets. The fact is that people can claim to be prophets who are not. The claim to have a prophetic revelation can carry some authority in a given society, so one can see that the temptation to claim to be a prophet might be great.

There are a number of ways that these societies deal with the question of false prophecy. They acknowledge that someone could be making a false claim, but they also note that some people can be deranged or mentally impaired. Many societies believe that people who are suitable to be prophets, because of some natural openness to the other world, are also susceptible to demon possession. They may believe that they are speaking for a great god, when, in fact, they are possessed by a demon.

The law of the prophet in Deuteronomy 18:9–22 suggests two similar explanations for false prophets. Either the prophet is simply lying (God did not speak to him or her), or the prophet is prophesying for another god.

The story of Micaiah ben Imlah in 1 Kings 22 offers another alternative. In this story, the kings of Israel and Judah are deciding whether or not to go to war. They have assembled about four hundred prophets, who all of whom tell them that they should wage the war. They decide to consult one more prophet, Micaiah, a man who is not supportive of the northern king. When he arrives on the scene, he tells them that they will lose. One of the prophets who is in favor of the war challenges him. Micaiah's response is surprising: he claims that Yahweh, who wants the king to die in battle, has sent a "lying spirit" to the four hundred prophets so that they would tell the king that he would be victorious! This story makes God the deliberate source of false prophecy.

1 Kings 19:1–18: Elijah on Horeb

This story immediately follows the previous one. It depicts parallels between Elijah and Moses.

In Case You Were Wondering

Beersheba is at the southern boundary of Judah. Elijah enters the same wilderness that the Israelites had wandered after leaving Egypt.

A mantle is a cloak.

Looking Closely at the Text

How many parallels between Elijah and Moses can you find in this material?

Sheer Silence

The first part of this chapter compares Elijah to Moses. Moses spent forty years in the wilderness, and Elijah spends forty days and nights. Both prophets receive a message from God at Horeb or Sinai, and both of these prophets experience wind, earthquake, and fire while on this mountain. Can you find other parallels?

These similarities only make the main difference between the two experiences more apparent. While Moses heard God's message in the midst of the wind, earthquake, and fire, Elijah does not! Throughout Israelite literature, some sort of cosmic storm, with wind, lightning, and earth-shaking thunder, accompanies God's appearance. At the very least, Yahweh's appearance is associated with a "glow" or fire.

Elijah finds God in "sheer silence." This word is very rare in Hebrew, and you will find it rendered differently in various translations. We're not sure if it means absolute silence, or a very small sound, such as a whisper. What we are sure about is that it is quiet, and rather unlike Yahweh, who usually makes a grand entrance. Why does the account make such a point of this element of Elijah's experience? Is it to highlight that Elijah is different from Moses? Is it to convey the idea that God is found in unexpected places? The text never says, and the uniqueness of this element makes it hard to interpret.

The first part of the story gives the impression that what is central to it is Elijah's personal experience of God. But, as you see, this spiritual experience has national significance. Elijah, and his successor Elisha, will validate the leaders of the revolution who will get rid of Ahab's evil dynasty. Elisha will

The Bible in the CHRISTIAN TRADITION

Prophecy, Mysticism, and Revelation

Some of what the Old Testament accepts as legitimate religious activities remains suspect even by modern Christians. For example, what would you think if the Catholic Church picked the next pope by casting lots? There is a whole tradition of Christian theological discussion concerning the legitimacy of lot-throwing.

Although the New Testament attests to the continuation of prophets in the early Church (see, for example, Romans 12:6 and 1 Corinthians 12:10), the fact is, different contemporary denominations have different approaches to the Christian prophets. Some of the Pentecostal churches are more open to certain elements of prophetic activity, such as healings and channeling the spiritual world (for example, by speaking in tongues). Others, while admitting the possibility of prophecy, have no official place for prophets. Notice, for instance, how the word *possession* usually connotes demonic possession, not a possession by a good spirit sent by God.

However, while certain branches of Judaism would state that prophecy ceased with Daniel, Christians remain open to the phenomenon. In some ways, the Christian mystical tradition has preserved elements of the prophetic tradition. Christian mystics sought a more direct experience of God, often by living a life of piety, prayer, and asceticism. This direct experience of God mirrors the direct revelations in the biblical prophets. Sometimes these experiences included visual and auditory elements. Some of the mystics recorded their visions, much like the recorded oracles of the biblical prophets.

Like the prophets, the mystics maintained that the revelations that they had received were not for their personal benefit, but were meant to help the Church at large. Sometimes, the experience included messages for the Church. At the very least, these mystical experiences were supposed to lead to a more moral, self-sacrificing life.

You could compare some of the visions of the Christian mystics with biblical prophets. You might look, for example, at the mystical visions of Joachim of Fiore or the revelations of Julian of Norwich. Would you consider these mystics to be Christian prophets?

Today, the mystical tradition is not as pervasive as it once was, but there have been various apparitions, particularly of Mary, which have included messages for the Church, such as those at Lourdes, Fatima, or at the shrine of Our Lady of Guadalupe. Are these messages modern-day prophetic revelations or something else? How would you make the connection between the biblical prophetic experiences and these apparitions, or how would you explain how they are distinct?

succeed Elijah and anoint both Jehu, a very zealous worshipper of Yahweh, and a foreign king, Hazael of Aram, who will be an ally to Israel's revolutionaries. Notice that Elijah is called to address a concrete, historical problem. His actions, performed on behalf of God, will benefit the faithful and oppressed among the Israelites. Although Elijah finds God in the "sheer silence," the text reveals that God is not silent at all when the people suffer.

2 KINGS 2:1–14: THE ASCENT OF ELIJAH

THE TIES THAT BIND

Elijah anoints Elisha as his successor, but most of the intervening stories tell of various wars fought by Ahab and his son.

The Enoch Traditions

Look up the name "Enoch" in the Old Testament and you won't find much. Outside of the genealogies in Genesis and 1 Chronicles, there is no reference to him. However, during the Roman period, a lively interest in this biblical character arose.

Outside of the genealogy at the beginning of Luke's gospel, there are two references to Enoch in the New Testament. Hebrews 11:5 reflects what we know about him from Genesis, that is, an example of someone who is rewarded for his faith by ascending into heaven: "By faith Enoch was taken so that he did not experience death; and 'he was not found, because God had taken him.' For it was attested before he was taken away that 'he had pleased God.'" Jude 1:14, on the other hand, quotes a prophecy of Enoch as if it were scripture, a prophecy not found in the Bible.

That quotation in Jude can be found in one of three books of prophecy by Enoch that were circulating during the Roman period. Although we do not know when the final form of these books took shape, fragments of the Enoch text have been found among the Dead Sea Scrolls. These pseudepigraphical books utilize the figure of Enoch as the mouthpiece for fictional oracles and revelations that addressed various elements of Hellenistic Judaism.

These Enoch traditions were held in high esteem throughout the early centuries of the Common Era, including their depiction of the fall of the angels. Some of the New Testament writers and early Christian theologians reflect the Enoch traditions. Although these traditions fell out of favor in the western Church, they remained in high esteem in Ethiopia. Recent renewed attention to the Enoch traditions has helped biblical scholars trace their influence on ancient Christianity and Judaism.

IN CASE YOU WERE WONDERING

"Let me inherit a double share . . ." The eldest son inherited twice as much as his younger brothers. What is significant here is that Elisha is not referring to Elijah's property, but to his "spirit," or prophetic power.

LOOKING CLOSELY AT THE TEXT

1. What further parallels can you find between Elijah and Moses or Elisha and Joshua?

2. How does Elijah die?

ELIJAH'S ASCENT INTO HEAVEN

This chapter provides even more parallels between Moses and Elijah. Both prophets can part large rivers. Both anoint a successor. Most importantly, both die in exactly the same place, just across the Jordan River from the city of Jericho.

Within Jewish tradition, both men also had similar deaths, what today we call *ascension*, which means that a person is taken up bodily into heaven. Their bodies are not separated from their spirits when they die. In the ancient world, ascension was believed to be a reward for righteousness or special service to the gods. Such persons did not have to suffer the bodily pains of a real death.

Jewish tradition holds that only three people ascended into heaven: Enoch, Moses, and Elijah. The case for the first two is not so clear. The tradition about Enoch is based on Genesis 5:24, "Enoch walked with God; then he was no more, because God took him." For Moses, the fact that his burial site was unknown was taken as a sign that he had ascended bodily into heaven (Deuteronomy 34:6).

The story of Elijah has no such ambiguity. It was not a random tornado that picked him up and blew his body some distance. In fact, the chapter later states that some of the prophets thought this was what had happened and offered to look for his body (2 Kgs 2:16–17). But Elisha knew that the "whirlwind" was really God's way of bringing Elijah to heaven. The text says that Elisha even saw chariots and horses, as if God had sent a limousine down to get Elijah.

Elijah remains a central figure for both Jewish and Christian traditions. According to Jewish tradition, Elijah is supposed to return at the end of the world. In traditional Passover celebrations, an extra place is set "for Elijah," just in case this is the year he returns. In the New Testament, the account of the Transfiguration (told in Matthew 17:1–8, Mark 9:2–8, and Luke 9:28–36) depicts an appearance by Moses and Elijah to Jesus, while he is praying on a mountain in the wilderness, probably to foreshadow Jesus' own ascension into heaven.

READING PROPHETIC BOOKS

This section of the textbook is organized differently than the previous material. We are going to look at some prophetic books which are collections of oracles. They don't read like a story, so they require a different reading strategy: you have to unravel the puzzle of the oracles.

You may be wondering why I don't just tell you what they are saying. Let me tell you a story of my own. I hated the prophets! When I started my doctoral program, I said I was interested in everything but the prophets. It was not because I hadn't had classes on the prophets: I had studied them several times. But every time I had studied the prophets, a teacher told me what they were saying, and I memorized that and passed the tests with flying colors. Then I promptly forgot everything I learned. In those classes, I didn't really need to read the prophets myself; reading them was only confusing. I just had to focus on what the teacher told me the prophets were saying. I ended up concluding that the prophets were confusing and boring.

Years later I had an instructor who taught me how to understand what the prophets were saying. I finally realized that the prophets were brilliant, creative intellectuals. Their use of poetry is amazing, and the way they use irony is masterful. Their play with images, their shocking actions—all these devices make the oracles fun to read. But first you have to know how to read them.

What I will do here, then, is give you some background information on a prophet. I will suggest some passages to read, and I will have you practice reading prophetic oracles, in order to help you develop a habit of reading this type of material. In this chapter we will look at Amos and Hosea, two prophets from the period of the divided monarchy, but you can use the skills you learn here to read any of the prophets.

How to Read a Prophetic Book

Another difficulty that we have with prophetic oracles is that they can all sound alike to a modern reader. This is what the prophets used to sound like to me: "Blah, blah, blah, you're bad!" "Blah, blah, blah, God is angry!" "Blah, blah, blah, you're all going to die!" It didn't matter to me whether it was Isaiah or Ezekiel; all the prophets seemed to say the same thing.

Reading stories about the prophets is a breeze compared to reading the prophetic books, such as Isaiah and Jeremiah. Let me explain why. The books we think of as "the Prophets" are primarily collections of oracles. Occasionally, the redactor adds stories about the prophet, but the main element in these books are clearly the oracles themselves.

Focus on METHOD

Form Criticism and the Prophets

One of the most prominent methods used in biblical interpretation is "form criticism," a method that helps scholars think about how biblical material was spoken and heard by the ancient Israelites. It is a very complex method, but I want to highlight some of its main points.

A "form, or a "formula" is a phrase that tells an audience how to read or hear what follows. Let me quote an example you all know: "Once upon a time . . . ." As soon as you hear these words, you know that what follows is a fairy tale. It would be silly to use this phrase in a newscast or a history textbook.

A form can also tell the audience something about the social location of the speaker. Today, a minister starts a speech with the words, "Dearly beloved, we are gathered here today . . ." In ancient Israel, prophets said, "Thus says the LORD . . ." Others can use these forms, but when they do, they either take on another role or use the forms derivatively. This social aim of form criticism is called the *Sitz im Leben* or "setting in life."

Every society is filled with "forms," although not all forms are words. Have you ever channel-surfed? You can do so because you know the visual and verbal "forms" of various television programs. The screen for a home-shopping network looks quite different from that of a crime drama. Even with a genre, such as music videos, distinct forms differentiate the country music channel from the rock-video station.

When we study the Bible, we can only recover the verbal forms. We can't "see" if a prophet looked different than a priest, or if the delivery of a prophetic oracle had a different visual setting than the reading of the law. We can, however, detect patterns in the words. These patterns are "forms."

The patterns tell us what kind of material we have. You have already learned some biblical forms, such as laws and psalms. In future chapters we will examine the forms of proverbs and the short story. These forms give us a small clue into how these varying materials were spoken and heard.

See if you can find some forms in your everyday life. Are there any parallels to these forms in the Bible?

These oracles are separated from the events and situations that prompted them. In a book such as Amos, the collection of oracles has no apparent order. They are not chronological. They are not thematic. The collector simply assumes that you know who Amos was, when he lived, and what the issues were in his day. How should we read prophetic books today?

FINDING AN ORACLE

It can be difficult to figure out where one oracle ends and another begins. Scholars have recognized some typical phrases that open some oracles; these phrases are called *prophetic forms*. If you know these phrases, you can at least start to distinguish one oracle from another. Here are the most common prophetic forms we see in the Bible:

Messenger formula. A messenger formula begins with the phrase "Thus says the LORD." It comes from the way royal messengers communicated in ancient times. Let's say a king wanted to send a letter to another king. He sent a messenger, who would "read" the letter to the other king. The messenger would begin by saying, "Thus says the king," and then he would read the letter in the first person as the king had written it. So when a prophet says, "Thus says the LORD," what follows is usually a direct speech by God that the prophet is announcing. This is by far the most common form of prophetic oracle, and it shows that the primary job of the prophet is to be God's messenger. Sometimes these oracles end with another stock phrase, ". . . says the LORD."

Vision report. Sometimes prophets have visions of things that represent an oracle. A vision report describes what the prophet sees and what the vision symbolizes. For instance, Amos has a vision of a basket of fruit. In Hebrew, the word for *fruit* is spelled the same way as the word for *end*, so the "fruit" means the "end" is coming (Am 8:1–3).

Symbolic act. Sometimes a prophet acts out something that symbolizes an oracle. For example, in Jeremiah 27 the prophet walks around Jerusalem with a yoke on his back. This symbolizes that the people are going to be "yoked" when they are conquered by the Babylonians.

Woe oracle. This oracle is more difficult to recognize, because different translators render it differently. In Hebrew, this oracle begins with a particle pronounced, "Oy!" Sometimes this is translated as "woe," "alas," or "ah." Whenever you see one of these words, an oracle is beginning, and it will be an oracle of doom.

Call narrative. Many prophetic books have a chapter that describes how the prophet was commissioned as a prophet. Since prophets are God's messengers, they are "called" into service by God. The "call narrative" describes this event.

Oracles against foreign nations. Many prophetic books also have a section where some of the oracles that a prophet spoke against nations *other than* Israel or Judah are gathered together. Some prophets spoke oracles against Babylon, others against Assyria, and so on. These oracles, when collected together within a prophetic book, are called "oracles against foreign nations."

Prophets could also use forms from other settings to make a point. For example, in Ezekiel 19, the prophet sings a funeral song for the princes of Judah who are still alive. This would be similar to printing the obituary of your enemy, even though that person has not died.

Oracles Are Poetry

The prophets also used poetic language when they spoke. In fact, prophetic speech is closer to poetry than it is to prose. They used images and metaphors to describe people, places, and God. As we saw in an earlier chapter, Israelite poetry is characterized by sparse wording; the fewer words, the better. In addition, the material is arranged in parallel lines, so these oracles may seem repetitive.

Prophetic speech was supposed to get people to act differently, so the prophets often used exaggeration or hyperbole, irony, or sarcasm, and sometimes even shocking images and ideas. They would not speak about the percentage of people who might be destroyed if an enemy attacked; *everybody* was going to be killed. The disaster would not ruin a few crops; the whole land would be *utterly desolate*.

Unraveling an Oracle

Between the poetic metaphors and the persuasive rhetoric, it may be hard to figure out what the prophets are saying. I have found that it is helpful to ask a simple series of questions whenever reading an oracle:

1. Determine whether this is an oracle of doom (predicting disaster) or an oracle of salvation (predicting restoration).

2. Identify any prophetic form that might be present. This might help determine if there are one or more oracles.

3. If this is an oracle of doom, ask:

> ▸ Who is being condemned?
>
> ▸ Why are they being condemned (that is, what specifically have they done wrong)?
>
> ▸ What's the form of the punishment (loss to an enemy, plague, drought, and so on)?
>
> ▸ Will everyone be destroyed, or will there be a remnant which is saved? If there is a remnant, does it survive because the people somehow deserve to survive, or are they just the lucky few?

If this is an oracle of salvation, similar questions can be asked: who is saved, when, and why?

4. Finally, pay attention to the view of God. What metaphors are used for God: warrior, judge, and so on? Does God govern only one of the nations, all twelve tribes, all people, and so on?

We will try these questions on the books of Amos and Hosea.

AMOS

The book of Amos is the earliest collection of oracles that we have. It is a good place to start, because there are many different prophetic forms in the book. The messages are easy to follow, if you use the series of questions that I have suggested. Amos uses poetry, metaphor, imagery, and even hyperbole, so you can see how prophetic speech is different from other kinds of speech.

Before you start reading Amos, let me give you some historical background. Amos prophesied around the years 783–746 BCE. He was from the southern kingdom of Judah, but, as he tells us in chapter 7, God called him to go to the northern kingdom of Israel to deliver oracles there. Because he lived during the divided monarchy, you may want to refer to the chart of the two kingdoms.

It was a time of relative peace and prosperity in the north. Israel was facing no major enemies, and its economy was booming. Yet Amos is a prophet of doom, predicting disasters because of the sinfulness of the people. See if you can figure out what they're doing wrong and how God will punish them.

Read Amos straight through. Don't worry about the details, and don't stop if you don't understand. Just get a general idea of how the book is arranged and what sort of material is in it.

Reflecting on the Reading

1. What did you notice about the way the book is arranged?

2. Where was it easy to follow and understand?

3. Where was it difficult to understand?

4. Could you find any particular issue(s) that Amos was concerned about?

Dissecting the Book

Now that you have a general idea of the book, pick one or two oracles to examine in greater detail. You could pick from the following list, or determine for yourself where an oracle begins and ends.

Amos 1:3–10

Amos 4:4–13

Amos 5:18–24

Amos 6:1–7

Amos 7:1–6

Amos 7:10–15

Answer the following questions concerning your passage:

1. Is this passage an oracle of doom or salvation?

2. Does it contain any prophetic form?

3. If this is an oracle of doom, who is being condemned? Why are they being condemned? What's the form of the punishment?

4. If this is an oracle of salvation, who is being saved, when, and why?

5. What is the view of God, and God's relationship to the nation, presented by the oracle?

Putting It Back Together

As you examine each oracle in turn, do you see patterns that you missed before? Are some of the passages that you first found confusing now clearer? I expect that there are still plenty of things that you have questions about, but I would hope that you have a better sense about the issues that Amos addressed.

Here are some things you may have noticed in the book. First, Amos does not claim that the Israelites were worshipping other gods or that they were neglectful in their worship of Yahweh. In fact, he pictures the people as rather pious, keeping the sacrifices and going to the temples with regularity. So what is the problem? Is Amos opposed to the rituals at the temple?

I'd have to say yes and no. As a southern prophet he may have objected to the northerners going to temples other than the one in Jerusalem. But he certainly objected to the people's belief that observing ritual obligations *alone* made them "good." They thought that it didn't matter how they acted toward each other, because they participated in temple rituals. Amos sees hypocrisy in this attitude. People who go through the motion of worshipping God, while still oppressing the poor, show that they "don't get it." Sacrifice without justice is empty ritual. Where do you find this issue addressed?

The main sin of the people is their treatment of the poor. We see this theme repeated in various parts of the book. Notice that Amos's primary audience had to be the rich citizens of the north. Where do we find clues as to Amos's audience? They controlled financial matters. They also controlled the judicial system and the bulk of the agriculture. The sins of the elite, Amos reports, are bringing the nation to ruin.

Amos also claims that these people should have known better, because God had sent them signs of the divine anger. What were those signs? Periodic drought, regional famine, and scattered pestilence or disease. In other words, God sends signs through natural disaster. Remember that Amos prophesied "two years before the earthquake" (Am 1:1). This was a huge earthquake that devastated large portions of Israel. Amos's oracles might have been preserved in part because he was seen as one who predicted this disaster. His oracles of God's impending judgment helped people make sense of this horrible tragedy. Where else does Amos talk about natural disasters?

Lastly, were there any sections in this book that struck you as clever, interesting, or bitingly ironic? Amos is a truly brilliant speaker. Take the beginning of the book, for instance. The book opens with oracles against foreign nations. He starts by condemning all the countries around Israel, one-by-one. You can feel the crowd growing as he condemns the Phoenicians, insults the Philistines, and prophesies against the Edomites. If you're an Israelite, this is great entertainment! Next he turns against those rotten people in Judah, who think they're the chosen ones just because they have the Davidic king and the temple in Jerusalem. Then, just as he has a whole audience thinking, "This man is a true prophet!" he turns the focus on the audience themselves. "For three transgressions of *Israel*, and for four, I will *not* revoke the punishment" (Am 2:6). The oracle of condemnation that follows is more than twice as long as the oracles against other nations. It's a fantastic rhetorical device. Prophetic oracles were clearly a kind of public performance with a real audience.

Many of Amos's oracles are like this. He uses catchy images and twists of fate that a live audience would have enjoyed, such as the image of the person who runs into his house to escape a lion, only to get bitten by a snake (Am 5:19). One way to appreciate his language is to think about how these oracles might be worded today. What images and twists would have a similar impact? Or you might want to re-create how Amos would have actually proclaimed the words of your oracle. Where was he? What was the audience doing? What did he do to keep them listening?

HOSEA

Hosea was a contemporary of Amos. He began his ministry during the reign of Jeroboam II, but he was still around when Assyria had become a real threat to the northern kingdom's existence.

As Assyria advanced on the northern kingdom, Israel went through a period of political instability. Kings came and went at a rapid pace, each one trying some new way to keep the Assyrians at bay. They tried paying high tributes to the Assyrians, forming a coalition to resist them, but it was to no avail.

Unlike the southerner Amos, Hosea was from the northern kingdom. The book has the highest percentage of rare words of any book in the Hebrew Bible, perhaps because he speaks in a northern dialect. As a result there is more uncertainty about how to translate the text than we experienced with Amos.

Again, read Hosea straight through, without worrying about the details. Get a feel for the issues that concern him and the metaphors that he uses. See if you can notice any differences from Amos, even in your first read-through. Again, I will suggest some individual oracles to analyze using the same method that we used with Amos. This will help you practice your skills in interpreting prophetic oracles, a good thing to develop before we move to the longer prophetic books of Isaiah, Jeremiah, and Ezekiel.

REFLECTING ON THE READING

1. What did you notice about the way the book is arranged?

2. Where was it easy to follow and understand?

3. Where was it difficult to understand?

4. Could you find any particular issue(s) that Hosea was concerned about? Were these the same as or different from Amos?

5. Did you find prophetic forms in Hosea?

DISSECTING THE BOOK

Now that you have a general idea of the book, pick one or two oracles to examine in greater detail. Answer the same questions that we used for analyzing the oracles in Amos.

Hosea 1:2–8

Hosea 4:4–14

Hosea 7:11–13

Hosea 8:5–13

Hosea 11:1–9

Hosea 14:1–7

PUTTING IT BACK TOGETHER

Hosea talks a lot about sex, adultery, and whoredom! From God's opening command, that he take a wife of "harlotry," to Hosea's condemnation of Israel's whoring after other gods, this prophet revels in metaphors derived from sexual misconduct.

One of the first issues that biblical scholars face in interpreting Hosea is how the various parts of the book interrelate. Chapters 1 through 3 describe Hosea's marriage(s) and children. Chapters 12 through 14 describe God's love and compassion for Israel, while, in between, chapters 4 through 11 contain prophetic indictments of the northern kingdom.

Let's turn first to chapters 1 through 3. Are we supposed to read Hosea's marriage to Gomer literally? Did God actually command him to marry her? If so, then this is a symbolic act, that is, an action that symbolizes the oracle that Hosea is trying to convey. Or did Hosea's oracles stem from his personal experience of being married to a promiscuous woman? Some exegetes have suggested that Hosea's experience of loving someone who was unfaithful led him to depict God's covenant with Israel in this way. Or is the "marriage" a literary device, an allegory, and not a description of an actual marriage? The reality is hard to determine.

What is clear is that marriage and adultery are used throughout the book as a metaphor for God's covenant with Israel and Israel's unfaithfulness to that covenant. Just as a wife owed her husband complete fidelity, so too Israel owed Yahweh its absolute allegiance. Therefore, the prophet condemns the nation for worshipping other gods.

> My people consult a piece of wood,
> and their divining rod gives them oracles.
> For a spirit of whoredom has led them astray,
> and they have played the whore, forsaking their God. (Hos 4:12)

Hosea's God is emotional, in love with this partner. The divine love is expressed both in the passages lamenting Israel's infidelity and in those pericopes where Yahweh mourns for the honeymoon period or anguishes over having to punish the wayward child. "How can I give you up, Ephraim? How can I hand you over, O Israel?" (Hos 11:8). The use of the marriage metaphor to explore the covenant between God and Israel becomes a rich vehicle for the prophet to express the complex theological issues facing Israel in its final days.

Although the notion of a metaphor that expresses God's love for the people in very concrete ways may sound appealing to us, we have to remember the reverse side of this metaphor. It presumes the subservience of women to men, especially their husbands. It accepts the man's role in punishing his wife, including the use of physical force. In the hands of Hosea, this is not the depiction of a loving marriage, but rather an abusive, dysfunctional one. When modern readers forget the metaphoric nature of the language, and that the metaphor has to be interpreted within ancient Israel's understanding of marriage, the text can seem to support domestic violence as some sort of divinely sanctioned activity.

Moving beyond Hosea's use of the marriage metaphor, it should be noted that Hosea and Amos have some striking similarities. Both are concerned with social justice and the treatment of the poor. Both denounce empty ritual. Both predict impending doom. What else did you notice?

In other ways, Hosea is quite distinct from Amos. Did you notice the lack of prophetic forms in the book? It is not clear why this is so. Perhaps Hosea performed his oracles differently from Amos. Or maybe the final redactors simply did not preserve the formal elements of prophetic speech. Hosea is rich in metaphors but does not use the element of irony that Amos was noted for. What other differences did you find?

While Amos did not depict the Israelites as particularly idolatrous, Hosea does. In chapter 4 he condemns the priests, and then the people, for worshipping idols. In chapter 8 he goes after the national religion of the northern kingdom, stating that Samaria's "calf," that is, the image they used to represent Yahweh in the national temples, has been rejected.

The Assyrian threat lies close to the surface of Hosea, as opposed to the economic prosperity underlying Amos's text. In 7:11–13, Hosea warns the nation against making an alliance with Egypt, even though Egypt would have also wanted to stop the Assyrian advance. The names of Hosea's children symbolize the imminent fall of the nation. "I will put an end to the kingdom of the house of Israel" (Hos 1:4). In this light Israel's whoring refers in part to their dealings with foreign nations. "For they have gone up to Assyria, a wild ass wandering alone; Ephraim has bargained for lovers. Though they bargain with the nations, I will now gather them up. They shall soon writhe under the burden of kings and princes" (Hos 8:9–10). Although they tried to buy off the Assyrians, God will punish the people for their disloyalty.

Mixed in with the oracles of condemnation, however, are oracles of restoration and hope. Scholars wonder if the oracles of salvation are original to Hosea or later additions. Similarly, many oracles seem to address both Judah and Israel; are the references to Judah also original to Hosea? While it is impossible to answer these questions with certainty, we can say that the effect in the final form of the book is to humanize the portrayal of God. This is not a God who relishes destruction, but one who seems conflicted about the inevitable events pending for the nation. This ambiguity, and even vulnerability, on the part of Hosea's God makes the book attractive to many readers.

So which do you like better: the God of Amos or the God of Hosea? Is Hosea's God loving and passionate or abusive and controlling? Was Israel wrong for trying to avoid the impending disaster by paying tribute and making alliances, or should the people have trusted Yahweh to save them?

PROPHETS THEN AND NOW

I would hope that one thing your reading of these prophets has shown you is that they addressed a real audience about real issues. Elijah helped the people during a grave economic disaster. Amos spoke in a time of prosperity to a people caught up in their own gain. Hosea addressed a nation whose enemy was mobilizing against it.

Yet there is something in each of these prophets, as in all great literature, which continues to speak beyond their historical contexts. The prophets assert a connection between what one believes and how one acts. They exhibit concern for all members of society, including the poor and marginalized. They address the significance of national politics and the role of government in creating a "national ethic." They challenge views of the environment and natural disasters. They depict a God who feels both love and anguish. Lastly, the prophets of doom reflect on how fragile the world is. In one instant peace and prosperity can be swept away. Yet, even in the face of disaster, the oracles of salvation hold out a picture of hope.

FOR REVIEW

1. What is a prophet?

2. What is an oracle?

3. Describe three of the features of Israelite prophets.

4. What is the most common prophetic form?

5. Pick three different forms, and describe them.

6. Why is it useful to know about prophetic forms?

7. How was prophetic speech like poetry?

8. Why did prophets use exaggeration or hyperbole?

9. What is the aim of a miracle?

10. How is Elijah like Moses?

11. What are three main topics in the book of Amos?

12. How does Hosea use the metaphor of marriage?

FOR FURTHER READING

There are many excellent introductions to prophetic literature, including those by Joseph Blenkinsopp, *A History of Prophecy in Israel*, revised edition (Louisville, KY: Westminster John Knox, 1996); Alexander Rofé, *Introduction to the Prophetic Literature* (The Biblical Seminar 21; Sheffield: Sheffield Academic, 1997); David L. Petersen, *The Prophetic Literature: An Introduction* (Louisville, KY: Westminster John Knox, 2002); and Marvin A. Sweeney, *The Prophetic Literature* (Interpreting Biblical Texts; Nashville, TN: Abingdon, 2005).

For an accessible example of the importance of cross-cultural analysis of prophetic phenomena, see Thomas W. Overholt, *Channels of Prophecy: The Social Dynamics of Prophetic Activity* (Minneapolis, MN: Fortress, 1989). For more recent sociological analyses of Israelite prophecy, see, among others,

Joseph Blenkinsopp, *Sage, Priest, Prophet: Religious and Intellectual Leadership in Ancient Israel* (Library of Ancient Israel; Louisville, KY: Westminster John Knox, 1995); and Victor H. Matthews, *Social World of the Hebrew Prophets* (Peabody, MA: Hendrickson, 2001).

Original texts on prophecy in the ancient Near East can be found in Martti Nissinen et al., *Prophets and Prophecy in the Ancient Near East* (SBLWAW12; Atlanta, GA: SBL, 2003), while studies of these texts can be found in Martti Nissinen, editor, *Prophecy in Its Ancient Near Eastern Context: Mesopotamian, Biblical and Arabian Perspectives* (SBLSymS 13; Atlanta, GA: SBL, 2000).

On the problematic nature of Hosea's marriage metaphor, see Renita Weems, *Battered Love: Marriage, Sex, and Violence in the Hebrew Prophets* (Overtures to Biblical Theology; Minneapolis, MN: Fortress, 1995) and chapter 5 of Gale Yee's *Poor Banished Children of Eve: Women as Evil in the Hebrew Bible* (Minneapolis, MN: Fortress, 2003).

10 JUDAH STANDS ALONE

Ah, Assyria, the rod of my anger —
the club in their hands is my fury!
(Isa 10:5)

CHAPTER OVERVIEW

In the last chapter we focused on prophets working in the Northern Kingdom during the Divided Monarchy. We used that material to develop an approach to interpreting prophetic oracles.

Now we turn to southern prophets who respond to the Assyrian crisis and the fall of the northern kingdom, namely Isaiah and Micah. They spoke forcefully about the implications of this disaster for their own nation's relationship with Yahweh.

This chapter will provide the following:

▸ A survey of the historical background of this turbulent period of Judah's history

▸ A discussion of the complex redactional layers evident in this material

▸ An explanation of why Isaiah and Micah responded differently to the issues facing the nation

By the end of this chapter you should gain confidence in reading prophetic material within its historical context.

Disaster upon Disaster

Judah and the Assyrian Crisis

Micah prophesied in Judah during the rising threat from the Assyrians. He lived about twenty miles outside of Jerusalem, and so his perspective is shaped by those who were not centered on the king and the temple. Isaiah, on the other hand, was a court prophet. He was an advisor to the kings of Judah, and the vision that he has when he is called to be a prophet takes place inside the temple itself. His oracles reflect the perspective of someone focused on the twin pillars of the nation: the monarchy and the temple. Isaiah lived during three significant crises in Judah: the Syro-Ephraimitic War, the fall of Samaria, and the siege of Jerusalem.

The Syro-Ephraimitic War

Although Israel arose as a nation during a time that Assyria and Babylon were fighting each other for control of Mesopotamia, once Assyria gained the upper hand, it set its sights toward the west. Many empires of the ancient world wanted to control Egypt, probably because of its stable, agricultural economy. Between Assyria and Egypt lay the various countries of the Levant.

The peoples of the Levant knew about the advance of the Assyrian army. Many of them realized that they would be unable to resist such a powerful army. This left nations with three options. First, they could pay tribute to the Assyrians and become a vassal state. Second, they could form an alliance with Egypt, in whose interest it was to stop the Assyrians before they reached Africa. Third, they could form their own coalition of forces.

Several of the nations in the Levant chose this last option. In particular, the Arameans in Syria, centered around the city of Damascus, and Israel, whose main tribe was Ephraim, led the formation of a coalition of forces. They had hoped that Judah would join them; after all, success depended on gathering the greatest number of troops. But Judah refused.

Syria and Israel attacked Judah in order to try to unseat their king, Ahaz, and force the Judahites to join them. This foray is called the Syro-Ephraimitic War. The Syro-Ephraimitic War, then, occurred when Syria and Israel attacked Judah to try to force them to join a coalition that would resist the Assyrian advance. Confusing? You bet!

We will see Isaiah delivering oracles to Ahaz addressing whether he should join their coalition.

Focus on METHOD

Ideological Criticism

Ideological criticism refers to those methods of interpretation that try to uncover the unexpressed ideologies that lie behind the text. Originally it began as an outgrowth of class analysis utilizing Marxist theories. Now ideological criticism has expanded because of the recognition that other categories of human existence, such as gender and race, are also important features of social status.

For example, if you listen today to talk radio, you'll hear people talking about the "feminist (or gay or liberal or conservative, and so on) agenda." Popular pundits "unmask" the ways in which certain groups promote their "agenda." In a sense, the pundits are doing ideological criticism. Notice its negative connotation, however. Pundits never accuse anyone of a hidden agenda if they agree with his or her position. *Ideology* also often has a similar negative connotation. Most of us like to think of ourselves as "ideologically free."

The difference between modern claims that someone has an agenda and ideological criticism is that the latter does not assume that all ideologies are bad. In fact, these scholars would maintain that everyone has an ideology (an agenda, if you will), and that we only resist those with which we disagree.

Recognizing this fact is important because it reminds us that ideologies can be invisible. Think about some of your own strongly held beliefs. What principles do they assume as "natural"? For instance, do you assume that belief in one God is naturally superior to belief in many gods? If so, does anyone (including yourself) benefit in terms of prestige, money, or status if everyone in your society agrees with you? Could a polytheist accuse you of having a "monotheistic agenda"? That question may seem silly, but, in fact, you're thinking like an ideological critic.

In this approach to biblical texts, there is an assumption that at least one factor behind a text's composition serves some group's purpose or interest. This ideological purpose is usually masked, and it is, therefore, more influential because it is not overt. Ideological criticism tries to bring these motivating factors to light.

Ideological criticism looks at three elements of the text. It uncovers the text's production within its historical, ideologically-charged context. For instance, it would ask what other competing ideologies were at play when Isaiah was advocating against the making of foreign alliances.

Second, it would analyze the text to show where the hidden ideology makes itself evident. It might seem that Isaiah's view of God's transcendence is based simply on theological or religious principles, but ideological criticism uncovers the political motivation that benefits from insisting on this view of God.

Third, the method looks at the text's use by various reading groups, each with a particular ideology that it is trying to advance. The use of Isaiah's texts focusing on divine transcendence might be used by a contemporary group, such as Christian ministers or priests, to underscore their own status within contemporary society.

You might want to use ideological criticism to unveil the differences between Isaiah and Micah. Do they have different presuppositions about God and the nation? Do their differences stem from different social locations? Do their oracles advance the worldview of the group to which they belong? What groups today would prefer the message of Isaiah to that of Micah, and why? Who might prefer Micah?

The Fall of Samaria

Every attempt to ward off the Assyrian attack by the northern kingdom failed. Israel tried tribute, alliances with Egypt, and a coalition, all to no avail. In 722 BCE, after a three-year siege, the capital of Israel fell.

When the Assyrians conquered a nation, they dispersed the elite throughout their empire. This broke up any factions that could have mounted a revolt.

As a result of the fall of Samaria, the elite of the ten tribes of Israel were scattered throughout the Assyrian empire, and peoples from other parts of the Assyrian empire were settled in and around Samaria, forming an ethnically-mixed population. From the perspective of the elite in Judah, the nation of Israel was gone. The nation had fallen.

The fall of Samaria caused those in the south to question God's role in this disaster. They would have viewed the original population as their kin, even if they had a separate government, perhaps similar to the way North and South Koreans regard each other. We know that the city of Jerusalem increased in size by about fifty percent at this time, probably as the result of a flood of refugees. These refugees would have also wondered about Yahweh's role in their city's fall. Their voices would have been added to those wondering where Yahweh was.

Of course, for some who spoke from a southern perspective, there was a quick answer: the fall of the North was Israel's punishment for their rejection of the temple at Jerusalem and their failure to recognize the legitimacy of the Davidic monarchy.

What is interesting, however, is that the prophets from this time period, whose words have been preserved, were those who warned Judah that what happened to Samaria could just as easily happen to them. These prophets viewed the disaster as a warning, a lesson from which Judah must learn.

This relief, dating to 700 BCE, depicts Israelite captives leaving the city of Lachish.

Hand-carved at the end of the eighth century BCE, Hezekiah's Tunnel connected the city to the water wells so that they could be accessed during a time of siege. Shown here is a modern-day view of the tunnel's entrance.

THE CITY IS SURROUNDED

It is clear from archaeology that Hezekiah, the king of Judah at the time when the Assyrians had reached Jerusalem, knew that the city most probably would be besieged. (You may want to review the discussion of siege warfare in chapter 7.) Jerusalem had no source of fresh water within the city walls, so Hezekiah had a tunnel built to reach a spring in the caves under the city. Archaeologists have found the inscription that the workers who completed this tunnel, made. This tunnel left the city in better shape to resist a siege.

The book of 2 Kings also tells us that Hezekiah shut down sacred areas outside of Jerusalem (2 Kgs 18:3–4). The text describes this as evidence of his faithfulness, but we know that it was also a way that kings prepared for a siege. By shutting down certain shrines, they were better able to defend key cities.

You may want to read 2 Kings 16–20 as background for Isaiah and Micah. These chapters describe the reigns of Ahaz and Hezekiah, along with the fall of Samaria. Notice that the Deuteronomistic Historian mentions Isaiah in connection with Hezekiah. The material is repeated with some variations in Isaiah 36–39 and 2 Chronicles 29–32. In addition, this is one event from Israel's history for which we have written records from non-Israelites. The Assyrian annals talk about the siege of Jerusalem and their subjugation of Hezekiah.

As you can see, then, there is an abundance of sources for this period in Israel's history. The problem with this abundance, however, is that the sources do not agree on what happened. How many times was the city besieged? Was Jerusalem actually conquered by the Assyrians? Did the Assyrians stop the siege because of revolution back home? Or did the angel of death kill the Assyrian soldiers in their camp? For our purposes, these details don't matter. What all the sources seem to agree upon is that Jerusalem was not destroyed by the Assyrians, nor was the population exiled. For the citizens of Jerusalem this was a miracle, God's reward for the faithfulness of Hezekiah, who heeded the words of his prophet, Isaiah.

LAYERS UPON LAYERS: ADDITIONS TO PROPHETIC BOOKS

Let's review what we have learned to this point. Prophetic books are difficult to understand because they don't explicitly state what the prophet is talking about or where he is. Moreover, the prophet is using elevated speech: poetry, hyperbole, metaphor, and so on. It can all sound the same. In addition, we don't always know where one oracle ends and another begins. Oracles are not arranged in any particular order. And there's another problem: we can't be guaranteed that everything in a prophetic book was spoken by that prophet. This situation is especially true for the books of both Isaiah and Micah.

In light of these complexities, it's important to think about the process by which these books were created. This process was not an issue for the ancient audience: the "problem" is a modern one.

In the ancient world, authorship was a more fluid concept. The identity of the author of a given text was rarely preserved. Notice that we keep referring to the "Deuteronomistic Historian" rather than "Joe" or "Michael." Ancient authors not only freely used earlier material, but it would have been considered an insult if they hadn't. It would have been tantamount to dishonoring your elders; so the Chronicler uses large sections of the Deuteronomistic History, in part to show respect for that work.

Scribes who copied texts were the learned ones in their society. Their job was to transmit traditions, texts, information, and so on. Sometimes, in order to do this responsibly, they had to add material and explanations so that the original message was understood. They weren't human copy machines; they were active participants in the transmission of traditions. Collections of prophetic oracles show some signs of these explanatory additions. Some sections of Amos, for example, extend his message to the nation of Judah.

In addition, prophets at this level usually had a following. Think about Elisha's relationship to Elijah. He is a disciple of Elijah and clearly takes on Elijah's role and powers at his master's death. The master of a group of prophets is the "father," and the disciples or apprentices are his "sons."

The prophets whose words have been preserved probably left a legacy of disciples. These prophets would view their own prophetic spirit as having been an "inheritance" of the powers of their founder. For them, when they prophesy, even if it is one hundred years later, they prophesy in name of their founder. For example, oracles from the disciples of Isaiah would be preserved as part of the "oracles of Isaiah."

Oracles that were not fulfilled were especially susceptible to further interpretation and subsequent additions. This was true for many of the oracles of restoration. Later authors would use these oracles as the basis of or inspiration for their own vision of an ideal world. However, this is also the case in oracles of condemnation, which might have been made broader and less historically specific so that they could address later audiences. When you read an oracle, then, you must be aware that it may be from a later addition to the book.

Isaiah: Fitting Assyria into God's Plan

Isaiah of Jerusalem

We will now turn to an even more complex book than the ones previously examined: the book of Isaiah. It would be impossible to read the whole book within the space of one class, so I will suggest some of Isaiah's "greatest hits."

Let me start by telling you about Isaiah and his book. The prophet Isaiah lived and worked at a slightly later date than Amos, and for a much longer period of time (from around 742–701 BCE). He lived in Jerusalem and was consulted by the kings of Judah. He was clearly from the Judean upper-class, and his oracles show he had a great interest in the temple and the monarchy.

The oracles from Isaiah, as well as the account of his advice to Hezekiah, are contained in the first thirty-nine chapters of the book of Isaiah. The rest of the book, chapters 40 through 66, comes from a much later time period, more than 150 years later. In these chapters, later Israelites wrote in the name of the earlier prophet. Chapters 40 through 55 date from the end of the Babylonian exile; they are called Second Isaiah. Chapters 56 through 66 come from the early days, when Israel was resettling into the land, and is called Third Isaiah. We will look at Second and Third Isaiah in other chapters, but know that whoever added them also may have added material to the first part of the book.

Because this is prophetic material, we will use the same approach to the book that we used with Amos and Hosea. The oracles I have selected represent the book's main concerns. Read all of the oracles in the following list. Then pick one or two to examine more closely. This time, however, I will follow this list with my discussion of each pericope. At the end I will provide an overview of the book's main themes.

Isaiah 6:1–13: The Call of Isaiah

Isaiah 7:1–17: The Sign of Immanuel

Isaiah 31:1–9: Make no alliances

Isaiah 10:5–19: Assyria is God's weapon

Isaiah 2:5–22: Oracle against Israel

Isaiah 5:1–7: The Song of the Vineyard

Isaiah 3:16–4:1 and 10:1–4: Oracles against the elite

Isaiah 9:2–7 and 11:1–9: The reign of the perfect king

ISAIAH 7:1–17: THE SIGN OF IMMANUEL

Let's begin with a couple of oracles that demonstrate Isaiah's historical context. The first one deals directly with the Syro-Ephraimitic War. You may also be asked to read 9:8–22 in conjunction with this oracle, since both talk about Israel joining forces to attack Judah.

IN CASE YOU WERE WONDERING

Aram and Damascus. Damascus is the capital of the Arameans. Aram is north of Israel.

LOOKING CLOSELY AT THE TEXT

1. Why is Ahaz afraid?

2. What is the function of the woman and the child in this passage?

HIS NAME SHALL BE IMMANUEL

A few years ago there was a commercial for some wonderful new car that didn't need certain types of regular maintenance checks. The commercial showed a pregnant woman standing next to the car, and the voiceover said something like, "even when her child is ten years old, you will still not have needed to have your car serviced." The pregnant woman was a way to mark time.

The pregnant woman in Isaiah 7 fulfills the same purpose. Jerusalem is about to be attacked by the coalition from the north. Isaiah delivers an oracle to Ahaz, king of Judah, a war oracle that tells him not to fear this attack.

This oracle is followed by God, via the prophet, offering Ahaz a sign that what has been predicted will happen. Remember the sign that Saul was given after Samuel told him that he would be the first king of Israel. Ahaz looks pious by turning down the offer, but here's some friendly advice: if God asks you to do something, just do it. Don't be polite.

Isaiah gives Ahaz a sign, which isn't really much of a sign. It's a timeline. He points to a pregnant woman. Scholars have suggested it was Ahaz's wife, since the child will be given such an exalted name. Another option is that the prophet points to his own wife, who according to Isaiah 8:3 may have also been a prophet. You may remember that part of Hosea's marriage included giving his children names that symbolized his message. *Immanuel* (often spelled "Emmanuel") means "God is with us," which certainly sums up Isaiah's message.

The Bible in the CHRISTIAN TRADITION

The Virgin, Text Criticism, and Jewish-Christian Relations

Not all of the results of traditional Christian interpretations of biblical texts have been positive. The belief that Isaiah 7:14 predicts the virgin birth of Jesus is one such case. Notice that in the context of the book of Isaiah, this passage is not about the woman at all. The woman and her child are merely a literary device to mark off time in the oracle.

The assumption that this text refers to Mary comes from a text critical problem. The Hebrew text identifies the woman as a "young woman." It is the Septuagint that translates the word as "virgin." Matthew 1:23, reading with the Septuagint, states that this verse is "fulfilled" in Mary's conception of Jesus. Christians can debate what the author of Matthew 1:23 meant by that text, but that is a separate question from the meaning of the text in the book of Isaiah.

The problem for Christians comes with the assumption that Isaiah 7:14 has only one meaning, and that all other claims to what it signifies are wrong. This is exactly what happened in the Middle Ages. Christians believed that this text was so obviously about Jesus that anyone who would deny it must be evil or opposed to God's plan. Consider who in the Middle Ages would have disagreed with this interpretation of the passage. Of course, the answer is "the Jews."

A few Christian scholars able to read Hebrew realized that the Hebrew text does not have the word "virgin." Some of them asserted that Jews must have changed the original wording of the text, which was faithfully preserved in the Septuagint. Jewish leaders, they posited, changed the Scriptures so that their own people would not convert to Christianity upon realizing that Jesus was predicted in their own Scriptures.

You need to understand that these debates about Isaiah 7:14 were taking place in a world of increasing hostility of Christians to both Jews and Muslims. In the High Middle Ages, Christians, under the direction of the papacy, burned Jewish books and translations. They justified this violence by saying that these books were keeping Jews from converting to Christianity. It was not a great leap from this violence against Jewish property to violence against Jewish persons. As efforts to convert Jews increased, so too did violence against them when those efforts failed.

This justification of violence is a sad element of the Christian tradition. Adding to the tragedy is the fact that, with the discoveries of ancient biblical texts found at Qumran, we now know that "young woman" is the original wording of the passage in Isaiah.

The question of the relationship between the meanings of texts in the Old Testament to the use of those texts in the New Testament will be explored further in a future chapter. Here I want to raise another question: what is Christianity's responsibility when biblical interpretations lead to injustice, oppression, and especially violence? This is not just a problem with this text. We could look at the interpretations of the slave laws or the curse of Eve, for example, to find other examples of interpretations that have led to violence. Can a church affirm an interpretation of the Bible as "correct" while ignoring the effects of that interpretation? Should some interpretations be viewed as "wrong" not because they are not theoretically possible, but because they are too easily misused?

Either way, the birth of the child is not what is being predicted. It is a rhetorical device to mark time. We don't know when children were weaned, although certainly much later than they are in modern industrial societies. The oracle states that the child would have reached the age of some sort of moral reasoning, so perhaps within five to eight years of the oracle's delivery. Isaiah says that within that span of time, the nations of Aram and Israel, whom Ahaz fears, will have already been destroyed.

ISAIAH 6:1–13: THE CALL OF ISAIAH

Although this passage does not open the book of Isaiah, it describes Isaiah's call as a prophet. Pay particular attention to the oracle that the prophet is called to deliver.

IN CASE YOU WERE WONDERING

Seraphim. These appear nowhere else in the Bible. The Hebrew word at its root means "to burn," so these beings are associated with fire. Isaiah has them where other texts have cherubim.

Purification by fire. Purification rituals require either water or fire. For example, metals are purified in fire, and people are purified by water. Here, however, the prophet, who is experiencing a vision, is purified with fire.

Turn This word can also mean "repent."

LOOKING CLOSELY AT THE TEXT

1. Where is Isaiah when he has the vision? What does this suggest about him?

2. To whom is God speaking in verse 8?

3. Summarize the mission that God gives Isaiah.

KEEP LISTENING, BUT DO NOT COMPREHEND

I once liked this passage: the vision in the temple, the angels singing, "Holy, holy, holy," the prophet accepting his commission—that is, I liked it when I believed it ended with Isaiah saying, "Here am I; send me!" I wanted to be like Isaiah.

And now? Well, now I realize what he got himself into. Look at the "oracle" that God gives him. God is giving him a mission: to make sure that the people do *not* understand that they are sinning, because God does *not* want them to repent; Yahweh has no plans to heal them.

While you may have missed that message, Isaiah certainly didn't. His immediate reaction is a stunned, "How long?" Really, God, how long do you expect me to make sure they keep on sinning?

If Isaiah thought that God's answer was going to bring him some hope, he was sorely mistaken. "Until cities lie waste without inhabitant, and houses without people, and the land is *utterly* desolate" (6:11). Although some commentaries view the reference to the "holy seed" in verse 13 as a reference to a remnant who will survive the divinely decreed disaster, it actually is part of the condemnation: even the seed will be burned out of the ground in which it is rooted, like the stump of a felled tree.

We so often associate Isaiah with the poems describing the reign of the peaceful king and the hope in God's restoration, that we can forget that most of the book predicts unrelenting doom. Isaiah is no Pollyanna prophet whistling while Jerusalem burns. He's the one running around yelling, "You deserved it!"

This text may be an example of typical prophetic overkill ("You're *all* going to die"), except for one thing. It describes what happens to the northern kingdom, at least from the perspective of the elite. The land was destroyed and emptied of its core members. The elite who survived were sent away (v. 12) so that a vast land lay "empty." Isaiah 6 provides one way to express God's role in this unhappy event. It admits that the people had not been properly warned because God chose not to warn them.

Notice also that the passage addresses the embarrassment to Isaiah. If Isaiah was such a great prophet, why didn't he know what the people needed to do to save themselves? By stating that his commission included the guarantee of their demise, Isaiah is off the hook.

I date the call to later in the prophet's career, a date which helps explain its placement later in the book. Modern audiences tend to think of prophetic calls as singular experiences, similar to an ordination ritual. But the fact is that prophets could have multiple encounters with God, each one for a different purpose. Remember the story of Micaiah ben Imlah in 1 Kings 22 who is already a prophet, but still sees God sending out the lying spirit. Isaiah's call can be seen as his commission for a particular task, rather than as a ritual of initiation into the prophetic office.

ISAIAH 10:5–19: ASSYRIA IS GOD'S WEAPON

This oracle has two sides to it. On the one hand, it describes Yahweh's use of Assyria in the punishment of the northern kingdom. On the other hand, it predicts disaster for Assyria because of its over-reaching pride. See if you can find each element in these verses.

In Case You Were Wondering

Calno, Carchemish, Hamath, and Arpad. These are all Syrian cities destroyed by the Assyrians.

Looking Closely at the Text

1. How does God's view of Assyria's victories differ from Assyria's views?

2. What evidence is there in the text for the date of the oracle?

3. Who is speaking in verses 13–14?

4. Explain the metaphors in verse 15.

5. What will be Assyria's punishment?

The Pride of Assyria

This is a complex set of oracles. Although it could be divided into three parts (verses 5–12, 13–14, and 15–19), those parts are interrelated. Look at verses 5–6 and 15, which open the first and third sections of the oracle. In both of them Assyria is described as God's weapon or tool by which divine judgment is brought to bear on Israel.

The middle section contains "his" speech, that is, the speech of a personified Assyria or of its king. This speech depicts the arrogance of the Assyrians, who believe that their victories are due to their own power. This arrogance is a fitting image for the Assyrians, who loved to display images of their military victories in large reliefs.

The juxtaposition of these two parts shows that the biblical author knew that the Assyrians did not claim that they had been sent by Yahweh; from their perspective, they're just great warriors. It is the prophet who reveals the truth behind the boastful pride of Judah's enemy: their source of power is Yahweh.

The proof of this is in the punishment that awaits Assyria. Yahweh will turn on the tool, this boastful ax, and destroy it. Notice the specific images of this destruction: fire, a wasting disease, and the stripping of the land. In other words, God will send the same disasters on them that they visited on those they conquered.

This oracle clearly postdates the fall of Samaria, which is mentioned explicitly in verse 11. The reference to a "wasting sickness among his stout warriors" may express the hope of those in Jerusalem during the siege. As you may recall, one of the things that people inside a city hoped for was a disease in the military camp that would decimate their enemy. The book of 2 Kings 19:35 states that the siege of Jerusalem ended when God sent an angel into the Assyrian camp one night who killed "185,000" troops. Yes, the numbers are exaggerated, but the reference to the avenging angel may be a euphemism for a "wasting sickness" sent by God, that is, some kind of plague or deadly virus that killed a significant number of the Assyrian troops. The Assyrian annals do not mention such a disease, but it may have played a part in the cessation of the siege.

ISAIAH 2:5–22 AND 5:1–7: ORACLES AGAINST ISRAEL AND JUDAH

The first oracle contains Isaiah's view of the sinfulness of the northern kingdom of Israel. Note the types of sins which he catalogues.

The extended metaphor in the second oracle compares the nations of Israel and Judah to a vineyard that the Lord has planted. In the hands of Isaiah, the vineyard becomes a metaphor about God's judgment.

IN CASE YOU WERE WONDERING

Diviners and soothsayers. These were illegitimate prophets, either because of the way that they received their oracles or because they were prophets for foreign gods.

Israel is a plant. Prophetic texts often use the image of a plant for the nation.

LOOKING CLOSELY AT THE TEXT

1. List the sins for which the people will be punished.

2. Who and/or what will be the object of this punishment?

3. How is God depicted in this passage?

4. Can you tell why God wants to destroy the vineyard?

HIDE FROM THE TERROR OF THE LORD

Let's start with the oracle in chapter 5. The poetic skill evident in this passage is typical of Isaiah. The metaphor is transparent: it describes God's role in establishing the nation and its walled cities. The metaphor justifies God's decision to destroy them.

The oracle is addressed to the southern kingdom which is asked to render a judgment over whether the garden deserves to be destroyed. It's a rhetorical device. The audience is expected to agree with the divine prosecutor. The end of the oracle turns the tables on the audience when, in verse 7, Judah seems to be included in the decision. It's similar to Nathan getting David to decide the case about a rich man who takes a poor man's ewe lamb, only to have David realize that he's just pronounced a judgment against himself.

The oracle of condemnation in chapter 2 contains elements typical of Isaiah of Jerusalem. First, its view of God is very exalted. This is a warrior God who brings terror on the enemy. There are references to God's glory and majesty (verse 19), which contrast with the lowly status of humans (verse 22). This view of God echoes the emphasis on God's holiness in Isaiah's call narrative.

The people are condemned for arrogance and pride, a condemnation we see repeated against various groups in first Isaiah. The women of Judah are condemned for haughtiness in chapter 3, as are the landowners of Judah in chapter 5 and the Assyrians in chapter 10. Condemnation of human pride is the flip side of Isaiah's exalted view of God. Core to this prophet's message is the necessity of remembering the essential difference between God and humans. In contrast, Israel trusts in its wealth, the strength of its army, and, most foolishly, in the power of other gods.

The poetry of the passage is again typical of Isaiah. Even his oracles of condemnation have a certain beauty about them. Notice the refrain repeated in verses 10, 19, and 21. It describes people running in terror before an invading army; their only hope is to hide in a cave or a niche in the rock, and hope that the soldiers miss them. However, in this oracle, the enemy is God in "his" glory and majesty, rising to terrify the earth. It is remarkable how the phrase "glory and majesty" can sound so threatening in the hands of a poet such as Isaiah.

The oracle predicts the north's fall, along with the destruction of its allies. Verses 12 through 16 extend the condemnation to Phoenicia and Aramea. This oracle certainly dates to some time prior to the fall of Samaria, perhaps around the time of the Syro-Ephraimitic war.

ISAIAH 31:1–9: MAKE NO ALLIANCES

In light of Isaiah's exalted view of God, we can now turn to his foreign policy, which can be summed up in one sentence: make no alliances.

IN CASE YOU WERE WONDERING

Egyptian horses. Egypt was basically the arms factory of the ancient world. Since the ancient versions of tanks were chariots, the Egyptian horses were the engines that literally gave these weapons their horsepower.

Looking Closely at the Text

1. Why shouldn't Judah go to Egypt to equip its army?

2. How do the references to animals function in this text?

Yahweh Will Protect Jerusalem

Notice how this passage again contrasts human arrogance with divine power. Here the poet lambastes those in his own country who think that the weapons which they purchase from the Egyptians will be able to save them. Verse 3 parodies their false hope in Egypt; after all, the Egyptians are human too.

This image contrasts with Yahweh's ability to defend the city with no human help. God is compared to a lion that is so confident in its strength that not even a whole band of shepherds could scare it away. In other words, God does not quake at the sight of a coalition of kings who band against Judah.

God is also described as a bird hovering over Jerusalem. That image sounds comforting, until we look at ancient iconography. The image referred to is not little bluebirds, twittering comfortingly over the city. It is probably a reference to a bird of prey, such as a vulture or a hawk, ready to devour Judah's enemies.

Both of these animals, the lion and the vulture, are associated with the warrior goddess in Canaanite religion. In iconography, she rides the back of a lion. In an ancient mythic text unearthed in modern Lebanon, the goddess Anat hunts down her enemy with a vulture-like assistant. This particular warrior-goddess is known for her enjoyment of bloody violence. These animals, then, connote God's warrior nature.

The final verses deliver the punch line. God alone can defend this city. No other help is needed. In fact, this warrior God will enjoy sending terror on the Assyrians who won't even be able to find a rock to hide behind. In light of this imagery, an alliance with Egypt is like trying to empty the ocean with a spoon.

Isaiah 9:2–7 and 11:1–9: The Reign of the Perfect King

Isaiah's more famous oracles are those predicting the reign of an ideal king. Notice the way these texts exalt this future monarch.

In Case You Were Wondering

The day of Midian. This phrase refers to a miraculous military campaign in the days of the judges.

A stump out of Jesse. This is a reference to the Davidic line.

LOOKING CLOSELY AT THE TEXT

1. What can you tell about the identity of the child in chapter 9?

2. What can you tell about the person described in chapter 11?

3. What are some of the features that these two texts have in common?

THE PEACEABLE KINGDOM

If you read descriptions of ideal kings in the ancient Near East, you would be accustomed to seeing the kind of exalted language that you find in this text. An ideal king not only brings economic prosperity and domestic security to his land, his reign results in good crops and a cessation of natural disasters. If a king is great enough, no wild animals will wander into the city, there won't be any wasting sicknesses, and all the females in the realm, from cattle to humans, will be fertile. Why? Because an ideal king is a blessing from the gods.

These two poems express the prophet's hope that the nation's current suffering would someday come to an end. He expresses his confidence that God will restore the promises to Judah, and, since he's a royal prophet, he envisions that this restoration will be centered around the Davidic monarchy. For Isaiah, a restoration without a Davidic king would be like a chariot without a horse, going nowhere.

As a royal prophet, Isaiah would view the monarchy as an essential conduit for God's blessings to the nation. Notice that these two poems focus on the justice and righteousness associated with the king: there can be no justice in the land without a king to insure it. It's quite a different view of the monarchy than we saw in the Deuteronomistic History.

The titles attributed to this future monarch, listed in 9:6, are remarkable for the way the poet piles them up, but in and of themselves they are not unique. Psalm 2:7 and 45:6 both call the king the son of God or simply "God" (although the reference in Psalm 45 may be harder to detect depending on which translation you use). It might help to remember that this Hebrew word can also be translated "divine." It's really not that different from Christian views of saints who go to heaven and become, in a sense, divinized. Since Christians would not view the heavenly quality of saints as threatening to God, so too the king's divination is simply a way for the community to talk about his connection to Yahweh.

Isaiah 9 is written from the context of war. The prophet envisions a day when the soldiers can burn their bloody, defiling clothes and settle down in peace. Chapter 11 might share this context: an oracle of hope in the midst of apparent defeat. Imagine hearing these poems in Jerusalem at that time, on a hot and sticky day when you are starving, quite literally. The Assyrian army is camped outside your city walls. All night long you can hear their battering rams striking the walls. The city is infested with rats and snakes; animals lie in wait to eat your newly dead, at times competing with the humans who want to get their fill of the corpses first. Your king sits holed up in his palace, praying in the dark, terrified because he can do nothing. He has already stripped the gold off of the temple walls, trying to buy some peace. He is worthless.

Then, off in the distance, you hear a voice, the voice of a singer, the voice of Isaiah. He's singing one of his songs again. You expect that it will be another of his diatribes reminding you how you deserve all this. But this time he's singing about a child, a baby, a prince. He paints a beautiful picture, one that you know is utopian; things will never be that great, but you can dream. You can still remember that Yahweh is strong enough to defend this city after all.

Reading the Book as a Whole

Did you notice any differences between Amos or Hosea and Isaiah? Can you describe those differences? Did they define sin in the same way? Did they have the same view of God? Was their use of language the same?

There are some similarities between these three prophets. They all use similar prophetic forms. They despise empty ritual and condemn the oppression of the poor. They use metaphors and poetic language, and they are full of prophecies of doom.

There are some important differences between them as well. Isaiah's oracles are usually longer, more elaborate, and the use of metaphor more drawn out. Isaiah is also more concerned with helping the king than either Amos or Hosea had been. Isaiah advises Ahaz and Hezekiah, even if the "advice" consists of telling them that what they are doing is wrong. Isaiah clearly wants the monarchy and the temple to continue, and his oracles are designed to help that happen.

Isaiah also uses hyperbole to a much greater degree than Amos. In chapter 6 he prophesies complete doom for the whole nation. "Even if a tenth part remain in it, it will be burned again" (Isa 6:13). Yet in other oracles he envisions a glorious future, embodied in a future king. This king's reign will be so just that all of nature will respond. "The wolf shall live with the lamb, the leopard shall lie down with the kid, the calf and the lion and the fatling together, and a little child shall lead them" (Isa 11:6). Both kinds of hyperbole effectively convey the prophet's core message: God calls people to account for their sins but also rewards the just.

Just as the nation of Judah was not completely destroyed in the days of Isaiah, so too the promises of a righteous and powerful king did not materialize. If we think that prophets simply provided a blueprint for the future, Isaiah's faulty predicting might lead us to think that he was a false prophet. However, it is important to remember that prophetic speech is not like other kinds of speech. Isaiah wants us to hear his words as poetry, not as historical description or as a manifesto for the future. Isaiah's main purpose was to look at his world through God's eyes.

Isaiah's world was one of great international turmoil. In chapter 7 he advises Ahaz not to join a coalition against Assyria, because in the span of less than ten years that coalition will have failed (Isa 7:16). In chapter 10 Isaiah announces that God had used Assyria as a weapon to punish Israel (Isa 10:5–11). Chapter 31 contains a warning not to seek military aid from Egypt. Isaiah's messages are not concerned with sin in general, nor with some distant future, but with the fate of the nation of Judah in his own day.

Isaiah's view of God draws on images taken from these conflicts. Often God is portrayed as one who sends war as punishment (for example, Isaiah 10:5–11) and is ready to inflict defeat on the sinful (for example, Isaiah 5:26–30). Making alliances with other countries is condemned, because it insinuates that God cannot defend the city. At other times, God is depicted as a king sitting on a throne in judgment (Isa 6:1–8).

God's reward for Israel will come through the Davidic monarchy. God will provide a future king who will bring in true justice and lasting peace. In this sense, then, Isaiah has many messianic prophecies: he predicts the coming of a blessed king, whose name, "Immanuel," communicates the close connection between God's kingship and human kingship.

These prophecies of salvation have always captured the imagination of their readers. In part this is a testament to the beauty and artistry of this material. Later Israelite and Jewish readers still believed in the "truth" of these oracles, especially those about a future king or messiah. Isaiah is one of the most quoted books in both the Dead Sea Scrolls and the New Testament. The poetry of this great prophet remains a source of hope for Jews and Christians today.

Micah: The Prophet from Moresheth

Micah also lived during the reigns of Ahaz and Hezekiah. He too delivers oracles that address the rising threat of Assyria, the fall of the northern kingdom, and the politics of his own government. Yet he does so in ways noticeably distinct from his contemporary Isaiah.

The superscription of the book tells the audience that he's from Moresheth, a town approximately twenty miles outside Jerusalem. Some scholars have conjectured that his voice stems from rural landowners, the lower classes of Judean society. Yet, the level of learning evident in his oracles speaks against such a simple conclusion. He may not have been from the capital city, but he certainly had enough learning to draw on Israel's traditions, enough artistry to compose (in either oral or written form) the powerful poetics of his oracles, and enough status and following that his oracles were preserved. Micah is no country bumpkin.

His oracles are critical of Jerusalemite leadership. Even if he came from a wealthy land-owning family, the policies of the central government still impacted those outside of the city rather harshly. Taxation, for example, would have been felt more severely by those landowners. The closure of cult sites outside of Jerusalem would have affected those communities directly.

Moreover, as the Assyrian army advanced, it devastated the countryside. Assyrian armies would have eaten the crops, while picking off the smaller villages one-by-one. The men defending their ancestral lands would have been the first to die by Assyrian swords and their wives the first to be raped. The landowner's, only other option was to abandon their ancestral land and join those awaiting the siege in Jerusalem.

It is no wonder, then, that Micah focuses on different aspects of the political situation than Isaiah does. As you read through the book of Micah, make note of these differences.

Finally, be aware that scholars agree that Micah contains a lot of material that was added some time after the prophet lived. What they don't agree on is precisely which oracles belong to which layer. As you read, you may notice that some of the oracles are addressed to both Israel and Judah; these seem to be original. It is not clear when the oracles of restoration originated. Were they part of Micah's message, or were they added by a later disciple? Are there any oracles of condemnation that you would date to a later period, and why?

Because this is a short book, I will ask you to read through all of it. However, this time I have grouped together oracles that address common themes:

Micah 1:2–7 and 5:10–15: Oracles against improper worship

Micah 6:1–8: Using the language of the courtroom

Micah 2:1–5; 3:1–4; and 6:9–16: Condemnation of the greedy

Micah 3:9–12 and 7:1–17: Oracles addressed to the leadership of Israel and Judah

Micah 4:1–4 and 5:2–5a: Oracles of restoration

MICAH 1:2–7 AND 5:10–15: AGAINST IMPROPER WORSHIP

These two oracles involve worship practices that the prophet felt were illegitimate.

IN CASE YOU WERE WONDERING

High places. This is a phrase which usually refers to open air shrines where sacrifices could be made. Sometimes the phrase is used for installations that have a temple building as well.

The Scroll of the Minor Prophets

In the Hebrew version of the Bible, there are three Major Prophets, Isaiah, Jeremiah, and Ezekiel, plus one scroll on which can be found twelve Minor Prophets. The arrangement of the Major Prophets is obvious: they're in chronological order. But that of the Minor Prophets is not so clear.

There have been several attempts to uncover the principle behind the precise ordering of these books. It must be kept in mind, however, that our earliest manuscripts of the Minor Prophets do not completely agree on their order. In general, all of them have the Minor Prophets in rough chronological order. This means that the prophets of the Divided Monarchy come first (although Amos is placed after Hosea), then those of Judah alone, and so on. Within these rough divisions, the final redactors may have used catch words or other connectors to determine their order.

The problem with this schema is that we cannot rely on it to date the individual books. For example, Jonah is placed among the prophets of the Divided Monarchy. This makes sense, because Jonah is set some time before 612 BCE, when Nineveh was destroyed. However, most biblical scholars would date the text's composition to the postexilic period, as we will see in a later chapter.

This textbook gives sample readings from nine of the fifteen prophetic books. Let me summarize the other six for you:

Nahum. This short book consists of oracles against Assyria, focusing especially on the city of Nineveh. This places at least parts of the book prior to 612 BCE.

Zephaniah. The superscription places this prophet in the reign of Josiah, a contemporary of the young Jeremiah.

Obadiah. This shortest book in the Old Testament is an extended oracle against the Edomites who helped the Babylonians defeat Jerusalem, which suggests an exilic date.

Malachi. This prophet prophesied during the early post-exilic period.

Joel and Habakkuk. There is much debate about the dates of Joel and Habakkuk. The superscriptions of both books lack references to any historical king or time period.

Sorceries. These are rituals with which the prophet does not agree, especially those associated with false prophets.

Images, pillars, and sacred poles. These were all objects found in temples that could represent a god's presence.

Looking Closely at the Text

1. Who will be responsible for the destruction of the sacred places?

2. In 5:10–15, is the prophet speaking to Israel, Judah, or both?

Yahweh Is Coming

This short collection of oracles opens with a powerful image of Yahweh coming out of the temple in order to destroy the temples and high places of both Israel and Judah. This is a god so powerful and glorious that mountains melt beneath the divine feet.

The two passages suggest that God is angry with several aspects of their ritual systems. In the first passage, it seems that God is angered by the mere existence of multiple shrines, a conclusion made clearer when you realize that the passage condemns the "high places" (plural) of Judah in the original Hebrew.

Archaeology has shown that there were, in fact, multiple sacred sites in both Israel and Judah at this time. Although excavations cannot usually determine what god(s) were worshipped at each installation, the Bible tells us at least some were devoted to Yahweh. Notice that in neither chapter does Micah accuse the people of worshipping other gods. It is the multiplicity of the shrines that seems to be the problem.

In the second passage, it is what is inside the temples that is at issue. The passage condemns a variety of items used to represent a god's presence in a temple. Again the Bible attests to the fact that statues, standing stones, and sacred trees existed at various times throughout both nations, even within the temple of Jerusalem. Archaeological excavations have uncovered examples of some of these, such as the twin standing stones in a temple built into a Judean fortress at Arad. At this temple, an inscription was found that mentions Yahweh and an altar that matches the law in the book of Exodus.

The Bible also tells us that, after the destruction of the northern kingdom, Hezekiah shut down these high places and cleaned out the Jerusalem temple. It is interesting, then, that Micah does not seem to reflect those events. The first oracle, which must predate 722 BCE, predicts the destruction of these sacred areas, while the second one predicts the collapse of the whole nation.

Yahweh and His Asherah

Did the ancient Israelites believe that Yahweh had a wife? While that question would have seemed preposterous just fifty years ago, recent excavations have forced biblical scholars to reconsider the question.

The Bible mentions the *asherah* many times. Some of those citations refer to an object found within the temple of Jerusalem. In those cases, the wording suggests that the *asherah* was some kind of stylized tree. It was wooden. When it was set up, it was "planted"; conversely, when it was taken down, it was "cut down." It was destroyed by burning. The Deuteronomist did not like having *asherim* in the temple.

We saw in an earlier chapter that "Asherah" was also a goddess. She was the consort of El, the head god of the Canaanite pantheon. She was associated with the feeding of wild animals. In iconography, the goddess who feeds wild animals is herself like a tree, holding the branches off of which the gazelles feed. The question this fact raises is: did the *asherim* in the temple represent the goddess *Asherah*?

Recently inscriptions have been found linking Yahweh with Asherah. Both inscriptions are prayers for blessing. One reads "I bless you by Yahweh of Samaria, and by his Asherah," while the other reads, "Blessed be Uriyahu by Yahweh; his enemies have been conquered by Yahweh's Asherah." These indicate that the *asherah* was associated with Yahweh.

The inscriptions do not answer the question whether the *asherah* was a goddess to whom it was believed Yahweh was married, or whether it was a symbol of God, representing a different aspect of Yahweh. The grammar supports the latter view more than the former.

If the *asherah* represents Yahweh, then it would symbolize a feminine manifestation of Yahweh. There are a few references to God as female scattered throughout the Old Testament, such as some mothering images. In addition, some of the warrior language may reflect the kind of fighting for which warrior goddesses were responsible. We will see female imagery attached to Yahweh in the Wisdom literature, but there the feminine aspect is separated from God, a kind of divine helper.

Most scholars, however, favor the view that the *asherah* represented a divine consort to Yahweh. The blessing formula suggests that both "Yahweh" and "Asherah" are gods. In the Hebrew Bible we find many masculine metaphors attaching to God: *he* marries Israel, brings storms like Baal, rules over the divine council like El, and so on. If the Israelites thought of God as primarily male, then it should not be surprising that many Israelites would have thought he had a wife.

Micah 6:1–8: Using the Language of the Courtroom

This oracle opens with God bringing a lawsuit against the people. The scene contains God's defense and the people's response.

In Case You Were Wondering

Balak and Balaam. These enemies confronted Israel during the wilderness wanderings. Balak was a king of Moab who hired a prophet from Mesopotamia, Balaam, to curse the Israelites.

Shittim to Gilgal. These are references to the Conquest.

Looking Closely at the Text

1. How are verses 1–5 related to verses 6–8?

2. Who is speaking in verses 6–8?

Israel on Trial

The opening verses of this passage utilize images from Israel's judicial system. God is like a prosecutor bringing up charges against the land. The reference to "Israel" in verse 2 suggests that it may be addressed to the northern kingdom.

God does not mount much of a case. The heart of the message is a reminder of all the good things that God has done for the people in the past. The implication is that the people are ungrateful. But notice that, by referring to military successes in the Wilderness and Conquest eras, the poet implies that God could save them again if Yahweh chooses.

The reference to Balaam is also significant. Balaam was a famous prophet in the ancient Near East, and the book of Numbers relates how the king of Moab had hired him to curse the Israelites, so that they would not be able to destroy Moab. Balaam was unable to complete the job because Yahweh made him bless Israel instead. This text attests to the unavoidable nature of a true prophetic experience.

The second half of the passage seems, at first glance, to be unrelated to the first. While it may have originally been a separate oracle, it now reads as the response of those who have realized their sin. They ask what kinds of sacrifices are needed to atone for their sins. They are even willing to sacrifice their own children to make amends.

With echoes of Amos, Micah states quite clearly that what God requires of people is a change in their whole way of life. They must act with justice, an idea fleshed out in other oracles. They must stay true to the covenant (love kindness) and remember their place (walk humbly with God). Is Micah rejecting the whole sacrificial system or just seeing those sacrifices as empty without associated ethical behavior?

Micah 2:1–5; 3:1–4; and 6:9–16: Condemnation of the Greedy

These passages display Micah's concern for poor landowners. Scholars have connected this concern with his location in a smaller town outside of Jerusalem. It is probable that these outlying areas felt the economic constraints resulting from the Assyrian advance more acutely than those living within Jerusalem.

In Case You Were Wondering

A taunt song. This is a musical parody designed to mock or shame its subject.

Statutes of Omri. Omri was a northern king who founded a particularly strong dynasty. In fact, Israel was known as the "house of Omri" in certain international circles.

LOOKING CLOSELY AT THE TEXT

How are the punishments in these oracles fitting for the sins that they describe?

BOILING UP THE POOR IN A CALDRON

These three oracles are addressed to those who have cheated people and treated the poor unjustly. In some ways they echo concerns we found in the book of Amos. The nation addressed in the first oracle is unnamed. The second one is directed to both Israel and Judah, while the third focuses only on the northern kingdom.

Let's start with the last one. In chapter 6, the prophet focuses on those who have used rigged scales. In an economy heavily reliant on bartering, false scales could net quite a profit. But, why would the prophet mention Ahab and the house of Omri, a dynasty no longer in power? Perhaps it is because of their association with unjust oppression, mirrored in the account of Ahab's seizure of Naboth's vineyard (1 Kings 21).

The oracle in chapter 2 refers explicitly to illegal seizures of property. Remember that many Israelites believed that God had granted particular land to specific tribes, clans, and families. Israelite law tried to ensure the preservation of property within strict family lines. The heavy tribute levied on Israel and Judah by the Assyrians, as well as the expense of military preparations, resulted in a heavy tax burden on the landowners. Those who could not pay faced bankruptcy and thus lost their ancestral land either to the government or to private creditors. Micah condemns those making a profit from such economic hardship.

The middle oracle uses the most symbolic language of the three. It likens this economic oppression to cannibalism. The oppressors slaughter and butcher the people, just as cattle are slaughtered and butchered. This oracle is aimed at both Israel and Judah. Apparently economic oppression is an equal opportunity sin.

Notice the way the punishments pick up on the themes of the indictments. Those who have seized others' lands will have their own lands parceled out to a foreign invader (2:4). Those who have boiled the people will be cut off from God (3:4), an image associated with death in the Psalms. Those who have gained by using false scales in the marketplace will suffer agricultural collapse (6:15). God will have the last word.

Micah 3:9–12 and 7:1–7: Oracles Addressed to the Leadership of Israel and Judah

These texts target those in charge. From rulers to chiefs, priests to prophets, officials to judges, no leader escapes Micah's condemnations.

In Case You Were Wondering

Sentinels. These guards sat on the city walls to warn the people if an enemy approached. They had to be very trustworthy.

Looking Closely at the Text

1. What is the source of the people's false hope in chapter 3?

2. How many images of betrayal can you find in 7:1–7?

There Is Nothing to Rely On

Both of these oracles turn their gaze on the leadership of Israel and Judah, and both undercut those things on which the people may rely. In some ways, these oracles pick up the same sentiment of the last oracles: they castigate those who hold power over others. Here, though, rather than focusing on economic power, they cover various aspects of ancient city life.

The first oracle condemns the rulers, priests, and prophets for thinking that God is on their side. What Micah represents here is the attitude of the Jerusalemite elite, such as Isaiah, who believe that everything will be fine if they simply rely on God. Do you think Micah would have considered Isaiah to be one of the prophets who falsely declares "Peace" (3:5)?

The picture of desperation in chapter 7 is powerfully drawn. The oracle opens with the voice of one desperately hungry, yet with no hope of finding food. The focus switches in verse 2 to the question of trust. There is no one who is trustworthy: neither rulers, nor friends, nor even a lover. The picture that the oracle paints is that of a society completely unraveling.

Notice that the two oracles end differently. The first one predicts that the whole land will be made utterly desolate because of the treachery of the leaders. In the second, the prophet expresses confidence in his own salvation, although it is impossible to guess what he is imagining if society at large is in disarray.

Even so, the ending of this oracle points us to another feature of the book of Micah: its oracles of restoration.

Micah 4:1–4 and 5:2–5a: Oracles of Restoration

One of the big questions that arise with these oracles of restoration is their date. Are they original to the historical Micah or are they the result of secondary additions to the text?

In Case You Were Wondering

"In the days to come" is a phrase found in the Prophets to refer to some distant future. It is usually followed by a vision of a perfect world.

Looking Closely at the Text

1. What aspect of the nation is the focus of the restoration in 4:1–4?

2. What does the reference to Bethlehem in 5:2 communicate about what is being restored in this oracle?

3. How are these poems like the material we saw in Isaiah?

4. Are these views consistent with Micah's perspective in the oracles of condemnation?

In Days to Come . . .

Once again, we come upon beautiful poems that describe a glorious future for the whole nation of Israel. In fact, the first oracle widens its circle to include the reordering of all of the nations around Jerusalem. The second one presents another picture of an ideal king, one who rules with justice and under whom the people will live in peace and fullness.

In some ways, these two passages pick up themes we have seen in the oracles of condemnation. They focus on the restoration of justice and the security of the people at large. They reflect the hopes of people suffering horrible military aggression, picturing, for example, a day when the blacksmiths can melt down the weapons of war and turn them into farming tools. They depict images of agricultural abundance shared justly.

However, there are other elements in the text that suggest a later and different hand. We noted above that Micah's condemnations were rather critical of Jerusalem's leaders. Nor were those oracles that condemn the high

Ploughshares and Swords: Tracing Scriptural Echoes

One of the things that biblical scholars like to do is trace the influence of certain biblical texts on others. This helps them date the material. Here is an exercise that you can try. Look at these three texts.

Isaiah 2:3–5	Micah 4:2–5	Joel 3:9–12
3 Many peoples shall come and say, "Come, let us go up to the mountain of the Lord, to the house of the God of Jacob; that he may teach us his ways and that we may walk in his paths." For of Zion shall go forth instruction, and the word of the Lord from Jerusalem.	2 and many nations shall come and say: "Come, let us go up to the mountain of the Lord, to the house of the God of Jacob; that he may teach us his ways and that we may walk in his paths." For out of Zion shall go forth instruction, and the word of the Lord from Jerusalem.	9 Proclaim this among the nations: Prepare war, stir up the warriors. Let all the soldiers draw near, let them come up.
4 He shall judge between the nations, and shall arbitrate for many peoples; they shall beat their swords into plowshares, and their spears into pruning hooks; nation shall not lift up sword against nation, neither shall they learn war anymore.	3 He shall judge between many peoples, and shall arbitrate between strong nations far away; they shall beat their swords into plowshares, and their spears into pruning hooks; nation shall not lift up sword against nation, neither shall they learn war anymore; 4 but they shall all sit under their own vines and under their own fig trees, and no one shall make them afraid; for the mouth of the Lord of hosts has spoken.	10 Beat your plowshares into swords, and your pruning hooks into spears; let the weakling say, "I am a warrior."
5 O house of Jacob, come, let us walk in the light of the Lord!	5 For all the peoples walk, each in the name of its god, but we will walk in the name of the Lord our God forever and ever.	11 Come quickly, all you nations all around, gather yourselves there. Bring down your warriors, O Lord. 12 Let the nations rouse themselves, and come up to the valley of Jehoshaphat; for there I will sit to judge all the neighboring nations.

It might be tempting to presume that whichever prophet lived earlier wrote the first version. The problem with this approach is threefold. First, we have no idea when to date Joel. Second, the historical Isaiah and Micah were contemporaries. Third, the books of both Isaiah and Micah have secondary additions, so even if we could determine that one was younger than the other, this would not mean that these passages were necessarily from them.

The question is: what are the options for thinking about how these passages might be related? Here are four options for you to consider:

1. One of the three can be the source, which the other two are quoting. If this is the case, then it would be unlikely that the version in Joel is the original since that would presume Isaiah and Micah both changed it in the same way.

2. If Joel were first, then either Isaiah or Micah changed it, and then the other one quoted the changed version.

3. There was one common source for all three prophets, perhaps a famous proverb or a psalm that all three are quoting.

4. There is a common redactor for at least Isaiah and Micah who added this in both texts.

Can you think of other options? Based on the texts alone, what relationship between the three do you find most likely?

places paired with an exaltation of Zion. It seems incongruous that Micah would think that Israel's hope lay in the preservation of the Zion priesthood and the Davidic monarchy.

In between these two oracles comes a clearer hint that this material stems from a later hand. In 4:10, the text states:

Writhe and groan, O daughter Zion,
    like a woman in labor;
for now you shall go forth from the city
    and camp in the open country;
    you shall go to Babylon.
There you shall be rescued,
    there the Lord will redeem you
    from the hands of your enemies. (Mic 4:10)

The reference to an exile to Babylon leads many biblical scholars to date this material to a later hand. The oracles of restoration are images created by those who were preserving Micah's oracles a couple of hundred years later. They may have picked up on hints of restoration in his own speeches, expanding them to relate the prophet to the events of their own day.

We will focus more on this phenomenon of secondary additions to prophetic works in the next two chapters. However, there are two things I would like you to remember at this point. First, though material may have come from a later hand it is no less integral to the final form of the book. Often these additions pick up on ideas that may have been hinted at or ambiguous in the earlier layers, pushing them in a particular direction. Second, just as multiple authorship is not viewed as a threat to the authority or canonicity of texts in the Pentateuch, so too multiple authors in the prophets do not undermine the sacred nature of the text for many strands of Judaism, as well as Christian denominations. After all, God can inspire two or three people as easily as one.

Putting It Back Together

In summary, the book of Micah contains a number of oracles from a contemporary of Isaiah living in a town outside of Jerusalem. The book is difficult to dissect for a number of reasons. First, as you may have noticed, the book contains very few prophetic forms, making it more difficult to determine where one oracle ends and another begins. Second, there is evidence of secondary additions to the text. While some of these are quite clear, others are debatable. Third, we know little about Micah himself. We do not even have a prophetic call narrative to tell us how he came to be a prophet. The redactors of the book probably assume that the audience knows who he is. Fourth, since it is such a short book, it is more difficult to get a picture of Micah's unique perspective than is the case with Isaiah or even Amos.

In spite of these factors, a couple of trends can still be noted. Unlike Isaiah, which focuses on the fate of the elite, this book looks at the events of the Assyrian crisis from the perspective of small landowners. As such, it condemns the various leaders of the nation for their treatment of the poor and vulnerable. Also, Micah sees little hope in Zion. He condemns illegitimate worship practices; not because he regards the temple of Jerusalem as the people's sole saving grace, but because ritual without righteousness cannot save the nation.

In spite of his critique of the elite, Micah was influential enough for his oracles to be not only preserved but also expanded and updated as Judah went through its own crisis. Was their preservation a result of Micah's elite status? His oracles reveal that he was educated and well versed in Israel's history. Or were his oracles saved due to a large following of disciples who preserved his words? It is hard to say, although it's probably a mixture of both.

No matter why we have this book, we can be grateful for it. Its images of economic justice are a profound reminder even today that those who follow Yahweh are called to live a life of justice and to care for those more economically vulnerable than they are. Only in such righteousness can one say with the prophet, "But as for me, I will look to the LORD, I will wait for the God of my salvation; my God will hear me" (7:7).

CHASTISEMENT AS A CONFESSION OF FAITH

It is difficult to appreciate the amount of faith that Isaiah and Micah must have had. The events of their day called into question Yahweh's justice, power, and even existence. Yet these prophets provided the people with ways to make sense of the disasters that they were experiencing. Let's summarize their common theological strategies.

First, they both maintain God's power. They view Yahweh as the one responsible for the fall of Samaria. Although some may see that as attributing violence and evil to God, for the prophets, the fall was necessary to maintain God's power.

Second, both prophets preserve God's justice by assigning blame to the people. By using the language of the courtroom, the prophets reinforce God's right to destroy the nations. The depiction of the people as overwhelmingly sinful renders God even more just in enacting a sentence on criminal behavior.

Third, both provide enough images of God's reliability that later hands felt justified adding oracles of restoration. Micah made clear that one of the issues facing the people was the question of whether anything was reliable anymore. For both Isaiah and Micah, God is reliable, whether by virtue of the covenant promises that are eternal or by virtue of God's divine nature. Either way, divine reliability is a source of hope.

Finally, by focusing on God's justice, both prophets allow for the possibility that God still loves the people. The acts of destruction are not signs that God's love for Israel has changed; rather they are simply things that must be done. Ultimately what God desires is a strong nation, one built on righteousness and centered on proper worship of this patron deity. The oracles of restoration flesh out the implications of God's plan to exalt this chosen nation.

FOR REVIEW

1. What are the three major crises behind the oracles in Isaiah?

2. What further challenges to contemporary readers do the additions to prophetic books pose?

3. How do the social locations of Isaiah and Micah differ, and how do those differences affect their messages?

4. What are some of the major concerns of Isaiah of Jerusalem?

5. What are some of the major concerns of the book of Micah?

For Further Reading

The best place to start further study of most prophetic books is with commentaries. Your instructor can suggest the best current ones. You can also find articles and book essays on individual passages. One way to find these is to use a journal titled *Old Testament Abstracts*. It is published three times a year, and it contains references to and summaries of everything that has been published on the Old Testament in a given period. Since the material comes from all over the world, not all of it will be available to you at your library, but because the publication contains summaries, you can determine if a given book or article addresses the issues that you are researching.

For an overview of ideological criticism, see Gale Yee's article on the method in *Dictionary of Biblical Interpretation: A-J*, edited by John H. Hayes (Nashville, TN: Abingdon, 1999) pages 534–37.

A good introduction to the history of ancient Israelite religion can be found in the two-volume work by Rainer Albertz, *A History of Israelite Religion in the Old Testament Period* (OTL; Louisville, KY: Westminster John Knox, 1994); it is not aimed at beginners, but it does provide an overview of many of the issues that we have discussed here, as well as extensive bibliographies prior to 1992.

There are many studies of the temples outside Jerusalem, most of them in technical archaeological reports. However, you will find that the articles in *Biblical Archaeology Review* summarize the conclusions of archaeologists in understandable ways. In addition, its photography is particularly engaging.

For more information about whether Yahweh had a wife, see Saul M. Olyan, *Asherah and the Cult of Yahweh in Israel* (SBLMS 34; Atlanta, GA: Scholars Press, 1998) who also uses ideological criticism to uncover the motivation of the Deuteronomists' polemic against Asherah. See also John Day, *Yahweh and the Gods and Goddesses of Canaan* (JSOTSup 265; Sheffield: Sheffield Academic, 2000) and William G. Dever, *Did God Have a Wife?: Archaeology and Folk Religion in Ancient Israel* (Grand Rapids, MT: Eerdmans, 2005).

11 Why, Oh Lord?

Have you completely rejected Judah?
Does your heart loath Zion? Why have you struck
us down so that there is no healing for us?
(Jer 14:19)

CHAPTER OVERVIEW

Thus far we have explored literature that paints a picture of what life was like during the monarchy. But when the city fell, the people who survived were exiled. The Babylonian exiles were not allowed to live in Judah. Instead, they were settled in Babylon, often working for the government. This chapter captures the voices of two prophets and one poet who watched their world crumble. You will hear their anguish, frustration, and devastation, even though they came from different social groups. You will see their struggle to make sense of a world in collapse.

Although we touched on the events of the exile in a previous chapter, we will review that history here. The new setting in exile led to changes in prophecy, theology, and Israelite society. We will survey these changes before turning to biblical texts from the exile. This chapter will provide the following:

> An examination of the history behind these texts

> An exploration of the theological issues that arose as a result of the fall of Jerusalem

> An opportunity for these authors to speak for themselves

Although much of the Old Testament bears the stamp of the exile, we will focus on the three books that provide first-hand witnesses to the fall of Jerusalem: Jeremiah, Lamentations, and Ezekiel. These texts show a way to maintain belief in God's presence without denying the exiles' experience of loss and anger.

THE LITERATURE OF THE EXILE

JUDAH'S FATE

It is a challenge when describing the exile to give enough details that people can understand the material, but not so much that they are overwhelmed. The history I will describe is summarized in the timeline. You may want to refer back to it, especially when you read Jeremiah and Ezekiel.

You may remember that the northern kingdom, Israel, fell to the Assyrians in 722 BCE, and then the Assyrians besieged Jerusalem (while Isaiah was a prophet). Soon after this event, Assyria was attacked by the Babylonians, which ended Assyrian control of the Levant.

The Babylonians were similar to the Assyrians. They spoke the same language and worshipped the same gods. Like Assyria, the Babylonians wanted to control the Fertile Crescent, so they began attacking the nations in the Levant on their way to Egypt.

Egypt had steadily grown in strength during this period, and it chose to fight the Babylonian army before it reached Africa. Judah's fate was tied to this conflict. The Judahite king, Josiah, an ally of Babylon, died fighting the Egyptians. All four kings who succeeded him were put on the throne either by the Egyptians or the Babylonians. The following chart illustrates this turbulent time:

King's Throne Name	Also Known As	Dates He Ruled	Supporting Power
Jehoahaz	Shallum	609 (3 months)	Babylon
Jehoiakim	Eliakim	609–598	Egypt first, then Babylon, then he rebelled against Babylon
Jehoiakin	Jeconiah	597 (3 months)	Exiled to Babylon
Zedekiah	Mattaniah	597–587	Babylon, then Egypt

Notice that Jehoiakin was exiled to Babylon in 597. The Babylonians besieged Jerusalem because of an uprising under his father. Jehoiakin surrendered to the Babylonians in order to save his city. He did not go alone into exile. The Babylonians also took "his mother, his servants, his officers, and his palace officials" (2 Kgs 24:12), which would have included high-ranking priests and prophets. This exile of the elite is called the First Deportation. By keeping Jehoiakin in Babylon where he could be executed at any moment, the Babylonians hoped to ward off rebellion in Judah.

It did not work. Although Zedekiah ruled without much incident for several years, by 589 he had turned to Egypt in hopes of winning Judah's independence. The Babylonians responded by, once again, besieging Jerusalem. This siege lasted about eighteen months (2 Kgs 25:1–2). The walls were finally breached in July, 587. The destruction that ensued culminated in the annihilation of the temple.

The population of Judah was decimated. A large number of people were killed. The poorest people remained in the land, but they lived under a foreign government and had no temple. Some people fled. The book of Jeremiah tells us about one group that went as refugees to Egypt. The rest, including leaders, were exiled, but this time the exiles had no hope of return.

LIVING AFTER THE FALL

When we examined siege warfare, we considered what it would have been like to live through such an event. We have also talked about how the fall of the nation affected the way the Israelites told their history. The fact is that the fall of the nation led to changes in all aspects of the Israelites' world: where they lived, what they thought about society, and even how they wrote.

WHO'S ON FIRST?

Have you ever been part of a large group of people when something goes wrong? Let's say you and your roommate plan a party that flops: the music is terrible, the food is bad, people leave early, and, to top it off, a fight breaks out. What do people tend to do in situations like that? They often blame each other. Does this sound familiar?

Nations do this too. After the destruction of New York's Twin Towers on September 11, 2001, a common question was, why did this happen? Who is to blame? We ask these questions, not just because we humans are petty (although that is true, too), but because we know such events will happen again if we do not understand their causes.

The exile may have happened more than 2500 years ago, but the people of Judah had the same questions. They too wondered who was to blame. Was it the bad diplomacy of the king? Was it the weakness of the army, the ethical character of the people, or the impropriety of the priests?

Inherent in these questions is a more hopeful one. They wondered how they would avoid such a fate in the future, if they ever returned to being a nation again. They did not reject the need for a king or priest, but they did question how each position could be lived out more in accord with God's will. Sometimes the prophetic texts that we will look at will assign blame. Other times they will paint a picture of a society restored to its proper order.

FROM TEMPLE COURTYARD TO SCRIBAL DESK

This change in setting affected all of literature, not just the prophetic books. Traditions were committed to writing that might have been otherwise lost. These included parts of the history of the monarchy, the preservation of various laws, and the collection of proverbs. In poetic books, earlier poems were expanded, often with laments or prayers for the future. In short, writing became an important tool for the production and preservation of Israel's traditions.

One of the many groups affected by the exile was the prophets. During the monarchy, if prophets wanted to deliver a message, they went to a public square, a temple complex, or a royal court, where they could speak to a live audience. But how do you deliver an oracle in exile? There were no public spaces open to exiles suitable for delivering such a speech. We see prophets turning more and more to writing. Jeremiah spoke, but that book tells the audience that a scribe, Baruch, recorded Jeremiah's oracles. The book of Ezekiel was primarily a written work. As a result, oracles became longer, visions more detailed, and prophetic forms changed.

HOW CAN WE SING?

For a people whose religious life centered around one particular place, the destruction of the temple left many to wonder how to express their faith. While scholars disagree about what religious practices changed during the exile, rituals other than those performed at the temple became more prominent. These included prayer, mourning, fasting, and various rituals performed at home. While Israelite belief in Yahweh continued, even as it adapted to new circumstances, some rituals may have been influenced by the religious practices of the Babylonians. Let me give a few examples of religious adaptation:

▸ Some exilic texts, such as Ezekiel, give prominence to observing the Sabbath. As a day of rest, this was a religious act that could still be observed during the exile.

▸ Acts of piety that were distinct to Jews also became an important way for the exiles to express their identity. Circumcision, for instance, which was not practiced by the Babylonians, set Jewish men apart. Later Israelite texts focused on dietary restrictions, such as kosher laws, as another way Jews maintained their identity.

▸ Elements of Babylonian religious practice pop up in Israelite texts from this period. These include the adoption of the Babylonian calendar, and the use of Babylonian mythic images in descriptions of Yahweh's actions.

IS ANYBODY OUT THERE?

As with any great tragedy, the exile led people to think about God. I suspect that it even led some people to stop worshipping Yahweh. After all, why worship Yahweh if Marduk had so clearly defeated Israel's God? Those who retained their faith had to admit that the experience of exile changed their understanding of God. Exile added new images to their experience of God, images that are often far from comforting.

The texts we will look at have the issue of theodicy at their heart; *theodicy* involves speculation on the relationship between human suffering and a good God. Who is this God who would allow this to happen? What is God's involvement in the fall of the city? Is God involved in human history, or does Yahweh simply not care? How can those who have experienced defeat worship God? Rethinking the nature of God often results in rethinking the nature of humanity and human experience.

We will see that this speculation continued far beyond the exile. Long after the return to the Levant, Israelites still wondered about the nature of God in light of human suffering. The texts in this chapter show some of the ways that Israelites, in the midst of the fall of the city, dealt with human suffering, while still maintaining that God is directly involved in human history.

Siege and Destruction

Jeremiah: In the Eye of the Storm

Jeremiah was a prophet in the city of Jerusalem during the final years of the nation. It would help you to read 2 Kings 24—25 as a backdrop to both Jeremiah and Ezekiel. Jeremiah began prophesying before the fall, during Josiah's reign, and continued until the fall of Jerusalem. His book comes down to us through the hands of later redactors, writing during or after the exile.

Redactional Layers in Jeremiah

We saw in the book of Isaiah that later disciples added chapters of material to the original collection of oracles by the historical Isaiah. The book of Jeremiah has similar additions, except that these additions permeate the book. While there are clear chunks of material produced by later hands (such as the account of the fall of the city from 2 Kings), there are also revisions to oracles and additional texts scattered throughout the book. Portions of the Greek version of the text are significantly different from the Hebrew version. Most experts on the book of Jeremiah no longer try to delineate discrete layers of redactional additions.

Yet, it is also true that some of the material coheres, especially with respect to style and theology. In general there are at least three blocks of material in Jeremiah:

- **Original poetic oracles. Many of the oracles in chapters 1—20 have a core that dates back to the prophet. These oracles have a poetic style similar to Amos.**

- **Biographical information or the "Baruch Layer." One of the distinguishing characteristics of Jeremiah is the amount of biographical information it contains. The book tells us that the prophet had a scribe named Baruch who recorded Jeremiah's oracles and re-created an original collection of oracles after the king burned the first copy (Jeremiah 36). We will see that this**

material has two rhetorical effects. First, it helps the audience identify with the prophet, so that they hear his oracles from his perspective. Second, it highlights the role that scribes played in preserving prophetic material.

- **A Deuteronomistic layer. Much of Jeremiah has echoes in Deuteronomistic material. When you read the Temple Sermon in chapters 7 and 26, you may notice some typical Deuteronomistic phrases. While a few scholars argue that this indicates that Jeremiah had been part of the Deuteronomistic group, it is more likely that the book was redacted by someone from that group or someone influenced by them. The fact that the poetic material is less Deuteronomistic argues against the view that Jeremiah himself was a Deuteronomist.**

There are also smaller units of material that may have come from later redactors. For instance, there are a series of laments placed in the mouth of the prophet. Were these laments that Jeremiah or his scribe preserved, or were they added later to depict the anguish that these events caused for the righteous? There is also something called the "Book of Consolation" in chapters 30—31 which contain a number of restoration oracles. Were these from Jeremiah himself, or were they later additions? Unfortunately we can only speculate.

The book is a difficult one to read. It is hard to discern what came from Jeremiah himself and what disciples added later. The collection has no chronological order, and many oracles are impossible to date.

The book provides some context for the life of the prophet. He was from a minor priestly family, one that did not serve at the temple of Jerusalem. He was apparently not a member of the elite classes. The book further notes that he never married, a rare thing in the ancient world. His prophecies, which urged surrender to the Babylonians, led to his arrest for treason. After the fall of the city, Jeremiah told the people to stay in the land, but Judean leaders took him to Egypt.

The oracles I have selected represent the book's main concerns. Your instructor may choose to use different ones. Either way, the overview that I provide at the end of the section will highlight the book's main themes.

Jeremiah 1:4–10: Jeremiah's call narrative

Jeremiah 16:1–13: Jeremiah's life as a sign

Jeremiah 27:1–28:17: Babylon as part of God's plan

Jeremiah 15:15–21 and 20:7–18: Jeremiah's laments

Jeremiah 7:1–20 and 26:1–24: An oracle delivered at the temple

Jeremiah 18.1–12 and 19:1–13: The image of the potter-God

Jeremiah 31:15–34. A new covenant

Jeremiah 1:4–10: A Prenatal Call

The book opens with an oracle describing Jeremiah's birth. While it is probably an introduction to the book as a whole and, therefore, part of the last layers of the text, the point of the oracle is to present Jeremiah as a man created by God to be a prophet.

Looking Closely at the Text

1. What does it mean for Jeremiah to be a "prophet to the nations"?

2. Whom does Jeremiah's reaction to God's call remind you of?

"I Knew You"

This oracle is a bit confusing. It is not delivered to Jeremiah while he is still in the womb. It is an oracle that Jeremiah receives much later, and in it God tells Jeremiah that he was created to be a prophet. In other words, the oracle asserts that Jeremiah had no other purpose in life but to be God's prophet. We will see in later oracles that many people thought that Jeremiah was a false prophet. By placing this text at the beginning of the book, Jeremiah's function as a true prophet is emphasized.

His importance is shown in another way. Notice that he objects to God's commissioning of him. He tells God, "Truly I do not know how to speak." Did you remember another prophet who initially refused God's call, because he also felt he could not speak well enough? It was the Israelites' great leader, Moses. The redactor of Jeremiah is highlighting this connection between Moses and Jeremiah: Jeremiah is a "prophet like Moses."

Something differentiates Jeremiah, however. He is a "prophet to the *nations*." What does this mean? Presumably it means that God's word extends beyond the boundaries of Judah. As Judah's history became more entangled in the fates of other nations, some of Israel's prophets realized that Yahweh's power had to extend to these other nations. Isaiah asserted God's control over Assyria. In Jeremiah that control includes the appointment of a prophet who can either curse or bless nations other than Israel.

The extent of the prophet's power is asserted in the final two verses. God literally puts his words into Jeremiah's mouth. God transforms Jeremiah's speech, so that it will be as effective as God's: by speaking God's word, the divine decrees will come to pass. Jeremiah has God's power to pluck up and pull down, to destroy and build nations other than Judah.

JEREMIAH 16:1–13: JEREMIAH'S LIFE AS A SIGN OF DOOM

This oracle of destruction talks about the futility of having children who will only suffer and die in the wars that will soon come.

LOOKING CLOSELY AT THE TEXT

How is Jeremiah's personal life related to his message?

JEREMIAH'S LIFE AS A SIGN

God demanded that the prophet dedicate his whole life to predicting disaster. God tells him not to marry or have children, because there is no hope for the future. The bodies of the dead will be heaped up in piles, and the destruction will be so vast that no one will be left to mourn for the dead.

The passage presumes that the audience knows how Judeans mourned for the dead. Ritual mourning was important in ancient Israel, not just because it offered comfort to those who had suffered the loss of a loved one, but because the people believed it also brought some kind of relief to the dead. The prophet refers to this ritual mourning in verses 5–8. What this oracle predicts is not just widespread destruction but also eternal suffering for the dead.

The punishment will be twofold: widespread death for some and exile for those who survive. There is no hint of a remnant or of any restoration after the disaster. The situation is so hopeless, the oracle contends, that anyone who truly understands what is to come would avoid marriage and family. There is no hope for future generations.

The final passage of the oracle contains an ironic twist. The Israelites are accused of "going after" other gods. God will punish them by "hurling" them to those other gods, not as worshippers but as servants or slaves.

Notice the contrast with Hosea. The marital status of both prophets is a symbol for a core message of their book. God commanded Hosea to marry a promiscuous woman to symbolize Israel's infidelity. Jeremiah is commanded to avoid marriage to symbolize Judah's desolation. Hosea (and Isaiah) has children whose names indicate the nation's future. Jeremiah's Judah is so far beyond hope that he is commanded to father no children.

JEREMIAH 27:1–28:17: SURRENDER TO BABYLON!

These two chapters give a clear picture concerning why Jeremiah was despised by the citizens of Jerusalem. When he talks about "serving" Babylon, he is advocating surrender to the enemy.

IN CASE YOU WERE WONDERING

A yoke. This is a heavy crossbar placed on the shoulders of oxen, by which they pull plows and other heavy farm equipment.

The fourth year of Zedekiah (Jer 28:1). This date seems to contradict the fact that this oracle comes at the beginning of Zedekiah's reign, but the general sense is that it occurs before the siege of the city.

Hananiah. This must have been another famous prophet at this time.

Jeconiah. A prophet, also known as Jehoiakin, whom the king exiled to Babylon in the first deportation.

"Amen." This is a Hebrew word that means something like, "So be it!" When Jeremiah responds to Hananiah's prophesy by saying "Amen," he is being sarcastic.

Looking Closely at the Text

1. Why would Jeremiah be considered a false prophet in his day?

2. Where does the confrontation between Hananiah and Jeremiah take place, and who is there listening to them?

3. What does Hananiah predict in 28:2–4? How does Hananiah's message differ from Jeremiah's?

4. Do you think Hananiah's death was caused by God?

Accepting the Yoke

This long passage, probably from a later layer of material in the book, is important for two reasons. First, it depicts the controversy among the prophets that existed in the days of Jeremiah. We see that prophets were delivering conflicting oracles, and that the people had to judge who the true prophet was. Second, the passage also conveys the heart of Jeremiah's message: that the Babylonian crisis was a punishment from God for Judah's sins.

Let's start with the first theme: true and false prophecy. Jeremiah was not from an important family. He was an odd man, who had dedicated his whole life to predicting disaster, going so far that he never even married. Yet, the disaster that he described in such vivid terms did not come. Year after year, the city stood. Bodies were not being heaped up, and, although some people had been exiled, most of the population remained. He was publicly humiliated when Hananiah broke the yoke from around his neck.

Hananiah's oracle seems reasonable: yes, the king is in exile, but things will be fine. God will remove this heavy burden from the nation and bring back his anointed to rule over the land once more. What was Jeremiah's response to Hananiah? A rather limp, "We'll see." How long did the people have to wait to see who the true prophet was? Well, Hananiah did die within one year, but the city remained standing. It was at least six more years before the city actually fell and all the disasters that Jeremiah predicted came true.

The second issue, concerning Jeremiah's message, would have also been startling. Today we can sit back and say, "Those stupid Jerusalemites! Why didn't they see that God would punish them for their sins?" But put yourself in Jerusalem at that time. Jeremiah is touting submission to the Babylonians as its only hope. His behavior can be compared to someone during World War II claiming that Hitler was sent by God and that the only "righteous" thing to do was to surrender to Hitler. Would you have agreed with this idea?

Jeremiah was accused of treason. His message was not popular in a time when Babylon was the clear enemy, and the one thing that people could agree on was that Babylonian power was destroying the nation. After all, this was the empire that held captive the royal family and their officials, within a sword's reach of death. Is it any wonder that Jeremiah was imprisoned for his oracles?

JEREMIAH 15:15–21 AND 20:7–18: JEREMIAH'S LAMENTS

The book of Jeremiah contains a series of individual laments that the prophet sang bemoaning his fate. In these examples, see if you can identify what he is upset about.

IN CASE YOU WERE WONDERING

Forbearance. This means to refrain from demanding something that is due to you, like a debt.

A deceitful brook. This is an image that connotes lack of trustworthiness. You can't count on a deceitful brook.

LOOKING CLOSELY AT THE TEXT

1. Try to put these two oracles in your own words. What exactly is Jeremiah lamenting about?

2. What is the view of God in these passages?

THE LAMENT OF THE PROPHET

Some people find the laments of Jeremiah, sometimes called his "confessions," to be the most moving part of the book. Through his anguish, we get a glimpse into what the prophets gave up in order to serve God. If anyone wonders why people like Moses and Jeremiah were reluctant to become prophets, these laments tell you.

The passages we have looked at so far portray a tormented Jeremiah. He had to deliver an unpopular message, whose predicted results were long in coming. He suffered because of his message, and he was mocked as a false prophet. Yet, over and over again, he claims that he had no choice: he was forced into this way of life.

These laments echo the form and content of the individual laments we looked at in the Psalms. Like the laments in the Psalms, the lamenter does not hold back: Jeremiah accuses God, pleads for vengeance, and curses his own birth.

What I find interesting about these poems is that Jeremiah is not lamenting the fate of the city, but rather he is vexed by his own situation. He does not pray to God to deliver the city or stop the impending disaster. Instead, Jeremiah asks God to take revenge against Jeremiah's enemies. It seems a little petty, considering that the whole nation is about to be destroyed.

The laments also make me wonder how much Jeremiah believed in what he was saying. After all, he accuses God of deceiving him. He claims that his accusers are right: the disaster is not coming, and God had picked him out to make him a lying prophet. We talked about God doing this in 1 Kings 22 when he sends a lying spirit into the mouths of all the prophets except Micaiah ben Imlah. Jeremiah accuses God of doing the same thing to him.

Although the laments may not be what we would expect the prophet to be concerned with, they do serve to make the prophet a sympathetic figure. In addition, the prophet becomes a model for how the audience should re-

Focus on METHOD

Rhetorical Criticism

Rhetorical criticism is another one of those methods of biblical interpretation that mean different things to different people. Some define it as a method that focuses on material meant to persuade the reader; it examines the techniques that the writer uses in service of that persuasion. Others view it as an examination of the literary style of the text itself, regardless of audience or intent.

We have seen in our discussion of historical inquiry that every text has a point of view. Although some texts have the express purpose of persuasion, the fact remains that all texts involve at least a subtle form of persuasion. They reflect someone's point of view, even when the author tries to write from the point of view of another person. For our purposes, then, rhetorical criticism examines all of the ways that an author presents a viewpoint.

Prophetic writing is a natural location to utilize rhetorical criticism. Clearly these texts have a point of view, and they are overt in their attempt to change people's behavior. A rhetorical analysis of an oracle would examine the way the oracle is persuasive. Take, for example, the oracles against foreign nations that we read in the book of Amos. We talked about how the oracles would have attracted an audience and led them to view Amos as a true

prophet, before the prophet's condemnation of them turns the tables.

In exilic prophetic texts, elements of the persuasive nature of oral oracles remain. Individual poetic oracles, such as Jeremiah 3:21–22 or Ezekiel 19:1–14 utilize the same kinds of prophetic speech patterns found in pre-exilic prophets. The confrontation between Jeremiah and Hananiah (Jeremiah 28) and the disputation of the proverb in Ezekiel 18 present moments of oral persuasion.

These two books also have rhetorical elements in their literary arrangements. Both books flesh out the personalities of Jeremiah and Ezekiel so that the prophets function as characters within their own prophetic books. This literary device creates the mechanism by which the audience experiences the exile through these two figures.

Here is an exercise you might do. Read Jeremiah 37—44 and Ezekiel 3—5. How do the different characterizations of these men affect the way you think about the role of the prophet and the nature of God during this national crisis? This analysis will make you aware that the personification of these prophetic figures fits the overall rhetorical purposes of each of their redactors.

spond to unjust suffering: complain. Remember that the audience of the final form of the book lived after the fall of the city. The laments encourage their own prayers to God.

JEREMIAH 7:1–20 AND 26:1–24: DOES GOD DWELL IN JERUSALEM?

These passages address the question of God's presence within the city of Jerusalem. Here the prophet argues against those who claim that God's presence in the temple will save the city of Jerusalem. Both passages have evidence of Deuteronomistic influence.

IN CASE YOU WERE WONDERING

A den of robbers. In the New Testament, Jesus quotes Jeremiah, who uses the phrase to describe those who have false ideas about the temple.

Shiloh. This was a city where the ark had been located before the monarchy. The Philistines destroyed the city of Shiloh, capturing the ark. The city of Shiloh had not yet been rebuilt in the time of Jeremiah.

LOOKING CLOSELY AT THE TEXT

1. Where does Jeremiah deliver this oracle?

2. What are the "deceptive words" in which the people trust?

3. According to Jeremiah 7:5–6, what must the people do so that God will dwell with them?

4. In Jeremiah 7:15, what will God do to the people in order to punish them for their sins?

5. How does the version of this incident as preserved in chapter 26 differ from the version in chapter 7?

THE TEMPLE SERMON

Jeremiah 7 is sometimes called "the Temple Sermon." Jeremiah goes to the temple in order to refute the idea that God's presence in the temple is enough to protect the city from impending disaster. There he addresses the people who talk about the temple ("This is the temple of the Lord") as if it will magically save them from the Babylonians.

From our review of Israel's history, you may understand why people would have believed this. God had promised David that the monarchy would last forever and that the temple would be a part of this eternal promise. This promise seemed to be affirmed during the Assyrian siege when the city of Jerusalem was miraculously saved.

Jeremiah tells the people that their hope is in vain. God's presence, his "dwelling" was not some magical force field that would deflect enemy attack. What was Jeremiah's evidence for asserting this? It was the fate of Shiloh. Although God had "dwelt" there, the city had been destroyed. Jeremiah invites the people to travel to the ruins of Shiloh if they are so sure of God's protection.

Jeremiah then refutes the idea that God's covenant with Judah is unconditional. For Jeremiah, the covenant depends on the moral behavior of the people. Jeremiah 7:9 echoes the Ten Commandments: he asserts that the people have broken the commandments, and can no longer expect God's presence to save them. Shiloh was destroyed as punishment for the people's wickedness. Jerusalem will be destroyed as punishment for their sins.

Chapter 26, probably from a Deuteronomistic redactor, differs from chapter 7 in two important respects. First, it focuses on God's reason for sending the oracle. God desired repentance, not destruction. Second, it tells the audience about the immediate reaction to this oracle. By juxtaposing these two elements in chapter 26 the redactor highlights the stubborn sinfulness of the people. Even the deliberations about whether to kill Jeremiah in verses 11–24 cast King Jehoiakim and his officials into a terrible light.

JEREMIAH 18:1-12 AND 19:1-13: GOD IS LIKE A POTTER

God is compared to a potter who creates a vessel, judges whether it is good or bad, and either keeps it or destroys it. This image is known from an Egyptian creation account where the sun god, Ptah, is a potter who makes the world on a pottery wheel.

IN CASE YOU WERE WONDERING

The valley of the son of Hinnom at the entry of the Potsherd Gate (Jer 19:2). According to Jeremiah 7:31, this was a place where child sacrifice was performed.

The Topheth. This is probably the sacred precinct where the child sacrifice was performed.

LOOKING CLOSELY AT THE TEXT

1. How does the metaphor of the potter address the problem of evil?

2. How is Jeremiah 19:1–13 related to 18:1–12?

God Is the Potter, Israel the Pot

This oracle has two parts. In the first part, Jeremiah goes to a pottery maker's, and learns how God is like a potter. In the second part, Jeremiah delivers an oracle of destruction to Jerusalem using the image of pottery to illustrate the coming destruction. The graphic descriptions of death in Jeremiah 19:7–13 have a basis in reality. In siege people do resort to cannibalism, while unburied bodies become food for wild animals.

The image not only tells us something about what is predicted (that the destruction of Judah is coming), but it also tells us something about God. Just as the potter creates vessels out of clay, so God has created nations. Just as the potter must judge his work, so God judges the nations. And just as the potter can destroy what he has created in order to fashion something better, so God has the right to destroy nations and begin again.

The metaphor breaks down, however, when the oracle focuses on the sin of Judah. In chapter 19, the nation is "bad," not because it has been made poorly, but because it is acting badly by worshipping other gods and practicing child sacrifice. We talked about child sacrifice when we looked at Abraham's near sacrifice of Isaac. For those who performed child sacrifice, it was a ritual that expressed a person's belief that all good things came from the gods. The bones of the sacrificed children were placed in pottery jars and buried in the sacred area.

We also mentioned that the Israelites, as well as many other peoples in the area, practiced substitution, that is, they sacrificed a lamb in place of the firstborn child. Some people believed that it was a greater sacrifice to actually offer up the child, and in times of crisis, some people offered their child (rather than a lamb) so that the gods would look favorably on them. Both Jeremiah and Ezekiel condemned those who practiced child sacrifice, an indication that in these years of national crisis, some people hoped to avert disaster by sacrificing their children.

The passage uses irony to describe the punishment. Not only will child sacrifice not avoid disaster, but it will cause Yahweh's anger to burn so fiercely that the dead bodies will be heaped up in the very place where the bodies of the dead children, slain to avoid the disaster, are buried. The oracle that starts out with the picture of God, the potter, culminates in the portrayal of the dead heaped on top of pottery jars containing the bones of sacrificed babies. Death of the firstborn will not protect the city from the death that awaits them.

Jeremiah 31:15–34: A Vision of Restoration

Although much of the book of Jeremiah contains oracles of destruction, some of the later passages in the book contain oracles of restoration. These oracles, so different from the tone and style of the rest of the book, were probably added by Jeremiah's followers. They presume the fall of Jerusalem, and reflect the concerns of a later community. They witness to Jeremiah's continued importance to later generations.

In Case You Were Wondering

Ramah. This was a city in the north.

Rachel. She was one of Jacob's wives, and mother of some of the northern tribes.

"The parents have eaten sour grapes, and the children's teeth are set on edge." This proverb expressed the Israelites' belief that God could punish people for sins that their ancestors had committed.

The heart. This symbol represented the inner part of a person. If something is "written on" someone's heart, it is an innate part of them.

Looking Closely at the Text

1. Whose restoration is predicted in Jeremiah 31:15–22?

2. Whose restoration is predicted in 31:23–25?

3. How will the people be different after the restoration than they were before it?

"I Will Write It on Their Hearts."

Jeremiah's vision of restoration contains a powerful image: the law written on people's heart. Reading this passage centuries after it was first written, we still understand the concept that the poet was trying to convey.

The text begins with an image coming out of city laments: the weeping goddess; but, as is common in Israel, the goddess is replaced with a personified nation. Just as poets sometimes refer to the northern kingdom by the name "Jacob," the prophet uses the image of Jacob's wife, Rachel, to symbolize the desolate city. The restoration results from God's merciful response to her tears.

The first section of the oracle focuses on the restoration of the northern kingdom, while the second section depicts the restoration of Judah. Even though Israel had split off from Judah almost four hundred years prior and had fallen more than a century before Jerusalem, the oracles of restoration recognize that the nation is not completely healed without the restoration of both Israel and Judah.

Jeremiah 31:27 uses both planting metaphors and the image of the inscribed heart to describe the restoration. Sandwiched in the middle of the passage is a brief hint that the exiles are struggling with the question: for whose sins are we suffering? Will God punish the innocent for the sins of their ancestors, or will each generation be given its due? For Jeremiah, each generation is judged on its own merit.

In the last verses of the oracle, the author addresses another question: how can this restoration succeed when the nation has already failed? For Jeremiah, this restoration will include a "new covenant" in place of all previous covenants. The description of this new covenant implies the creation of a new kind of person, one for whom the law is internal.

READING THE BOOK AS A WHOLE

The persona of Jeremiah is a central element in the book. You might be thinking, "Well, yeah! It has his name, doesn't it?" But remember when you read the book of Amos. Did you get much of a feel for the personality of Amos? The book of Amos tells us a few things about his life, but not much. We don't know if he was married, if he was sad or angry when people didn't listen to him, or if he was ever arrested.

In the book of Jeremiah, the prophet's personality is essential to the message. We not only read his oracles, but we learn where he was when he delivered them, what the consequences of his preaching were, and even how he felt about being a prophet. Other than the book of Jonah, this characteristic is quite distinctive among the prophetic books.

Why is the book of Jeremiah so different? It could be that the people who preserved Jeremiah's oracles had more information about him than collectors of Amos had about him. But I think there's a more fundamental reason. We read about the last days of Jerusalem through the experience of the man, Jeremiah. He does not provide a disinterested reporting of events. In fact, if we hear the oracles of Jeremiah and fail to feel his loss, frustration, and outrage, then we've missed the point. Jeremiah's experience symbolizes the effect of these events for the audience.

Taken as a whole, the book deals with the theological problems that the exile posed for the nation: why did the city fall, and where was Yahweh? Jeremiah's oracles were unheeded before the fall of the city. God's message in these oracles is that the city falls because of the people's sinfulness. The devastation inflicted by Babylon is God's just punishment for the people's sins. Therefore, the only faithful response to the siege of the city is surrender to the Babylonians.

As prophecies often are, that oracle was a radical message. Put yourself back in that besieged city for a moment. You are surrounded by brutal soldiers who offer sacrifices to idols. You know that when the city faced a similar crisis under the Assyrians, King Hezekiah followed the advice of his prophet, Isaiah, and placed his trust in Yahweh. You also know that the city was delivered by some miracle. Even though you and your children are starving, you have faith that God, who is present in the temple, will come to your aid if you have enough faith.

Then along comes this man, who claims he's a prophet, saying your faith in the temple is all a lie! Moreover, he goes around telling people to surrender to the enemy. Would you have listened to him? I don't think I would have.

The book exalts Jeremiah by stressing how many people opposed him. He was arrested by the authorities. People wanted to kill him; he was opposed by other prophets, the priests, and the royalty. Yet he remained completely dedicated to God and faithful to the message he was charged to give. Within the book are poems in which Jeremiah complains to God about what he has been called to do. Even though Jeremiah asserts that God must have picked him out to be a lying prophet, the rhetoric of the book depicts Jeremiah as a true prophet who suffered unjustly.

The book also addresses the question of theodicy: what does the fall of the city tell us about the nature of God? You may have to read between the lines to see this issue, but here are three examples:

Is God reliable? The oracle that Jeremiah delivers in chapter 7 addresses the question of God's reliability. Didn't God promise to always be with Israel? Jeremiah answers, "No." But this answer does not mean that God is weak or fickle. Rather, the fall of the city demonstrates that the people have misunderstood the covenant. They thought it worked like a magic ring of protection. Jeremiah points out that God's promise depends on their behavior: they must live their lives in accordance with God's laws. *They* are the ones who have been fickle and unreliable, not God. But even though Israel turns its back on God, Yahweh continues to speak to the people. Jerusalem's fall forced them to reexamine their actions and their relationship with God.

Is Yahweh only Israel's God? A subtle theme in the book is the issue of God's love for other nations. Jeremiah contends that God's reign is over all people, not just Judah. God's use of Babylon to punish Israel is placed within that context. The Babylonians are not a symbol of evil's growing power in the world. They also are a people that God has created, a nation that God governs. Israel's purpose remains central for global salvation, but the ultimate goal of God's plan extends beyond its national boundaries.

Is God in control? The image of the potter represents Jeremiah's answer to the question of God's control. Israel has forgotten that the creature is far inferior to the creator. Just as a pot cannot object if the potter decides to destroy it and make a new one, so Judah has no right to wonder if its destruction is justified. God's power makes such a question ridiculous.

Finally, the book of Jeremiah offers some hope for the future. The book of Jeremiah focuses on a new covenant, written on the hearts of the restored people (Jer 31:33). The new covenant will be so ingrained within God's people that they cannot help but follow it.

LAMENTATIONS

THE CITY IN TEARS

Israel was not the only ancient city to have suffered great loss. The ancient world was a brutal place. Mesopotamia had a long history of war, because control of the fertile river valleys meant life or death, in light of the arid land that surrounded them. The history of Mesopotamia is filled with accounts of invading peoples seeking to control the rivers.

One of the earliest types of literature from Mesopotamia is city laments. These were poems written in response to the destruction of a great temple city. They described the brutal destruction of that city, in part from the perspective of the city's patron goddess, who wept over the loss of her people. Shorter laments were used in temple rituals. These laments are found in various accounts throughout Mesopotamia's history.

There are no city laments in the Bible, but some of the poetry from the exile reflects elements of Babylonian laments. One of the most prominent adaptations of the city lament in Israelite texts was the replacement of the weeping goddess with the weeping of the city, personified as a woman. Although we also see elements of the city laments in Psalms, Jeremiah, and Ezekiel, the book of Lamentations comes closest to the city laments.

The book of Lamentations is placed directly after Jeremiah in Christian Bibles, although in Jewish Bibles it is found among the Writings. For a long time Jeremiah was thought to be the author of Lamentations. While it reflects the lamenting style we saw in the book of Jeremiah, its author was probably not the prophet.

The book of Lamentations has many elements that derive from Mesopotamian city laments. The poems describe the fall of a major city, and they address the role of God in that fall. The images and anguish of the poem reflect the style of the Mesopotamian texts.

Since the book is only five chapters long, you may want to read the whole thing. The book is probably comprised of five short poems, even though they are not set off clearly from each other. These poems were probably written soon after the destruction of Jerusalem, and they convey the sadness, horror, and anger of the people.

LAMENTATIONS 1:1–2:22: TWO LAMENTS OVER ZION

Lamentations 1:1—2:22 contain the first two poems of the book. In Hebrew, each verse of each poem begins with a different letter of the alphabet, indicating two separate poems. The language of the poems recalls the language of the psalms, especially the description of those who rejoice in Jerusalem's destruction. These poems do not present an account of the fall of the city, so they should not be read as if they are describing the order of the events. They are poems or, more probably, songs.

IN CASE YOU WERE WONDERING

The city speaks. Some of the direct speech in the poems is the voice of the personified city.

LOOKING CLOSELY AT THE TEXT

1. What aspects of the city's fall do these poems emphasize?

2. Who is to blame for the fall of the city?

THE CITY CRIES

These poems are not told from God's perspective. Instead, they tell us how the fall felt to the people who were there. Because the poems use an acrostic structure, verses that logically would go together are in separate places. The poems are more like a collage of images, rather than a single painting.

Some verses focus on the experience of war. For instance, both Lamentations 2:11–12 and 2:20 describe starvation and cannibalism. Lamentations 2:21 recalls those killed in battle, while 1:19 depicts the starvation of the city's leaders. When the city speaks, she laments the suffering of *her* people in maternal tones. This city mourns for her dead.

Some verses describe life after the fall. The city is empty; its glory is gone. No longer are there sounds of festivals, ritual worship, or victory songs.

The enemies of Jerusalem, here unnamed, laugh at the former city, rejoicing at her downfall. I can relate to the poet's anger: I remember, after the destruction of the World Trade Center in New York City on September 11, 2001, seeing images of some people in other countries celebrating as the towers fell. Many Americans were angered by this reaction. Similarly, the people of Judah were incensed that others took joy in their suffering.

While the first poem describes Zion's fate, the second poem turns to the question of blame. Although at one point false prophets are blamed (Lam 2:14), the bulk of the poem accuses God for the city's destruction. Anyone who has read the Mesopotamian city laments would be familiar with this type of language. In those poems the goddess rails against the chief male god who has destroyed her city. She accuses him of being unfair, overly angry, or simply unreliable. She begs him to allow her to restore the city, because he gets no benefit from people who no longer worship him. Rarely, however, do these poems claim that a god was justified in destroying the city because the people had sinned.

In contrast, Lamentations follows Israelite prophets in attributing the fall to Judah's sins, which provoked God's anger. Yet, even granting this difference between the city laments and the book of Lamentations, the city still blames God for not sending prophets to warn the people. She accuses God of being too angry. "The LORD has become like an enemy . . . and in his fierce indignation has spurned king and priest" (Lam 2:5 and 6). She even accuses God of unjust cruelty

> Look, O LORD, and consider!
> To whom have you done this?
> Should women eat their offspring,
> the children they have borne? (Lam 2:20)

The book of Lamentations does not run away from the emotions such destruction causes. It does not censor the anger or tell its poets that these are not "proper" or "correct" views of God. It understands that even a partial, and maybe even flawed, experience of God is still an experience of God. In the heart of such destruction, isn't it amazing that people continued to pray to this God, continued to hope that someday the temple would be rebuilt, so that they could praise the Lord again?

EZEKIEL: WATCHING THE WHIRLWIND

Ezekiel lived during the same years as Jeremiah, but while Jeremiah was an old man during the siege of Jerusalem, Ezekiel was probably in his thirties. What makes these two prophets so different, however, isn't their age. Ezekiel prophesied from Babylon, while Jeremiah was in Jerusalem. This means that Ezekiel was among the highest classes of Jerusalemite society, while Jeremiah was among the lowest. Although both men were priests, Jeremiah came from a family who no longer served as priests, while Ezekiel was probably from a family who served in the temple of Jerusalem.

These differences affect their theologies. While Jeremiah characterizes sin as the breaking of the covenant, Ezekiel depicts sin as ritual defilement. While Jeremiah has little hope in the temple, Ezekiel focuses on the changing nature of God's presence in the temple, both in the oracles of destruction and restoration. While Jeremiah's laments allow us to empathize with his struggle, Ezekiel's almost tacit obedience distances the prophet from his audience. Lastly, while Jeremiah's God feels anguish over the city's destruction, Ezekiel's God acts out of concern for the divine reputation.

While it might be surprising to find such differences in the Bible, they occur within a broad area of agreement. Both prophets agree that there is only one God. Both agree that God punishes each generation for its sins. Both agree that God will restore the nation and create a new covenant. You will find many other examples of agreement, but within that agreement, these prophets show us that the Israelites had many theological responses to tragedy.

The book of Ezekiel, while containing oracles that might have been delivered orally, was probably mostly a written work. There are many pieces of evidence that point to its literary character. For example, the book is well organized:

Ezek 1:1—23:49	Oracles of destruction
Ezek 24:1—33:20	Oracles against foreign nations
Ezek 33:21–22	Report of the fall of the city
Ezek 33:23—48:35	Oracles of restoration

In addition, the visions scattered throughout the book are very long (the last one extends for nine chapters), inviting meditation over the pictures they are trying to paint. The book tells us that God made the prophet mute, a hint that the oracles were primarily written. Many of the oracles in the book are dated, a literary device for a reading audience. Lastly, the book is unified by a number of images and visions that reappear throughout the book. The most prominent of these is the vision of God on a moveable throne, an image that opens the book.

Scribes and Scrolls

Sociologically we would expect a rise in writing during the exile. The loss of social settings for the oral deliverance meant that oral traditions were in danger of being lost without some other mechanism for preservation. The fact that the Babylonian exiles came from the elite classes of Judah meant that the literacy rate was much higher among the exiles than it was in the nation as a whole.

Evidence within both Jeremiah and Ezekiel confirm the rise of literary forms. The material in the book of Ezekiel has the markings of a growing literary tradition. The book of Jeremiah describes the prophet directing Baruch to preserve his oracles on a scroll.

As written scrolls became an increasingly important vehicle for preserving traditions, the scribal class grew in status. Again, Jeremiah attests to this. The most positive figures in the book, other than Jeremiah and Baruch, are scribes.

The ancient Israelites developed a writing tradition within a culture that remained primarily oral. Therefore, their writing reflects this oral context. For example,

traditions remain fluid and authorship is not a central concern.

Yet, writing did affect other elements of Israel's traditions. Writing crystallizes the viewpoints of those responsible for the material. It is not surprising, for example, that the book of Jeremiah views scribes in a relatively positive light. Similarly, the fact that many oracles of restoration feature a Davidic king is to be expected, given that the remnants of the Davidic court had the means to preserve their texts through the exile.

These new productions also give evidence of a tension between the authority of an oral tradition versus that of the written word. The ancient audience was aware that because a tradition was written down, it was not necessarily more objective or "true." You can imagine that some people, for whom the oral tradition had prominence, treated the written texts of the elite with suspicion. Thus we see in Ezekiel 18 a disputation about the authority of an oral proverb, while in Jeremiah 36 the fragility of a combustible scroll is countered when the prophet authorizes a new version.

The following passages convey Ezekiel's main themes:

Ezekiel 1:1–28: The vision of the chariot throne

Ezekiel 8:1—9:11 and 11:22–25: God abandoning the city

Ezekiel 16:1–63: The city as a defiling wife

Ezekiel 18:1–32: The question of guilt

Ezekiel 20:1–31: A history of sin

Ezekiel 37:1–14: The vision of the dry bones

Ezek 43:1–9; 44:1–3; and 47:1–12: A vision of restoration

EZEKIEL 1:1–28: GOD'S CHARIOT THRONE

The book begins with a description of God's throne in the Jerusalem temple. Ezekiel's vision is usually referred to as a "chariot throne" because it has wheels and flies away. I have a colleague who has her students draw this throne as they are reading its description.

In Case You Were Wondering

The river Chebar. This was a smaller stream that ran off the Euphrates River in Babylonia.

The Chaldeans. This was the Hebrew name for the Babylonians.

Four faces. These are not the same thing as "four heads." The creatures that Ezekiel describes have one head with four faces.

Beryl. This is a crystal, which in some forms is considered a precious gem. Both emeralds and aquamarines are examples of beryl.

Looking Closely at the Text

1. How does this passage mirror Isaiah 6?

2. How is the text's description of the vision arranged?

God in the Temple

This is one of the most influential passages in the book of Ezekiel. The author is taking a well-known prophetic motif, the image of God in the temple (Isaiah 6), and expanding it. We will see Ezekiel repeatedly expand well-known images and motifs, in order to produce often startling passages. In this way, the prophet both recognizes his connection with Israel's past and also expresses how past traditions must now be seen in a different light, because of the exile.

The chapter is a vision: Ezekiel does not actually go to Jerusalem to see God, but he sees it through a prophetic experience. The first creatures that Ezekiel describes are the cherubim, as he calls them in 9:3. The reader sees this vision through Ezekiel's eyes. As his eyes travel up the image, our eyes follow. If you tried to draw this description, you would find it increasingly difficult to do so as the passage progresses. The further his eyes travel up the vision, the less able he is to express what he sees. He can only tell us what the vision was "like," because God's presence is ultimately indescribable.

Ezekiel's vision unifies the book. God is present in the temple at the beginning of the book, but the sins of the people defile the temple, and, in chapters 8—11, God must leave. The city, now without divine protection, is doomed to fall. At the end of the book (chapters 40—48), the prophet has a vision of the restored temple whose central scene is the return of God on the chariot throne. The movement of sin-punishment-restoration is marked by the three appearances of the chariot throne.

EZEKIEL 8:1–9:11: THE BEGINNING OF THE END

This passage describes some of the sins that led to the city's downfall.

IN CASE YOU WERE WONDERING

The image of jealousy, which provokes to jealousy. This an odd phrase that appears in a few places in the Bible, referring to God's presence in the temple. The reference to "jealousy" may derive from the demand for the exclusive worship of Yahweh.

Jaazaniah, son of Shaphan. This person must have been famous to the original audience, but it is no longer known who he was.

Tammuz. This was a Babylonian god or mythic figure associated with an annual journey to the world of the dead. Part of the ritual commemoration of Tammuz included ritual mourning.

LOOKING CLOSELY AT THE TEXT

1. How is this vision related to chapter 1?

2. Why does God leave?

THE MARK ON THE FOREHEAD

Ezekiel has many visions; in this one he is taken by the hair to the city of Jerusalem and plunked down in front of the wall of the inner court of the temple. God commands him to dig through the wall, and, when he does, he sees terrible things happening in the heart of the temple. What he observes is the ongoing worship of other gods in the holiest part of the temple complex. This would be like a Catholic priest finding satanic rituals being performed in St. Peter's at the Vatican!

Then Ezekiel is allowed to witness the start of the destruction of the city. God calls six "men." In Babylonian religion, different gods had different duties. Those who wrote carried a writing case. Others, who fought for the great gods, carried swords. Today many people think of the Israelite versions of these figures as angels. We are never told how many people are marked. The "man" simply returns and states that the job is done. But earlier in the passage God commands the "men" to fill the temple courts with the slain: it must have been a large number.

Immediately following this passage, God leaves the city. As long as God dwells in the city, the people are safe; but God is forced to leave, because of the defilement that is taking place within the sanctuary. While this abandonment is

Divine Abandonment in the Ancient Near East

Ezekiel's audience would have known that God's abandonment of the city signaled its unavoidable fate. The oracles that follow Ezekiel 8—11 are a kind of ancient version of watching a movie like "Titanic." The motif of divine abandonment was ubiquitous in the ancient Near East. From Sumerian laments commemorating the fall of important cities to Babylonian stories of Marduk leaving his throne, Mesopotamian texts often attributed urban collapse to the abandonment of the city by its god.

The city laments rarely give a reason for the god's departure. The presumption is that the god has every right to do so and does not need a reason. As the city slowly collapses, the citizens pray for help. They are often aided in this process by a patron-goddess who weeps for her "children." Their efforts are futile.

Babylonian texts use the motif of divine abandonment to explain events in their city's history. The Marduk Prophecy provides an explanation for the city's defeat at the hands of the Assyrians. The Assyrians had taken the Marduk statue from Babylon when they had overtaken the city. They set it up in a subordinate position to the statue of their main god, Assur, in their own national temple. The text depicts Marduk as the one who wishes to leave his city.

A city's need for a god is highlighted perhaps most starkly in the *Erra Epic*. In this poem, Erra, a god associated with sudden death, convinces Marduk, the god of Babylon, that his statue in the temple needs renovation. Marduk hesitates to have it restored because he does not want to abandon his throne. Marduk describes the destruction that occurred the last time his throne was abandoned. This time, Erra volunteers to occupy Marduk's throne, which leads to another series of disasters.

These last two texts show that divine abandonment is associated with the removal of whatever objects signified the god's presence in the temple. The Marduk Prophecy deals with the capture of the statue of the god. In the *Erra Epic,* even though the Marduk statue probably remained within the temple precincts, its removal from its place in the temple threatened the city's security.

not permanent, the city will suffer horrible devastation as a result of God's departure. The audience knows that from this point forward the city is doomed.

EZEKIEL 16:1–63: THE DEFILED CITY

This passage also personifies the city as a woman. But, once again, you will see Ezekiel expanding a metaphor almost to the breaking point. The language is graphic, violent, and designed to make the reader uncomfortable.

IN CASE YOU WERE WONDERING

"Whoring" and "adultery." These terms are sometimes used interchangeably for female promiscuity.

LOOKING CLOSELY AT THE TEXT

1. In what state does God find the child?

2. How is this passage similar to material in Hosea?

3. How is the personification of the city different from that in Lamentations?

This relief, circa 640 BCE, shows Assyrian officials recording loot taken from a conquered city.

THE ADULTERESS

Were you at all uncomfortable when you read this? Some people are shocked by its interacting images of sex and violence. Such a reaction is evidence that this literature is truly powerful, enough to make an audience uncomfortable 2500 years later!

Ezekiel *wants* to shock his audience. He takes up a common metaphor, as you may recall from your study of Hosea, but embellishes it with graphic details. The metaphor was a way for the Israelites to understand the notion of covenant. God's relationship with Israel is like that of a husband to his wife. But here Ezekiel focuses on the husband's right to control and even punish his wife.

This passage plays on ancient assumptions about the status of women. By personifying the city as a woman, the audience recognizes that the city is of a lower status than God, the husband. For ancient writers who wanted an image of something that is great compared to something that is small and undeserving, the images of husband and wife worked perfectly. The passage assumes that we agree that God, as husband, is justified when he hurts his wife, and that stoning is a just punishment for adultery.

The city's adultery occurs, in part, when the leaders of the city make alliances with Egypt and Babylon. Leaders had to swear before the other people's gods when they made an alliance, so the Jerusalemite leadership had to swear by the gods of Egypt and Babylon when they made their alliances. By not trusting in the power of Yahweh and swearing by other gods, the city as a whole "committed adultery" against its exclusive covenant with Yahweh.

While other prophets use this same motif, Ezekiel's use of it is unrelenting. First, the oracle is very long. Second, the images intensify as they are repeated; English translations often use euphemisms for the sexually graphic Hebrew terms that Ezekiel uses. But the ultimate insult to the city is when the prophet compares it to Samaria and Sodom, stating that even those cities are embarrassed by Jerusalem's bad behavior!

Ezekiel uses images of defilement to describe sin. The baby is born in blood and wallows in its blood, until God comes and purifies it. The prophet is saying that Jerusalem has always been a defiled city, and that it only became pure enough for a covenant with God because God purified it. The sexual images are also images of ritual defilement: going after other gods renders the city unclean. The practice of child sacrifice also leads to Jerusalem's defilement.

The punishment matches the historical experience of Judah. How does Yahweh punish Jerusalem for its adultery and defilement? By having Babylon and other enemies attack it. The city's "lovers," that is, the countries from whom the city sought safety, were the ones that ultimately destroyed it.

The end of the passage expresses two major themes of the book of Ezekiel: shame and God's reputation. The passage presumes that what will keep the city from sinning again is a proper sense of "shame." For Ezekiel, shame has a positive effect. The experience of shame means that the people realize how little they deserved all the things that God has done for them. Shame is recognition of God's otherness.

God also acts so that people will know that "I am the LORD" (Ezek 16:62). God wants all people to recognize the divine nature. For Ezekiel, the most important fact of God's nature is that God is infinitely greater than any human. To "know" Yahweh is to know that God, personified as a male, can do all things and that people are nothing without God.

EZEKIEL 18:1–32: WHO IS GUILTY?

This oracle takes up the question of guilt: can persons be punished for the sins of their ancestors? We saw that the book of Jeremiah addressed the question briefly. Ezekiel gives it fuller treatment.

Looking Closely at the Text

1. According to Ezekiel 18:4, who shall die for sin?

2. Docs Yahweh enjoy punishing people?

The Buck Stops Here

This passage is very easy to follow. Yahweh states at its beginning that only the people who commit a sin will be punished. He then goes through several different cases to show how this principle works. Although the passage talks about individuals, it really addresses the question of the guilt of a whole generation of people, such as those in the city of Jerusalem. The idea that each generation is punished for its own sins was controversial. The Deuteronomistic Historian believed that a generation could suffer for the sins of people three generations prior.

Ezekiel uses *life* and *death* as a shorthand for reward and punishment. Righteous behavior leads to "life," while sin leads to "death." He uses these terms in the same way that they are used in the wisdom literature. "Life" represents all the good things humans hope for: wealth, good health, a large family, and so on, while death represents the opposite. But in light of the Babylonian threat, these terms can also be taken literally. If the city as a whole had repented, then God would have saved the city

Which brings me to the question: how would this passage have been read or heard by people living in exile? The book of Ezekiel reached the form in which we have it after the city had fallen, and so its audience was the exiles. These exiles must have wondered why tragedy had happened. It would have been comforting to think, "It wasn't my fault! It happened because my parents/grandparents/great-grandparents had sinned." Ezekiel 18 responds: *you* sinned! By including a discussion of repentance, he reminds the exiles that if they had repented in time, they could have avoided the disaster. In other words, Ezekiel's discussion of guilt does not let the exiles off the hook. They sinned; they suffer.

Ezekiel 20:1–31

Ezekiel retells the exodus story, but with some unsettling twists. Are you getting used to his manipulation of older traditions? Read closely, and perhaps you will be shocked again.

In Case You Were Wondering

To consult the Lord. This phrase means that the elders came to get an oracle from God.

The date. This refers to August 14, 591 BCE, before the siege of Jerusalem.

"My name." This term means the same as saying "my reputation." God repeats that Yahweh acts to protect the divine reputation.

To profane. The meaning of this is similar to the act of defilement.

My eye spared them. This phrase means that God ignored their sins.

Sacrifices on hills and groves. These sacrifices were generally associated with the worship of other gods, such as Baal and Asherah.

Looking Closely at the Text

1. How does this version of the exodus differ from what you read in the Pentateuch?

2. How does Ezekiel characterize Israel's sin? What words are repeated?

3. What is God's motivation in this chapter?

A History by Which They Cannot Live

The first thing you may have noticed about this passage is how repetitive it is. Ezekiel is pointing out a repeating pattern of sin and defilement. As in chapter 16, Ezekiel asserts that sin, especially the sin of worshipping other gods, leads to defilement.

In contrast, what God offered to Israel was a path to life. Again we see an interconnection with earlier parts of the book: the result of righteous behavior is "life." God is saying that the people have been given the blueprint for success in the law God gave them, yet time after time, Israel has proven itself unwilling to follow it. The passage uses metonymy, a figure of speech in which a part of something is meant to represent the whole thing. Here, the Sabbath represents the whole law.

What does God finally do? Look at verses 25–26 carefully.

Moreover, I gave them statues that were not good and ordinances by which they could not live. I defiled them through their very gifts, in their offering up all their firstborn, in order that I might horrify them, so that they might know that I am the LORD.

What is the passage saying here? It says that, as their punishment, God gave them laws that, when they were obeyed, would cause the people to defile themselves. Once again the prophet uses metonymy: child sacrifice represents a whole collection of laws that "were not good." The verse asserts that God commanded them to do things that would cause them to sin. (Of course, the irony is, these are the only laws that the people actually follow.) Why would Ezekiel make such a claim?

For Ezekiel two theological problems arose because of the fall of the city. One was the question of God's power. Perhaps, people wondered, Yahweh was not strong enough to defend the city. Those who felt this way would have ceased worshiping Yahweh.

If, however, Yahweh was strong enough to defend the city, then a second question arises about God's justice. Perhaps Yahweh was not a god that people could count on. Perhaps Yahweh was mean or quick to anger. In the ancient world there were many gods who were known for having quick tempers.

This passage addresses both of these concerns. First, it asserts that everything that happens to Israel happens because God intends it. In fact, God's choice of Israel reflects divine power: God "acts for his name's sake" by picking the most lowly and unlikely people to make into a special nation. If God can make them great, then the whole world will know that Yahweh is a great and powerful god.

Second, the passage paints a picture of Israel's utter defilement. God's anger is fully justified. In fact, what is *not* justified is the fact that God had ever cared for this people. As in chapter 16, the people's repeated reprieves from punishment show that what is abundant is God's mercy, not anger. In other words, God is fully justified in allowing the city to fall.

In the context of the book as a whole, this passage does a third thing. By stating that the laws Judah was using at the time of the fall of the city were bad laws, Ezekiel lays the foundation for his vision of restoration at the end of the book. One of the major components in Ezekiel's restoration is a new set of laws, which will govern the renewed nation and protect God's presence from further defilement. By stating so strongly that the current laws were bad, Ezekiel prepares the readers of the book to accept a new set of laws by which the restored community can live.

What is lost in this view of God is the question of God's justice. Is it right for God to give laws that "are not good"? Isn't God tricking people? For Ezekiel, it is far more important to reestablish God's power (yes, the deity can give bad laws), than it is to protect God's goodness (but Yahweh wouldn't do so because that would not be just). We are left with an unsettling view of God, but one that clearly calls the audience to think seriously about God's sovereign power. It is only when Ezekiel's audience recognizes what God *can* do, that they can begin to appreciate fully what God chooses to do.

Ezekiel 37:1–14: The Dry Bones

In this oracle of restoration, Ezekiel compares the fallen nation to a field of dry bones. While this image may be familiar to those who know the contemporary song of the same name, try to read the passage in the context of the themes examined so far.

In Case You Were Wondering

Sinews are tendons, fibers that attach muscle to the bone.

Looking Closely at the Text

1. How are the bones brought to back to life?

2. According to Ezekiel 37:11, what do the bones represent?

Them Bones

Did you find yourself singing that old song, "Them bones, them bones, them dry bones"? Some Christians like to think of this passage as an image of resurrection, but it is not. The text couldn't be clearer in stating that the bones represent the nation of Israel. The image says that Israel is as dead as bleached-bare bones in the wilderness, like a skull found in the middle of a desert.

Some scholars suggest that what he sees is a battlefield littered with the un-buried corpses of slain soldiers. The passage also picks up on the interplay between life and death that we have seen in other parts of Ezekiel. Here, the nation is utterly dead, yet God commands Ezekiel to "prophesy" to them. Through this prophetic act the dead bones come to life.

Once again the passage ends by stating that the goal of this command is knowledge of God. "Then you shall know that I, the LORD, have spoken and will act" (37:14). What will the people "know"? They will know that God speaks and things happen. There are many parts of Ezekiel that resemble the Priestly writer, with his focus on ritual purity and defilement. Here, the connection between divine speech and divine action resembles the Priestly creation account in Genesis 1:1—2:3 that we will examine in a future chapter.

What differs here is the function of the prophet as the vehicle by which this change is accomplished. The passage graphically illustrates that the real power of the prophetic word comes directly from God. From Ezekiel's mouth comes God's word that acts.

EZEKIEL 43:1–9; 44:1–2; 47:1–12: A VISION OF RESTORATION

These texts are part of the long closing vision of the book. In Ezekiel 40—48, the prophet has another vision of the temple. This vision presents an ideal picture of a perfect temple, and consequently, a perfect city.

IN CASE YOU WERE WONDERING

Mortal. This is the title that God uses to address Ezekiel throughout the book. The literal phrase in Hebrew is "son of man," which here simply means "human." It contrasts with the usual title for a prophet, "man of God."

The Arabah and the sea. Ezekiel 47:8–11 refers to the Dead Sea and the land around it.

LOOKING CLOSELY AT THE TEXT

1. What does Ezekiel see coming to the temple from the east in Ezekiel 43:2–3?

2. According to Ezekiel 44:7, how long will God now dwell with the Israelites?

3. Put Ezekiel 44:1–2 into your own words.

4. In chapter 47, from where does the flowing water start and where does it end up?

5. According to Ezekiel 47:12, how will the trees that line the river differ from normal trees?

A WHOLE NEW WORLD

Jeremiah's vision of restoration focused on the change in the people. Ezekiel's vision is quite different. Ezekiel does not imagine any fundamental change in human nature. For Ezekiel, people can still defile, and, according to other visions in the book, they are still unable to earn God's grace on their own. The only difference is that once they experience God's grace, they will feel shame and "know" Yahweh.

For Ezekiel, the restoration will be effective because God chooses to interact with humanity differently. The vision of the restored temple uses the language of sacred space to describe this difference. God is going to "fix" the world, so that human sin can no longer defile the sanctuary. Ezekiel's temple guarantees a separation between human and divine realms. If you read the rest of the vision, you will see that it includes the reorganization of the whole nation of Israel, so that each person is in his or her proper place in relationship to the temple. In the passages that you have read, notice that not even the royal family can enter God's sanctuary.

Once the main outlines that separate sacred and profane are laid out, God can return to the temple. The permanent locking of the gate, through which God both left and returned, symbolizes God's permanent, eternal presence there. The locked gate also serves to permanently lock out anything that could defile God.

The passage ends with a vivid portrait of the life-giving quality of God's presence. Once the temple is built and the nation arranged around it properly, a river flows out from the temple that is so life-giving that it turns the Dead Sea into fresh water. A sea that once brought death now brings life!

The passage is *utopian*, meaning that it presents a vision of something that is impossibly ideal. First, the description of the temple exceeds the boundaries of Mount Zion. Second, it would have been impossible for the nation to have been rebuilt as Ezekiel imagined it. Third, no matter how humans build, they will never produce a freshwater river that can change the water of the Dead Sea. This is a vision, not a prediction of the future. This vision reminds the exiled audience that God still wants a relationship with them that can lead them to life.

The book ends with the renaming of the city. No longer will it be called Jerusalem. "The name of the city from that time on shall be, 'The LORD is There'" (48:35). This final verse sums up the primary concern of the book of Ezekiel: God's presence for the nation.

PUTTING IT BACK TOGETHER

Like the book of Jeremiah, the book of Ezekiel is concerned with the "God question." Theological problems raised by the exile were even more acute for Ezekiel than for Jeremiah. After all, Ezekiel came from the "elect" in Israel, the priests who were chosen to serve at the temple in Jerusalem. These priests ministered to God's "presence" in the sanctuary, and the book of Ezekiel approaches the "God question" by talking about divine presence and absence. Let me give you some examples.

God should be present in the temple of Jerusalem. At the beginning of the book, as well as at the end, the prophet "sees" God sitting on the throne in the temple.

The Bible in the CHRISTIAN TRADITION

The Visions of Ezekiel Live On

While the book of Ezekiel may not be widely read today, that has not been true for most of Christian history. Ezekiel's visions, in particular, were continually re-used by Christian communities. For example, the vision of the dry bones was an important symbol of hope for slaves in the United States.

The chariot-throne vision was an important image in both Jewish and Christian interpretation. Jewish exegesis utilized the chariot-throne within its mystical traditions. Christians read the vision as an allegory or symbolic picture of the Bible itself. This interpretation has two parts:

- In the first part, the four cherubim represent four sections of both the Old Testament (as organized in the Septuagint and the Vulgate) and four corresponding sections of the New Testament:

Law	Gospels
History	Acts of the Apostles
Wisdom	Epistles
Prophecy	Revelation

- In the second part, the four faces are symbols of the four gospel writers:

Man or angel	Matthew
Lion	Mark
Ox (sometimes depicted with wings)	Luke
Eagle	John

Sometimes these four symbols are depicted with wings to connect them more closely with the cherubim in Ezekiel's vision.

Another one of Ezekiel's visions that became especially important for Catholics is the vision of the locked door in Ezekiel 44. Early Christian interpreters saw this as a symbol of Mary, the mother of Jesus. How is a locked gate like Mary? An ancient title for Mary is *theotokos*—God-bearer. The presence of God, as Jesus, dwelled within Mary. Just as the temple was God's dwelling on earth, Mary was a temple housing God in the form of Jesus. In some paintings of Gabriel's annunciation to Mary, a small temple in the background expresses her role as the temple of Jesus.

In the Catholic doctrine of Mary's perpetual virginity, Mary was set apart for God and remained set apart for God. When God entered the temple in Ezekiel's vision, God permanently locked the door of the temple. Similarly, Christian theologians noted that God made Mary's womb a dwelling for Jesus, "locking" it behind him. The Old Testament image reminds Catholics that this doctrine is an expression of their understanding of the nature of Jesus (truly God).

God's presence can move. This throne has wheels. We see God leaving the temple in Ezek 11:22–25. Where the presence goes is debatable, but it is clear that God is no longer in Jerusalem.

The city cannot stand without God to protect it. With God gone, the city can no longer expect divine protection. Ezekiel's visions focus on how God's presence is essential for the city's safety.

But why does God leave? For Jeremiah, God leaves because the people had broken the covenant. Ezekiel agrees that God leaves because the people have sinned, but he uses ritual language to describe what they have done. For Ezekiel, each sin defiles the land; in other words, sin leads to impurity. Once impurity builds up, then the whole land is defiled, and God can no longer reside there.

Ezekiel 18 maintains that the people who had committed these sins were his own generation. The idea that people can suffer for the sins of their parents and grandparents is rejected. Rather, Ezekiel says that his own generation is utterly debased. Their sin and defilement had built up so acutely that God was justified in leaving.

The book of Ezekiel uses shocking images to make this point. The sexually-charged imagery of Ezekiel 16 uses an old concept (that Israel's covenant with God is like that between a husband and a wife), but pushes it until the audience squirms. The notion that God would give Israel laws that would cause the people to sin focuses the audience's attention on the crisis regarding God's power that needed to be addressed.

Ezekiel plays with images of defilement and shame in order to convey the idea that Israel needs to "know" God. To "know" Yahweh is to know that God can do all things and that people are nothing without God. "Knowing" God and realizing how limited people are should cause shame. While there is something negative about shame, for Ezekiel it ultimately has a positive effect. If Judah feels shame, then the people must be realizing how little they deserve all the things that God does for them. Shame is the recognition of God's undeserved grace.

Ezekiel was also concerned with the question of God's power. Just as Jeremiah likens God to a potter who has every right to destroy what he creates, Ezekiel portrays God's power with complete control of events in Israel's history. Again, the book emphasizes God's power in shocking ways:

God never acts because Israel deserves it. In chapter 16, Israel is likened to a baby wallowing in its own birth-blood. It cannot act for good or for ill. Israel has always been defiled and defiling. Anything God has done for Israel is a free act of God.

God's restoration of Israel is also undeserved. In chapter 37, Israel is compared to dried-up corpses, nothing but bleached bones in the desert. Again, the people can do nothing to prompt God's care for them, not even repent. God's restoration is solely a free act.

The book repeatedly states that God acts for "his name's sake." The exile threatened God's international reputation. God's actions reveal divine power. God blesses the people of Israel *because* they are nothing. If God can make them great, it will be obvious to all people that Yahweh is a powerful god.

God's power is not limited by "ethical" principles. In Ezekiel 20:25, Ezekiel is prepared to give up some of God's goodness in order to preserve God's power. The no-good laws focus on divine prerogative.

The emphasis on God's power in both Jeremiah and Ezekiel shows that it was a huge question for the people at the time of the exile. Ezekiel leaves us with an unsettling view of God; one that calls even today's audience to think seriously about God's sovereign power. But it was an urgent issue for the Israelite audience in the time of exile.

The themes of divine grace and power carry through into the final vision of God's return to a restored temple. While Jeremiah's vision of restoration focused on a changed people, Ezekiel's focus remains on God's free acts. For Ezekiel, the restoration will be effective because God *chooses* to interact with humanity differently. God provides a new temple design, one that guarantees that Israel's sins can no longer defile it. The permanent locking of the gate, through which God both left and returned, symbolizes God's permanent eternal presence in the temple. The passage ends with a beautiful image of the life-giving quality of God's presence. The river that flows from the temple and turns the Dead Sea into fresh water symbolizes that God's presence for Israel is life-giving. This is a utopian vision, one that expresses the prophet's hope for Israel's future in concrete images.

GREAT LOSS, GREAT GOD

The poet Mark Doty once wrote, "Great grief, great God," meaning that great mourning can only occur when there is an abundance of something that you love, and love always has its source in God.

I think in some ways that these texts demonstrate this paradox. Yes, they are about horrible events in Israel's history; and, yes, these events caused the people of Israel to question the existence, power, and character of God. But in the midst of that struggle, these texts provide images that can speak to all those who suffer. They contain the voices of people praying their anger, accepting blame, and envisioning a future. They develop a picture of God who feels rage at our rebellion and a God who forgives, even when people do not deserve forgiveness, a God who both punishes and restores. Even if God's people are as dead as bones bleached white on a desert floor, God will bring them back again.

For Review

1. Who was exiled in the first deportation?

2. How was the second deportation different from the first deportation?

3. How did the fall of Jerusalem affect the way the Israelites thought about their society?

4. How did the exile affect Israelite literature? Give one example.

5. How did the exile affect the way Israelites worshipped Yahweh? Give one example.

6. Where was Jeremiah during the years 597–587?

7. Why wasn't Jeremiah "popular"?

8. According to Jeremiah, why would the city fall?

9. What does it mean to have the covenant "written on your heart"?

10. What is the book of Lamentations, and how does it address God's role in the fall of the city?

11. How does the book of Ezekiel address the question of God's power?

12. Give one example of Ezekiel's use of shocking language or ideas.

13. Define what Ezekiel means by these three phrases: "God acts for his name's sake," "Israel will know Yahweh," and "Israel should feel shame."

For Further Reading

For an understanding of the way the exilic setting may have affected Israel's theology, see Daniel L. Smith-Christopher, *A Biblical Theology of Exile* (Overtures to Biblical Theology; Minneapolis, MN: Fortress, 2002). On the way the rise of writing affected issues of a tradition's authority, see Susan Niditch, *Oral World and Written Word: Ancient Israelite Literature* (Library of Ancient Israel; Louisville, KY: Westminster John Knox, 1996), and various essays and articles by Robert Carroll, including "Inscribing the Covenant: Writing and the Written in Jeremiah," in *Understanding Poets and Prophets: Essays in Honour of*

George Wishart Anderson, edited by A. Graeme Auld (JSOTSup 152; Sheffield: Sheffield Academic, 1993) pages 61–76.

A fascinating collection of essays on the book of Jeremiah is *Troubling Jeremiah*, edited by A. R. Pete Diamond, Kathleen M. O'Connor, and Louis Stulman (JSOTSup 260; Sheffield: Sheffield Academic, 1999).

Two interesting studies of how the book of Lamentations addresses the theological issues raised in disaster are Tod Linafelt, *Surviving Lamentations: Catastrophe, Lament, and Protest in the Afterlife of a Biblical Book* (Chicago/London: University of Chicago Press, 2000), and Kathleen M. O'Connor, *Lamentations and the Tears of the World* (Maryknoll, NY: Orbis, 2002).

On the theme of divine abandonment in Ezekiel, look at John F. Kutsko, *Between Heaven and Earth: Divine Presence and Absence in the Book of Ezekiel* (Biblical and Judaic Studies 7; Winona Lake, NY: Eisenbrauns, 2000). Two collections of essays on Ezekiel that explore more recent approaches can be found in *The Book of Ezekiel: Theological and Anthropological Perspectives*, edited by Margaret S. Odell and John T. Strong (SBLSym 9; Atlanta, GA: SBL, 2000) and *Ezekiel's Hierarchical World: Wrestling with a Tiered Reality*, edited by Stephen L. Cook and Corrine L. Patton (SBLSym 31; Atlanta, GA: SBL, 2004).

OVERVIEW

THE SECOND TEMPLE PERIOD

When the LORD restored the fortunes of Zion,
We were like those who dream (Ps 126:1).

WHERE WE HAVE BEEN

The texts that you have just read reflect Israel's history as an independent nation. The books of Joshua and Judges related how Israel came to possess the land. Samuel described the establishment of the monarchy, and Kings narrated the history of that monarchy.

Many different types of literature flourished during the monarchy. Prophecy gave voice to a religious critique of Israelite society. Histories of Israel's ancient origins were written down, and law codes were embedded in ancient revelations.

Yet, Israel and Judah were not strong enough to survive the great empires of the Fertile Crescent. Israel fell to Assyria in 722 BCE, and Judah was exiled to Babylon in 587 BCE. Historians note that many other nations of similar size were defeated by these two powers; they were too weak to survive.

The Bible tells us that Israel and Judah were weak internally as well; the people were not unified. The twelve tribes had split into two nations. Within both nations the rich oppressed the poor. Not even the worship of Yahweh could unite them. Some Israelites worshipped other gods, while those who worshipped Yahweh disagreed about how this should be done.

The fall of the temple of Jerusalem was a bitter pill to swallow. Everything these people had trusted in, all of the things that gave them their identity, were gone. They should have eventually passed out of world history as a distinct people, as did the Moabites and the Philistines.

But they did not. Rather than give in to the religious polytheism of their conquerors, the Israelites re-affirmed their belief in Yahweh. By explaining

In the year 20 BCE, Herod the Great renovated and expanded the Second Temple. This model shows the temple as it stood until the year 70 CE, when it was sacked by the Romans.

their loss as the result of worshipping other gods, they laid a firm foundation for what set Israel apart from countries like Moab, Philistia, even Babylon: the belief in one particular God.

WHERE WE ARE GOING: THE SECOND TEMPLE PERIOD

Israel not only survived the exile; it was able to build on the insights that the experiences of exile had provided. Even so, only Judah was rebuilt after the exile. What had been the nation of Israel (the northern kingdom) was now called Samaria, inhabited by an ethnically diverse population. Because the history from this point on is only that of Judah, I will refer to the people as *Jews*.

Most of the texts that you will read for the final section of the textbook were written during the Second Temple Period of Israelite history. "Second Temple Period" refers to the time during which a rebuilt temple stood in the city of Jerusalem, that is, from approximately 538 BCE to 70 CE. This 600-year period can be divided into smaller sections.

THE PERSIAN PERIOD (538–332 BCE)

The Persian empire, centered in modern-day Iran, conquered the Babylonians in 539 BCE. The Persians took over Babylon's empire, and, for a time, they extended their rule even into Egypt. In 538, their leader, Cyrus, issued a proclamation that allowed all of the peoples who had been exiled to Babylon to return to their homelands. The Persians, however, did not allow the countries it controlled to have political independence; the people of Judah could not reestablish the monarchy. Instead, the Persians appointed governors to rule for them.

Jerusalem was re-settled during this period; the temple was rebuilt around 520 BCE. The prophecies in Haggai, Zechariah, and the later chapters of Isaiah date from this period, as do the books of Chronicles, Ezra, and Nehemiah.

THE GREEK PERIOD (332–165 BCE)

If you ever took a World History course, you may remember something about Alexander the Great. His center of power was Greece. From there he created an empire that included parts of southern Europe, northern Africa, and the Fertile Crescent. He acquired the Fertile Crescent by defeating the Persians in 332 BCE.

Judah fell under Greek rule. The Greeks also allowed the Jews to live in their own land, but Greek rulers held political power. While the Persians allowed countries a degree of cultural freedom, the Greeks tried to impose their culture on the people they ruled. This process is called "Hellenization."

Many of the later books in the Old Testament show the influence of this Greek culture, including Ecclesiastes (Qoheleth) and Sirach (Ecclesiasticus). The book of Daniel reflects the turmoil felt by those who opposed Greek religion and culture.

THE MACCABEAN PERIOD (165–63 BCE)

The last of the Greek rulers to control Judah, Antiochus IV Epiphanes, was especially cruel. During his rule, a Jewish family, the Hasmoneans, led a successful revolt. The nickname of their leader was "Maccabee" or "The Hammer." Judah experienced a brief period of independence under the Hasmoneans.

This family appointed themselves as both kings and priests of the temple. Some Jews did not think that they had the right to do this. One of these groups left Jerusalem in protest and established their own community at Qumran. They produced the Dead Sea Scrolls. Other Jews welcomed the revolution, as is reflected in 1 and 2 Maccabees and Judith.

The Roman Period (63 BCE–70 CE)

Jewish independence did not last long. As Roman power grew, Judah came under Roman rule. Again, foreign oppressors ruled Judah. After many uprisings, the Israelites ceased to exist as a political entity in 70 CE, when the Romans destroyed the Second Temple. From this time until after World War II, there was no nation of Israel. Jews lived in the *Diaspora*, a term that refers to the scattering of Jews outside of the Levant after the Babylonian Exile. Although the Roman Empire lasted well past 70 CE, the destruction of the Second Temple marks the end of the Roman Period of Israel's history.

Most of the Old Testament books were written before the Roman period, although we have many other Jewish texts from this period, which are found outside of the Old Testament. In addition, some of the earliest New Testament books were written in the Roman Period before the Second Temple was destroyed. These texts tell us that this was a period of hostility, oppression, and war.

The Arch of Titus was built in the Roman Forum in 81 CE to commemorate the defeat of Judea. Carved panels in the structure depict the Roman triumph over the Jewish rebellion and show such scenes as Roman soldiers carrying the great menorah away from the temple.

Summary

It may be difficult to remember all of these names and dates. The following table summarizes the main periods of the Second Temple Period:

Name of the Period	Years	Some Old Testament Books Written in That Period
Persian Period	538–332 BCE	Haggai, Zechariah, Ezra, Nehemiah
Greek Period	332–165 BCE	Ecclesiastes, Sirach, Daniel
Maccabean Period	165–63 BCE	Judith, 1 and 2 Maccabees
Roman Period	63 BCE–70 CE	Wisdom of Solomon

What It Is Like Here: Society and Literature in the Second Temple Period

The following chapters will fill in the details of the history we have just sketched. They will also explain the important issues facing the community during each period. However, it might be helpful to get a brief glance at the world you are about to enter.

Who Is on Top?

Although the Jews wanted to restore the monarchy, they were unsuccessful. Persia, Greece, and Rome did not allow such independence. Sometimes these other nations picked Jews to rule for them, but it was always clear that the foreigners were on top.

We know that in the Greek and Roman periods, the Jewish population was divided about how much they should adapt to and cooperate with these foreigners. Hellenistic culture was quite different from the cultures of the ancient Near East. While many Jews opposed adopting Greek customs, those who did were often treated better and rose to positions of influence.

Temple and Priests

The one thing that unified Jews at this time was the temple in Jerusalem. Religion became more important than nationality for providing Jews with a sense of identity. We will see that the "law" also became very important now. As you may recall from the first part of this book, many of the laws in the Pentateuch were about proper worship and cultic purity. These ritual laws provided a way for Jews everywhere to express who they were.

As you might guess, this meant that the priests at the temple remained important leaders. They helped the community interpret, define, and express this sense of identity. Many texts from this period reflect the essential role that law, priests, and the temple played for the Jews.

Prophecy and the Future

Prophets still delivered oracles, but without the political protection they experienced in the monarchy, they found it dangerous to express views other than those of the ruling powers. The Old Testament does not preserve many prophetic texts after the initial rebuilding of the temple. This does not mean that prophecy ceased; we know it is still important in the New Testament period. It means that, for reasons unknown, the Old Testament does not preserve these later prophets.

A new type of literature appears in the Old Testament at this time which literature scholars describe as "apocalyptic." The word comes from the Greek word meaning an "unveiling," that is, a "revelation." *Apocalyptic literature* consists of a secret revelation given to an individual that describes, often in symbolic form, some cosmic conflict. Sometimes this conflict involves the end of the world.

Apocalyptic literature may have grown in popularity in the Second Temple Period because of the people's prolonged experience of oppression by foreign rulers. Their suffering led them to the following conclusions:

1. God is less involved in their current history.

2. God has a future plan to save the righteous.

3. Current suffering is a test to determine who is righteous and who is wicked.

We will see that this reasoning matches the views found in Jewish apocalyptic writings

STORYTELLING

History writing fades without a monarchy. While there are some historical books from the Second Temple Period, most only tell about a small part of Israel's history. Ezra and Nehemiah recount the events of the early Persian Period, while 1 and 2 Maccabees, two separate books, give two accounts of the revolution under the Hasmoneans. Only the books of Chronicles tell a longer history.

With no kings to fill the pages of the histories, stories of more ordinary people become treasured. We will devote a whole chapter to these entertaining tales. Not all of them come from the Second Temple Period, but most of them, such as Esther, Tobit, and Judith, certainly do. They reflect the recognition that, even without a king or national independence, the people continued to experience God in their lives.

12 RESTORING A NATION

Go out from Babylon, flee from Chaldea,
declare this with a shout of joy, proclaim it,
send it forth to the end of the earth; say,
"The LORD has redeemed his servant Jacob!"
(Is 48:20)

A CHANCE TO SET THINGS RIGHT

CHAPTER OVERVIEW

This chapter focuses on texts that reflect Israel's return from exile. We will start by looking at the historical events that shaped the Restoration Period of Israel's history. This chapter will provide the following:

▸ An examination of the issues facing the nation as it was rebuilt

▸ A survey of the prophets who addressed these issues

▸ An exploration of the rise in monotheism

▸ A discussion of writers re-interpreting their own traditions

Once the people were allowed to return to the Levant, new questions arose: who were the true descendants of the Israelites? Who should run the nation? How can the old traditions be honored and God's wrath avoided? Throughout these accounts we will see that Israel's experiences led to new and sometimes conflicting views of God's relationship to nations other than Israel.

How Were the Israelites Returned to Their Land?

The Babylonian exile lasted almost fifty years, from 587 to 538 BCE. The average life expectancy in the ancient world was, at most, forty years; so, by the time the exile ended, many of the people who had been adults when Jerusalem fell were dead. Many Jewish children had been born and raised in a foreign land. It looked as if the children living in exile were being punished for the sins and mistakes of their parents and grandparents. People, who did not deserve to, were suffering God's wrath.

Salvation for the Israelites came from an unexpected place: the East. The Persian empire under Cyrus conquered the city of Babylon in 539 and quickly gained control of the whole Babylonian empire.

Cyrus had a different policy for dealing with peoples that he conquered than the Babylonians had. He wanted people to live in their own land and worship their own gods. He issued a proclamation in 538, called the *Edict of*

Age in the Ancient World

It is hard to imagine a world in which forty is considered a ripe old age, but this was the case in the ancient world. An analysis of a typical near-eastern grave site revealed that thirty-five percent of the skeletons were of children under the age of five; fifty percent of the skeletons were under the age of eighteen. Throughout the ancient Near East, life expectancy for women was even shorter: usually around thirty years of age. This is because of the risk to women that pregnancy and childbirth produce.

The most common type of death throughout the ancient world was that brought about by infection. Without antibiotics, infections could ravage a weak body. In addition, plagues could wipe out large segments of the population. Although we do not have similar statistics for the ancient world, statistics for Medieval Europe, where life expectancy was the same, show the tragic effect that plague could have on life expectancy. During the years of the plague or Black Death, life expectancy dropped to around eighteen years. There is no reason to think the statistics wouldn't have been analogous for ancient Israel. Some historians have even suggested that the burning of cities during military conquest was

done as much to prevent the spread of disease as it was to punish the conquered population.

People who did reach adulthood could live a long life, the statistics on average of life expectancy are skewed by the high level of infant and childhood deaths. Even so, the people who reached adulthood would have had limited resources to address health issues, such as dental health, loss of eyesight, and simple viruses. By the age of forty, women who had worked at grinding would probably suffer permanent back problems. Skeletal remains show that teeth were worn down because of the poor quality of grains and the amount of stones in the bread, the common staple of the ancient diet.

Think about how the reality of a short life expectancy might be reflected in ancient texts. For example, there are few references to female menopause in the ancient world, since only a small percentage of women lived long enough to experience it. A girl of fifteen would be middle aged. Old age, even if that was defined as fifty or sixty years of age, would be a divine blessing. Elders were revered in ancient Israel because they were so few, and they were, therefore, considered blessed.

The clay Cyrus Cylinder, dating to 536 BCE, records the Edict of Cyrus, *which permitted the Jews in Babylon to return to Judah and rebuild the temple.*

Cyrus, which allowed exiles to return to their homelands. One of the nations that he restored was Judah; thus begins the Persian Period of Israel's history.

We call the first part of the Persian Period the *Restoration Period*, because it involves the events and conflicts that arose when the Israelites were trying to rebuild their nation. It is a period filled with conflict. The Jews faced numerous challenges: which traditions should be maintained and which ones should be changed? Who will have the most say in the rebuilding? Who should head which projects? These issues led to problems among different groups of Jews.

Who Are the New Israelites?

Many exiles welcomed Cyrus. They saw his policy as the means by which God would restore the nation. For these people, Cyrus's proclamation was a direct call from God.

There was, however, one problem: not all of the exiles wanted to return. We know from ancient records that some Jews living in Babylon had reached financially secure positions. They owned houses, had freedom of movement, worked for the government, and had adopted elements of Babylonian culture. Some even had enough money to lend to other Jews; some started using the Babylonian calendar, gave their children Babylonian names, and adapted Babylonian astrology to their belief in Yahweh.

In contrast, Jerusalem was an unknown land to many of the exiles. It was a land still devastated by the Babylonian invasion. Jerusalem had not been rebuilt, and farms outside of the old city limits were sparse and poor. The exiles would literally have to rebuild the city brick by brick. Moreover, farming in the

Levant was less reliable than in the irrigated farms in Babylon. Since Jerusalem was a city on the edge of the empire, those trained in reading, writing, and finance would find work there scarce. Nor would government posts there be as plentiful and prestigious as working in Persia or Babylon. It is no wonder that many exiles chose to remain where they were.

Those who did return would have been pious people, for whom there was something to gain by living in Jerusalem. For example, the descendants of the kings of David would have wanted to return in order to reestablish their claim to the throne. Priests who wanted to serve at the temple of Jerusalem would have desired to return, as would landowners wanting to reclaim their ancestral lands and those who strongly believed that the land was given to Israel by God.

When the exiles returned, the Levant was not uninhabited. While the Babylonians had exiled Judah's rich and the powerful, many of the poor had remained behind. Sometimes the Bible refers to this group of people as *the people of the land*. A struggle ensued over who would be the leaders of a restored Judah: would it be the returning exiles or the people of the land? Each side felt hostility toward the other. The view of the people of the land was that the exiles did not deserve to rule the country again, since their ancestors' sins had led to the country's downfall. In the eyes of the returnees, the people who had remained in the land were not God's chosen ones and were, therefore, suspect, since many had married outside the kinship lines of ancient Israel. Some returning exiles accused the inhabitants of the Levant of being "foreign."

The question of who could rebuild the temple fueled the conflict. As the returning exiles made plans to rebuild the temple to Yahweh, Samaritans volunteered to help. The *Samaritans* were the people living in what had once been the northern kingdom of Israel. You may remember that the Assyrians had exiled

The Samaritans

The history of the Samaritans is a long and interesting one, extending from the biblical period through today. There is still a small group of Samaritan Jews, who claim to have descended from Israelites of the northern kingdom who survived the Assyrian invasion. In contrast, ancient texts from other Jewish groups assert that the Samaritans were the descendants of, at best, mixed blood unions between Jews and others who were settled in the north by the Assyrians.

Although prophetic visions of restoration hope for the restoration of all twelve tribes of Israel, by the Persian period it is clear that there were two distinguishable groups claiming to be Jewish, the Judeans and the Samaritans. This is confirmed by letters from the Jewish colony at Elephantine in the fifth century BCE, written to both the Samaritan and Judean priests.

The Samaritans maintained a distinct temple from that of Jerusalem. It appears that the Samaritan temple was built in the latter part of the Persian period on Mt. Gerizim in Shechem. It was destroyed in the Hasmonean period around 128 BCE. Remains of the temple have not been found, although some scholars conjecture that it may have been a tent shrine, in keeping with the instructions for the Tabernacle.

The Bible of the Samaritan Jews consists of the Pentateuch only. Ancient fragments of this Pentateuch are invaluable for text critics, because they give witness to a very old text tradition of this section of the Bible.

Hostilities between Judean and Samaritan Jews festered from the period of Restoration until the fall of the Second Temple. Some of these hostilities resulted in violence. For example, in 52 CE, Samaritans killed some Jewish pilgrims in southern Galilee. These hostilities lie behind the references to the Samaritans in the New Testament.

many of the Israelites and repopulated the area with people from all over the Assyrian kingdom. We do not know much about these people, but it is clear that, by the Restoration Period, they were worshippers of Yahweh for whom the rebuilding of the temple at Jerusalem was important.

The exiles refused to let the Samaritans help. The exiles viewed these people as "foreign" and, therefore, not qualified to participate in this religious activity. The two groups fought so much that the Persian government put a stop to the rebuilding of the temple. It was almost twenty years later that the inhabitants of Judah were allowed to begin the rebuilding of the temple.

THE GROWING IMPORTANCE OF THE TRADITIONS OF ISRAEL

The group that ended up with the most power in the Restoration was the returning exiles. They were the descendants of the rich, educated, and elite of pre-exilic Israel. They were the ones who had preserved in writing some of Israel's traditions during the exile. Their claim for control over the restored Israel was based on their connection to the past.

It is not surprising, then, that written traditions became very important in the Restoration Period. All of the biblical material that we will read for this chapter makes connections with the past. We will see religious leaders reading the old law code to the people (Nehemiah), new prophetic oracles being written in the name of earlier prophets (Isaiah), and the history of Israel being retold using older written accounts (Chronicles).

During this period, the formation of the Bible, as a collection of sacred books, began. Written traditions were now regarded as having an authority coming from God. The community experienced God in written texts. As the book of Ezra shows, one of the first of these divinely revealed texts was the written law.

ISRAELITE SOCIETY IN THE PERSIAN PERIOD

Historians do not know as much about the Persian period as they do about other periods in Israel's history, because there are fewer extant texts from Persia than from Mesopotamia or Egypt. Historians are especially in the dark with respect to Persian religion. We know that the Persians' main god was named Ahura Mazda and that he was depicted as the god of the whole world, but we do not have much information about the Persian religious system as compared to other civilizations in the Fertile Crescent. As a result of this general lack of direct information, much of what historians reconstruct is based upon inferences in other texts.

Focus on METHOD

The Canonical Approach

The Canonical Approach describes a theological stance that a reader may take when approaching the biblical text. It is not a specific method of biblical interpretation, although its articulation has led to new movements in biblical inquiry.

Canonical criticism has been used to label two separate but interrelated tasks. One task seeks to reconstruct the process by which biblical books came to have authoritative status. In this task, the focus is historical, but it traces the history of a given text beyond its mere production to the change in its status within various faith communities. This field has seen a number of important studies on a previously ignored aspect of the text's history.

More often, however, the canonical approach refers to those interpretations that read a particular biblical text within the context of the canon as a whole. This approach, started by Brevard Childs, sought to describe the way many "people in the pews" read the text. He noted that Christians, for example, usually do not read a book like Isaiah in isolation from New Testament uses of the text. He notes that if one is doing theological inquiry, then one should ask theological questions and use a method appropriate for that inquiry. For him, awareness of a text's placement within the larger canon is an essential element of most Christian theological endeavors.

His approach to biblical theology has had wide influence, although different theologians use this approach in different ways. Three of the most prominent understandings of it are: (1) the examination of conscious re-use of material; (2) the focus on the history of interpretation of a text within a given community of faith; and (3) the effect that canonical placement has on a reading community. Let me examine each of these in turn.

Recent work on the Bible has looked at ways in which later authors and redactors make references and allusions to earlier texts. This conscious echoing, or rereading (in French, *relecture*), tells the audience that a given work is supposed to be read within a larger literary context. Biblical texts are not simply self-referential, but they tease out ideas present in earlier traditions. For some scholars, this tendency to connect originally isolated literary pieces can be seen in the final formation of the Twelve Minor Prophets and the book of the Psalms. An abundance of intertestamental allusions across the canons of the Old and the New Testaments affect the reading tradition. This awareness invites the interpreter to read the text within ever-widening literary contexts.

While the formation of the final form of the text provides one guide to reading, for a community of faith another guide is the interpretive tradition of which it is a part. Catholics read the Bible through the lens of people such as Thomas Aquinas. Lutherans are informed by Luther's own attitude toward biblical interpretation. In the nineteenth and twentieth centuries, biblical scholars needed to free themselves from traditional interpretations so that they could move forward in their appropriation of new methods of biblical interpretation. Now, however, there is a desire to recover some of that interpretive tradition. In some ways, this movement echoes the post-modernist approach which encourages readers to be aware of the interpretive context that informs their work. However, in the canonical approach, this focus aids the reading community's theological discussion of a given text. Canonical approaches can highlight the history of the interpretation of the text as part of this theological endeavor.

Third, some canonical critics focus on the a-historical or unintentional meaning created by putting disparate texts together. These scholars are not trying to make a historical argument that a later author is consciously using earlier material, but they note that a book like Isaiah is read differently simply by being placed in a collection with New Testament texts. Think about it: would you read Isaiah differently if it weren't in the Bible? For these scholars, examining materials under the rubric of "canonicity," their presumption is that the divine author intended the juxtaposition of various literary texts.

If you were going to read Isaiah 52—53 using a canonical approach, you would assume that it is a sacred/canonical/authoritative text. You might look at allusions in the chapters to earlier biblical traditions, especially those in Isaiah, and then at references to these chapters in later biblical texts. You might also trace the history of the text's interpretation, focusing, perhaps, on how the liturgical uses of these texts developed and affected theological reflection. Lastly, you would interpret the text as part of the canon as a whole.

The Persian government was not as benevolent as some texts might have you believe. Although the Persians did allow exiles to return to their homelands, they did not let them have political independence. Instead, they organized their empire into districts, each with an appointed governor. These governors were usually chosen from the native population, but they were always people who supported Persian rule. In Israel this meant that, while some people hoped for the restoration of the Davidic monarchy, Israelites were ruled instead by governors such as Nehemiah, a Jew appointed as governor by the Persians.

It is not clear how much legal freedom Persians allowed people in the districts to have. There seems to have been some attempt by the Persians to collect the laws of the peoples that they governed, but whether this was a common practice is debated. Many biblical historians see the initial impetus for the formation of the Pentateuch in this Persian policy.

The Persians did allow local religious institutions to exist, although they may have granted this privilege to those who cooperated with them. These local temples probably paid a tax to the Persians, and they certainly existed only at the whim of the Persian government.

We see the first clear references to the office of the high priest, variously named the "great priest," or the "head priest," in Persian period texts. In texts that date to the Restoration Period, the ancestry of this head priest is traced to Zadok, the priestly family that ran the temple of Jerusalem during the monarchy (see, for example, 1 Chr 6:8–15, plus Hg 1:1). However, later texts call these priests Aaronides, meaning that they traced their ancestry back to Moses' brother, Aaron (see Sir 50:1–17). Although these genealogies are not incompatible in the final form of the Bible, at the least, they represent two different traditions about the founder of this office.

Since the authority of the local political ruler was quite limited, the high priest came to have considerably more power in postexilic Jerusalem. In fact, some scholars refer to Judah's form of government as a "Citizen-Temple Community," one in which the temple was the main social, economic, and administrative institution. It is true that the temple came to wield a great deal of authority, since it could collect taxes, punish religious offenses, set up an independent legal system, preserve written traditions, provide for education, and handle health issues in the city.

GOD OF THE WHOLE WORLD

New human experiences lead to new understandings of God. The experience of living among other peoples for almost fifty years changed the way the Israelites talked about God. When they had been an independent nation worshipping a national God, they appropriately focused on Yahweh's unique relationship with Israel. But the exile led Jewish authors to grapple with the question of God's relationship to the rest of the world.

Texts from the Restoration Period emphasize that Yahweh is not just the *best* god; Yahweh is the *only* god. Earlier texts that condemned idols carried the same implication. The Psalm literature that praised God as creator also implied that God controlled everything. Prophetic texts that talked about Babylon as God's instrument to punish Judah suggested that God alone was truly divine. But the period of the Restoration was the one that focused on the full implications of belief in one God.

Monotheism and Polytheism (Or, What Exactly Is a God?)

What does it mean to be monotheistic? While the simple answer is that it means to believe in the existence of only one god, this answer begs the question, what is a "god"? Does monotheism require a particular kind of god, one with no manifestations as separate persons? (This would be the view of Islam; to them the Christian doctrine of the Trinity looks like a reduced polytheism.) Does it mean that there is only one being in heaven, "God"? This is not the view of Christianity, Judaism, or Islam, all of whom believe in the existence of angels.

So, how is an angel different from a god? Traditional Christian definitions would say that angels are created beings, which implies that the only thing that could be a "god" would be something that is eternal (not created and not capable of dying). Yet, the historian of religion will admit that in most polytheistic cultures, many of the gods and goddesses were created. In ancient Egypt, for example, the sun god begins creation by making all of the other gods.

In the Second Temple Period, God was viewed as more transcendent. Subsequently, texts from this period have angels doing things that earlier Israelite texts ascribe to God. This rise in angelology, however, may also be the result of the rise in monotheistic thinking. It is more difficult to imagine a single god personally involved in the day-to-day events of human existence than it is to think of patron gods and goddesses within polytheism. The notion of "guardian angels," for example, replaces the function of personal deities.

Some divine functions are too important to leave to minor heavenly beings such as angels. In the writings of ancient Israel, we will see texts addressed to Wisdom. Was she a separate goddess for the Israelites or simply the personification of an aspect of God? If the latter, how is that different from Christian notions of "persons" in the Trinity? When is an individual aspect of a god experienced as a separate god? These questions about the definition of "god" help us to remember the essential task of theology.

Historically, we can understand why monotheism is not the most common form of religious belief in the ancient world. Some theological problems arise with monotheism. The particular features of Jewish monotheism were heavily influenced by Hellenistic philosophical thought. The great Greek philosophers of the fourth and third centuries BCE defined "God" as not only "one," but also as "perfect," meaning indivisible, uncreated, with nothing left to develop. This is where notions of God as omniscient, omnipotent, omnipresent, and omnibenevolent come from. But you can see that if God is all of these things, then explaining the presence of evil in the world becomes more difficult.

The prominence of angels and demons in ancient Christianity was one way that these communities could understand the seemingly contradictory nature of divine acts. Christian philosophers and theologians have struggled with this question of the nature of God for centuries now. But even without surveying those attempts, it is easy to see why remnants of polytheism have remained even until today.

The belief that there is only one God is called *monotheism*. This emphasis on the existence of only one true God came to characterize Judaism. From the Restoration Period onward, more and more Jewish texts make monotheism a central element of their conception of the divine world. Both Christianity and Islam, which are partially dependent on these traditions, accept monotheism as an essential component in their religions. All three religions would agree with the statement in Isaiah, "I am the LORD, and there is no other" (Is 45:18).

TEXTS FROM THE RESTORATION

The texts for this section come from both the prophets and the historical books. All of them were written during the Persian Period, and they reflect the issues that arose during the restoration of Judah.

A READING FROM THE PROPHET ISAIAH

Not all of the oracles in the book of Isaiah came from the prophet who lived during the reign of King Hezekiah. In fact, much of the book was written at least 150 years later. The material in Isaiah 40—66 was written during the Persian period. It circulated as prophecies in the "name of," or "in the spirit of" Isaiah. In other words, these were prophecies Isaiah would have proclaimed if he had been alive at that time. Whenever someone writes as if they are a figure from the past, it is called *pseudepigrapha*. This is a common style of writing in ancient times as well as today. For instance, in the novel *Burr* by Gore Vidal, published in 1973, Vidal writes as if he is Aaron Burr, who lived from 1756–1836. No one would accuse Vidal of forgery or deception; assuming Burr's voice is not an act of deception on the part of the author.

Scholars refer to Isaiah 40—55 as "Second Isaiah" to designate that a later follower of Isaiah wrote the material; chapters 56—66 come from a slightly later time and are called "Third Isaiah." How do we know they were written later? One reason is that the chapters refer to Cyrus by name and to the events during the Restoration with very specific details, and, while it is possible that Isaiah of Jerusalem could have predicted these events, it is more likely that they were recorded at the time that Cyrus was in power.

The chapters themselves indicate that they were meant to be regarded, not as orally delivered oracles, but as poems written "in the spirit of" Isaiah. As you read, notice that there are none of the prophetic forms that you found in earlier prophets. There is no mention of the prophet's experience of God. There are no messenger formulae, no vision reports or symbolic acts, and certainly no call narrative. It is as if the prophet has simply disappeared. This is not true for the prophets Haggai and Zechariah, who were alive during the Restoration. Their books use prophetic forms. By omitting prophetic forms, the followers of Isaiah are acknowledging the absence of the prophet.

As you read the texts from Isaiah, notice how beautiful the poetry is. These are not short proclamations; they are long poems that use all the artistry known to the best poets of the day. Even in translation, the skill of the poet shines through.

ISAIAH 40:1–11 AND 52:7–10: PREPARE THE WAY OF THE LORD!

These oracles represent God's call to the exiles to return to the land. Remember that many exiles did not want to return. These texts are written by someone trying to encourage people to return to Jerusalem.

IN CASE YOU WERE WONDERING

Comfort. This term refers to the restoration of the people after God's punishment.

"The LORD has bared his holy arm" (Isa 52:10). This is a reference to God's military strength.

To redeem. This means "to pay off the debt." Someone who is redeemed is released from debt and slavery.

LOOKING CLOSELY AT THE TEXT

1. Who is being addressed in these two oracles?

2. How is God depicted in these passages?

A JOYFUL ANNOUNCEMENT

"How beautiful upon the mountains are the feet of the messenger who announces peace!" (Is 52:7). I'll bet you didn't know there was a praise of feet in the Bible! It sounds funny when you think about it, since these messengers probably had ugly, dirty feet. Yet here the poet is praising them. Why?

It is because he is praising the message. It's similar to wanting to kiss a lottery ticket when you find out you've won. The image is that of the messenger bringing word to people living in and around the ruins of Jerusalem that Cyrus is allowing the exiles to return.

Chapter 40 notes that this exile has been too long. "She has received from the Lord's hand double for all her sins" (Is 40:2). In other words, a punishment that should have lasted one generation (twenty to twenty-five years) has lasted for two generations (forty-eight years).

Notice that it is the personified city that is the primary addressee in these passages. God wishes to console the city more than the exiles. In other words, the city has deserved the punishment less than the people who had lived there.

The poet often refers to the city as "Zion," reminding the audience of the city's function as a sacred city. The city is also personified as female, as we have seen before. In other places in Second Isaiah, the city is called a "daughter," and in chapter 40 she is paralleled to a "mother sheep" (Is 40:11).

While God is portrayed as a loving shepherd in Isaiah 40:11, in both of these chapters, Yahweh is also a warrior king, leading the people back home. The references to the wilderness in Isaiah 40:3–5 recall the way God led the Israelites out of slavery in Egypt during the exodus.

In summary, the poet uses images and ideas known throughout Israel's history (the personified city, God as a warrior, the exodus through the wilderness) as he writes in the spirit of an ancient prophet (Isaiah) to express the unexpected joy of the exiles' return from Babylon. In this way the poet expresses the communities' dual experience of being both connected to the past and undergoing a new present.

Isaiah 44:6–20 and 45:1–19: Yahweh Is God Alone

These passages show how the unexpected policies of Cyrus led the author to acclaim that Yahweh is God of all people.

In Case You Were Wondering

Stylus, planes, and a compass. These are some of the tools used by carpenters, metalworkers, and builders.

Looking Closely at the Text

1. What does Isaiah 44 describe?

2. In Isaiah 45:1, what is Cyrus called?

3. According to Isaiah 45:4, why does God help Cyrus?

4. Does Cyrus know that Yahweh is directing his actions?

5. In how many verses of Isaiah 45:1–19 does God say, in one way or another, that there is only one God?

YAHWEH ALONE

The message in these verses is clear: there is only one true God and it is Yahweh. Notice how the prophet ties this idea to God's work as creator, especially in Isaiah 45:9–12. The logic here may be somewhat hard to follow, but the argument is simple. First, it asserts that God created all things, including all human people. If God created everything, then God controls everything. Those, then, who would question that Yahweh sent Cyrus, a Persian, are like a pottery jar which claims that its potter couldn't possibly make a different kind of pot.

Cyrus is the key to the new emphasis on monotheism. To the exiles, Cyrus's Edict is so unexpected that it must be a miracle. Second Isaiah asserts that this surprising event is God's way of rewarding the Jewish exiles for their patient acceptance of their punishment. Remember that Cyrus's Edict was not directed just at Jews; *all* those exiled by the Babylonians were allowed to return. But for Second Isaiah this whole event is being orchestrated by Yahweh in order to reward only one of those groups: the Israelites. The Edict is evidence that Yahweh controls all of world history.

Second Isaiah makes a startling claim. Isaiah 45:1 states, "Thus says the LORD to his anointed, to Cyrus." Do you remember what the word *anointed* is in Hebrew? It is the word *messiah*. Second Isaiah says that Cyrus, a Persian king who does not even worship Yahweh, is a messiah. Remember that the word *messiah* also meant a future king of Israel, but so far we have only seen descendants of David referred to as *messiahs*. During the exile, the Jews hoped that one day they would return to their land and have a new king. The poet sees Cyrus as a king sent by God who would return them to their land.

The poet notes that Cyrus has no idea that God controls what the king is doing. God speaks directly to Cyrus in Isaiah 45:4. "For the sake of my servant Jacob, and Israel my chosen, I call you (Cyrus) by your name, I surname you, though you do not know me." If God can appoint the oblivious Cyrus to be the "anointed," then Yahweh must certainly be the one and only god.

In chapter 44 Second Isaiah ridicules the gods of other countries by claiming that they are nothing but wood and metal. Isaiah 44:9–20 describes the Babylonian process of making statues that represented the gods, although he does so with a clearly polemical stance. He uses his knowledge of statue making to show that the gods, whom the Babylonians worship, do not exist. The statue maker, who uses some of the wood to make the statue and some to cook his food, should see that his creation is not a god. Since the Israelites did not use statues to represent God's presence in the temple, they would find this argument convincing.

In summary, Second Isaiah asserts that Yahweh is the only true God in three ways. First, Yahweh is the God who has created everything. Second, Yahweh controls world history, a fact made clear in Cyrus's miraculous policy of allowing the exiles to return. Third, the gods worshipped by other peoples do not exist; they are nothing more than wood and metal statues. Yahweh is the only God.

Isaiah 42:1–9 and 52:13–53:12: The Suffering Servant

The poems best known to Christians from Second Isaiah are those which describe a "suffering servant." Sprinkled throughout chapters 40—55 are a series of poems celebrating Yahweh's servant, who suffered more than he has deserved.

In Case You Were Wondering

God is speaking. The speaker in both passages is God.

"Former things." This is a phrase used by post-exilic prophets to refer to earlier prophecies and histories.

A marred appearance. This phrase means he looks bad. For instance, a boxer often has a "marred appearance." Other kings are surprised when God exalts this servant, who had been "beaten up."

Looking Closely at the Text

1. According to Isaiah 42:1 and 42:3, what will the servant "bring forth"?

2. Who is being addressed in 42:6–9?

3. Find images associated with royalty in 52:13—53:12.

4. Who do you think the "we" is in these verses?

5. Can you reconstruct the explanation for the servant's suffering that this passage is trying to address?

The Suffering Servant

Like many Christians, whenever I hear these texts, I think of Jesus. Christians make this connection because Jesus suffered on the cross, not because he

The Bible in the CHRISTIAN TRADITION

Is Jesus the Suffering Servant?

While most Christians would assert that Jesus is the Suffering Servant, most biblical scholars will say that Isaiah is not referring to Jesus in these passages. Can both statements be true?

The writer of Second Isaiah had a particular person or group in mind when he wrote the poems describing the Suffering Servant, such as a future ruler or ruling family, whom he felt did not deserve to suffer through the long exile.

By the time that the texts in the New Testament were written, many Jews read prophetic texts as referring to future events; this is a common move observed in the Dead Sea Scrolls. After Jesus suffered and died on the cross, early Christians found in Second Isaiah a way to make sense of Jesus' horrible death.

You might think that the gospels would have quoted these poems often, especially when they described Jesus' death, but there are only a few direct quotations from Second Isaiah in the New Testament. The most direct quote is found in Matthew 8:17, where it explains why Jesus spent so much time healing people: "This was to fulfill what had been spoken through the prophet Isaiah, 'He took our infirmities and bore our diseases.'" The connection between the Suffering Servant and Jesus' death on the cross is clearly made in a later text, 1 Peter 2:22–25. Christian post-biblical tradition made the most of these links. From an early period, texts from Isaiah have been included in the liturgy at Advent and Lent.

So in what way is the Suffering Servant Jesus? Nicholas of Lyra in the fourteenth century provided the Church with a very helpful way to think about this problem. He introduced the notion of a "double literal" sense. Texts in the Old Testament have their own literal meaning. But when Old Testament texts are quoted in the New Testament, they take on a new literal meaning in that context. Let me show you what that means.

- The literal meaning of the Suffering Servant when read exclusively in the context of the book of Isaiah is that it is a royal figure or group.

- The literal meaning of the Suffering Servant in Matthew 8:17 and 1 Peter 2:22–25 is that he is Jesus, the Christ.

- Therefore, for Christians the Suffering Servant is both a royal figure or group in the Restoration Period *and* Jesus Christ: the figure has two literal meanings.

This way of reading avoids the heresy of "supercessionism." Supercessionism involves the assertion that the original meaning of the text is superceded or nullified by the later meaning. A supercessionist reading of the Suffering Servant would say that, although the Israelites thought this poem was about a figure in the past, we know that it is exclusively about Jesus.

Instead of supercessionism, Catholics talk about the *sensus plenior*. This phrase is translated as the "fuller sense" of the text, and it is a shorthand way to refer to the fact that Catholics believe a text can have multiple meanings. Throughout most of Christian history, biblical exegetes have talked about the text as having multiple meanings. By the high Middle Ages, Christian theologians, such as Thomas Aquinas, concluded that every text has a literal meaning. (This is the basis for resisting supercessionism.) But they also realized texts can mean more than one thing. The Suffering Servant is a great case in point. The literal meaning is set in the context of the period of the late Exile. The Servant as Christ, however, is an additional meaning or "fuller" meaning of the text.

Many Christians, including Catholics, then, would hold that the Suffering Servant refers to a figure at the time of the late Exile and to Christ. Both meanings are part of the divine revelation of the text, and neither is less "holy" or "canonical," although the literal meaning is what must be affirmed.

had sinned, but in order to take on the punishment that others deserve for their sins. Because of Jesus' suffering on the cross, which "pays back" the debt created by sin, people have access to eternal life. Jesus pays the price so that the rest of humanity can go to heaven.

When someone suffers a punishment or takes on a debt that another person owes, it is called *redemptive suffering*. The New Testament writers understood Jesus' suffering in this way, in part because they already understood about redemptive suffering from Second Isaiah.

However, Isaiah is not talking specifically about Jesus here. Although many of the images sound as if they refer to Jesus, not all of them do. In fact, it would be rather odd for a poet living five hundred years before the birth of Jesus to write about him, and even more strange for people to have kept reading these texts if they did not know who they concerned. These poems had an original meaning about life in the exile, which was later understood to also be meaningful when referring to Jesus. What did the suffering servant originally represent?

Scholars debate this question. The identity of the servant in Second Isaiah is contradictory. Texts such as Isaiah 44:1 state that the servant is Israel. Other passages, such as the two poems you have read, depict the Servant as an individual who suffers *for* Israel's sins.

Scholars have many theories, which are too complex to explore here, to explain the contradictions. What *is* clear from the poems are the following points:

▶ The Servant suffers.

▶ The Servant does not deserve to suffer.

▶ The Servant's suffering pays God back for the sins of others in Israel.

▶ Because of the Servant's suffering, Israel is redeemed.

If you were an exile, you might see yourself or your leaders as the servant. We can easily imagine that there were people, especially among the "people of the land," who claimed that these exiles had no right to return to their old positions of power. They had obviously sinned. After all, they were the ones who were being punished in exile, and their ancestors had been the ones in charge when the nation initially fell.

The poem answers these charges by asserting that the servant is suffering for *their* sins, and that God intends to reward him for that sacrifice. These poems are able to explain the length and hardship of the exile, while allowing the exiles to maintain their innocence and to claim that they deserved to rule the nation again.

The Servant poems use specific images that focus on the royal family or on a particular person with a claim to the throne:

▸ The Servant will be in charge of bringing justice.

▸ His rewards (exaltation, being among the great and dividing spoil) are the rewards of kings.

▸ Those who notice his restoration are other kings.

▸ The people describe themselves as "sheep" (Is 53:6), which suggests that the servant is the shepherd (king).

But the poems remain ambiguous. The Suffering Servant could have been the exiled Israelites, the leaders among the exiles, especially the royal family, or an individual, such as someone with a claim to the throne. It is the ambiguity of the passages that leave the poems open for reinterpretation. Because the prophecies were not fulfilled by a human king or any human group (Israel did not bring justice to all the nations and the people continued to suffer), the Israelites continued to hope for someone who would bring about a glorious reign.

Haggai 1:1–2:9 and Zechariah 3:1–4:14: Prophets of the Restoration

We know about life in Judah after the exile both from historical accounts contained in the books of Ezra and Nehemiah, as well as from two prophetic books whose oracles deal directly with the rebuilding of the temple, Haggai and Zechariah.

In Case You Were Wondering

King Darius. He was a Persian king who ruled approximately twenty years after Cyrus. The oracles in Haggai were delivered in 520 BCE.

Satan. He is not the devil here. Instead, he is one of God's angels, whose job it is to charge people with crimes against God. In Zechariah 3 he is charging the high priest, Joshua, with being too impure to serve at the rebuilt temple.

"I rebuke you." This phrase means that God does not agree with Satan's charge and declares Joshua innocent.

A brand plucked from the fire. This means that Joshua was saved from a destroying punishment.

Festal apparel and a turban. These were part of the priestly garments.

The Branch. This was a title usually given to a king, but here applied to the high priest.

The lamp stand or menorah. This was a large, seven-branched oil lamp that stood outside of the Holy of Holies in the second temple. It burned olive oil, not candles.

The olive trees. They pour oil directly into the bowls on the menorah. As far as we know, there were no olive trees in the second temple.

Looking Closely at the Text

1. What are the issues that Haggai appears to be tackling

2. What problem does Zechariah 3—4 address?

Problems in the Restoration

The rebuilding of the temple did not go smoothly. The returnees did not have enough resources to rebuild the temple. The problems of rebuilding were complicated by a drought. Haggai urged on the people by claiming that the drought was punishment for their delay. The only way that they could increase their profits was by continuing the construction of the temple.

The Jews placed their hopes in two leaders: Zerubbabel, who was a descendant of the Davidic kings, and Joshua, who was a descendant of the Zadokite priests. These two men represented the restoration of both the monarchy and the priesthood. Many of the oracles in Zechariah focus on these two men, both called "messiahs."

Zechariah 1—8 contains a series of visions. As you may recall from the visions in Amos, prophetic visions are highly symbolic. The prophet sees something that symbolizes the message that he or she should deliver. Zechariah "sees" a lamp stand flanked by two olive trees. The two olive trees symbolized the two people who were anointed into their office with olive oil: the king and the high priest.

Zechariah 3 deals with the question of whether these leaders deserve to be reinstated to positions of power. The charge against Joshua is that he is defiled; his "filthy" clothes are a symbol of his impurity. God does not deny that he has become defiled, but Yahweh asserts that Joshua can be purified and restored to the role of high priest. Joshua retains the "right of access" that his ancestors had; that is, he is pure enough to be allowed into the interior of the temple complex.

The oracle addressed to Zerubbabel in Zechariah 4 focuses on the king's role as temple builder. As you may recall when we looked at the reign of Solomon, only kings built temples in the ancient Near East. Zechariah 4:8–10 depicts Zerubbabel as a royal temple builder. The oracle ends by affirming that Joshua and Zerubbabel, priest and king, were both "branches" and messiahs.

We do not know what happened to these men. Apparently Zerubbabel was unsuccessful in reestablishing the monarchy. Did the Persian government see him as a threat and remove him? Was he unable to get enough support from the Jews to be effective? Did drought and famine make national restoration impossible? We have no way of knowing.

HISTORIES OF THE RESTORATION: CHRONICLES, EZRA, AND NEHEMIAH

Chronicles, Ezra, and Nehemiah are sometimes referred to as the *Chronicler's History*. All three share a similar writing style, date, and theology, although different people probably wrote them. You might think that the gaps in Israel's history could be filled in by the historical accounts of this time period, but when you turn to these accounts you find that they raise more questions than they solve.

The history in Chronicles focuses on the same period of Israelite history as found in the Deuteronomistic History. Chronicles starts with the creation of the world, but covers the history from Adam to Saul with genealogies only. In addition, it only tells the history of Judah (not of the northern kingdom, Israel), using large chunks of material from Samuel and Kings to retell this history. The historian tells us about historical events from the death of Saul onward but ends at the Edict of Cyrus. Chronicles does not include the history of the Persian Period. It can be outlined as follows:

1 Chronicles 1—9	Genealogies covering the history of the world from Creation until the reign of Saul
1 Chronicles 10	The reign of Saul
1 Chronicles 11—29	The reign of David
2 Chronicles 1—9	The reign of Solomon
2 Chronicles 10—36	History of Judah until the Edict of Cyrus

The events surrounding the restoration of the city and the temple are recounted in Ezra and Nehemiah, two leaders whose historical relationship is unclear. These two books are counted as one in the Hebrew tradition. Although there is no agreement about the overall structure of Ezra-Nehemiah, the material that they contain can be outlined as follows:

Ezra 1—6	Restoration of the temple
Ezra 7—10	Restoration of the worshiping community
Nehemiah 1—7	Restoration of the wall of Jerusalem
Nehemiah 10—13	Restoration of the community around the law

Details in the mission of Ezra suggest that he may have come after Nehemiah became governor, although the biblical account places him before Nehemiah. We do not have enough information to resolve these chronological problems, although the two books give an overall picture of the issues that the foundling community faced as it tried to rebuild.

The Chronicler's History makes clear that a burning question the community faced was: who were the true Jews? The answer to this question determined who would be full citizens in the restored nation: who could own property, who would have access to the court system, who could have full status in the temple? Ezra and Nehemiah represented those who defined "Israel" very narrowly. Only those who could prove a pure line of descent from the landowners of the monarchy could be full citizens. This is why genealogies became so important in the literature from this period.

One of the major problems was the fact that many people, both exiles and those who had remained in the Levant, had married non-Israelites. Ezra and Nehemiah tell us that men were forced to divorce non-Jewish wives and disinherit their children if these men were to be granted full rights of citizenship (Ezra 9:1–2 and Nehemiah 13:23–31). Neither account states what would have happened to the women and children, now among the class of "widows, orphans, and resident aliens."

NEHEMIAH 8:1–8: THE READING OF THE LAW

In this passage Ezra, here both scribe and priest, reads an ancient law code to the people. As part of the restoration, he leads the people in renewing their covenant with God.

In Case You Were Wondering

The date. The date of this passage is around the year 444 or 443, almost one hundred years after the Edict of Cyrus and more than seventy-five years after the oracles of Haggai.

Names, names, and more names. The Chronicler's History is obsessed with names, since these names and genealogies were an essential part of how they defined who was truly a Jew.

Looking Closely at the Text

1. What does Ezra read to the people?

2. Who came to the assembly?

3. According to Nehemiah 8:7, what did the leaders who were with Ezra do for the people?

Renewing the Law

You may remember that, at the beginning of this course, I said that the Pentateuch is the earliest section of the Bible, dating to approximately 400 BCE. This would be during the Persian period.

We know that the Persians at some point requested a copy of the law codes from some of the peoples that they governed. Although it is not clear how widespread this policy was, it may have been the reason that the people in Judah assembled their laws together as we have them in the Pentateuch.

Nehemiah 8 depicts Ezra, here a scribe and priest, reading a "law of Moses" at a ceremony in which the people are renewing their covenant with God. What Ezra reads must be shorter than the Pentateuch, since he can read the whole thing in one day, but Ezra is still the "traditional" figure associated with the formation of the Pentateuch.

We do know that texts from later in the Persian period refer to "the law of Moses" as a binding law. When those texts give details about that law, we can usually find those laws in the Pentateuch. For example, in the next set of readings, Ezra 9:1–2 states that God forbids marriage with foreigners. These laws are found in Exodus 34:15–16 and Deut 7:3. The passage describing Ezra's reading of the law is one small example of a typical change in post-exilic literature. Post-exilic texts tend to define piety as adherence to specific Jewish laws. This public declaration of the law to all of Israel means that no Israelite can claim that they do not know the law.

Ezra 9:1–10:17, Nehemiah 13:23–27, and Isaiah 56:1–8: Who Is a Jew?

These three passages deal with the question: can someone who is not descended from the monarchic Israelites be a Jew? The section from Isaiah comes from the restoration period, close in date to Ezra and Nehemiah. You will see that two different answers were circulating at that time.

In Case You Were Wondering

To forfeit something. This means that you give up your property and/or civil rights because of a crime you have committed.

Benjamin (Ezra 10:9). He comes to represent Jews living north of Judah in the post-exilic period.

Sanballat. He was the Persian-appointed leader of the Levant who ruled from the territory of Samaria.

A eunuch. This is a castrated male, that is, a man whose testicles have been removed or mutilated. This procedure was sometimes done to male slaves who served women and to some prisoners of war. Deuteronomy 23 says that eunuchs cannot worship Yahweh at the temple.

Looking Closely at the Text

1. How do Ezra and Nehemiah deal with the presence of foreigners among the community?

2. How does Isaiah 56 differ from Ezra and Nehemiah on this issue?

Dissolving Mixed Marriages

I remember learning once that Jews trace their heritage through their mothers. I do not know how widely this is true, but I do know that this was not the case in ancient times. Lineage passed from father to son. The prohibitions against marriage in Ezra and Nehemiah assume this.

In addition, I remember being confused when somebody said that they were "Jewish" as to whether they were talking about their ethnic heritage or their religious identity. I now realize that the term itself is ambiguous. One person can be talking about nationality, while another is referring to religious identity.

This is an ancient problem, although it took a slightly different form in the days of Ezra. The Bible does not doubt that people who are ethnically Jewish have the right, even the obligation, to participate fully in the worship of Yahweh. The question that the biblical texts do not agree on is whether it is essential to be ethnically Jewish in order to fully worship Yahweh. What do I mean by "fully worship"? The question seems to center on whether people who were not ethnically Jewish could enter the courtyard of the temple set aside for Jews and whether they could participate in the sacrificial rituals.

The issue had political consequences as well. If only Jews could own land in the Levant, then Jewish identity had an economic element. If there were special laws that protected Jews within the land, then non-Jews would not have had the same rights. If Jews and non-Jews paid different taxes, then the categories were important.

Some biblical texts like Ezra and Nehemiah consider ethnic purity an important element. Although the texts do not specifically address the question of whether a non-Jew can convert to the Jewish religion, they imply that Jews who married outside their ethnic group were no longer full members of their community. Other texts, such as the one from Isaiah, do accept conversion. They specifically deny that one's ethnic background should limit one's right to worship Yahweh. After reading the passages in Ezra and Nehemiah, it becomes clearer how daring the statement in Isaiah 56 is.

Most Jews and Christians today are probably more comfortable with the views expressed by Isaiah. Of course, people should not be excluded from worshipping God because they are physically challenged or because they have a different ethnic background. It is important to understand the equally dominant viewpoint found in the Chronicler's History, however, because it helps us understand why marriage with foreigners is such a prominent element in the literature from the Second Temple Period. Why would Ezra and Nehemiah want Jewish men to divorce foreign wives?

In the United States questions of ethnic identity have loomed large. Ethnic identity can be at odds with our country's need to function as a unified nation. The United States has sometimes been defined as a "melting pot," since some ethnic identities here have tended to lessen as various groups have interacted. This was the goal of integration. Some ethnic groups have sought to resist this movement, in part by putting pressure on young people to marry within their own ethnic group. Today we talk about pluralism, rather than integration.

Young people can also feel pressure to marry within their religious group. I know in the 1960s, my relatives had a hard time when their children married people who were not Catholic. Back then the question was whether you could marry a Protestant. Now marriages between Christians and Jews, Muslims, and Buddhists are more common, although each combination offers its own challenges.

Ezra and Nehemiah address both issues: can you marry outside your ethnic group *and* can you marry outside your religious group and remain truly Jewish. Like today, the problem faced by the people is one of group identity. Notice that the "foreigners" that Ezra actually mentions are mostly peoples living in the Levant (Ezr 9:1). These would be people indistinguishable to the Persians since their language, dress, and physical features would be similar to the people living in Judah. (All of the people of the Levant would speak a form of Aramaic from this period on. This is reflected in some of the texts dating to this period, such as Ezra and Daniel, that switch between Hebrew and Aramaic.) For those agreeing with Ezra, the Jews needed to define who they were over and against other neighboring groups.

From the perspective of the returning exiles, the biggest source of confusion was with the Samaritans. These were the people living in the area that once comprised the northern kingdom of Israel. The Persian government had placed the whole Levant under the rule of one governor who ruled from Samaria. The Samaritan Jews had more rights and more visibility to the Persians than did the Jews who returned to Judah from exile. The exiles did not consider the Samaritans to be Jewish, since the resettlement of diverse people after the Assyrian Conquest in 722 meant that the Samaritans had been an ethnically diverse group for almost 300 years. Yet the inhabitants of Samaria, who worshipped Yahweh, considered themselves to be Jewish; they were not religiously diverse.

The fear of marriage with Samaritans comes out most clearly in the passage from Nehemiah. The threat to Nehemiah's community was that Samaria would simply swallow up Judah. In addition, the Samaritans had long before broken away from the Davidic monarchy, and they would not have seen Jerusalem as the only, or even primary, place where Yahweh could be worshipped. This meant that those people in Judah who viewed the return of the Davidic monarchy and the rebuilding of the temple of Jerusalem as essential elements of the restoration would have seen the Samaritan form of Judaism as unacceptable.

Although we have examined why a text like Nehemiah might advocate resistance to foreigners, we are left with the challenge of how to read the texts today. The texts point to the tension between wanting to be open to others, yet wanting to maintain your own identity. Let's go back to our contemporary examples. Does marrying someone who is not Christian threaten the religious identity of your children? Is it important to maintain ethnic traditions within the United States, or is it better to be a "melting pot"?

1 Chronicles 22:2–16 and 28:1–19: Rewriting History

The person who wrote Chronicles used the books of Samuel and Kings as primary sources of information. We can most clearly detect Chronicle's point of view in those passages where the author changes what is found in those two sources. Look at these two accounts about David's involvement in the building of the first temple. See if you can detect where changes have been made.

Looking Closely at the Text

List the ways that 1 Chronicles 22 and 28 differ from their parallels in Samuel and Kings.

Cleaning up Israel's History

Much of what you find in the books of Chronicles sounds familiar, especially if you have read the Deuteronomistic History. The Chronicler simply uses long sections of Samuel and Kings in writing this history. The Chronicler, however, has a different reason for telling Israel's history. The reason is not to explain why the nation fell, as we saw in Samuel and Kings. Instead, Chronicles emphasizes those parts of Israel's past that the author wants to see restored in his own day.

The material you read is a small part of the long passages that the Chronicler devotes to the building of the *first* temple in Jerusalem. You now realize that in the Restoration Period, when the Chronicler was writing, the big issue of the day was the *re*built temple. Most of the changes that the Chronicler makes to the earlier history entail lengthy additions to the information about how the temple was built and who could serve at the temple. The Chronicler focuses on this material because it was such a pressing issue in his day.

A second major change in this material is that actions performed by Solomon in the books of Kings are here done by David. In Kings, Solomon has the temple plan. Here the temple plan is divinely revealed to David. In Kings, Solomon gathers the workers and material. Here David does so. Chronicles wants to increase David's involvement in the building of the temple.

Throughout the books of Chronicles, the author says only good things about David. He makes him the center of Israel's history, by stating that all of the most important elements of Israel were begun during his reign. He depicts him as a prayerful king.

He also leaves out any stories that would raise questions about David's moral character. For instance, the Chronicler does not retell the story of David and Bathsheba. Moreover, in Chronicles, David designates Solomon to be the next king long before David is an old man, and, in chapter 28, David's strength and wisdom as an old man contrast sharply with the feeble old David depicted in 1 Kings 1. For Chronicles, David is a hero, whose righteous behavior people should imitate.

This is a common move in Israelite literature from the Second Temple Period. There are many Jewish texts from this period, most not in the Bible. Many are "rewritten Bible," meaning that they are retelling stories we now find in the Bible. These rewritten histories usually make the Old Testament characters more pious and moral than they appear in the Bible. Chronicles is an early example of this type of literature.

Rewritten Bibles and Jewish Midrash

As certain Jewish texts became more fixed in form, the only way to present another version of the material that they contained was by rewriting their accounts. In some ways, this is what the books of Chronicles do: they rewrite the Deuteronomistic History. There are other examples of "rewritten Bible" found outside of the canon, such as the book of Jubilees, which covers the history of Israel from creation to events at Mt. Sinai, and the Temple Scroll, which provides another book of law revealed to Moses on Sinai.

Often times, these rewritten versions "clean up" the moral issues found in earlier texts. They give witness to changes in attitudes toward biblical characterization (a biblical figure must be moral), as well as the view of God (who is often more remote in these versions).

Within early Judaism, the Targums were translations of biblical texts into Aramaic, the language spoken by most Jews from the Persian period on. These translations, however, included paraphrases and explanations of the biblical texts. Sometimes these translations "cleaned up" the text. For example, the translations avoid anthropomorphism by eliminating any reference to God's body and, at times, replacing God with an angel.

Another form of early biblical interpretation came to be known as *midrash*, a term derived from the Hebrew verb "to seek." It has come to have two meanings. First, it is often used to denote interpretations of Jewish rabbis in antiquity. Second, *midrash* has come to mean a mode of interpretation that results from juxtaposing seemingly similar words, phrases, or events found throughout the canon. This mode of interpretation assumes that the primary author of Scriptures is God. These freer associations are legitimized because hidden meanings have been imbedded in the text by the divine author. Some of these interpretations were collated into various collections of midrashic interpretation, such as *Genesis Rabbah*, a collection of midrashic interpretation of Genesis.

The benefit of reading midrash is that it reminds the modern reader what a serious commitment to divine authorship might look like. In addition, the results of midrash often reveal parallels between biblical texts that can be missed if we read each one as a discrete unit. It parallels Christian attempts to find the "fuller sense" of the text, although it does so in a distinct way from the Christian interpretive tradition.

REWRITING HISTORY, ENVISIONING A FUTURE

The literature from the Restoration Period reveals how hard it is for a community to come together again to build a new future. The people of Judah were still reeling from the devastation of the exile. Each group blamed the other for the disaster, and they lived in fear that God's wrath threatened them at every turn. Sometimes this fear prevented them from realizing their dreams.

Where is God in all of this? The later chapters of Isaiah depict a vision of a world unified under the rule of a restored Jerusalem. There is only one God and this God controls all of human history. In Haggai and Zechariah, God actively participates in the reestablishment of Judah. Yet, these plans seem to have failed. The monarchy was not restored. Money did not flow into the temple, and all nations did not see Jerusalem as the center of the universe. Even the temple was not run according to Isaiah's visions: foreigners were excluded from full participation in the temple rituals.

The Chronicler's History shows a more common attitude toward God at this time: the one and only God was a distant figure, sitting in heaven, ready to judge the sins of the people. God has given the people a law through Moses that they should follow. Yahweh has appointed priestly lines from long ago who can interpret that law for the people. The Lord has decided in ancient days who should own land and which family should be king. The people need only follow those ancient outlines in order to do what is right.

In one way, the theology of the Second Temple Period gives us a more contemporary view of God: God is the one and only God who creates and controls all things. But monotheism raised a thorny question for the Jewish people: can God be Lord of all, and yet choose some over others? If there is only one God, can there be a chosen people? Who is right: Isaiah or Ezra?

FOR REVIEW

1. When did the exile end?

2. What do we call this period of Israel's history?

3. Why didn't all of the exiles return to Judah?

4. Describe the conflict between the exiles and the people of the land.

5. Why wouldn't the returning exiles let the Samaritans help rebuild the temple?

6. What is monotheism?

7. When was Isaiah 40—66 written?

8. Give some examples of Persian Period texts that interpret or use earlier material.

9. How does monotheism affect the question of God's relationship to the world?

For Further Reading

There has been increasing interest in the Persian period of Israel's history. Most influential in this regard has been the work of Joel P. Weinberg; the major elements of his historical reconstruction can be found in *The Citizen-Temple Community* (JSOTSup 151; Sheffield: JSOT Press, 1992).

A useful tool for examining Chronicles' use of earlier traditions is John C. Endres, et al., *Chronicles and Its Synoptic Parallels in Samuel, Kings, and Related Biblical Texts* (Collegeville, MN: Liturgical/Michael Glazier, 1998). A very important study of Ezra-Nehemiah is the one by Tamara C. Eskenazi, *In an Age of Prose: A Literary Approach to Ezra-Nehemiah* (SBLMS 36; Atlanta, GA: Scholars Press, 1988). Similarly influential studies of the Chronicler are H. G. M. Williamson's *Israel in the Books of Chronicles* (Cambridge, MA/New York: Cambridge University Press, 1977); Mark A. Throntveit's *When Kings Speak: Royal Speech and Royal Prayer in Chronicles* (SBLDS 93; Atlanta, GA: Scholars Press, 1987); Peter Ackroyd's *The Chronicler in His Age* (JSOTSup 101; Sheffield, GA: JSOT Press, 1991); and Sara Japhet's *The Ideology of the Book of Chronicles and Its Place in Biblical Thought*, second revised edition (BEATAJ 9; Frankfurt/New York, Peter Lang, 1997).

Mark S. Smith has written extensively on the development of Israelite views of God; one of his recent works, that traces the rise of biblical monotheism up to the time of Second Isaiah, is *The Origins of Biblical Monotheism: Israel's Polytheistic Background and the Ugaritic Texts* (Oxford/New York: Oxford University Press, 2001).

For a recent collection of essays addressing the identity of the suffering servant, both within the history of interpretation and today, see *The Suffering Servant: Isaiah 53 in Jewish and Christian Sources*, edited by Bernd Janowski and Peter Stuhlmacher (Grand Rapids, MI: Eerdmans, 2004).

Brevard Childs has written extensively on the canonical approach to Scripture. One of these is *Old Testament Theology in a Canonical Context* (Philadelphia: Fortress, 1985). On the subject of the formation and authority of the canon, see Lee Martin McDonald, *The Formation of the Christian Biblical Canon* (Nashville, TN: Abingdon, 1988) and Joseph Lienhard, *The Bible, the Church, and Authority: The Canon of the Christian Bible in History and Theology* (Collegeville, MN: Liturgical Press, 1995).

13 THE WISE SHALL BEHOLD ALL OF CREATION

The LORD by wisdom founded the earth;
by understanding he established the heavens.
(Prov 3:19)

CHAPTER OVERVIEW

Now we are ready to go back to the creation of the universe. Remember that this book started in the middle of the book of Genesis with the stories about the patriarch Abraham. We did this because creation accounts are among the most sophisticated material in the ancient world. To be sure, the storylines are easy to follow, but the "information" the authors are trying to convey is the realm of scientists, philosophers, and theologians: in a word it is the subject of the *wise*!

The material that we will explore in this chapter comes from the most intellectual stratum of Israelite society. In the introduction we will consider the connection between Israelite philosophy, better known as Wisdom literature, and descriptions of the creation of the world. This chapter will cover the following topics:

❯ The content of proverbs

❯ The social context of Wisdom literature

❯ How ideas of creation are central to the Wisdom tradition

❯ The figure of "Lady Wisdom"

The biblical texts we will read will show the connections between Wisdom literature and creation accounts. By the end of this chapter, you should be able to identify some of the ways in which God's work as creator and sustainer of the world was understood by the ancient Israelites.

Your instructor may choose to cover all or part of this chapter earlier in the course. The material on Genesis 1—11 could go with the material on the patriarchs. Alternatively, the Wisdom material could follow the discussion of Solomon, since the Wisdom traditions are associated with him. I have placed it at this point so that it is closer to the short stories in the next chapter, many of which display Wisdom themes, as well as nearer to the final chapter where I discuss skeptical wisdom.

WHERE IS WISDOM FOUND?

WHAT IS A PROVERB?

A *proverb* is a short, popular saying that expresses a common observation about life. Often these short sayings use images or metaphors. Proverbs were an important part of Israelite society. They reflected Israelite values, encapsulating how people should live, what they should value, and how they could succeed.

From a cross-cultural perspective, proverbs often have a degree of authority, especially within oral cultures. The proverbs developed over time and represented traditional social values. They were often accepted as universal truths, and they could be used in arguments as ways to settle debates. Rarely are the truths of a proverb questioned, although we saw this happen in Ezekiel and Jeremiah.

In Hebrew, the word that we translate as *proverb* was also used for a wide variety of forms, including riddles and comparisons. In the longer canon of the Bible, three books contain collections of Israelite proverbs: Proverbs, the Wisdom of Solomon (also known as Wisdom), and the Wisdom of ben Sirach (also known as Sirach or Ecclesiasticus). Other proverbs are scattered throughout the Bible.

Most Hebrew proverbs have a standard form. They are short, usually only two lines long, and they use parallelism. Sometimes these parallels contrast the good and the bad or the wise and the foolish:

> The wise of heart will heed commandments,
>> but a babbling fool will come to ruin (Prov 10:8).

> The mouth of the righteous is a fountain of life,
>> but the mouth of the wicked conceals violence (Prov 10:11).

The form of these proverbs makes them easy to remember.

These proverbs developed, in part, as a way whereby older men taught younger men about their future rights and responsibilities. The sayings were collected by scribes or sages, a learned class in ancient Israel. Much of this material focuses on becoming respected members of society. This includes teaching the rights and responsibilities of being a rich landowner.

If you were to read long portions of proverbial literature, you might notice that it addresses a specific audience. Take a look at these proverbs from Sirach:

> He who acquires a wife gets his best possession,
> a helper fit for him and a pillar of support (Sir 36:29).

What can you tell about the person being addressed? Here are a few things you might notice:

The audience is male. There are no parallel passages in the proverbs advising women about husbands.

The audience is young. At least they are inexperienced with respect to women.

The speaker is trying to teach his audience. We call this kind of literature "didactic" because it has a teaching purpose.

Now read two more proverbs:

> Do not rely on your wealth,
> or say, "I have enough."
>
> Do not follow your inclination and strength
> in pursuing the desires of your heart (Sir 5:1–2).
>
> The merciful lend to their neighbors;
> by holding out a helping hand they keep the commandments.
>
> Lend to your neighbor in his time of need;
> repay your neighbor when a loan falls due (Sir 29:1–2).

Can you tell anything else about the audience?

They are rich. Or, at least, they will inherit riches.

Many of the proverbs presume that the audience has access to money.

Focus on METHOD

Contextual Approaches

One element of historical research that has long been recognized is that the cultural context of the historian affects what persons notice, what they deem as important, and how they explain what they discover. For example, the increase of women in an academic field such as history has led to an increased awareness of the role women have played in all eras of human history.

Sometimes, being a member of an oppressed group also makes one aware of how certain biblical texts have been used for both good and ill. The biblical slave laws are a case in point. As a white Christian, I was content to dismiss the laws permitting slavery in ancient Israel as an historical curiosity. To me it was something that was "okay back then."

It wasn't until I began reading some African-American biblical scholars that I became aware of the use of these laws (and other biblical texts) by Christian slave owners in the nineteenth century to justify the owning of slaves.

While gender and race are important lenses through which to look at the Bible, social class also informs an interpreter's context. Traditionally biblical scholars came from the elite classes. If we think about the society of rich males of the late nineteenth and early twentieth centuries, we can understand that some of the elite perspectives of Israelite proverbs might sound like universal truths to them. It has been the entry of various social classes into academia that has furthered our understanding of the economic location of the authors of these proverbs.

"Contextual approaches" is an umbrella term that covers any criticism that makes use of the context of the interpreter as an important element in biblical interpretation.

The aims of the contextual approach can include the following:

- Highlighting overlooked elements in the text
- Reading the text from the perspective of those oppressed within the text
- Uncovering the use (or misuse) of the text by those in power to maintain a system of oppression (This often includes uncovering how the context of privilege has affected these interpretations.)
- Providing reading strategies for oppressed groups both to identify oppressive elements in a text and to counteract those elements

Oftentimes contextual approaches can be expressly theological in that they are interested in the meaning and use of the Bible today.

This approach is important for all interpreters because it makes the interpreter aware of her or his own bias. Such awareness can prevent the interpreter from misreading the text. In addition, contextual approaches offer new readings of the text that any one individual's perspective may have missed.

You might want to look up passages in Proverbs that deal with the poor and loss of wealth. Would someone who was poor have written the same proverbs? What kinds of proverbs might slaves, for instance, have passed on to their children? How would they differ from those preserved in Proverbs?

WHAT IS WISDOM?

A dominant theme in books such as Proverbs, Wisdom, and Sirach is the pursuit of wisdom. The aim of this didactic material is to encourage people to become "wise."

Being wise is not the same thing as being smart; sages wouldn't be Jeopardy winners. While sages were certainly well-educated, this fact alone did not make them wise. For the Israelites, wisdom included the ability to make judgments when the path wasn't clear and knowing what is just when choices are not good. Remember that when Solomon was granted wisdom, his wisdom was displayed in judging the case of the two women who both claimed the same child (1 Kings 3:16–28). He did not determine that case because he found more facts, but because he was a wise judge of human nature.

In many wisdom texts there is an intimate connection between the king, his role as judge, and wisdom. As chief judge of the land and the one who insures justice for the people, the king needed wisdom, more than strength or power. While this suggests that wisdom literature originated in royal circles, the wisdom books clearly contend that all people should strive to be wise.

Chaos Theory

To better understand wisdom and creation, it helps to look at their opposite: foolishness and chaos. Let's start with foolishness.

Fools are people who squander their talents. A fool, for example, would be someone who wins the lottery but who ends up homeless because she or he spent that money wastefully. A fool is also someone who does not discern the right path, marries someone for their looks, or chooses friends because they are rich. But remember, if wisdom is not the same as being smart, foolishness is not the same as being ignorant. In fact, a fool is someone who should "know better," what used to be called "willful ignorance." Therefore, as the wise person is righteous, so the fool is sinful. Why is foolishness sinful? To understand this concept, we have to turn to the concept of God as creator.

Chaos Monsters

In the ancient Near East, including Israel, the opposite of creation was not "nothing-ness," but "chaos." It is clear that the ancients did not regard creation as just an event in the past. God did not create a bunch of atoms floating around in space and then disappear to let them bump into each other "willy-nilly." The bulk of the creation accounts describe God's imposition of "order" onto matter. God acts as creator primarily by bringing order to the universe.

For the Israelites, the threat to God's creation does not come in the form of annihilation. They were not afraid of becoming "nothing" again. The threat came in the loss of this order, what today we call "chaos." God creates by imposing order onto chaos and sustains creation by keeping chaotic forces at bay.

Countries throughout the Fertile Crescent represented this struggle between creation and chaos with similar images. One of the images commonly used is that of water. Creation is like fresh water. It brings life and allows humanity to thrive. Chaos is like salt water. It looks like fresh water, but its looks are deceiving. If you water your plants with salt water, they will die. Add salt water to fresh water, and it destroys the life that fresh water nourishes. Mixing salt and fresh water destroys their order, their distinction; in short, it turns an ordered element chaotic.

Sometimes in the ancient Near East, a god, goddess, or monster represented chaos. One such deity was named "Sea" (salt water). Another god was

To Live and Die in Jerusalem

Death is a big thing for Christians. A major focus of Christianity is the afterlife; after all, Christians confess that Jesus came in order that people might have eternal life. When Christians think about that afterlife, they assume that it includes a system of reward and punishment, through the mechanisms of heaven and hell (as well as purgatory and limbo, for some Christians). When I first started studying the Old Testament, I assumed that the biblical view of the afterlife was the same for all. It didn't take long to realize that this assumption was not accurate.

Outside of those who ascended into heaven, like Elijah, all of the dead go to a place called *Sheol*. Translated as "Hades" in the Septuagint, this is a place that does not seem to distinguish between the righteous and the wicked. Look at the view of the dead nations in Ezekiel 32:18–31, a funeral song that the prophet sings for the not-yet-dead Pharaoh. Sheol is crowded with the slain soldiers of Israel's neighbors.

In a variety of Old Testament texts, Sheol does not sound very pleasant: it is dark, cut off from communication, and often called the "Pit." These descriptions stem from Israelite burial practices. The elite Israelites buried their dead in family tombs which resembled caves. These caves, sealed off from the world by large stone doors or rocks, had benches carved into the walls on which a corpse would be placed. Once the corpse had decomposed, the bones would be gathered and placed in a box, called an ossuary. These ossuaries would be stored in the niches in the walls of the cave.

Biblical texts, such as 1 Samuel 28, suggest that at least some of the dead became gods or "elohim." Archaeological evidence shows that people were buried with items that they used in life: food, jewelry, lamps, and so on. We know that offerings to the dead were a regular practice of cultures surrounding Israel. Biblical texts, such as Deuteronomy 26:14 forbid this ritual, belying the fact that some Israelites probably offered sacrifices to the dead. Therefore, there was some sense that the dead lived on.

The earliest reference that we have to a judgment of the dead can be found in the Hellenistic text Daniel 12:2: "Many of those who sleep in the dust of the earth shall awake, some to everlasting life, and some to shame and everlasting contempt." We do not know if this view of post-mortem judgment developed in Israel or as the result of Hellenistic influence. This and other Hellenistic texts are influential on the New Testament understanding of death.

Shown here are archeological remains of Israelite tombs at Katef Hinon, near Mount Zion in Jerusalem.

"Death." In the myths, these gods threaten the earth, engaging in battle with a god of the rains. This god defeats them, bringing order and abundance to the world. The creator god also sometimes fights a sea monster in an effort to sustain life on earth. We will see Israelites using some of these images in their texts as well.

Modern Chaos

Understanding that chaos threatens our world is a profound insight. Think about it. What makes the world "livable"? All sorts of things have to remain in a delicate balance. The earth's temperature must stay within a limited range. There must be no contaminated fresh water, the right mix of oxygen and other elements in the air, enough plants, and the right balance of animals. Predictions of global warming, fear of asteroids, or acid rain all reflect our own awareness of the need for natural order. For the Israelites, God's work as creator did not end at some point in the past. If creation means "ordering," then God creates continually by sustaining this order, this delicate balance. Each day, each moment, God creates.

Order is also required for the flourishing of human society. Our capacity for violence, selfishness, and pride also threaten God's order. Think about a war-torn or famine-riddled country where the social order has failed. Or think of the city of New Orleans after Hurricane Katrina. What are the features of such a world? If you were to look at such a place, you would see human institutions, such as family, church, education, health-care, and so on, all withering in the face of violence, greed, and social collapse. Christians ponder, is that the "life" God has intended for us?

Israel captures this sense of loss when it expresses the results of foolish behavior. The fool experiences a poor marriage, loss of wealth, poor health, and early death:

> Those who despise wisdom and instruction are miserable.
> Their hope is vain, their labors are unprofitable,
> and their works are useless.
> Their wives are foolish, and their children evil;
> their offspring are accursed (Wis 3:11–13)

While the texts talk about these things as if they happen to each individual fool, what they are really addressing is the collective behavior of a foolish society.

Fools are those who oppose God's plan and work for chaos. Putting their own personal satisfaction above the good of human society, they disrupt the delicate balance by which God sustains society.

LADY WISDOM

Israel also used personification to represent wisdom, the image of Lady Wisdom. A personification is the representation of an abstract thing or idea as a person. Some countries in the Fertile Crescent depicted this principle as a god or goddess, just as they did for the concept of chaos. For Israel, however, a figure such as "Lady Wisdom" became a literary device, a metaphor, not a real being or goddess.

Wisdom is personified as a woman in part because the Hebrew word for *wisdom* is feminine. It is a rich metaphor for Israel, because it can be used in so many ways. For instance, since the audiences of the written proverbs were men, the texts about Lady Wisdom use the language of romance. A wise man "pursues" her, seeks her, and woos her. She is God's partner, intimately connected, but not equal in status. She can be contrasted with a personification of foolishness, Mistress Folly, who is seductive, a temptress, beautiful on the outside but sinful on the inside. You can imagine how the imagination of a young male audience might be captured by these metaphors.

You will also find that many proverbs focus on male-female relationships. While this is a fundamental element of human society, it is also a way for the sage to flesh out the effects of the pursuit of wisdom. For Israel, wisdom has a direct effect on how actual men should interact with real women. In other words, the pursuit of wisdom is not simply contemplation or study. It is a way of living.

There are many descriptions and hymns of praise to wisdom throughout the wisdom literature. These texts express the connections between wisdom and creation. In Proverbs 8:22 Wisdom says, "The LORD created me at the beginning of his work, the first of his acts of long ago." Sirach 1:4 states, "Wisdom was created before all other things, and prudent understanding from eternity." Wisdom 9:9 addresses God saying, "With you is wisdom, she who knows your works and was present when you made the world; she understands what is pleasing in your sight, and what is right according to your commandments."

THE ETHICAL ELEMENT

At first glance, it may look like the proverbs have nothing to do with God.

> Where there are no oxen, there is no grain;
> Abundant crops come by the strength of the ox (Prov 14:4).

> Better is a dinner of vegetables where love is
>   than a fatted ox and hatred with it (Prov 15:17).

> "Bad, bad," says the buyer,
> then goes away and boasts (Prov 20:14).

You do not have to read far in any of the proverbial books to find repeated references to God. The ancient Israelites believed that God created the world, and that this creation was not slapped together any-which-way. God created with a design, a purpose. Therefore, all humans can know something about God by observing creation. Unlike the prophets, and even much of the historical material, the proverbs assume that the experience of wisdom does not depend on some kind of "appearance" from God, but that everyone can come to know how to be wise.

We also sometimes misunderstand the term *creation*. First, we sometimes think of creation as a single event in the past. The Israelites included God's work of sustaining the world as part of creation. Second, when we think of "creation" today, sometimes we think only of "nature": plants, earth, animals, and so on. We forget that "creation" also includes human nature and human

The Bible in the CHRISTIAN TRADITION

Is God Male or Female?

Many people today picture God as a wise old man with white hair and a beard, a picture based, in part, on the description of God in Daniel 7:9. Although Christ became a man when he was here on earth, Christians know that God does not have a body, so God cannot literally be a man.

St. Thomas Aquinas notes that all language about God is metaphorical. God is so far beyond human comprehension, and our human language is so limited, that anything we say about God only approximates the reality of God's essence.

Christians find that it is important to think of God as a person. It is a way to express the fact that God loves humanity and has an intimate relationship with people. Christians use the language of "personhood" to serve their understanding of God's love for humanity.

The Bible uses many human metaphors for God, and many of these are male metaphors. For instance, in calling God the husband of Jerusalem, the author is using a clear male image. In addition, Christians refer to God as "he," because to call God "it" impedes our ability to affirm God's love.

Sometimes, however, the Bible uses female images to describe God. For instance, Deuteronomy 32:11–13 uses images of a mother bird and a nursing mother to describe God's care for Israel. Similarly, Hosea 11:4 describes God as a nursing mother, bending down to feed her child.

The most enduring female image for God is Wisdom. We see in this chapter that Wisdom is an aspect of God's work in creation. Wisdom 7:25 states this explicitly,

"(Wisdom) is a breath of the power of God, and a pure emanation of the glory of the Almighty." Wisdom is personified as a woman. Therefore, God's plan in creation, the purpose and meaning of creation, is consistently depicted as a female aspect of God. The use of both male and female images for God is one way the Israelites affirmed that these images are metaphors. God is not literally male or female.

When Christian theologians think of Jesus, they recognize that Jesus was a man with a male body. But Jesus as *Christ* is both fully human (and literally male) as well as fully divine (neither male nor female). The New Testament affirms that the divine aspect of Christ is also not literally male when it equates Christ with Wisdom. The beginning of John's gospel, for instance, uses descriptions of Lady Wisdom from Proverbs and Wisdom to describe Christ as God's "Word." Colossians 1:15–20 also uses language of Lady Wisdom to praise Christ, depicting the involvement of Wisdom/Christ in creation.

Christian mystics have maintained the use of male and female images of God and Christ as a way to penetrate the mystery of God's nature. For example, Julian of Norwich, a mystic from the fifteenth century, had visions of Christ as mother. Therefore, while Jesus states that his followers can address God in prayer as "Our Father," neither Jesus nor later Christian tradition claim that this is the only way we can address God. Both Scripture and tradition affirm that we can apply female images, such as mother and Lady Wisdom, to all three persons of the trinity: God, Christ, and the Holy Spirit.

society: families, cities, politics, culture, religious expression, even love, hate, pleasure, and so on. You'll see that much of the wisdom literature calls for observation of these human elements in order to "know" God.

This knowledge of God and God's creation resulted in an "ethic" in ancient Israel, a structure within which the Israelites determined what was morally right and wrong. In ancient Israel, wisdom included knowing how God wanted people to live. In order to avoid being a force of chaos within creation, people should act within the bounds created for them by God.

The Israelites believed that God created human society to have a certain "order." For the Israelites, landowners had more privileges than the landless. Some people were created to be slaves. Men were created to "rule" over women. Notice the social order in the following series of woes:

> Under three things the earth trembles;
>> under four it cannot bear up:
> a slave when he becomes king,
>> and a fool when glutted with food:
> an unloved woman when she gets a husband,
>> and a maid when she succeeds her mistress (Prov 30:21–23).

As you can see, sometimes Israel's understanding of God's order seems offensive to modern ears. I bristle when I hear proverbs such as, "He who loves his son will whip him often" (Sir 30:1), and "A silent wife is a gift from the LORD" (Sir 26:14). How did this work within its ancient context?

A wise person lives a righteous life. Righteousness, or justice, is defined as living in accord with God's created plan, living as God has created each person. While we may define righteousness differently from the Israelites, the Proverbs teach its ancient audience how to find God's purpose for them.

When we look at wisdom literature in this way, we understand that the Israelites saw God in every aspect of their lives. God created people to have friends, and so everyone has a responsibility for how they choose and treat their friends. God created marriage and family, so people have a responsibility to pick partners, not on the basis of looks or riches, but with the purpose of cooperating with God in their personal lives.

While we might reject many of the ways the Israelites understood God's "order," we understand the reality that some people have more advantages from birth than others. The proverbs provide a constant reminder that those who have gifts and talents have a religious responsibility to use those gifts and talents as God intends them to be used. In Israel, if you were born to become king, then you were also called to live more ethically, to become wiser, and to worship God more diligently than any other person in your kingdom.

The Wisdom of Creation

We will look at a wide variety of texts in this chapter. First, we will look at some proverbs and hymns that connect wisdom and creation. Next, we will examine the view of creation in the book of Genesis and some psalms. By the end of these readings, you should have a better sense of the importance of a fully developed "theology of creation."

THE WISDOM BOOKS

While you have learned about the date and historical background of Genesis and Psalms, we have not yet talked about the date and composition of wisdom material. We will start with the earliest of these books, Proverbs.

The book of Proverbs is a collection of wisdom material, much like Amos is a collection of oracles and Psalms is a collection of songs. Most of the materials in Proverbs are short proverbs, although there are also longer discourses and poems. All of these resemble poetry in that the writers use parallelism, brevity, and metaphors.

The date of Proverbs is unknown. It is unclear when each proverb was written, or when this collection was put together. When we look at this type of literature in the ancient Near East, it often comes out of royal circles, partially serving the education of princes and royal advisors. But proverbs can be in use long after they were created, sometimes long after the metaphors they use stop making sense. The universal nature of their language makes them adaptable to many situations.

The dates of the Wisdom of Solomon and the Wisdom of Ben Sirach are much easier to determine. These were both composed after 200 BCE. They show remarkable continuity with Proverbs. They also address a privileged male audience, define wisdom as the comprehension of God's purpose in creation, and personify wisdom as a woman.

The book of Job tells the story of a righteous man who experiences horrible disasters. (We will examine the book more fully in a later chapter.) Conversations between Job and his friends on justice, sinfulness, and human suffering make up most of the book. Its date is also unknown. It does not contain proverbs like the other three books, but it does include many reflections on wisdom, justice and creation.

PROVERBS 7–8: A PICTURE OF LADY WISDOM

This passage presents Mistress Folly and Lady Wisdom. As you read it, make note of specific ways the poet contrasts the two.

IN CASE YOU WERE WONDERING

Sister. This is a term of endearment. Husbands and wives would call each other brother and sister.

Lady Wisdom and Mistress Folly. These are not phrases that appear in the Bible. They are used by scholars to indicate the personification of wisdom and folly. Mistress Folly is never named, while Lady Wisdom is simply called "Wisdom."

Looking Closely at the Text

1. In Proverbs 7:1–5, who is being addressed, and who do you think might be talking?

2. In what ways are the females in chapters 7 and 8 similar? How are they different?

3. Who is speaking in Proverbs 8:4–36?

4. Name or describe three characteristics of Wisdom.

5. When did God create Wisdom?

6. Where do you find images of death and life?

Mistress Folly and Lady Wisdom

This passage illustrates the use of personification to contrast foolishness and wisdom. The surface meaning of the texts is clear, but the reader is asked to ponder what these two portraits symbolize.

Let's start with the portrait of Folly. On the surface, you have a clear picture of a "loose" or immoral woman. She is sexually promiscuous (a prostitute). She cheats on her husband (adulterous). She is seductive, making it easy for an immature man to say yes to her.

But remember, this passage is not really about women. (If you want to see an almost identical description of an actual loose woman, see Proverbs 9:13–18.) This passage is about the ways the young can be distracted from pursuing a wise and just life. The poet recognizes that there are things that seem to promise "happiness," that are seductively attractive, and that are easy enough to attain. But, he says, they are a sham! That strong ox of a man is being led to his "death."

Wisdom is also seductive. She calls out to young people, but pursuing her is not so easy. To pursue wisdom requires self-discipline, diligence, and self-control. Yet, she reminds her audience that the rewards are great, better than silver or gold.

Take a look again at Proverbs 8:22–31. Here the poet connects wisdom with creation. The image is of a helper, almost like an architect (master worker) who designs the universe that God fashions. Wisdom is a metaphor for God's plan of creation, coming before the act of creation. But wisdom does not disappear once the world comes into existence. God's plan is still there, and those who seek to understand and attain it, find true happiness and fullness of life (Prov 8:34–35).

What strikes me most in this passage, however, is the pure joy of it all. We will read in Genesis 1 that God deems creation "good," but here we feel that goodness, that sense that God creates, not out of necessity, but out of sheer joy. Wisdom, God's plan, "rejoices" in the inhabited world, "delights" in humanity. If you were to ask this poet why God created humans, I think he would answer, "Because we are delightful to God." No wonder then that the poet ends this section by saying that the one who understands this is truly "happy."

Job 28:12–28 and Sirach 1:1–20: In Praise of Wisdom

These are two of the many poems in the Bible that praise wisdom. Try to figure out what the poet is saying about wisdom.

In Case You Were Wondering

Ophir. This was an area, either in southern Arabia or eastern Africa, known for its gold.

Chrysolite. This is a precious metal.

Abaddon. This is another name for Sheol. It comes from the Hebrew word for "destruction."

Looking Closely at the Text

1. How do these poems connect wisdom to creation?

2. Why do the texts associate wisdom with the fear of the Lord?

Wisdom Is the Fear of the Lord

These two poems are just two of the many passages in wisdom literature that praise wisdom. In the course of that praise, the author describes wisdom. The section that comes from one of Job's speeches stresses its mystery: only God can truly comprehend wisdom. The second passage is a reflection on wisdom that opens the book of Sirach. This poem also asserts that God alone can fully comprehend wisdom. These two passages demonstrate that, while humans should pursue wisdom, its fullness is beyond their comprehension.

Both texts associate wisdom with God's acts as creator. This idea is a bit more obscure in Job. When it says, "When he gave to the wind its weight . . . ," and so on, in Job 28:25–26, the passage describes God's creation. By referring to a part of creation, it infers the creation of all things. This is a literary device called *metonymy* in which a reference to part of something is used to signify the whole thing. The connection with creation is much clearer in Sirach 1:1–20. Sirach states, "Wisdom was created before all other things" (Sirach 1:19). All of creation reflects God's wisdom.

Most striking in these two passages is that both define wisdom as "fear of the LORD." This definition of wisdom is found throughout the proverbial literature. What does it mean?

"Fear of the LORD," as you may recall from our discussion of Deuteronomy, is the proper attitude humans should have toward God. The word translated as "fear" also connotes awe and respect. It is the recognition that God is much greater than humans, and the acknowledgement that the blessings God gives are gifts, not anything owed anyone. Within the context of the praise of wisdom, "fear of the LORD" also means that a truly wise person recognizes that (1) God alone truly comprehends wisdom; (2) wisdom is a reflection of God as creator; and (3) humans cannot attain wisdom apart from God. The pursuit of wisdom is the quest to know God, and true knowledge of God results in fear, awe, and respect.

Lastly, both Job and Sirach suggest that humans benefit in very concrete ways from the pursuit of wisdom. Job states that wisdom surpasses all human wealth (Job 28:15–19). Sirach 1:14–20 traces wisdom's rewards from the womb. She "inebriates" people, fills their savings accounts (storehouses), and gives them health, glory, and long life. We will see in a later chapter that the Israelites knew that these things did not happen literally. They are metaphors for a variety of benefits that come from the pursuit of wisdom and the fear of the LORD.

PROVERBS 30–31 AND SIRACH 7:18–36: THE CREATION OF A TIERED REALITY

These passages describe social hierarchies that were viewed by the Israelites as divinely created. The first passage comprises the final two sections of the book of Proverbs and addresses poverty and wealth, as well as an ancient view of the perfect wife. The second passage demonstrates the social location of Sirach's audience. See whether you agree that these social realities are divinely ordained.

In Case You Were Wondering

Agur and Lemuel. We do not know anything about these people. There is no King Lemuel in Israelite tradition.

Three things and four. A common literary device in the proverbial literature is to give a few examples of something that the sage is trying to illustrate. Notice how the examples can mix phenomena from nature and from human interaction.

Looking Closely at the Text

1. What is the purpose of the series of questions that opens Proverbs 30?

2. How does the sage feel about social inversions?

3. Are these texts correct that people are preordained into a particular place in society?

4. What are some of the characteristics of the good wife in Proverbs 31? Does this match what we know about married women in other parts of the Old Testament?

5. What can you tell about the audience of Sirach 7:18–36?

Divinely Ordained Hierarchy

If you ever thought that the Bible teaches that all people are created equal, you might have to revise that conclusion based on the proverbial literature. This material reflects the fact that the Israelite audience did not believe in the social equality of everyone. For them, each person is born into a particular "niche." Those social categories included a person's social class (rich or poor; landowner or slave), gender (male or female), and the jobs for which they were eligible based upon their birthright (king or priest, for example).

If you are born into a specific social class, then acting in a way contrary to that class is tantamount to opposing God's created order. You become a force for chaos. The earth itself trembles when a servant girl usurps the role of her owner (Prov 30:21–23). Women who are barren are depicted as a gluttonous

Sheol that is never satisfied (30:15–16), while a king strutting about is stately like a lion (30:29–31).

The passage in Sirach provides a clear example of how one can flesh out the intended audience of this kind of material. Here the audience is a male (v. 19 and 26), with excess money (v. 18). He owns slaves (20–21) and possibly cattle, children, and daughters whose marriages he'll need to arrange (22–25). He is still subservient to the priest (29–31), and he accrues honor and righteousness by treating those under him (the poor, the sick, and even the dead) with generosity and kindness.

But notice that these passages do not question this social order. The rich man is not exhorted to undermine the institution of slavery. He is not told to let his daughter choose whom to marry. In fact, anyone who does things that in any way subvert this social order is a force of chaos and death.

For contemporary readers who view this material as sacred, there is a challenge: must they accept the worldview of Israel's wisdom tradition? Has God created some people not only to be poor, but also to be evil if they try to get out of that poverty?

Look at the description of the good wife in Proverbs 31:10–31. What assumptions about women's behavior does this text make? What are women "honored" for? Some scholars have pointed out that this text does subvert the traditional patriarchal view of other Israelite texts. This woman works, and she buys property (v. 16). Other scholars note that her actions serve to exalt her husband and that the things for which she is honored tend to be the traditional roles for a woman. What do you think about this text? Would you want it read at your wedding, for example? Why or why not?

Genesis 1:1–2:3: Speaking a World

This material and the material in the next section will probably be familiar to most of you. In fact, advertisers presume it is so familiar that references to the seven days of creation and the Garden of Eden abound in commercials. But sometimes these popular uses of the story of creation make it difficult to read the account in the Bible closely and carefully. So, if you are familiar with this material, try to read it as if you were hearing it for the very first time.

Most scholars see a combination of two creation accounts in Genesis 1—3. The first account runs from Genesis 1:1 to 2:3 and was written by the Priestly source. The second one, written by the Yahwist, goes from Genesis 2:4 to 3:24. You may notice some repetitions and contradictions between these two texts.

In Case You Were Wondering

Dome or firmament. The Israelites believed that the world existed in a kind of bubble surrounded by water. This bubble had hard "walls" that kept this water at bay. Humans could see the wall above in the canvas of the sky. These walls are called "the dome" in some translations and the "firmament" in other translations.

Looking Closely at the Text

1. How does this text view the created world?

2. What is this passage trying to say about the purpose and nature of humanity?

The Account of God as Creator

Whole books have been written on the first three chapters of Genesis alone! Much of what Christians understand about this material flows out of Augustine's writings (d. 430 CE), especially the views of original sin, free will, and the definition of "good." But a discussion of Augustine's teaching on Genesis 1—3 is best left for a different course. Our purpose here is to help you read the Old Testament, as it was understood by the original audience.

Sometimes readers can get hung up on the details of the creation account. For example, hasn't it been proven that the world was not created in seven days, but over the course of thousands of years?

While it is certainly possible for God to have created the world in seven days, the audience is no more required to read "seven days" literally than it is to take literally that God has a mouth that speaks. The "week" is a way to express that creation is ordered, taking place with a certain rhythm and symmetry.

Today Catholics and many Protestants affirm that Genesis 1—3 is not trying to present a scientific account of creation. For example, as long as Catholics affirm that creation is a deliberately designed act of God, one that has a purpose, then scientific conclusions as to how this plan was achieved are not contradictory. Therefore, if science proves that it took far longer than six days for humans to appear on the earth, this conclusion does not contradict the biblical message that human creation was part of God's design.

Genesis 1:1—2:3 presents a well-designed, purposeful creation. The "order" is made clear when you notice the sequence of the days. First, God creates realms for creatures, and then he inhabits those realms with creatures.

Days	Realm	Creature
1 and 4	Light and dark separated (day 1)	Sun, moon, stars (day 4)
2 and 5	Waters separated, creating the sky (day 2)	Fish and birds (day 5)
3 and 6	Dry land separated from water (day 3)	Animals and humans (day 6)

Notice though that these "creations" consist in the arrangement and ordering of elements.

One of the greatest advances in biblical studies has come from the discoveries in the past one hundred years of ancient texts from the Fertile Crescent. Among these texts have been creation accounts from Mesopotamia and Egypt. These myths, while certainly quite different from the Bible, with their belief in many gods, are still similar to Israelite texts in both general outline and specific details. They help us understand the biblical texts much better. For instance, Genesis 1:1—2:3 presents creation as the result of God's effortless work in the course of seven days. It is similar to an Egyptian story of creation in which the sun god, Ptah, speaks, and what he says comes into being. Both texts are trying to express the belief that their god is so powerful that every word he speaks comes to pass.

Thomas Aquinas, a famous thirteenth-century theologian, notes that the first three days of creation encompass acts of separation and distinction (for example, light from dark, dry land from water, and so on), while the second three days entail "ornamentation" or filling up these created spaces. What Aquinas noticed about creation as an act of distinction is a common element in creation accounts in Mesopotamia, as well. In the Mesopotamian myth, *Enuma Elish*, the creator god, Marduk, fights a chaos goddess named Tiamat. Genesis 1:2 uses the same word, translated as "the deep," to describe the pre-created world's watery chaos. When Marduk defeats Tiamat, he splits her body like a clam shell and with it makes the dome, or firmament, around the earth. God forms a similar dome over the earth, although not from the body of a dead goddess. After the battle, Marduk sets the world in order, and then he rests in his temple. Genesis 1:1—2:3 ends with God observing Sabbath and resting on the seventh day. While these myths have significant differences, they both feature creation as the act of imposing order over chaos. The Mesopotamian myth helps us better understand what Aquinas and others had noticed about the biblical creation account.

The creation of humans in Genesis 1:1—2:3, however, is quite distinct from ancient Near Eastern texts. For both Egypt and Mesopotamia, humans

Creation in the Ancient Near East

I love reading the creation accounts of the countries in the Fertile Crescent. They are interesting, both for the places where they agree with the biblical account as well as where they diverge. They help me to think about all the different purposes that a creation account can serve, and they raise questions for me. What does it mean to be human? What is the relationship between the human and divine realms? What is the relationship of the divine realm to the world?

Some of the Mesopotamian creation texts emphasize the debasement of the human person. For example, in some Mesopotamian texts the creator god makes humans by mixing clay (or dirt) with the blood of a rebellious god. Notice that this vision of humanity explains both its rebellious and spiritual natures. All of the texts, including the biblical ones, presume that humans exist only because the gods want them to.

Many creation texts in the ancient Near East view creation as the result of a battle between the forces of order and the forces of chaos. This is seen most clearly in the Babylonian *Enuma Elish*, but it is also reflected in the Ugaritic myths about the storm god, Baal. Why would ancient people view creation as a battle? Perhaps because they experienced things that harmed them, such as drought, plague, death, and disease, as constant threats that they had to fight against. The warrior/creator god led this fight.

A common pattern of Mesopotamian creation texts is the assumption that there was a problem with the first group of humans. The creator god decides to wipe them out, and, as a result, sends a flood to do so. In the *Epic of Gilgamesh*, a popular text in the ancient world, the hero seeks the secret to immortal life from the only person who has achieved it, a man who had survived the Flood. In the course of their conversation, this survivor tells Gilgamesh the story of the Flood. Many of the details of this account match the versions in the Bible.

Sumerian king lists also include references to the Flood. In those lists, the kings who lived before the Flood were semi-divine and lived long lives. After the Flood kings were only human and lived for a normal length of time. The biblical text contains remnants of a similar pattern. Before the Flood the people lived long lives, and Genesis 6:1–4 states that "sons of God" could impregnate human women. After the Flood there is a clear divide between the human and divine realms, and, in texts other than P, the humans seem to be quite like us. These ancient near-eastern myths, then, help us understand some of the details of the biblical texts.

were debased, hideous, and annoying. But in Genesis, humans are created in the "image and likeness of God," a phrase linked to their dominion over the earth. *Image* was a word used for a statue of a god that represented the god's presence in a temple. In addition, in human society, the king was the "image" of the god, meaning that his rule was really an extension of divine rule. Genesis 1 extends the use of *image* to all humanity. Humans signify God's presence on earth. With this privilege comes great responsibility: they must care for the whole earth. It is because they take on this task that God's creation is completed, and God can "rest" on the seventh day. Sabbath is the culmination of God's creation, and the Israelites would have understood that reference to the Sabbath as divinely ordaining their own worship practices.

The view of humanity is quite different in these passages than in Genesis 2:4—3:24. The fact is that, for many Christians, it is hard to read Genesis 1:1—2:3 without thinking about Genesis 2:4—3:24. I know I can't. But consider this: what would be our view of human nature if we only had the creation account in Genesis 1:1—2:3? What would be our view of women? What would be our view of human sinfulness?

Genesis 2:4–3:24: Forming a Messy World

Let's turn to the second account of creation. In many ways it is quite different from the first account. Instead of God's effortless creation through speech, we have God forming a man out of the earth and a woman out of man's rib. In place of the creation of the universe, only the creation of people and animals is described. And rather than humans created in the image and likeness of God, there is human sin and disobedience. See what other differences you notice.

In Case You Were Wondering

Eden. The Garden of Eden is God's garden. It was common in the ancient Near East for kings to have lavish gardens: quite an extravagance in a dry land. God's garden contains the headwaters for four major rivers: these rivers were the source of fresh water for the world.

Adam. The Hebrew word *adam* can be translated "human being" or it can be made into a name, "Adam." Different Bibles will translate this word differently. He is created outside of the garden and then placed there, as a quasi-head-gardener.

The tree of life and the tree of the knowledge of good and evil. There were two special trees in God's garden. The tree of life gave mortal creatures eternal life, probably by preventing them from aging. Apparently Adam and Eve could eat from this tree until they sinned. The tree of the knowledge of good and evil is the forbidden tree. Jewish and Christian scholars have both speculated about the nature of this tree and why humans could not eat it.

The serpent. While Wisdom 2:24 identifies the serpent as the devil, the book of Genesis never says this. It is more probable that this serpent was like a chaos monster.

Looking Closely at the Text

1. What is this passage saying about men and women?

2. Who is more to blame for eating the fruit: the man or the woman?

3. How does God punish the serpent, the woman, and the man?

4. Why does God banish Adam and Eve from the Garden of Eden?

A Story of the Creation of Humans

Creation narratives express a community's fundamental beliefs about the world. When I refer to Genesis 1—3 as "narratives" or "stories," I mean that the author is not writing about the beginning of the world like a philosopher or scientist. He is relaying it in the form of a story. In later philosophical treatments of creation, the philosopher is careful to make all the pieces work together properly.

But, sometimes, timelines and philosophical discourses, while true and factual, miss the very message they want to convey. Sometimes a story reveals more of the "truth" than a timeline can. Let's say you wanted to tell someone about your family. You could simply tell them facts: how many people there are in your family, where they have lived, what jobs each person has had, and so on. But these facts alone might not tell the whole picture. Some things might be better explained by telling stories about your family. Are the stories more or less "true" than the facts? Of course not. They just express different truths.

It was common for cultures in the ancient Near East to have a variety of creation "accounts" at any given time. Sometimes they were written for different audiences or situations. Sometimes they reflected different groups' values. The fact that there were various creation accounts, however, was not a problem to the ancient audience.

Genesis 1:1—2:3 and 2:4—3:24 stress two different aspects of creation. Genesis 1:1—2:3 focuses on God as the creator. In these verses, God is the only "actor," that is, the only one doing anything. This author is concerned with accurately portraying God's role in creation. Therefore, the passage stresses the following points:

> God creates effortlessly.

> Creation is not the result of a battle against another god.

> God creates out of divine goodness.

> Creation participates in divine goodness.

> Humans, created in the image and likeness of God, reflect God's nature more than any other creature.

> The purpose of creation is to worship God, who now enjoys Sabbath rest.

In contrast, Genesis 2:4—3:24 concentrates on humanity in its relationship to God. The story stresses the divide between human and divine nature. We will see that this theme runs through the first eleven chapters of Genesis. The theme serves as an introduction to the idea that humans are quite unlike God.

There are many ways that the second creation story expresses humanity's feeble nature. Consider for instance, the following details:

› Adam is created out of clay or dirt and needs God's breath to become alive.

› Adam is created to serve God, that is, "to till and keep" God's garden (Genesis 2:15).

› Adam cannot do his work by himself; he needs a helper.

The most obvious way that the story expresses human unworthiness is by talking about human sinfulness. God gives Adam one simple command, a command that should have been easy to obey, yet Adam and Eve were unable or unwilling to do this one thing.

Notice too that the serpent's claim that they will become like God convinced Adam and Eve to eat the fruit. Their actions reinforce the main theme of the narrative: humans are decidedly *not* like God. The passage reflects the view that part of God's plan for creation is a certain hierarchy. That hierarchy is subverted when an animal tells a human what to do, a husband follows the lead of this wife, or humans ignore God's direct command. The narrative defines sin as striving to be like God; that is, not accepting humanity's place in the universe as creatures and servants of God.

God banishes the humans from the garden to prevent their further attempts to become like God. To insure this does not happen, God puts more barriers between the human and divine realms:

› Humans cannot eat of the life-giving tree.

› Human acts of creation (producing crops and bearing children) are cursed, so that humans cannot "create" effortlessly.

› Humanity's "natural" state (symbolized by their nakedness) must be covered over.

The greatest divide between humanity and divinity, however, is mortality: humans die. In Genesis 3:19, God reminds Adam that "you are dust, and to dust you shall return." In Genesis 3:22, God worries that humans might become immortal; they are banished from the garden in order to prevent this from happening. The theme of death is further elaborated in Genesis 6:3 where human

The Afterlife of Genesis 2–3

The sinfulness of the first couple, who represent the whole human family, is the basis for later Christian understandings of original sin. *Original sin* describes the fallen state of human nature, human separation from God, and the loss, which affects every person born into the world, of the original harmonious order of creation. Some of the effects of original sin are washed away by the waters of baptism. Baptismal water is a fitting symbol, in light of the biblical use of fresh water as a symbol for creation and for God's gift of life. Although the Israelites did not talk about "original sin," the story of Adam and Even certainly contains the view that humans are inherently sinful, that the world's order has been damaged by their foolish sins, and that they are deemed righteous only through the grace of God.

While Christian theologians developed the doctrine of original sin, both Jewish and Christian circles developed other elements of the Adam and Eve tradition. For example, some Jews in the Middle Ages viewed the woman created in Genesis 1:26 as Adam's first wife, Lilith. She was depicted as a demon-like figure who wanted to steal babies. Some Medieval Jewish homes had amulets to protect infants from Lilith.

Some of the most popular elements of the Adam and Eve story, such as the account of the fall of the angels and Satan as a tempter, come from a post-biblical textual tradition called *The Life of Adam and Eve*. This text, extant in several ancient languages, was quite widespread in the early centuries of the Common Era.

The text describes the life of Adam and Eve after they were expelled from the Garden in far more detail than the biblical text. Although there are many different versions of this text, at the center of the tradition is the couple's attempt to return to the Garden. At one point Adam and Eve decide to repent. Satan tricks Eve into thinking that their repentance has been accepted by God, and so she stops her acts of repentance. When Adam realizes that Eve has been tricked, he turns to Satan and asks him why he keeps tempting them. It is at this point that Satan recounts the story of how some angels were cast out of heaven for not bowing down to Adam as the image of God.

These post-biblical traditions had widespread popularity. Their influence can be found into the Renaissance and beyond. Even today, many people assume that the account of the fall of the angels is in the Bible.

life is limited to 120 years. In this way, God's statement in Genesis 2:17 ("in the day that you eat of [the tree of the knowledge of good and evil] you shall die") foreshadows the reality that outside of Eden, humans experience death.

Although this account in Genesis does not depict creation as God's imposition of order over chaos, it does stress human folly. The serpent, a symbol of both eternal life and of the wisdom goddess in the ancient world, "entices" the humans into doing something foolish through shrewd trickery, similar to the ways of Mistress Folly. Adam and Eve are foolish when they attempt to preempt the quest for wisdom by snatching that knowledge from the fruit meant only for God. Folly is understood to be the wrong-headed and willful belief that humans can be like God. Their foolish behavior results in shame, suffering, disharmony with nature, and, ultimately, death. Adam and Eve are "every person," the foolish couple who should have known better.

Genesis 6:5–9:17 and 11:1–9: Creation Continues

These passages contain Israel's account of the Flood and the story of the Tower of Babel. Both stories complete the theme of creation begun in Genesis 1—3.

It is not until the end of chapter 11 that the world is organized in the way the Israelites knew it.

In between the account of creation and the Flood comes the story of the intervening generations. The second generation shows that human sinfulness was not a unique feature of the first couple: their son, Cain, kills his own brother, Abel, out of jealousy. Just as with Adam and Eve, God both punishes and protects Cain.

Most of the material from Genesis 1—11 that you are not reading, however, is comprised of genealogies. Occasionally these genealogies note the beginnings of elements of human society, such as hunting, metal working, and music.

In Case You Were Wondering

Ark. In Genesis the ark is a large boat. Do not confuse it with the Ark of the Covenant. In Hebrew, there are two different words for *ark*.

Bitumen. This is a sticky substance, like tar, that seals wood against water seepage.

Mount Ararat. The precise identification of this mountain is debated; it may be in Armenia.

Bow. There is a play on words here. The sign of God's covenant with all of humanity is the rainbow. In Mesopotamian stories of creation, after the god battles a chaos monster, he hangs up his "bow" (as in, bow and arrows) in the sky. The rainbow represents God's weapon against chaos.

Shinar. This is an area in Mesopotamia that includes Babylon.

Babel. This word sounds a lot like the Hebrew verb, "to confuse." The author is making a play on words.

Looking Closely at the Text

1. How does the account of the Flood pick up images of creation and chaos?
2. How do the accounts of the Flood and the Tower of Babel continue the themes of the separation of divine, human, and animal realms?

Dividing Heaven from Earth

When we think of "the creation" in the Bible, we usually think of Genesis 1—3. In the ancient Near East, however, they would have considered all of Genesis 1—11 as "the creation narrative." The Mesopotamian creation stories, which focus on human sinfulness, include a worldwide flood which almost destroys humanity. The account ends with the gods establishing a sharp divide between heaven and earth.

Genesis 6:5—9:16 intertwines two versions of the Flood story. Here is an easy way to untangle them. Highlight all those paragraphs which call God *God* with one color, and all those paragraphs which call God *Lord* with another color. Then read consecutively the paragraphs of the same color; do so for each color. You should have two complete accounts of the Flood. The account that uses *God* is from the Priestly source, who wrote Genesis 1:1—2:3, and the other one is from the Yahwist, who is responsible for Genesis 2:4—3:24. Both versions agree that the Flood is part of the creation account.

The Flood depicts humanity as overwhelmingly evil. The accounts do not describe the nature of human sinfulness, but they suggest that people had become utterly evil. Only the righteous Noah and his family escape this description.

Notice that the accounts stress the interdependence of divine, human, and animal realms. The animals need humans to build the boat, while the humans need God to tell them how to build it. Conversely, the story ends with humans worshipping God through animal sacrifice.

The problem of human sinfulness that resulted in the Flood is further resolved by sharper boundaries between God, humans, and animals. The account culminates in the first covenant in the Bible. In this covenant, God makes clearer the distinctions between creatures and God. God promises not to "curse the ground" on account of human sinfulness (Genesis 9:21). In addition, although humans must still refrain from murder (9:5–6), they are allowed to kill and eat animals. In turn, animals "fear" humans. Thus the separation among created things is completed.

While the divide between heaven and earth is not explicitly mentioned in this passage, two things suggest that it still weighs on the minds of the authors. First, in the covenant that God makes with humans, God promises that there will not be another attempt to destroy the earth. The presumption is, then, that God could do so. Just as God is creator, so Yahweh has the power to return the world to an oceanic chaos. Second, God utters the covenant after smelling the sacrifice that Noah offers to God. While this is not the first sacrifice in the Bible, it is clearly one that exemplifies Noah's righteousness. Sacrifice was a way that humans expressed their subservience to gods. The importance of this sacrifice is better seen in the Mesopotamian version of this story. There the man who offers the sacrifice is granted eternal life after this one sacrifice.

This illustration of the Tower of Babel is from the Dore Bible, a famous Bible illustrated by Gustave Dore and published in England in 1866.

The final story within Israel's creation complex explicitly takes up the theme of the division between heaven and earth. This story of the Tower of Babel is not found in the creation stories from the ancient Near East. This is a story of "urban" sin, the sin of big business, the sin of a human community and its collective pride.

In Hebrew, the name for the city is a play on the name of the city of Babylon. The Babylonians had large structures called *ziggurats* within some of their temple precincts. While there is a lot of debate today about what the ziggurats represented to the Babylonians, it is clear that the author is making fun of them when he asserts that they were attempts to reach heaven.

There are two ways in which this act was seen as sinful. First, the story continues the theme of foolish human attempts to cross the divide between the human and divine worlds, and, as such it is a fitting conclusion to the creation material. Notice that for the Israelites human cooperation, in and of itself, is not necessarily a good thing. The punishment not only explains why there are many different languages in the world, but it also explains how the barriers that impede global unity are punishments from God for human pride.

Second, the text states that people wanted to build a tower so that they could stay together and not be scattered across the earth. However, as early as Genesis 1:22 and 1:28, God had commanded both humans and animals to "fill the earth," a command repeated after the Flood narrative (Genesis 9:1). Human fear of being "scattered abroad" directly conflicts with God's command. The result of God's punishment is not just the confusion of languages. God insures that the command to fill the earth is honored. "So the LORD scattered them abroad from there over the face of all the earth" (11:8).

PSALM 8; 74; 89:6–19; 93; 136:1–9; ISAIAH 40:12–14 AND 21–22; JOB 9:4–13; 25:1–26:14: ISRAEL REFLECTS ON CREATION

While these texts are not full creation accounts, they are some of the many texts throughout the Old Testament that reflect on creation. You will see that some of them agree with the account of creation in Genesis 1:1—2:3, while others have elements not found in Genesis. What may be most surprising is how few direct references there are to the story of Adam and Eve.

In Case You Were Wondering

Leviathan. This was the name of a chaos monster. It appears in other myths from the Levant as a seven-headed sea serpent.

Rahab. This was also a chaos monster, although its origins are less certain.

Looking Closely at the Text

What images in these psalms echo images of creation and chaos?

Israel's Many Ways to Describe Creation

There are many references to God's work as creator throughout the Bible. Some, like Psalm 136, sound very similar to Genesis 1:1—2:3. Others, however, seem to reflect other views of creation. For instance, while Genesis 1—3 has no battle between God and chaos, texts like Psalm 74:13–14 and 89:10 refer specifically to God's defeat of a chaos monster (Leviathan or Rahab). Psalm 93 focuses on God's control over the Sea, while several other texts stress only God's creation of the firmament and the heavenly bodies. Sea, stars, sun, and moon were gods in other countries; these creation accounts focus on God's power over otherwise "divine" elements.

Most of these texts refer to creation, not because it happened long ago, but because God's acts as creator are perceived as ongoing. Look at Psalm 74, for instance. The psalm is a communal lament during the siege of a city. In the midst of the people's plea to God, the psalmist describes God's defeat of chaos. In this way, the psalmist draws a parallel between the enemies and chaos monsters. The Israelites appeal to God to act as creator, because their hope lies in divine opposition to chaos.

Creation also functions as hope in Psalm 89, Job 9:1–13, and Job 25:1—26:14. These texts deal with the unjust suffering of the innocent (David and Job). The hope of the innocent rests in God's ongoing work as the creator who keeps the world in order.

References to creation also describe God's power. This is most obvious when God defeats chaos monsters, but it is also seen in Job 25:4–6 and Psalm 8, where the authors' recognition of God's creative power leads them to realize how "small" humans are in comparison. While Job stresses humanity's lowly state (people are called maggots and worms), Psalm 8 recognizes God's grace. "When I look at your heavens, the work of your fingers . . . what are human beings that you are mindful of them, mortals that you care for them? Yet you have made them a little lower than God, and crowned them with glory and honor" (Ps 8:3–5).

For contemporary Jews and Christians, these texts demonstrate three important features of the Old Testament's witness to creation:

There are a variety of images for creation. Just like the Israelites had different "stories" by which they communicated the truths of God's work as creator, so people today have different "stories," both the "scientific" account of creation, as well as the biblical accounts of creation.

Creation is an ongoing activity of God. These texts demonstrate quite clearly that creation is not an event in the past, but it is a present reality, and also a hope for the future. God "fights chaos" and "imposes order" every day this world exists.

Creation both humbles and uplifts humans. The creation accounts clearly demonstrate that humans are not God. Every time humans try to act like God, they work on the side of chaos and oppose Yahweh's creation. But humans are also honored within this creation, uniquely created in the image and likeness of God. With this honor comes responsibility to maintain God's harmonious balance in the world.

The Wisdom of God's Creation

Creation accounts are important not because they give us the "facts" of creation, but because they speak about God and humanity. For the Israelites, these texts expressed their hope in God's care for them, which they experienced by observing God's hand in creation. This observation is the work of the wise. The Israelite authors maintained that anyone who looked to the stars in the sky, the majesty of the sea, the joys of a family, or the blessings of friendship could be among the wise ones who understood the ethical implications of seeing God as creator.

For Review

1. What is a proverb?

2. What do we know about the person addressed in the proverbs?

3. Why is having wisdom more than just being smart?

4. What is wisdom? What is a fool?

5. Why is foolishness a sin?

6. What is chaos, and how is it symbolized?

7. What is Lady Wisdom?

8. How is wisdom connected to God?

9. How does Wisdom help in creation?

10. Why is wisdom defined as the "fear of the LORD?

11. In what ways is creation an ongoing activity of God?

12. What are some of the things that the creation accounts are trying to express about the nature of God and humanity?

FOR FURTHER READING

There are many excellent introductions to wisdom literature. Among them are Richard J. Clifford, *The Wisdom Literature* (Interpreting Biblical Texts; Nashville, TN: Abingdon, 1998); James L. Crenshaw, *Old Testament Wisdom: An Introduction*, revised edition (Louisville, KY: Westminster John Knox, 1998); Anthony R. Ceresko, *Introduction to Old Testament Wisdom: A Spirituality for Liberation* (Maryknoll, NY: Orbis, 1999); and Roland E. Murphy, *The Tree of Life: An Exploration of Biblical Wisdom Literature*, third edition (Grand Rapids, MI: Eerdmans, 2002).

For a comparison of ancient near-eastern creation accounts, see Richard J. Clifford, *Creation Accounts in the Ancient Near East and in the Bible* (CBQMS 26; Washington, DC: Catholic Biblical Association, 1994). Regarding the mythic elements in biblical literature, see Bernard F. Batto, *Slaying the Dragon: Mythmaking in the Biblical Tradition* (Louisville, KY: Westminster John Knox, 1992).

For a study connecting wisdom and creation traditions, see Leo G. Perdue, *Wisdom and Creation: The Theology of Wisdom Literature* (Nashville, TN: Abingdon, 1994).

There are many studies of contextual criticisms under a variety of names and perspectives. Two classic collections of essays in this vein are *Voices from the Margin: Interpreting the Bible in the Third World*, edited by R. S. Sugirtharajah (Maryknoll, NY: Orbis, 1995) and the two-volume *Reading from This Place*, edited by Fernando F. Segovia and Mary Ann Tolbert (Minneapolis, MN: Fortress, 1995). Susanne Scholz has assembled a collection of shorter essays accessible for undergraduate students in her volume, *Biblical Studies Alternatively: An Introductory Reader* (Upper Saddle River, NJ: Prentice Hall, 2003). Because this is currently a vibrant field, some of the best material can be found in journal articles and book essays.

14 A NICE LITTLE STORY

Pleasant words are like a honeycomb,
sweetness to the soul and health to the body.
(Prov 16:24)

THE ART OF THE STORYTELLER

CHAPTER OVERVIEW

Everyone likes a well-told story, one with suspense, interesting characters, and a vivid setting. In this chapter, we will look at some of the best short "stories" of the Old Testament. This chapter will provide the following:

▸ A review of the art of storytelling in ancient Israel

▸ An examination of the ways that stories can express theology

▸ A survey of five of the best short books in the Old Testament

With each story we will think about God's role in the book.

ISRAELITE STORIES

When we hear the word *story* we sometimes assume that it means "made up." This is not always the case; some stories describe actual events. Even when we hear about events that actually happened, we best remember those events when they are told in a manner which makes them "real." Good authors tell us the "story" of an event or an idea.

I am using the word *story* in this chapter, because I want to focus on how texts communicate ideas. As you read one or more of these biblical books, instead of asking, "Did this happen?" ask, "Why is this material told to us in this manner?" As you raise the question, you will come to realize that these books have many elements of a good story.

THE PLOT THICKENS

The most important feature of many well-told stories is a gripping plot. A typical plot introduces a problem or tension, the tension builds, and is finally resolved. For example, in the Snow White story, the problem is the Queen's jealousy of Snow White. The tension between the queen and Snow White builds, until the queen tries to kill Snow White with the poisoned apple. Resolution comes when the prince awakens Snow White with a kiss.

As you read a biblical story, see if you can graph or outline the plot. Some stories begin rather slowly; that is, they do not introduce the problem right away. Others seem to drag at the end; they give us more information after the problem has been resolved. This might indicate that what we think is the story's problem is different from what the Israelites saw as the problem.

Good plots are self-contained. While they might make some assumptions about what a reader knows, they do not expect the reader to have extra information. The story of Snow White presumes that you know what a queen is, but it does not expect you to know what happened to Snow White after she married.

As you begin reading these biblical tales, you will enter a self-contained world. The authors expect you to have some general knowledge about Israelite history and culture (knowledge which you now have and which is why we turn to these stories at the end of the course). On the other hand, the authors do not expect you to know more about Esther, for instance, than the book tells you.

Focus on METHOD

The Bible and Literary Theory

We have talked a lot about the literary artistry of the biblical texts. This literary quality can be understood better through the lens of different modes of literary analysis. New Literary Criticism applies theories of reading to the biblical texts.

There are many different literary methods that scholars have used to unpack the way that a text communicates to a reader. One helpful way to organize these methods is to think about the elements involved in this form of communication.

Textual communication involves at least three stages. There is (1) an author who creates a (2) text that is (3) "read" by a reader. (Theorists use author-text-reader to describe a variety of phenomena, including artwork: the artist is the "author" and the art piece is the "text," which is "read" by the viewer. This theory, therefore, is not dependent upon reading; it is equally valid for a work that is performed or heard.) This schema raises the question, where is "meaning" located? When I say, for example, "This text means . . . ," what kind of a claim am I making? Let me go through each of the three options and relate them to different literary theories.

If I believe that *meaning* is something that stems from an author, I would see it as something deposited in a text by this author. My reading would be an act of excavation, in which I would "uncover" the meaning deposited by him or her. Therefore, I would focus on the author's historical setting, or I might try to delve into the psyche of the author. I might look at what the author said about the text. Notice that this approach presumes that there is one (or, at least, a limited number) of answers to the question, what does this text mean? Disagreements about the text's meaning are adjudicated by appeal to the author. We see this approach behind some forms of psychoanalytic analysis and something called "New Literary Criticism."

But can a text mean more than an author intends? Think about popular songs, for example. Sometimes a song can mean a lot to you for reasons different from that which the author intended. "Let It Be," sung by many Christians in honor of Mary, the mother of Jesus, was actually Paul McCartney's tribute to his own mother. Does that mean any other use of the song is somehow "wrong"? Of course not. Pieces are deemed "art" because of their ability to "speak" to a wide audience.

Some methods of literary analysis focus on the text alone. The analysis of the text proceeds without reference to the author or its historical setting. The text is viewed as an artifact whose elements communicate independently of its author's intentions. Structuralism is one literary approach that focuses on the text itself. Narrative analysis and some forms of rhetorical criticism do the same. These theories view multiple interpretations as not only legitimate but expected.

Other theorists have pointed out that texts mean nothing until they are read. Meaning is created by a reader in the act of reading. Methods of analysis that highlight the role of the reader, such as reader-response criticism, start with the reader's conclusions about the text's meaning, and then they look at the text to trace the source of that conclusion. This approach is not interested in determining whether or not a reader's interpretation is valid; if meaning is in the hands of the reader, then there are no external criteria to determine validity. In some ways, contextual approaches to the text, such as feminism and class analyses, focus on the reader in a similar way. For example, some feminist biblical interpretations do not make the claim that biblical authors were concerned about gender issues; rather, it is the effect of the text on modern readers that becomes the focal point.

When literary criticism first arose, scholars would choose one approach and stick to it to the exclusion of all others. Today, people realize that the act of reading/interpretation is too complex to divvy up so sharply. Literary analysis is best done by recognizing that reading is the result of the interplay of an author's intentions, the text's structure, and the reader's social location.

THE WELL-TOLD TALE

Good authors embellish their stories with humor, irony, and word play. Snow White could be quite boring in the hands of an inexperienced storyteller. A good storyteller, however, will add to the suspense, delay the resolution, or enhance the tale with humor, twists, or intriguing images.

The biblical stories you will read represent some of the best literature produced in ancient Israel. The author of Jonah uses subtle touches of humor and irony. Esther's author delays the final resolution. Ruth's author plays with words that have double meanings. Some of these literary devices will be hard for you to detect, since they depend on the wording in the original Hebrew text. Some will become clearer the more often you hear the stories. These subtle embellishments keep audiences coming back to them again and again.

One type of embellishment that was more commonly used in the ancient world than today is symbolism. Some of the characters in these stories are both individual characters *and* representatives of different groups in Israel. For instance, Judith is a symbol of the nation of Israel. Jonah is a symbol of those within Israel who believed God only saves Israelites. Sometimes the characters play with a reader's assumptions about what they symbolize. Ruth is a foreign woman but her actions contradict the usual portrayal of foreign women in the Old Testament.

The use of symbols gives these stories a meaning beyond the simple plot. The book of Jonah might be considered trite if it only told us about one incident in the life of some ancient prophet. It has universal meaning, however, when read as addressing the question: whom will God forgive?

READING BETWEEN THE LINES

The best stories hint at a world beyond the text. Characters might say things that are unexpected. A change in scenery might change a tranquil mood into one of danger. A well-worded phrase might cause you to think that the storyteller is telling you something important, such as how people "should" behave, or what it means to be "beautiful."

Good authors communicate themes in subtle ways. Rather than stating the theme, an author will "imply" it through images, scene choice, and dialogue. When authors imply meanings, they anticipate that readers will "read between the lines." In fact, authors expect readers to understand a story's themes from both what is said and what is left out.

Sometimes authors use deliberate ambiguity. They leave elements of their stories unclear. This literary device draws in the reader, who must fill in the gaps or decide among various options. Authors use odd comparisons or unexpected sequences in the narratives, in order to slow down the reading process and encourage the reader to take notice. One of my professors used to say that just where the text doesn't make sense is precisely where you can find the most theological meaning.

Biblical texts invite us to read between their lines, and you have already developed some ways to read between those lines. You can work more on those skills using these texts. Notice how things are worded, where the action slows down, and when the author does not tell us something that we would expect to be told.

What Should We Expect in an Israelite Story?

Readers are expected to notice elements of a story that are out-of-the-ordinary, unexpected, or surprising. We need to remind ourselves what *Israelite* audiences would have expected. They told stories differently than we do.

We talked about literary style during our exploration of Genesis, but it is helpful to review some of those points here.

Hebrew narratives are sparse. In other words, Hebrew authors liked to give the most information they could using the fewest words. They did not describe what people looked like, what they wore, or what their surroundings involved, unless that particular element was important for the plot.

Hebrew stories focus more on actions than words. People were known by what they did rather than what they said. Sometimes what they "did" was speak; in those cases, the writer could insert a whole speech, but only if it was necessary for the plot.

The Bible rarely tells us a person's inner thoughts or motivations. We do not know why most biblical characters do what they do, although we can sometimes infer it. The biblical authors do not reveal any more about their characters than they would know in real life.

Parallelism is important. We have seen that individual lines of Hebrew poetry often contained parallelism, that is, the repetition of an idea using similar terms or opposing images. Hebrew stories did not use parallel lines; instead, they sometimes contained parallel scenes. The audience was supposed to notice which scenes were placed next to each other and when the actions of one character were repeated or mirrored by another character later in the story.

Later Israelite stories contained references to earlier texts. This is a new idea. We previously noted that in the Second Temple Period some texts, such as the earliest form of the Pentateuch, some prophecies, and the Deuteronomistic History, were seen as having authority. The tales that were written in the Second Temple Period make subtle allusions to some of these texts. A minor character might have the name of someone from long ago. A major character might refer to events in Israel's history in a prayer. Poems might combine verses from earlier psalms. Many of these may be too subtle for you to notice, but they are fun to tease out if you are able to do so.

These were the expected elements of Hebrew narrative. Take notice when they are changed or ignored. You might also get in the habit of asking the following questions:

▸ Does the story have a particular setting and why?

▸ Who is speaking and when?

▸ Is there anything described that is normally ignored?

▸ Am I told what a character is thinking? Why is this important?

▸ What scenes are placed next to each other?

▸ Are there any actions that are repeated by different characters?

▸ Are there any references to earlier episodes of Israel's history, prophecies, psalms, or laws?

INSIDER/OUTSIDER

In every one of these stories Israelite characters interact with foreigners.

▸ Ruth is from Moab, but lives with her Israelite mother-in-law.

▸ Jonah preaches to the Assyrians.

▸ Esther marries the Persian king.

▸ Tobit lives in exile.

▸ Judith leads her city to victory over a foreign army.

In each of the stories the relationship between Israelites and foreigners adds to the tension in the text. These stories each deal with the problem of how a group views the outsider, the person who does not belong to the group.

There are two different views of the "insider" in these texts. In the earlier texts, Ruth and Jonah, the Israelite characters, are not distinguished by their morality or piety. As you read about Ruth and Jonah, ask yourself how the author is defining what it means to be an Israelite.

In the later texts, Esther, Tobit, and Judith, the Israelite characters, are set off from other characters by their acts of piety. While less obvious in the short version of Esther, in the longer version, as well as in Tobit and Judith, the Israelites pray, fast, observe dietary laws, and practice penance rituals. This is typical of Jewish books from the Greek period and later. Clearly, by this time to be a "Jew" meant you had to act in certain ways that were different from the way most other people acted.

When it comes to the way foreigners are portrayed, we see much greater variety. All of the books presume some prejudice on the part of the audience. Sometimes that prejudice is negative. In Esther, the foreign king is foolish and his officer is evil. In Judith, the foreign general is lustful. The foreign king in Tobit persecutes the Jews. Other books highlight the worthiness of foreigners. Ruth is nobler than any other character in her book. The book of Jonah takes seriously God's universal rule.

Notice what each book says about what it means to be an Israelite and how it depicts God's relationship with foreigners.

WHERE IS GOD?

In most of these stories God is in the background. Sometimes the stories tell us something explicit about God. When they do, it is important to take notice. But at other times we only know God through what the characters say or how the plot develops. In order to understand what the author is telling us about God, we must read between the lines.

This hiddenness of God makes the stories more like the Wisdom material. Except for the book of Jonah, these are not stories of prophets with direct revelations or military heroes fighting under the influence of "the spirit of God." Instead, most of these are stories of ordinary people doing the best that they can. The books convey the sense that God is responsible for their successes, but not through miracles or some other divine intervention. Instead, the events work themselves out according to the workings of the created world.

Some of the texts, like Esther and Judith, feature women who know how to succeed in their tasks: they are wise. Their opponents are foolish men, who think that their power is invincible. For these reasons, some of these short stories are referred to as "wisdom tales." See if you can notice other elements of the wisdom tradition as you read.

TELLING STORIES

This section will have a different format. I am going to provide a brief introduction to each of five short biblical books. I think you will find the plotlines easy to follow. If there is any major issue that you should know about before reading the book, I will explain it to you. Otherwise, use the notes in your Bibles to answer questions about specific details. Rather than answering questions to check your reading, write a short outline of the plot for each book.

After the introduction, I will suggest things you might think about as you read. These suggestions will help you "read between the lines." Your goal is to figure out why the author is telling this story in this particular way. What is the story telling you about God, human nature, morality, human history?

Some of these texts are controversial: you or your fellow classmates may not agree with everything they say. One person may think that a particular character is admirable, while another person may find the character's actions troubling. It will not always be easy to "peg" a character, and many of these stories have elements of ambiguity.

One final note: you might have trouble finding these books. Jonah is in the prophetic section in all of your Bibles. However, the other books might be in various places depending on what Bible you are using:

Catholic Bible. If you are using a Catholic Bible, Ruth is placed between Judges and 1 Samuel; Esther, Tobit, and Judith are among the last few historical

The Bible and the Arts

Often those who study the Bible come to think that the main vehicle for biblical interpretation is the work of biblical scholars. But the truth is that scholarly influence is largely indirect. Think about how most people's views of the Bible develop. One common source of their view is preaching, sermons and homilies given by pastors, ministers, priests, and rabbis who have been informed by biblical scholars.

Another common source for biblical interpretation is works of art. By *art* I mean all of the fine arts: painting, sculpture, drama, music, and so on. Oftentimes artistic interpretations work their way into people's imaginations in a powerful way. Think about a painting of a biblical scene or a scripturally-based movie that has had an impact on you. How does this artwork affect the way that you read the biblical text?

You might want to explore this impact further. Look at a number of paintings of Judith, for example. Use an internet search engine to locate the images. As you look at each one, consider what the piece is conveying about Judith's thoughts or feelings as she is about to cut off Holofernes' head. I have had students put together virtual art exhibits of the books in this chapter as a way for them to literally see the powerful role that art plays in our interpretations.

Another helpful exercise is to create an artistic interpretation of a particular book. When a person thinks about creating a painting based on Tobit, for instance, he or she has to decide what the book means and how to translate that meaning into a different medium. I have found that students understand biblical texts on a whole new level after they try to put them into their own artistic language. Try it yourself: produce an artistic interpretation of one of these biblical stories. How do you understand the story differently after doing so?

books. If you want to read the Hebrew version of Esther, you should read it in a Jewish or Protestant Bible.

Protestant Bible. In the Protestant Bible, Ruth follows Judges. The short version of Esther is in the historical books. Judith and Tobit are in the Apocrypha. (If your Bible prints the Apocrypha, it is usually between the Old and New Testaments.) While you will find the extra material that is in the Greek version of Esther in the Apocrypha as well, it is easier to read the longer version in a Catholic Bible.

Jewish Bible. A Jewish Bible will have the short version of Esther. Both Esther and Ruth will be among the Writings or Ketuvim. A Jewish Bible will not have the books of either Judith or Tobit, even though these books also had Jewish authors.

RUTH: A RIGHTEOUS WOMAN

The book of Ruth is the most women-centered book in the Old Testament. It is the story of two widows: Ruth, a Moabite, and Naomi, her Israelite mother-in-law. The opening verses rush through the tragic tale of how the fate of these women came to be intertwined, but the book focuses on their survival.

The story is set in the time of the Judges, before Israel is a monarchy. The economy is based on agriculture, and all of the laws prohibiting women from owning

property are in effect. Ruth and Naomi, who have neither husbands nor sons, have no hope for the future. At least that's what the audience first believes, until a "redeemer" appears. This term, *redeemer*, comes from an ancient Hebrew law that provides a way for a widow to have sons if her husband dies.

Read the law of levirate marriage in Deuteronomy 25:5–10.

Let me help you make sense of that law. Let's say a male friend of yours died before he had fathered any sons. Your friend's brother (or closest male relative if he had no brothers) was required to sleep with his brother's widow until she bore a son. This son would be the legal heir of your dead friend, although he is the biological son of your friend's brother. "Legal" means that the son would inherit your friend's property, not the property of your dead friend's brother. The living brother is the "redeemer" because he provides for the widow of his dead brother.

This is an illustration from the Doré Bible depicting Ruth the Moabite gathering corn from the field.

The only hope for Ruth and Naomi is to find a living male relative on their husbands' side of the family willing to perform the role of the "redeemer." Men were not usually anxious to do this, because it meant that their own sons would inherit less. You'll see this tension in the story. Boaz is a distant relative of the women's dead husbands. Although he ends up being the "redeemer," there is a closer relative unwilling to take on this role.

We do not know when this story was written. It may have been written during the monarchy because of the reference to David near the end. It may have been written during the Restoration period as an objection to the decree to divorce foreign wives. The use of the law of levirate marriage from Deuteronomy may suggest a later date, but you'll also see that this law is not exactly the same in Ruth as it is in Deuteronomy. Most probably this was a story that was told and retold over the course of many years. The version we have may contain elements from several different time periods.

What should you notice about the book? The first question to ask is why is this story of two poor women preserved? The end of the book may hint at an answer. The author has emphasized the "foreignness" of Ruth; how does that feature of her character add to the theme of the book?

The second question that scholars debate is whether Ruth or Naomi is the main character of the book. The book is titled "Ruth," but this title was added much later. Who is more active in the story? Who reaps the most rewards and whom does God care for more? Which character is more life-like, more interesting, more "unexpected"? Don't assume that everyone will agree on the answers to these questions: that's what makes these questions so fascinating.

Finally, notice that some of Naomi's actions raise some questions. When Ruth tells her that she has been gleaning in Boaz's field, Naomi knows that he is a potential redeemer. Why, then, did she tell Ruth and Orpah that there was no one to redeem them in Bethlehem? Given the fact that Naomi nurses Ruth's baby, how old is Naomi? If she has not yet hit menopause, how would this affect her willingness to bring back Ruth and Orpah to Bethlehem?

JONAH, THE RELUCTANT PROPHET

I think the funniest book in the Old Testament is the book of Jonah: it is a satire or comedy. Jonah is a silly character, the fool who should know better. Even his name is funny. Women were more often named after animals than men were, and the name "Jonah" means "dove." Therefore, it's a name more typical of a woman than a man.

This painting of Jonah being cast into the sea is from an illuminated Armenian manuscript dated 1266 CE.

Those of you who have heard of Jonah might think of how he was swallowed by a whale, a kind of biblical Pinocchio. But the book is not really about that episode. The "big fish" (not necessarily a whale) is a vehicle to advance the plot. The original audience probably pictured a chaos monster, such as Leviathan.

The story of Jonah is really about the question, can and will God forgive everybody who truly repents? The city of Nineveh had been the capital of Assyria. The Assyrians were known for their brutality; their kings used to display bloody war scenes to show how great they were. The original audience of Jonah would have reacted to the name *Nineveh* similarly to the way Jews today react to the word *Nazi*. In other words, the question that the book would ask today is, if Hitler and the Nazis had truly repented for what they did, would God have forgiven them?

Jonah is a prophet, commanded by God to tell the people of Nineveh to repent. As you read about Jonah's various reactions, keep in mind that Nineveh is not in Israel. The audience knows that the Assyrians would eventually destroy the northern kingdom of Israel.

The setting of the story has to be before the year 612 BCE, when Nineveh was destroyed. There is a brief reference to a prophet named Jonah in 2 Kings 14:23–27; if this is meant to be the same person, then the book is set in the reign of Jeroboam II (786–746 BCE).

We do not know when the book of Jonah was written down however. Just because it was set in the reign of Jeroboam II does not mean it was written then. Most people agree that the book was written after Nineveh fell. Some people think it was written in the Restoration Period to object to the policies against foreigners, under the leadership of Ezra and Nehemiah. If the author intends the reader to associate Jonah with the reference in Kings, then the book has to have been written after the Deuteronomistic History was circulating. However, there is nothing in the book that requires a specific date.

As you read the book, ask yourself, is the reader supposed to identify with Jonah? Why is he portrayed as he is? Is he a sympathetic character? What things does he do or say that are admirable? What things are troublesome? Can you compare or contrast Jonah's behavior with various foreigners in the book?

This biblical book pays a lot of attention to God. How is God portrayed? Are all of God's actions good, or are some troubling? What is the role of "nature" (animals, weather, and plants) in the book, and what do the actions of "nature" tell us about God?

Most importantly of all, notice that the book ends with a question. By ending the book with a question that Jonah does not answer, the author is saying that the reader becomes Jonah, since you must supply Jonah's answer. How does it feel to have to answer for Jonah here? How does the author expect you to answer that final question?

ESTHER, QUEEN OF PERSIA

The book of Esther recounts the story of a Jewish woman who marries the king of Persia after the exile. The story has an "exotic" feel, because the storyteller has to interrupt the story at certain points to explain Persian customs. These explanations tell us that he does not expect his audience to be familiar with life in Persia.

It might be hard to keep all of the characters in the book straight. Esther and Mordecai are Jews living in Persia. Mordecai, Esther's relative, works for the king. The king has an impossibly long Hebrew name; I find it easier to call him by his Greek name, Xerxes, or simply "the king." The king has many wives, including Vashti and Esther. He also has a conniving officer named Haman. The story follows Haman's growing hatred of the Jews; Esther is the one person who can save her people from Haman's evil plans.

This text had to have been written after 486 BCE, because the king portrayed in the story ruled some time after that. There is no historical evidence for a Jewish queen nor of a systematic killing of Jews in Persia. Scholars debate whether it

The Bible in the CHRISTIAN TRADITION

The Sign of Jonah

When most people think about Jonah, they picture the prophet sitting in the belly of a whale. Yet most biblical scholars would tell you that this event is not the most important part of the book. Why is there such a divide between popular opinion and professional conclusions?

This is one example of how the artistic tradition has hugely influenced popular perceptions. Look up images of Jonah on the Internet. Notice the percentage that depicts Jonah inside a fish.

So why were artists so focused on the fish? Most of these artists were Christians, and they knew that Jonah is mentioned in the New Testament (Matthew 12:38–42 and Luke 11:29–32). In these texts, Jonah's three-day sojourn in the belly of the fish is used to foreshadow Jesus' three-day stay in the tomb. This is referred to as the "sign of Jonah."

Now, return to your images of Jonah, and look at them in light of this information. How many depict Jonah as a kind of Christ figure? Do any use crosses, light, or other elements associated with Jesus? Do any of the paintings depict the fish as a chaos monster, such as Leviathan? These versions are trying to convey the cosmic nature of Jonah's struggle as a pre-figuration of Christ's victory over sin and chaos. What else do you notice?

This example demonstrates that artistic pieces often combine images derived from the biblical text with a tradition of interpretation stemming from a variety of sources.

was written later, during the Greek period, which would explain why the readers would be unfamiliar with Persian customs. In addition, Jews experienced more religious persecution in the Greek period than during the Persian period.

The text comes to us in two versions. The Hebrew version is shorter and absolutely does not mention God in the whole text. The Greek version is longer, and it includes prayers and acts of piety by the characters. Protestants and Jews consider the shorter text as canonical, while Catholics and Orthodox Christians accept the longer version. Read both, and see if you think length makes a difference.

On the surface, this book is preserved because it records the origins of the Jewish festival of Purim. This is the only mention of this festival in the Old Testament, and it remains a minor holiday in Jewish tradition today.

Beneath the surface, however, this book has larger themes. When you "read between the lines" you realize that the king is a rather comic character. On the one hand he is the most powerful man on earth, but notice how often someone else gets him to do what they want him to do. Is he really that powerful? The book of Esther is a tale of the struggle over power, from Queen Vashti's defiance of the king's order to Haman's attempts to be honored by the king to Esther's rescue of the Jews.

The author uses irony to depict the subversion of the apparent power grid of the story. In other words, although it looks like the king has absolute power, in fact, he is almost powerless. Haman, who thinks he will be honored, is hanged on his own gallows. What ironic twists can you find in the story?

Think about the characterization of Esther and Mordecai. Some people view Mordecai as the real hero of the story, because of his role in advising Esther. Notice the lineage of Mordecai and Haman; what does their lineage suggest about what they represent? Others see Esther as the heroine, because of the risks she takes to save her people. Still other people are critical of Esther because she does not tell the king that his view of his own power is warped; to them Vashti is the heroine. What do you think?

Purim and Other Jewish Holidays

Most Christians are probably aware of the fact that the Jewish festival of Passover is based on the texts in Exodus. Some may even know that a complete reading of the Torah is accomplished each and every year in synagogue services. Readings from the Pentateuch are coupled with readings from the prophetic books, usually a chapter in length each time. This prophetic portion is called the *haftorah*, which means "completion" or "concluding portion."

On certain festival days, however, one of five smaller scrolls is read. These five books are called the *megilloth*.

Holy Day	Biblical Reading
Passover	Song of Songs
Weeks or Pentecost	Ruth
Ninth of *Ab* (date of the destruction of the temple)	Lamentations
Booths or *Sukkoth*	Qoheleth
Purim	Esther

These books remained important in Jewish tradition because of their connection with the Holy Days.

The festival of Purim comes straight out of the book of Esther. It celebrates the day that the Jews were saved from the violence of the Persians. The contemporary celebration includes noisemakers used to drown out Haman's name every time it is mentioned in the text.

Another minor holiday that is known to Christians is Hanukkah. Hanukkah is a feast that celebrates a miracle that God worked for his people. When the Hasmoneans won independence from the Greeks, the temple needed to be ritually purified before it could be used again. This ritual required eight days for completion, but there was only enough purified oil to last one day.

However, the oil miraculously lasted all eight days. The eight days of Hanukkah commemorate this miracle of light. The Hanukkah menorah has nine candles: eight that represent the eight days of Hanukkah, and one larger candle used to light each smaller candle on successive days. This is in distinction from the menorah in the second temple that had seven lamps or candles, a version of which is mentioned in Zechariah 4:1–3.

Hanukkah is one Jewish holiday that is not described in Jewish Scriptures, since the stories of the revolt are found in the two books of Maccabees (also written by Jewish authors), which are not in the shorter Tanakh. However, the holiday has become popular, in part, because of its proximity to Christmas.

This wall painting dating to 245 CE is from the Dura Europos, the oldest known synagogue (circa 300–272 CE) which was excavated in 1932 on today's border between Syria and Iraq. The painting depicts scenes from the Book of Esther.

As you think about power, also think about the role of God in the book. You might conclude that God's role is different in the two versions of the story. How does this affect the theme of power in the book?

Tobit, the Afflicted

Tobit is a work of fiction. The author has mixed up the historical and geographical information as a clue to the reader that this story is set during a fictitious exile. It presumes an audience, like Esther's, who understood what it meant to be persecuted for following their faith. This suggests that the book was written sometime in the Greek period.

The story tells of the trials of two families living in exile. Tobit, Anna, and their son, Tobias, live in one city, while another Israelite family, Raguel, Edna, and their daughter, Sarah, live in another city. Both families are facing large problems: Tobit is blind, and Sarah's husbands keep dying. Tobias, with the help of an angel in disguise, is able to resolve the problems of both families.

The story contains elements typical of folktales, such as irony and coincidence. The book also contains medical advice, a love-sick demon, a description of wedding customs, and even the one and only pet dog in the Bible. These elements bring color to the story.

The author has also used parallel scenes. Notice, for instance, that Tobit and Sarah pray for death at the same time. The story contrasts the demon with the angel. Tobit's blindness and his healing both come through animal products. Can you find other examples of parallels in the story?

One of the fascinating elements for me is the portrayal of women acting within everyday families. Notice the way that Anna and Edna are able to sway their husbands and how Anna must work once Tobit is blind, which makes her vulnerable to unfounded accusations by her husband. Notice also that no one ever knows that Sarah is tormented by a love-sick demon. How do the servants explain her husbands' deaths in 3:8–9? What is her father doing on the night of her wedding to Tobias (8:9)? These details alert the reader to the life of shame that Sarah was forced to endure.

Why is this story in the Bible? As entertaining as it is, does it have any "great" message for the reader? I think it does. Think about God's role in the book: God acts without ever "appearing" in the story. God seems to be both everywhere and nowhere at the same time. How does the author communicate this? What do you think about the view of God in the story?

Judith, the Warrior

I predict that many of you will either love the story of Judith or hate it. Judith tells the tale of a pious Jewish widow who saves her city through trickery and violence. I think that the author clearly wants us to view Judith as a heroine, but I find that many of my students have difficulty admiring the way she saves her city. See what you think about the morality of her actions.

This tale is fictitious. It starts by locating the story during the reign of Nebuchadnezzar, king of Assyria in Nineveh. In fact, this man was not king of Assyria; he was the king of Babylon. In addition, the city of Nineveh had been destroyed before the real Nebuchadnezzar had attacked Judah. If you started a story today by saying, "When George Bush was king of the Canadians, ruling from the island of Atlantis . . ." the reader would know that the story was fiction.

The book was most probably written during the Maccabean period, making it one of the latest books in the Old Testament. Judith's name is a symbol: it means "Jewish woman." Judith's goodness is demonstrated by acts of pious devotion above and beyond what is required by the law. She represents the pious nation who has been persecuted by evil foreigners. The fictitious city, Bethulia, symbolizes Jerusalem.

The story seems to start slowly. Judith is not introduced until chapter 8. The main character of the first seven chapters is Achior, a leader of the Ammonites. The author is setting up a parallel between what the foreigner, Achior, says

This illustration from the Dore Bible shows Judith taking the head of Holofernes (Jdt 13:8).

about Yahweh, and how Judith acts because of her faith in Yahweh. The figure of the enemy's general, Holofernes, connects the two halves of the book.

The book invites you to look at what various characters say about Yahweh and to decide who is right. After you read the book, you may want to consider these questions: what do the people and the elders of the city imply about God in Judith 7:23–31? Do you think Judith is right when she attributes her victory to God in Judith 13:15? Does the general ever say anything "true" about God?

The book is not just about what people say; it is about what they *do*. Judith is the heroine because she does more than just pray for God's help. She brings about God's victory. This seems to be a main point of the story, but this theme raises hermeneutical questions. Is the book encouraging women to act like Judith? Does it assert that the end justifies the means? Is it okay to deceive and kill people, if you are doing it for God? On the other hand, in what ways is Judith wise? If Judith represents the nation, how does the author think the nation should act?

GOD'S CARE FROM LEAST TO GREAT

These stories do not necessarily hit us over the head with their theology. Instead, they tell great stories, with intrigue and interesting characters. Through the stories of individuals' struggles and victories, God is to be seen. These tales provided the Israelites with a model for seeing God in their own lives. From the struggles and minor victories of the most destitute people to the ways the more powerful stayed true to God while interacting with foreigners, Yahweh was there. For the Israelites, God acted through each of them individually and all of them collectively. This is what it means to profess a belief in a God of history: God acts in the lives of all: the weak (Naomi) and strong (Judith); foolish (Jonah) and pious (Judith); foreign (Ruth, Achior), native (Jonah, Judith, and Naomi), and stranger in a strange land (Esther and Tobit).

FOR REVIEW

1. List three things you should notice as you read.

2. How do these stories reflect wisdom themes?

FOR FURTHER READING

There are several excellent introductions to literary approaches to the Bible, although many of them are either highly technical or theoretical. A classic study that has stood the test of time is Robert Alter's *The Art of Narrative* (New York: Basic Books, 1981). See also Adele Berlin, *Poetics and Interpretation of Biblical Narratives* (Bible and Literature 9; Sheffield: Almond, 1983); J. Cheryl Exum and David Clines, editors, *The New Literary Criticism and the Hebrew Bible* (JSOTSup 143; Sheffield, KY: JSOT, 1993); and J. P. Fokkelman, *Reading Biblical Narrative: An Introductory Guide* (Louisville, KY: Westminster John Knox, 1999). John Barton has compared the presuppositions behind various literary approaches with other classic approaches to the Bible in *Reading the Old Testament: Method in Biblical Study*, revised edition (Louisville, KY: Westminster John Knox, 1996). For a concise discussion of the different loci of meaning, see Gale Yee, "The Author/Text/Reader and Power: Suggestions for a Critical Framework for Biblical Studies," in *Reading from This Place*, volume 1, edited by Fernando F. Segovia and Mary A. Tolbert (Minneapolis, MN: Fortress, 1995) pages 109–18.

The commentaries on these biblical books are great sources to explore them further. An introduction to this type of literature can be found in Lawrence M. Wills, *The Jewish Novel in the Ancient World* (Myth and Poetics; Ithaca, NY/London: Cornell University Press, 1995). However, there are also many excellent articles and book essays. You can use your library databases, such as ATLA or Old Testament Abstracts, to find recent ones; your instructor or reference librarian can help you with these. One collection of essays for the nonspecialist, including essays on Ruth, Esther, and Judith, is Alice Bach, editor, *Women in the Hebrew Bible: A Reader* (New York: Routledge, 1999).

Because we talked about artwork in this chapter, it is also helpful to know about three internet search engines related to this issue. First, Art Concordance catalogues images available on the internet especially from museums. It catalogues them by the name of biblical characters. So to find paintings of Ruth, simply click on "Ruth," and you'll have plenty of works to choose from. Second, Fr. Felix Just, a New Testament scholar, has a website with a portal to biblical art. Art Concordance is one of the sites that he lists, but there are several others as well. Third, the search engine Altavista allows you to search images. You pull up a lot of nonbiblical material when you type in something like "Ruth," but the search results provide you with thumbnails so you can preview which ones you would want to look at further.

15 An Orchestra of Voices

Just as you do not know how the breath comes to the bones in the mother's womb,
so you do not know the work of God, who makes everything.
(Eccl 11:5)

Unity and Diversity in Scripture

Chapter Overview

In this final chapter we will explore how God's revelation in the Old Testament contains many different messages. This chapter will be devoted to passages that seem to contradict biblical messages that we have already surveyed. This chapter will provide the following:

❯ An examination of the effects of Hellenism on ancient Judaism

❯ A discussion of the skeptical wisdom tradition

❯ An introduction to apocalyptic literature

This chapter deals with a major theological issue for most Christians: does the Bible have a unified message, and, if so, what is its source?

THE MAIN MELODIES OF THE OLD TESTAMENT

Have you ever listened to a symphony? The composer weaves together various melodic themes to present a complex musical idea. Each symphony has various movements, that is, sections that sound to the untrained ear as if they are completely different pieces of music, played one after another. However, for the composer, these various movements comprise a unified piece of complex music. A symphony is a good metaphor to describe how the Old Testament is a unified whole, even though this unity is not the result of a single theme or melody.

Certainly there are some ideas in the Old Testament that are more prominent than others. Let's review a few of these:

Covenant. This is a theme we see biblical authors return to again and again. In the Pentateuch and the historical books, God makes covenants with Noah, Moses, Abraham, and David. The prophets remind the people that their relationship with God is based on a covenant, one that places demands on how they should behave.

Creation. This is major theme in the Bible, especially in wisdom texts, psalms, and, again, the prophets. All of existence is the result of God's actions as creator. In Israelite texts, creation is contrasted with chaos, a lack of order that renders all things meaningless. God creates not only at some time in the past but throughout every single moment of existence.

Revelation. This concept is depicted in a variety of ways in the biblical texts. Sometimes revelation is direct, such as when God talks to Moses on Mt. Sinai, or when the prophets receive God's word. Sometimes divine revelation is mediated through angels or through God's created world. But at every point in Israel's history, people understood that God communicated with them.

Can you add other prominent themes to this list?

The three themes that I mentioned all suggest the reliability of God and God's direct involvement in human history. All three also come out of Israel's cultural context. Other nations in the Fertile Crescent also talked about the ways their gods revealed themselves, their gods' work as creators, and even the special relationships particular gods had with certain cities and nations.

In this chapter, we will look at texts that raise questions about these dominant themes, because pessimism is also part of Israel's cultural heritage. There are Babylonian texts that question their gods' care for humanity. In addition, Greek speculative thought influenced Israelite understanding of their own traditions in the Second Temple Period. The texts we will look at in this chapter contain

Focus on METHOD

Postmodernism and Deconstructionism

Whether or not you realize it, you live in the postmodern age. You live in a world where claims for objective truth, certitude, and universal principles are met with skepticism. Some people say that this skepticism is part of the degeneration of our age; they long to return to an age of certainty. But the fact remains that there have been a number of things that have contributed to this "methodological doubt."

As we have discovered in previous chapters, people have come to realize that much of what passed for "universal truths" were simply the conclusions of a select and homogenous group of scholars. In twentieth-century America, university education became available to a much wider group of people than previously. The significant rise of women and minorities within academia was one contributing factor to the realization that there were more ways to think about intellectual conclusions than had previously been assumed.

Postmodernism refers to those intellectual movements that recognize that all knowledge is constructed by individuals within specific cultural contexts. It highlights the subjective element involved in all claims of knowledge and truth. It also avoids evaluative statements. For example, postmodern art critics would not distinguish between "high" and "low" art; graffiti is as much art as is a classical oil painting.

One movement within postmodernism is deconstructionism. Both terms have a variety of meanings, but in our context deconstructionism refers to three primary approaches to biblical interpretation. First, deconstructionism seeks to uncover the ways in which interpretations that result in claims for objectivity and truth mask attempts to establish privilege for a particular group. For example, a claim that the Bible objectively calls for wives to obey their husbands is viewed by a deconstructionist as an attempt to maintain patriarchal authority by attaching it to a text viewed as sacred by those involved in the oppression. A deconstructionist attitude asks, whose interests does a particular interpretation serve?

Second, deconstructionism also seeks to uncover the ways in which the text masks the attempts of the group that produced it to maintain their own power. A deconstructionist analysis of the Deuteronomistic History would view the text as an attempt by a small group of Levites to assert their own ideology by the way they tell their history.

Third, deconstructionism also uncovers the ways in which the dominant "paradigm" of the text, its central ideology, is often undercut by its own text. For example, the claim of the absolute authority of men over women in a prophetic metaphor such as Ezekiel 16 (the city as God's whoring wife) betrays male anxiety over their inability to completely control women's behavior.

For some biblical theologians postmodernism and deconstructionism can pose a problem. In some forms they seem to reduce the biblical text to nothing more than political propaganda, the products of self-interest. However, in traditions that allow for the full range of human activity in the production of biblical texts, such human motivation does not limit God's ability to use the texts as vehicles of authentic revelation. The view that the texts are revelatory is a statement of faith in the activity of God; it is not an assertion about how the texts were produced.

Both postmodernism and deconstructionism avoid sweeping universal statements, even within biblical theology. In fact, deconstructionism begins by stressing the element of "difference"; we know things as individual phenomena specifically because they are unlike other phenomena.

Even if people today have never read deconstructionist theory, its influences are wide-reaching. For example, many biblical scholars today reject the notion that there is one or even a limited number of biblical themes or ideas. They point out the variety of voices in the text, and they stress that any attempt to reduce these voices does violence to the text that we have received. These approaches to biblical interpretation have resulted in a much more accurate appreciation of the variety of texts in the Bible and, thus, in a more nuanced and accurate assessment of the Bible's contribution to theology.

Israelite reflections that challenge their own traditions. We will see that this type of reflection often resonates with our own experience of God and the world.

HELLENISTIC JUDAISM

I bet most of you have heard of Alexander the Great. He was a brilliant Macedonian general whose control of the ancient world extended from Greece to Persia, which included all of the countries that we have learned about in this course.

Alexander's conquest changed more than the political makeup of the area. The Greeks had an active policy of colonization, by which they introduced Greek culture into the countries they controlled. This practice is called *hellenization* (coming from the Greeks' name for their country, *Hellas*), and it resulted in a systematic introduction of Greek politics, religion, and culture throughout the empire. This process commenced with the introduction of the Greek city, or *polis*, into the colonized areas, which was subsequently a vehicle for introducing the Greek constitution, religion, education, and entertainment. By the end of the Greek era, Hellenistic influence in Judea can be found in everything from wedding practices to funerary customs.

Israel's contact with Hellenism marked the first time that the Israelites had to interact with a culture so different from their own. Greek religious thought at this time had moved away from the mythic tales of Homer to the speculative thought of Socrates, Plato, Aristotle, and others. Here was a group who replaced the "stories" of their own narrative theology with speculative contemplation on the nature of God. We can see the influence of Greek thought on Jewish texts dating from this period and later. For example, you will find that God is more remote, more transcendent, in Jewish Hellenistic texts, a result of speculation on the perfection of God.

Hellenistic education introduced several distinctive elements of Greek culture, especially philosophy and literature. In the literary realm, Jews adapted Greek forms of writing. In addition, Hebrew ceased to be a living language. Many Jews living outside of Judea, by now a sizeable and influential group, were Greek-speakers. Jews in Alexandria, Egypt are credited with requesting the translation of the Bible into the Greek language that they spoke. In Judea, Aramaic had replaced Hebrew as the language of the people.

After Alexander died, his empire was divided up among three of his generals. It was a turbulent time for Judea, caught as it was at the border between the Ptolemies in Egypt and the Seleucids in Syria. In the third century alone, there were five major wars between these two groups.

Judea was first controlled by the Egyptian Ptolemies. After 198 BCE, Seleucid rulers in Syria gained control of the area. These rulers were very aggressive in their policy of colonization. Some Jews found the Greek presence appealing, and they cooperated with their Greek rulers as a way to advance their own status. Others greeted the new culture with hostility. Their resistance led them to embrace those elements of their Judaism that contributed to their distinct identity. These included keeping kosher, practicing circumcision, and observing other purity laws.

ANTIOCHUS IV EPIPHANES

The last Seleucid ruler was Antiochus IV, who gave himself the epithet, "Epiphanes," which means "manifest (as a god)." Although Hellenism had been met with mixed reactions prior to his rule, his hostile policies proved to be the final straw.

It is not known why Antiochus introduced the first solely religious persecution that Judea had ever known. Rather than introducing Greek religion as an addition to Judea's native Judaism, Antiochus IV outlawed the practice of certain Jewish rituals, such as circumcision and observation of the Sabbath. He forced Jews to commit acts abominable to them, including sacrificing to idols. Moreover, he desecrated the temple by setting up a statue of Zeus and sacrificing pigs there. (The Greeks had long included pigs as part of their own sacrificial system.) As the Jewish community struggled to make sense of these events, Antiochus became the defining icon for an evil enemy to God.

THE MACCABEAN REVOLT

Antiochus's heavy hand also spawned a revolution, first on the edges of Judea and eventually reaching to Jerusalem itself. This revolution was spearheaded by a man and his five sons, who were part of the Hasmonean family. These men, under the leadership of the eldest brother, Judah, whose nickname was "Maccabee," were able to organize Jewish resistance to Greek rule. Although this revolution took some time to succeed, when it did, it ushered in a brief period of Jewish independence in the Second Temple Period.

By this point in Judea's history, the high priest had become the most important figure in Judean society. The Maccabean rulers also assumed the office of high priest as part of their political power base.

The Hasmonean period was marked by some ironic contrasts. On the one hand, these rulers and their followers opposed Greek hegemony. They sought to reestablish Jewish religious practices and to encourage the flourishing of

The Origins of the Dead Sea Scrolls

When the Hasmoneans took over both political and religious power in Judea, not all Jews met them with open arms. In fact, there were groups who viewed Hasmonean control of the temple to be sacrilegious. Although there is some disagreement about the history of these groups, a consensus remains that one of these groups abandoned the city of Jerusalem and settled near the Dead Sea at a place now called Qumran.

This group was led by a man referred to as the "Teacher of Righteousness." A recently translated text reveals that this movement stemmed from debates over Jewish law and ritual procedures. This community felt that the temple's purity had been compromised. They believed that the only option left to them was withdrawal from the whole system.

In the 1940s their texts were found hidden in clay jars in caves along the cliffs near the Dead Sea. Some of these texts described elements of their lifestyle, elements that associated them with a group that Josephus, a Roman-period Jewish historian, called the "Essenes." Today, scholarly references to the Dead Sea Scrolls, the community at Qumran, or the Essenes, all refer to this group.

The texts found at Qumran were of a wide variety. They include the following:

Biblical texts. The most important scrolls were copies of biblical texts. Fragments of every book of the Tanakh except Esther have been found among the scrolls. The reason that this discovery is so important is because, for many biblical books, these are by far the earliest copies that we have. For some, the next oldest manuscripts come from a synagogue in Cairo dating to the tenth to the thirteenth centuries CE. The biblical texts among the Dead Sea Scrolls are amazingly similar to manuscripts of the same texts copied down 1000 years later. Apart from the fact that there was no indication of vowels yet in Hebrew writing during the Roman period, most variations from later manuscripts have to do with spelling and minor word changes. However, some biblical books, such as Psalms, had clearly not yet reached their final form when this community came into existence.

Sectarian texts. The scrolls also include texts that people from the Qumran community wrote for their group. These texts help to fill out the complex structure of Judean society at this time. This community was an apocalyptic group, meaning that they awaited God's intervention into human history and viewed the world as a battle between the forces of good and the forces of evil. One scroll, sometimes called the War Scroll, describes clashes between these forces of light and darkness. Another text, sometimes called the Community Scroll describes how members of the community were supposed to live.

Other Jewish writings. There were also copies of other popular Jewish writings, such as the book of Jubilees. There are also Hebrew fragments of two apocryphal books, previously preserved primarily in Greek: the Wisdom of Ben Sirach and Tobit.

The texts from Qumran help us understand the development of the biblical canon. They fill in information on the social history of Judea during the Roman Period, and they provide background for the New Testament period. While they may not provide the key to unlock the secrets of the Bible, as some tabloids like to claim, they remain invaluable to biblical historians.

Jewish identity. On the other hand, their world was one still heavily influenced by Hellenism. They lived in Hellenistic palaces, gave their children Greek names, and wrote in Greek literary style. Hellenism had become so internalized that even those seeking to bring back the "good old days" no longer viewed certain elements, originally introduced by the Greeks, as foreign.

ISRAELITE LITERATURE IN THE HELLENISTIC PERIOD

Jewish literature of this period looks a bit different than its pre-Hellenistic counterparts. One change that pervaded all the literature was a move away from

Pictured is a view of the sandstone formations at Qumran in which cave number four is located. In this cave, fifteen thousand scroll fragments have been found.

ambiguity, replacing it with a more dualistic worldview. *Dualism* is a system of thought that organizes reality within a schema of opposites. For instance, human behavior is either good or bad; moral ambiguity is not appreciated. Whether dualistic thought is an idea imported from Greek speculative thought or simply a general trend, evident throughout the entire ancient Near East at this time, is debated. However, it is clear that Jewish Hellenistic literature is more dualistic than most previous literature.

Literary genres also changed at this time. This included adaptation of older literary forms:

Wisdom. The wisdom tradition flourished under the influence of Greek speculative thought, but it did so with a willingness to entertain the possibility of the capriciousness of God and the futility of human action. This change produced what some scholars label "skeptical wisdom."

Rewritten Bibles. As we saw in our discussion of Chronicles, some texts rewrite earlier versions of Israel's historical traditions. These rewritings often protect the moral integrity of Israelite heroes and heroines, producing a more dualistic version of their own traditions.

In addition, new literary genres appear:

Apocalyptic texts. We will examine the elements of apocalyptic literature later. Here, suffice it to say that this literature, which picks up elements of Israelite prophetic and wisdom traditions, utilizes them in new ways, in order to explore the ultimate meaning of human suffering.

Biblical interpretation. We have many Hellenistic Jewish texts that preserve explicit attempts to interpret earlier texts. Some of these quote verses from a particular biblical book in order, each quote followed by an explanation. At Qumran, they called these *pesharim*, meaning "interpretations." By the time of rabbinic Judaism, these pesharim had developed into two distinct forms: halakah, which was a controlled system of interpreting legal texts, and haggadah, a more associative interpretation of non-legal material, especially narrative. This latter material is sometimes called *midrash*.

Translations. Our earliest extant translations of the Bible into languages other than Hebrew also stem from the Hellenistic period. The two translations that had the most impact on subsequent interpretations were those into Aramaic (also known as the *Talmud*) and those into Greek (the *Septuagint*).

Thus, Hellenistic Judaism is marked by a period of lively literary production. This literary tradition demonstrates the creative response of the Jews to an oppressive dominant culture.

INTRODUCING COUNTER MELODIES

ISRAELITE SKEPTICAL LITERATURE

For a long time, biblical scholars assumed that one of the changes that resulted from the influx of Hellenistic thought was the rise of texts questioning the ethical presuppositions of classical Israelite literature. Although this explanation is now recognized as too simplistic, the fact remains that some later Israelite texts are less confident that virtue and right action lead to rewards in this life. The fact that good people were being persecuted for their piety might have affected the way that the Israelites thought about their own wisdom traditions.

These skeptical texts often resonate with contemporary audiences, who also recognize that bad things sometimes happen to good people and that sometimes the wicked prosper. Rather than leading to doubt about God's existence or nature, however, this literature uses this experience as a catalyst to contemplate God's incomprehensibility. Notice that skeptical wisdom, along with apocalyptic literature, and Hellenistic tales avoid blaming Israelites for their own suffering.

It Is All in Vain: The Theology of Ecclesiastes

The book of Ecclesiastes questions many Israelite beliefs about the meaning of life, especially as seen in wisdom literature. As you may recall, wisdom literature presumes that God has created the world with a certain order, and it is the job of the wise to discern this order and live accordingly. The wise person will be rewarded with long life, prosperity, a good reputation, and so on.

The author of Ecclesiastes knows this tradition, yet he notes, "There are righteous people who perish in their righteousness, and there are wicked people who prolong their life in their evildoing" (Eccl 7:15). In other words, the system doesn't work.

Read the whole book of Ecclesiastes. You will see that Ecclesiastes questions the meaning of life in light of this universal human experience.

In Case You Were Wondering

Vanity. The word *vanity* in Hebrew means "a vapor, a breath, something that vanishes into thin air." It does not mean pride or thinking better of yourself than you deserve. When you see the word *vanity* in the text, think "emptiness" or "wasted effort."

Teacher. This is just one of many translations for the author of the book of Ecclesiastes. Jews call the author, *Qoheleth*, the Hebrew word translated here as "Teacher." The Hebrew means, literally, "a woman who assembles," and the assembly is usually a religious congregation. Sometimes the word comes into English as "Preacher," to get this sense of the religious community. Although the narrator says that he is a son of David who becomes king, the book was written during the Greek period, long after the monarchy. Both the royal association with Solomon and the female voice of the narrator tell you that this is a wisdom book; and, like Proverbs, it is associated with Solomon in the words of Wisdom herself.

Looking Closely at the Text

1. Name three things in chapter 2 that the Teacher examines to find meaning in life.

2. In Ecclesiastes 3:16–21, what is the problem as the Teacher sees it?

3. According to a repeated refrain in the book, why should people enjoy all their toil?

4. What does the poem in Ecclesiastes 11:7—12:8 describe?

5. Is the perspective on the meaning of life in Ecclesiastes depressing, realistic, or comforting?

EVERYTHING IS JUST A PUFF OF SMOKE

Many of my students suspect that the author of Ecclesiastes was in serious need of some antidepressants! To some people he sounds as if he's on the edge of despair in his search for the meaning of life. His own experience tells him that all human effort is pointless.

Readers throughout the centuries have had trouble with the pessimistic themes of this book. Jewish rabbis in the first century debated whether it should be included in the canon. The final six verses of the book, a clear addition, may preserve an early attempt to bring the message of the book into line with other biblical texts. Yet, despite the odds, this is part of the Jewish and Christian canons.

Let's look at the main topics that the Teacher explores. First, he sees a problem with the tradition that he has inherited. Ethical behavior seems to have no pay-off in this life. You can be righteous and still die young. You can be wicked and make lots of money. Human behavior is neither rewarded nor punished; the system presented in books like Proverbs does not work. I think we could agree with him on this point.

Second, the Teacher has a cyclical view of history, a view common in Greek thought. What does this mean? It means that, instead of believing that human history is moving toward some final point, he believes that history repeats itself. "What has been is what will be, and what has been done is what will be done; there is nothing new under the sun" (Eccl 1:9). This is the point of the poem about "time" in 3:1–8; I find it amusing that today we sing those words as if they are meant to be a comfort. Instead, these passages imply that human history has no inherent meaning.

Third, like most Israelite texts, the book does not posit an afterlife that rewards or punishes human behavior. The Teacher mentions Sheol in Ecclesiastes 9:10, but it adds nothing to human purpose: "Whatever your hand finds to do, do with your might; for there is no work or thought or knowledge or wisdom in Sheol, to which you are going." His view of death is perhaps best captured when he wonders whether humans have any different experience of death than animals (Ecclesiastes 4:16–22). Today, we hear people assert the same thing.

Finally, if human behavior has no consequences, then there must be a problem with God. The Teacher repeatedly asserts that God is behind the whole "vain" system. "Consider the work of God; who can make straight what he has made crooked?" (Eccl 7:13). This is why the author repeats a number of times that God's ways are unknowable: he cannot figure out why God acts as God does.

The Teacher examines all that he touches upon—human experience, ethical behavior, human history, the reliability of God—in light of the finality of death, in order to try to find meaning for life. But he repeatedly comes up empty. The words *vanity* and *vain* mean that everything has as much meaning as a puff of smoke or a passing fog. All human existence adds up to "nothing."

Is there any hope in this book? Not much. The only thing that the Teacher can endorse with confidence is that God has given us whatever we have, our "toil," our families, all the small and simple pleasures in life. If these are our only consolations, then we better enjoy them. He denounces those who try to get more benefit from these things, as if these "things" give life meaning. He notes that if you look at things as an end in themselves, then you will never be satisfied with them when you get them; you will always want more. So he is not advocating a life of decadence or excess. He is saying, stop and look at what you have. This is it, that's all there is for you. So, if you want to find happiness, you had better find it here.

But notice that the author never asserts that God is not involved in human lives. He never posits the existence of other gods or evil powers that bring harm to humans. He never slips into atheism. He simply concludes that he cannot understand God's ways.

Many readers find this comforting. The author's skepticism resonates with their own experience, and they appreciate the text's honesty. To have such a viewpoint represented in the Bible affirms this human experience and communicates that even those who question God's justice and the goodness of the natural order are part of God's people. They do not have to hide or change those feelings; they can bring them to God.

Pessimism and *Gilgamesh*

Because Ecclesiastes is so unlike other biblical books, biblical scholars asserted for a long time that it had to be the result of influence from some foreign culture. However, there has been a recent recognition that these skeptical attitudes can be found within the literature of the Fertile Crescent.

An example of such skepticism is the epic poem *Gilgamesh*. We mentioned the text earlier in the book, because it contains an account of the Flood story that is similar to the one in Genesis. However, this account is only a small part of a much larger work.

The poem focuses on a king's quest for the meaning of life. As the poem opens, the citizens of the city of Uruk complain to the gods because the behavior of their king, Gilgamesh, has become too disruptive for them. The gods send a wild man, Enkidu, whose own intensity is a match for Gilgamesh. As a result, the two become fast friends, and they set off on a series of adventures. In the course of these escapades, they insult the goddess, Ishtar, who kills Enkidu.

Enkidu's death causes a crisis for Gilgamesh. He cannot understand what purpose life serves if we are all simply destined to die. "When I die, shall I not be like Enkidu? Woe has entered my belly. Fearing death I roam over the steppe" (Tablet IX, column i, in *ANET*). He decides to seek out the one human who has been granted immortality, Ut-Napishtim, the Babylonian Noah, in order to find out how he can also avoid death. Gilgamesh finds Ut-Napishtim, who eventually gives him the key to eternal life: a plant that provides eternal youth.

After all of his journeys, Gilgamesh has finally succeeded in his quest to avoid death. He sets off for home, sure that his life has meaning. At the base of the mountain he boards a ferry to cross the river, where he drops the plant, which is eaten by a fish. . . .

That's it, the end of the story (although some later versions add material not related to this main tale). Gilgamesh realizes that he cannot avoid death and that human life is limited by the gods. Once back in Uruk, he builds a temple to Ishtar and accepts the limitations on his life.

The epic of *Gilgamesh* shares Ecclesiastes' honest assessment of the limits on human power. Both explore the meaning of life in light of the fact that we all die. On the way to see Ut-Napishtim, Gilgamesh stopped at a tavern. There he met a barmaid, who responded to his quest by saying,

Thou, Gilgamesh, let full be thy belly, make thou merry by day and by night. Of each day make thou a feast of rejoicing, day and night dance thou and play! Let thy garments be sparkling fresh, thy head be washed; bathe thou in water. Pay heed to the little one that holds on to thy hand, let thy spouse delight in thy bosom! For this is the task of [mankind]!" (Tablet X, column iii, *ANET*).

Notice how similar this is to Eccl 9:7–9:

Go, eat your bread with enjoyment, and drink your wine with a merry heart; for God has long ago approved what you do. Let your garments always be white; do not let oil be lacking on your head. Enjoy life with the wife whom you love, all the days of your vain life what are given you under the sun, because that is your portion in life and in your toil at which you toil under the sun.

Did the author of Ecclesiastes know the epic of *Gilgamesh*? Perhaps; it was a very popular text, even in the Hellenistic period. But at the very least, these texts demonstrate that this questioning of the meaning of life was part of the ancient world's literary tradition.

God on Trial: The Book of Job

Unfortunately, the book of Job is too long for me to require you to read the whole thing, but reading the beginning and end of the text will give you a good idea of the issues that the book addresses.

In order to help you understand the selected chapters, let me first describe the structure of the whole book. The book begins by describing how Job becomes an innocent sufferer. For the story to work, you must accept the fact that Job in no way deserves his suffering. The bulk of the book contains cycles of speeches by Job, his friends, and one young man, who all debate whether Job deserves his fate. In the course of the debate, Job calls on God to prove, as if in a court of law, that he deserves what he is suffering. At the end of the book, God finally appears and addresses Job directly.

Job 1–2 and 40:6–42:17: Who Is God in the Book of Job?

Read the opening chapters, which describe why Job suffers, and the end of the book, which contains God's response to Job. As you read this last part, ask yourself, did God give Job a good answer?

In Case You Were Wondering

Uz. This is a land located to the east of the nation of Israel. Job is not an Israelite.

Satan. Here, once again, Satan is not the devil. He is the "district attorney" for the divine court. His role is to find people who have sinned and bring the evidence to God, who then decides on a proper sentence.

Behemoth and Leviathan. These are the names of two chaos monsters.

Looking Closely at the Text

1. Why does God allow Satan to hurt Job?

2. When God finally confronts Job, what is the response that is given?

3. How does Job react to God's speech?

4. Is God "just" in this text?

From Satan to the Devil

We have seen throughout this course that the Israelite view of angels changed over time. In the texts of Genesis and Exodus, angels are often indistinguishable from God, while in post-exilic texts, like Zechariah, angels act as intermediaries between the human and divine realms.

There is a similar development of the view of hostile forces, such as demons and the devil. Demons persist as an unnamed entity of hostile beings that can possess people and cause other difficulties. It is only in later texts that some of the demons develop individual personalities, names, and duties.

The most prominent evil force ends up being Satan. His name originally meant "adversary" or "the accuser," and it stemmed from his role, which was to find and prosecute cases of undetected or unpunished sin. I call him the Law and Order of the heavenly realm. In Zechariah we see him accusing the high priest of impurity, and in Job we see him patrolling the earth and bringing cases to God. There are no texts prior to the Hellenistic period that claim that he is a fallen angel or that he tempts humans or causes them to sin.

Yet, many people today assume that the full story of the fall of the angels is in the Bible. The fact is that, although some Hellenistic Jewish texts may allude to a devil in the way that we think of him, the earliest example of the story of the fall of the angels is in a Roman-period text, sometimes called *The Life of Adam and Eve*. This text, preserved in several ancient languages, describes the details of Adam and Eve's life after they had been kicked out of the Garden of Eden, in more detail than in Genesis. For example, some versions describe the first time Eve experiences labor pains.

One episode in the texts recounts Adam and Eve's attempt to repent for their sins. Adam decides that they should each stand in a river for an extended period of time as a form of repentance. On the day before their repentance is to be complete, Satan comes to Eve and tells her that Adam has said that God has forgiven them

and that she can come out of the water. When Adam arrives the next day and finds Eve out of the water, he asks Satan why he insists on tempting them to sin (notice that this text assumes that the serpent who had tempted Eve in the garden was also Satan). Satan then proceeds to tell the story of the fall of the angels.

He notes that when God created Adam, he placed him in heaven as the image of God. This element stems from two details in Genesis 1—2: first, that humans are created in the image of God (Gen 1:27) and that Adam is created outside of the Garden and later placed within it by God (Gen 2:7–8). The *image* of a god was a term applied to a cult statue that represented the god's presence in a temple. Here Adam, the image, is set up in heaven, and God requires the angels to bow down to him. Some of the angels, led by Satan, object, saying that they had been created before Adam and that he should bow down to them. For their refusal to worship God's image, Yahweh throws them out of heaven. Satan states that from that point on, he vowed to make life as difficult as possible for humans.

This story was widely popular for many years, and it has become part of the Christian tradition. Yet Christian exegetes have long struggled with the fact that this account is not in the Bible. In the patristic period, theologians tried to identify what biblical text referred to this fall. Some claimed that it occurred before the opening of Genesis. Others said that the reference to the "sons of God" in Genesis 6:1–4 alluded to the angels' fall. Still others viewed the reference to the fall of the day star in Isaiah 14:12–21, in Latin translated as "Lucifer" or "Light-bearer," as the indication of this event. The fact remains that the story itself is found outside of the Bible.

As you can see, our contemporary view of Satan developed over a long period of time. We can trace some of that development within the biblical texts, while others come from non-biblical Jewish and Christian literature.

GOD, THE MASTER OF CHAOS

Readers of the Bible have been bothered by this text for years. God simply does not play fair: Job's suffering is the result of a bet between Satan and God! Not only that, but when God finally shows up to speak to Job, God never tells

Job why he's suffering; Job is as clueless at the end of the book as he was in chapter 2. (I might like the book better if I could rewrite God's final speech.)

It helps me to remember that the book of Job is probably fiction. It has always been placed among the wisdom books, not among the historical books. The issue that Job addresses is theodicy, the problem of innocent suffering in light of God's goodness and power. As we saw with the exilic literature, this is a universal human question. Let's look at the answer offered in the book of Job.

The author sharpens the book's focus by making sure that the reader knows that Job is absolutely innocent. If you had read the whole book, you might have found the arguments of Job's friends convincing: everybody sins, no one is blameless, and, therefore, Job also must have sinned. By starting the book with the wager between God and Satan, the author is not letting the reader fall back on this common argument. In other words, the author is saying that it is a fact that some people suffer who do not deserve to. Perhaps we don't need to be reminded of this today, but in the ancient world people assumed that human suffering was a punishment from God, for either their own sins or for the sins of their ancestors.

Let's put the problem of unjust suffering in the context of creation theology. In biblical parlance, the opposite of creation is chaos. God created the world in such a way that justice is rewarded. If even one person suffers unjustly, then this is contrary to God's creative work. It is the result of the forces of chaos. Job's suffering may mean that God is losing control over the universe.

Once again, the beginning of the book denies such a conclusion. The reader understands that Job's suffering is something God wants. We may object to the idea that God would have someone suffer so that the deity can win a bet, but we must recognize that the text clearly leaves God in control.

At the end of the book there is a description of the chaos monsters, Behemoth and Leviathan. How is the description an answer to Job's suffering? First, their descriptions are the culmination of a longer poem in which God describes similar elements of creation. Notice that the animals that God describes tend to be wild animals, ones that do not directly benefit human society. One can assume, then, that God's descriptions of Behemoth and Leviathan are further examples of this aspect of creation.

Look closely at the way the chaos monsters are described. There is a certain awesome beauty in these poems. They do not frighten God, although they certainly frighten humans. Instead, they are described as God's playthings, Yahweh's pets. How is this an answer to Job?

The existence of the chaos monsters reflects Job's innocent suffering; both are evidence of chaos in the world. The book asserts that God's creation does not stand in opposition to chaos. Rather, God creates chaos as well. Why does God do so? The answer that the book of Job gives is that God does so because it is amusing, as is a bird on a leash (Job 41:5) or a wager between friends.

Job is satisfied with this answer, even if we may not be. The text does seem to suggest that God finds innocent suffering amusing, a conclusion I find abhorrent. On the other hand, it rightly points out that nothing stands outside of or is opposed to God's work as creator. In making such an assertion, the author further reminds the reader that God has a reason for what happens in the world, even if humans cannot understand it.

ELEMENTS OF APOCALYPTIC

In Greek the word *apocalypse* means a "revelation." *Apocalyptic literature* describes a secret revelation, often communicated through an angel, that contains many symbols; this revelation discloses an ultimate reality, such as the real nature of heaven or the ultimate purpose of human history. It often reflects a dualistic worldview.

APOCALYPTIC AS RESISTANCE LITERATURE

Hollywood loves apocalyptic themes: *The Matrix, Lord of the Rings*, even *Constantine,* all have elements of apocalyptic literature. In our culture, these movies function as action-horror films. In some of them, such as *War of the Worlds*, the apocalypse is something to be avoided.

This is not how this material has functioned in all cultures, however. Many apocalyptic texts are produced by oppressed groups. For them, apocalyptic literature functions as a form of resistance literature.

The Old Testament contains eschatological texts, such as portions of the book of Daniel, that envision an end-time, when humans will see God bringing the created world to its fulfillment. Sometimes people think that these texts predict the future, and they try to figure out when the world is going to end. They are misreading the purpose of these texts. They are not predictions of the future, but symbolic visions of the nature of God and the purpose of history.

African-American scholars have noted the ways in which African spirituals resonate with the themes of biblical apocalyptic literature. Brian Blount, for example, traces the use of biblical texts by nineteenth-century slaves. Slaves could preach on texts advocating resistance to an evil leader and apply the themes directly to their own lives. Often the subversive nature of this preaching was missed by white slave-owners who did not object to their slaves being Christians. I have to admit that I had been reading apocalyptic literature for a long time without "getting it." But when I thought about the way that slaves could sing a song like "Swing Low Sweet Chariot" as a protest against unjust oppression, I was finally able to read apocalyptic material in a new light.

These texts are not advocating some passive submission to the forces of evil. They are not suggesting that people sit back and wait for God to save them. Nor are they saying that the resolution to life's problems will arrive in the future. Instead, they are presenting an alternative understanding of the universe, using powerful mythic symbols. This alternate worldview allows the audience to express their belief that the power structures that dominate their world are not ultimately real. The dominant culture's message, that the oppressed have no power, is false. The idea that God is on the side of the victors is absurd. This alternate view feeds the efforts of the oppressed group to maintain group identity and personal dignity in the face of shameful destructive experiences.

If you have a chance, try to read the tales of Daniel and his friends in chapters 1—6 as resistance literature written during the oppressive regime of Antiochus IV. How do these tales of miraculous resistance address a Jewish community whose sons were being martyred for their faith?

The End of the World As We Know It

The book of Daniel, written in the final turbulent years of the Greek period, is a complex text. It is clearly the result of a long tradition. The version in the Hebrew Bible has parts written in another language, Aramaic. The edition in the Greek Septuagint is longer than the Hebrew version, with two chapters perhaps originally written in Greek. In addition, the book mixes two types of material. Eight of the chapters (using the longer version of the text) are stories of Daniel and his friends in the Babylonian court, while the other six describe visions that Daniel has of the end of the world.

A common element in apocalyptic literature is pseudepigrapha, when an author assumes another persona. Often ancient apocalyptic texts were written as if they were visions that had been given to someone in Israel's past, such as the books of Enoch. The book of Daniel uses this literary device. The author, who lived during the reign of Antiochus IV Epiphanes (175–163 BCE), assumes the persona of "Daniel," a wise man who serves in the court of the Babylonian king around the year 530 BCE. The Jewish audience would have accepted this pseudepigraphical element as an expected part of apocalyptic literature.

The first six (or eight) chapters set up the literary context for the six chapters of visions. These narratives about Daniel highlight the unjust oppression that he and his friends are experiencing at the hands of cruel foreign rulers. This oppression, which was not typical of the Babylonians, threatens their group's existence, and they resist through acts that maintain their distinct identity.

The audience, living through the persecution of Antiochus IV, would have identified with the book's hero. They would have recognized that the text spoke to what they were experiencing.

DANIEL 7–12: VISIONS OF AN END TIME

While the stories about Daniel are very interesting, I would like to concentrate on the chapters that describe Daniel's apocalyptic visions. Daniel's visions, revealed through angels, describe the "time of the end." Their date is determined by the fact that the visions are correct up to the reign of Antiochus IV, but incorrect after that.

Numerology in the Bible

We have seen in several places that numbers functioned as symbols in ancient Israel. For instance, numbers in parallel lines of poetry are not meant to be read literally. Some important numbers that we have encountered are the numbers *7* (perfection or completion) and *40* (which means a long time or large amount).

In addition, Hebrew had no separate system of designating numbers. Instead, each letter of the Hebrew alphabet was assigned a numeric value. The first letter of the alphabet, *aleph*, was used for the number *1*, the second letter, *beth*, for the number *2*, and so on. Therefore, any Hebrew word could be "added up" to give the numeric value of the word. In the book of Revelation, for instance, the author adds up the values of the letters for the Roman emperor Nero, and gets the number *666*, although some early manuscripts preserve the number *616* here (Rev 13:18). Within the Christian tradition, then, the number *666* came to be associated with the anti-Christ.

We don't always know what numbers meant to their original audience, nor what the source of their symbolism was. For example, the number *3* is always a good number, but scholars debate why. For the modern reader it is important to remember that these numbers were not meant to be read as literal computations, but rather as part of the mythic symbolism that pervades these texts.

IN CASE YOU WERE WONDERING

Apocalyptic literature. This literature is highly symbolic, and it presumes that the reader knows what each element symbolizes. The animals are symbols, as are the metals, the horns, even the numbers.

Daniel. The hero of the book is portrayed as a young man who works within the court of eastern kings. The references to him in the book of Ezekiel (14:14; 20; and 28:3) suggest that he is a mythic figure within Israelite tradition.

The kings. The book tries to date the visions by reference to the king who was in charge. The list of kings in the book, however, does not match near-eastern history. As with their parallels in the books of Esther and Tobit, Daniel and his friends maintain their Jewish identity by acts of piety, such as fasting and not eating impure foods. They are persecuted for this.

Gabriel. The name given to the angel who is often depicted as a messenger.

Michael. The name of the warrior angel. Here he seems to be the one in charge of Israel.

Media. This was a nation east of Babylon and north of Persia. Some of the kings in the Exile came from Media, so Daniel depicts it as a separate power.

The abomination that desolates (Dan 9:27). This term refers to the image of Zeus which Antiochus set up in the temple.

Looking Closely at the Text

It would take too long to lead you through the details of these visions. Instead, allow yourself to get an overall impression of the visions, their use of images, and the interaction between heavenly beings and Daniel.

Decoding the Symbols

When I teach these texts, I find that students either love this material or they hate it. I've always been someone who has tended to hate it. What's the point of all those symbols and complicated visions? Just tell me what you want me to know!

Scholars have debated why this literature uses so many symbols. Some thought it was because the literature was so critical of people in power that its authors wanted to "hide" what they were saying. But if you had lived back then, the symbols would have been obvious to you (believe it or not).

The purpose of the symbols is probably to communicate that these texts are not to be read literally; these are visions, dreams, imaginative verbal pictures that paint an ideal resolution to history. They are extended allegories, using symbols that stem from the mythic traditions of the ancient Near East. By tapping into those mythic symbols, the authors convey the idea that this struggle for justice has cosmic consequences. We do the same thing in contemporary films. Think about the symbols of death and fertility in *The Lord of the Rings*, or the symbols of water and fire in *Constantine*.

The book of Daniel was written during a time when Jews were being persecuted. The author sees Antiochus's reign as one in a series of ever-worsening persecutions. In chapter 7, for instance, each nation that has ruled over Judah is represented by an animal (a lion, a bear, a leopard, and a monstrous beast), each one more terrifying than the previous one. The book of Daniel addresses the question of God's power and goodness in light of the series of tragedies that the Jews endured in the Second Temple Period. Remember that first they were ruled by the Babylonians, then the Persians and Medes, and then the Greeks. Although Daniel 9 includes a prayer by Daniel for forgiveness of sins, as a whole the book depicts the Jews as righteous and pious. Daniel represents the suffering, innocent nation. He fasts and observes the kosher laws of the Torah, even when kings threaten to kill him, just as Judah remained true to the Torah even when ruled by other nations.

Apocalyptic literature, such as Daniel 7—12, addresses the problem of this innocent suffering. Ecclesiastes and Job look at theodicy from the perspective of the individual. Daniel looks at the question from the perspective of the community. As the author of Ecclesiastes did, the author of Daniel could have concluded that history has no meaning or purpose, that one should avoid struggle, and that one should enjoy whatever God gives to enjoy. Instead, this author implies that history does have a purpose, one that remains hidden from human understanding for now, but one which will be revealed at the end of time.

Contrary to Hollywood versions of these texts, they were meant to be read as visions of hope. They do not give in to the despair of Ecclesiastes, nor do they relish cosmic destruction. Instead they provide hope and are symbols of God's ultimate purposes for humanity. With that in mind, let's look at some of these texts in more detail.

Daniel 7 is probably the most influential of Daniel's visions. Notice how the vision is structured:

> ‣ He describes four beasts that represent four kingdoms: Babylon, Media, Persia, and Greece. The horns on the last beast symbolize individual Greek rulers.

> ‣ Next, he has a vision of heaven. The "Ancient One" is Yahweh who, with other heavenly beings, decides the fate of the world (similar to what God does at the beginning of Job).

> ‣ Next, God decides to take power away from Greece and give it to the "holy ones," led by "one like a human being" (Dan 7:13). In other words, Daniel 7 envisions a day when God will remove power from evil nations and give it to angels (holy ones), who will rule the earth for God. When will this happen? After "a time, two times, and half a time" (7:27), symbolic language.

Let's focus for a moment on the "one like a human being." In Hebrew, this phrase is "one like a son of man." He is "like" a human ("son of man"), but he is not a human. The chapter later confirms this when it says dominion will be given to "the people of the holy ones of the Most High" (Dan 7:27). Jewish apocalypses often include a figure like this, someone (angelic or human) sent by God to fight the final battle against evil and/or rule over the new kingdom after evil is vanquished. New Testament texts, such as the gospel of Mark, call Jesus the "Son of Man" because they see him as the one who would rule God's new kingdom.

Daniel 8 describes another animal vision, explained by Gabriel: the ram with two horns is a land east of Mesopotamia with two nations, Media and Persia. The goat is Greece, and the first large horn is Alexander the Great. Once again the vision ends with Antiochus. In this chapter, Gabriel states that these visions describe the "time of the end" (8:17). Chapter 8 depicts a series of persecutions that reach their apex in Antiochus. The "end" expresses the author's hope for the end of persecution.

Daniel 9 contains Daniel's prayer of forgiveness on behalf of the people. While this chapter contains no vision, the prayer elicits Gabriel's description of the future, which again culminates in the desecration of the temple by Antiochus ("the prince who is to come").

> The troops of the prince who is to come shall destroy the city and the sanctuary. Its end shall come with a flood, and to the end there shall be war. Desolations are decreed. He shall make a strong covenant with many for one week, and for half of the week he shall make sacrifice and offering cease; and in their place shall be an abomination that desolates, until the decreed end is poured out upon the desolation (Dan 9:26–27).

Although the book of Daniel addressed Judah's suffering under Antiochus, this suffering did not destroy faith; it added to it. Rather than deny God's work in history, persecution led the author to affirm that God has a purpose in history, one that makes suffering meaningful.

Daniel 10—12 contains a complex fourth vision. This vision assumes that you know many of the details of the Greek period, some of which remain unknown to this day. Once again, the vision culminates in the reign of Antiochus IV Epiphanes, although it does not accurately portray his death. This fact leads scholars to assume that the book was written just before Antiochus's death. Once again the vision is clearly about the end of suffering. The author has lost hope that suffering can be avoided in this life. He recognizes that humans are only free from suffering in the kingdom of God.

What makes this section so interesting is that it is the first place in the Bible where we have a clear indication of belief in the resurrection of the dead. "Many of those who sleep in the dust of the earth shall awake, some to everlasting life, and some to shame and everlasting contempt" (Dan 12:2). The

The Bible in the CHRISTIAN TRADITION

The Unity of Scripture

The Catechism of the Catholic Church states a principle that is common among Christian denominations. "Through all the words of Sacred Scripture, God speaks only one single Word, his one Utterance in whom he expresses himself completely" (CCC 102). Sometimes Christians think that this means there is a dominant theme in the Bible, one message. I think this assumption has led to erroneous interpretations of some biblical texts. If people assume that the Bible must have a single message, when they encounter texts with a different message, they often try to convince themselves that the text they are reading does not say what it does. For instance, the claim in Ecclesiastes that all human toil is pointless is often "explained away" as an exaggeration.

The search for universal themes, however, is a misunderstanding of the true meaning of the unity of revelation. The unity of revelation comes, not from its content, but from its source. Let me try to explain this statement from the Christian perspective.

God is One, Eternal, Perfect. God's revelation, since it is an expression of God's essential nature, must also be One, Complete, Perfect. The unity of revelation is a statement about the nature of God.

Humans are many, mortal, and imperfect. We cannot perceive God completely or perfectly. This means that we cannot perceive God's revelation perfectly.

The Bible is a vehicle to God's revelation in human words. It preserves, in a reliable and authoritative way, human experience of God's revelation. This means that the human experience of God's revelation is true, good, and beautiful, but still limited, contingent, and partial.

Human limitation means that each text tells us something about God, but no single text can tell us everything about God. Just as we need a community of believers, each with their own perspective, to come to a more complete (though not perfect) understanding of God, so too

we need a variety of texts about God in the Bible. Like a complex symphony, Christians believe that God has provided a text rich in its diversity. To try to reduce that diversity to one theme is like trying to capture a symphony in a single line of music.

Catholics believe that Scripture is not the end or the fullness of God's revelation. The fullest manifestation of God's revelation is Christ, but even in Christ humans still have only limited experience of this revelation. Christ helps humanity see God's plan for humanity more clearly, but we remain human, limited in our capacity to experience the fullness of God.

Christians believe that the saints in heaven have a better, unmediated experience of God. In Catholic tradition, this "better view" is sometimes called the Beatific Vision. Christ helps his believers understand what it is they hope for. The Beatific Vision is central to Christian hope in the resurrection and the immortality of the soul.

This journey in the experience of God's revelation serves as a model for how Christians understand the relationship between biblical revelation, Christ, and the fullness of revelation. What is known about God through the Bible is understood better because of Christ. Yet, even with God's revelation in Christ, Christians assert that humans will know revelation better still at the end of time.

Part of what we will "know" better is God's purpose for creation. We have said before that many Christians believe that history is not just one meaningless event after another, but part of God's plan for humanity. The Bible reveals something about that plan, but it also implies that there is yet more to know. We call the idea that there is an ultimate reality beyond the human realm *eschatology*; Christians believe that they will experience this reality at the end of time. This is what the Nicene Creed means when it says, "We look for the resurrection of the dead, and the life of the world to come."

resurrection of the dead to reward or punishment gives meaning to Israel's struggles. For the original audience of the book of Daniel, this belief, that their suffering had meaning and that their faithfulness would be rewarded, gave them a way to make sense of the horrors of the reign of Antiochus. Daniel expresses their hope for a better world.

Theodicy, Despair, and Hope

I am glad that we have texts like Ecclesiastes, Job, and Daniel in the canon. They affirm my experience of the world as a place that sometimes does not make sense. They recognize that there is horrible unjust suffering in the world, and that, all too often, the wicked prevail.

But they do not let me off the hook from believing in God because of this suffering. God may seem distant, an old bearded judge sitting on a throne, as in Daniel 7. Yahweh may seem long gone, or like someone you have to yell at to get attention, as in Job. The deity may be incomprehensible and unknowable, as in Ecclesiastes. But, in spite of that, all three texts say that God is there, in control, and still caring, even if our puny human minds cannot comprehend it.

The book of Daniel offers the most hope. It suggests that if we could just get high enough to see the whole sweep of human history, what looks like a world overrun by evil beasts is really only one melody in the great symphony of creation. Moreover, that symphony will not end on a minor chord. It will end with a triumphal song of God's eternal reign.

For Review

1. What do the themes of covenant, creation, and revelation in the Old Testament suggest about God?

2. Why does the Bible contain many different themes and messages?

3. Describe three main topics that the Teacher explores.

4. What does the word *vanity* mean in Ecclesiastes?

5. Why does Job suffer?

6. How are the descriptions of Behemoth and Leviathan an answer to Job's plight?

7. What is apocalyptic literature?

8. How does Daniel 7—12 address the problem of innocent suffering?

FOR FURTHER READING

I've compared Ecclesiastes to *Gilgamesh*, but for its connection to Egyptian literature see Shannon Burkes, *Death in Qoheleth and Egyptian Biographies of the Late Period* (SBLDs 170; Atlanta, GA: SBL, 1999). On the Greek background of Daniel 1—6, especially, see Paul Niskanen, *The Human and the Divine in History: Herodotus and the Book of Daniel* (JSOTSup 396; London/New York: T & T Clark, 2004).

There are many books on Job. Two that deal directly with the God's final speech are David Penchansky, *The Betrayal of God: Ideological Conflict in Job* (Literary Currents in Biblical Interpretation; Louisville, KY: Westminster John Knox, 1990) and Leo G. Perdue, *Wisdom in Revolt: Metaphorical Theology in the Book of Job* (JSOTSup 112; Bible and Literature 29; Sheffield, KY: Almond, 1991).

For an introduction to apocalyptic literature, including Daniel, see John J. Collins, *The Apocalyptic Imagination: An Introduction to Jewish Apocalyptic Literature*, second edition (Grand Rapids, MI: Eerdmans, 1998). Brian Blount's work can be found in *Then the Whisper Took on Flesh: New Testament Ethics in an African-American Context* (Nashville, TN: Abingdon, 2001); although it focuses on the New Testament, much of what the author describes can be applied to Daniel as well.

There are an amazing number of studies of the Dead Sea Scrolls. Geza Vermes has remained a standard source for both an introduction to the scrolls and for a translation of them. See *The Complete Dead Sea Scrolls in English* (New York: Penguin, 1997) and *An Introduction to the Complete Dead Sea Scrolls* (Minneapolis, MN: Fortress, 1999).

On the development of the Adam traditions, see Gary A. Anderson, *The Genesis of Perfection: Adam and Eve in Jewish and Christian Imagination* (Louisville, KY: Westminster John Knox, 2001). On the Satan traditions, most recently, see T. J. Wray and Gregory Mobley, *The Birth of Satan: Tracing the Devil's Biblical Roots* (New York: Macmillan, 2005).

Deconstructionist and post-modern theories are recent additions to methods of biblical interpretation. Many of the studies are heavily theoretical, making them too abstract for the non-specialist. However, I have found that students find A. K. M. Adam's (editor) *Handbook of Postmodern Biblical Interpretation* (St. Louis, MO: Chalice, 2000) a handy entryway into the variety of post-modern approaches to the Bible. John Collins speculates on the implications of post-modernism on the classic historical-critical approaches to Scripture in *The Bible after Babel: Historical Criticism in a Postmodern Age* (Grand Rapids, MI: Eerdmans, 2005).

Epilogue

Cracking Open
a Familiar Book

Of making many books there is no end,
and much study is a weariness of the flesh.
(Eccl 12:12)

What Have I Learned?

If you were taking my class, I wouldn't be writing this section. I'd be making you answer the question. But since I can't interview every single one of you, I'll provide the most common responses that I get to this question: what have I learned?

The most common answer I get is awareness that reading the biblical text is not a simple process. Many of my students come into class assuming that the meaning of the text is clear, and that I'm just trying to make it more complicated. What they don't know is that what was "clear" to them was their own interpretation. They later realized that their interpretation was not the only way to understand the text. They came to appreciate how much more the text engaged them once they understood its background and implications.

The second most common answer that I get is that students realize how valuable it is to engage people who have different views of the text than they do. Whether they discover this by working in groups in which they challenge each other, or by doing a research paper through which they encounter conflicting interpretations of the text, they come to understand where their own interpretation fits in. Sometimes they even change their mind about a text or a topic.

The third answer comes out of classroom work, but it is something that is replicated beyond the classroom. My students find that thinking about the Bible on a creative level adds to their appreciation of the text. By engaging the imaginative part of their minds, whether through producing their own creative pieces or through analyzing different creative appropriations of the text, they come to realize that the Bible is a collection of artistic literary pieces. This process gets them beyond what I call the boring question (Did it happen?) to the important questions (What does it mean? What does it evoke in the audience?).

All these important interpretive skills can also be applied to many aspects of your world. Whether you are reading a novel, watching a movie, or listening to music, you are now more informed consumers of contemporary forms of communication.

By examining multiple voices in the Old Testament, students learn that the Bible is a collection of discrete texts. But there is a final issue that many Christian readers want to address, and that is this: is there a "Christian" reading of the text? This is an important question in contemporary American society, since you will find many claims about the Bible being made in the public discourse.

READING WITH THE CHRISTIAN COMMUNITY

THE BIBLE AS A GUIDE FOR LIFE

Many of my students assume that the Bible is some kind of moral guide. It's not surprising that people might think that; after all, that's how it's often used. But is that the main purpose of the Old Testament? On the one hand, surely the Bible must make a difference to how Jews and Christians live their lives, but just how does it do that?

One of the problems of viewing the Bible as a moral guide is that it seems to disregard the vast number of texts that do not address that issue. It's one thing to look at a biblical law, for instance, and say, that's how we're supposed to act now, but what about a description of an ancient battle, or a list of genealogies, or a description of Israel's land-holdings? Aren't those also part of the Bible?

A second problem is that sometimes the text holds up things as good (or at least acceptable) that today we reject. How are the texts that describe Israelite slavery, polygamy, or the slaughtering of non-Israelites a moral guide? The conclusion that the Bible is a moral guide is problematic.

The Old Testament Is the Bible of Jesus

Some people read the Old Testament because it helps them understand the New Testament. Israelite texts from the Greek period and later show how Jewish thought was affected by Hellenism. In the New Testament you read about different groups in Judea: Sadducees, Pharisees, scribes, Essenes. These groups disagreed about how much Jews should cooperate with Roman forces.

More importantly, however, these were the texts treasured by Jesus, his first followers, the writers of the New Testament, and their audiences. They would have believed that the Pentateuch, some of the historical books, and most of the prophets, at the very least, were sacred. We see this belief reflected in their speech and writing. For example, the writers of the New Testament explain who Jesus is by recalling Old Testament texts.

Some Old Testament themes are particularly prominent in the New Testament. Here are a few examples of Old Testament themes reinterpreted by the earliest Christians:

Messiah. This term originally referred to any Israelite king. But as the Jews became more oppressed, they hoped for the arrival of a glorious leader who would deliver them from their suffering. Christians saw Jesus as the messiah, who rules the "kingdom of God."

Son of Man. This term originally meant a "human being," but it came to be a title for a figure who would help God bring a final resolution to the people's suffering. Jesus' triumph over death offered Christians tangible hope of a resurrection in which the wicked are punished and the righteous are rewarded.

The Suffering Servant. This title was a metaphor used in the book of Isaiah for those who had suffered during the exile. Early Jewish writers used these poems to describe anyone who takes on the suffering of others in order to save them. For Christians Jesus' suffering on the cross "redeems" humanity; that is, he takes on the suffering of others to save them from sin.

Beloved Son. The term "beloved son" comes from the story of Abraham's near sacrifice of Isaac. The "beloved son" is the one you most want to protect, the one most difficult to give up for some greater good. When God calls Jesus the "beloved son" it reminds Christians that Jesus is God's great gift to humanity.

Sacrifice. There were many different kinds of sacrifice in ancient Israel: sin offerings, the offering at Passover (sometimes called the "Paschal lamb"), holocausts or whole burnt offerings, and so on. As the most important act of worship in Jewish life, the practice of sacrifice generated metaphorical language which permeates Israelite texts. We saw this in Second Isaiah when the Suffering Servant is called a "sin offering." In the New Testament, Jesus is sometimes called a "sin offering," sometimes a "Paschal lamb," and sometimes he is the "high priest" who offers the sacrifice.

GOD IS REVEALED IN ALL OF SCRIPTURE

The Old Testament is more than just "background reading" for the New Testament. Do you know what Marcionism is? Marcion was a Christian who was born around 110 AD. He believed that the revelation of God in Jesus meant that the Old Testament was no longer sacred. The Church has always maintained that Marcion was wrong.

Instead, Christians believe that the Old Testament remains fully revelatory in its original meaning. This is why I have tried to instill in you the habit of reading the Old Testament on its own terms. Too often Christians only hear Old Testament texts in church, where the lectionary focuses on readings in which Christ is prefigured. This is a perfectly good setting for reading the Old Testament, but it is not the only way to read it.

One of the most common claims that Christians make is that the Old Testament is important either because it predicts Christ in its prophecies or because Jesus "fulfills" the Old Testament. For example, the Catechism of the Catholic Church states rather typically, "Christians . . . read the Old Testament in the light of Christ crucified and risen" (CCC 129). What does it mean to read the Old Testament "in the light of Christ"? Some people think that it means finding predictions of Jesus behind every Old Testament passage. While Christians do read some texts as predicting Jesus, Catholics do not believe that every Old Testament passage must be read in this way. To read "in the light of Christ" is much more subtle and far more profound than that.

Christians believe that all of Scripture is a vehicle of God's revelation, seen most perfectly in Christ. But God is revealed in all parts of Scripture, not just those explicitly about Christ.

READING WITH THE TRINITY

Who is the God that is revealed in the Old Testament? Christians believe that God is *triune*, meaning that God has one nature, but three "persons" within that nature. In other words, Christians know God as both "one" and as "three persons." The precise meaning of this idea is a mystery that is difficult to explain, but it remains a fundamental teaching of Christianity. When Christians read the Old Testament, they read it with a belief in the Triune God.

So, how is the God of the Old Testament related to the Holy Trinity? Is the God of the Old Testament the same as "God the Father"? Or is the Old Testament's God a different person of the Trinity (God the Son or the Holy Spirit)? Or is God the Trinity as a whole?

I think that most Christians would say that the God of the Old Testament is God the Father, and in a sense that is true. Jesus explains who "the Father" is with reference to the Old Testament. For instance, when the young Jesus is found teaching people in the temple of Jerusalem, he calls the temple his "Father's house" (Luke 3:41–51). In Matthew 11:25–27, Jesus addresses God as his Father who has revealed all things to him, his Son. In the passages where Jesus teaches his followers to pray the Lord's Prayer (Matthew 6:9–15 and Luke 11:2–4), he calls the God whom the disciples know from the Old Testament as "Father."

But it is more accurate to say that the God of the Old Testament is the Triune God, that is, Father, Son, and Holy Spirit. This has been the Church's interpretation throughout its history. For example, many Christian interpreters read passages where God speaks of "us" as evidence of the trinity.

Each person of the trinity is in some way revealed in the Old Testament. But seeing the trinity in the Old Testament is not a matter of dividing up the canon and assigning each part to a different "person." Rather it is a statement that reflects our belief in the unity of God's persons within the Godhead. In other words, where God "speaks," it is done as a trinity. God's actions are actions of the Trinity as a whole.

In other words, the Old Testament is not only a story about God the Father. It is also a "story" about God the Son and about the Holy Spirit. Christ is in the Old Testament, not as a future event that is predicted, but as an inseparable part of God who reveals. What God reveals in the Old Testament is revealed by, through, and about the Father, Son, and the Holy Spirit.

Scripture as Revelation

Christians believe that Scripture is a vehicle for *Revelation*. Revelation is God's self-disclosure to humanity. Scripture provides one way that humans know about God. This is the fundamental theological purpose of Scripture.

Scripture's revelation does relate to Jesus, because Jesus is also an example of God's self-disclosure. The God-head or unified God is revealed in the Old Testament. Christians read the Old Testament to know God better and to understand their existence and behavior in light of that divine revelation.

Revelation also relates to moral or ethical behavior. It is only by knowing who and what God is, that humans can begin to think about the question, what is the proper response to God? Scripture's role as a moral guide, then, isn't so much in providing a list of dos and don'ts as it is in revealing the God who sets standards for human behavior.

For Those on a Journey of Faith

For those of you who are Christian, let me add a final note. I hope you have learned that God wants to communicate with us, just as we are, in our own language. We do not have to be perfect to be chosen by God. We do not have to understand God perfectly to say something true about God. We do not have to learn how to "talk like a theologian" to speak about God. God's revelation comes to us in our own language: in histories, prophecies, stories, proverbs, and songs. All human expression testifies to God.

I hope that you appreciate the Old Testament's unique witness to God's revelation. While some texts can be troubling or difficult to understand, the Old Testament offers a wealth of images about Yahweh and God's relationship to us. It invites us to read these texts and pray them throughout our whole lives.

I hope that you see that this relationship with God has some demands. It is not enough to believe; we must also act with justice, love, and humility. We must act together as a community of believers. God calls individuals to be part of a "people," a people who worships together, suffers together, and rejoices together.

I hope that you will understand that we are on a journey; we have not yet "arrived." Our knowledge of God is imperfect; our speech about God is inadequate; our faith in God wavers. But we are on the road. The Old Testament is an essential part of that journey, not as something that we must leave behind or "get through," but as something that transforms us.

If we are on a journey then we know that we are not at the end. We have only just set out. We meet Jesus in the New Testament. We understand who we are as church in our "post-Scriptural" world. And we wait, hope, and know that what God's promises, while partially fulfilled, will yet be fully realized.

GLOSSARY

Abrahamic Covenant. This is the term used to refer to God's promise to Abraham that he would become a great nation in the land of the southern Levant. This promise was inherited by Abraham's descendants.

Allegory. This is a literary device in which the literal meaning on the page is a set of symbols for another concept or subject. For example, the characterization of Jacob may be a symbol set for the characteristics of the nation of Israel.

Altar. This is a structure on which sacrifices were made. Although there were incense altars, most mentions of altars in the Bible refer to the place where meat offered to a deity would be burned.

Amen. This is the Hebrew word for "it is true" or "so be it." It is used as a liturgical response in Judaism, Christianity, and Islam. The word has the same Hebrew root as "faith" and is also connected with a word meaning "truth."

Anat. This is the name of a very important Canaanite goddess, who was known primarily for her warrior attributes.

Annal. This is a list of national or royal events catalogued by year.

Anoint. This term refers to a ritual action in which oil is poured or smeared on someone's head. This ritual marks the transition into a particular office or position. It is used as a central part of the coronation of a king and for designating a high priest.

Apocalyptic literature. Coming from the Greek word meaning "a revelation," apocalyptic literature contains a secret revelation, often to a mythic figure from the past, using mythological symbolism. It often has a dualistic worldview, and looks for some resolution for unjust suffering by a righteous group.

Apocrypha. This is the name for the extra books that are in the Septuagint, but not in the Hebrew Bible; it is also used by those who hold that these texts have religious value but not religious authority.

Ark of the Covenant. This is a gold-covered box used by Israelites which represented God's presence. The Bible preserves various traditions of its contents, although its origin is traced back to the time of Moses. In the Temple of Jerusalem it was the footstool of God's empty throne, formed by the cherubim. Its ultimate fate was not preserved.

Asherah. (1) This consort of El was a Canaanite mother goddess who fed the wild animals in the steppe. (2) This is the name given to a wooden object that was often set up in the temple of Jerusalem; the Deuteronomistic Historian objected to its presence. It may have represented either Yahweh's feminine, goddess-like aspects or a consort of Yahweh.

Ashtart. The name of a young Canaanite fertility goddess and a daughter of El; she may have been an occasional partner of the storm god, Baal.

Baal. *Baal* is actually a title meaning "lord or master" that can be ascribed to many male Canaanite gods. The biblical references to Baal denote a young storm god and warrior. One of his epithets was "Rider on the Clouds," and his weapons included the thunderbolt. Because storms were essential for agriculture, he was associated with fertility.

Ban. Although the term translated as "ban" can also refer to items dedicated to God, according to the book of Deuteronomy, this was a set of rules governing wars fought within the Promised Land. It required the Israelites to kill all living things, thus purifying the land of anything foreign or impure.

Canaan. This is an area of land, inhabited by Canaanites and "sea peoples," along the eastern shores of the Mediterranean Sea. It would include the southern Levant.

Canon. Originally meaning "rule," this term refers to an authoritative list of books accepted as Holy Scripture by religious communities.

Chaldeans. This is the Israelite name for the Babylonians.

Cherubim. This is the name for heavenly beings of a minor order found throughout the Fertile Crescent. They were composite figures, combining both animal and human elements. Their job was to protect the major deities. Israelites carved cherubim figures onto the lid of the Ark of the Covenant and the walls of the temple, and they included free-standing cherubim in the Holy of Holies. These latter cherubim are sometimes referred to as God's throne or seat.

Circumcision. This procedure, which is the sign of the covenant between God and the descendants of Abraham, removes the foreskin of the penis, the body part responsible for producing the heirs of the land promised to Abraham.

City-state. This is a form of political organization in which a king rules over a walled city and its surrounding lands and cultivated fields.

Clean. This is a term referring to a person or item that can participate in rituals. It does not refer to hygiene.

Concubine. This is a wife who comes from a lower socio-economic status. A man does not need to pay a bride-price for her; she has no dowry; and her children do not inherit land, unless they are formally adopted by their father as heirs.

Conquest. This is the name given to Israel's invasion of Canaan. The book of Joshua depicts it as the result of a quick and effective military campaign.

Contextual criticism. This is a modern method of biblical interpretation that recognizes the importance of the reader's cultural context in the production of interpretations of the Bible.

Court History. This is a source used by the Deuteronomistic Historian in composing the account of the reign of David. It extends from 2 Samuel 9—20, and it contains the stories of David's sins, and the unraveling of his family.

Covenant. This is a pact, agreement, or contract between God and humans, often including a promise.

Davidic Covenant. This term refers to God's promise to David that there would always be an offspring of David on the throne of Israel. It is often coupled with a belief in God's residency in the temple of Jerusalem.

Dead Sea Scrolls. These were a collection of scrolls placed in pottery jars and hidden in eleven caves above the Dead Sea during the Roman period. They were probably hidden there by a sectarian group that lived in a complex nearby. The texts written by this group reveal them to be strict adherents of Jewish law, who separated themselves in protest with the way the temple was being run during the Hasmonean period.

Decalogue. This is a term for the Ten Commandments (see below). It means literally "ten words," referring to the ten prohibitions that were revealed to Moses on Sinai.

Deuteronomist. This term refers to one of the sources of the Pentateuch, found primarily in the book of Deuteronomy. It represents northern traditions, but its date is disputed. It is either a "pious fraud" composed in the time of Josiah, or it preserves northern traditions from the latter part of the Divided Monarchy. It has a distinctive style of exhortation, and it limits sacrifice to one place which is ministered by the tribe of Levi.

Deuteronomistic History. This is the name given to the following books: Deuteronomy, Joshua, Judges, 1 & 2 Samuel, and 1 & 2 Kings. It tells the history of Israel from the death of Moses until the fall of Jerusalem, from the perspective of the laws in the book of Deuteronomy. Although it may have existed in earlier editions in the days of Josiah, and perhaps Hezekiah, the final form of the collection dates to the early Exile.

Diaspora. Although this term is sometimes used to refer to the Exile, it more properly refers to the scattering of Jews throughout the world. This movement of Jews to areas outside of the Levant began as early as the monarchic period, but it increased markedly at various historical points: the fall of Samaria (722 BCE); the fall of Jerusalem to the Babylonians (587 BCE); and the destruction of Jerusalem by the Romans (70 CE).

Divination. This is the term for the process of discerning a divine message by manipulating physical objects or interpreting omens.

Dualism. This is the name for a worldview that explains the presence of evil in the world by positing the presence of opposing divine forces, one controlling good and one controlling evil. Human experience is seen to be a result of the struggle between these divine forces.

Eden. This is the biblical name of God's garden. It is a place of abundance and the source of fresh waters. In Genesis 2, humans are created to guard and tend this garden.

Edict of Cyrus. Cyrus was a Persian king who defeated Babylon and allowed those peoples exiled by the Babylonians to return to their homelands and rebuild their temples. This proclamation, dated to ca. 538 BCE, announces that policy.

El. This is the head god of the Canaanite pantheon; El is described as an older male who rules like a king over a divine council.

Elohim. This is a Hebrew word translated as "God" in the Bible.

Elohist. One of the sources of the Pentateuch, this northern source is probably an edition of the Yahwist source. It shares the Yahwist's style and theology, but it highlights northern traditions and prophetic activity. It refrains from calling God "Yahweh" until the divine name is revealed in Exodus 3.

Empty throne. The Temple in Jerusalem represented God's presence by having an empty throne above which God invisibly dwelled. The seat of this throne was formed by the cherubim wings, while the Ark of the Covenant was the footstool.

Ephraim. This is the name of one of the major tribes in the northern kingdom of Israel. Some biblical texts refer to the northern kingdom as "Ephraim."

Etiology. This term refers to a story about something that happened long ago that helps explain why things are the way they are today.

Exile. (1) This is the name for a forced emigration of a group of people as the result of defeat in war. (2) This is the period in Israel's history when the elite were forced to live in Babylon; it lasted from approximately 587–538 BCE.

Exodus. (1) This is the name of the second book of the Bible. (2) It is also a term used to designate the series of events culminating in the deliverance of the Israelites from slavery in Egypt.

Exodus pattern. This phrase refers to the general outline of the exodus event: slavery in Egypt, a miraculous deliverance, and the giving of the law in the wilderness. Israelite writers could refer to any element of this pattern and expect that the audience would understand it in the context of the whole pattern.

Fertile Crescent. This is the area that extends from the Persian gulf, along the twin rivers of Mesopotamia (the Tigris and the Euphrates), down along the Mediterranean coast, and over to the Nile valley in North Africa.

Firmament. In Genesis 1, God makes a dome-like border that keeps the chaos waters out of the created world.

Form criticism. This is a modern method of biblical interpretation that originally investigated remnants of oral traditions in the texts. In its current use it also includes formulaic language associated with written material.

Fortified city. This term refers to any city that has city walls. Most major cities in the Levant would have been walled to protect the citizens in the event of siege warfare.

Gabriel. This is the name of a divine being or angel who delivers messages from God.

Genealogies. These are lists of off-spring. Most Israelite genealogies record the core members of their society or heads of households. Women and minor sons are rarely included in Israelite genealogies.

Gilgamesh. This is a widely read, popular epic poem from Mesopotamia that tells the tale of a semi-divine king who goes on a quest to find the meaning of life.

Glory. According to some biblical texts, such as the Priestly Writer, this was the aspect of God that dwelled in the temple of Jerusalem. It is associated with brilliant light.

Hallelujah. This is a Hebrew phrase meaning, "Give praise to Yah(weh)."

Hanukkah. This minor Jewish holiday celebrates the time when the temple was rededicated after its desecration at the hands of Antiochus IV Epiphanes. The Jews only had enough oil to last for one day, but the oil miraculously lasted for the eight days required for the purification.

Hebrew Bible. This is a name for the Jewish version of the Old Testament. This book is arranged in three sections: Torah or Law, Nevi'im or Prophets, and Ketuvim or Writings. Together they are known as the *TaNaK*.

Hebrews. This is a term used for the Israelites when enslaved in Egypt, as recounted in the Book of Exodus. The term may have derived from the ancient word *Habiru*, designating a lower social class.

Hellenization. This is a process of colonization used by the Greeks, whereby they introduced Greek thought, political structure, and religion to the regions that they controlled.

Hermeneutics. This term refers to the study of the methodological principles of interpretation, often including the theory by which readers bridge the gap between what the text formerly meant and what it means to contemporary readers.

Holiness. Ultimately an attribute of God, something is "holy" if it is fit to come near to God, either in the temple or in heaven. The original Hebrew word means "separate," which connotes the belief that items or people who are holy must remain separate from anything that can contaminate them or make them less holy.

Holocaust. This is a sacrifice in which an animal is completely burnt as an offering to God.

Horeb. This is the name that the Deuteronomistic traditions use for Mt. Sinai.

Hyksos. This is the name for the western Asian invaders that took over the Egyptian throne during the Second Intermediate Period.

Hymn. This is a type of psalm, usually in the form of a communal song of praise.

Iconography. In archaeology, this term refers to pictures or images found on ancient artifacts such as seals, commemorative steles, and wall decorations.

Inerrant. This is a term literally meaning "free from error." This term is used by religious groups to connote the trustworthiness of the revelation contained in Scripture. For some groups, this term means that everything in the Bible is factually true, while for others what are inerrant are the truths necessary for faith and salvation.

Inscription. This term refers to the wording or text on an ancient artifact, such as a stele, coin, or seal.

Inspiration. This term is used to denote the belief that the Bible is the product of the interplay of both divine and human authorship. Different religions and denominations have different models for describing this interaction.

Irony. This is a literary device often used in the Old Testament in which what is expected to happen either does not happen or happens in an unexpected way. This device often highlights an incongruity between the actual result of a sequence of events and the normal or expected result.

Israel. (1) This is a national, ethnic, and religious coalition of twelve tribes which, during the United Monarchy, were ruled over by a single king. (2) This is also the name for the northern kingdom during the Divided Monarchy comprised of ten tribes ruled over by a single king.

Judge. This is the term for an Israelite leader during the period of the Tribal Confederacy. Judges are described as charismatic leaders whose power is attributed to the "spirit of God." The book of Judges preserves stories of a select few who led the tribes in various battles.

Kosher. This term is given to those edible items that are not ritually defiling; they can be eaten without making the person ritually defiled.

Lady Wisdom. Lady Wisdom is a personification of wisdom in the Bible. She appears in a variety of texts as a divine being or principle that aids God in creation, helps human kings rule, and entices young men to pursue her.

Lament. This is a type of psalm or literature in which the speaker complains about or mourns over some disaster or setback. In the book of Psalms, the most common type of psalm is the individual lament. There are also laments over the destruction of cities in the Bible and the wider ancient Near East.

Lectionary. This term refers to a regular cycle of biblical readings for church services. Several Christian denominations share a lectionary cycle, with some minor variations.

Levant. This is the inhabitable land along the eastern edge of the Mediterranean Sea.

Leviathan. This is the name of a chaos monster, sometimes depicted with seven heads, associated with the Sea. In creation accounts, the creator god defeats or subdues Leviathan in the process of creation.

Literary criticism. This is a modern method of biblical interpretation that examines the literary artistry of the written text.

Maccabees. This is the nickname given to the Hasmonean family who brought a brief period of national independence to Judea during the Hellenistic period. It may derive from the Hebrew word for "hammer."

Manna. This is a term given to the food that God sent to the Israelites when they were traveling through the wilderness. Tradition says it tasted like coriander.

Marduk. This is the name of the Babylonian storm god. He was the head deity of the Babylonians at the time of the Exile. Their creation epic, *Enuma Elish*, recounts his victory over the forces of chaos.

Messiah. This Hebrew word, meaning "anointed one," most often refers to a royal figure. Any king, present or future, could be a "messiah." Occasionally it was also used to designate the high priest.

Metaphor. This is a literary device in which something is referred to under the guise of something else. The word that symbolizes the intended subject communicates parallels between the intended subject and the symbol. Calling the king a "shepherd" is a metaphor that connotes the king's care for God's flock, Israel.

Metonymy. This is a literary device in which a reference to part of a thing is meant to reference the whole thing. For example, references to Ephraim are used to reference the whole northern kingdom.

Michael. This is the name of a divine being or angel who is sometimes depicted as leading God's army and, at other times, as having charge over Israel.

Midrash. This is a Hebrew word meaning "to investigate." It describes the method by which the ancient rabbis interpreted Scripture in order to make it yield interpretation not apparent in a surface reading.

Mishnah. This term refers to rabbinic law as collected and organized into categories about 200 CE. It represented the culmination of the oral tradition of centuries. Worked out in Palestine, it became the basis of the Talmuds, which are commentaries on the Mishnah.

Monarchy. This is the name given to the period from 1020 to 587 BCE, when Israel was ruled by a king.

Monolatry. This is the belief that other gods exist but only one should be worshiped.

Monotheism. This is the belief that there is only one God.

Mosaic Covenant. This is the group of laws, including the Ten Commandments, that was given to Israel by God through Moses. God's blessings on Israel are dependent on Israel's obedience to these covenant stipulations.

Name. (1) According to some biblical texts, such as the Deuteronomistic History, this was the aspect of God that was present in the temple of Jerusalem. (2) A person's "name" is their public reputation; God's name refers to God's international reputation.

Nathan's Oracle. Located in 2 Samuel 7, this oracle contains the outline of the Davidic Covenant. In it God promises David an eternal dynasty, from which will come the builder of the temple in Jerusalem where God will dwell.

Old Testament. This is a collection of literature produced by the ancient Israelites, deemed sacred by some contemporary communities of faith.

Parallelism. This is a literary feature found commonly in Hebrew poetic, prophetic, and proverbial literature. It entails saying things twice, in parallel lines. Often the B line, or repetition, uses rarer or more specific words than the A line.

Passover. This is the name for a biblical holy day that celebrates the day that the angel of death passed by the houses of the Hebrews, killing instead the firstborn of the Egyptians. It marks the beginning of the people's deliverance from slavery. It is often associated with the Feast of Unleavened Bread.

Patriarchs and Matriarchs. This is the name given to the founding fathers and mothers of the tribes of Israel. This term is used for the main figures in Genesis 12—50.

Patriarchy. This is a term referring to any hierarchical system that gives the males of the dominant ethnic group the highest social status. It is often justified as part of the natural order. Israelite society was patriarchal.

People of the land. This is a phrase used in some biblical texts to refer to a particular social group, probably those people left behind when the elite were exiled to Babylon.

Pericope. This term refers to any self-contained unit of a text.

Personification. This is a literary device that depicts an abstract concept as a character or person. For example, the concept of divine wisdom is personified as a woman.

Plague. This is the name given to the series of natural disasters which God brings upon the Egyptians during the period of the exodus.

Pogrom. This is an organized massacre of helpless people, often referring to a massacre of Jews.

Postmodernism. This term refers to an intellectual movement that questions the assertions of objectivity associated with modernism. Postmodernism notes the subjective features of all human knowledge, and it treats with distrust all claims of objectivity.

Priest. This is the name for the officiant at sacrifices. Priesthood in Israel was dynastic. Although there were priestesses in Egypt and Babylon, the Israelites had an all-male priesthood. Priests could become holier than any other person, thus legitimizing their right to come closer to God's presence in the temple.

Priestly Writer. This term refers to one of the four sources of the Pentateuch; this source has a distinctive style and theology. The writer, who avoids using the divine name until Exodus 3, limits sacrifice to one place and its performance to the descendants of Aaron. It is responsible for such things as genealogies, accuracies in ritual practice, and travel notices. Although classically dated to the late Exile or early Restoration period, its date is currently debated.

Promised Land. This term refers to a section of land in the southern Levant, also known as Canaan, which was promised by God to Abraham.

Prophet. This term refers to one who is an intermediary with the divine realm, who delivers messages from the divine realm, and who could intercede on behalf of the people. In Israel, prophetic experience could include hearing voices, spirit possession, visions, or dreams.

Prophetic forms. These are methods of stylistic phrasing, most of which stem from the oral stage of prophetic utterances. These include the messenger formula, the woe oracle, the vision report, and the symbolic act.

Proverb. This is a short saying that encapsulates social wisdom; an aphorism. In Israel proverbs were usually preserved in parallel lines, and had a certain authority as obvious truths.

Psalm. These are the words of songs, many of which had their origin in temple services.

Pseudepigrapha. This is a literary device in which authors write as if they are another person, usually someone from the past.

Purim. This is a minor Jewish holiday whose origin is recounted in the book of Esther. It celebrates a day when the Jews living in Persia were allowed to defend themselves against attack.

Purity. This term refers to the avoidance of ritual contamination. It is important to the Hebrews because impurity effectively prevented much religious and social activity. Impurity could be "caught" by contact with the dead, from prohibited foods, or from contact with bodily fluids and various diseases.

Qoheleth. The Hebrew name for the book of Ecclesiastes, this name is the title given to the narrator. It means "one who assembles," or "preacher," although it is feminine in form.

Rahab. (1) This is the name of a chaos monster whose defeat is attributed to Yahweh in some biblical texts. (2) This woman in the book of Joshua was rewarded by God after hiding the Herbew spies.

Raphael. This is the name of a divine being or angel associated with healing.

Redaction criticism. This is a modern method of biblical interpretation that focuses on the way the final author (redactor) has arranged, changed, and supplemented earlier written material.

Redactor. This is the name given to the final editor of any biblical book. In classical redaction criticism of the Pentateuch, scholars debated whether this redactor was the Priestly Writer, or a fifth author who wove together the four written sources.

Redemption. This term originally referred to paying off a debt. For example, debt slaves could be redeemed if their debt was paid. Sins against God are redeemed, in part, by sacrifice which makes restitution for an offense.

Redemptive suffering. Also known as vicarious suffering, this is a term that refers to the act by which someone takes on the punishment that someone else deserves. By doing this, the redeemer makes restitution for another person's offense.

Restoration period. This term denotes the time period between the Edict of Cyrus and the dedication of the second temple. It was a time marked by internal Israelite conflict over the political organization of the renewed nation.

Revelation. This term refers to God's self-disclosure to humanity. In Christian theology, Scripture is a vehicle for God's revelation.

Sabbath. This is a holy day for the Israelites which celebrated God's rest at the end of creation, but it also reminded the Israelites that God had delivered them from slavery. It began at sundown on Friday and lasted until sundown on Saturday, the last day of the week.

Sacrifice. This term refers to any physical offering to a god. Sacrifices can take the form of meat which is burned, or of grains, produce, oil, or wine which are set before the god. Some peoples in the Levant also sacrificed the firstborn human child, but this practice was often condemned in Israelite texts.

Samaritans. This is the name of the people living in what had been the former northern kingdom during the restoration and second temple periods. Those returning from exile in Babylon viewed these people as foreign and ineligible to participate in the rebuilding of the temple.

Satan. This is the name of a divine figure or angel whose original job was to patrol the earth searching for undetected sin. This divine being would then bring those cases before God, who would judge them. Satan becomes a figure who tempts humans to sin only in the late Hellenistic period.

Second Temple Period. This period of Israel's history covers the years during which the second temple that was built in Jerusalem stood. During this period, Judah was governed by the Persians, the Greeks, the Maccabeans, and then the Romans.

Septuagint. This is a term used for any ancient Greek translation of the Bible. Its Old Testament was organized into four parts: the Pentateuch,

History, Wisdom, and Prophecy. The collection was more expansive than the Hebrew Bible, containing more books and sometimes longer versions of books than its Hebrew counterparts.

Shekel. This is a form of Israelite money, probably made of silver.

Sheol. This is the Israelites' place of the dead. It is not a place of reward or punishment, but simply where the dead reside. It is described as a pit, dark and cut off from communication.

Shiloh. This is the site of a pre-monarchic Israelite temple which was destroyed by the Philistines. The Ark of the Covenant had been housed at Shiloh.

Siege. This is a type of warfare in which an enemy surrounds a walled city, cutting off its food supplies. The attacking army tries to starve those in the city and breach its walls, while the people inside try to outlast the attack.

Source criticism. This is a modern method of biblical interpretation that looks for evidence that an author has used other written sources to compose his or her work.

Stele. This term typically refers to a carved or inscribed stone slab or pillar used for commemorative purposes.

Supercessionism. This is the term for the belief that the literal meaning of the Old Testament is negated or superceded by a later meaning. It is a heresy in most Christian denominations.

Tabernacle. This is a portable tent-shrine used by the Israelites in the desert as a substitute for a permanent temple.

Targum. This is an ancient Jewish translation of the Bible into Aramaic.

Tel. This is a mound formed from the repeated occupation of a particular site. Ancient cities were rebuilt on the same location, creating layers of occupation. Archaeologists attempt to dig through those layers to trace a site's history.

Temple. There is no word for "temple" in Hebrew; the word translated as "temple" is actually "house" or sometimes "palace." A temple, then, is the house of God, that is, a place where a real aspect of God's presence resides.

Ten Commandments. This is the name given to a set of ten prohibitions or "words" that Moses receives from God on Sinai. This list appears twice in the Pentateuch with only minor variations, once in Exodus 19 and once in Deuteronomy 5.

Textual criticism. This is a modern method of biblical interpretation that seeks to reconstruct the "original form" of the ancient texts.

Theodicy. This is a term given to texts that attempt to explain the presence of evil within a worldview that believes in only one beneficent God.

Theophany. This is a physical manifestation of God, usually accompanied by natural wonders such as storms, earthquakes, and volcanic action.

Torah. This is a term that literally means "teaching," and it is the Hebrew name for the first five books of the Bible. It is sometimes translated as "law."

Tribe. This is a large group who traces their ancestry back to a common ancestor.

Trickster. This is a folk character who is apparently weak or powerless, yet who succeeds by tricking or duping the one(s) in power.

Unleavened bread. This is a high holy day in the biblical calendar, often associated with Passover. Unleavened bread has no yeast, and so it does not need time to rise before baking. Matzoh bread is an example of unleavened bread.

Utopian. This is a term that refers to proposing or advocating ideal social, political, or religious schemes which are often impractical.

Vulgate. Originally Jerome's official Latin translation of the Bible, the term is now used for a series of Latin versions approved for liturgical use by the Roman Catholic Church.

Wadi. This is a dry river bed common in arid environments.

Wilderness Narratives. These are the accounts of Israel's history during their time in "the wilderness," that is, between their sojourn in Egypt and their entrance into Canaan.

Yahweh. According to biblical texts, this is God's proper name, rendered in some translations by the word "Lord." Its meaning is debated, although it may mean, "the one who creates."

Yahwist. This is the name given to the earliest of the four sources in the Pentateuch, classically identified as a southern writer composing during the United Monarchy. This source uses the divine name "Yahweh" throughout Genesis. It is marked by lively story telling, an anthropomorphic god, and sacrifices made in multiple sites by various people.

Ziggurat. Part of some Mesopotamian temple complexes, this building resembles a stepped mountain. It is not known what function it served, although ritual activity occurred in a room at the top of the edifice.

Zion. This is the name of the hill within the city of Jerusalem on which the temple was built. References to "Zion" are an example of metonymy, where "Zion" refers to Jerusalem as the sacred center of the nation.

APPENDIX

MAPS

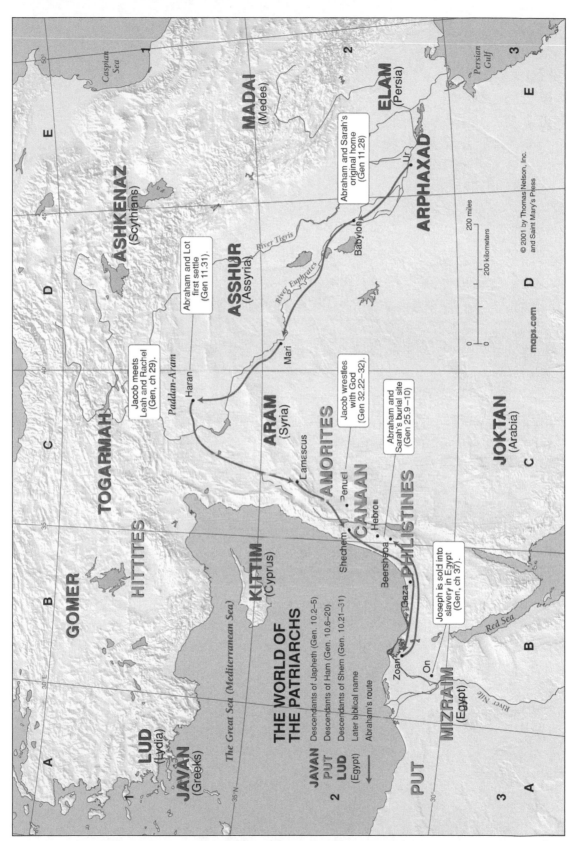

467

THE WORLD OF
THE PATRIARCHS

JAVAN   Descendants of Japheth (Gen. 10.2–5)
PUT   Descendants of Ham (Gen. 10.6–20)
LUD   Descendants of Shem (Gen. 10.21–31)
        Later biblical name
        Abraham's route

GOMER

JAVAN
(Greeks)

LUD
(Lydia)

TOGARMAH

HITTITES

ASHKENAZ
(Scythians)

MADAI
(Medes)

KITTIM
(Cyprus)

The Great Sea (Mediterranean Sea)

ASSHUR
(Assyria)

ARAM
(Syria)

AMORITES

CANAAN

PHILISTINES

MIZRAIM
(Egypt)

PUT

ELAM
(Persia)

ARPHAXAD

JOKTAN
(Arabia)

Caspian Sea

Persian Gulf

Red Sea

River Nile

River Tigris

River Euphrates

Paddan-Aram

Haran

Mari

Babylon

Ur

Damascus

Penuel

Shechem

Hebron

Beersheba

Gaza

Zoan

On

Jacob meets
Leah and Rachel
(Gen, ch 29).

Abraham and Lot
first settle
(Gen 11.31).

Abraham and Sarah's
original home
(Gen 11.28)

Jacob wrestles
with God
(Gen 32.22–32).

Abraham and
Sarah's burial site
(Gen 25.9–10)

Joseph is sold into
slavery in Egypt
(Gen, ch 37).

© 2001 by Thomas Nelson, Inc.
and Saint Mary's Press

200 miles

200 kilometers

maps.com

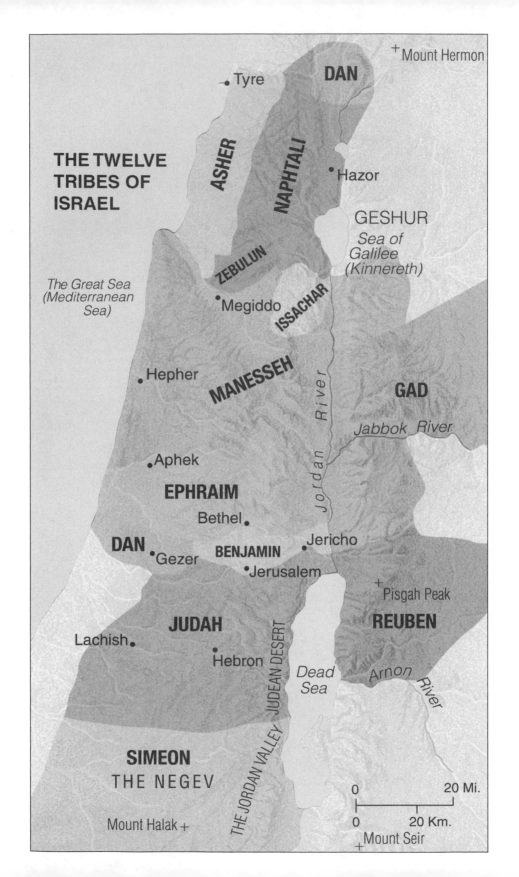

THE TWELVE TRIBES OF ISRAEL

Mount Hermon

Tyre

DAN

ASHER

NAPHTALI

Hazor

GESHUR

Sea of Galilee (Kinnereth)

ZEBULUN

The Great Sea (Mediterranean Sea)

Megiddo

ISSACHAR

Hepher

MANESSEH

GAD

Jabbok River

Jordan River

Aphek

EPHRAIM

Bethel

Jericho

DAN

Gezer

BENJAMIN

Jerusalem

Pisgah Peak

REUBEN

JUDAH

Lachish

Hebron

Dead Sea

Arnon River

THE JORDAN VALLEY

JUDEAN DESERT

SIMEON

THE NEGEV

Mount Halak

0   20 Mi.

0   20 Km.

Mount Seir

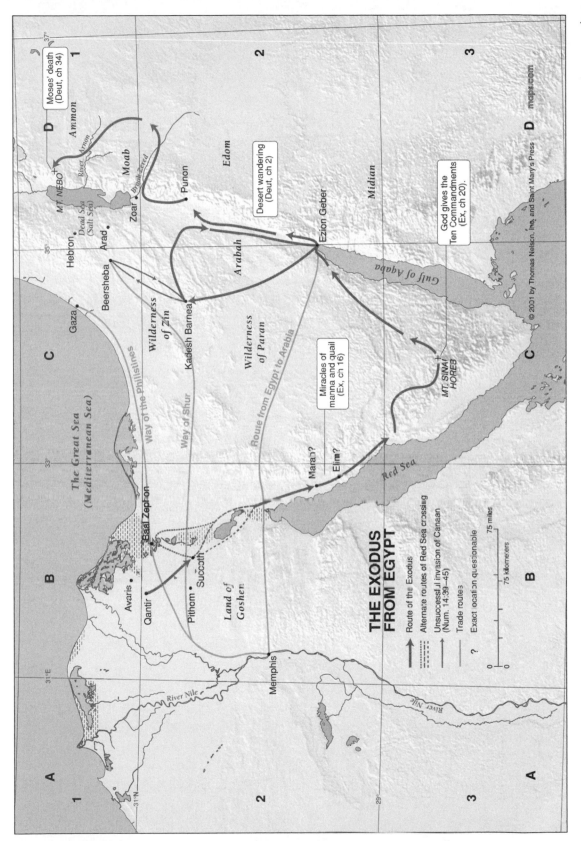

THE EXODUS
FROM EGYPT

Route of the Exodus

Alternate routes of Red Sea crossing

Unsuccessful invasion of Canaan
(Num. 14:39–45)

Trade routes

? Exact location questionable

0   75 miles

0   75 kilometers

Moses' death
(Deut, ch 34)

Desert wandering
(Deut, ch 2)

God gives the
Ten Commandments
(Ex, ch 20).

Miracles of manna and quail
(Ex, ch 16)

Ammon

Moab

Edom

Midian

River Arnon

Brook Zered

MT. NEBO

Dead Sea
(Salt Sea)

Zoar

Punon

Hebron

Arad

Beersheba

Gaza

Wilderness
of Zin

Kadesh Barnea

Wilderness
of Paran

Arabah

Ezion Geber

Gulf of Aqaba

MT. SINAI
HOREB

Way of the Philistines

Way of Shur

Route from Egypt to Arabia

The Great Sea
(Mediterranean Sea)

Baal Zephon

Succoth

Pithom

Land of
Goshen

Avaris

Qantir

Memphis

River Nile

River Nile

Maran?

Elim?

Red Sea

© 2001 by Thomas Nelson, Inc, and Saint Mary's Press

maps.com

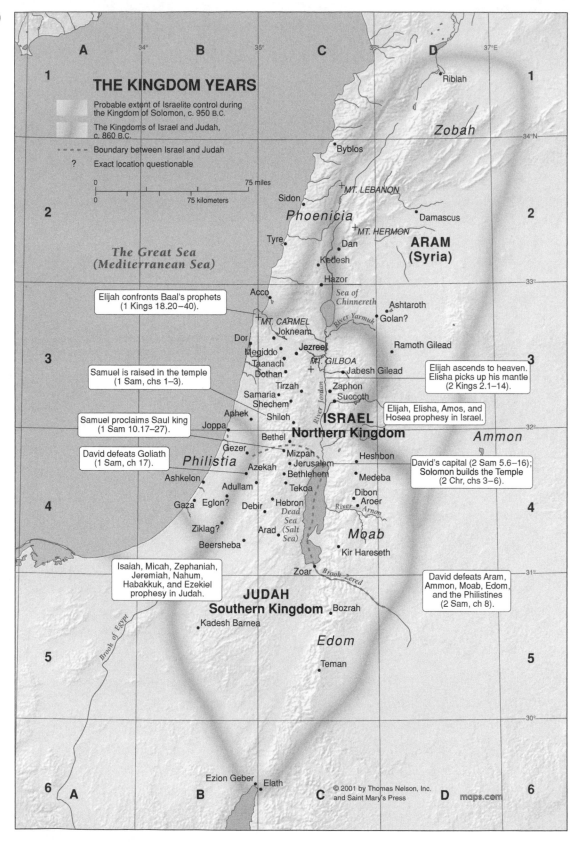

470

THE KINGDOM YEARS

Probable extent of Israelite control during the Kingdom of Solomon, c. 950 B.C.

The Kingdoms of Israel and Judah, c. 860 B.C.

- - - - Boundary between Israel and Judah

? Exact location questionable

0 — 75 miles
0 — 75 kilometers

A B C D 1

Riblah

Zobah

34°N

Byblos

MT. LEBANON

Sidon

Phoenicia

Damascus

2

MT. HERMON

Tyre

Dan

ARAM (Syria)

The Great Sea
(Mediterranean Sea)

Kedesh

33°

Hazor

Acco

Sea of Chinnereth

Ashtaroth

Elijah confronts Baal's prophets (1 Kings 18.20–40).

MT. CARMEL

Jokneam

Golan?

River Yarmuk

Dor

Megiddo

Jezreel

Ramoth Gilead

3

Taanach

MT. GILBOA

Dothan

Jabesh Gilead

Elijah ascends to heaven. Elisha picks up his mantle (2 Kings 2.1–14).

Samuel is raised in the temple (1 Sam, chs 1–3).

Tirzah

Zaphon

Samaria

Succoth

Shechem

River Jordan

Aphek

Shiloh

ISRAEL

Elijah, Elisha, Amos, and Hosea prophesy in Israel.

Samuel proclaims Saul king (1 Sam 10.17–27).

Joppa

Bethel

Northern Kingdom

Ammon

32°

Gezer

Mizpah

David defeats Goliath (1 Sam, ch 17).

Philistia

Azekah

Jerusalem

Heshbon

David's capital (2 Sam 5.6–16); Solomon builds the Temple (2 Chr, chs 3–6).

Ashkelon

Bethlehem

Medeba

Adullam

Tekoa

Dibon

Gaza

Eglon?

Debir

Hebron

Aroer

4

River Arnon

Ziklag?

Arad

Dead Sea (Salt Sea)

Moab

Beersheba

Kir Hareseth

31°

Isaiah, Micah, Zephaniah, Jeremiah, Nahum, Habakkuk, and Ezekiel prophesy in Judah.

Zoar

Brook Zered

David defeats Aram, Ammon, Moab, Edom, and the Philistines (2 Sam, ch 8).

JUDAH

Southern Kingdom

Bozrah

Brook of Egypt

Kadesh Barnea

Edom

30°

5

Teman

Ezion Geber

Elath

maps.com

6 A B C D 6

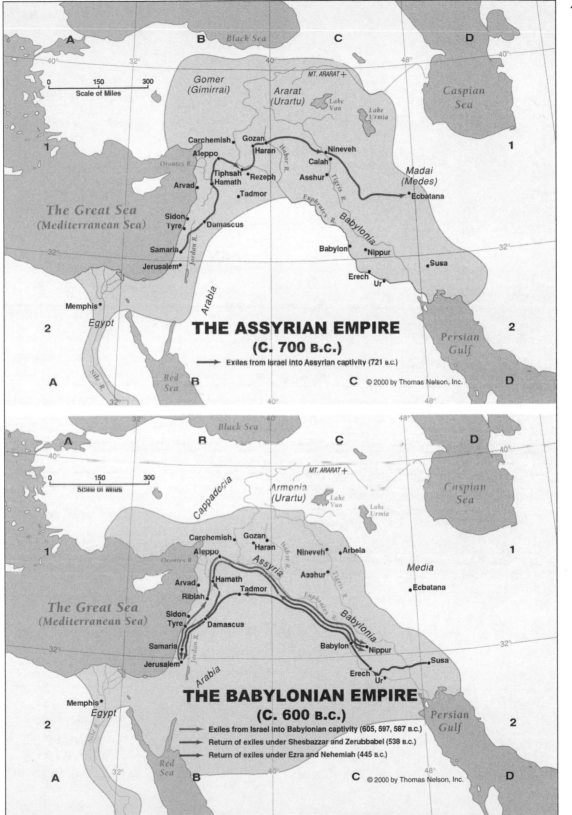

THE ASSYRIAN EMPIRE
(C. 700 B.C.)

→ Exiles from Israel into Assyrian captivity (721 B.C.)

© 2000 by Thomas Nelson, Inc.

THE BABYLONIAN EMPIRE
(C. 600 B.C.)

→ Exiles from Israel into Babylonian captivity (605, 597, 587 B.C.)
→ Return of exiles under Shesbazzar and Zerubbabel (538 B.C.)
→ Return of exiles under Ezra and Nehemiah (445 B.C.)

© 2000 by Thomas Nelson, Inc.

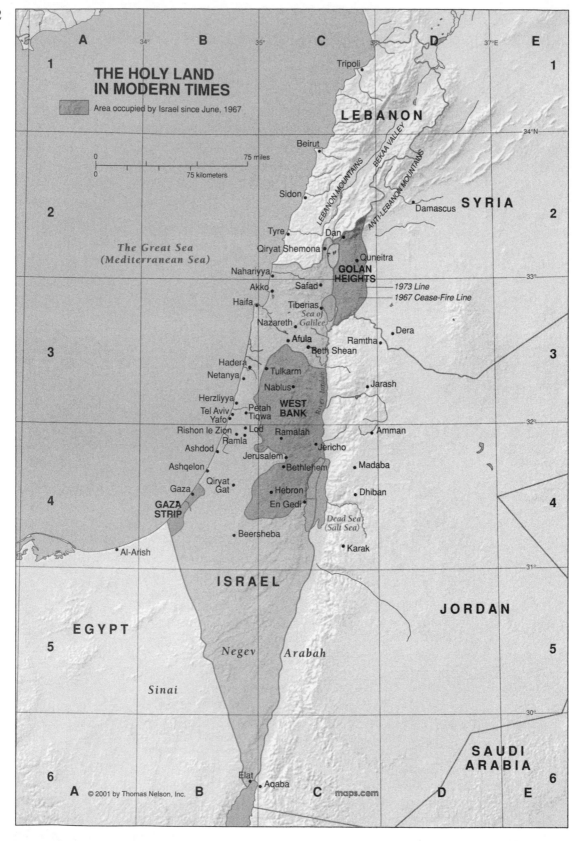

THE HOLY LAND IN MODERN TIMES

Area occupied by Israel since June, 1967

0 _____ 75 miles
0 _____ 75 kilometers

A   B   C   D   E
34°   35°   36°   37°E

LEBANON

Tripoli

Beirut

34°N

Sidon

LEBANON MOUNTAINS   BEKAA VALLEY   ANTI-LEBANON MOUNTAINS

SYRIA

Damascus

Tyre

Dan

Qiryat Shemona

Quneitra

The Great Sea
(Mediterranean Sea)

Nahariyya

GOLAN HEIGHTS

33°

Akko

Safad

1973 Line
1967 Cease-Fire Line

Haifa

Tiberias

Sea of Galilee

Nazareth

Dera

Afula

Ramtha

Beth Shean

Hadera

Tulkarm

Netanya

Nablus

Jarash

Herzliyya

WEST BANK

Tel Aviv
Yafo

Petah
Tiqwa

River Jordan

Lod

Rishon le Zion

Ramalah

Amman

32°

Ramla

Jericho

Ashdod

Jerusalem

Bethlehem

Madaba

Ashqelon

Hebron

Dhiban

Gaza

Qiryat
Gat

En Gedi

GAZA STRIP

Dead Sea
(Salt Sea)

Beersheba

Karak

Al-Arish

31°

ISRAEL

JORDAN

EGYPT

Negev   *Arabah*

5

Sinai

30°

SAUDI ARABIA

6

Elat
Aqaba

A   © 2001 by Thomas Nelson, Inc.   B   C   maps.com   D   E

SIMPLE INDEX

NOTES

NOTES

NOTES

NOTES

NOTES

NOTES

NOTES

NOTES